TEA

TEA

CONSUMPTION, POLITICS, AND REVOLUTION, 1773–1776

JAMES R. FICHTER

CORNELL UNIVERSITY PRESS
Ithaca and London

Publication of this book was made possible by a generous grant from the Hong Kong Research Grants Council.

First published 2023 by Cornell University Press

Library of Congress Cataloging-in-Publication Data

Names: Fichter, James R., author.
Title: Tea : consumption, politics, and revolution, 1773–1776 / James R. Fichter.
Other titles: Consumption, politics, and revolution, 1773-1776
Description: Ithaca : Cornell University Press, 2023. | Includes bibliographical references and index.
Identifiers: LCCN 2023034826 (print) | LCCN 2023034827 (ebook) | ISBN 9781501773211 (hardcover) | ISBN 9781501773228 (pdf) | ISBN 9781501773235 (epub)
Subjects: LCSH: United States. Continental Congress. Association. | Tea trade—Political aspects—United States—History—18th century. | Tea—Political aspects—United States—History—18th century. | Tea tax (American colonies) | Boston Tea Party, Boston, Mass., 1773. | Protest movements—United States—History—18th century. | United States—History—Revolution, 1775-1783—Causes.
Classification: LCC E215.7 .F5 2023 (print) | LCC E215.7 (ebook) | DDC 973.3/115—dc23/eng/20230810
LC record available at https://lccn.loc.gov/2023034826
LC ebook record available at https://lccn.loc.gov/2023034827

To my family, Bronwyn, Emily, Rose, and Robert

Rally Mohawks! bring out your axes,
And tell King George we'll pay no taxes
On his foreign tea;
His threats are vain, and vain to think
To force our girls and wives to drink
His vile Bohea!
    —allegedly sung at the Green Dragon Tavern when rallying for
       the Boston Tea Party

For since the Government o' th' City
Hath lade devolv'd on a Committe
Whose Sov'reign Right to rule the Nation,
Has Tar & Feathers for Foundation;
. . .
Fair Reas'ning & Fair Trade are hiss'd at,
As het'rageneous to a free State;
To cheat the King is Public Spirit,
Republicans will aver it,
And prove by Syllogistic Juggle,
True social Virtue is to smuggle.
    —John Drinker, 1774[1]

Contents

Figures and Tables

Figures

Tables

Acknowledgments

This book has been fifteen years in the making. It began as a side project, grew into an article, and then became a book. As such it has accumulated many debts. I am grateful to the many colleagues who read it in whole or in part, and I am especially grateful to colleagues who commented on or discussed it, including David Smith and Mark Hampton at Lingnan University, Kendall Johnson at the University of Hong Kong, Frederic Grant Jr. and my colleagues in the Hong Kong American history reading group. Barbara Clark Smith provided detailed commentary. Mary Beth Norton commented extensively on an earlier draft while finalizing her own book, 1774, and read other bits later on. She entertained queries with a grasp of sources that only a scholar deep into similar material could provide, allowing me to see whether there was "something there" at many points. I am especially grateful to the peer reviewers for extensive and thoughtful commentary.

Major funding for this project was provided by a grant from the Research Grants Council of the Hong Kong Special Administrative Region, China (Project No. HKU 17615318). Additional support was provided by the University of Hong Kong, the International Center for Jefferson Studies at Monticello, and Lingnan University.

The editors and staff at Cornell University Press, Sarah Grossman foremost among them, have been especially helpful and understanding, and this book is the beneficiary of many other pairs of hands at Cornell and elsewhere.

I owe a profound debt to myriad archivists for their usual indispensable work but especially to those who, during COVID, transformed themselves into research librarians, looking up and emailing documents I could no longer consult in person and answering queries. This includes Jayne Ptolemy and Terese Murphy at the Clements Library, University of Michigan; Lara Szypszak and others at the Library of Congress; Elizabeth Bouvier and Christopher Carter at the Supreme Court Judicial Archive (Massachusetts Archives); Katie Clark at the Historical Society of Pennsylvania; Carley Altenburger at the Winterthur Museum, Gardens & Library; Micah Connor at the Maryland Center for

History and Culture; Kenneth Carlson at the Rhode Island State Archives; Edward O'Reilly at the New-York Historical Society; Maurice Klapwald at the New York Public Library; Abby Battis at the Beverly Historical Society; the Harvard University Archives reference staff; Jennifer Keefe at the Massachusetts Historical Society; Amelia Holmes at the Nantucket Historical Association; Mary Ellen Budney at the Beinecke Library, Yale University; Douglas Mayo at the Rockefeller Library, Colonial Williamsburg; the staff at the Albert and Shirley Small Library, University of Virginia; Lindsay Sheldon at the Washington College library; Brian Burford at the New Hampshire State Archives; and Jacob Hopkins at Swem Special Collections, College of William and Mary.

Many others contributed along the way, including Emily Matchar, who copyedited an earlier draft; Jeremy Land and Chris Nierstrasz, who helped interpret a thorny source; and Vanessa Ogle, David Naumec, Donald C. Carleton Jr., and Robert Allison, who helped with research queries.

This work would have been impossible without the labor of research assistants based in Hong Kong, the United States, Britain, and Canada. They combed distant archives and worked on large datasets. These include JP Fetherson, Sophie Hess, Xiao Wenquan, Zachary Dorner, Alexey Kritchal, Katherine Smoak, Tsui Yuen, Christopher Consolino, Neal Polhemus, Enyi Hu, Eric Nichol, Angie Nichol, Daniel Hart, Jordan Smith, Tina Hampson, Virginia Clark, Benjamin Sacks, Jessica Auer, Michelle Farais, and Mark Markov.

I am especially grateful to my family for putting up with me as I worked on this.

Note on Currency

British money in the 1770s was given in pounds (£), shillings (s), and pence (d).

A price of 5 shillings and 3 pence might be written as 5/3 or as 5s3d. Five shillings was written 5/. This book uses both the "5/" and "5s" notation styles.

British money was a non-decimal currency. 12 pence = 1 shilling and 20 shillings = 1 pound.

Colonies issued their own currencies, which traded, sometimes at significant discounts, against one another and the pound sterling. In 1774 five shillings in Massachusetts money was worth 3/8 in sterling and £1/6/10 in South Carolina currency. Sources are not always clear about which currency was being used. Currencies are clarified in this book where possible.

Spanish silver dollars were a common method of payment. These traded against pounds sterling. In 1776, Congress and some states issued paper dollars which were supposed to be exchangeable at par with silver dollars. That year, dollar-denominated price controls appeared. This paper currency depreciated in 1777 and onward as Revolutionary authorities printed money. The level of depreciation in 1776 remains unclear.[2]

Introduction

The Boston Tea Party was not, despite what you may have read, unanimously acclaimed; even some Patriots were appalled. The ensuing Patriot boycott and prohibition on tea did not endure; both ended before Congress declared independence. The Tea Party did not turn Americans away from drinking tea. In 1800, the average American drank a least as much tea as his predecessor in 1770. The Tea Party did little to create US national identity; that process took decades. Giving up British material culture— "unbecoming British"—took just as long. Tea boycotts were disagreements among fellow Britons; they were incredibly porous and did little to alter consumption.[1]

This should not be surprising. In the eighteenth century, trade between states did not automatically end when they were at war, nor did consumers easily make market decisions on political grounds. In the Seven Years' War (1756–1763), Philadelphia, New York, and Rhode Island merchants traded with enemy French ports, enriching themselves and providing colonial consumers with cheap rum and sugar.[2] The British state struggled to stop this trade, for many merchants and colonists saw this as business, not treason. Politicizing trade and consumption was difficult in 1760. So, too, in 1774.

Yet tea mattered deeply in the Revolution. Destroying it was the Patriots' way to protest taxation without representation, the East India Company's monopoly, and parliamentary infringement on colonists' British rights. After the destruction of the tea in Boston in 1773, destroying tea could signal support for the Tea Party. When, in 1774, Parliament's Coercive Acts punished Boston and mandated the East India Company be reimbursed for the destroyed tea, burning tea showed solidarity with Boston and resistance to Parliament. Congress's Continental Association banned tea imports (and all imports from Great Britain and Ireland) beginning December 1, 1774, banned consumption of said goods after March 1, 1775, and banned exports to Britain, Ireland, and the British Caribbean after September 10, 1775. Patriots claimed the Association bound all colonists, whether they signed it or not.[3] Hanging, drowning, and burning tea symbolized conformity to the Association, support for Congress, and acceptance of Patriot legitimacy. The Association was the most important expression of pre-war support for the Patriot cause and America's founding attempt at prohibition. This was one set of ways tea mattered.

Like Prohibition 150 years later, the tea ban was a failure. It failed because of another way tea mattered: as a drink for North America's growing consumer classes. Because of this, Patriots enforced their ban on tea in word more than deed. Merchants sold tea under the counter, and colonists drank it in private. The boycott fizzled out. When Congress re-authorized tea in April 1776, it reasoned that because so many colonists ignored prohibition the ban was meaningless. Like the colonial officials who had tried enforcing the ban on trade with French Caribbean fifteen years earlier, Patriots found colonists had a greater appetite for consumption than politics.

Tea was no less symbolically important for this, and tea's central, symbolic role in the Continental Association linked to other issues, such as how Patriots mobilized the populace and controlled the distribution of information. Signing the Association functioned like a test oath, even as Patriots policed actual consumer compliance lightly. Checking whether colonists lived up to their claims about not consuming tea and British manufactures would have alienated the populace. By contrast, news of tea protests, emphasizing popular enthusiasm, printed in Patriotic newspapers, and distributed in the new Patriotic postal system, could build support for the "common" cause. The Association was signed in a public performance designed to mobilize the public. Tea burnings were often reenacted a second time in print. Even if townsfolk did not burn all their tea and no one in power ever heard of their protest, the spectacle acted out Patriotism and built a sense of shared experience. But one must read Patriotic accounts of these events with care.[4]

Tea protests were not signs of American "national consciousness," as Timothy Breen argues.[5] Abstention did not make US citizens. Breen, one of the most influential scholars on the intersection of consumption and politics in the American Revolution, brings new insights to the study of consumer politics. His work, however, relies heavily on examples of colonists denouncing tea and other consumer goods. These denunciations usually occurred only when a colonist was caught. But is being caught evidence of the ban's enforcement? Or of its violation? Breen does not say, but the few who were caught imply a larger body of consumers who were not. Breen also relies on Patriotic newspaper reports without any awareness that Patriots, like other political actors, presented self-serving accounts of events to the public. Tea renouncements and Patriotic essays were public speech about non-consumption, precisely the ideological content from which Breen attempted to distance himself. Much of this speech used the idea of virtue to connect private non-consumption to the public good, but the evidence that colonists were virtuous enough to affect the public weal is lacking. Breen provides little evidence for what colonists did about the things they supposedly boycotted—not a single merchant's papers are consulted, nor are diaries used to show how colonists behaved during non-consumption. Yet appreciating the gulf between public pledges and private commercial and consumer behavior is fundamental to any understanding of the revolutionary era boycotts or the Association.

Histories of the Association usually ignore how non-consumption worked on the ground. Without this, how can we say that non-consumption "mobilized people"? Mobilized whom? To do what? To what degree? To what end? The Patriot wish that non-consumption were popular is not proof that it was. If such mobilization created a "national consciousness," why would that be an American one? The road from destroying the tea to the "making of America" or declaring independence was indirect, and the bonds of identity and ideology that would unite Americans were only just begun. Here, Breen "assumes the nation before the fact." The emergent United States was contested and changing. It included twelve colonies in 1774 and added Georgia and parts of Quebec in 1775, while declining to aid rebels in Nova Scotia and remaining strikingly friendly to Bermuda. It excluded Boston in 1775, lost Quebec and New York City in 1776, and omitted Florida for a generation. It is not the America we know. Late colonial tea politics played out among fellow Britons and were played out before US independence.[6]

The Association constituted economic policy, with the boycott often seen as a way to coerce Britain economically. For merchants, the most important provisions of the Association were its bans on trade with Britain, Ireland, and the British West Indies, and its ban on the slave trade. This, and the anti-merchant tone of some Patriot rhetoric, has led some scholars to see a farmer-versus-merchant or plantation-owner-versus-merchant dynamic in the Association.[7] In this reading, farmers and plantation owners used the Association to claw back wealth from merchants.

Patriot enforcement of the Association certainly focused on merchants. But Patriots made compliance in merchants' self-interest. Surviving committee records suggest that Patriots generally did not inspect merchants' books without suspicion or cause. A merchant's ledger might contain embarrassing information about other Patriots and was best kept shut. Committees rarely sought out individual consumers for violations. Congress and the committees never admitted to turning a blind eye, which would have sapped the motivation of the true believers who boycotted sincerely. Yet few, if any, of the colonists to whom merchants recorded selling banned tea in 1775 were caught because Patriots rarely looked.[8] Patriots talked against tea but enabled those merchants to continue selling what they had on hand. The main barrier to selling tea was limited supply, not Patriotic action against retailers or lack of colonial demand.

This is to say that non-importation was an "effectual security" against non-consumption (the logic behind the Boston Tea Party), despite Congress's claim that it was the other way around.[9] Congress flattered colonists by saying it relied on their virtue, and could point to its own success blocking new imports as "proof" that colonists were virtuous non-consumers.

The Association banned all tea (no matter when or from whence it arrived), making it a totem. It banned most other goods by place and time: woolens were not banned, just British and Irish ones imported after December 1, 1774. The Association thus allowed a version of some of the most-consumed imports (cloth, sugar, coffee, and rum) to be imported and sold.[10] Looking at a merchant's ledger, it is impossible to tell whether the "coffee" or "merchandise" consumers bought complied with the Association (or with British trade regulations). Only tea was banned, no matter when and whence it came.

Consider, by way of contrast, Madeira wine, which one imagines could have been a bigger part of boycott politics. British merchants dominated the Madeira trade. Parliament taxed colonial wine imports. And the Association banned wine imported from the "Wine Islands." Madeira was a distinct type of wine, meaning that a ban on wine from the island of Madeira was, in effect, a ban on Madeira as a commodity. Boycotting Madeira could have become a symbolically straightforward way to engage in consumer politics. It was not. For non-consumption applied only to wine imported after December 1, 1774. Colonists could drink Madeira still on hand, which was convenient since colonists preferred to buy Madeira young and age it themselves. So they could drink older wine they had already aged and wait out the Association as they aged their youngest purchases. In October 1775, Thomas Jefferson settled his bills upon leaving Philadelphia after the Second Continental Congress. This included paying his Madeira tab, which he accrued while non-consumption was in effect. Jefferson was scrupulous about the Association and took care not to consume tea and other banned goods during the ban. But there was no contradiction here, as this particular Madeira was permitted.[11]

No one at consumer protests smashed bottles of Madeira, discarded their sugar canisters, or burned British-made woolens; such goods were allowed for sale and use, if already imported. They may also have been too valuable to destroy. And the articles of the rich: fine clothes, furniture, chariots, and paintings, these baubles of Britain were put away in response to Patriots' sumptuary orders, not burned. Tea was the lone good to which non-consumption applied without exception. Its boycott became a sign of support for the Association as a whole, and tea and the tea canister became street protest icons in a way that Madeira, rum, sugar, and coffee could not be (it was hard to tell banned and permitted coffee apart just by looking). Even tea was often set aside, not destroyed. This is not quite the boycott we had imagined.

Individual merchant violators of the Association, especially violators of non-importation, did get in trouble. Andrew Sprowle led the Virginia Meeting of Merchants, a sort of chamber of commerce, in signing the Continental Association in November 1774. In December 1775, he was caught ordering goods from Britain. Patriots discovered this from reading his mail, a procedure they reserved for persons they already suspected. Sprowle had attracted suspicion by quartering Governor Dunmore's troops. His "unfriendly disposition" when answering the Norfolk County committee's queries left him shunned in August 1775.[12] Thus, broader suspicion that he opposed the common cause drew attention to violations of the Association, not the other way around.

Merchants had economic reasons to comply with the Association. The ban on exports to Britain started eight months after the ban on imports, holding merchants' future sales of goods in Britain hostage to their present compliance with non-importation in the colonies. Non-importation from Britain and Ireland, in turn, was easily enforced—local customs ledgers recorded all legal arrivals, and Patriots inspected these books. This motivated merchants. When John Norton's *Virginia* arrived in Yorktown with tea in November 1774, Patriots threw the tea overboard; then, for a real punishment, they prevented Norton's agents from loading tobacco for the return. Norton, who lived in London, begged for forgiveness and thereby secured tobacco cargoes for subsequent ships. His motivation was financial. Delaying non-exportation allowed Virginia merchants to collect large amounts of tobacco this way, effectively collecting debt from the colony's plantation owners.[13] The Association did not curtail New England and mid-Atlantic colonies' substantial trade with Continental

Europe and the non-British Caribbean. And it allowed South Carolina's rice exports to continue. All these trades were far larger than the tea trade. A merchant who imported tea and other banned goods risked these other businesses being boycotted.

War and Parliament's 1775 trade restrictions affected non-consumption under the Association. The Continental Association might have ended up being more forcefully anti-merchant or more broadly enforced, but less than two months after non-consumption began, war replaced the boycott at the center of Patriot attention. Restrictions on consumption remained in force after the Battles of Lexington and Concord. However, they were no longer core symbols of resistance or indicators of what Patriots planned to do next. Defense associations, wherein one publicly pledged to defend the King or Congress with arms, mattered more. Militia musters displaced tea parties. Guns and powder horns eclipsed tea canisters as symbols, allowing colonists to turn tea back into an apolitical consumer good. Jane Merritt describes this as tea's repatriation, but sometimes just ignoring the politics of tea and British goods was enough to ensure they remained an important part of post-revolutionary US consumer culture.[14] Patriot press releases continued to talk of non-consumption, particularly of tea, but a considerable space existed between what Patriots said about tea in the press and what colonists did about it.

In 1775, support for Congress mattered more than support for the boycott. This is not surprising. But the way wartime politics severed the link between the consumer politics of 1774 and independence in 1776 is easily missed. The wartime politics of 1775 saved the Patriot movement. The consumer protests of 1774 were, on their own, fraught and probably insufficient. Boycotts are difficult to sustain. A prior boycott had collapsed in 1770, setting the Patriot cause back considerably. Such a collapse happened in 1775, too. Had that collapse been in peacetime, when the boycott was the primary form of resistance to the British government, it would have implied Patriot acquiescence. Instead, the war was a stronger and more direct way to resist Parliament and fight for the common cause, and it let non-consumption collapse almost unnoticed.

War elevated merchants' political value. Merchants had been smuggling in arms and ammunition since late 1774. After the Battles of Lexington and Concord, smuggling became vital to the cause. Weeks after non-exportation began, Congress's Secret Committee allowed exemptions to its trade regulations for merchants returning from Europe with arms, a smuggling business that overlapped significantly with the tea trade. Smugglers brought foodstuffs (especially salt for preserving meat) and other goods past Royal Navy patrols. These importers ameliorated shortages and price spikes that threatened Patriot popularity.[15]

Congress had secured merchants' non-importation by offering them continued exports to Britain until September 1775. Once this "carrot" expired, Parliament helped perpetuate (or perhaps took the blame for) non-importation by passing the Prohibitory Act in December 1775. This act withdrew the King's protection from all shipping belonging to the thirteen colonies, making any colonial vessel a lawful prize to British privateers and helping a weak Congress enforce its own ban on imports from Britain.

Finally, the congressional reauthorization of tea consumption also allowed new tea to be brought into the colonies, provided it was British tea taken as prize, a loophole allowing merchants to explain away any tea kept in East India Company crates. The allowance for seized goods likely provided cover for a significant smuggling trade between British-occupied New York City and upstate New York, beginning in late 1776. By this time, riots about tea and food centered not on eschewing but demanding them. Rioters objected to shortages and high prices and demanded more consumer goods [16]

Beyond consumer politics, the Association was an act of political economy, and here Patriots worked to ensure that tea did not become a symbol of their own economic misrule. There was a risk of this, since non-consumption and non-importation threatened colonists' standard and cost of living. Patriots responded by regulating prices, but the worry that escalating tea prices might backfire on Patriots was a through-line from late 1773 to late 1776.

This book breaks new ground in several areas, bringing in new sources, new locations and events, and new interpretations of old ones. It reveals the survival and ultimate consumption of the East India Company's tea in Boston and Charleston and their importance in the politics of 1774. It eschews a Boston-centered frame that can overdetermine events. It analyses tea advertisements, tea prices, and merchant ledgers to reconsider the relationship between merchants and the Association. It reveals both the continuation of tea consumption during the tea ban and the importance of the war in ending non-consumption. In many histories of the Revolution, we read that the Association takes effect, and then our attention turns to the fighting at Lexington and Concord without finding out what happened to the Association. Only in the last decade has anyone noticed that the tea ban ended at all.

This book is also intimately connected to two recent books. It concurs strongly with the analysis in Jane Merritt's *The Trouble with Tea: The Politics of Consumption in the Eighteenth-Century Global Economy*. Merritt's book appeared after the early drafts of this one were complete. Merritt was the first to note how the tea ban ended, an analysis this book develops. Both books agree that in 1773–1776, tea consumerism triumphed over politics. Whereas Merritt examines a century, this book thoroughly examines the years 1773–1776. The second book is Mary Beth Norton's *1774: The Long Year of Revolution*, which examines the period between the East India Company's tea shipments and the Battle of Lexington. *1774* and *Tea* agree on the political importance of tea, with this book also examining how tea politics played out in wartime.[17]

Colonists did not uniformly aspire to make tea a political symbol. In 1774, Patriots struggled to politicize tea, a product that retained an apolitical consumer value. In seeing tea bonfires as the mass participation of consumers who refused to consume, it is easy to take Patriot assertions that anti-tea rallies "spoke" for the people at face value. Tea rallies were acts of "conspicuous nonconsumption," which is to say they were performances. Ignoring the performative aspect occludes colonists' ambivalence toward politics and makes it easy to overlook the coercion that helped some to agree that Patriots and Sons of Liberty spoke for "the People." Tea was an important symbol, and rhetoric about tea must be taken seriously on its own terms and also examined critically, lest one mistake Patriots' wish for a ban for the actual deed.[18]

Careful chronology is also vital. The period from the Boston Tea Party to the Declaration of Independence was revolutionary. It is easy to blur the rapid political changes pertaining to tea between 1773 and 1776 into a single, monolithic, anti-tea moment. Worse, one could equate the political significance of tea in 1773–1776 with its significance in earlier periods of the imperial crisis.[19] But Bostonians who drank tea on the night of the Tea Party could not be "defiant" of Patriot authority (as one prominent historian of the Association has claimed) because Boston Patriots had not yet banned tea. It is also easy to blur geographical differences, creating a pan-Continental image of a period when colonies were different. This risks an anachronistic teleology toward independence inappropriate for events in 1774 or 1775. It sacrifices local differences and changes over time for a static, undifferentiated sense of Patriot opposition to tea. It accounts poorly for the politicization of tea and, worse, completely ignores the process by which tea ceased to be political. Tea changed twice in the Revolution— first into a political good, then back to a non-political one.[20]

Boston was not the only city to have a tea party in 1773. Others, like Charleston, South Carolina's, were just as important. The East India Company's tea survived both tea parties, and it is time to re-examine them (chapter 1). Tea protests and smuggling had a history in the colonies before 1773 (chapter 2). In 1774, tea politics took many turns, summarized in chapter 3. One of these turns was the attempt to reimburse the East India Company for its losses in Boston Harbor (chapter 4). This failed. In the second half of 1774, Patriots turned to stopping legal tea importation (chapter 5) and discouraging tea consumption (chapter 6). Patriot print sources—committee press releases, essays, news of protests carefully reworked by Patriotic editors—flooded the public sphere. For non-consumption to work, for colonists to feel they truly shared a common cause and worked in concert with people hundreds of miles away, the Revolution had to be publicized.[21] Oddly enough, a useful antidote to this is the advertisements for tea that often appeared in the very newspapers that denounced the drink (chapter 7). Patriotic propagandists continued to attack tea, alleging that it harmed human health, that it was being forced upon the colonies by the King (chapter 8), and that it was a womanish drink (chapter 9)—the suggestion being that if women were strong enough to give up tea, any man who could not stop was a wimp. Yet even formal prohibition of tea consumption (March 1, 1775 to April 13, 1776) was lightly enforced (chapter 10) and widely violated (chapter 11), leaving Congress to effectively repeal the ban (chapter 12).

PART ONE

Late Colonial Tea Consumption

CHAPTER 1

The Tea Party That Wasn't

The *London* carried 70,000 pounds of the East India Company's tea across the Atlantic Ocean to South Carolina, anchoring in Charleston Harbor on December 2, 1773. In response, Christopher Gadsden and his Sons of Liberty put up notices against the tea's landing, roused men in the taverns, and called for a meeting the next day.[1]

Charlestonians met in the Great Hall of the Exchange, the center of city life. Standing where Broad Street met the harbor, its public arcade opened in multiple directions onto both road and sea.[2] The customs house was inside, the vaulted basement provided storage, and the great room above suited public gatherings. Faced with the "UNCONSTITUTIONAL" act of "raising a revenue upon us, WITHOUT OUR CONSENT," colonists debated what to do. Several of the wealthier men took the Patriotic side and signed an agreement against the tea:

> We, the underwritten, do hereby agree, not to import, either directly or indirectly, any teas that will pay the present duty, laid by an act of the British Parliament for the purpose of raising a revenue in America.[3]

Several—but not all.

Next, the meeting summoned merchants Roger Smith, Peter Leger, and William Greenwood Jr. They were the Company's consignees, the men designated to receive and sell the tea on the Company's behalf. They faced, in their words, a "great majority" against landing the Company's tea, and against landing any duty tea at all. Peter Timothy, editor of the *South Carolina Gazette*, claimed the consignees refused to receive the tea, but Timothy sometimes shaded the truth for the Patriotic cause. The consignees did not land the Company's tea then and there, but they did not give up their roles as consignees, either. After the meeting, the consignees promised the Company they would do "every thing in our Power (Consistent with the Safety and Future Welfare of our Family)" to advance the Company's interests. They remained in their roles another two weeks. They also noted that the meeting decided "to Wink at every Pound [of tea] Smuggled in," so as not to actually run out of it. This created a glaring "Inconsistency," and, Leger and Greenwood reported, the "Merchants in general have determined against it."[4]

The next day, a committee deputed by the meeting waited on the rest of the city's merchants, asking them to sign the non-importation agreement. According to Timothy, "upwards of" fifty signed. Others contrived to be absent when the committee called, or put them off with requests for "a little more time to consider of the matter." Some radical planters and landholders helped these merchants along by agreeing not to "import, buy or sell" duty teas, or buy from any merchant who did.[5]

It is easy to overestimate these early agreements, which were partial and full of loopholes. Merchants who did not sign could ignore them. The planters' agreement against buying tea allowed them to drink the tea they had already bought. Timothy never indicated exactly who signed, and we do not know whether those who did sign were influential, representative, or even involved in the tea trade.[6]

The East India Company had sent tea to South Carolina. That the *Company* sent tea was new, but Charleston merchants had been ordering tea from third parties in London for years: all of it taxed by Parliament, all of it originating from East India Company auctions—20,000 pounds of tea in 1772. Leger and Greenwood agreed to take on the Company's tea in 1773 in part because "nothing was said against the Importation of tea" at the time. When one of Smith's business ventures advertised duty tea for sale in autumn 1773, it did so without incident. Any move against the *London's* tea framed in terms of the East India Company or taxation without representation made sense only if all this other tea legally imported from Britain were also stopped. This was why the non-importation agreement emphasized teas "that will pay the present duty" rather than just the Company's shipments. "Junius Brutus," writing in the *South Carolina Gazette*, urged fellow colonists to go further and undertake "a *total disuse of India Teas*" until the tax was repealed and proposed that any tea on hand be "made a *public bonfire* of." In this he included tea on the *London*, other

British tea, and tea smuggled from other countries. It was not a good sign for Junius Brutus, however, that three merchant firms advertised tea in the same issue of the *Gazette* that ran his letter.[7]

Charleston merchants formed a Chamber of Commerce, which met on December 9 and selected a leadership of twenty-one prominent merchants. The chamber was not inherently conservative; rather it sought a stronger voice for merchants in "Disputes relative to Trade and Navigation" and took up the concerns of the broader group of merchants who had been importing tea from Britain, seeking equal treatment from the Company and from Patriots. As Leger and Greenwood explained, "When every Merchant Imported his own teas, and Calmly paid the Duty," there was no trouble. But "the moment it appeared" the Company would send its own tea directly to a select few in Charleston, "every [other] Man out of Trade held up against it. Right or Wrong," fearing a large shipment directly from the Company would ruin their own part of the business. Charleston merchants similarly objected to a Patriot ban on legal tea that left smuggled tea untouched. As Smith, Leger, and Greenwood reported, "Unless Smuggling is altogether Prevented and every Man" who imports tea, whether legally or illegally, "be on a[n equal] footing, they [i.e., other merchants] will as usual Import" tea. This put paid to the agreement then circulating not to import duted tea.[8]

Patriots soon realized how ineffective their early efforts had been. On December 3, upstairs in the Great Hall of the Exchange, radicals had argued their case. But downstairs, merchants landed "private" "parcels of tea" from the *London* and two other vessels, paid the duties at the customs house in the same Exchange, and carted the containers right by "the meeting of the people, in their conveyance to the respective owners." Even Timothy admitted merchants "had not *desisted* from *importing Teas* subject to the odious Duty."[9]

Charlestonians could not even agree what the December 3 meeting had agreed upon. So, a new "General Meeting" was called for December 17, with various groups organizing in advance. Timothy claimed the "unpopular" side had "*very few*" advocates, that the meeting unanimously agreed that the tea on the *London* "ought not to be landed," and that the consignees should not receive it. But William Henry Drayton recalled differently. "Many friends to liberty and opposers to the views of Administration, considered the East-India Company in the light of a private merchant; and therefore, were of opinion, that no exception ought to be taken to the landing of their tea; since, none had been taken to landing [tea] from private merchants in London." Tea had "always been landed, and had paid the duties here." Why fuss now?[10]

The consignees made their case, arguing that it was "unjust" "to the Company" to allow "others and not them to Order teas to be Shipt here" and that banning some but not all tea sent from Britain was uniquely "Injurious" to the consignees. A ban on Company tea also violated their right to manage their business and property how they pleased "by depriving us of the Liberty of Receiving on Commission" tea from the Company. At minimum, the consignees argued, the Company's tea should be landed and stored, pending the Company's advice, and they deployed "every Argument and all the Interest in our Power" to that end.[11]

The consignees failed. The December 17 meeting upheld the ban on the *London*'s tea.

Lacking legal authority, the meeting enforced this by coopting tea importers to the Patriot cause. The consignees finally resigned their role as custodians of the Company's tea. They noted to the Company that they did this under duress, lest they become "Enemys to our Country and be Subject to the insults of many rascally Mobbs Convened in the Dark high charged with Liquor to do every act of Violence their mad Brain could invent." This was the truth, or at least part of it. But the consignees also gave up their role to preserve their core business. For Leger and Greenwood, this entailed selling Carolina planters' rice and indigo in Europe and European dry goods in Carolina. Roger Smith preserved his slave-trading business. But, keen to avoid a reputation for unreliability (reputation was key for merchants corresponding overseas), the consignees emphasized to the Company that giving up the tea was a last resort.[12]

The meeting also put other tea merchants, whether legal importer or smuggler, on the "same footing" by resolving that Carolinians had six months "to consume all the Teas now on hand," after which "no Teas should be used." News of resistance to the Company's tea in Boston, New York, and Philadelphia arrived that day and may have inspired a stronger stance. But the meeting was not as harsh as it seemed and was merchant-friendly in important ways: it adopted the Chamber of Commerce's request that the legal and smuggled tea be treated equally and even took on a secondary request of the Chamber: providing lag time for merchants to sell what tea they had on hand. Tea exports from Britain to North and South Carolina fell from 22,916 pounds in 1772 to 13,655 pounds in 1773 (excluding the Company's tea on the *London*) as merchants anticipated that vessel's arrival. Tea prices rose in several North American ports in late 1773 and may well have risen in Charleston, too. Holding the Company's tea off the market kept tea prices high—but merchants could take advantage of these high prices only if they avoided Company tea and abided by any other Patriot trade restrictions. As a sweetener, merchants could even import a little bit more: the meeting resolved that tea "ought" not to be imported but set no clear date for non-importation to start, with a final determination pushed off to a later date. This was a negotiated solution.[13]

Patriots wanted to turn this solution into a proper non-consumption agreement. Their "general agreement," "to be entered into by every [white] Inhabitant of this province"—male and female—built off the meeting's resolve that "no Teas ought to be imported from any Place whatsoever, while the offensive Act remains unrepealed," and bound signatories not to "import, buy, sell, or use" tea or similarly taxed goods. Signatories also promised not to buy "any" other goods from merchants who imported dutied tea. This agreement, however, was put off and only adopted later.[14]

Though the consignees had given up their role in the tea, the ship's master, Alexander Curling, could not. Curling had given bond in England for the tea's delivery to America. He could get his bond money back only by returning to England with a customs certificate from the Americas showing he had landed the tea there. Charleston Patriots had found a way to work with the consignees and other merchants, but they used British navigation laws to make an example of Curling. Curling had attended the meeting on December 3. When he laid out his "Difficulties" returning to England, he was told that it was his problem. The consignees hoped he could return without "Forfeiting" the bond, but for Patriots, forcing Curling to forfeit the bond could deter future captains from carrying dutied tea in the future. According to law, Curling had twenty days after the London's arrival to unload it, or else the customs collector would impound the tea for non-payment of tax.[15]

As the deadline approached, the Sons of Liberty sent Curling anonymous letters, threatening to burn his vessel unless it pulled away from the wharf. They sent the wharf owners and the owners of nearby vessels similar missives promising a violent denouement.[16] But nothing happened.

On December 22, Customs Collector Robert Halliday seized, landed, and stored the tea for non-payment of duty with the assistance of the sheriff and his men. This was the great step the Massachusetts Patriots prevented by throwing Boston tea shipments into the harbor. It took five hours, from 7 until after noon, to store the London's tea in the northernmost cellar of the Exchange, during which time, "There was not the least disturbance." Lieutenant Governor William Bull claimed, "The warmth of some was great, many were cool, and some differed in the reasonableness and utility" of fighting the collector. Bull thought the merchants might even have been able to sell the tea, had they not been so "hasty" to back down. Gadsden's Sons of Liberty explained that they were surprised it had happened so early in the morning.[17]

Such was the Charleston Tea Party—the tea party that wasn't.

Charleston's was one of four tea shipments the East India Company sent to North America in 1773. Each met a different fate. Bostonians, fearing tea might later be sold if the customs collector impounded it, boarded the Dartmouth,

Eleanor, and *Beaver* and tossed their tea in Boston Harbor—the Boston Tea Party. Less well known, the *William* wrecked on Cape Cod while bringing tea to Boston. The *Polly* brought tea to Philadelphia, but threats of violence and 8,000 people (the "greatest Meeting of the People ever known in this City") compelled the captain to return to England before entering the Port of Philadelphia's customs area. The *Nancy* brought tea to New York, but only in April, months after the moment had passed.[18] Of these cities, only in Boston was tea destroyed.

Reception of the Boston Tea Party

Charleston's response to the tea is not considered as canonical or remembered with the same intensity as the Boston Tea Party—either by the American public or historians. Compared to Massachusetts Patriots, South Carolina Patriots can look "embarrassed" by how their tea party turned out. "Since the Bostonians have destroyed their Teas," Leger and Greenwood concurred, "our People seem more dissatisfied & are now sorry they sufferd it to be landed." And yet its landing "under the direction of the Collector," rather than the consignees, ameliorated this. The Charleston committee claimed to be certain the landed tea would not be drunk. As Timothy explained, the people "were perfectly quiet" when the tea was landed because they "*did*" and "*do still* confidently *rely*, upon its remaining locked up." If only "the Bostonians could have trusted to their own Virtue, Suffered the Tea to be Landed, & refused to purchase any part of it, as you have done in Charles Town," South Carolina's Henry Laurens wrote, then "the Laugh & derision would have been turned against Administration" rather than Boston.[19]

Charleston Patriots relied on more than virtue. The tea could be released if the customs collector auctioned off the tea. Colonists and customs officials negotiated authority at the waterfront, and so Charleston Patriots reached understandings that prevented the tea's release, keeping it in the Exchange at least for the next several months. First, the Charleston consignees had given up their role in the tea. Second, merchants were deterred from bidding on the Company's tea by the threat not to buy other goods from them. At the same time, merchants who had tea and did not bid on the Company tea would be able to sell their remaining supplies at inflated prices. Third, His Majesty's collector of customs awaited instructions from London, perhaps with an off-the-books understanding to let the matter rest until then. In the interval, Charleston Patriots could shore up support for tea non-importation.[20]

The Boston Tea Party was exceptionally violent in part because Boston Patriots could reach no such understandings with Boston consignees and customs collectors. No one had died, but, as John Adams pointed out, people could have. Other colonists, even other Patriots, objected to its general destructiveness. Because of this, the Boston Tea Party did not rally colonists to a common cause in 1773. It divided them.[21]

To be sure, some Patriots approved. "Huzzai" wrote Samuel Chandler in his journal when news of the Boston Tea Party reached him. Some colonists had tea parties of their own. Three nights after Boston, Patriots in Marshfield, Massachusetts took tea from a local ordinary and a deacon's cellar. They brought the tea to a hilltop, placed it on a stone, prayed, and burned it. The spot is now canonized as Tea Rock Hill. In Charlestown, Massachusetts, Patriots collected tea and burned it in the town center before a crowd. John Hancock claimed, "No one Circumstance could possibly have Taken place more effectually to Unite the Colonies than" sending the Company tea, which is "universally Resented here."[22]

Yet many colonists were outraged by the destruction of the tea. The conservative Massachusetts Provincial Treasurer, Harrison Gray, thought the destruction of the tea "gross immoral" "malignant atrocious" and literally "*diabolical*." Patriot elites also disapproved, including George Washington, Benjamin Franklin (who called the Tea Party "an Act of violent Injustice"), Patrick Henry, and Richard Henry Lee. Henry Laurens was not surprised "wily Cromwellians" went to extremes in Boston and preferred Charleston's "prudent" approach. James Madison preferred Philadelphians' "discretion." In Philadelphia, the crowd that sent the *Polly* back to England voiced its approval of the Boston Tea Party, but the committee disapproved on behalf of the "substantial thinking part" of society. Conservative Peter Oliver falsely imagined that Boston was "generally condemned." The ever-elusive silent majority would be a common conservative fallacy in the years ahead, but disapproval of the Tea Party was real.[23]

Colonists responded to the destruction of the tea in many ways: support, opposition, ambivalence, and indifference. Connecticut Reverend Israel Holly noted "the divided sentiments among us" on the matter. Judging from the resolves they passed in the weeks after the Boston Tea Party, New England towns did not reach a consensus. Watertown and Montague, Massachusetts, supported the destruction of the tea; Freetown and Marshfield, Massachusetts opposed it. Littleton, Massachusetts was so divided it abolished its committee of correspondence altogether. Yet most town resolves made no mention of the destruction of the tea. These resolves opposed the Tea Act and/or urged a tea boycott. Some scholars read these positions as endorsements of the Tea Party. But town resolves were lengthy lists of positions the towns agreed upon. If they had wanted to explicitly endorse destroying the tea, they could have done so by simply adding another resolve to their list. Instead, their silence spoke to their division on the matter. Bostonians were divided, too. Merchant John Rowe, the owner of the tea ship *Eleanor* (but not a recipient of the tea), served on various Patriot committees concerned with the tea. He noted, "The affair of Destroying the Tea makes Great Noise in the Town." It was "a Disastrous Affair & some People are much Alarmed," one way or another.[24]

Marshfield's *Resolves* condemned Boston's destruction of the tea, demanded the perpetrators be arrested, and implied opposition to the little Marshfield tea party. But then fifty Marshfield Patriots repudiated these resolves in the *Massachusetts Spy*. In this tit-for-tat Marshfield foreshadowed the crisis of authority that many colonies would face as men on each side claimed men on the other no longer spoke for them. It also pointed to the appeal of uniting and expanding one side of the dispute and imposing one faction's views upon the other, rather than even trying to speak for the whole across a widening political spectrum. The Boston Tea Party's canonization in later years (and the little canonizations that went with it, like Marshfield's Tea Rock Hill) was an example of winners writing history. They reimagined a deeply contested event into an uncontested one, making one faction's views appear to be a consensus. The idea that colonists broadly supported the destruction of the tea is a myth.[25]

Colonists across North America disagreed about the virtues of destroying the Company's tea. It should not be surprising that an attack on property would alarm well-to-do and middling Patriots, or that, since the American Revolution divided colonists, the event that sparked it divided them, too.[26] Destroying the tea was popular politics, in the sense that it involved the lower orders, but this does not necessarily mean that it was "popular" in the sense of having broad approval from the populace. When Timothy described Patriots as the "popular" side, his was a deliberate and common Patriot obfuscation of these two senses of the word.

Two signs of the continued divisiveness of the Tea Party were Patriots' attempts (1) to argue that it could have been worse and (2) to blame others. If the tea on the *Dartmouth*, *Eleanor*, and *Beaver* had not been destroyed, the customs officers' unloading of it, backed by troops and opposed by an angry crowd, would have led to "bloodshed." And in any case, Bostonians only had to go to such extremes because, as Boston printer John Boyle explained, the consignees had "frustrated" the efforts of "The People . . . to preserve the property of the East-India Company, and return it safely to London." As the Continental Congress explained nearly a year later, the tea was destroyed "because Governor [Thomas] Hutchinson would not suffer it to be returned." Customs officials came in for blame as well. Boston committeemen said much the same in their letter to the Philadelphia and New York committees, making no mention of the option of storing the tea. But to deny the Tea Party was their fault was to concede that it was blameworthy.[27]

History and Memory

The dominance of the Boston Tea Party in historical memory obscures the various ways Patriots approached the tea in other cities and the various ways colonists responded to Boston Patriots. Reactions to both mapped poorly onto later political categories like Patriot or Loyalist. Destroying the tea engendered varying measures of support, opposition, division, ambivalence, and indifference. Tea was not always the most important issue in the winter of 1773–1774. Connecticuters were more likely to care about their colony's Western expansion than the tea in Boston Harbor. Virginians were exercised about Dunmore's War, and colonists everywhere were concerned about renewed war with Native Americans.[28] The meanings and prominence colonists gave tea and the Tea Party were contingent on future events and varied locally, making the through line, from the Boston Tea Party to independence, a misleading overlay of priorities belonging to a later time.

The destruction of the tea in Boston was influential: news of it reached Philadelphia on December 24, just as events there crescendoed, pushing radicals on.[29] Patriots lionized the Philadelphia case and ignored Charleston's. Subsequent events gave Boston's actions even more importance. Parliament singled out Boston and Massachusetts for punishment in the Coercive Acts, even though tea had been refused in other colonies. Further tea protests in support of Boston after the Coercive Acts became known have been read as support for the Tea Party itself, which was not always true. Tea, by then, had already acquired other meanings. Colonists could rally around Boston in 1774 by burning tea because of the Coercive Acts and despite the Tea Party.

Such complications are forgotten because the Boston Tea Party itself was soon forgotten. The Massachusetts provincial congress did make December 15, 1774, a day of thanksgiving. The next day was the first anniversary of the destruction of the tea, and this thanksgiving hinted at the Tea Party. But Patriots could not celebrate the destruction of the tea—a criminal act—on a holy day. Instead they gave thanks for the common cause "throughout the continent" supporting Boston, and hoped God would restore "harmony and union" between the colonies and Britain. Sermons from this thanksgiving day examined the broader imperial crisis, not the destruction of the tea. By this time, revolutionary attention was moving from tea to gunpowder and militia drills. By 1776 the December 15 commemoration was subsumed by Evacuation Day and the Fourth of July. As Al Young has reminded us, by the end of the American Revolution the Boston Tea Party was no longer commemorated even in Boston. There were no monuments to it. Nor, indeed, was the event even called the "Boston Tea Party" until the 1830s, when it was resurrected in a new wave of historical remembering.[30] At the time, colonists called it "the destruction of the tea."

Yet the Tea Party (a term of convenience that is hard to give up) remained part of private and family history. Perhaps some wrote themselves into the event or misremembered the actions of others as their own, and families recalled progenitors in the best light. The family of William Russell, who claimed to have been a Tea Partier, recalled, perhaps with embellishment, that when he came home from Boston Harbor, he dusted the remaining bits of tea off his shoes into the fire and emptied his tea canister, writing "COFFEE" on one side and "NO TEA" on the other. Samuel Fenno claimed that after destroying the tea he abstained from tea for the rest of his life—remarkable given that his son made a living buying tea in China. Claims of permanent abstention reveal an anachronistic sense of the Tea Party's meaning: jumping from protest against the *Company*'s tea to general abolition and extending that abolition over time. In 1773 it was unclear whether other duty tea would be boycotted, let alone smuggled tea or tea imported into the independent United States. These participants described their roles in destroying the tea as though it were already the "Boston Tea Party" as remembered in the 1830s—a virtuous past seeding an American national present. But the destruction of the tea was a British colonial protest against Parliament, taxes and monopoly, and, for the "rascally" sort who "Convened in the Dark high charged with Liquor," fun.[31]

Famous Last Words

One example of this gap between history and memory is the story of Pennsylvania Sargent Robert Dixon. Dixon served in the invasion of Quebec. In November 1775, outside the Quebec City walls, a cannonball shot off his leg, fatally wounding him. According to one captain's journal, a doctor operated, and "advis'd him to drink tea." "I would not if it would Save my life," were the "Noble spirit'd" soldier's alleged words. He died not long thereafter. John Joseph Henry told another version, claiming the wounded Dixon was carried to the house of an "English gentleman" where the doctor saw him, and the "lady of the house" offered tea. "No, madam," Dixon replied, "it is the ruin of my country."[32]

This story was about nobility in death, but surely Nathan Hale's purported, "I only regret that I have but one life to give for my country" was a better exit line. At least nine fellow soldiers noted Dixon's death in their journals. None heard what he said firsthand. They noted his death because it was interesting, perhaps writing for an audience back home. Such anecdotes had to be ben trovato, not necessarily true. Colonial soldiers, like other Britons, also collected interesting "last words." Dixon's last words, set in Quebec, evoked General James Wolfe's then-famous "I die happy" (upon hearing the French were retreating from Quebec in 1759). Yet of the nine accounts, only the two diaries above mentioned tea. One of the other accounts noted Dixon, an early casualty, died with "great composure and resignation." Yet another noted the "agonies" of his injury and amputation.[33]

Dixon's last words were said to be about incipient American nationalism. According to Henry, Dixon refused tea because of his principles about taxation without representation, "ideas and feelings" which he shared with his "countrymen." "Hence it was, that no male or female, knowing their rights, if possessed of the least spark of patriotism, would deign to taste of that delightful beverage." Henry made opposing tea a way to be American, but this was probably spurious. Henry was an embellisher who dictated his memoir thirty-six years later, and then to his daughter, whom he was trying to impress. Henry and Dixon had served together from Lancaster, Pennsylvania, and Henry may also have found it useful to make Dixon a Lancaster war hero to counter the county's reputation for revolutionary ambivalence and pacifism.[34]

If Dixon did think tea was the "ruin of my country," what country was that? What country did an Anglo from German-speaking Lancaster fighting a colonial civil war in French-speaking Quebec represent? Pennsylvania? America? Britain? What were the relationships between these places? Rhode Islander William Humphrey, who also served at Quebec, described his as the "Provincial" side, not the American one. Sometimes he called opposing troops "English," but he also thought Provincials at Quebec "died in a glorious cause" each and every one "worthy of bearing the name of Englishman." Indeed, some men born in Britain fought on the Provincial side. Taken prisoner after the New Year's Eve raid on Quebec, some of these "old country" men changed sides and enlisted in the King's service. Later, some of these same men deserted the King. Meanwhile, Rhode Islander James Frost privateered the St. Lawrence River on behalf of the Crown. Both sides jockeyed for the support of the French-speaking habitants. (With many habitants wary not of "Britons" or

"Americans" but of their old enemy, *les Bostonnais*.) Imputing, as Henry did, latter-day American nationalism to 1775 misses the ambiguous and sometimes quite different loyalties and motives at play.[35]

If anything, the war detracted from tea's symbolic appeal. Destroying and boycotting tea could, in 1774, be seen as symbolic self-defense against unjust laws, like the Tea Act and Coercive Acts. But warfare provided literal forms of self-defense, which crowded out boycotts as ways to support the common cause. Among symbolic acts, militarily inflected ones, like commemorating the fallen (especially General Richard Montgomery, martyred at Quebec), had a potency that non-consumption could not match.[36] Perhaps the tea in Dixon's story implied rebels would keep their principles until death, but it was also just odd: in a story about Dixon giving up his life, a real sacrifice, renouncing tea was a distraction.

Dixon's story hinted at the other things tea could be. Tea could be tyranny, but also a medical aid (when the doctor carried it), a domestic refinement (when served by the lady), "delightful" (according to Henry), and possibly consumed (since it was available). The province of Quebec did not implement the Association. When Continental troops took Montreal, tea and British goods remained available. Merchant David Salisbury Franks retailed tea to Anglophone and Francophone residents of the city—"Enslow the baker" and Madame Sanguinet—selling larger amounts to other merchants, who presumably sold it retail, in all just over one hundred pounds of tea in the first two months of Patriot rule. Franks was also paymaster general for Continental forces in Montreal. There is no evidence he sold Continental soldiers tea, though his ledger is incomplete. Continentals taken prisoner after the raid on Quebec differed on whether to drink tea. Jeremiah Greenman accepted a present of "Sugar & tea & some money" from the Loyalist (and fellow Newporter) Frost. Henry Dearborn described fellow prisoners receiving port, sugar, and "several pounds of tea," but returning the tea "as the majority thought that it would have been imprudent for us to have drank it." John Joseph Henry recalled sick prisoners collected alms to buy tea. Henry bought tea, too, despite claiming no Patriot would "deign to taste" it.[37]

Popular myths that the destruction of the tea was universally acclaimed or that colonists turned away from tea to coffee in the Tea Party do not help our understanding. A trend in American historical writing to emphasize the Revolution's popularity and downplay Loyalists, a trend only recently arrested, has exacerbated these myths, allowing the Tea Party's association with the Revolution (which entailed, among other things, a civil war) to seem consensual.

Removed from memory and nation-building, it is easier to see the destruction of the tea as just the destruction of some tea. Colonial consumers liked tea and could not agree on whether to stop drinking it. This division was why the tea had to be destroyed.

Tea: The "Invincible Temptation"

Colonists drank tea. By the early 1770s, colonists of almost all classes, save slaves (and possibly indentured servants), consumed it. Housemaids, laundresses, and other domestics drank tea, sometimes borrowing against future pay to buy it. "[E]ven the very paupers" drank tea twice a day, wrote one contemporary. Philadelphia and New York poorhouses provided tea. Inventories of colonial wealth reveal even relatively poor colonists had tea equipage. Tea was drunk in cities and in country towns. Mohawk and Delaware Indians drank it, and some Native Americans had imported teacups. Tea was part of daily meals in middling homes and at the upper echelons of society. At Rhode Island College (later Brown University), the steward provided "tea, coffee, and chocolate" for breakfast and supper.[38]

Tea was a mass consumer good, consumed by at least one-quarter of the free adult population daily and a broader swath less often. Other scholars have estimated colonial tea consumption at between 0.5 and 0.75 pounds per capita per year.[39] These are estimates because most tea in the colonies was smuggled and, therefore, unrecorded.

In their thirst for tea, colonists were very British, for tea was also a mass consumer good in Britain. Inmates at English poorhouses bought tea with their earnings, and the working poor considered tea a necessity. Different classes consumed tea differently, but all social classes in Britain consumed tea by the 1770s. This can be seen in the statistical data and in the mid-century boom of upper-class writers moaning that the lower classes were reaching above their station by drinking tea. Consumption levels in England reached 1.4 pounds per capita per year in the 1770s.[40]

What did tea mean in the colonies? T. H. Breen argues that the wide distribution of tea and other consumer imports in late colonial North America made these items usable in consumer protests. Colonists who were barred from voting might still be consumers and could participate in politics as consumers. In tea there was the potential for a political movement of consumers who refused to consume.[41]

Growing tea consumption made tea protests possible, but tea's popularity also suggested consumers were unlikely to give it up. The breadth of tea consumption made a boycott hard to organize: it had to be broad and sustained to be meaningful, and it had to be stronger than consumers' desire for tea.

This was why Patriots made sure the Boston Tea Party of 1773 was not a boycott: tea was too popular to boycott.[42]

Writers opposing the destruction of the tea pointed this out. If colonists disliked tea, they could avoid it. As Virginia Attorney General John Randolph noted, "If a Commodity which is not approved of be brought to Market, no One will purchase it," leaving little to fear from the tea being landed if it were truly "not approved of." But, as Robert Carter Nicholas asked in reply: "why should we expect to find a larger Portion of public Virtue amongst" Bostonians than anyone else? "Many . . . would have refrained from buying, but other probably could not." Boston Patriots had to destroy the tea because they could not trust other Bostonians to boycott it. Similarly, Massachusetts Patriot James Otis worried New Englanders generally would refuse to "renounce" tea—and that Patriots would have to do it for them. Organizing against the *Polly*, Benjamin Rush worried that if the tea were landed, "it will find its way amongst us." So Philadelphia Patriots sought to stop the tea's landing rather than stop its sale. A desire to buy duties tea was assumed to encompass most colonies. As one candidate for the Virginia provincial convention explained, the assumption in Boston was that if the tea were landed, it would be "sold" somewhere: "if not in New England, to the other colonies in America."[43]

In Boston, Charleston, and Philadelphia in December 1773, Patriots, having railed in the press against tea for months, had to stop the Company's tea to save face. If colonists bought and drank that tea after Patriots had argued so vociferously against it, Patriots would appear to have little hold on the broader populace. As Samuel Adams explained, "Our credit is at stake."[44]

Worse, the abundant and affordable Company tea shipments came during high prices and shortages. Smugglers and legal importers anticipated these shipments by reducing their purchases. As the London firm Hayley and Hopkins explained:

> The India Company are just shiping a large Quantity of Tea for America upon their own Account, for which reason the Merchants here have unanimously agreed not to execute any orders for that article this Fall, as when the Companys Quantity arrives, Tea must be cheaper in America than in England, and you'll be able to supply yourself cheaper than we can ship it. what you order of that article is therefore ommited, which we hope you'll approve.[45]

Supplies fell and prices rose in November and December 1773 in anticipation of the Company's tea flooding the market, which shortage made Company tea even more appealing. One report to the Company's directors exaggerated that "there was no tea then to be bought" in Boston in November 1773. Reverend Samuel Cooper, an influential figure in the Boston Patriotic movement, worried a large supply of tea from the Company, at a time of high tea prices, would be an "almost invincible Temptation" for tea sellers. Nicholas also noted the "Temptation of purchasing [Company tea] at *Half Price,*" compared to what tea had recently sold for.[46] Consumers, having endured a shortage, might like buying more for less.

This shortage led to a paradox: Patriots were both against tea and against it being expensive. In December 1773, "AN OLD PROPHET" advised readers in the *Pennsylvania Gazette* "TO USE NO TEA." Then he argued that the real problem was how expensive tea was, which only mattered if people used it. If "any Person should give to the Sellers more than the usual Price for Tea, he ought to be held up as a mortal Enemy to *American Freedom*" for bidding up the price. A committee confirmed that prices for bohea tea were high and announced that Patriots had pressured retailers not to exceed six and a half shillings a pound (Pennsylvania currency, which was about 3/11 sterling). This was an admonition against further price increases, but not a price cut. Philadelphia wholesale prices had risen 50 percent over 1773, from 4 to 6 shillings per pound, but the margin between 6/ and 6/6 still left retailers profit.[47] The committee blamed engrossers for the shortage, but the admonition to "USE NO TEA" failed to lower demand enough to bring the price back down. (See figure C.1.)

Locking up, destroying, and sending back the Company's tea worsened shortages and prices, risking the Patriots' position with a people yet to support the boycott fully. Patriots needed to appear to address high prices. Price controls did not end shortages, but they deflected blame and made Patriots look like they were doing something. Thus Worcester Patriots denounced merchants for importing tea and for charging "extortion[ate]" prices in March 1774, even as the Patriots' own discouraging attitude toward importation worsened prices. The Little Compton, Rhode Island town meeting reacted to rising bohea prices more straightforwardly by refusing to buy from anyone who charged the new price. It is sometimes thought that because Patriots used price controls they did not fully understand supply and demand. Yet ideas of supply and demand were well established enough for a provincial rector like Samuel Seabury to note that non-importation would raise prices. Price controls, rationing, and "virtue"—the logic of the moral economy—let the Patriots appear heroes, lest the logic of the market economy condemn them.[48]

Drinking the Company's Tea

The biggest myth about the Boston Tea Party is that it destroyed all the tea the Company sent to Boston. The *William*'s tea was salvaged from Cape Cod and brought to Castle William, on an island just two miles from town. Jurisdictional quibbles had prevented officials from storing the tea from the *Dartmouth*, *Eleanor*, and *Beaver* at the castle. After the tea on those vessels was destroyed, saving the *William*'s tea became easier. One of the Boston consignees, Jonathan Clarke, rode out to the cape to oversee salvage. He took the key decision to send the *William*'s tea to Castle Island rather than to Boston proper, informing the other Boston consignees from Cape Cod on December 31, 1773. The castle was an obvious refuge; the other consignees were already holed up there to escape the Boston mob.[49]

On January 1, 1774, the consignees informed Boston customs officers that they would not bring the tea to town or report it at the custom house, as legally required, since it was "utterly out of our power to receive and Sell said Teas." His Majesty's Customs should take whatever "steps" were needed, they added.[50]

This looked like a resignation, and at least one contemporary writer reported that the "gentleman Consignees refused to receive" the tea at the castle. But it was actually a feint, as it allowed customs officers to determine it "our Duty to take possession of said tea" when the tea arrived on January 3 without having to wait the standard twenty days to seize it for non-payment of duty. (One way we know it was a feint is that throughout 1774 the consignees, not the customs commissioners, corresponded with the Company about the tea. Despite myriad claims they had resigned, none of the consignees in any of the cities receiving the tea were truly done with it until the tea was gone—sold, send back, or destroyed. As long as the tea lingered, their reputations as merchants necessitated they do the best they could by it.)[51]

Before making any final determination, Collector Richard Harrison and Comptroller Robert Hallowell sent the surveyor and searcher out to the castle to inspect the tea. They found fifty-four chests and one barrel of tea out of the original fifty-eight chests sent. Deeming the tea "unsafe in the Kings Store in this Town," and fearing the tea would be "destroyed was it to come up the Harbour," customs officers looked for a way to secure it. They first asked Admiral John Montagu to provide protection, then asked Governor Hutchinson and Lieutenant Colonel Leslie, who commanded the regiment at the castle, to store the tea at the castle. The castle offered one of the most secure points in the entire colony. The governor and the colonel agreed, coming to a jurisdictional compromise whereby customs personnel got "the Key of the Room in which it [the tea] is Lodged at the Castle." There it stayed, protected by the army and navy and "in the Custody of the Officers of the Customs for the Security of the Duty thereon," the very outcome the Boston Tea Party was meant to avoid. (See figure 1.1.)[52]

The Boston Tea Party was a forceful refusal of Parliamentary authority. It was also initial and partial, occurring after news reached Boston that "most of the Cargo" had been saved from the *William*. By tossing the remaining tea into the harbor, Boston Patriots sent a message for Patriots on the Cape to do the same and drowned out news that some of the tea had survived with news that the rest had not.[53]

The Boston committee had two public relations problems: hiding news of the salvage of the *William*'s tea and maintaining the right legal distance from the destruction of the *Dartmouth*'s, *Eleanor*'s, and *Beaver*'s tea. Thus, in their letter to the New York and Philadelphia committee (carried by Paul Revere), Boston Patriots pretended they did not know the "people" who "immersed" the tea. They added that the *William* has been "cast on Shore on the back of Cape Cod," omitting that any of the cargo was saved while implying but never saying that the *William*'s tea might be lost. News that the Company's tea had reached dry land in Massachusetts risked enervating the Patriot movement in New York and Philadelphia, where other tea ships were daily expected. It risked implying the destruction of the tea was ineffective and creating a precedent for storing tea elsewhere.[54]

The idea that the *William*'s tea was lost spread from Philadelphia to Charleston, where Peter Timothy informed readers of the *South Carolina Gazette* that "none" of the *William*'s tea was landed. The Boston Tea Party was so effective in obscuring the fact that a customs collector had seized the Company's tea that Boston Patriots could chide Charleston Patriots for permitting the same thing. "How great therefore was our Chagrin," the Boston committee wrote of the landing of the *London*'s tea, to hear that the "Grand Cause was neglected, & your best Intentions render'd abortive?" The New York Sons of Liberty wrote similarly.[55]

News of the safe storage of the *William*'s tea did appear in some newspapers. Writers speculated on what this meant. One Boston writer claimed that because Jonathan Clarke had aided the salvage, storage in Castle William was part of the "original design" to sell it. He promised that "watchfulness will be kept upon this tea." The *New-York Journal* noted the tea "seems to be a matter of consideration, among the consignees" at the castle, wondering, "What shall be done with it?"[56] But the legal details of its storage remained unclear, and the entire story was largely buried. It received nowhere near the attention that the destruction of the tea did, one reason most people today have never heard of it.

As 1774 dawned, the story of the East India Company's tea in North America was not over. Undestroyed Company tea loomed over Boston and

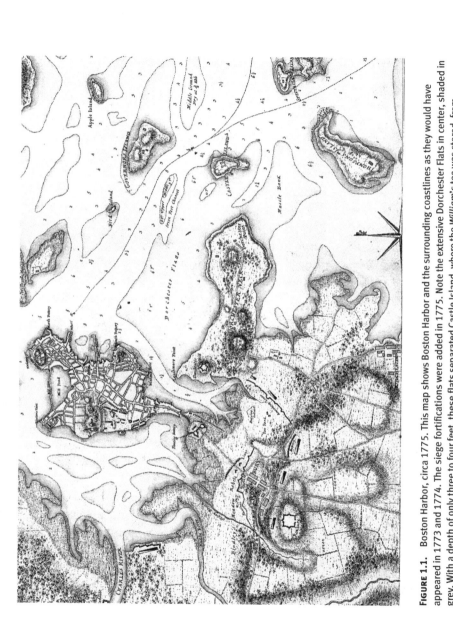

Figure 1.1. Boston Harbor, circa 1775. This map shows Boston Harbor and the surrounding coastlines as they would have appeared in 1773 and 1774. The siege fortifications were added in 1775. Note the extensive Dorchester Flats in center, shaded in grey. With a depth of only three to four feet, these flats separated Castle Island, where the *William*'s tea was stored, from Dorchester Neck. East India Company tea was salvaged from the neck and flats after the Boston Tea Party. Note, too, the flats' distance by road from the central settlement in the Town of Dorchester (several structures of which can be seen at the bottom edge). Source: Page, "Boston, Its Environs and Harbour," Library of Congress, Geography and Map Division.

Charleston—ready to be landed, sold, and drunk, unraveling the Patriot myth that colonists did not want it. It was not the Tea Party alone that shaped the coming year. It was the interaction between the lingering uncertainty of the surviving tea and the potency and urgency of destroying tea that affected colonial politics. The ongoing choice between selling or destroying the remaining Company tea set up a series of all-or-nothing choices in 1774 to repudiate or validate the Tea Party. This affected subsequent tea protests, responses to the Port Act, and the emergent tea boycott. The political turn against tea was a Patriot triumph, but as a vanguard of revolutionary action it required constant vigilance because it was fragile, tentative, partial, and ultimately temporary.

Patriots did well to be concerned, since most of the *William*'s tea was drunk. Some of the 10,000 pounds of tea on the *William* was consumed on Cape Cod in 1774 (where the ship wrecked); most was sold in Boston in 1775, drunk by Massachusetts Loyalists and British soldiers and sailors defending them. (And lest the reader imagine that these consumers do not "count," recall that in 1773 Patriots were concerned with keeping Company tea away from everyone, whatever their politics.) The 70,000 pounds of tea from the *London*, locked up in Charleston, was also drunk. South Carolina Patriots sold it off in 1776 and 1777 to help fund the state. This was a far cry from the idea that only Tories drank tea. In both locations, war upended the peacetime constraints that had prevented the teas from being sold, just as it would upend the logic of non-consumption under the Association.[57]

Colonists destroyed 90,000 pounds of Company tea in Boston Harbor, but between Boston and Charleston they drank nearly as much. Meanwhile, most of it, the 423,556 pounds sent on the *Polly* and *Nancy* to Philadelphia and New York, went back to England, even as large amounts of smuggled tea continued to come into those ports. The Boston Tea Party was significant—it catalyzed the Revolution—but it was not, on its own, representative of what happened to the other tea, or of what it meant.

The stories described above remind us that events did not always proceed as the canonical understanding of Boston Tea Party would have us imagine. The full story was more complex. Authority on the waterfront was still negotiated in 1774. Tea prices affected (and revealed of success of) consumer politics and boycotts, but not always in straightforward ways. Merchant compliance with Patriot demands could derive from ideology or coercion, but also self-interest. Public pronouncements and newspaper coverage of protests and boycotts were often propagandistic, but merchants' advertisements and account books belied this rhetoric. As such, the response to tea was contingent upon local choices, choices that could and did unfold differently in different cases, sometimes even preserving tea cargoes.

Colonists, Patriot and Tory, were united in consumerism, and merchants were the men who best spoke to that consumption. In 1774, 1775, and 1776, politicians had a lot to say about consumption. Patriots banned the import, sale, and consumption of tea and British consumer goods, and sought to leverage colonial non-importation, non-consumption, and non-exportation in their feud with Parliament. Parliamentarians, in turn, restricted the colonies' trade with the rest of the world. The fight with Parliament would go on for years after the Declaration of Independence, but even before independence, Patriots relented on tea; they lifted the ban on April 13, 1776, conceding that colonists saw and treated tea as a consumer good, not a political symbol. After independence, Americans' tea consumption grew with their affluence.

The story of tea was not simply one of Patriots dashing it from Tory lips. Despite the propaganda, colonists from all political perspectives sometimes bought, sold, and consumed tea after the Tea Party. Colonial attitudes toward tea, 1773–1776, changed over time (because of the Coercive Acts, the Association, the war, and other events). They varied by political camp and by geography. The distinction between smuggled and legal tea complicated these attitudes further. Yet all these complications were ultimately overwhelmed by a desire to continue consuming, one of the many things colonists shared with one another and with Britons in 1776, even if they could not seem to share the same country any longer. In politicizing consumption Patriots got, as in so many other areas, more than they bargained for, as consumers, like other categories of colonists, had notions of their own.[58]

CHAPTER 2

Before

Tea consumption and tea politics before 1773 help contextualize the events of 1774. Tea was both legally imported and widely smuggled in the colonies, and this smuggling was part of a larger British phenomenon. Parliament addressed British and colonial smuggling in the Townshend Acts (1767), which proved a commercial failure in Britain and a political failure in the colonies, sparking colonial boycotts in 1769 and 1770. The North ministry tried to fix the problems of the Townshend Acts and set the colonial tea trade on a more-secure footing with the Tea Act (1773). It failed.

Tea Smuggling and Britain

British home demand drove tea smuggling. European ports shipped tea to Great Britain, where, despite the English East India Company's formal monopoly on tea imports, high taxes and high Company shipping costs gave smugglers an advantage. British taxes could more than double tea's price in the 1760s: bohea auctioned in London at 2s1d a pound in 1767 before tax, with an after-tax cost of 4s5d. By contrast, in Amsterdam, bohea cost 1s10d. The Netherlands was not the only low-tax location for tea: the Danish government charged a 1 percent tariff on re-exported tea and a 2.5 percent tariff on tea for Danish consumption. European East India Companies also had lower shipping costs than their English rival—the Dutch East India Company (VOC) since 1740.[1] Between 1765 and 1774, the English East India Company (EIC) auctioned roughly 6.8 million pounds of legal tea a year for home consumption within Great Britain. In addition, conservative estimates give another 4 to 6 million pounds of tea smuggled into Britain annually, for a yearly demand of 11 to 13 million pounds. This suggests a per capita tea consumption level of 1.31 to 1.55 pounds of tea annually. If the Company's theory that sales of smuggled tea exceeded sales of legal tea were correct, this estimate would be low. Certainly, high British taxes were self-defeating. In the decade between 1766 and 1776, British tea tariff revenue fell 10 percent, despite population increase and "growing consumption of Tea by all ranks of People."[2] The rest was smuggled.

Colonial tea volumes were much smaller. On average 373,000 pounds of legal tea were imported into North America per year between 1768 and 1772, one-sixteenth of the British average. Estimating smuggled tea volumes is difficult. London tea merchant William Palmer thought colonists consumed 3 million pounds of tea a year; merchant Samuel Wharton gave 5 million; Massachusetts Governor Thomas Hutchinson gave 6.5 million. Large estimates were used to justify large tea-trading concessions (Wharton for his brothers in Philadelphia, Hutchinson for his sons in Boston) and should be taken with a grain of salt. Hutchinson also estimated that five-sixths of the tea imported in 1770 was smuggled, which implied, based on records of legal tea imported that year, a colonial market of less than a million pounds of tea. But the estimate that slightly more than half of British tea was smuggled is also a good low-bound estimate for the colonies. Assuming half the tea in the thirteen colonies was smuggled in 1768–1772 would put per capita consumption at about 0.34 pounds of tea per year and annual consumption at about 746,000 pounds. We might also make a higher-bound estimate that colonial tea smuggling comprised three-fourths of colonial supply—giving an annual demand of 1.49 million pounds at a per capita level of 0.69 pounds of tea a year. Even this estimate means the British market for smuggled tea was three to five times greater than the colonies'. But at least, in ignoring Parliament and smuggling tea, colonists were being British.[3]

Smugglers surrounded Britain. Tea came from France, the Austrian Netherlands (present-day Belgium), the Netherlands, various German states, Sweden, Denmark (which then included Norway and the Faroe Islands), Portugal, and Spain. The Channel Islands provided excellent smuggling depots. Between 1772 and 1782, three-quarters of the tea brought to Europe by all the European East India Companies was smuggled into Britain.[4]

The VOC was foremost among the European companies, importing between 18 and 21 million guilders a year of Asian commodities. In the 1770s, about 40 percent (by value) of VOC imports were retained in the Netherlands;

60 percent were re-exported to Britain, Germany, and the Baltic. Not all European tea ended up in Britain. Dutch and German demand for tea was significant, and even poor Amsterdammers consumed tea.[5]

Dutch and British traders also trafficked tea from other European companies around the North Sea and the English Channel, making the Netherlands a contraband entrepôt. When colonials spoke of "Dutch" tea, they referred to tea smuggled through this network. The term "Dutch tea" should not be taken literally.[6]

Some Dutch tea came from Sweden. The Swedish East India Company (SEIC), run by a mix of Swedes, Britons, and others, imported Asian goods for re-sale abroad. Foreigners could buy tea at the SEIC auction in Gothenburg, and the Company made sure to publish its auction catalogs early enough to allow foreign buyers to attend. Swedish tea demand was important, but the Company re-exported over 90 percent of its tea, most reaching Britain and North America via intermediaries.[7]

Denmark re-exported 81 percent of its Chinese imports in 1753–1770. Only Danish merchants could buy the Danish Asiatic Company's tea, but after marking it up, they sold it to British or Dutch middlemen. It would be a mistake to assume that these re-exports went only to Britain. Some went to the German Baltic and was probably consumed in Germany. Before the 1780s, the Danish and Swedish companies imported between one-quarter and one-third of the tea destined for Europe, in some years carrying more tea than the English Company did. They were significant suppliers to Britain and the Continent.[8]

France was another source. In the western side of the English Channel, the little Breton town of Roscoff became a major exporter of tea and eau de vie to Devon, Cornwall, and Ireland. On the eastern side of the Channel, Archibald Hunter, part of an Anglo-American family, hoped to enter Dunkirk's smuggling trade, where tea re-exports were big business. Hunter explained that the town's "monied men . . . find their advantage in buying" tea at Dunkirk and selling it on to Britain, and that June—when the cutters arrived with tea from the European companies' auctions—was "the only time in the year to make money here." Hunter explained how Virginians could join their English cousins in smuggling. Virginians might smuggle to France by loading tobacco off the books after officially clearing customs in Virginia. Colonial vessels were supposed to stop in Britain before landing in France, but doing so put them at risk of seizure in France. So they could stop at Madeira and take wine to Falmouth, then go to France, or arrive in France with false papers making it look like they had come from the Channel Islands. After acquiring cargo in Dunkirk, they might leave the French port in a storm, pretending they had been blown to sea, taking "all kinds of India Goods," including tea, back to Virginia.[9]

Colonial Tea Smuggling Networks

Colonial smugglers only needed to draw up existing commercial networks, which made colonial tea smuggling so ubiquitous one writer thought the "whole Navy of England" could not stop it. The Netherlands was an attractive place to sell colonial cargoes and get products (besides tea) for the return. In Hamburg, Gothenburg, and other European ports, British factors—merchants who received and sold goods on commission—filled colonial orders for tea. Sometimes colonial firms sent one of their own. The Hunters had stationed Archibald Hunter in Dunkirk since 1770, selling Virginia tobacco and shipping European goods home. In 1774, he tried smuggling tea to Britain. "I shall endeavor to send you some tea," he wrote to James Hunter in London. Colonial smugglers also used British finance. When Nathaniel Hammond was dispatched from Newport to Gothenburg for tea in 1770, he brought a bill of exchange drawn on the London firm Hayley & Hopkins.[10]

Merchants also shipped tea to European colonies in the Caribbean, from whence it was smuggled to British North American and Caribbean colonies. Dutch St. Eustatius and Danish St. Thomas (opened to shipping of all flags in 1764) supplied tea to North America. A vessel that traveled between Nevis and Rhode Island might put in a clandestine stop at St. Eustatius for tea. The Caribbean was an important area for colonial shipping; its supply of sugar and coffee and its demand for lumber, foodstuffs, and cloth complemented North American markets. A little tea could be slipped in along the way, for colonial tea smugglers were often regular traders who smuggled a little on the side. This was what Newporters Samuel and William Vernon did when they sent Captain William Tanner in the *Dolphin* on a surreptitious voyage to Hamburg, with instructions to proceed on to Sweden, load tea, and then take it to the Danish Caribbean island of St. Croix.[11]

Geography made smuggling hard to stop in North America. Ships offloaded illegal cargoes down the shore before officially making port, then proceeded to the customs house and declared whatever legal cargoes were aboard or arrived empty and claimed to be "in ballast." Other goods, like wine, were smuggled too. In Maine, the Chesapeake, and North Carolina, trade was too dispersed for customs houses to be effective; in other areas, customs houses were far from major points of trade. In South Carolina, over one hundred vessels claimed to be engaged in "coasting" trade within the province. Such coasters went uninspected, and nothing prevented them from going to the Caribbean and returning with tea. Thousands of coasting and fishing vessels went unchecked, never entering a customs house, able to collect tea in the Caribbean and redistribute tea across North America.[12]

Nor did customs officers, in the rare instances smugglers happened upon them, make much difference. In New York City, the customs house had only one vessel and three men on foot for enforcement, with the vessel often out of service. By late 1774, it was gone. Unsurprisingly, New York smuggling was extensive. Smugglers routinely bribed customs officers. When that failed, smugglers could use the routine apparatus of the customs service against them. Though customs agents did occasionally seize smuggled goods, these goods were then put up for auction, whereupon the smugglers could buy back their tea. Alternatively, smugglers fought back. In 1771, smugglers bringing tea into Philadelphia overpowered customs agents and locked them below deck in the officers' own vessel. Customs collector John Malcom claimed that he was the only man in the Boston Customs House who dared "Stoping Large Quantitys of the Dutch and French East India Companys Tea." Notably, he was tarred and feathered twice in the winter of 1773–1774.[13]

Such attacks on customs collectors were quintessentially British. In Bristol and Salisbury, English gangs attacked collectors seizing smuggled tea. In the latter, customs collectors were left "Weltring in their Blood." Smugglers beat officers who seized tea in Reading "very cruelly." In Wells, a supervisor commandeered dragoons to seize smuggled tea, but the smugglers gave him chase, took the tea back, and wounded the supervisor, "beating out one of his Eyes." The Commissioners of Excise considered tea smuggling in Britain a matter of "great Magnitude & Enormity," a trade taking up about one hundred vessels and utilizing large armed gangs who passed inland and were dangerous.[14]

British Tea Tax Reform and Failure, 1768–1772

How to solve the smuggling problem? Parliament could cut the tea tax to make smuggling unprofitable. A lower tax on a larger trade might even bring in more revenue—which is what happened when Prime Minister William Pitt passed the Commutation Act in 1784. Chancellor Charles Townshend tried something similar in 1767. His Indemnity Act dealt with two taxes. The first was the 25 percent duty on East India Company tea sold at the London auction. Townshend refunded this if the tea was re-exported to Ireland or North America. In its place, the Revenue Act set a new tea tax to be levied in colonial ports at 3d per pound. For bohea priced at 3s per pound, this represented a tax cut of two-thirds. Townshend kept this duty for British consumers, but eliminated the inland duty on black and singlo teas (1s per pound, previously charged in addition to the 25 percent duty). The rebated 25 percent applied to the colonies, and the cut in inland duty applied to Britain. The Indemnity Act had an almost immediate effect: in July 1767, the price of bohea in England fell from 2/9 to 2/1. British merchants sent out 500,000 pounds of tea to the colonies that year and over 800,000 the year following, a record. Townshend wanted to establish the precedent of colonial taxation. He also provided for a new customs board based in Boston to implement the tax in North America. This was cumbersome. It has been easier to tax tea before it left Britain.[15]

US historians remember the Townshend Acts for their effect on the colonies: their new taxes on lead, glass, paint, paper, and tea; the North American customs administration; and the vice-admiralty courts created to interdict smuggling. But in terms of revenue, the acts focused on Britain, where most tea was consumed and smuggled. Combatting smuggling in Britain might even put European smugglers out of business.

Townshend's new tax was low enough to make legal tea competitive. In 1766, before Townshend's reforms, bohea had auctioned in London at 3s per pound, compared to 1/11 in Holland. The 1767 tax cut, which amounted to about 7d to 1s a pound (depending on the auction price), bridged most of that gap. But while the Townshend Act enabled the Company to compete, the Company failed to do so. The Company cut its tea prices, but not enough, leaving market share to smugglers. This is despite the Company importing 44 million pounds of tea between 1768 and 1772 to take advantage of the Townshend Acts. Increased imports necessitated lowering auction prices further to move volume. Failing to make sufficient price cuts, the Company saw no increase in sales volume. By 1773 the Company had a backlog of 17 million pounds of tea. The prime minister, Lord North, thought this a three-year supply. Legal tea sales declined between 1769 and 1773, even as the Company cut its bohea prices, due to smuggling. With lower prices and lower sales volumes, tariff revenue plummeted. This hurt the Company, since the Indemnity Act required the Company to reimburse the government for tariff revenue lost in the tax cuts. The Company's half-baked execution of its "business plan" left it owing about £300,000 for lost import duties. Before the inland duty was reimposed in 1772, the Company also had to reimburse merchants who purchased its tea but could not sell it on because of its high price. This cost the Company another £560,000.[16]

The Company failed to manage inventory. It should have radically cut tea purchases and prices as its backlog grew. It also should have imported a different assortment of tea—notably, congou, a black tea the Company imported in small amounts, despite its benefitting from the cut in inland duty. The reimbursements the Company would be expected to make in 1772 had been spelled out in 1767, making these costs foreseeable once the Company's sales volume fell short. With £2 million of capital tied up in inventory, even selling tea at a loss would raise needed funds.[17] Instead, the Company, too big and too connected to fail, just got a government bailout.

This pointed to the problem at the heart of the Company: it could not function like a business. On paper it did not have to; it was supposed to have a monopoly on supplying the British market with Asian goods. But there were many other European East India Companies. While they all had formal state monopolies, their respective European states were linked by trade, making the East India Companies function more like national champions than monopolies. The East India Companies competed with each other in a European and trans-Atlantic marketplace. The EIC and VOC had been vying in the tea trade since at least 1685. These firms often relied on the political competitiveness of their government patrons rather than the economic competitiveness of their businesses. When the VOC and EIC wanted to stop the rival Ostend Company, the Netherlands and Britain applied diplomatic pressure to kill it. Market competition was harder, but companies that pursued it profited. During the Indemnity Act the Scandinavian companies shifted their focus to green teas and congou.[18]

The East India Company even suffered from competition against itself. Crew and officers of its vessels unloaded some of its tea in Ireland, the Channel Islands, or France before reaching London. This tea was smuggled into Britain untaxed. Smugglers evaded customs agents to land Company tea and India goods in the Thames. Merchants bought legally imported tea, re-exported it to Ireland for the tax rebate, then smuggled it back to Britain. Much of the jump in re-exports to Ireland was part of this tax fraud. From an average of 301,000 pounds of tea exported to Ireland in 1763–1767, re-exports tripled to 924,000 pounds of tea annually in 1768–1772.[19]

The Colonial Response to the Townshend Acts

In the colonies, Patriots objected to the Revenue Act in the winter of 1767–1768, even though, for tea at least, it represented a tax cut. The colonial smuggler liked the old taxes that had kept out the legal competition. In the summer of 1768, Patriots wrote against the Revenue Act. But in the first eighteen months of the law (July 1767 to December 1768), legal tea imports increased 42 percent in Philadelphia and 100 percent in New York as merchants stocked up. Patriots also resisted customs officers by force, as had occurred in Britain for years. Custom houseboats were burnt, seized goods "rescued," officers

Table 2.1   Tea legally imported into North America, 1768–1772 (pounds weight)

	1768	1769	1770	1771	1772
Newfoundland	3,168	1,564	5,838	4,781	3,949
Quebec	4,360	3,913	7,786	10,340	9,721
Nova Scotia	570	454	13,248	5,358	4,399
New Hampshire	0	0	11,179	0	2,032
Massachusetts (including Maine)	298,251	95,567	48,070	265,884	113,456
Rhode Island	3,446	15,393	17,988	17,754	3,079
Connecticut	0	0	0	0	0
New York	352,488	16,986	147	344	530
New Jersey	0	0	0	0	0
Pennsylvania	146,763	112,159	65	0	128
Delaware	0	0	0	0	0
Virginia and Maryland	40,743	43,112	17,251	25,034	85,279
North Carolina	53	166	786	238	0
South Carolina	28,693	21,238	1,032	26,974	22,138
Georgia	6,754	5,250	2,980	5,864	10,420
East and West Florida	2,551	1,818	918	2,799	2,435
Bahamas	347	788	347	0	0
Bermuda	0	0	0	170	0
Total:	888,187	318,408	127,635	365,540	257,566

Source: PRO CUST 16/1.

tarred and feathered. In 1768, John Hancock openly landed wines without going through customs, then registered his vessel "in ballast." Not one of the various witnesses who saw it was willing to testify against him. This omertà enabled smuggling. Boston Patriots launched a non-importation movement, pledging not to import objectionable goods from Britain, including tea. New York and Philadelphia merchants joined in early 1769. But merchants in regional ports, like Halifax, Portsmouth, Providence, and Newport did not. Those towns saw spikes in legal tea imports, which then supplied New England demand despite Boston's non-importation (see table 2.1). Maryland merchants kept their movement weak, and tea imports increased in the Chesapeake in 1769 despite the Virginia Resolves. Tea imports continued in South Carolina, too. While some merchants signed non-importation pledges, non-signers still imported, including Thomas and Elisha Hutchinson (sons of the governor) and Richard Clarke & Sons in Boston, all of whom would be among the East India Company's tea consignees in 1773. In 1769 the Hutchinsons brought in roughly 50,000 pounds of tea, half of Massachusetts's legal supply. Benjamin Woods Labaree, in his canonical *The Boston Tea Party*, thought these men "obstinate," but they had buyers, and tea imports continued across the colonies. Were they not just practical? The Hutchinsons' tea was carried on a ship owned by John Hancock, a Patriot with a pragmatist's nose for money.[20]

Maintaining the leaky non-importation regime into 1770 proved difficult. Boston Patriots marked "Importer" on the doors of merchants known to import goods and taunted customers. At a January 1770 merchants' meeting, merchants caught breaking non-import pledges were boycotted, but legal tea continued to come. Boston Patriots had extracted pledges of non-consumption from colonists, which they sought to renew. But the renewed vows of non-consumption did not last. Patriots had to lock up the Hutchinsons' tea in May 1770 to keep Bostonians from buying it. Yet in 1770, non-importation did operate effectively in other colonies. Legal tea imports collapsed in New York, Pennsylvania, the Chesapeake, and South Carolina. In South Carolina, even the future Company consignees, Leger and Greenwood, ceased tea imports from Britain. This prevented colonists from drinking dutied tea whether they wanted to or not.[21]

But non-importation struggled in Boston, as John Mein showed. At the January merchants' meeting Patriots had denounced John Mein for his defiance of Patriot authority. Mein, a printer, responded a few months later by publishing public information from the custom house: which ships had brought in which goods that year. Mein listed 32 vessels arriving from Britain and Ireland, many with banned goods. Eleven vessels brought 146.5 chests of tea, including John Hancock's ship *Lydia*, with seventeen chests of duited tea for six different buyers and his *Paoli*, which brought in another 38 chests.[22] Though Hancock offered to return some goods, the tea stayed. The official Patriot reason was that it was difficult to smuggle tea to England.

Mein's exposé suggested Patriotism really was the last refuge of the scoundrel. It detracted from the Patriots' self-image as virtuous upholders of colonial rights and gave credence to the Tory line that Patriots were hypocrites who asked others to sacrifice while they profited. Out-of-colony merchants and newspapers began to ask, Why should our merchants eschew imports, if all it did was create scarcity for Bostonians to exploit?[23] Boston Patriots controlled the Boston crowd, ensuring that their friend Hancock was not attacked for smuggling tea, while Mein was attacked and financially ruined.[24]

Yet merchants still turned against non-importation. Mein's publication, combined with the Repeal Act, which ended Townshend's duties on most goods, except tea, left little will to continue. A sunset clause in the Townshend duties meant the tea tax was set to expire in 1772. Because Parliament repealed the duties on some goods, non-importation is sometimes remembered as a success, however its leakiness suggests it was not. New York merchants ended non-importation in July 1770. Boston ended it in September, Philadelphia in October,

South Carolina in December. All claimed still not to import British tea. However, colonists in Massachusetts, the Chesapeake, and the Lower South reverted to importing tons of it.[25]

Between the Townshend and Tea Acts

Boston took 40 percent of all legal tea shipped to North America between 1768 and 1772. This was well known enough for the Sons of Liberty to have to deny it. Merchant vessels from London might have several vessel co-owners and bring in cargo for several different cargo owners, which made it easy for merchants of all political leanings to be invested in vessels carrying dutied tea, including, as the comptroller of customs noted, "Mr. John Hancock the Patriot." Hancock's clerk, William Palfrey, disputed this in print, but Hancock's vessels did carry over 80,000 pounds of dutied tea for various owners between 1768 and 1772. Hancock was hardly the only one. William Dennie was invested in tea ships as well (he would seek the Boston consignees' resignation in 1773). So were Bostonians Joseph Jackson and Gustavus Fellows and Salemite John Derby. Loyal merchants like George Irving and Thomas Boylston were invested, as were London and Nantucket men. Some, including Hancock, also smuggled in tea from the Netherlands.[26]

Dutied tea importations rebounded in the Chesapeake and South Carolina, too. After non-importation ended, Leger and Greenwood initially held back from ordering new teas from London. But once they realized other Charleston merchants were importing dutied tea, they resumed their own imports, bringing in an average of 20 chests of dutied tea per year.[27]

Meanwhile, smuggled tea was dominant in New York and Philadelphia, cities that received almost no legal tea. Joseph Reed, a Philadelphia Patriot, estimated Pennsylvania tea consumption at hundreds of thousands of pounds per year, entirely smuggled. Political virtue and commercial expediency drove mid-Atlantic merchants to maintain ties with the Netherlands and import Dutch tea. Bohea prices spiked from a baseline of roughly 2/6 sterling in New York and Philadelphia in 1769 to 4/10 in Philadelphia and 6/4 in New York in 1770, before returning to around 2/6 in 1772 as Dutch and British tea were eventually able to meet colonial demand. One of the "lessons of history" from the Townshend Act boycotts would be that non-importation could affect consumer prices.[28]

The other "lesson of history" driving Boston Patriots in 1773 was the fear that so-called non-importers and non-consumers would cheat.[29] Merchants like the Clarkes and the Hutchinsons had violated the Townshend Act boycotts.

This was one reason for the Company to ship tea to them in 1773. Similarly, Patriots confronted the Boston consignees so acrimoniously that year because those consignees were the only recipients of the Company's tea in 1773 to have flagrantly violated non-importation in 1769 and 1770. Boston consumers had violated the boycott in 1770, too, to the point that Patriots had to keep tea away from them, a logic of non-consumption by force majeure which would inform how Boston, Charleston, and Philadelphia Patriots responded to the tea ships a few years later. All this cheating was blamed on the merchants, leaving unsaid the obvious follow-on: merchants sold tea because colonists paid good money for it. If the new tea boycotts were to be more extensive or better enforced than the old ones, then they risked a greater effect on prices, too.

The Tea Act, 1773

The 1773 Tea Act continued Townshend's Revenue and Indemnity Acts within the colonies. The rebate on tea re-exported to the colonies persisted, as did the 3d per pound tax in colonial ports. (However, higher taxes on tea in Britain ensured smuggling there.) The Company was encouraged to re-export tea to the colonies without auctioning it in London; thus, cutting out London middlemen and lowering prices, though colonial merchants could still get tea from their regular London suppliers if they so chose. In 1773, colonial smugglers could buy bohea in Holland for 1s9d per pound and sell it in the colonies for 2s7d (a markup of nearly 50 percent). The EIC instructed its consignees to sell bohea in the colonies at 2s per pound, which would have taken away much— but perhaps not all—of the smuggler's profits. Historians disagree whether the Company would have undersold smugglers. It had failed to do so in Britain under the Townsend Acts, and the EIC with its high shipping costs would have struggled to undersell the VOC permanently.[30] By setting a floor below which it would not sell, the Company left room for smugglers should Dutch wholesale prices fall, as they did in the spring of 1774. But the Company anticipated success: the tea it sent to the colonies in 1773 was more than double the volume of all legal tea sold in North America the previous year.

In 1772, the Company faced severe financial difficulties: it defaulted on customs payments and loans to the Bank of England. A general credit crisis, ironically begun when a bank shorting East India Company stock defaulted, made things worse. The Company now governed parts of India; tax revenues there were low, and expenses were high. Its British importing business was strained: of the various Indian and Chinese items it brought in, tea was becoming its main product but remained widely smuggled. Smuggling suggested a yet-uncaptured British tea market, but the Company was burned by its 1767–1772 attempt to capture market share.

By 1773, solutions to the Company's money problems centered around halving dividend payouts (a step its rentier shareholders took with great reluctance) and a bailout loan of £1,400,000 from the British government.[31] The Tea Act, which sought to increase the Company's exports to North America, was passed in this context.

The Company initially planned to draw down its tea stockpile by exporting to Europe. One estimate suggested that if the Company sold 11.5 million pounds of tea to Europe, it could generate over £1,400,000—enough to cover the loan from Parliament. The tea probably could have sold if granted full drawback on all duties. But sales at such volume would depress prices. And as long as taxes on tea remained high in Britain, the tea sold to Europe would be smuggled back into Britain, just like the tea re-exported to Ireland had been.[32] The Company decided to sell tea in North America instead.

Yet the colonial market was too small to affect Company finances meaningfully. The Company shipped roughly 600,000 pounds of tea to the colonies in 1773, 3.5 percent of its total tea on hand.[33] Though passed just months after the Company's bailout, the Tea Act offered only a marginal improvement to the Company's cash flow. It is easy to assume the Tea Act was meant to address the Company's financial problems, but it was not, for those problems had already been addressed.

In addition to cutting dividends, borrowing, and seeking new markets, the Company improved its inventory management. It had 17 million pounds on hand, but this figure is misleading. The Tea Act required the Company to maintain 10 million pounds of tea on hand as a condition of allowing direct Company exports to the colonies. The surplus beyond that of 7 million pounds could be sold off over time. Between 1774 and 1783, the Company imported 48.1 million pounds of tea and sold 59.4 million pounds. The difference was drawn down from supply. The Company sold an average of 5.944 million pounds of tea a year between 1774 and 1783, roughly what it had been selling in the 1760s, just with less additional tea on order. The Company paid off its government loan by 1776. Meanwhile, the King's duties grew handsomely (the Company estimated that in these years a chest of hyson tea generated nearly three times as much revenue for His Majesty's Customs as it did profit for the Honourable Company). By the time of the Commutation Act in 1784, which lowered tariffs on tea consumed in Britain, the Company had too little tea to meet the increased demand for legal tea. So the Company bought up supply on the Continent—25.5 million pounds between 1785 and 1787—and increased imports from China to

12 million pounds a year. The broad tax cut and the Company's purchase of European supplies finally put British tea smugglers out of business.[34] Had Parliament done this ten years earlier, it likely would have put American tea smugglers out of business, altering the course of the imperial crisis. The Company's financial problems were resolved without North American help.

Though not much for the Company, the tea shipped to North America in 1773 was a lot for a colonial merchant. So the Company held the merchants in the four receiving cities jointly responsible for the cargo. It limited consignees to a 6 percent commission, of which their London referrals took a share. Having a capped commission and a capped sales price on one hand, and facing, once Patriots turned the populace against them, uncapped losses across all their businesses on the other, quitting the tea consignment business made sense. The four Philadelphia consignee firms, who managed a larger shipment, could expect to share no more than £2,400 sterling profit.[35] The Boston consignees held out—driven, at least initially, by their belief in the Boston market for legal tea.

Commissions would only be paid upon sale, motivating consignees to sell tea fast and in bulk, perhaps even at auction, to every retailer and wholesaler they could. The Company did not send tea anywhere else in the Americas, leaving potential buyers for the consignees' cargoes spread from Quebec to the Antilles. Manhattan consignee Henry White hardly knew every merchant, even in Albany. So Albany merchants would order tea from their usual New York suppliers, who knew them and accepted their credit; in turn, the latter would get it from consignees like White or wholesalers in London. The North American consignees competed with the wholesalers who bought tea at Company auctions in London. This prevented White or any other North American merchant from taking over the legal tea market. However, the price cap of 2 shillings a pound for bohea would hurt smugglers.

The Problem with the Colonial Response

The colonial response to the Tea Act was unexpected in Britain. Townshend's colonial tea duty had been levied uneventfully in 1771 and 1772. The ministry thought the continuation of a tax cut and the chance to remove expensive London middlemen were boons to the colonies. Peter Oliver, who served as chief justice in Massachusetts, pointed out that the Tea Act was enacted with a "lenient Principle," a liberality that tried to improve the common man's lot to reduce smuggling rather than interdicting smugglers with force. Thomas Hutchinson, relying on his experience importing and selling dutied tea—which he did until 1773—originally thought the tea would be landed in 1773 without trouble.[36]

This was in part because tea did not seem too important. Tea was widespread but represented only 2.9 percent by value of the goods legally shipped from Britain to the colonies. Woolens, by contrast, comprised 37 percent of English exports to the colonies. Fabrics of all sorts represented over half of all English shipments to the colonies. Neither the Townshend nor Tea Acts touched these vital goods, which supplied British workers with jobs and colonists with warmth. Instead, those acts tinkered with taxes on paint, tea, glass, and other "luxuries." But the Tea Act disappointed expectations that Townshend's tea tax would be sunset. It renewed attention to colonial taxation. And Patriots objected to the Company's monopoly. As Governor William Tryon of New York explained to Lord Dartmouth, secretary of state for the colonies from 1772 to 1775, even "if the tea comes free of duty, I understand then it is to be considered as a monopoly of dangerous tendency . . . to American liberties . . . let the tea appear free or not free of duty, those who carry on the illicit trade will raise objections."[37]

The complaint of monopoly was bizarre. It argued that the Company's tea would push out other tea, dominate the colonial market, then allow the Company to raise prices. Lower prices would thus cause higher ones, or so the reasoning went. But the Company could not raise prices in the colonies much beyond what merchants would bid for it in London without creating a new smuggling problem, and it could not raise prices of the tea it sold in London and the Americas without losing market share (and costing His Majesty customs revenue), problems highlighted by the Company's failures in 1767–1772. The VOC still existed, smugglers sold Dutch tea in Britain, and colonists were good at smuggling it. Patriots who worried that the Company's de jure monopoly (which had existed for a century) would become a de facto one overlooked these points.

Nor was the Dutch tea that Patriots preferred a principled, ideological alternative. The European East India Companies, like the English one, were formal, state-sanctioned monopolies. The Netherlands did not tax tea re-exports, but Sweden and Denmark maintained just the sort of low, nominal taxes that Patriots opposed. Colonists had no elected representatives in Parliament, but they did not have elected representatives in any other European government, either. At least in Parliament they had colonial agents. Some of these polities had abolished representative politics altogether. The Netherlands had a recognizably representative government. But France and Denmark had absolutist monarchies, and Sweden's king sidelined the legislature with a constitution that made him, as the *New York Journal* noted, "absolute Sovereign" in 1772.

And, of course, there was the Great Qing, which taxed all tea as it left China. This was, quite plainly, taxation without representation.

Few colonists knew what taxes smuggled tea bore. VOC tea was the least bad, and the catch-all term, Dutch tea, concealed ideologically problematic French, Danish, and Swedish tea. Perhaps, since these European states did not rule North America, their tea seemed innocuous. Or perhaps Dutch tea was re-imagined as a serviceable ideological alternative by smugglers and consumers who wanted to protest the Tea Act without giving up tea.[38]

One of the central questions nagging at histories of the tea protests has been: How much action was driven by ideological principle, and how much was driven by the self-interest of smugglers? To this we might add the self-interest of consumers. Before 1773, widespread smuggling and leaky boycotts were good businesses for smugglers and consumers. Before 1773, smuggling and boycotts were revolutionary actions for Patriots. Yet in the years ahead, as politicians sought an effective ban on all tea, and as many merchants and consumers still trafficked it, tea's career as a political symbol and as a consumer good pulled it in competing directions.

PART TWO

Campaigning against Tea

December 17, 1773–February 28, 1775

CHAPTER 3

Tea Politics

In 1774, tea became a symbol of the colonies' political transformation. The questions of 1773–1774—what to do about the Company's shipments, how to respond to the Coercive Acts, and whether to join the Association—all involved tea. "It is Tea that has kept all America trembling for Years. It is Tea that has brought Vengeance upon Boston," Rev. William Tennent wrote. Tea was, for James Duane, "the fatal cause of our present Misfortunes." It symbolized Company monopoly, unrepresentative taxation, and parliamentary infringement on colonists' constitutional rights. In Boston, destroying the Company's tea was a way, Patriots thought, for colonists to defend their rights at a time when they had only symbolic ways to do so. Elsewhere, burning or drowning tea, even Dutch tea, showed fellow feeling with Boston in destroying its tea, especially in early 1774 when that destruction was still contested. In the summer, tea destruction became a way to form common cause with Boston and oppose the Coercive Acts, though to friends of government, it just looked like rioting.[1]

Radicals' response to the Company's tea varied across North America and was initially confined to the four cities receiving that tea: Boston, New York, Philadelphia, and Charleston. Boston radicals banned all tea sales (English and Dutch) after January 20, 1774. This had many virtues. It made up for Patriots' allowing English and Dutch tea into the city previously. The ban on Dutch tea pleased legal tea dealers and removed suspicion that smugglers would benefit.

The ban was also practical, as English and Dutch teas were hard to differenti-ate. And it made the high prices, which the Tea Party worsened, impossible to discuss in the press.[2]

At the same time, the surviving Company tea from the *William*, brought to the Castle on January 3, remained a threat. If sold, the *William*'s tea stood to upend Boston Patriots' claim that the Tea Party and tea boycott reflected popular will. As "An Enemy to Tea, dutied and undutied," explained the *Boston Evening Post*, "if undutied Tea should be admitted," dutied tea would inevitably be introduced as well, and this would allow the consignees to "disperse" across Massachusetts "the East India Company's' Tea now at the Castle." Importers in Rhode Island, New Hampshire, Halifax, and Boston would follow, allowing the Company to make new shipments of tea to Halifax for redistribution to "differ-ent parts of America." The ban on consuming any kind of tea neutralized these threats. While the full cargo from the *William* would have to travel between the castle and Boston by the main shipping channel, small amounts might be taken from Castle Island to Dorchester Neck. A ferry linked the island and the neck, and the two were nearly connected by sand bars at low tide. (See figure 1.1.) A ban on all tea made it harder to pass off parcels of this tea as "smuggled." And long as Boston Patriots kept the populace riled up and the ban reasonably well enforced, the consignees had little incentive to hazard the tea in town. Previ-ously, Boston Patriots had banned tea imports to choke off tea sales. Now they banned sales to choke off imports of tea.[3]

In South Carolina, as in Massachusetts, Patriots had not stopped dutied tea in 1772, with opposition to the Company's tea in 1773 catalyzing efforts to ban all British tea in early 1774 and to eventually ban Dutch tea, too. The Tea Act made British tea, whether shipped by the Company or private merchants, price competitive with Dutch tea, so both had to be opposed. Opposition to Dutch tea followed to keep merchants on the same footing and prevent British tea from being sold as Dutch.

In Charleston, a January 1774 "general meeting" was supposed to finalize Carolina Patriots' positions on non-importation and non-consumption. Patri-ots timed the meeting to coincide with the seating of the colonial legislature, but Lieutenant Governor Bull prorogued the legislature until March, allow-ing time for things to calm down. Bull had effectively forestalled Charleston Patriots from implementing the non-importation or non-consumption of du-tied tea for several months. Given enough time, perhaps the tea, safely in the Exchange, might even be sold.

With the legislature prorogued, Charleston Patriots formed a general com-mittee of forty-five men. It spoke for Charleston as a city and South Carolina as a colony and, most important, coordinated the different parts of the Patriot movement. A quorum of fifteen men, most likely Charleston-area men, could act for the whole if the others were away. The increased cohesion was vital, for radicals blamed the divisions within the South Carolina Patriot movement for their situation. As the Boston committee reminded its Charleston counterpart, "By Uniting we <u>Stood</u> & by dividing we <u>fell</u>."[4]

The committee, chaired by Christopher Gadsden, included a number of Patriotic planters; merchants; the printer Peter Timothy; and, crucially, the erstwhile East India Company consignee Roger Smith. The general committee was to (1) "diligently" watch the Exchange to prevent the sale of the Company's tea and (2) review the resolves of the previous December against importing and using tea (about which there still seems to have been disagreement).[5] By including Smith, the committee ensured he would not assist in the sale of the tea and enabled him to inform on the other consignees should they attempt a sale. Including large number of merchants was a practical way to help watch the Exchange. Over the next half year, the general committee took power from the colonial legislature. The committee called a "general meeting" at the Liberty Tree for March 16, 1774, to deal with tea matters left over from the December 17 meeting. The March meeting was ostensibly open to "Every Inhabitant of the Town or Country"—that is, the free white men—and claimed to represent all of South Carolina. Practically, only colonists who lived in Charleston or had the time and money to travel from the country could attend. This left the meetings dominated by plantation owners (who could stay in their townhouses), merchants, and Charleston tradesmen, while excluding poorer, backcountry settlers, who tended to be more disaffected from the Patriot cause. This meeting was less representative than New England town meetings. Yet Charleston's meeting did include men from the towns' lower orders. Fliers went up for a meeting of "Mechanicks" (i.e., the Sons of Liberty) to convene the night before the meeting, and the Sons organized themselves for the general meeting the next day. On March 16, the Sons of Liberty successfully persuaded the general meeting to declare that "NO TEAS" (taxed or smuggled) be imported effective April 16, 1774, and created an "Agreement" to this effect, which was circulated for signing.[6]

South Carolina merchants tried to delay. They avoided the "publick Meetings," hoping the meeting's resolves would bind only attendees. (As Christopher Gadsden put it, they "separated themselves from the general Interest.") But the committee asked the merchants to sign anyway. The merchants quibbled. Some argued that smuggled (and hence untaxed) tea be allowed. Others argued that if taxed items were to be boycotted, then non-importation should include wine and coffee, a point first raised the previous December. Their points were logical (wine and coffee were taxed without colonial representation). These were also "poison pills" meant to scuttle agreement. Gadsden reassured Samuel Adams that these "overvirtuous" and "treacherous" sallies failed.[7]

In New York and Pennsylvania, the boycott of British tea dating from 1770 continued, with residents using only Dutch tea. British tea broadly had already been stopped before the Company tea ships were turned around in those ports. The New York "Association of the Sons of Liberty" declared non-consumption in December 1773 but limited the order to dutied tea, of which there was none. Mid-Atlantic colonies sustained non-importation of British tea had put them at the vanguard of tea politics in 1772. But in 1774 they did not ban Dutch tea, even as other colonies did. Bans on Dutch tea first emerged in colonies where dutied tea had previously been available: South Carolina, Massachusetts, and the Chesapeake, and those bans came fastest in Boston and Charleston, where Company tea was still on hand, an unsold, ever-present threat. New York and Philadelphia imported Dutch tea for much of 1774, even as other colonies banned it. This can make these ports seem politically laggard; yet importation of Dutch tea was crucial in helping to lower colonial tea prices, which was useful since high prices might incentivize new shipments of British tea.[8]

The ministry's response to the Boston Tea Party, the Coercive Acts, escalated the conflict. The response encompassed four separate laws. The Boston Port Act closed the port of Boston until the destroyed tea was paid for. The Massachusetts Government Act rewrote that colony's charter to make it more amenable to law and order. The Administration of Justice Act allowed British officials accused of crimes in the colonies to be tried in Britain (fearing unfair trials in the colonies). The Quartering Act allowed soldiers to be housed in unoccupied homes.[9] Colonists often added to this a fifth intolerable act, the Quebec Act, which expanded Quebec's territory and its French Catholic colonists' privileges as far as the Ohio region. The prime minister also sent General Thomas Gage to take over as civilian governor and military commander in Massachusetts. By linking repayment for the Company's tea in Boston to laws affecting all of the colonies, the Coercive Acts made tea a symbol of resistance to Parliament across the continent.

The Coercive Acts had myriad consequences. One overlooked consequence was the inflammation of tea politics in Boston and Charleston. The acts made the unsold Company tea even more hated. Worse, by not providing a way for the tea to be reshipped to England, the acts left the Company's tea trapped in these ports, providing an existential motivation for Boston and Charleston Patriots. These Patriots had to maintain a level of radicalization sufficient to keep the tea from being sold, lest sales undermine a now-much-higher-stakes cause.

Boston port closed on June 1, 1774, putting thousands out of work and threatening them with starvation. Whiggish colonists across the continent united against ministerial policy. They fasted and prayed. They sent food. They advocated for a boycott of Britain. And, as George Washington and Benjamin Franklin, they overcame doubts about the Boston Tea Party. Patriots in many colonies responded to the Coercive Acts with more tea parties. Because the Port Act was seen as a way to compel tea duties to be paid in the future, the protest of tea became a way to object to taxation without representation and to the Coercive Acts. As the symbolic value of tea protests grew, colonists became less picky about what tea they burned. Patriots tried to forbid all tea importation and burn whatever tea they had as a sign of opposition to Parliament and solidarity with Boston.[10]

Patriots proposed banning imports and exports with Britain and the consumption of British goods. Stopping tea imports symbolically supported broader non-importation, and destroying tea supported broader non-consumption. Such symbolism grew in value as provincial Patriots struggled to unite around non-importation. They needed to unite, since there was no sense in one colony boycotting unless neighboring colonies joined; otherwise the boycott would merely divert business elsewhere. Thus the need for a Continental Congress to form a common response to the Coercive Acts.

A ban on tea in the colonies was far from certain. Various attempts at encouraging non-importation and non-consumption stalled in the summer of 1774. The Boston committee of correspondence tried and failed to get merchants to countermand fall orders, which might be landed in Salem to get around the Port Act, but merchants quibbled; it was too late, the goods were needed, it would not effectively punish Britain, the capital was already committed. So the committee circulated a Solemn League and Covenant with a rapid non-importation deadline of October 1 among inland towns in June 1774. The committee hoped to leverage support of outlying towns to pressure Boston to join. But only seven towns took up the Covenant. Others agreed to a boycott in principle but objected to this one: they needed time to prepare, and Boston would have to join first.[11]

Non-importation faced an uncertain future in Philadelphia, too. News of the Port Act reached Philadelphia on May 14. But on May 20, a meeting of Philadelphia merchants and lawyers decided to wait on other colonies before acting. Questions emerged. Non-importation affected merchants importing from Britain, not Europe, so some dry goods merchants wondered why should they "risque their whole property, while others are totally excepted from any risque"? Others worried a trade stoppage might create mass unemployment. Why make Philadelphia as poor as Boston? Letting Congress decide about non-importation also suited Philadelphia and New York conservatives, who mistakenly hoped the body would kill the idea entirely.[12]

The Port Act was front-page news in Charleston by June 3, and the Charleston committee sought to gather support from the province with a general meeting, to sit on July 6. Gadsden lamented the colony's laggardness in banning tea. The "overhasty breaking through and forsaking the first Resolutions [respecting tea] without previously Consulting or so much as acquainting our Committee therewith disgusted many," he wrote, and was the "principal and most successful" means to "deter us from Farther Engagements." But the Port Act had unified Charleston Patriots once again. While some questioned the wisdom of non-importation and non-exportation, Timothy informed the Boston committee that "even the Merchants now seem generally inclined to a Non-Importation" of British goods. The Charleston committee thought that "the people here in general" supported non-importation but that non-export remained more difficult. The July 6 gathering met at the Exchange, the same place Carolinians had met the previous December and where the South Carolina Provincial Congress would meet in 1775. Its Great Hall was an amenable meeting spot, and it sat above the customs warehouse storing the *London*'s tea. Both sides of the non-importation issue ultimately agreed to permit the colony's congressional delegates to vote as needed on non-importation and non-exportation to reach inter-colonial agreement in Congress. It is unclear whether the presence of so much Company tea affected this.[13]

Responding to the Coercive Acts, Patriots outside Boston, New York, Philadelphia, and Charleston entered into tea politics. In several colonies, Patriots marked June 1, 1774, as a solemn day. The Virginia House of Burgesses voted its sympathy with Boston by declaring June 1 a day of "Fasting, Humiliation and Prayer." In response, Governor Dunmore dissolved the House. House members met at Raleigh Tavern and "recommend[ed] it strongly" not to import tea. They agreed to consume no East India goods personally until the Coercive Acts were repealed. Fredericksburg inhabitants also agreed to neither use nor sell tea. The moderate Loyalist Robert Beverley III agreed that the ministry acted "tyrannically & oppressively [sic] in the Measures they are pursuing," even though the "Bostonians certainly acted imprudently and unjustly in the Destruction of the Tea." That summer, Chesapeake radicals began destroying regular, dutied tea and turning around tea ships. When Virginia delegates reassembled as an (illegal) Virginia convention in August, they passed the Virginia Association, also known as the Virginia Non-Importation Agreement, which forbade the importation or use of "tea of any kind" and began non-importation of British goods on November 1, 1774. They also recommended an immediate end to tea consumption and selected delegates to an inter-colonial congress. Virginia's congressional delegation proposed its association as a model for Congress.[14]

It was unclear what significance this congress would have or what, if anything, it would decide on. It was even unclear whether Congress would become a lawmaking body. As Congressman John Routledge pointed out, Congress had "no legal authority." "Congress" in 1774 meant a meeting or gathering, not a legislature. No colonial legislature was called a congress. Prior congresses—the Albany Congress of 1754 and the Stamp Act Congress of 1765—recommended measures to colonial legislatures and issued declarations; they did not make law, which might have been why some conservatives misjudged the potential of this congress. Few congressmen were elected by properly constituted legislatures. Most, as in Virginia, were chosen by provincial conventions. Though some colonial legislatures subsequently validated conventions' decisions, it was unclear in the summer of 1774 how authoritative and legitimate the colonies' conventions and the inter-colonial congress would be. The legitimacy of these bodies was deeply contested. The conventions and Congress, largely lacking conservative voices, were more radical than the colonial legislatures or the populace as a whole and fundamentally unable to represent the spectrum of colonial opinion. Though Joseph Galloway (a moderate in 1774, later a Loyalist) attended the Continental Congress, men like Virginia Attorney General John Randolph, who thought conventions unconstitutional, did not. And many colonies— Quebec, Nova Scotia, Bermuda, the Bahamas, Georgia, the Floridas, and the entire British Caribbean—were unrepresented. By dividing radical colonists from the rest, it was easier for Patriots to unite this rump as though it were a whole. Conservatives' absence made Patriot action easier. There were other layers of irony here: Patriots worried that their colonial charters were not secure from Parliament, but conventions and congresses, by circumventing elected legislatures, damaged those charters, too, a point Gage made, in vain, to the Massachusetts provincial congress.[15] Meanwhile, by largely failing to attend these conventions, conservatives accelerated the radicalization they abhorred.

Congress met from September 5 to October 26, 1774. On October 20, it promulgated its Continental Association—a non-import, non-export, and non-consumption agreement. Non-importation of tea and British and Irish goods was set to begin December 1, 1774—moved back from November to allow importing merchants to receive the last of their fall goods. The tenth article of the Association added a further grace period until February 1, prior to which importers could buy back seized cargoes, mirroring how customs officials dealt with interdicted goods. As Patrick Henry explained, "We don't mean to hurt even our Rascalls," "if We have any." Non-importation banned some British Caribbean goods but allowed rum and some sugar from the British West Indies—a major loophole, though one which did not benefit merchants based in Britain. Non-consumption of English goods and Dutch tea was to begin on March 1, 1775 (to give merchants time to sell off goods imported before December 1). Non-consumption of British tea would begin immediately. Non-exportation to Britain, Ireland, and the British Caribbean would begin September 10, 1775. These provisions were to stay in place until the Coercive Acts, the tea tax, and all other duties on colonial commerce were repealed.[16]

Supposedly, non-importation would pressure merchants in Britain, who would then pressure Parliament. Some colonists thought trade with Britain was unnecessary: "we can do much better without it than they Can," explained the Worcester committee, though coastal towns may have been less sanguine. As Lieutenant Governor Bull explained, colonists hoped to bring Britain around "by their sufferings." Some hoped the boycott would influence the outcome of the 1774 parliamentary election. It did not. (The election was completed before the Association was implemented.)[17] Such thinking over-estimated colonial trade's value to British merchants and those merchants' political influence.

Congress sacrificed the economic effects of the boycott for inter-colonial political expediency. To be economically viable, the Association would have to inflict more pain on Britain than North America. Yet the delay in non-export allowed tobacco to be supplied to Britain and food and wood to be supplied the British Caribbean for nearly a year. Non-import was supposed to deprive British merchants of a market. Yet colonial merchants placed their 1775 orders in late 1774, robbing non-import of its punch. The size of the free colonial population (roughly one-quarter of Britain's) also meant that the colonies had never been the main market for British merchants. Instead, by limiting exports to Britain in 1775 to merchants who had *already* complied with non-import in 1774, the Association ensured local merchants heeded non-import to maintain their access the export market. Thus customs records show thirty vessels departing Annapolis in June 1775, compared to twenty-four departures the previous June, with all the arrivals from Britain in June 1775 carefully "in ballast" to be Associationally compliant and to take on exports. Delayed non-export bought colonial merchants' and planters' support of the Association. The Association reflected North American political needs more than transatlantic economic ones.[18]

Patriots also thought their past protests and boycotts had been reasonably effective: the Stamp Act protests of 1765 seemed to have gotten the Stamp Act repealed, and the Townshend Act boycott, though it eventually collapsed, appeared to have gotten some taxes repealed, though not the tax on tea. Thus the appeal of a new boycott in 1774, as a means to affect change through political mobilization. Patriots outside Congress also continued to campaign for a boycott, as in Massachusetts Patriots' Suffolk Resolves, which declared an immediate cessation of trade with Britain, "especially of East-India Teas," and disobedience to the Massachusetts Government Act.[19]

Across the continent local revolutionary committees formed to enforce the Association. This was a radical departure from how previous congresses had worked, driven by Patriots' desire to improve upon previous non-importation attempts and ensure this boycott did not collapse because of non-compliance. The Association seemed voluntary: committees asked individual householders to sign. But signatures were coerced, and non-signers were punished, often by being proscribed and having their businesses shunned. This effectively changed the Association from a private agreement between signatories into a law that ruled everyone. The transfer of power from chartered colonial legislatures to revolutionary conventions, committees, and congresses was the real revolution of 1774. Tea became a symbol of this, burning it a way for colonists to oppose the ministry, the Tea Act, the Port Act, and the other Coercive Acts, and also a way to support Boston, the Association, the "common cause," and Patriot authorities.[20]

Writing in April 1774, South Carolina plantation owner Henry Laurens anticipated and initially recoiled from the consequences of extra-legal rule. Voluntary agreements were fine. But the resolve that "no Tea shall be Imported" necessarily involved imposing the resolution on others. "What right have we to Resolve that no Tea Shall be Imported, bought, or Sold? The desired End, might have been obtained, by a Resolution, that *We* will not Import, buy, or Sell. Restrain our Selves, but make no attempt to lay violent & illegall prohibitions on our fellow Subjects." A voluntary association is "acceptable & pleasing," but a resolve acting *as law* "Sounds a general alarm & Serves to Arm those who are Inimical to the freedom of America." Laurens denounced the Coercive Acts as "Violent, Arbitrary, & unjust," but wondered what his fellow Carolinians were up to. "Surely some Judas has been working among you." Indeed, the original agreement, proposed at the previous December's meeting, asked each signatory to sign for "him or herself" only—here, men could not even bind their wives, much less all society. John Greenough, who salvaged the Company's tea from the *William*, likewise asked how could "private Persons and Societies" determine "what is lawfull prudent just and right for a Man to say and do and what is not?" To concede to the rule of "Indian Liberty Sons" would be "Liberties destroyd."[21] But Greenough had a financial interest in the tea and Laurens, then in London, was out of step with his fellow Carolinians, who did not pursue polite voluntarism, but imposed non-importation and non-consumption on others. Revolutions are not made by consensus.

Laurens did point to a major shift in Patriot thinking. Previous non-importation agreements had failed because, the reasoning went, they lacked teeth. Patriots would not make the same mistake again. The decision to impose non-importation by force was a deliberate toughening.

Tea politics in 1774 were very different from tea politics in 1775. In 1774, Patriots labored to politicize and mobilize the population, and tea helped with this. Politicizing tea and mobilizing people against it (as a stand-in for the ministry) was a slow and incomplete process. Tea remained widely advertised through 1774, often in the same newspapers that carried anti-tea essays or resolutions not to drink it. In 1775, with the Association up and running, tea non-consumption became a test of colonial obedience to Patriot rule, but an increasingly shallow one as war and its preparations took center stage after April 1775.

Patriots shifted their attention to control of gunpowder instead of tea. The struggle had begun in September 1774 when Governor Gage saved the powder stored in Somerville, Massachusetts, and relocated it. This Powder Alarm drew thousands of militiamen from across southern New England to Boston. In December, Patriots from Portsmouth, New Hampshire, seized powder from Fort William and Mary. Gage tried to take powder at Salem in February 1775 and sent troops to Concord to capture colonists' gunpowder in April, resulting in the Battles of Lexington and Concord on April 19. The next day (and unaware of the fighting in Massachusetts), Virginia Governor Dunmore seized the gunpowder from the Williamsburg magazine, sparking militia activity and unrest there. South Carolina Patriots seized powder in Charleston on April 21. As news of the fighting of Lexington and Concord spread, so did seizures of powder, a more practical and urgent way to support (and show support for) the Patriot cause than burning tea. Other questions colonists asked in 1775—whether and how to fight a war, whether to become independent, what form of government the new states should take—had little to do with tea, and tea faded from public consciousness.[22]

In response to the boycott, Parliament passed a series of acts restricting colonial trade. These escalated the conflict and confirmed colonial fears that the Coercive Acts were a model for future laws. North was sure a boycott "could never last." Yet, rather than letting the boycott fail, he punished the offenders. If the colonies "refused to trade with Great Britain, Great Britain would take care they should trade no where else."[23] The New England Restraining Act of early 1775 forbade New England to trade abroad except with England, Ireland, and the West Indies. The Trade Act (April 1775) extended these restraints to Pennsylvania, New Jersey, Maryland, Virginia, and South Carolina. The Prohibitory Act (December 1775) banned all trade in the rebellious colonies and authorized naval and privateering vessels to capture their shipping. A response to the fighting, including the colonial endurance at Bunker Hill and the congressional invasion of Canada, it came into effect on January 1, 1776. The act transformed the politics of colonial consumption: if Parliament banned British trade with the colonies, to continue non-importation was to obey Parliament's ban. Congress repealed its tea ban a few months later.

CHAPTER 4

Paying for the Tea

Some colonists thought the Boston Tea Party was excessive and the tea should be paid for, preferably by someone else. Governor Hutchinson assumed wealthy radicals like John Hancock would pay. Failing that, Hutchinson sought others. Massachusetts Chief Justice Peter Oliver claimed some colonists thought "justice demanded Indemnification to the owners of the Tea." Provincial Treasurer Harrison Gray noted "the sober thinking part of the town" "disclaimed" the destruction of the tea, though Boston town and Massachusetts colonial governments took "no steps" to "show their dislike." In London, Benjamin Franklin recommended the colonial government pay, lest Parliament be "compulsive." Others in Britain thought similarly, and the idea had precedent: in 1766, the Massachusetts General Court had compensated victims of the Stamp Act riots. But Samuel Adams suppressed Franklin's advice: radicals had little interest in acknowledging fault. Loyalists hesitated to pay, too. In the Marshfield Resolves, the town's Loyalists demanded that neither "the Province in general" nor "the Town of Marshfield" pay. They instructed their representative in the Massachusetts legislature to oppose payment by the colony. Only those "acting, aiding and assisting or conniving at the Destruction of said Teas" should pay, not honest, law-abiding subjects.[1]

Making amends for the tea tossed into Boston Harbor could help de-escalate the conflict and reconcile the two sides. Amends entailed reimbursing the East India Company and prosecuting offenders since the Tea Party, an "Attack upon

Property" in John Adams's phrase, was a crime.[2] Boston Patriots blocked both. Lord North, the prime minister, failed to understand the Tea Party's unpopularity in North America and missed the opportunity this offered. After a decade of Patriot complaints about ministerial overreach, finally friends of government could lament Patriot excess in the press. Moderate Patriots wanted to pay for the tea; payment was thus a wedge issue that could divide Patriots. Yet North never tried to divide and rule Patriots. Rather, his Coercive Acts attempted to divide Massachusettsans from other colonists. But because they were extreme and harmed innocent and guilty Massachusettsans alike, these Acts had the opposite effect, encouraging colonial unity. North suffered from a catastrophic failure of political imagination: he saw Massachusetts as a place to be ruled, not a place for politics. The Coercive Acts shifted colonial attention from Patriot excesses to ministerial ones, and colonists raised money for Boston, not the Company. Yet the idea of compensation survived: Continental Congress debated it in the fall of 1774, and in the winter of 1774–1775 Dartmouth and the colonial agents still in London discussed it.

Failure of the Massachusetts Courts

The first way to remedy the Tea Party was to prosecute offenders. Fearing this, Boston committee of correspondence members discussed plans for defending one another from arrest. But arrests proved difficult. The most plausible eyewitnesses—the commanders and crew working the *Dartmouth, Beaver*, and *Eleanor* when those vessels were attacked—proceeded to a notary public the day after the Tea Party and swore affidavits that "solemnly Protest[ed]" the attack but claimed not to recognize any attackers. Radicals had a mafia-like extra-judicial control over Boston. They terrorized Boston's streets, prevented arrests, and intimidated witnesses. The crew thus protected the rioters to protect themselves: the documents would impeach crew testimony that subsequently identified tea partiers; this kept the crew safe from Patriot mobs. Seamen were part of the Boston crowd, and the *Dartmouth, Beaver*, and *Eleanor* crews had to survive daily life in Boston Harbor and make their next sailing with these men.

Individual tea partiers might also be witnesses. But their identities were unknown to authorities: out-of-towners might have already left, and Bostonians had been disguised. Governor Hutchinson's government operated without modern innovations like police or racketeering statutes. The government had no civilian force to maintain order, no detectives to investigate crime, and no way to guarantee witness safety. It struggled to link Patriot leaders to what was a highly organized crime, particularly since some of the most prominent leaders of the movement, including Samuel Adams, John Hancock, and Joseph Warren, made sure they were seen lingering in the Old South Meeting House and *not* at the wharves while the tea was destroyed. Such men would remain free unless the Massachusetts attorney general could "flip" street-level rioters on their leaders. And flipping was impossible as long as the master, mate, and boatswain of the *Eleanor* all said the attackers were "unknown" to them. Putting the mob out on the street, meting out violence to their enemies, and protecting their own kept Patriot leaders out of jail and allowed the Boston committee to portray the destruction of the tea as a spontaneous act of "the People."[3]

Demonstrating their power on the night of January 25, 1774, a 1,200-strong Boston mob tarred and feathered John Malcom. No one was ever prosecuted for this crime. The alleged catalyst for the attack was the claim that Malcom had assaulted George Robert Twelves Hewes, a Boston shoemaker. But there are several reasons to think the attack sent a larger message. First, were the goal to avenge a comrade, a few punches would have sufficed. But they publicly tortured and brutalized Malcom for hours. Second, Hewes and Malcom were on opposite sides of the Tea Party. Hewes probably helped destroy the tea; Malcom had worked for His Majesty's Customs. Third, customs workers like Malcom were potential witnesses in any court case about the destruction of the tea. Two customs officers were on each of the three tea ships when the crowd arrived to destroy the tea. The crowd set them onshore before beginning their work. These men had not signed affidavits failing to identify the tea partiers, and they presented a legal risk for Patriots. Making an example of Malcom, one of the more energetic customs officers, shut up other officers who might identify members of the crowd. Fourth, Malcom himself indicated a link between his beating and the tea. He asked the Company for compensation for the "hardships he underwent in consequence of the Company's' exporting Tea" to Boston. Finally, the January assault was the second attack on Malcom; he had already been tarred and feathered earlier that winter in Maine for seizing a vessel guilty of smuggling tea, which suggests the real reason for the attacks was not the fight with Hewes but that Malcom was a customs officer who did his job as imperial authorities expected, rather than negotiating with colonists, as others expected.[4]

Boston Patriots were done negotiating—a concept that implies give and take. After the Tea Party, they dominated Massachusetts with political violence and silenced their opponents. The mob dragged Malcom from his house in the night, beat him, and brought him to the customs house, demonstrating customs agents were unsafe at home and work. They stripped him to his waist and warmed him with hot tar and "comic" feathers. They carted him around town in humiliation: from the customs house to the "Liberty Tree," where they freely beat him when he would not curse the governor and resign his commission, to

Copp's Hill, to the Charlestown ferry, and the customs house again, flogging him when he refused their demands. At the gallows they threw a noose around his neck and threatened to hang him unless he recanted his commission. When he would not, they beat him half to death with clubs, flogged him some more, and then threatened to cut off his ears. During the night, the mob made Malcom toast each member of the royal family with a bowl of tea until he vomited. After three bowlfuls, they thrust a "drenching Horn" in his mouth and forced another nine down—a nice touch for a customs officer who had failed to stop the Tea Party. The ordeal lasted four hours, at the end of which Malcom, stripped naked in a winter so cold Boston Harbor had frozen over, was frostbitten and nearly frozen stiff. Doctors did not think he would live. It took him three days to warm up again. The tar and the cold had stripped his skin, which came off "in Stakes." He brought the pieces to England to prove his endurance for the Crown.[5]

This was a dominance ritual. Malcom was harassed, debased, and expected to shut up and take it. Customs Commissioner Henry Hulton was "pelted by the Mob" in the summer of 1773 and told not to complain. "I took it quietly, and said nothing," he wrote. "And I am told they now say I am such a patient, quiet Gentleman, they will trouble me no more." Malcom's beating was worse because he did not take it quietly. Malcom's debasement complete, Hutchinson reported to London that "there is no spirit in those who used to be friends of government." The consignees had fled to the harbor-island Castle William before the Tea Party. Colonel Leslie thought them "likely to remain" in the castle, "for the Mob threatens them much if they go to Town." Protected by a regiment from angry crowds but not from this "very cold place," they stayed for much of the winter. Some escaped to the countryside, but Governor Hutchinson thought "not one of them dare to appear in Town though their business suffers greatly." The *William*'s tea's arrival increased their opprobrium, the Patriotic *Boston Gazette* suggesting that the consignees would have been better off with a "Mill-Stone tied round their Necks, than suffer'd the Tea" to come to the castle. The concern they might bring some of this tea with them may have made it even harder for the consignees to go to town. Visiting his in-laws in Plymouth, Elisha Hutchinson suffered "base treatment." "My friends [had] advised me to go to Court," which entailed going to Boston, Thomas Hutchinson Jr. wrote. Fortunately for him, in the days before the attack on Malcom, his friends "generally advised me the contrary."[6]

In early March, a series of near-daily events underscored Patriot street power. On Friday, March 4, John Hancock gave the annual Boston Massacre oration, whipping up the populace. On Sunday, March 6, the *Fortune* arrived from London with a private shipment of tea, which "Indians" destroyed the next day. "The owner of the Tea" on the *Fortune* was "very silent" about this, wrote Hutchinson. "I think if they could find out who were the immediate actors they would not venture at present to bring any Action in the Law against them," lest the crowd chase them to Castle William, too. That evening, exhibits for the Boston Massacre memorial were illuminated, showing the bodies and severed heads of Henry VII's tax collectors in a pool of blood, axe nearby, with portraits of Governor Hutchinson and Chief Justice Oliver adjacent.

Lieutenant Governor Andrew Oliver's funeral came the next day. The mobs following the funeral train were so abusive Peter Oliver thought it unsafe to attend his brother's burial. None of the Company's consignees had yet been able to return to Boston. When General Gage arrived in Boston in May 1774 he found Hutchinson, Oliver, the customs commissioners, and the consignees either in the castle or dispersed to the countryside. Oliver explained that the radicals' philosophy, *inter arma enim silent leges* (in times of war, the law falls silent), worked.[7]

Radical power in government complemented radical power on the streets. Radicals dominated the Massachusetts Assembly (which chose the governor's council), the Boston town meeting, and its committee of correspondence. The town meeting, in turn, elected grand jurors. The governor and his attorney general, Jonathan Sewall, sought criminal charges for the Tea Party, but grand jurors elected for their politics had to approve these charges. Past grand jurors had been celebrated for refusing to indict Patriots. In the summer of 1774, grand jurors elected to serve in the Suffolk County Superior Court included Patriot Paul Revere and John Hancock's brother, Ebenezer. Hutchinson hoped to prosecute tea rioters on charges of breaking open a shop or ship (punishable by branding), but the prosecution failed. He tried to offer a reward for information and, when his Patriot-selected council rejected this, asked Sewall to investigate and present the matter to a grand jury. But, as Hutchinson explained, "Grand Jurors for that town . . . were among the principal promoters of the meetings which occasioned the destruction of the tea, and were undoubtedly selected to prevent any prosecutions."[8]

Patriots intimidated witnesses. The presence of active radicals on the grand jury was a form of witness tampering, for a witness could expect grand jurors to point him out to the mob later. Informers, especially customs informers, were targets for angry mobs. So witnesses forget what they saw, and grand juries did not indict. Criminal charges, while technically available, were practically impossible.[9]

As agents of the East India Company, the Boston tea consignees could have filed a civil suit for damages. Rumors the Company would file reached Hancock's ears in February. The Company sent out a "Letter of Attorney" in April, empowering consignees to recover damages, but no record of any suit survives. A civil suit faced similarly hostile juries and frightened witnesses, as well as plaintiffs afraid to come to Boston.[10]

The best solution was the Vice-Admiralty Court, which provided for a trial by judge (and was assailed by Patriot writers because of this). The Vice-Admiralty Court was a civil court. Tea consignees could have sued on behalf of the Company, and customs officers could have sued for violation of trade laws. But both scenarios required plaintiffs to be in Boston.[11] One of the most important reasons to continue frightening the consignees was to keep them from the courthouse. There is no evidence any case was filed.

Patriots further undermined the courts by attacking judges, especially Chief Justice Oliver. Patriots escalated an old issue—Oliver's decision to take a salary from the Crown rather than the colony—after the Tea Party. Thomas Hutchinson Jr. thought attention on Oliver would "Screen the poor Consignees" from Patriot ire, but his father noted the attacks on judges were meant to "prevent a trial of those concerned in the tea riots." Certainly, pressure on Oliver made it harder for such a case to proceed. Jurors used the salary issue to prevent Oliver from presiding over the Suffolk County Superior Court in February 1774. Patriots in the colonial legislature impeached him. Others threatened murder. The "flame is kindling fast against" judges, Thomas Hutchinson Jr. wrote, "it is thought it will not be safe for them to come to Court unless they comply with every demand made of them."[12]

The inability to produce witnesses had stopped criminal prosecution for the destruction of the government schooner *Gaspée* in Rhode Island in 1772. That had been a more-direct affront to parliamentary power than the destruction of private property in Boston Harbor.[13] Despite rewards for information, investigators could not definitively name anyone involved in the *Gaspée* attack. An investigation into the destruction of the tea was unlikely to fare better. This was a change from earlier days when the court system *had* worked, most notably in the Boston Massacre trial. But now grand jury nullification would also stop prosecution in Greenwich, New Jersey, in 1775 as well. Failure to prosecute demonstrated the weakness of the customs administration, the courts, and the empire.

But perhaps the central weakness, in the ministry's eyes, was Massachusetts. A criminal conspiracy threatened the colony. It lacked rule of law. Judges could not preside in court; grand jurors voted politically; the governor's council refused to offer rewards for information about plainly criminal acts; and public beatings of crown officials intimidated plaintiffs and witnesses from appearing in court. Patriots, for their part, saw this as the democratic elements of the colony's constitution (town meetings, governor's councils, and grand jurors) constraining imperial power. But is there either law or democracy in organizing a crime and then voting yourself innocent?

The Ministry's First Response: Tea Party as Treason

As news of the Boston Tea Party reached London, the ministry formulated a response to secure the "Dependence of the Colonies upon this Kingdom." Demanding Bostonians pay for the tea was an early and important goal, but not payment merely for payment's sake. Payment was punishment and, more importantly, a way of "reducing [Massachusetts] to a state of obedience to lawful authority." Reports of Massachusetts lawlessness—especially the attack on Malcom—underscored the view that Patriot rioters needed to be brought to heel. Combined with a sense that this lawlessness was not merely the selfish acts of smugglers (as it was in England) but organized in deliberate rejection of parliamentary authority, the ministry came round to the idea that Boston had to pay monetarily because, punitively, Boston had to pay.[14]

The ministry initially focused on criminal prosecution. Massachusetts courts had jurisdiction and were unlikely to indict. But one crime could be prosecuted in England: treason. The Treason Act of 1543 allowed for treason committed outside England to be tried in England. If the Tea Partiers could be charged with treason, the problems of Massachusetts courts might be avoided.[15] And perhaps, with Patriot leaders in England, Boston would calm down.

The charge of treason was a political and legal escalation. The destruction of the tea was a property crime, for which treason was not a straightforward charge. When Hutchinson had wanted to bring treason charges, his council stood him down, focusing Massachusetts prosecutorial interest on the Tea Party as a property offense. Treason charges validated the Patriots' claim that the Company's tea shipments were not simply commercial ventures but political ones. Elsewhere, friends of government had tried to de-escalate the politics of the Company's tea shipments. John Penn of Pennsylvania never even reported the tea ship *Polly* being turned around there. Dartmouth, alarmed at being kept in the dark, explained that what happened to the *Polly* was an "insult that has been offered to this kingdom by the inhabitants of Philadelphia." Penn replied that he had understood the Company's tea was a "private adventure of their own in which the government had no immediate concern." This point was made about the Company's tea in Charleston in service of getting the tea landed. Now the ministry pushed in the opposite direction as its friends, validating Patriot efforts to turn questions of private property and local crime into questions of imperial authority, legitimacy, and power.[16]

To stretch legal reasoning far enough to allow treason charges, Attorney General Edward Thurlow and Solicitor General Alexander Wedderburn argued that the Tea Party could be considered treason because it was "an attempt, concerted with much deliberation and made with open force . . . to obstruct the execution of an Act of Parliament imposing a duty on tea" and to restrain trade, which amounted to "the levying of war against His Majesty." After examining testimony and evidence in February 1774, they listed several Patriots leaders as chargeable for calling on one of the tea consignees to give up his role, for their role in the Boston town meeting of November 29 (which resolved to block the tea's landing and set a watch on the ships to ensure no tea was brought ashore), and for the watch itself. These acts "were of such a nature & criminality as to have fixed a deep degree of Guilt upon those who were the principal Ring-leaders," Dartmouth explained. All members of the Boston committee of correspondence were chargeable. If the town selectmen or the Massachusetts Assembly authorized these acts in their official capacity, they were chargeable too.[17]

Charging treason required proving intent. Destruction of private property was not prima facie treason. Prosecutors would have to prove that the Tea Party was not an anti-tea riot, a mob organized by one merchant to impoverish another, common criminality, or even a political protest but, according to Thurlow and Wedderburn's reasoning, an organized effort to stop effective enforcement of the law equivalent to "War against His Majesty." The November and December town meetings were certainly part of an organized effort to subvert the Tea Act. But connecting those meetings to the Tea Party proved impossible. Thurlow and Wedderburn could find no evidence any meeting authorized the Tea Party. Rather, according to witnesses interviewed in England, the November 29 meeting was specifically concerned that the "Tea would not be destroyed." One reason the Patriots put a guard on the ships had been to prevent such precipitous action, pending the tea's hoped-for return to England. The meeting on December 16 ended not with a determination about the tea, but with Samuel Adams's lament that he did not know "what more they could do to save their Country." Perhaps this was a signal to destroy the tea. But it was impossible to prove this or to connect any of the meetings to the destruction of the tea in court.[18]

To bring a charge of treason amounted to over-charging for political reasons. Treason would have been more plausibly charged had the Tea Partiers attacked the King's officers. But they had not even broken into the His Majesty's Customs House. They attacked privately owned tea on privately owned ships. And why charge the Boston committee but not the committees in New York, Philadelphia, and Charleston, which had also stopped the implementation of the Tea Act? Singling out Boston was a political choice intended, as Lord Apsley noted, to "mark out Boston and separate that Town from the rest of the Delinquents." It was not a choice based on legal reasoning.[19] Meanwhile, according to Thurlow and Wedderburn's logic, the tea smuggling gangs that roamed the English countryside were committing worse treason than the Bostonians, yet remained ignored.

More basically, if destroying the tea obstructed the Tea Act, then perhaps it was a violation of the Tea Act, or of the Navigation Acts generally, not treason. Thurlow and Wedderburn's description of the Tea Party made it sound like smuggling. But it is hard to see how destroying the tea violated even the Tea Act, which did not mandate tea be imported or forbid attacks on private property. The Patriots worked around British mercantile law. They destroyed the tea because of the otherwise successful functioning of the Tea Act. The destruction of the tea in Boston fulfilled the conditions of the Tea Act by leaving no tea to be landed. The problem, of course, was the destruction of the tea. The attorney general was well to be worried about the rule of law in Boston, but spurious, excessive, and political charges hardly ameliorated this.

Even Thurlow and Wedderburn warned at the end of February that testimony available in England was insufficient to sustain a treason charge. After interviewing ten witnesses in the Privy Council, Dartmouth and the attorney general gave up on treason for the time being. Most "witnesses" had seen nothing. The attorney general had queried travelers from Boston—had they had seen anything? Of the ten queried, only seven were in Boston on the day of the Tea Party; of those, only one saw the destruction of the tea. This "eyewitness," Hugh Williamson, was a doctor who had walked down to the water's edge to watch. He (wisely) did this from a fifty-yard distance and could identify no one: he was too far off, the actors were disguised, and, hailing from Bristol, Rhode Island, he would not have recognized them anyway. Francis Rotch and James Hall, owner and master of the *Dartmouth*, respectively, also traveled to England. But they were not with the vessel when it was attacked. Captain Scott of the *Hayley* had been in Boston but had not witnessed the event. It is not clear if the Privy Council even tried to interview crewmen. Thurlow and Wedderburn utterly failed to connect the actions of the Boston Patriot leadership to the destruction of the tea.[20]

Punishment: The Boston Port Act

Believing Boston had in its official capacity aided treason, but unable to charge treason, the ministry brought in the Boston Port Bill. The bill punished Boston as though the town had committed treason. Parliament's collective punishment of Bostonians was somewhat logical since the town was operating under a sort of omertà about the Tea Party. The Port Act shut Boston's port until the tea was paid for. This bill converted payment for the tea from restitution to submission, a goal supported by the King, driven by North, adopted by Parliament, and pursued by General Gage, who was sent out to replace Hutchinson as governor.[21]

The Port Act was vague. It stated that Boston could re-opened only when "full satisfaction" had been made to the Company, a know-it-when-you-see-it concept that was not specified further. Perhaps this was left to Gage, but he did not explain it. In their farewell address to Hutchinson, Massachusettans offering to pay for the tea asked, a mere three days before the act took effect, when "the sum and manner of [paying] it can be ascertained."[22] Would the charge for the tea be limited to the real loss to the Company (booked at £7,521 and change), or would it include the lost duty and commission charges as well (which raised the price to £9,659 and change)? Should they pay in specie, in Massachusetts currency, or sterling? In barter, notes, or bills of exchange? Should they pay in Boston or London? Should the East India Company be paid directly? The consignees? Gage? Would Gage open the port immediately, or should townsfolk, who needed to know where their livelihood would come from, expect him to wait for approval from London? The bill demanded "reasonable satisfaction" to the customs and other officers harassed in the winter of 1773–1774. This included Malcom, but who else? How much money for them? Who would decide? How would these payments be made? Gage and the ministry held Boston for ransom but refused to say what the ransom was because they were waiting for the Town of Boston to ask.[23]

A second, vital, and unstated part of this was the *William*'s tea now stored in Castle William. The Port Act stipulated that re-opening Boston required "peace and obedience to the laws" such that "the trade of Great Britain may safely be carried on there, and his Majesty's customs duly collected." This meant that Patriots would have to allow the *William*'s tea to be landed and taxed after Boston was re-opened and dutied tea to be landed as a matter of course. There would be no more tea parties on vessels like the *Fortune*, either. And with the Company's tea safely landed in Boston, Collector Halliday could sell off the much larger supply of Company tea in the Charleston Exchange. This in turn would likely kill much of the opposition to Company tea and the

Tea Act generally. Why reject Company tea in New York and Philadelphia if it was coming in by the tens, perhaps hundreds, of thousands of pounds in other ports? Paying for the tea could quickly grow into an existential defeat for the Patriot movement.[24]

It is unclear whether all this was planned. The sale of the *William*'s tea went unmentioned in parliamentary debates about the Port Bill. Treasury, Dartmouth, and the East India Company were informed separately about the tea's survival. The implications of that survival may also have been unclear since, while Parliament debated the Port Bill, Dartmouth urged repeal of the Tea Act. Repeal could have allowed the *William*'s tea to be returned to Britain (it was only through the Tea Act that the Company could ship un-auctioned tea directly to the Americas). The possibility of repeal may explain why the Port Act did not mention the *William*'s tea directly.[25] Yet requiring the sale of the *William*'s tea fit perfectly in the Port Act's larger aim: to defeat the Patriot movement by forcing the continent's most vociferous Patriots into a humiliating stand-down.

Vagueness—in an otherwise specific act—belied the idea the Port Act was about making the Tea Party's victims whole (its official justification) instead of punishing Boston. Repayment was a pretext for the long-overdue (in North's mind) chastisement of Boston. The town's unruliness included the Stamp Act riots of 1765, the *Liberty* riots of 1768, the Boston "Massacre" of 1770, and the destruction of the tea. The Port Act was deliberately not proportional to the crime. If payment were not made, it did not re-open the port after a set time, meaning the harm to Boston would far outstrip the harm done to the Company. For North, the goal was submission.[26]

The brief period between news of the act reaching Boston (May 10) and port closure (June 1) made it impossible to pay quickly enough to keep the port open. As the Loyalist addressers of Governor Hutchinson lamented, even if payment were possible, there was no time: the townspeople had to "suffer" together before any relief. If payment, not punishment, were the priority, the threat of punishment could have been left dangling over Boston for some months, and Parliament (or Gage) could have specified how much money was required. As Patriotic South Carolinian John Lewis Gervais explained: "If your political engineers had been skillful, a reimbursement for damages would have been first demanded, and punishment held, *in Terrorem*, in case of refusal."[27]

Instead, the town was held ransom in a situation seemingly analogous to the debtor's prison: imprisonment kept the inmate from earning money for his release, but his suffering forced friends or family to pay on his behalf. Closing the port put much of Boston out of work and hobbled the town's and colony's ability to pay. But, unlike the analogy of debtor's prison, North would not take just anyone's money. He turned down the offer of Robert Murray, a

New York merchant then in London, to help pay for the tea. Hayley and Hopkins and other British firms trading with North America offered partial payment to delay the Port Act. North rejected it. Other reports suggest British merchants trading to Boston offered a £16,000 security. They would pay the Company on Boston's behalf and collect from Boston later. The Lord Mayor of London offered £20,000 security, provided the Port Act was not introduced. These offers made some economic sense—it was not uncommon for one merchant to act as "security" for another, and the East India Company had asked various merchants in Britain to act as security for the North American consignees. That promise may not have extended to insuring the cargo against a riot, but merchants trading to Boston seem to have thought some sort of shared guarantee was in their self-interest. Yet North would only take the money if the merchants would guarantee "the future peaceable conduct & entire acquiescence" of Massachusettsans in taking British tea and obeying British laws, a knowingly impossible demand.[28] The ministry was choosy about who paid because money coming from official bodies—the town of Boston or the colony of Massachusetts—would mean those bodies had been cowed and could, as institutions, be expected to help enforce the law and secure residents' good conduct.

Gage was similarly choosy. Bostonians offered to ransom the city at the end of May and again on June 8. When they asked Gage how much money was needed, he sent them away without an answer because they had no official or personal responsibility for the tea's destruction. Gage would tell the Assembly or the town of Boston—but only if either body asked. When Gage urged Bostonians to raise funds "to pay for the tea" in October (a point he also raised with the Continental Congress), he was not so much seeking funds as seeking a collective acknowledgment of guilt (or a collective agreement by these bodies to punish the guilty).[29]

One unintended consequence of collectively punishing Boston was that the ministry made the position of conservative merchants, some of its most important allies in Boston, untenable. The Port Act "has had every evil consequence that was anticipated," lamented Joshua Winslow to a friend in London. Among "persons chiefly punished are the very ones who should have been excluded from the operation of the act"—friends of government, who, he thought, should have been allowed the use of the port while it remained shut to others. Merchants like Winslow were attacked from both sides. The ministry impoverished them by closing the port, while Patriots harassed them for speaking up for the ministry, which Winslow came to regret. He should "have been silent and at the least have fallen in with the many," because if he could not escape the Port Act, he could have at least escaped the Patriots.[30]

The Company hardly needed the money. The Company asked Parliament in February 1774 to reimburse its loss of £9,659 6s 4d in Boston. In comparison, it had received a £1.4 million bailout loan from Parliament in 1773. It also had considerable surplus tea, meaning any tea that was returned would be hard to sell. The merchants who offered a £16,000 security explained that the Boston tea was "of a bad Quality"; much of it was "'Out of Time, that is Tea, which has been repeatedly offer'd for Sale" at the Company's auctions in London, "and so often refused" it "could not be again ever offer'd for Sale." Other reports suggested the tea was "Damagd tea not fit for merchants," some of it three years old, some moldy and "not merchantable." "Many of the off[ic]ers in the Company Service Say the tea was Extream Bad." The *Pennsylvania Gazette* picked up on allegations the tea was "three Years old," "mouldy and unwholesome." Reimbursement for unsellable tea was a neat trick.[31]

Yet these claims served an agenda and must be taken with a grain of salt. While it is easy to imagine the Company kept its newest and best teas back in London, it is hard to imagine the Company paid to ship half a million pounds of tea with no reasonable prospect of sale. The teas from the *William* and *London* were ultimately drunk with no complaint—but in wartime conditions when consumers had little choice. It is difficult to assess the tea's quality in part because eighteenth- and twenty-first-century tastes, and even grades of tea, are so different. If the tea was truly spoiled, the irony worked twice. First, the Company, presented with an opportunity to expand, had sabotaged itself by sending bad product. Second, the Boston Patriots did not have to be so exercised about it. The ministry saw no urgency in the Company's demand and made no payment. Refunding the Company was a cudgel against Boston; it did not matter to the Company's finances.[32]

Treatment of Boston as a unit punished the innocent with the guilty. This was contested in Parliament. Edmund Burke spoke out against collective punishment. Hutchinson, he pointed out, had not called out soldiers or ships, so why should citizens who had not participated in the destruction of the tea suffer for it? It was unclear that so many Bostonians were involved as to implicate the whole town, or even how many participants were Bostonians.

Nor are these points clear today. Benjamin Labaree's *Boston Tea Party* claims that "most" participants were Bostonians but provides little evidence. We know that men from neighboring towns joined, and some participants were seamen who subsequently went to sea. A crowd gathered to watch the destruction of the tea, but it would be a mistake to assume, as Labaree did, that watchers granted "silent approval"—some mix of shock, horror, and approval probably informed them.[33] Reliable estimates of crowd size for the Boston Tea Party are hard to come by, but even the 1,200 souls who tarred and feathered John Malcom were not a large enough gathering to indicate, on its own, that the event was broadly approved of. Twelve hundred people comprised only 8 percent of the whole city. In assessing the popularity of street politics, one needs to be wary of conflating "popular," as in involving the lower orders, with "popular," as in more liked than not. However Bostonians felt about destruction of the tea, we cannot derive approval from workingmen's participation or crowd size alone.

For precedent to the Port Bill, North pointed to the collective punishments of Glasgow, Edinburgh, and London, all of which were fined (not shuttered) for failing to apprehend criminals. So Rose Fuller, Jamaica plantation owner, West India lobbyist, and MP for Rye, recommended fining Boston £20,000 to pay for the Tea Party. But North dismissed fines—his own precedent—as "lenity." Fuller's fine would have covered the Company's damages, compensated Malcom and others, and capped the hardship to Boston. It was significantly larger than the £2,000 levied on Edinburgh during the Porteous riots, where someone died. Certainly, the cost would have been a serious punishment for the town. William Dowdeswell, who led the Rockingham Whig opposition in Parliament, pointed out that any policy that punished Boston should have been extended to New York and Philadelphia, where the Company had incurred losses in the form of shipping costs, and to Charleston, where he thought the tea was rendered "rotten and useless" by being placed in a "damp cellar." He, too, was ignored. So, to get repayment for a Company that did not need it, and to make sure the guilty paid, North punished the innocent and the guilty together. Even attempts to make the Port Act more palatable by pairing it with a repeal of the Tea Act—a pairing suggested by MPs disposed to make peace with the colonies rather than punish them—failed.[34]

The Boston Port Act was punitive, but the rest of the Coercive Acts were not primarily meant to punish or even confront but to remedy perceived defects in colonial governance. The Massachusetts Government Act made the Massachusetts Council appointed by the Crown rather than elected by the lower house and restricted town meetings, which were seen as a source of disorder. These provisions reflected a sense that Massachusetts was overly democratic and have been the focus of scholarly attention. Yet twenty-one of the act's twenty-four provisions focused on the courts, which the ministry also saw as overly democratic. The act empowered the governor to appoint the attorney general, judges, sheriffs, and other court officers unilaterally. Most of the act's provisions focused on juries. Grand juries were to be chosen by governor-appointed sheriffs, not elected by town meetings, preventing Patriot interference in criminal prosecutions. General Thomas Gage would go out as civilian governor and military commander with four regiments of reinforcements in support of these changes. The Administration of Justice Act allowed officials charged with capital crimes committed in the course of their duties to be tried outside the colony if the governor felt they would not receive a fair trial in Massachusetts. It did not provide for the trial of suspected tea partiers outside of Massachusetts. Such a possibility, though discussed, was dropped.[35] Other acts, such as the Quartering Act and the Quebec Act (sometimes lumped with the others), were similarly reformatory.

The core flaw in the ministry's reasoning was not understanding the key theater for quelling colonial unrest was the colonies. Colonists' protests against taxation without representation argued that the colonies were important polities. And voices from these polities suggested alternative paths. The few remaining colonial agents in London, along with colonists like Henry Laurens, lobbied against the Port Bill. Dartmouth maintained correspondence with Joseph Reed and Thomas McKean, both of whom served on revolutionary committees.[36] But Dartmouth and North were in a Westminster bubble—they did what sounded good to other MPs, not what played well in North America.

North and Gage missed key avenues to advance the ministry's cause in colonial politics by embarrassing Patriots. Patriots practiced victimhood politics—portraying the ministry and its taxes as oppressive and the colonists as victims. The destruction of the tea made Patriots aggressors, but North and Gage could not embarrass Patriots by decrying Patriot aggression—perhaps because these men were nobody's victims. In the Revolution, conservatives struggled to match Patriot rhetoric. And so, rather than pursuing a more lenient course (to portray the Patriots as aggressors), or pursuing measures that might set Patriots against each other (like fines), North's harsh, collective punishment returned Patriots to their role as victims at the hands of an evil ministry. North saw himself as a rationalizer eliminating the barriers to effective government. But he reacted to the wrong target: the destruction of the tea rather than the discord among Patriots that destruction created. And in ignoring concerns about the Coercive Acts, North united colonists across North America, who wondered what colony would be next.

Despite the punishment of Boston, efforts to charge individual tea partiers continued. Dartmouth explained in March that the ministry wanted to suspend Boston's trading privileges and also to see the "ringleaders in destruction of tea to be punished." After it proved impossible to try people in England, Dartmouth hoped Gage could bring prosecutions in Massachusetts. The "one thing I much wish" is "punishment of those individuals who have been the ringleaders," he told Parliament in April. He gave Gage copies of all available information. It was "difficult . . . to establish such a connection between the Acts of the body of the People [in town meetings, etc.] and the destruction of the Tea" to charge treason in England. However, lesser charges might still be brought in Massachusetts. Gage should go ahead "in the ordinary Courts of Justice within the Colony" if "there is a probability of their being brought to punishment." This was "a very necessary and essential Example to others." Dartmouth listed the men known to have led attacks on the consignees when the Company's tea first arrived: Joseph Warren, Samuel Adams, Benjamin Church, William Mollineux, Thomas Young, and others. This was an obvious place for Gage to start his own investigations. However, Dartmouth cautioned Gage not to bother bringing a case unless he was confident of victory. If the "prejudices of the people" made conviction impossible, it was better to avoid a trial than risk "disgraceful" defeat, and Warren and Adams had already alibied themselves for the Tea Party itself.[37]

Gage provided Peter Oliver with all the testimony gathered in London. In late June Oliver thought the time "not yet favorable" for prosecutions and recommended delays. Attempts to gather evidence continued, but in early July Gage reported that he could not gather enough to prosecute: "tho' I hear of many Things against this and that Person, yet when I descend to particular Points, and want People to stand forth in order to bring Crimes home to individuals by clear and full Evidence, I am at a Loss." The problem, Gage continued, was "the usurpation and Tyranny established here, by Edicts of Town Meetings enforced by Mobs, by assuming the sole use and Power of the Press, and influencing the Pulpits. By nominating and intimidating of Juries, and in some Instances threatening the Judges." These would be difficult to stop, and they prevented a "free and impartial course of Justice whereby Delinquents can be brought to Punishment," which was "the chief thing wanting." Despite "thousands" of people involved in the Tea Party or "spectators of it," Gage lamented that "only one witness could be procured to give testimony against them, and that one conditionally that the delinquents should be tried in England"—far from the madding crowd. Oliver also hoped Gage would send men to England for trial. But English courts had no jurisdiction. Gage was as powerless to round up tea partiers as Hutchinson had been.[38]

Despite the Massachusetts Government Act, Gage's writ extended no farther than his troops, making the act pointless. Parliament expected "obedience and due submission to legal authority." But Patriots responded to the Massachusetts Government Act by shutting down the courts. Patriots forced sheriffs and deputies who issued writs under the new colonial government to renounce that government's authority. They forbade jurors from participating in the new courts. Mobs attacked or shut courts in Worcester, Taunton, Springfield, and Berkshire, Massachusetts, attacked the attorney general's home in Cambridge, and surrounded the lieutenant governor's home, forcing him to sign a letter of resignation. Gage wrote Dartmouth in September, "Civil government is near its end, the courts of justice expiring one after another." Three days later, Benjamin Hallowell lamented that the "civil authority in this country being now quite at an end, no courts of justice to be held, juries refusing to serve, and . . . rebellion has at last taken place." Four days later, the Suffolk Resolves demanded "no Obedience" to the new Massachusetts government. Massachusettsans, Dartmouth noted, "refuse obedience to the law." Boston Patriots of all classes resisted. Patriot William Tudor asked an out-of-work ship carpenter at the end of September, "This is very discouraging, pray don't you think it almost Time to submit, pay for the Tea, & get the Harbour opened?"

"Submit! NO," the carpenter replied.[39]

To Pay or Not to Pay

Efforts to prosecute tea partiers ended by September, but efforts to pay for the tea had been ongoing since May. Boston held a town meeting on May 13, the day Gage arrived. Harrison Gray, in attendance, thought "the general sense of the town was in favour of paying for the tea." But stalling was easy: Should the town or colony pay? Did the town need colonial authorization? Should the town borrow? The matter went to a committee. Merchant John Rowe sat on the committee and recommended payment. Rowe felt "the revenge of the ministry was too severe," but that Boston had little choice. Rowe, who served on revolutionary committees, joined merchants' meetings, and called on Governor Gage, was positioned to bring a moderate solution. He disliked the radicals' violence and the ministry's response. But the committee proved a bust: two other members who might have supported moderation, merchants Nathaniel Appleton and Thomas Boylston, avoided the meetings, leaving radicals dominant, as they dominated the town meeting as a whole.[40]

On May 18, Boston merchants and others circulated a proposal to pay for the tea. Loyalist George Erving offered £2,000 if others would contribute, offering to call on Governor Gage to find out how much the total would be. There are "many among us, who are for compromising," merchant John Andrews noted. Merchant John Amory recommended at the town meeting that Boston follow Erving's lead, but the suggestion was rejected and omitted from the town records "though he urged the matter much."[41]

Radicals delayed the committee's report. As Gervais had suggested, the brief lag between the Port Act's announcement and its implementation was the Patriots' weakest spot. The longer Patriots delayed consideration of payment, the more damage the act caused and the more blame accrued to the ministry. In the short term, implementation of the act also made it harder for the consignees to land the tea from Castle William, as that tea would have to be shuttled to another port of doubtful security elsewhere along the Massachusetts coast. Nothing was done at the May 18 meeting or at the next meeting on May 30. This was the last chance for Boston to pay before the Port Act took effect. Merchants and tradesmen pushed for repayment. But, as Bostonians filed in the door, Whigs told them not to mention payment. Instead, according to Gray, the radicals, "whose importance and political salvation depend upon the province being kept in a continual flame," urged waiting several months to form a congress.[42] There Patriots' martyrdom of Boston could rally the continent.

Conservatives lacked a ground-level organization outside of government capable of organizing payment. Erving's offer stood. Signers of the address presented to Hutchinson seconded it. They "disavowed" the "lawless" "outrage" of the Boston Tea Party, "yet, considering ourselves as members of the same community," offered to pay their share. Conservatives exhorted "all the Colonies on the Continent (the infant Settlements of Georgia and Nova-Scotia excepted) [to] join in paying for it."[43] But they did nothing to accomplish this. Hierarchically minded, they waited on Gage to name a price. Gage, in turn, waited on the Patriot-controlled town meeting, which left conservatives holding back their own actions on behalf of Patriots.

Of the 124 signatories to the farewell address presented to Hutchinson, about half were merchants. Some sold or advertised tea. One, Joshua Winslow, had been involved in the Company's tea now at the bottom of Boston Harbor. Boston's merchants wanted to pay for the Company's losses so they could stem their own. But the signers were a small minority—not even 15 percent—of Boston's import-export merchants (who would be hardest hit by the closure of the port) and a smaller minority of the town. The Patriots struck back with a broadside listing the names of Hutchinson's addressers and, helpfully for the mob, where their shops were.[44]

On June 2 some Tories and moderate Whigs agreed to pay for the tea. Like the May 18 petitioners, they were neither representative of nor accountable to the town. In response, the Boston committee of correspondence sent out its Solemn League and Covenant, calling for a boycott without the town meeting's approval either. "We have found from experience, that no dependence can be had upon *merchants*," wrote Charles Chauncy. They stand not for liberty and serve only "their own private separate interest. Our dependence, under God, is upon the *landed interest*." By farmers "not buying of the merchants what they may as well do without," merchants could be made to boycott England. Boycotts, explained John Andrews, make merchants less willing to pay for the tea. Why pay to open the port to trade if a boycott were coming?[45]

Moderates still wanted the town to pay for the tea. At the June 17 town meeting, one radical lamented that Bostonians "wanting to pay for the Tea . . . are too formidable." Arguing payment would legitimate the Port Act, radicals defeated the proposal. Writing in the press, Patriots claimed "not one" person had supported payment at this meeting and boasted of their "unanimity." Moderates tried again in the June 27–28 meeting, which rejected the Solemn League and Covenant and investigated the committee of correspondence for sending it out without meeting approval, but failed. The colonial legislature, moved by Gage to Salem, likewise refused to consider payment, and Gage's dissolution of that body on June 27 precluded future efforts. In the end, neither Boston nor Massachusetts paid.[46]

Here, the Company's tea in Castle William served as a one-way ratchet for escalation. In their letter to the Company in July 1774, the Boston consignees advised "that the Inhabitants did not at that time appear disposed to pay for the Tea," and that consignees were unable "to sell any of the Teas which had been deposited in the Castle."[47] (The consignees had not quit trying to advance and protect the Company's interests.) Closure of the port made it impossible to land the tea in Boston, impoverishment of the city made it hard to find buyers, and political odium made it worse. All this was good for Patriots. Though the Port Act might secure the tea's eventual sale, ironically, by shutting Boston's port, the Act prevented the tea's landing for the time being. Boston Patriots had an all-or-nothing choice: oppose the Tea and Coercive Acts, leave the port closed, keep the *William*'s tea out, boycott, and rally Congress. Or, accept the Tea and Coercive Acts, pay to open the port, receive the *William*'s tea, drop the boycott, and not bother with Congress.

Paying for the tea outside of government was "silly." A subscription solved nothing since radicals would refuse to contribute, leaving conservatives and moderates to bail out extremists, who would bear no cost for their actions. What would stop them from sticking moderates with the bill again? Individuals could afford to pay once, but the town or colony would have to start enforcing order afterwards, and this was best confirmed by the town or colony paying in the first place. This was why Gage wanted the town or colony, as institutions, to pay.[48]

Some colonists elsewhere encouraged Boston to pay. Members of the Philadelphia committee of nineteen did, even after the Coercive Acts, if it could end the "controversy" and preserve "constitutional liberty." Wealthy Quaker merchants in Philadelphia agreed, as did some New Yorkers. Abel James and Henry Drinker, consignees for the Company in Philadelphia, reported the "weighty and serious part of the [Philadelphia] Community"—that is, conservatives—thought "it would . . . have been for the best" had the Polly's tea been landed. James Pemberton, a conservative Quaker merchant, thought it was "agreed by most" that "Restitution" for Philadelphia sending away its tea "ought to be made," and that the town's radical newspapers mispresented public opinion on this.[49] It is difficult to know how much to credit conservatives' conceit of their own silent popularity.

On July 18, the Fairfax, Virginia County Resolves offered to help pay for the tea. If its destruction was "an Invasion of private Property, we shall be willing to contribute towards paying the East India Company." Fairfax also resolved to boycott the Company. The Fairfax Resolves, written by George Mason and endorsed at a meeting chaired by George Washington, were radical and influential, serving as a framework for the Virginia Association. They called for non-importation of British goods, a congress, and ending the slave trade. Fairfax Patriots paired this with paying for the tea. South Carolinian Henry Laurens likewise supported inter-colonial payment. "I truly hope, that payment will be made by the Colonies in general for the Tea which was destroyed in Boston. It will be of no consequence that the respective contributions are Small, provided they are general." Laurens suggested opening a subscription across South Carolina to share Bostonians' burdens, making payment "an American cause." He offered "from five to Fifty pounds Sterling" himself. Laurens, in London, was influenced by English outrage against the destruction of the tea. From London, payment seemed reasonable: the destruction was "at most a trespass" which could be "healed by paying for the Damages." The tea "must be paid for," he wrote. "I say must, not because an Act of Parliament enjoins it, but upon principles of honesty we ought not to impose Losses & hardships upon our fellow Subjects in the course of our Struggles for maintaining our Liberty."[50]

"A PHILAELPHIAN" made a strong case for payment in the Massachusetts Gazette. Paying was fair play. It was also "what every REAL friend to the cause of America must think [Boston's] indispensable duty. While we contend for liberty, let us not destroy the idea of justice. A trespass has been committed on private property in consequence of the Resolves of your town. Restore to the sufferers the most ample compensation." Convince your enemies "that you regard honesty as much as liberty, and that you detest libertinism and licentiousness." "[P]ay for the tea; it is but justice" and "ought to have been effected" already out of "virtue and TRUE patriotism." The "hint given you" by the Philadelphia committee should "have induced you to comply," and Boston's reasons otherwise "are indeed futile and puerile."[51] Then, with the tea paid for, Whigs could focus on parliamentary taxation without the taint of hooliganism.

The Patriot Response

Instead, radical Patriots urged a continent-wide boycott of Britain and tea, with a congress coordinating it. Patriots knew that payment meant submission. They worried that if "conscientious Americans" paid, it would justify the Port Act and tacitly accept the Massachusetts Government Act.[52] Patriots contested the constitutionality of these acts. The acts were legal according to the doctrine of parliamentary supremacy, but that doctrine seemed a dangerous imposition in colonies with charters and local legislatures that predated it.

Colonists outside of Massachusetts who disliked both the Tea Party and the Port Act chose sides, often against Parliament. The "chastisement of Boston," Penn explained to Dartmouth, was seen as "intimidation to all America," leaving Boston "suffering in the common cause. Their delinquency in destroying the East India Company's tea is lost in the attention given to what is here called the too severe punishment." Writing back to Virginia from London, William Lee opposed payment. One Middletown, Connecticut, resident noted that "even the old Farmers"—the Yankee skinflints "who were So sorry that So much Tea" has been "wasted" in Boston Harbor—"now Say they will Stand by the Bostonians." Parliament's destruction of constitutional order, collective punishment, and imposition of a military governor were troubling. While "it should be granted that the Bostonians did wrong in destroying the tea," Virginian Edmund Pendleton wrote, the Port Act and the Massachusetts Government Act were greater wrongs. Whether the Boston Tea Party was "warranted," explained residents in Hanover, Virginia, "we know not; but this we know, that the Parliament" by the Coercive Acts "have made us and all North America parties in the present dispute." What colony might be next? "[W]e shall not suffer ourselves to be sacrificed by piecemeal," but unite, George Washington wrote. Because of Parliament's "despotick Measures," the "cause of Boston . . . now is and ever will be considered as the cause of America." "UNITED WE STAND, DIVIDED WE FALL," wrote residents of Hanover, Virginia.[53]

Patriots objected to the collective punishment of Boston. As Charles Chauncy explained in one pamphlet, there were over 10,000 Bostonians who depended on the port for a living. Parliament had thrown them all out of work, loyal and rebellious alike, without evidence any had "more an hand in the destruction of the East-India company's tea [than] Lord North himself."[54]

The severity of the Port Act, which lacked a time limit, convinced others. "I was of your opinion formerly," John Lewis Gervais explained to Henry Laurens, that the tea which was destroyed at Boston should be valued and paid for; but that motion now requires reconsideration, since the heavy punishment inflicted upon that devoted town. . . . [F]ifty times the amount of the tea would fall short of the damage already sustained in consequence of the port bill; here is infinite distress brought upon a City, in which very few, if any, of the inhabitants are guilty,

and with no benefit to the Company for it. Either forgetting or unaware of the difficulty in getting Boston to pay, Gervais thought Parliament should have "called upon the people who were accused, to answer for themselves before they had either made such demand, or denounced vengeance . . . all the provinces upon the continent would, in such case, have united in this one voice, 'pay the damages;' now their voices are united" against Parliament.[55]

The anonymous author of "An Address to the People of Boston" (June 1774) took advantage of North's misstep to reposition Boston Patriots—who had destroyed thousands of pounds sterling in property—into defenders of property rights. Some colonists said of the tea, it was "but an act of justice we should pay for it." But if payment meant Parliament could pass acts like the Boston Port Act, then "An *American*'s property and liberty are become matters of indulgence, rather than right" and colonists "become slaves." The Port Act included specific provisions forbidding the loading or unloading of goods on Boston's private wharves. The Port Act damaged those assets and was the real attack on property. "We hear not a word of any private company appearing in this whole transaction [in Parliament], not a mention of private property, but Government takes the matter up, and chastises us by an Act of Parliament. Ships and troops are sent out on Government expense, and the whole plan of resentment is Governmental."[56] Private property was, in the author's view, just an excuse.

Practical considerations also facilitated the Patriot position. The tea was difficult to pay for. As Franklin explained, "1. Because of the Uncertainty of the Act which gives them no Surety that the Port shall be opened on their making that Payment. 2. No specific Sum is demanded. 3. No one knows what will satisfy the Custom house Officers; nor who the "others" are that must be satisfied, nor what will satisfy them; and 4. After all, they are in the King's Power how much of the Port shall be opened."[57]

Other pragmatic concerns inhibited payment. The Boston committee had the organizing capacity to raise funds but did not want to, and there was no other organ to step in. Moderates had neither the initiative nor the organization to act in this way. Fundraising efforts like what Laurens proposed never even began. After five months, which should have been enough time, there were still no parties anywhere in North America willing and able to send payment. Their lack of cross-colonial organizing was one of the reasons many moderates supported the creation of a Continental Congress in 1774; they mistakenly hoped that the gathering would become the moderate organization they lacked. But by blocking compromise, revolutionaries made moderation impossible.

Boston Relief

Patriots refused to pay for the tea but paid to support Boston. The committee of donations distributed that relief to people put out of work by the Port Act, while the town's overseers of the poor cared for the infirm and traditionally needy. The committee created jobs through a public works program and carefully thanked each donor. Encouraged in Patriot newspapers—the *South Carolina Gazette* solicited donations on its front page—and by Patriot committees up and down the coast, news of other towns' donations (and of the thank-you notes they received, commonly printed in local newspapers) drove further giving. Boston relief was a propaganda stunt and a serious project, a showy contrast between Patriot charity and Ministerial cruelty, allowing distant colonists to participate in Boston's cause. General Gage thought relief would die out, then Bostonians would pay. He was wrong. Collecting for Boston created a common cause in a way collecting for the East India Company could not. "We will no[t] think so basely of you as to Imagine you will pay for One Ounce of the Tea," South Carolina firebrand Christopher Gadsden wrote Samuel Adams in early June. When he sent rice for Boston relief at the end of the month, Gadsden reiterated: do "not pay for an ounce of that damn'd Tea."[58] The common cause of 1774 was Congress, the boycott, and, most of all, Boston relief.

Donations came from across the continent. Norfolk, Virginia's committee sent 715 bushels of corn, 33 barrels of pork, 58 barrels of bread, and ten barrels of flour. Bethlehem, Pennsylvania Moravians donated, as did the Bucks County committee of safety. Portsmouth, New Hampshire voted £200. "Their bountiful donations from one part of the country and another are daily flowing in upon us," wrote Charles Chauncy. "Waggons, loaded with grain, and sheep, hundreds in a drove, are sent to us . . . Two hundred and fifteen teirces of rice, part of a thousand devoted to our service, are arrived at Salem from South-Carolina." He added, "The cause for which we in this town are suffering, they look upon us as the common cause of all north-America, their cause as truly ours." A survey of ninety-eight provincial and local resolutions responding to the Port Act in 1774 could find only two that urged payment for the tea. Forty-seven raised subscriptions for Boston.[59]

Yet by the spring of 1775, Patriots faced a daunting prospect. Some 7,000 Bostonians depended on donations for their "daily bread," and the number of the poor grew.[60] Perpetual relief was neither intended nor practical, but it was necessary for the foreseeable future. Patriots expected the Association would force Parliament to re-open Boston but did not know when. The Association impaired the colonies' trade more than Britain's. The ministry felt little from non-importation in the spring of 1775 and expected it would collapse from cheating, as the last boycott had. How much longer could Boston relief last? The fighting at Lexington and Concord saved Patriots from this problem: the need for Boston relief ended when, after news of the battles, Patriots fled Boston. Meanwhile, fighting re-energized the common cause.

Paying for the tea was far cheaper than supporting Boston—reimbursement could have been paid from the £13,000 in cash received by March 1775—let alone the value of what colonists sent in kind, and Boston Harbor would probably have re-opened.[61] But colonists gave (and voted substantial sums to support their congressmen) because they trusted Boston not to pay for the tea.

Congress Considers Repaying the Tea

Congress did consider payment. The Pennsylvania provincial convention instructed congressional delegates to pay for the tea in exchange for ending the Coercive Acts and lifting duties. Fairfax County, Virginia supported a continental subscription to pay for the tea. Middlesex County, Virginia resolved similarly. New Jersey delegates were nearly sent with instructions not to pay for the tea, but the option for payment was ultimately kept. Virginian Thomas Adams thought "Americans" (perhaps the upcoming Continental Congress) would "undoubtedly tender the E India Co Payment for their Tea."[62]

Some thought Congress would get Boston to pay. While the Massachusetts delegation was in New York, the committee of fifty-one urged New York congressional delegates to see Boston make payment. Gage thought Boston would follow Congress's advice and took it as the "opinion of most of the other colonies" that Boston should pay. Massachusetts conservatives hoped Congress "might prevail on the Bostonians to make restitution to the East India Company." Payment would be a first step toward "accommodation," Gage wrote in October, adding, "without Such a Complyance I don't see what can be done," in lieu of war.[63]

The Continental Congress debated payment. John Jay made the proposal, seconded by Isaac Low and Edmund Pendleton. Pendleton recommended Congress "expressly justify" Boston in destroying tea, then pay on the condition that the Port Act be instantly lifted. The colonies would then boycott East Indian commodities until the Company refunded the money. Pendleton sought to break the repayment-versus-boycott dichotomy by doing both at once, as the Virginia convention and the New York committee of fifty-one had recommended. Low added that, were Boston port not re-opened after payment, it would afford Congress a victory over Parliament in public opinion.[64]

But the measure lost. Just why is unclear. Beverley Robinson, who was not present, explained that the "proposal to pay for the tea was defeated by [Samuel?] Adams.—He said it was proper the other colonies should pay for it, but, that Boston doing this, would confess a crime, where they should glory in a merit." But there were other explanations. One reason, never stated openly, was the survival of Company tea in Boston and Charleston. The Massachusetts and South Carolina delegations strongly opposed repayment, which would expose them to the threat of Company tea from the *William* and *London* being landed. Sales of this tea would bust any boycott of the Company. This was why Gadsden opposed paying for that "damn'd Tea." Whether other congressmen understood the importance of these cargoes is unclear, though Congress was aware of Bostonians' past consumption of duded tea.[65]

Finally, since repayment would not end the other Coercive Acts, boycott and resistance seemed the only ways to get all offensive acts repealed. This was especially true with the Tea Act, which might generate meaningful revenue without a boycott. Thus, Pendleton adopted Congress's opinion. If examined "abstractedly" the tea "ought" to be paid for. "Merchants sent their property . . . where they had a legal right to send it and it was destroyed[.] [N]o one could speak of its being wrong . . . to pay for it." But in the Port Act "thousands" of "innocent are condemned for the supposed Fault" of others. And since boycotts might provide an excuse to keep Boston closed (as the port was to be opened when "the Trade of Great Britain may be carried on there"), they could not reimburse and boycott.[66]

In its draft address to the people of Great Britain, Congress re-wrote the tea story, noting that Tea Party was a mere "trespass" "committed on some merchandise." Parliament's response was disproportionate. "Even supposing a trespass was thereby committed, and the Proprietors of the tea entitled to damages.—The Courts of Law were open, and Judges appointed by the Crown presided in them.—The East India Company however did not think proper to commence any suits, nor did they even demand satisfaction, either from individuals or from the community in general." The Massachusetts delegation knew it had been impossible for the Company to bring suit; whether Congress knew is unclear. The claim that restitution was a matter for a court, not a legislature, ignored Boston Patriots' organized criminal activity: their intimidation of witnesses, plaintiffs, and judges, their corruption of juries, and their closure of courts. Congress was similarly right that Parliament heard "unauthenticated ex parte evidence" without the "persons who destroyed the Tea, or the people of Boston" being able to respond, while omitting that the destroyers of the tea were secret and chose not to respond.[67] Patriot propagandists often massaged the truth, and readers without first-hand knowledge and living hundreds of miles away were left with half-lies.

The End of Reconciliation

Yet the idea of payment as a step toward reconciliation limped on. In January 1775, Gage still hoped Boston might pay. Between December 1774 and February 1775, payment was the starting point for discussions between Dartmouth and colonial agents in London, not because tea was the largest item under dispute, but because the Tea Party was the chronological starting point for what followed, and so it repeatedly crept into negotiations properly focused elsewhere. In December, Benjamin Franklin agreed that Boston should pay, but by early 1775 he pointed out the injustice of charging Boston for the tea after the city had already endured impoverishment. Britain might extract reparations or injure Boston; it could not have both. Britain kept asking, anyway. Only repeal of the Tea and Coercive Acts and a settlement of constitutional principles would satisfy Patriots, without which payment was unacceptable. Stragglers, like Reverend John Murray, representative from Boothbay in the Massachusetts provincial congress, still pressed that congress to pay for the tea. Murray argued, "they never could expect the smiles of Heaven on their resistance, till they had made compensation for that flagrant act of injustice." But his words fell flat.[68]

CHAPTER 5

Toward Non-importation

There were many copycat tea parties on the colonial seaboard in 1774. These can create the impression of widespread colonial resistance to tea. But these tea parties were not exclamation points upon a Patriot triumph. They were part of an ongoing struggle to control the harbor front and stop tea importation. The outcome of this struggle was not inevitable. Small amounts of British tea still came in. More might have, were it not crowded out by a continued supply of Dutch tea and were colonial merchants not under considerable pressure to conform to the Association.

At the start of 1774 the East India Company still had a chance to sell tea in North America. It failed. Upon news of the Coercive Acts, colonists targeted tea shipments from Britain in a wave of dockside protests. Yet public views on tea remained complex. Colonists stocked up before non-importation, and smugglers brought Dutch tea in. Colonial demand was significant enough for Nova Scotia and the Caribbean to be potential staging grounds for landing and taxing British tea for transshipment to more-rebellious colonies. In November and December 1774, committees began to enforce non-importation. Merchants submitted, but tea consumption continued in various regions. Dockside protests against tea imports simultaneously revealed colonial disapproval of Parliament and the Patriot need to continue stopping tea because colonists still liked it.

Nancy, London, William

In early 1774 the Company's North American losses were potentially minor: of the vessels sent to Boston, most of the *William*'s cargo was safe in Castle William, and the Company sought reimbursement for the tea destroyed on the *Dartmouth*, *Eleanor*, and *Beaver*. The *Polly* was returning from Philadelphia with its cargo, and the Company even hoped to be reimbursed for shipping costs.[1] The *London*'s tea was secure in South Carolina. The *Nancy* remained en route to New York. Between the *William*, *London*, and *Nancy* the Company might sell nearly half its shipment, with losses on the rest covered by the state.

Historians have overlooked the possibilities and potential consequences of landing or selling Company tea in 1774. Governor Hutchinson pointed to these, hoping, in January, that the *Nancy*'s tea would be landed in New York, as "it will cast a great damp upon the heads of the people which destroyed it" in Boston. It would also see the King's duties and the Company's purse paid. But he was more cautious with the tea under his charge, explaining to the East India Company after a rough start to March that landing the *William*'s tea could not be done as it risked "new tumults." The plotline from the Tea Party to the Coercive Acts was not inevitable. It was a product of choices made in Parliament and in the colonies. The other teas could have different, unpredictable afterlives, as shown by Mary Beth Norton's study of the 1774 debates over consuming the part of the *William*'s tea left on Cape Cod.[2] Surviving Company tea could inflame protests, embarrass boycotts, or move the geography of resistance away from Boston.

North, seeing the matter as a threat to imperial authority and seeing Boston as leading that threat, sought to cow Boston Patriots. The Coercive Acts would restore order across North America by finally dealing with Boston. This ignored significant opposition to Company tea in Charleston, Philadelphia, and New York and elevated the views of the most recalcitrant Patriots. The preference for coercion also ignored ways to divide and rule colonial Patriots from one another by selling the tea from the *Nancy* and *London* (or even the *William*) in other ports. The colonists' struggles to maintain a boycott in 1770 suggest such an effort to evade and demoralize Patriot boycotts could have worked. The King, hearing of the Tea Party, initially imagined the Company tea would sell elsewhere and "by degrees tea will find its way" to Boston.[3] But the ministry preferred the Port Act instead. The Port Act required Bostonians to pay for the destroyed tea (thereby accepting they were wrong to destroy it) and to allow the *William*'s tea to be offered for sale (thereby accepting the legitimacy of the Tea Act). It was meant to force the embarrassment and submission of Boston Patriots as ends in themselves, with the eventual flow of tea and commerce a by-product.

Captain Lockyer might have unloaded the *Nancy's* tea in New York had he reached North America first. In November, the consignees hoped to land and store this tea (but not sell it), which was initially acceptable to local Patriots. As the consignees elsewhere, the New York consignees were businessmen substantial enough to handle the trade and well-connected enough to secure the privilege. Abraham Lott was the provincial treasurer. Henry White was on the governor's council. Frederick Pigou's father was a director of the East India Company and the Bank of England. Yet on December 1 the consignees gave up their role in the tea and asked Governor Tryon to take over. The governor thought he could land and store it. The presence of General Haldimand, commander-in-chief of the British Army in North America, and his troops, helped. So did the HMS *Swan*, which Tryon set to escort the *Nancy* into New York harbor. On December 17, Local Patriots rejected landing and storage and demanded the tea be returned to Britain. Four days later, news of the Boston Tea Party encouraged a New York crowd to threaten to destroy the *Nancy's* tea unless it was returned. On January 3, Tryon wrote Dartmouth that "landing, storing and safe keeping of the tea when stored could be accomplished, but only under the protection of the point of the bayonet and muzzle of the cannon, & even then I do not see how the Consumption could be effected." The "Outrage at Boston" convinced Tryon that "the Peace of Society" and "good Order," trumped landing the tea, and that the best he could hope for was an outcome like at Philadelphia (where the ship was turned around), not like at Charleston. Tryon and the *Swan's* Captain Ayscough agreed that the *Nancy* should land outside the city's customs area at Sandy Hook, where the *Swan* would see her supplied for a return to Britain. The consignees concurred, explaining to the Company that this was the only way, otherwise "your property must inevitably be destroyed," and left a letter for Lockyer to this effect.[4]

But a governor and naval officer could not formally condone smuggling around His Majesty's customs, even if it would maintain order. So Tryon made no official announcement. Instead, Ayscough appeared at a coffeehouse and mentioned dining with Tryon. He "declared before a great Number of Merchants, that as soon as the Tea-Ship arrived at the Hook, he should go down and supply her . . . and inform the Captain of the Resolutions of the People."[5] This pleased Patriots.

The *Nancy* encountered a storm and put in at Antigua in February 1774. If the *Nancy* had been too damaged to continue, Lockyer would have unloaded the tea there. Masters were supposed to enter their goods at the customs house upon reaching the Americas, and, having given bond that he would, Lockyer had a financial reason to do so. Lockyer carried no instructions for Antigua, and there was no consignee there. He could have waited for the customs collector to impound and auction the tea, thereby paying the Company and the tax, but this may have left the fate of his own bond uncertain. When Captain Lockyer put in at Antigua, he avoided formal entry into the customs area at English Harbour and did not land his tea.[6]

British West Indians consumed tea.[7] In 1772 Jamaica and the Lesser Antilles imported roughly 35,000 pounds of legal tea. Antigua imported 6,000 pounds of British tea in 1774 without incident. The *Nancy*'s 211,778-pound cargo was considerably greater than this, but, roughly price competitive with smuggled tea, it could attract bidders from across the Caribbean and perhaps have been transshipped to North America as "smuggled" tea.[8]

This was possible since Antigua and New York operated under the same tariff regime. After first entry, tea moved between colonial ports without tax. The Revenue and Indemnity acts applied to Antigua and New York. These acts adjusted taxes for "British colonies and plantations in America," including the West Indies. The American Board of Customs and vice-admiralty courts applied to North America, not the Caribbean. But the Tea Act applied to both, and British Caribbean colonies paid the tea duty peaceably. There is no evidence Antiguans were hostile to Lockyer or his shipment.[9]

On Antigua, Lockyer learned of opposition to the Company's tea in various cities. A notice appearing in several papers in late December promised Lockyer would be "acquainted" with Patriots' "Sentiments." It declared the tea should not be landed and promised to resupply Lockyer for the voyage to England to avoid "Fatality." The authors did not know whether Lockyer would read this, but he probably did. On February 15, Lockyer wrote ahead to New York consignee Henry White proposing to load supplies outside the city and head for England without stopping at the customs house. White seems to have leaked this to the press, perhaps for his and Lockyer's safety. Lockyer took care to ensure he arrived in New York well after his letter did. Thus Lockyer carried the Company's tea from Antigua, where he knew it could be landed and taxed, to New York, where he knew it could not, for reasons that remain murky at best. Had Lockyer unloaded at Antigua, the ensuing years may have unfolded differently.[10]

The Company had provided for difficulties in New York. On January 7, the Court of Directors, having heard of opposition to its tea (but not of the Boston Tea Party), decided that any refused shipments should be redirected not to the Caribbean, but to Halifax, the next "properest Place for the Sale and Disposal thereof throughout America." During the previous boycott, tea had been "smuggled" from Halifax to Boston in 1770, and Nova Scotia merchants had proposed taking tea in 1773. Selling tea in a port without an active Patriot organization made sense. The Company appointed consignees in Halifax and informed its other consignees, writing Governor Tryon as well. Lockyer could have offloaded tea in *two* colonies outside the thirteen that would eventually rebel.[11]

Dartmouth supported the Company, instructing Nova Scotia's governor, Francis Legge, to "give all proper Protection & Assistance to the Agents of the Company in the landing those Teas, and all Facility in your power to the Sale of them." Dartmouth also authorized New York governor William Tryon to use force. When "every other effort has failed," Tryon could call on General Haldimand "to remove any unlawful obstruction to commerce." North also accepted Tryon's recommendation that it was "more prudent to send the tea back to England, than to risk the landing of it," in New York. The ministry did not give definitive instructions on redirecting the tea to Nova Scotia, leaving Tryon room to maneuver. For the ministry the primary point was not the tea, but preventing further "insult" to the kingdom, a point Dartmouth reiterated.[12]

Enter the New York consignees. They are often said to have "resigned," which meant they started cooperating with Patriots, not that they had no more to do with the tea. By March, Alexander McDougall and Isaac Sears, representing the "Liberty Boys," and White, representing the consignees, reached a "Secret" agreement to resupply the *Nancy* and send her to England without landing the tea. This suited everyone. Governor Tryon even sanguinely declared to his council that "we should have no Trouble with" the tea ship. The consignees avoided using their connections to prevail upon the governor for help. This avoided putting the kingdom's authority at stake and gave the colonial government plausible deniability. The consignees also avoided sending the tea to Halifax, which would have enraged Patriots, at no profit to the consignees, while endangered the consignees' other businesses, which, for Lott at least, included selling smuggled tea wholesale in 1774. The Company's tea would remain undamaged. Lockyer would still get paid. North could focus on the "ringleaders" in Boston without a distracting riot in New York. And the Sons of Liberty got an easier task. When Lockyer reached Sandy Hook on the night of April 18, 1774, Captain Ayscough and the *Swan* were away to Boston, absolving him of any obligation to intervene in defense of lawful commerce. In Ayscough's absence, the Patriots treated Lockyer well, and three consignees, White, Lott, and Benjamin Booth, advised him to proceed quickly to England. He sailed past Halifax.[13]

Nor did Lieutenant Governor Cadwallader Colden intervene (Tryon had left, too). Colden had not been ordered to intervene, and, as he explained to Dartmouth, "Neither the captain nor any other made the least application to me about the ship or her cargo." However, Colden added that while the *Nancy* was off Sandy Hook, another vessel, the *London*, Captain Chambers (not the

London bringing Company tea to Charleston), brought a cargo of British tea, resulting in a "riotous" tea party, suggesting the disorder over this cargo justi-fied inaction toward the *Nancy*. Neither Colden, Tryon, nor Dartmouth men-tioned the Nova Scotia plan in their correspondence, and the New York consignees' correspondence is lost.[14]

The one objection came from the ship's sailors, who were "unwilling to sail with her to London." The ship had hit a second storm after leaving Antigua, los-ing its mizzen mast, an anchor, and sustaining damage to its main topmast. As the *Nancy* set out, some sailors made a raft of "oars and boards" to escape on the tide. Perhaps they feared the ship was unlucky; perhaps they did not want to cross the ocean in a damaged ship. But the captain and the committee, which was watching from a nearby sloop (and empowered by Ayscough's absence), forced them to. The *Nancy* reached England on June 6, its crew thankfully alive.[15]

Meanwhile, in Charleston, the *London*'s tea remained in the Exchange await-ing "further orders." Lieutenant Governor Bull thought the tea might sell. Yet the Treasury, learning of the Boston Tea Party, put off the decision, instructing Robert Dalway Haliday, collector of the customs at Charleston, on February 5 that the tea "be kept in safe custody" while he awaited yet "further Orders."[16]

The Company did not want to wait. On February 16, it asked the Treasury to auction the Charleston tea. Proceeds would go to the Company after de-ducting customs duty. If the Company's property were to remain locked up at the King's pleasure, it requested "other Relief."[17]

The Treasury contemplated these "further orders." Lord North, the prime minister, served as the First Lord of the Treasury and Chancellor of the Ex-chequer. North could, through the Treasury, have directed Haliday to auction the tea, or have directed Haliday to decide about auctioning the tea himself. The Treasury could also have compensated the Company, if it thought the tea permanently lost, or have ordered the tea sent to another port for auction (this may have required an act of Parliament). The Treasury Board dithered and did nothing.[18] In early May, Treasury's February stand-by order arrived in Charleston. At the end of May Bull reminded Dartmouth that, aside from that order, no real "orders have been received for the Disposal of the Tea," leaving "no opportunity of judging what will be the behavior of the discontented, when it is produced at sale." Bull worried Charleston merchants might not bid up "to the true value of the Tea," but this would not necessarily have been a defeat. Low bids would hurt the Company, but would also make the tea cheaper, and therefore more attractive.[19]

The ministry put off selling the Charleston tea and accepted Colden's non-intervention with the *Nancy* despite chiding Penn for similar non-intervention with the *Polly* earlier. Though Charleston's protest of the Company's tea was an "Insult to the Authority of this Kingdom," the ministry eschewed conflict in Charleston and New York to single out Boston for punishment.[20]

It is impossible to know what would have happened if Haliday had auctioned the *London* tea, or if someone had tried to send the *Nancy* to Halifax, or if Lockyer had unloaded in Antigua. Such actions presented risks, but the ministry's caution in Charleston and New York shielded Patriots there from risk, too. Would the ministry have seen a partial sale of tea in Halifax or Charleston as embarrassing Patriots or embarrassing the kingdom? What would Patriots have thought and done? An accumulation of different men's choices in London and the colonies precluded selling these other teas. The ministry preferred to avoid embarrassment in other ports with the *Nancy* and *London* by focusing on Boston, where the success of the Port Act, which implied the sale of the *William*'s tea, was to solve all problems.

In the North American public discussion sparked by the Port Act in May 1774 the *William*'s cargo of tea went unmentioned. This was despite earlier awareness of that tea being stored in Castle William. The castle got a mention. Thomas Gage and Thomas Hutchinson arrived at and departed from, respectively, the castle in May. In mentioning that Hutchinson had moved to Castle William the *Pennsylvania Packet* noted the "Tea commissioners" were there, but not the tea.[21] Boston Patriots did not remind their fellow colonists of this tea—for doing so would have highlighted the risk that the tea might be landed and done little for the common cause.

Thus with the Port Act colonial attention turned from the surviving 1773 tea shipments to the destroyed ones. Colonists pondered Parliament's overreaching rather than Patriots'. One could now imagine a chain of causation, from the Tea Act to the destruction of the tea, to the Coercive Acts, and, soon, to the Continental Congress and Continental Association. Alternative outcomes hinting at the potential frailty of the resistance were ignored (such as selling the *William*'s and *London*'s tea). The *Nancy* was remembered as an example of successful resistance (like the *Dartmouth*, *Eleanor*, *Beaver*, and *Polly*) rather than for its potential to undermine resistance. Future tea protests were cast similarly, and the ministry lost the opportunity to undermine Patriots by selling Company tea. If the colonists' trade protests would collapse, they would have to collapse from within.

Protesting Tea Imports

Despite the failure to land Company tea anywhere in North America without it being seized by customs authorities, dutied tea continued to be sent from

England to North America on private account. Two of these tea cargoes, send to cities already riled up by protests against Company tea, were destroyed. These were the tea on the *Fortune* in Boston in March and on the *London* in New York in April. Other cargoes of tea, including tea arriving in Charleston on the *Suky and Katy* and at least one other vessel, landed quietly.[22]

The destruction of the *Fortune*'s cargo, like the *London*'s, was linked to the original Company tea shipments from 1773. Sometimes called the "Second Boston Tea Party," though contemporary actors did not use that term, the destruction of the *Fortune*'s tea was in fact more connected to the rescue of the tea from the *William* than the destruction of the tea from the *Dartmouth*, *Eleanor*, and *Beaver*. Patriots needed to ensure that the *Fortune*'s tea was not rescued like the *William*'s had been. A threatened rescue loomed over the affair. There were two points of concern: the tea's potential delivery to the castle and its potential early seizure by customs authorities. The key actors in preventing the first step were the ship owners and captain, who had the authority to decide where the *Fortune* should dock after it arrived in Boston Harbor on March 6. At least two of the shipowners, Thomas Walley and Peter Boyer, were members of the Sons of Liberty. These men, unsurprisingly, did not direct the *Fortune* to Castle Island, where its cargo could easily have been saved. Instead, they directed the *Fortune* to Hubbard's Wharf in town, where it arrived on March 7. The tea was destroyed that day. This prevented the second step. As Deputy Naval Officer Nathaniel Taylor explained, the tea was "devoted upon its first arrival to be destroy'd." Skipping the twenty-day wait prevented seizure by customs officers. This immediacy, sometimes puzzled at, makes more sense when we recall customs officers' swift seizure of the *William*'s tea. Whether Walley and Boyer had an active role in destroying the tea (which was owned by other merchants) or simply knew what would happen when the *Fortune* came to the wharf is less clear, but the tumult over the *Fortune* during a period of already-heightened street action in Boston also deterred the consignees from selling the *William*'s tea.[23]

In June news of the Coercive Acts catalyzed widespread dockside actions against British tea. Destroying the newly arrived tea showed solidarity with Boston and opposition to the Coercive Acts. The protests varied. In New Hampshire Edward Parry received tea in June and September. Patriots made him redirect them to Halifax. In Charleston tea imported in June on the *Magna Charta* and in July on the *Briton* was locked in the Exchange. In the Chesapeake, the *Mary and Jane* landed tea in August; committees demanded it be sent back. In Massachusetts, more than thirty chests of tea reached Salem in the *Julius Caesar* (they had been sent to Boston, but that port was closed), and were reshipped to Halifax. In Annapolis, tea arriving in October on the *Peggy Stewart* was burned along with the brig.[24]

By November, some colonies had implemented non-importation locally. Continental non-importation began in December. Action against tea imports continued. The *Britannia* reached Charleston on November 1, its tea tossed into the river as an *"Oblation . . . to* NEPTUNE." The *Virginia* reached Virginia on November 4; local Patriots threw the tea into the water and forbade it from loading tobacco. Later that month, more tea reached Virginia on the *Ross.* Patriots sought to stop it. Tea reached North Carolina on the *Sally;* Patriots asked that it be sent back. In December, Greenwich, New Jersey Patriots dressed as "Indians" burned tea landed from the *Greyhound,* in from Rotterdam and bound for Philadelphia (it was being smuggled past Philadelphia customs officers). These were the major attempts to stop tea shipments. Of these, all but the last carried British tea.[25]

These cases varied. Patriots destroyed tea, locked it up, sent it back, or redirected it. Sometimes, after an initial public objection to the tea, records of the tea disappear: perhaps the tea was landed, perhaps records were lost over time. Even attitudes toward tax payment varied. In Annapolis, the brig owner paid duty on behalf of the importing merchant, one reason Patriots burned the brig. Yet in New Hampshire, where Governor John Wentworth hoped getting the duty paid would establish a precedent, the Portsmouth committee permitted this to facilitate re-export. In Salem, the importers gave bond that the duty would be paid in Halifax (it was), and when the *William* wrecked on Cape Cod, Cape Coders debated whether, since the tea was un-taxed, they could drink it.[26]

What Did Tea Parties Mean?

Tea and tea parties were contested. There was no consensus even among Patriots about what to do with tea, and the broader public was even less unified, despite the appearance of broad, near unanimous support in the press. When the *Greyhound* landed tea in December 1774, violating the Association, a mob of young men burned the tea. Patriots were popular in Greenwich. The governor could not find a grand jury to indict the tea burners, even after replacing the sheriff with a King's man. The tea owners' action of trespass never saw trial. Nevertheless, Philip Vickers Fithian, who may have been a tea burner himself, noted little enthusiasm for tea burning in Greenwich. "Violent and different are the Words about this Uncommon Manouver," he wrote. "[A]mong the Inhabitants—Some rave, some curse, some condemn. Some try to reason; many are glad that the tea is destroyed, but almost all disapprove the Manner of Destruction."[27] Here was no consensus, even among Patriots, about how the Association should be fulfilled, but one has to look at a diary, not a press release, to find this.

One must be careful not to equate Patriots' ubiquity and vociferousness with their popularity. Tea parties were widespread, showing Patriots had a meaningful presence in many towns. These rallies were widely reported in contemporary prints, which cast these events as triumphs of a colonial consensus. But this is not quite proof that Patriots were liked and tea was not, for it is unclear whether Patriots were trying to move the populace with these rallies, or whether they had moved it.

Patriots continued to block tea landings because some colonists wanted to consume it. Thus the conservative Samuel Seabury thought New Yorkers lacked "virtue enough to prevent the tea from being bought and sold, once landed." The shortage of tea in late 1773, the failure of the Company's shipments, and the reduced importation of legal tea in 1774 kept supply low but had less effect on demand. Dockside tea parties were "popular" in the sense that they involved the lower orders. But this obscured (and was perhaps even necessitated by) the lack of consensus about non-consumption.[28]

Consider the *Geddes*, which brought tea to Chestertown, Maryland, on May 7, 1774. Kent County Patriots held meetings on May 13 and 18 "upon discovery of a late importation of the dutiable tea . . . for some of the neighbouring counties" in the *Geddes*. They invited the public "to declare their sentiments respecting the importation of tea" on May 18, at which meeting attendees *"unanimously"* agreed to the Chestertown Resolves, determining that buyers and sellers of this tea would be "stigmatized." Subsequently, in popular memory at least, Patriots led the Chestertown Tea Party. But the tea party never happened, and the response to the tea was significantly less effective than it appeared.[29]

We know the *Geddes* landed its tea. There are three pieces of evidence for this. First, the reference to a "late" importation meant it had been landed. Second, shipping records show the *Geddes* imported "E[ast] I[ndia]" goods (a catch-all that sometimes included tea). Third, the *Geddes* departed with a new cargo on May 24, which required the full inward cargo be entered first.[30]

James Nicholson, the sole owner of the cargo, likely sold some tea despite the Chestertown Resolves, since on May 16 Annapolis merchant Thomas Brook Hodgkin advertised "East-India goods" "Just imported" by the *Geddes*. Hodgkin's advertisement opens up an intriguing reading: that Nicholson realized his tea was troublesome, perhaps after the meeting on May 13, sold some to Hodgkin, then signed the Resolves on May 18 (the signatories of the Resolves are not named, but Nicholson was likely among them). The Resolves appeared to stop the *Geddes*'s tea from being sold, but in reality they were a promise not to sell tea anymore. Instead of stigmatizing Nicholson, county Patriots added Nicholson to their committee of correspondence.[31]

This is less jarring when one recalls that when the *Geddes* arrived, tea was not a focus of protest in Maryland. Hodgkin, like Nicholson, eventually became a Patriot. Nor did Marylanders know of the Coercive Acts when the Chestertown Resolves were written. News of the Coercive Acts reached Maryland on May 25, when the *Geddes* had already left. Kent County Patriots wrote their Resolves on May 19. They were published on June 2. Between these dates the committee added a postscript referencing the Coercive Acts.[32]

Kent County Patriots' press release cast their efforts in the best light, obscuring that the tea might be gone and that the importer was on their committee. This was good politics, letting Kent keep apace with other counties in its resistance to the Coercive Acts—and Kent's Patriots were politicians. As long as Nicholson would behave in future, other Kent Patriots overlooked his transgression. It was also good leadership. Confirming that the *Geddes's* tea had been sold would only embarrass the cause, so Chestertown Patriots encouraged future non-importation by implying they had already stopped the tea—a sort of "fake it 'til you make it."

Other Maryland Patriots seem to have let in tea before the Coercive Acts became known on May 25. Four vessels brought East India goods to Annapolis between April 16 and May 25. If they brought tea—and some likely did—there was no protest. In June "Amor Patriae" (probably printer William Goddard) noted the continuation of tea sales and that tea "has, not long since, arrived here from England." Indeed, four more vessels brought East India goods from England in the month after the Coercive Acts were known.[33] Tea advertisements appeared in the Maryland newspapers into July.

A facade of tea resistance obscured an ongoing tea market in the case of the *Peggy Stewart* as well. The *Peggy Stewart* arrived in Annapolis on October 14, and a mob forced one of the vessel's owners, Anthony Stewart, to burn the tea and the vessel. Stewart first publicly denied knowledge of the tea to try to save his brig. But Patriots then forced him and his partners to ask pardon for importing tea and to "voluntarily" burn it. The official Patriot story, printed in the *Maryland Gazette*, pretended Stewart burned his vessel freely. This helped maintain inter-colonial Patriot unity. Congress announced its Association shortly after the *Peggy Stewart* was burned. News of the *Peggy Stewart* fire and the Congress's Association followed each other around the continent. As the former was ostensibly an attempt to enforce non-importation, it was important it not sour readers on that part of the Association. Committeemen and firebrands on the spot disagreed about burning the brig; Patriots elsewhere would likely have been as divided if they knew.[34]

Locals knew. William Eddis, a customs collector who witnessed the affair, thought the idea of the owner voluntarily burning his brig an "absurdity." "I went to Annapolis yesterday to see my Liberty destroyed," lamented merchant John Galloway. But readers in other colonies were left with what Maryland Patriots put in the press. Thus Bostonian John Andrews could cheer with William Barrell: "burning the vessel with tea at Maryland has elevated their [Patriots'] spirits," even if he did not normally approve of burning ships.[35]

Maryland Patriots also confounded the timelines of the *Peggy Stewart* and non-importation. Charles Carroll of Annapolis "wholeheartedly endorsed" burning the *Peggy Stewart*. It was "what those who oppose the patriot cause might expect." Charles Grahame reluctantly agreed it was "what they must expect who import tea or contravene the resolution of the Congress."[36]

But the *Peggy Stewart* reached Annapolis before Congress had passed the Continental Association. Tea imports were not yet banned. To be sure, Annapolis Patriots had been urging an immediate boycott all summer. But in June, the Maryland convention chose to wait until other colonies joined (through the Association). This left the matter open—colonial-level Patriots failed to ban tea, but local Patriots still opposed it, making Thomas Williams's decision to ship 2,000 pounds of tea from London on the *Peggy Stewart* risky. It was his largest tea purchase, but he had reasons to make the attempt. He had debts to pay, for which a handsome profit would help. He also had advertised British tea (with no trouble) in May, which may have led him to expect the same in October.[37]

One reason to burn the *Peggy Stewart* was for private gain. John Davidson, a local customs official and rival merchant, encouraged the burning and was said, by the anonymous "Americanus," to be a "PRINCIPAL ABETTOR and PROMOTER" of the riot." Davidson had heard from his London partner, Joshua Johnson, of Williams's shipment. Johnson's comment that August, "I should not be surprised to hear that you made a bonfire of the *Peggy Stewart*" since she had "tea on board," was a wink and a nudge. A third partner, Charles Wallace, may also have taken a role in burning the brig. Wallace, Davidson, and Johnson supported the destruction of its rival's tea because they wanted to corner the pre-embargo market while they sold their tea. Williams's outsized cargo implied that market was considerable. With the *Peggy Stewart* destroyed, Eddis thought Annapolis commodities "scarce and dear" in November—ripe for Wallace, Davidson, and Johnson. This aspect of the story did not make the Patriotic press.[38]

Wallace, Davidson, and Johnson may have imported tea. "Americanus" thought Davidson's firm had imported tea "three months before" the *Peggy Stewart*. Customs records show Davidson and Wallace had imported "East India goods" on the *Kitty & Nelly,* which reached Annapolis on May 12. Their internal order books show tea allocated for retail at their Annapolis store and their satellite on the Patuxent. They took tea orders from Buchanan & Cowan, Clement Brooke, William Bond, and Charles Carroll of Carrollton, who ordered 80 pounds just before the Association took effect. Carroll warned the goods were "not to be bought unless All the Acts mentioned by the Continental Congress as unjust and oppressive" were repealed. Other buyers made no such caveats.[39]

Stocking Up

In 1774 word of the impending boycott encouraged colonists to stock up. The value of all British exports to the thirteen colonies in 1774 jumped 31 percent over the previous year, much of it driven by increased orders from New York and Philadelphia merchants. There were probably increased orders from Europe as well, including tea. Virginia Patriot Robert Carter Nicholas had not initially wanted to stock up, since it would blunt the boycott. But, as autumn approached, "I learned from different Parts of the Country that People were laying in Stocks of Goods for their Families; at length I thought it prudent to take Care of mine." General Gage reported, "Merchants are sending for double the Quantity of Goods they usually import." Continental Congressman Caesar Rodney wrote his brother Thomas, a merchant, that "every Body say[s] half the Quantity of Dry Goods never was before imported, as now are, and likely to be this fall." Bristol merchant Thomas Frank warned a colonial correspondent that filling orders was difficult: the orders already placed left little room on westbound ships. As a result, many merchants had enough stock to sustain normal sales for months, perhaps a year, after non-importation took effect.[40]

For importers, non-import could be an opportunity. In his advertisement for drugs and East India spices, Baltimore pharmacist John Boyd used the threat of non-importation to drive sales; since non-importation was "probable" buyers should "supply themselves before my present stock is exhausted."[41] Others took the opposite tack: If non-consumption were broken, whoever had the most goods would profit. "Depend upon it," Robert Shedden of Portsmouth, Virginia wrote back to Glasgow, "you will never have such another opportunity to make money by dry goods in this country."[42]

Most merchants disagreed with Shedden. As Bristol merchant Richard Champion noted, now that colonial merchants had ordered so much, the "Great Stock of Goods" in the colonies made non-importation in their "Interest." Without it, the colonial market would be flooded and the supply would "become a Burthen." Others concurred. Samuel Seabury noted that merchants, anticipating non-importation, "have imported much more largely than usual: This makes me suspect, that the bustle about Non-importation &c, has its rise, not from Patriotism, but selfishness": merchants needed scarcity to profit. For merchant, privateersman, and Son of Liberty Alexander McDougall, there was no conflict between doing good and doing well. "Stocks [of goods] have risen in favor of Liberty," McDougall assured Samuel Adams in June 1774, ignoring that large orders blunted the Association's effect on British merchants.[43]

Tea Smuggling

Dutch tea was smuggled into the colonies. No British tea was landed in Philadelphia or New York in 1774, but tea was still available. His Majesty's customs collectors and warships watched for smugglers around New York. In the spring of 1774 they caught a small sloop with Dutch tea—they secured the vessel without any trouble from Patriots just a few days after the *Nancy* arrived. Lieutenant Governor Colden placed his grandson Richard in the post of surveyor and searcher of the port. After turning down a £1,500 bribe, Richard made several seizures, but smugglers were hard to catch. They landed in the "numerous bays and creeks that our coasts and rivers furnish," and landed contraband in small boats. In July Ayscough's *Swan* took one, "a small pilot boat, with about one hundred and forty pounds of tea" near Sandy Hook. Enforcement weakened thereafter as customs officers began leaving their stations.[44]

British intelligence detected colonial vessels bringing tea and gunpowder from Europe. A 300-ton ship loaded arms, gunpowder, and tea in the Elbe in August 1774. Another vessel was loading at Hamburg in October. When Dartmouth ordered it intercepted, it was gone and three more vessels were loading. Dutch-flagged vessels also carried tea. Sir Joseph Yorke, British ambassador to The Hague, reported the New York vessel, *Catherine Elizabeth*, loaded with tea and liquors for Curaçao, which Yorke thought was "a mask" for the tea's real destination. Intelligence from Copenhagen reported a scheme to use a Danish vessel carrying timber to St. Croix to smuggle tea to "North America" among the "intervals of its Cargo."[45]

Tea came from farther south, too. The *Swan* seized tea from a vessel traveling from Lisbon. Lord Dartmouth received reports of smugglers entering the South Atlantic "to meet with French and other India ships [coming from China] in order to purchase tea of them." Yorke estimated 5,000 chests of bohea were shipped to the West Indies and North America between January and September 1774. Most chests concealed gunpowder. Yorke estimated that only 1,000 to 1,500 chests contained tea, and the rest held powder. But 1,500 chests was a lot of tea: The Boston Tea Party had destroyed only 290 chests.[46]

British detection of tea was a by-product of efforts to interdict gunpowder. Yorke originally thought tea smuggling too "trifling" to report, but arms in the tea crates got his attention. The Admiralty sent vessels to deter gunpowder shipments from the Netherlands. North American customs staff focused on interdicting arms as well. This left much of the Dutch tea imported in 1774 undetected, though hints of it appear. In 1774 the firm Scott and Fraser, based in Gottenburg, hoped to supply Newport, Rhode Island merchant Aaron Lopez with tea, in what seems to have been a standing arrangement. They supplied Captain William Tanner, *Dolphin*, owned by Patriots Samuel and William Vernon, with 68 casks and two boxes of tea in August 1774. Tanner told Gothenburg authorities he was clearing for "New England" rather than St. Croix, as he had previously been instructed. Smuggling required a captain who could successfully change plans on the spot. So when Archibald Graham brought tea from L'Orient, France, into Baltimore in December 1774, he changed plans and reported his cargo to the Baltimore committee, which secured his supply.[47]

Dutch Tea

The prevalence of Dutch tea in 1774 is one reason harborside tea parties should not be taken as evidence of a colonial consensus against the good. Some observers even thought opposition to Company tea would encourage colonists to consume more Dutch tea. "The colonists," Charles Lee wrote, "one and all, have entered into the most solemn obligations to send" the Company's tea "back to its exporters, and continue furnishing themselves from the Dutch." John Adams also thought "honestly smuggled" Dutch tea was a good alternative to English—the syllogistic juggle the epigraph at the start of this book mocked. Conservatives joked "Sawney Sedition" "published, threatened, prayed and lied to delude the inhabitants from buying British tea" to buying Dutch.[48]

How much Dutch tea entered colonial ports in 1774? The general downward trend in Philadelphia bohea prices is one sign that these volumes were substantial in 1774. (See figure C.1.) It would have taken hundreds of thousands of pounds of Dutch tea to accomplish this. One downward force on prices may have been partially decreased demand. But strikingly, while tea prices spiked during the boycott of 1769–1770, this time around tea prices spiked while the boycott was forming and before the Continental Association took hold. Mid-Atlantic colonies allowed Dutch tea to be imported, transshipped, and consumed throughout 1774. Unmet past demand (the tea shortage of 1773), increased current demand for Dutch tea in neighboring colonies that had just banned English tea in 1774, and stocking up to meet future demand in 1775 all mitigated against a substantial drop in demand for Dutch tea. This suggests that new supplies of Dutch tea played a crucial role in lowering prices. There is no evidence that New York and Philadelphia Patriots let in Dutch tea to affect tea prices. However, the Patriot leadership in these cities included merchants (Thomas Mifflin in Philadelphia and John Alsop, Isaac Low, and Philip Livingston in New York) who understood the effect that importing Dutch tea would have on price. Because 1774 tea prices in the Netherlands remained below earlier levels while mid-Atlantic tea prices remained higher, trade in Dutch bohea stood to be profitable. (See table C.1.)

Tea prices still occasionally spiked. The May spike, perhaps caused by consumer hoarding on rumors of a ban, seems to have inspired Amor Patriae to complain that while tea sellers "are publickly avowing the Spirit of Patriotism, they are privately" "advancing the Price of Tea no less than *Eighteen Pence* per pound, within a few Days!" He urged an "Inquiry" . . . into the "real Cause" of the rise, which he thought could not be caused by "*Scarcity*," since Dutch tea was ubiquitous, but only by "iniquitous Fraud." Though price rises might dissuade consumers, Patriots could not cheer publicly. To do so would seem callous or, worse, accept blame for hardship, since Patriot action had led to Company tea being locked up in both Boston and Charleston, and since, as John Randolph explained, the Company had been poised to offer tea "at Half the Price" other merchants were selling it. Instead, Congress included price controls in the Association, and colonial-level Patriots admonished merchants to keep prices steady. Patriots' paradoxical preferences—that tea be cheap and British tea be scarce—worked better if they looked the other way as New York and Philadelphia brought Dutch tea in.[49]

It was easier to stop British tea imports than Dutch imports because customs officers recorded legal tea imports multiple times. Legal tea was taxed (and therefore recorded) upon auction in Britain. The Tea Act then rebated this duty upon re-export to the colonies, which occasioned the documentation of these re-exports in British ports. Captain Chambers's shipment of tea from London to New York was caught, in part, because other people could find cockets to that effect in the searcher's office at Gravesend. The bonds that captains gave customs officials for shipping that tea were another form of documentation. Finally, tea legally imported from Britain was recorded in a public register at the colonial customs house. Patriots followed George Washington's recommendation to check these "authentick Lists" for British imports. Customs officers failed to stop smugglers, but they recorded legal trade well. (Tea imported to other colonial ports could, however, be transshipped without much documentation, one reason Patriots had to include as large a group of colonies as possible within the Association.) The Association's most important provisions banned not just tea but trade with Britain and the empire. They called for local committees to form and "observe the conduct of all persons touching this association." Yet the Association presumed the continuation of the British Empire, not independence. With British tea imports the Association tried to influence Parliament, to affect merchants in Britain, and to use imperial customs officials' records against the empire. By contrast, because there was no official register of smugglers, Patriots found Dutch tea imports harder to stop.[50]

But as article of consumption, the only practical distinction between English and Dutch tea had been price. With that gone, Patriots decided that the only way to keep out one was to avoid consuming either. Thus, after complaining about tea prices, Amor Patriae urged colonists to stop using the drink generally. This move against Dutch tea was gradual.[51]

In most colonies where Patriots opposed British tea in 1773 or 1774, they eventually opposed Dutch tea. In Boston, Patriots ignored Dutch tea during the Boston Tea Party. In the last quarter of 1773, twenty separate tea sellers advertised tea in the Boston papers, much of which was assumed to be Dutch. Only after the Tea Party did the town's tea sellers agree to stop selling all tea. One merchant, Cyrus Baldwin, was caught out and tried to advertise around the problem, noting his tea was "imported before the East India Company's arrived," but he soon stopped advertising tea.[52] After January 1774, Patriotic merchants no longer advertised Dutch tea in Boston.

Elsewhere Dutch tea carried on. In New York, John Watts, who had previously favored non-importation, opposed a general tea ban since it would hurt tea smugglers as much as legal importers (an inversion of the position merchants had taken in South Carolina, reflecting the prevalence of smuggling in New York). New York smuggling and tea advertisements continued. Samuel Seabury thought that "All that is imported," into New York—especially tea—"is smuggled from Holland, and the Dutch Islands in the West Indies." In Rhode Island, merchant Samuel Ward urged a general tea boycott at the end of December 1773 but got nowhere. In South Carolina, despite talk of non-importation in December 1773, Patriots only reached an "Agreement" that "NO TEAS" (English or Dutch) be imported at their March 1774 meeting. They set April 16, 1774 as the effective date, but it is unclear how broadly agreed or enforced this was.[53]

The Coercive Acts accelerated the move against Dutch tea. The just-dissolved House of Burgesses recommended an Association boycott of "any kind of East India commodity whatsoever" in May 1774, and in August the Virginia convention announced an immediate boycott of "tea of any kind" in the Virginia Association. Yet importing Dutch tea remained a lesser offense.

When British tea on the *Britannia* was destroyed in November in Charleston, a separate cargo of Dutch tea was merely sent back "with a Caution to the Shipper to venture no more this Way." Charleston Patriots thought this a virtue: "This proves that WE do not reject the *dutied Teas* in order to countenance the Importation of others," but they upheld separate treatment for the two.[54]

The Continental Association differentiated between Dutch and British tea, banning British tea imports immediately, but allowed Dutch tea to be imported until December 1, 1774 and consumed until March 1, 1775. In New York and Philadelphia, the most important market towns in the colonies, Dutch tea imports continued until the former date. Without Dutch tea, colonial tea prices would have been higher, perhaps high enough to make shipping more British tea worthwhile. To the extent that colonial merchants eschewed British tea, it was partly because Dutch tea imports stopped tea prices from rising high enough to make British tea worth the risk.

Undermining Non-Importation

Seventy thousand pounds of British tea were shipped to the thirteen colonies in 1774. This figure includes 30,000 pounds sent to New England in 1774 and 31,000 sent to the Chesapeake, much of which was not landed. It also includes the tea on the *Geddes* and perhaps other shipments and 3,661 pounds to Georgia, which was landed. This was a far cry from the 264,000 pounds sent to the thirteen colonies in 1772, but it suggested a small and enduring market for legal tea in post-Tea Party North America. To this must be added the 64,000 pounds of British tea which went to the British West Indies, the Floridas, Quebec, Nova Scotia, and Newfoundland in 1774.[55]

The early embargo was fragile, and tea from other colonies was sometimes brought into Patriot zones. The *Sally*, Captain Joshua Davis, arrived in Salem, Massachusetts, in June from Barbados and St. Eustatius with forty canisters of tea and was entered. Later that month the *Welcome*, Captain John Smithwick, arrived from Grenada with twenty more canisters. These teas had been imported into Boston previously, perhaps in 1773. They were then shipped to the Caribbean in early 1774, part of the winter New England-Caribbean run, to escape Boston's ban on tea sales. The sixty canisters shipped from the Caribbean back to Boston in the spring of 1774 and then diverted to Salem on account of the Port Act were probably the remains of larger cargoes. It is not even clear whether these teas were originally English or Dutch. But since they had already been imported once, they owed no further tax regardless and did not need to be mentioned by name in the "authentick lists" at the customs house. We know about them only because customs officers discussed these canisters in separate correspondence. This was why tea was difficult for Patriots to stop beyond the port of entry. Similarly, Boston tea vendor Isaac Winslow could obtain tea from his Newport brother-in-law, Simon Pease, undetected and try to return it the same way.[56]

Initially, Patriots were also hampered in enforcing their embargo because they did not have clear control of Salem. Between June and August 1774, the Massachusetts government relocated there. General Gage, the customs commissioners, and many soldiers were based in Salem. Patriots do not seem to have been aware of the *Sally* and *Welcome* teas, but the presence of soldiers in Salem helped ensure the tea that reached Salem in September on the *Julius Caesar*, which Patriots did know about, was reshipped to Halifax, not destroyed.[57]

Conversely, once implemented in the right choke-points, an embargo could hold back British tea distribution more broadly. The subsequent withdrawal of troops from Salem (in response to the Powder Alarm), Governor Wentworth's dwindling power in Portsmouth, and the continued closure of Boston empowered Patriots to force residents of northern New England to follow the Association. Likewise, when Charlestonians stopped the *Briton*'s tea, they prevented tea sent to St. Augustine via Charleston from reaching its destination.[58]

Tea could also be landed outside the embargo zone. East Florida governor Patrick Tonyn, hearing of the St. Augustine shipment held up in Charleston, suggested that St. Augustine replace Charleston as a redistribution point. If tea came to St. Augustine "as a mart, it would finds its way all over America." Law-abiding Floridians might thus end Carolinians' non-importation. But British merchants shipped only 2,543 pounds of tea to the Floridas in 1774, hardly enough for large transshipments into Patriot zones.[59]

This was because St. Augustine had "no proper Wharf or Landing place for Goods," as London merchant Thomas Nixon, whose vessel carrying tea wrecked in St. Augustine in 1773, explained. All the town had was a wood "platform carried from the Shore on the Beach which was built extremely slight, and by reason of the Worm which breeds in the Mud is continually wanting Repairs and is now very unsafe to land goods on." The town suffered from "great want of a good Wharf and Crane and also of Lighters and other Craft," and had a sand bar at its harbor mouth. With no facility to unload or receive large vessels, St. Augustine had to conduct its trade via "Coasting Schooners" to Charleston.[60]

The Caribbean was a promising place from which to distribute dutied tea into North America, as the *Sally* and *Welcome* showed. High North American tea prices meant merchants could buy dutied tea in the Caribbean and sell it in North America at profit. But new tea was not sent out from Britain to take advantage of this. For while dutied tea could be sold in the Caribbean and re-sold in North America at profit, Dutch tea could be sold even more profitably. Philadelphia consignee Gilbert Barkley travelled with the *Polly* and her cargo of East India Company tea back to London, where he offered to buy the *Polly*'s tea and re-sell it in St. Eustatius. This would have been a political coup in North America, whether it got Company tea in North American hands or simply eroded colonial confidence in Dutch tea's provenance. But the Company turned him down. Barkley wanted to buy the tea at a discount to allow him to compete with Dutch tea on the island, but the Company did not need to cut prices to sell a cargo which might sell at regular auction. The Company reasonably expected that by importing less tea, it could eventually sell all its cargoes at full price. Selling Company tea to the Caribbean for onward sale to North America made political sense, not business sense, a logic driven in no small part by the ongoing shipment of Dutch tea to the Americas. The Company Directors offered to introduce Barkley and Lord Dartmouth, but it is unclear whether Barkley ever broached the matter with the minister. As such, British tea shipments to the Caribbean remained stable at roughly 30,000 pounds weight between 1773 and 1775.[61]

Then there were the northern provinces. Earlier, King George III had thought, "When Quebec is stocked" with tea "it will spread Southward." But British shipments to Quebec were declining. British merchants sent 6,433 pounds in 1773, but only 3,489 pounds in 1774.[62]

Others focused on Nova Scotia. "An Enemy to Tea" had seen Halifax as a possible base for distributing tea across the continent. The *Nancy* never reached Nova Scotia, but Halifax received two cargoes of British tea reshipped from New Hampshire and a third from Salem. English merchants also sent tea directly to Newfoundland and Nova Scotia in 1774, more (27,757 pounds) than in the previous two years combined, some likely intended for sale farther south.[63]

Tea was contested in Nova Scotia. Most Nova Scotians came from New England. When the Portsmouth tea reached Halifax in July 1774, there was a gathering in response. Magistrate John Fillis objected, linking it to the "unjust and oppressive" Coercive Acts, and some merchants denied importer George Henry Monk use of their stores. William Smith, a merchant and judge, was offered a share in the tea; he declined as it was "against his principles." Yet the tea was landed, and Smith ultimately took a share.[64]

In September 1774, Smith received another tea shipment, probably the one redirected from Salem. John Andrews had thought Haligonians would give the tea an "unwelcome . . . reception." (He based this on speaking with Haligonians in Boston, who breathed "the same spirit of freedom as prevails through the continent.") This tea was, according to Halifax customs officials, "regularly landed."[65] Then Smith notified other Halifax merchants and called a meeting. Whether Smith intended to agitate or explain himself against a "prejudiced" populace is unclear. Magistrate John Newton declared the meeting illegal. Governor Legge stripped Smith and Fillis, whom Smith had consulted, of their posts and forbade further meetings, noting to Dartmouth that it was "persons taking upon themselves the authority of assembling any body of people" which has led to so much "disorder" elsewhere. Any potential Halifax tea party was stopped before it could begin. As Monk explained, "the Governor has effectually cut the throat of the Rebelious Faction, in this Country & destroyed the seeds of Sedition, sewn among the People, who were Irritated to Town Meetings &c on the arrival of some Tea, by a Mr. Smith."[66]

Nova Scotians had shipped some small cargoes of tea to Maine in earlier years, and they did try to re-export tea to New England in 1774. Nova Scotia merchants sold 300 pounds of tea to John Thomas, who carried it to Plymouth, Massachusetts, where Patriots destroyed it. Rumors surfaced of other men wanting "to buy Tea" in Halifax "and carry the same to Plymouth for sale." According to the publicly reported version of events, a 150-pound shipment from Liverpool, Nova Scotia to York, Maine, was seized by men disguised as Indians. However, the Tory Judge Jonathan Sayward, who lived in town and may have had something to do with the tea, noted in his diary that "two days after [this event] the tea was replaced" by persons unknown.[67] Other re-exports may have gotten through as well.

Nova Scotia merchants wanted to replace New Englanders. Legge pushed the possibility of Nova Scotians replacing New Englanders in Atlantic trade in 1774. Haligonian merchants caught more cod and shipped more to the West Indies as Salem and Boston vessels withdrew in 1774 and 1775. The Restraining Acts of 1775 allowed Halifax to trade with the British West Indies, and Dartmouth encouraged Nova Scotia's timber trade there. But Halifax, like St. Augustine, was too small for the job. The *Adamant's* two yearly voyages between Halifax and Britain were Legge's main means of communication with London— the town was a satellite of Boston, not readily made into a hub of its own. Halifax merchants (resident in a town of roughly 2,500 souls) could not engross Massachusetts's trade: Halifax entrances and clearances in 1773 were less than half those in Salem, let alone Boston.[68]

A few cargoes slipped into Patriot areas from outside. More could have. That they did not is not only an artifact of colonial resistance but also of the cost-benefit analysis of many merchants, an analysis which was affected by the price, and therefore the benefit, they could expect. Falling tea prices because of ongoing Dutch tea shipments to New York and Philadelphia reduced the benefits. Patriot enforcement against dutied tea increased the cost.

Performing Violations

Patriots caught some importers with tea. The records of these interactions, generated by the committees, reveal the fixed roles Patriots permitted importers to play. If they begged pardon and accepted committee authority, they might survive unscathed. If they defied the committees, they were punished.

Some importers insisted they had never ordered tea. The first time he was caught, Edward Parry accurately claimed the tea had been sent to him "without my advice or knowledge." In South Carolina, James Wakefield and William Donaldson claimed their tea was "quite unexpected," "[p]art of some *old* Orders, which through *mere Inattention,* had not been countermanded." Captain Ball of the *Britannia* declared himself "an entire Stranger to their [tea chests] being on board his Ship" until he was ready to clear from England, at which point he signed a notarized protest objecting to the tea.[69] This did not always work (Anthony Stewart denied knowledge of tea on board the *Peggy Stewart*), but by implicitly denying the tea was meant to defy Patriots' wishes, it usually lessened Patriot ire. "Accidental" tea importation was amusingly common in 1774.

The Charles County, Maryland committee thought the timing of Robert Findlay's tea importation suggested ill intent. His tea, shipped from London on the *Mary and Jane* in May 1774, came late enough that his supplier was "acquainted with the passing of the Boston Port Bill and also of the sense of America respecting" dutied tea. Findlay replied that the tea had been ordered in 1773, therefore not intended to defy post-Coercive Acts sensibilities.[70]

Robert Peter went further, insisting to the Frederick County, Maryland committee that legal tea imports had been normal when ordered: "he relied on the custom which had constantly prevailed in the Province of *Maryland,* since the partial repeal of the Revenue Act [1770], to screen him from censure, and to justify" his ordering dutied tea. Customs records suggest he was right. Peter followed this risky comment by emphasizing that he "submitted" to the committee's will.[71]

Except, we do not know what accused merchants like Peter said. Committee reports are the only evidence, and they were written by a body that served as prosecutor and judge and had a political agenda. We know committees sometimes lied, as with the *Peggy Stewart.* Committees likely paraphrased what their subjects said, perhaps liberally, a common eighteenth-century practice. Committees sometimes wrote out confessions for the accused to sign, with the appropriate amount of groveling and acquiescence added for them. Yet there were basic truths the committee reports reveal: they were unlikely to claim someone who had submitted was defiant or vice versa, for example. Committees' records thus show the committees' self-image superbly, committee opinions reasonably well, and the internal world of the accused poorly. Peter ordered tea; the committee summoned him to explain; he did. But what did submission mean to Peter? Did he intend to continue obeying? When he "submitted to the sentiments of the Committee, and declared an entire willingness to abide by their determination," he accepted they would write the definitive version of events. If Peter had any quibbles, he kept silent. He had other goods to sell.[72]

Patriots lauded obedient tea importers. The Frederick committee gave "thanks" for Robert Peter's "candid and disinterested behavior." New York Patriots treated Lockyer well. The committee conducted him to the wharf with church bells, a band played God Save the King, and huzzas and cannon salutes saw him off.[73] This demonstrated Patriot magnanimity and protected importers from mobs.

Pleased with obeisance, committees and mobs treated evasion firmly. Captain Chambers risked "his life" when he was caught lying about tea and hiding documents. Edward Parry's claim that his first tea shipment was a mistake looked implausible when a second shipment arrived. The second time, the town meeting was "agitated," a mob broke his windows, and Parry asked the governor for protection. In South Carolina, Patriots were furious because Maitland had *"promised*, upon *his Honour"* not to land tea, then did it. Maitland witnessed the tea affair in Charleston in 1773, and, working a regular Charleston-London shipping run, was no "Stranger" to "the Sense of the People" of South Carolina. "[S]ince *he* had brought in the Teas with his Eyes open," Patriots held him responsible for their landing. Consequently, James Laurens thought, "had he fallen into their [i.e., the mob's] hands it would have cost his Life." He escaped to the HMS *Glasgow* just as the mob boarded his vessel.[74]

Illegal, seditious, and possibly treasonous, the committees guarded their emergent legitimacy, watching for contemptuous language since they needed to be respected *as* proper authorities to function. According to James Laurens, Maitland had "spoken disrespectfully" of "Patriots & their Measures" and was "rather Imprudent in letting his tongue run."[75] In colonial honor culture respect for leaders implied acceptance of their legitimacy (one reason North took the Boston Tea Party, as an act of disrespect, so seriously). To keep face, the Charleston committee omitted Maitland's disrespect in its published account. Meanwhile, Alexander Urquhart arrived in Charleston with tea the day the mob attacked Maitland. But Urquhart held his tongue and was unharmed.[76]

The committee derived authority, in part, from speaking for the public and having its ability to do so accepted. Thus Wakefield and Donaldson refused tea because they "had no Intention to act counter to the Sense of the Community" as expressed by the committee. When Edward Parry sent his June tea shipment away, he explained (according to the committee, at least), "I am unwilling to irritate the Minds of the People."[77] These men performed the role the committees scripted for them: acceptance of the premise that committees expressed popular will and obliviousness to the possibility that importing tea implied its salability with no sense that the boycott might be less popular than imagined.

There was truth to apolitical importation. Merchants bought tea for money, not politics. Most importers brought mixed cargoes dominated by other goods, especially British manufacturers. Tea was ancillary to this, and most merchants gave up British tea to sell other goods and collect export cargoes in the booming pre-Association market.

When Edward Parry sent away his tea, he probably hoped to save his business sourcing masts for the navy. Likewise, when London merchant John Norton sent the *Virginia* to Virginia in 1774, it was to collect tobacco. The value of the tea onboard was trivial compared to the tobacco he hoped to load. Though Patriots destroyed the tea to hit Norton, they forbade the *Virginia* to load tobacco. Norton sought absolution in the Virginia papers. Hoping to "recover" his "esteem" among "friends and countrymen in Virginia," he apologized, and noted, sincerely or not, that Parliament had "not the least shadow of a right to tax America." Norton's other vessels loaded tobacco later.[78]

The Fiction of Legal Distance

Merchants complied in part because of Patriots' threats and force. This required the pretense of legal separation between committee and crowd. In many tea parties, regular participants disguised themselves. This amplified the menace: the impossibility of knowing who might harm them was one reason consignees cowered in Castle William. But, as public figures, committeemen could not disguise their identities. The Boston committee of correspondence met the day the *Fortune*'s tea was destroyed without deciding on an official course of action. But privately, John Adams knew ahead of time that the tea was "to make an Infusion in Water." The York County, Virginia committee explained that unnamed "inhabitants of York" (not the committee) boarded the *Virginia* and threw its tea "into the River." The committee "highly approve of . . . destroying the tea," but denied doing it. The Gloucester County, Virginia committee said it would have broken the law but found the tea "committed to the waves" before its mob could act. Dunmore was convinced the York committee had acted, but Virginia authorities could not prove it in court.[79] The York and Gloucester committees implicitly took credit while minimizing legal exposure.

In December, the Cumberland County, New Jersey committee took control of tea from the *Greyhound*. By this time the Association banned tea importation and required the tea to be auctioned for Boston relief. This would
have put the tea in circulation and reimbursed the owners. To the committee's "surprise," "the tea had been destroyed by persons unknown." The committee "entirely disapprove of the destroying of the above-mentioned tea,"
and promised "not [to] conceal nor protect from justice any of the perpetrators." As one local historian noted, the committee had to "at least publicly dis-
avow the act." But the committee had failed to protect the tea in its possession,
and at least two committee members were among the Greenwich tea burners. Criminal charges were filed, and the tea owners sued the committeemen
for damages. The grand jury refused to indict—the sheriff who selected the
jurors and the jury foreman were brothers of one of the accused, and the authority of the colony's courts collapsed before the civil case could proceed.[80]

The fiction of legal distance worked because it was not always fiction.
Maryland leaders had little to do with the burning of the *Peggy Stewart*, which
Congressman Samuel Chase and Barrister Charles Carroll both opposed, as
did a majority of those gathered to debate the matter. Committees did not
always control the Sons of Liberty, and the latter did not always control the
crowd.[81]

The understanding that Patriot elites did not always control crowds, and
that, were committees too lenient, crowds might act anyway, gave a certain
menace to committee actions. The existence of committees "presumed the
presence of the mob," as Barbara Clark Smith notes, and committees benefitted from mob violence. In some colonies, the angry mob and the sensible committee was a performance derived from court days.[82]

In such a performance, the violent and respectable parts of the Patriot
movement each had a role. When the Charleston committee ordered merchants to destroy tea from the *Britannia*, it was to preclude "direct action by
the people," as Pauline Maier suggests. A mob watched the importers dump
their tea into the river and gave "three hearty Chears after the emptying of
each Chest." But the committee was both restraining the crowd and "restraining" the crowd. In New Hampshire, when it became unclear when Parry's tea
would depart, customs officers reported that "two Drums began to beat, and
the immediate distruction of the Tea was feared . . . especially as the Committee that had Guarded her [the tea vessel] the preceeding night said it was with
the utmost difficulty they had saved the Vessel and Tea" from "a number of
Men with Tools [who] came down the Wharf that Night in order to scuttle
her." The committee and the "Men with Tools" appear distinct, but their hand-
in-glove work hastened the ship's departure.[83]

Sometimes committees wrote the mob out of the story, as in the events surrounding Anthony Warwick and Michael Wallace's tea importation. The Nansemond committee claimed in the *Virginia Gazette* that Warwick and Wallace had imported tea and, after questioning, agreed to "keep the tea safe, ready to be delivered up to the committee when required, and that none of it shall be sold or used." But the committee achieved this because of threats made to Warwick and Wallace while in Williamsburg a few weeks earlier. There, a member of the Nansemond committee had confronted the men. According to Loyalist William Aitchison, Warwick and Wallace's "lives were threatened." Patriots threatened the pair with tar and feathers. "Young Nicholas," son to Robert Carter Nicholas and a comptroller of customs to be, "spoke very Violently against them & asked how they durst insult the Majesty of the People." Virginia gentry, including Continental Congressmen Peyton Randolph, Edmund Pendleton, and Richard Bland, colonial treasurer Robert Carter Nicholas, and Burgess Robert Munford convinced the merchants to deliver their tea to avoid assault.[84] The congressmen seemed well-meaning. But could they hold off the mob forever? What would happen when the merchants went home? No one had to spell this out.

Colonists understood that Sons of Liberty and Patriot committees were armed and political wings of a common movement. As one Loyalist writer joked: "What, do you drink Tea? Take care what you do, Mr. C., for you are to know the Committee commands the mob and can in an instant let them loose upon any man who opposes their decrees, and complete his destruction." The Sons of Liberty, on their own, could be terrifying. Peter Oliver Jr. considered them "Sons of Anarchy," guilty of the "horrid Crime of Rebellion." Their menace facilitated the Charleston committee becoming, in Sarah Maitland's mind, the "Committee of the Usurped Power." Other Patriots softened things to broaden the movement's appeal. They said, Edward Parry volunteered to send his tea away. The Charleston committee, in a press release headlined "FACTS," falsely claimed that Maitland made a "*free* and *voluntary Offer*" of his ship's tea into the river "at his own Cost," obscuring the violence he faced. As merchant Henry Fleming explained, "whilst some are contending for Liberty they are willing to deprive others of every pretention to it from which I conclude every one here is a Tyrant as far as his power extends." Without conciliation from Parliament, "our property at least must be very precarious," under committee rule. This helped stop the importation of tea and English goods.[85] Stopping consumption however, was another matter and would draw in colonists not previously involved in the imperial crisis.

CHAPTER 6

Toward Non-consumption

In Charleston, South Carolina, the first week of November 1774 was full of anti-tea politics. November 1 marked the start of non-consumption, according to the province's association. The *Britannia* arrived with British tea that same day. Also on that day, schoolboys knocked on doors and collected (presumably Dutch) tea from families in town for the Pope's Day celebration to come. Then at noon on November 3, the crowd and the committee made importers from the *Britannia* make an "Oblation . . . to NEPTUNE" and dump their tea into the river.[1]

The climax came on November 5, Guy Fawkes Day, the anniversary of the Gunpowder Plot (an assassination attempt on James I) and the Glorious Revolution of 1688 (which deposed his grandson). It was also known as Pope's Day, a charivari or mock celebration, filled with ritual devils and popes, who were attacked to celebrate the people's deliverance from evil and burned to celebrate the defeat of Stuart Pretenders in 1715 and 1745. The events expressed local community, loyalty to the crown, and opposition to Stuart Pretenders, the French, despotism, and the pope. Its various meanings were contradictory and situational (everyone seemed to forget that the pope had sided with England in 1688). Elites tried to control celebrations, but plebs often dominated them. South Carolina Patriots rioted while in Boston British troops fired cannons from batteries, warships, and the castle. Charleston Patriots embraced this holiday as Patriotic *Britons* attacking a ministry they thought had betrayed the kingdom. Their "Brethren in England" had "over-looked" the message of the Gunpowder Plot and the Glorious Revolution, bringing in new tyranny with the Coercive Acts. On Pope's Day protest made them good Britons.[2]

Patriots drew upon the symbolic language of Pope's Day to express fears that the Quebec Act established Catholicism in North America, that the Co-ercive Acts stripped colonists of British rights, and that the ministry plotted to replace British freedoms and Protestantism with despotism and the Roman Church. These fears, however misplaced, drew upon meaningful events in the British past and were shared in other colonies.[3]

Charlestonians placed tea at the center of these celebrations. Bells rang in the morning, showing four effigies on a "rolling Stage": Lord North, Massa-chusetts governor Hutchinson, the pope, and the devil. The four were placed in front of Mr. Ramadge's tavern in the most heavily trafficked part of town, the pope in his chair with North and Hutchinson on either side and Satan behind, regarding his wicked minions. A lantern hung from the devil's arm "in the Shape of a Tea Canister, on the Sides of which was writ in capitals, HYSON, GREEN, CONGO AND BOHEA TEAS." On North's breast his goals were given as "To bring in the PRETENDER," "To ruin the King—By estab-lishing POPERY," and "To crush the last Remains of British Freedom." Men and women came out all day to view the spectacle, and some swore they saw the pope and the devil bow to acolytes in the crowd. Around eight in the morn-ing, the stage was rolled to the statehouse, then back to the tavern, where it stayed the day. Religious services were held in St. Michael's Church. Out in the streets, a second pope and devil, built by schoolboys, paraded through town. This pope had a lantern also, with illustrations on every side, one de-picting a burning tea canister, another an allegory of America spearing Lord North, who was kneeling upon a tea chest. An elaborate text was attached to each character, identifying their crimes. In the evening, the main stage rolled through town and out the gate to the parade ground, where a pole, tar, and feathers stood. The tea collected by the schoolboys was tossed on the float, and all was burned. The schoolboys' effigies were burned, too. The tea brought "on our Enemies in *Effigy*, that Ruin which they had designed to bring on us in *Reality*," wrote the *South Carolina Gazette*.[4]

On one level, these events enforced non-consumption: householders' tea was collected and burned. They also protested the Coercive Acts. The up-is-downism of a charivari also let the lower orders do what their superiors nor-mally did: inflict public punishment. Ritual public punishment was central to colonial discipline: executions, stockades, skimmingtons (punishments for sex-ual deviance and immorality), scarlet letters (for a variety of causes), and brandings were all intended to shame and embarrass and convey moral standards (as with John Malcom).[5] Here, Patriots punished the pope, prime minister, and the devil for their plot to destroy British freedom and reminded the populace that tea was forbidden.

In this protest, tea was generic. To be sure, the effigies of North and Hutchinson suggested British tea, but much of the tea colonists gave to be burned was probably Dutch. This simplified visual lexicon of protest let any tea become shorthand for Company monopoly, ministerial taxation, and the Coercive Acts. Newspaper accounts of tea rallies similarly did away with the distinction between English and Dutch tea, which let holders of smuggled tea burn it in solidary with Boston and holders of dutied tea burn it without awkward questions. This was different from the action on November 3, when Patriots had opposed the importation of British tea specifically.

Avoiding all tea was a practical choice for the Patriotic colonist who wanted to avoid consuming duplied tea. As "Mentor" argued in the *Newport Mercury:* "How can you be sure you drink no duplied tea, if you indulge yourself in drinking any tea?" Duplied tea "has certainly been landed, and where, and how far it hath already, or may be hereafter dispersed, none can say." Destroying all tea, Mentor explained, was a better performance, and "can bear the strongest and most striking testimony of our abhorrence of [the Ministry's] wicked plan."[6]

The campaign against tea proceeded in different colonies at different times. The Association eventually imposed uniformity upon this diversity, a process John Adams described as getting "thirteen clocks . . . to Strike together." In 1774, these clocks struck separately. On the one hand, Patriots' enthusiasm and their desire to stage events that showed the populace was with them encouraged tea parties and announcements of rapid non-consumption. On the other, the Patriots' own Continental Congress indicated that tea could be sold and drunk until March 1, 1775, and some colonists continued to treat tea as a purely consumer good. Opposition to tea in 1774 was changing, partial, and inchoate. As part of their campaign, Patriot sources made opposition to tea look impressive, and we must read such sources carefully to see the gradualism of and resistance to their ban. By November 1774, Charleston Patriots had been campaigning against tea for a year but were only just then implementing their Association's orders.[7] This chapter examines the fits and starts of the move toward non-consumption in 1774: the gradual disuse of tea, which involved frequent backsliding; the role of coercion in the Patriot campaign; the tea parties and the various non-canonical intentions behind them, which Patriots obscured; enforcement and continued consumption; the storage of large quantities of tea in 1774 (which risked being drunk in 1775); and the Loyalist response.

The Gradualism of Disuse

It is tempting to interpret swift bans on tea sales as signs of an emerging consensus against the product. In Massachusetts, some towns responded to the Boston Tea Party with bans on tea sales: forty towns by April 1774. But this was forty towns out of nearly two hundred, hardly an expression of general will. Only five of the towns banning tea banned all tea consumption outright: Worcester, Acton, Lunenburg, Charlestown, and Boston. The rest allowed Dutch tea sales to continue.[8]

It took nearly a year to ban tea in Massachusetts, too. This reflected the difficulty in convincing Massachusettsans to see tea as a political and not a consumer product. *Declarations* of support were easy: The General Assembly endorsed the tea boycott in the spring of 1774. But when John Hancock advocated in his Boston Massacre speech "total disuse of tea in this country, which will eventually be the saving of the lives and estates of thousands," his formulation—*"eventually"*—suggested people in "this country" were not doing it yet. In June, the General Assembly again resolved that colonists should "renounce consumption" of tea. The provincial congress advocated "total disuse" of tea in October.[9] These announcements were passed to the towns for enforcement, their repetition suggesting not every town heeded at first.

Haverhill announced its resolves against importing, buying, or consuming tea in August. Plymouth County Patriots resolved the same in September. Medford voted not to use tea at home and, in November, set up a committee to "Enquire if any person or persons Sells or consumes" tea.[10]

Across the colonies, a similar dynamic played out: a few places, like Middletown, Rhode Island, quickly resolved to "have nothing to do with the East-India company's irksome tea." Then, more colonists turned against tea with news of the Coercive Acts. At the end of May Philip Vickers Fithian noted Virginians who "Drank Coffee" for "they are now too patriotic to use tea." Now—not before. Even then, resolves against tea spread gradually: Windham, Connecticut in June, Patriots in various Virginia counties in June and July; the Virginia Association in August, the North Carolina provincial congress in September. The last deemed "all persons in this province not complying with this resolve to be enemies to their Country."[11] Yet it is still unclear just how well colonists abided by this command.

The campaign against tea was particularly drawn out in Portsmouth, New Hampshire, where the governor assisted tea arrivals and got some tea duties paid. After Parry's failed importation in June, the July town meeting resolved against importing, buying, selling, or consuming tea until the tea duty was repealed and Boston opened. But sales continued. In August, a woman endured riotous insults from a group of "boys and sailors" for selling tea. The town denounced the riot, and Governor Wentworth reported the few "who had tea have sold it without molestation." Wentworth thought tea sales would dry up "entirely" in a few months, and in September, Patriots compelled six Portsmouth residents to swear they would not sell tea. But it was harder for Patriots to accomplish this than Wentworth thought. On January 18, 1775, a merchant was discovered attempting to sell tea. Patriots claimed it had come from Salem. The owner burned his remaining sixty-pound supply in front of a large crowd—but how much had already been sold or used? The next week, the New Hampshire provincial convention recommended total disuse of tea, as, clearly, it was not yet wholly disused.[12]

Half Abstention

There is evidence of at least some tea disuse. The *Newport Mercury*, for instance, estimated a third as much tea was drunk in Newport in January 1774 as three months earlier. John Harrower, an indentured servant, wrote in June 1774, "As for Tea there is none drunk by any in this Government [Virginia] since 1st. June last." Nicholas Cresswell noted in July that after the election to the House of Burgesses, one of the returned members "gave a ball . . . Coffee and Chocolate, but no Tea. This Herb is in disgrace amongst them at present." William Reynolds reported using sage instead. In December, Harrower wrote in his diary, "I have not drunk a dish of Tea this six Mos. Past."[13]

Yet there is also evidence tea continued to be consumed despite the protests. Boston merchant John Andrews reported that "prodigious shouts" at the Old South Meeting House forced him to interrupt "drinking tea at home" to see what was the matter. After seeing what was the prelude to the Boston Tea Party, Andrews, who sided with the Patriots in 1776, "went contentedly home and finish'd my tea." In January 1774, with Boston tea dealers having already announced they would soon stop selling tea, future Loyalist William Vassall Sr. wrote to London, ordering "16 Pounds of very best Superfine Hyson Tea": "Send the very best" "for my Family," he added. Elihu Ashley found himself both drinking tea and discussing "Liberty Matters" (probably in response to the Coercive Acts) in Goshen, Connecticut, in May 1774. Efforts to bring in non-consumption in response to the Coercive Acts failed in New York and Philadelphia that same month. In June, provincial treasurer, erstwhile Company consignee, and newly minted member of the New York committee of 51 Abraham Lott traveled to Albany, drinking tea in Poughkeepsie and Albany, and selling tea in the latter. That August, Andrews mentioned having tea in his letters as though there were no political significance to it, and it was not until early September that he was finally drinking "coffee (not tea)." Virginia merchant William Allason's books show fifteen pounds of bohea on hand in October 1773, all of which was gone within a year. Despite the public abstention from tea, Nicholas Cresswell noted in Virginia he still "Drank Tea and Coffee at Captn. Sandford's" in Alexandria that October. On December 11, 1774, Patriots seized a parcel of tea in a Manhattan store, and nineteen chests the next day in Flushing, New York. This did not prevent New York merchant Jonathan Freebody Jr. from sending a tierce of tea (a large barrel) to Christopher Champlin in Rhode Island.[14]

The *Newport Mercury*'s estimate implied reduced but continued consumption. At Yale, some classes voted in December 1774 not to drink tea until the duty was removed and to boycott the bookseller James Lockwood, who probably sold it. These Yalies also threatened to shun classmates who did not join their boycott. But not every class voted this way, and even among classes that did, "three or four" students dissented. Providence reported an indeterminate "Number of Families in this Town have discontinued the use of Tea," which, read the other way, also meant an indeterminate number continued using it.[15]

Bringing in non-consumption among the general public before the Association's mandated March 1, 1775, start date was difficult. If a householder had already paid for tea, burning it did not affect British merchants or un-pay any duty that had already been paid, and it could be hard to convince colonists to take the loss. "What Good," asked one writer in the *Norwich Packet*, will come from burning tea colonists already had on hand? As Virginia attorney general and conservative pamphleteer John Randolph explained, to boycott tea "already in our Houses," whether it had paid duty or not, was more "the Overflowing of Zeal, than founded on any solid Principle." Some Patriots seem to have agreed. Halifax, North Carolina resolved "never to purchase directly or indirectly or use [tea] in any of our families"—"except what we now have." The questions of what to do with the tea from the *William* further confused matters. The *William*'s tea had not paid duty, and salvagers had been paid in tea. Should Patriots wipe out their pay, or allow Company tea to circulate? Only in November did the Barnstable County congress vote against "any kind of India Tea, whether Imported on Account of the East-India Company, or any other."[16]

Even avowed Patriots struggled to maintain a political view of non-consumption in 1774. Philip Vickers Fithian was a tutor in Robert Carter's household. The Carters, Virginia Patriots, claimed to have stopped drinking tea in May. But Fithian recorded in September that "Mrs. Carter made a dish of Tea." She passed it round the table until her husband sipped it, realized what it was, and, exclaiming "Poh!," tossed the dish out into the fire. It is hard to believe this was an honest mistake. Did Mrs. Carter accidentally ask the slaves to make tea? Did they not bring it out in a tea service? How were there tea leaves to brew? One wonders whether Mrs. Carter had forgotten her Patriotism or that Fithian was present. Certainly, Fithian ordered tea when the Carters were not looking at him. He drank tea when he traveled in 1774: in Maryland in April, Delaware in May, and Maryland again in October.[17]

Even protesters struggled to stop drinking tea. In January 1774, students at the College of New Jersey (later Princeton) had a tea party, tying a container with twelve pounds of tea left in it around the neck of an effigy of Governor Hutchinson, burning both in the yard. They "tolled the bell" and made "many spirited resolves." They did this "to show our patriotism," Charles Beatty explained. "Officers and Students" announced they would not drink tea.[18]

But in late February Beatty had tea with a Mrs. Nelson, an acquaintance in Princeton town, mentioning it to his brother Erkuries. That spring he also had tea with a Mrs. Beatty, probably Mary, his brother John's bride, and a Miss B. Sergeant, with whom he "spent the afternoon very agreeably." The Coercive Acts helped him back on the Patriot wagon again by June, when he joined a "fine frolick" of roughly forty students "all drest in white," who went to a house in town belonging to a man "who used to drink tea, and said he would persist in it." The students "made him deliver up his tea," and they burned it in the street before running off to intimidate a Tory. "I am as strong a Whig as the best of them," he assured his brother.[19]

And he was right, for the best of them waffled just as much. On July 6, 1774, John Adams made a long ride on the circuit to Falmouth, Maine. Upon reaching an inn he asked the proprietress if it were "'lawful for a weary Traveller to refresh himself with a Dish of Tea provided it has been honestly smuggled, or paid no Duties?' . . . 'No,'" she replied, "'we have renounced all Tea. . . . but I'le make you Coffee.' Accordingly," Adams reflected, "I have drank Coffee every Afternoon since, and have borne it very well. Tea must be universally renounced. I must be weaned, and the sooner, the better."[20]

In August, traveling through New York to Congress, Adams and the Massachusetts congressional delegation declined tea with the relatively conservative William Smith. But the next day they were joined by Alexander McDougall, leader of the New York Sons of Liberty, for breakfast at Patriot John Morin Scott's home. Scott served tea. In Pennsylvania, tea continued to be consumed, provided it was smuggled. This could be verified via customs records. In August, the Lancaster committee seized 349 pounds of tea belonging to Josiah and Robert Lockhart. The Lancaster committee noted the container markings and consulted the Philadelphia committee, which responded that the Lockharts' tea "never had paid any Duty" and had in fact been seized by customs officers as smuggled tea before being bought back by the owner at auction. Having "acquitted" the Lockharts, the Lancaster committee returned the tea. Tea was available in Philadelphia. William Caswell, the son of North Carolina congressman Richard Caswell, "Drank Tea" in Philadelphia on September 18, 1774. George Washington was still drinking tea at Congress, taking tea with Mrs. Roberdeau on October 22, 1774, two days after signing the Continental Association.[21] Perhaps the mid-Atlantic colonies' permissive attitude toward Dutch tea wore off on delegates. If so, they must have struggled mightily during the Second Continental Congress.

Tea burnings' symbolic meaning and generalized non-consumption required a leap of faith. That symbolism flattened distinctions between different kinds of tea and made tea politics seem grand rather than trifling. It was not clear to observers that this symbolism would eventually triumph. Writing in the summer of 1774, John Randolph doubted Virginians would ever refrain from tea.[22] And so for much of 1774, non-consumption remained perpetually in progress.

The Campaign: The Limits of Coercion

Public events like Charleston's Pope Day celebration connected everyday consumer choices to a grand political narrative. That contest between colonists and Parliament gave rallies and consumer tea boycotts "a Dignity, a Majesty, a Sublimity," as John Adams wrote of the Boston Tea Party. Thus Patriots marked January 20, 1774, the day no more tea was to be drunk in Boston, by burning two barrels of bohea in a bonfire in front of the Customs House, "amidst the loud Acclaims of a vast Concourse of People." And thus Henry Hulton contested the grandeur of the event by suggesting that only a "small Cask of damaged tea" was burned. These rallies involved the mass participation of consumers who refused to consume and were often performed twice: first in person and again in the press as acts of "conspicuous *non*-consumption."[23]

Yet the rallies were coercive. Seen as fights between neighbors, as conflicts between political or commercial rivals, or as the intimidation of one group of colonists by another, they seemed not majestic but petty and disturbing. Thus New Jersey farm girl Jemima Condict lamented the general upheaval in late 1774: "They say it is tea that caused it. So then, if they will quarrel about such a trifling thing as that, what must we expect but war?"[24]

The coercion was usually directed against merchants. According to Wentworth, the tea burned in Portsmouth, New Hampshire, in January 1775 was "burnt by the Populace." Patriots, on the other hand, claimed the trader was "so far convinced of his own Error" in trying to sell it that "he put it in the Fire himself in the presence of a large Number of Spectators."[25] The tea importers on the *Britannia*, made to drown their tea days before the Charleston Pope's Day celebration, "volunteered" their tea. Merchants sometimes had to pretend to be like this. This pretense was another level of submission. Radicals sometimes watched for absent Tories at rallies and marched the crowd to their homes. It was a rational choice to toe the Patriot line, burn a little tea in public, and pretend one was not coerced, making the mix of coercion and fervor that brought tea to the flame hard to discern.

Outright violence was used, as at the riot, which Anglican minister Jacob Bailey reported "raging up the river" from Georgetown, Maine, in October 1774. It "destroyed one hundred and fifty pounds of tea"—a supply so large it could only have belonged to a merchant. Nicholas Cresswell noted in Alexandria, Virginia, in October 1774 that "committees are appointed to inspect into the Characters and Conduct of every tradesman, to prevent them selling Tea or buying British Manufactures. Some of them have been tarred and feathered, others had their property burnt and destroyed by the populace." Governor Dunmore lamented at the end of the year that committees had brought the Association into effect "with the greatest rigour," inspecting and interrogating whatever and whomever, and "Stigmatiz[ing]" transgressors with an "Outrageous and lawless Mob."[26] But the threat of mob action—made plausible by a few choice examples—was usually enough.

Conversely, the campaign against tea could dissipate without committees and Sons of Liberty, as in Nova Scotia. In response to the July tea landing in Halifax, a "great number of respectable and popular Merchants, Traders and Inhabitants" of Halifax talked of boycotting British tea. Patriotic Haligonians promised "not to purchase any of the said Tea themselves" and to boycott anyone who did. But they were too few to physically block the tea's landing and lamented their "utter inability to prevent it." The captain who brought the tea to Halifax reported that it was "much against the Minds of the Inhabitants, who are determined not to purchase it," but admitted that "Tea is sold there" still. Nova Scotians even tried to hold a tea party in Windsor, Nova Scotia. In one version of the story, a tea chest was stored in a local magistrate's house. A crowd threatened to burn the house unless he surrendered the tea. But he refused and, without Sons of Liberty to press the issue, the crowd eventually cleared off. In another version, the tea was kept in a store and sent on by water to Cornwallis Township, frustrating the crowd. Some Patriots thought Windsor proof of the "Spirit of Liberty" in Nova Scotia. But while some Nova Scotians boycotted tea, enough consumed it for Governor Legge to report that, despite minor protests, "inhabitants in general have behaved with due decorum" and "tea has been disposed of, Purchased and dispersed thro' the Country." If the tea sold in Nova Scotia was "small," it was only because its "Inhabitants are but few."[27]

The following year, Legge noted that non-importation and non-consumption had failed in Nova Scotia. Many Nova Scotians were sympathetic to the common cause. Patriotic Nova Scotians wished "our American Brethren success in their glorious struggles to preserve their Rights and Liberties."[28] But geographical barriers inhibited armed rebellion (Washington was unwilling to risk sending part of the Continental Army over water), and the lack of Sons of Liberty and committees of correspondence prevented Patriotic Nova Scotians from imposing non-consumption on their neighbors.

Likewise, in the summer of 1774, with the Massachusetts government come to Salem and hence with General Gage, the customs commissioners, and soldiers about town, Salem Patriots were unable to stop tea consumption. The *Boston Post-Boy* even made a joke of it. Only after they were emboldened by the Powder Alarm and empowered by Gage's withdrawal of troops from Salem to Boston did Salem Patriots begin attacking tea vendors. In October, a "Negro fellow" brought a cask of tea from Boston to Salem. Salem Patriots obliged "the Fellow . . . to leave the Town immediately" and stored the tea in committeeman David Mason's home before burning it in front of hundreds of spectators. Patriots "obliged" other tea sellers (but not all) to surrender their tea. Who had been buying? The *Essex Gazette* assured readers that tea had long been "contrary to the Minds of the People in general," implying the buyers were few, but who knows?[29]

When Is a Tea Party Not a Tea Party?

Patriots performed and wrote about their tea parties as though they were signs of widespread, uniform, and already-accomplished tea resistance. This was sometimes just propaganda. Attending a tea party did not a true believer make. Though North Carolina women "burnt their tea in a solemn procession" and boasted of compliance, Scotswoman Janet Schaw thought their "sacrifice was not very considerable," suspecting they had burned a token amount and left the rest at home. In other instances wherein Patriots' called upon colonists to burn tea from their cupboards, it is similarly naïve to assume colonists surrendered "every ounce" of their tea, as they supposedly did in Lexington.[30]

Some riots were not as tea-focused as they seemed. Sylvester Gardiner encountered one at Georgetown, Maine, comprising "one hundred and fifty men, armed with guns and various weapons," "running about in search of tea." They "surrounded his house, demanded a sight of him, and insisted upon searching for tea" at midnight. The mob tossed his place and drank "several gallons of" his rum. Probably drunk before they arrived, they continued imbibing until several were "dead drunk," and the rest went home. Along the way they stole valuables. The revelers were there to drink and to attack and loot Gardiner as much as they were there to look for tea.[31] A "tea party" was just an excuse.

Tea party attendees sometimes stole tea. This was a known problem at the Boston Tea Party. One participant claimed to have been "careful to prevent any [tea] being taken away," which meant he knew to be on the lookout. One observer noticed that after the tea was tossed into the harbor, "small Boats were rowed towards the Tea" to take it, and warned off. (The tea supply was so large that, the morning after, Patriots were still trying to drown all the tea in the harbor with oars and paddles to ensure it was ruined.)[32]

Peter Oliver claimed that some of the Boston revelers "filled their Bags & their Pockets" with tea. Patriots caught a "Captain Conner," who had "ript up the lining of his coat and waistcoat under the arms" and had "nearly fill'd 'em, with tea," and who was "handled pretty roughly" for it. They caught, too, a tall, old man hiding tea in his pockets—the tea was thrown into the water. Others may have gotten through. Jonathan Clarke, salvaging the tea from the *William*, worried that Cape Cod residents would "think themselves licensed to steal" the Company's tea once they heard news of the rest of the tea being thrown in Boston Harbor. The Massachusetts Historical Society holds two sets of tea leaves said to be souvenirs taken from Boston Tea Party—if real, then clearly taking tea was possible.[33]

Boston tea partiers could let tea "fall" into their boots. Some insisted, perhaps a bit too much, that they destroyed it. Thomas Melvill found tea in his boots the day after the Boston Tea Party. According to his family, he kept a vial as a keepsake but did not drink any. William Russell claimed to have dusted his shoes over the fire to destroy every bit of tea. George Robert Twelve Hewes recalled men were lined up in formation and ordered to empty their shoes after destroying the tea. Well they did, since his wife asked about the tea when Hewes got home. "Well, George," she said. "Did you bring me home a lot of it?"[34]

Greenwich, New Jersey tea burner Henry Stacks stole so much tea at that town's tea party that his name became a joke: "Tea Stacks" for the heaps of tea he took. The joke marked townsfolks' tacit acceptance of Stacks's actions. After a mock-hanging of tea in Connecticut, local Patriots burned it, as it was "dangerous to let the said Tea hang all night, for fear of an invasion from our Tea-lovers." In the summer, colonists broke into Richard Nichols's shop in Salem, Massachusetts and took "a Quantity of Tea, a small Part of which" ended up "strowed in the Street." The rest disappeared, which might be why, when Salem Patriots found more tea that October, they hid it "for safe keeping" before burning it. The Charleston, South Carolina committee ordered Maitland to retrieve his tea from the Exchange and burn it, but changed its mind, likely fearing that opening the Exchange would risk theft of the Company tea kept there from the previous December.[35]

Like the apocryphal New England fishermen who, when the preacher told the crowd that everyone had gathered to pray, shouted back: "We came here to fish and not to pray!" rank-and-file tea partiers did not always share the motives of their leaders.[36] This was a point Patriot writers avoided. Patriot publications described crowds uniformly intending to destroy tea, not take it. But colonists did not attend tea parties for ideologically coherent reasons. Some came for a good riot, a stiff drink, or to steal tea, not, as it were, to pray.

Enforcement as a Sign of Consumption

Enforcing a rule implies its violation. Thus the schoolboys who went knocking on doors in Charleston, South Carolina found tea to collect—nearly a year after the tea ships of 1773. Sensing the problem, the *South Carolina Gazette* explained that the boys "made a considerable Collection of Tea" but found "three-fourths of the Houses without any."[37] Finding tea and not finding tea both became signs of Patriotism. But we may ask whether the three-fourths who turned the boys away had no more tea to give or preferred not to give it.

Catching a tea seller implied some colonists had already bought tea without being caught. Patriots found a sizable amount of tea in possession of a merchant named Graham on November 4, 1774, in Charlestown, Massachusetts. Charlestown merchants had agreed not to sell tea the previous Christmas. The (rather vague) explanation was that in "pursuing a Person who had been guilty of breaking the peace" a barrel and bag of tea "were stumbled on" at Graham's shop and later burned. Graham's barrel "contained parcels done up 1 to 2 oz. Bundles for a conveniency to retail," suggesting he had been and intended to continue selling it. Troubled to have discovered a tea seller they had not even known to look for, Patriots went back, searched his shop, and found enough tea "to fill a large hogshead," which they burned on the green in front of a tavern.[38]

It is unclear how much this tea burning deterred the peddlers who sold tea at taverns. "Indians" from Northborough traveled to neighboring Shrewsbury, Massachusetts to confiscate a bag of tea from a peddler in February 1774. They burned it in front of the tavern. This is impressive, but then one realizes that the most likely way for Northborough men to know about this tea would have been if the salesman had already sold some in Northborough. A mob took 100 pounds of tea off an itinerant trader in Lyme, Connecticut. But he seemed to have been "pedling about the country" for some time. In Haverhill—one of the "remotest Parts of our English Settlements"—a "pedling Trader" left his tea with the local innkeeper in the summer of 1774, thinking this it means of safekeeping, only for "honest Savages" to seize and burn it.[39] One is as struck by the burning as by the expectation that the tea would be safe.

Marylander John Parks was caught delivering tea to relatives in Pennsylvania. His home committee followed up, publishing Park's agreement to give up the tea. Parks gave his committee some tea, but the committee suspected his main supply remained. So the committee ordered him to burn his tea publicly and sentenced him to be boycotted. A crowd broke his doors and windows in as well.[40] This seems like effective enforcement, but the other tea remained at large.

Such enforcement of the boycott was, by definition, an indication of its violation. Yet it was impolitic for Patriots to admit this in public, a sensitivity which requires us to read public Patriot documents carefully. Consider the case of the laborer Ebenezer Withington. Despite Patriots' efforts to keep the Tea Party tea in Boston Harbor, Withington salvaged a half chest of it from the Dorchester marshes. This was either on December 18, two days after the Boston Tea Party, or December 25. Patriots caught him selling to "divers Persons" and burned his tea on New Year's Eve on Boston Common.

On January 3, Patriots began to give meaning to these events. That day Withington appeared at a town meeting, begging ignorance of the political significance of East India Company tea. Dorchester decided Withington "proceeded from Inadvertency" (i.e., carelessness) and meant no "Harm." The town resolved that his buyers hand over their tea, lest their names be posted, an announcement which soon appeared in the press. It is easy to be taken in by this gloss of a rock-ribbed Patriotic town straightening out a wayward neighbor, for it is at least partly true.[41]

Dorchester took pains to show "one common Cause" with Boston. The greatest threats to that show were questions about Dorchester's Patriotism. In November "Several Persons, who are deemed Enemies to this Country" (perhaps tea consignees or customs collectors) had fled Boston for Dorchester and other towns, making Dorchester seem a safe haven for the King's men. Dorchester promised them "just Indignation," but news of Withington's tea—which would have reached Boston no later than the bonfire on December 31—raised more questions.[42]

For at the same January 3 town meeting that interrogated "old Ebenezer Withington," Dorchester elected "Captain Ebenezer Withington" to its committee of correspondence. These were different men: Captain Ebenezer Withington was a town leader and Patriot. The other, his second cousin, was a "Labourer." However, the committee could not send letters to towns like Boston over Captain Withington's name, after Bostonians had just made a bonfire of the other Withington's tea, as the names were sure to be confounded. Helpfully, when "Narragasett-Indians" searched for the laborer Withington's tea, they accidentally searched the captain's house first—with his "consent." Finding nothing, they went to the right Withington thereafter. On January 3, the *Boston Gazette* printed this colorful vignette without mentioning Captain Ebenezer Withington's role in town, exonerating him to readers who knew, leaving the rest none the wiser. The same day the *Gazette* ran this story, Dorchester elected Captain Withington to its committee of correspondence and dealt with the laborer Withington tea. Captain Withington served as an assessor and selectman, represented Dorchester in the provincial congress in February 1775, and, that same year, served on the town's committee of inspection, preventing consumption of "East-India Teas."[43]

The town meeting was concerned with what the story of the other Ebenezer Withington would mean. It claimed "Satisfaction" that Withington was "discovered in Selling said Tea," for this meant they could stop him and disprove the claim that the "Tea said to have been destroyed, was [actually] plundered & thus privately Sold." But Withington privately sold the tea for a week or two before getting caught. Saying Withington's sales were inadvertent helpfully implied townsfolk's purchases were also inadvertent. The meeting was vague about how much tea he sold, and to whom, only demanding these unnamed buyers "deliver" up the tea, or have their names "publickly posted."[44] Despite the firm language, it is unclear whether townsfolk actually turned in their tea.

Withington was no "simple old man." He did not take the tea naively but most likely intended to sell it (a half chest was too large for private use). He rightly judged there would be buyers. Worth perhaps between 4 and 18 pounds sterling, this tea meaningfully added to a laborer's income. But he was not the only workingman in town and surely not the only person to comb the beach for loot. At the earliest, Withington found his tea the second day after the Tea Party. Family histories tell of a young John Robinson finding a half chest of tea on Dorchester's shoals the day before.[45] Who else combed these shorelines for tea? Withington lived "below Dorchester Meeting House" near Dorchester Bay. He found the tea in the "Marshes" on Dorchester Neck, a distance of two, probably three, miles. For people who lived or worked near Dorchester Neck, or the harbor islands, or who fished, such scavenging was easier. Dorchester hinted at the possibility that others took tea, declaring that "if any other Person or Persons" took tea, they should surrender it or face exposure. That is to say, if they got away with it, we would never know, and if they took the tea and later surrendered it, the town kept their names quiet.[46] (See figure 1.1.)

The tea was difficult to carry inconspicuously. Chests were heavy and cumbersome. A proper half chest held roughly seventy-five pounds of tea, with the wet wooden casing adding weight. Even half this would have been hard to carry unnoticed for several miles, and even harder to carry right into the center of town, especially if it had Company markings still on it. Withington was noticed. On his way home "Some Gentlemen belonging to the Castle" saw him with the tea. (The castle ferry connected to the Heights road, giving the consignees, customs collectors, and soldiers in the castle access to the flats.) The gentlemen spoke with Withington about the tea, explaining that while there was no legal "harm" in salvaging the tea, it could cause trouble with Withington's "neighbours."[47]

Dorchester told of political and moral renewal, a righteous town setting a hapless man on the right path. It told past and potential future buyers to desist. But this was a cleaned-up story. Dorchester named a single scapegoat who deferred to his betters (the gentlemen from the castle) in believing the tea was harmless, and then deferred to the meeting in learning it was not. The other Withington is named only to be exonerated. The townsfolk who bought tea, scoured the flats for their own, or saw Withington with his load, are nameless and easily forgotten. Enforcement of non-consumption was predicated on its broader violation, making virtue a work in progress—a progress that proceeded more smoothly when Patriots wrote up progress as virtue achieved.

Buying Tea

Enforcement took unexpected forms. One of the more striking approaches some Patriots took in 1774 was to buy back tea for destruction. Tea buybacks could help keep merchants on-side. These men were worth placating, as sustaining non-importation and non-consumption was easier with merchant support. Another approach was to store tea, awaiting the end of non-consumption. Both presented a challenge to enforcement.

On December 25, 1773 Charlestown, Massachusetts merchants resolved not to sell tea. They formed a buyback scheme that made losses communal. Merchants with large stocks of tea were to be bailed out by others, and the tea to be burned. Three days later, the town supported a buyback with its purse, buying tea from residents at cost and publicly burning it.[48] This was not the easiest way to get rid of tea—ideologically, symbolically, or financially—but by purchasing rather than confiscating tea, Patriots avoided alienating consumers or merchants.

The Fairfax Resolves recommended all tea present in Virginia by September 1774 be stored in committee-controlled warehouses. A subscription would buy the tea back, after which the tea would be "publickly burn'd." The Fairfax plan allowed importers to keep the value of their assets and Patriots to make public contributions to the cause, all while maintaining tea discipline. If an unpopular importer failed to raise a subscription, he got no buyback, and his tea rotted in the warehouse.[49] It is unclear if Fairfax implemented this plan.

A similar proposal was made to the Westerly, Rhode Island town meeting on February 2, 1774. A merchant known for his "indisputable and reputable character" offered to sell the town a "considerable quantity" of Dutch tea. Perhaps fearing the offer might seem self-interested, he promised, as a good Patriot, to sell it cheaply to encourage "a dislike" of tea among the public. (A unique logic.) The *Newport Mercury* claimed the town "unanimously" agreed, reporting the "hopeful prospect of seeing speedily a total disuse. 'Twas supposed the above tea would be destroyed," though there is no record of the tea's purchase or destruction in Westerly town records.[50]

Perhaps the idea of reimbursing Patriotic tea owners echoed the idea of reimbursing the East India Company too closely to get traction. The practice remained uncommon.

Storing Tea

Storing tea was common. It is easy to notice the repeated performances of destruction, from the Boston Tea Party on, and miss the tea that was not destroyed. In Salem, Massachusetts, the tea delivered to that town in October was publicly burned, but the tea which local vendors surrendered was stored, not destroyed. Such public storage helped make non-consumption (and later consumption) collective actions. In December, the Caroline County, Virginia committee "Ordered every person in this County carry all their Tea to some one of the committee who are desired to seal It up & take a memo. of the quantity." The Wilmington, North Carolina committee announced "all the Tea, in the stores" of Wilmington and Brunswick "is locked up, never to be offered for sale." Thomas Richardson of George Town, Maryland, turned over 100 pounds of tea to the Frederick County committee "to be safely stored." The committee in Northampton County, Virginia let residents "deliver their TEA to Colonel L. Savage, to be by him Kept . . . until the General Association shall be dissolved," or have it burned at the Court House. Savage had stored 416 pounds of tea by

January 1775. In Baltimore County, Maryland, the committee stored 176 cases and chests and 16 quarter-chests arriving in December 1774. Worried British cruisers might get the tea, in 1775 the committee relocated the tea to continue guarding it.[51]

Storage was sometimes contested. The Newburyport, Massachusetts committee locked up tea in the winter of 1774–1775. Perhaps eyeing a petition for its release, a local shipbuilder, Eleazer Johnson, led workers to grab it and burn it in Market Square. Fearing such an end, William Holliday, a merchant in Dunmore County, Virginia, demanded to know what the committee "Intend to do with his tea." Holliday wanted "to sell [tea until] the first of March" as per the "general Association."[52]

From a merchant's perspective, the safest approach was to hold on to the tea privately and simply promise not to sell it. During the prohibition of 1775, vendors sometimes had sizable quantities of tea on hand, held back only by their word. Patriot authorities knew about some of these supplies. In New York, Philadelphia, and other major market towns, merchants petitioned throughout the year for permission to sell. The Patriotic Thomas Greenough hoped his son John would keep his tea from the *William* "Secreted untell some future time"—rather than destroy it.[53] Of course, tea held without the committee's knowledge was more easily sold off under the table, too. Merchants held over an unknown quantity of tea this way.

Just how much tea was held in committee warehouses is elusive; Eleazer Johnson's destruction of the tea in Newburyport, not the committee's storing it, occasioned a newspaper item. Had the committee guarded it successfully, we might never have known it existed. Patriots faced an overhang of tea stored in 1774 as they began prohibition in 1775, but the extent of it was only partly known to them and is even less clear to us.

Loyalists' Alarm

What did Loyalists make of all this? Reacting to the prospects of non-consumption and the Association, they feared the Association would be used to silence and control them. Coercive enforcement of non-import, non-export, and non-consumption would mean colonists were "required to support our liberties by dealing out terrors and threats amongst our fellow citizens." "Will you submit to this slavish regulation?" protested Samuel Seabury. "You must.— Our sovereign Lords and Masters"—Congress—"have ordered and directed it." Tea drinkers "shall be considered as Out-laws, unworthy of the protection of civil society, and delivered over to the vengeance of a lawless, outrageous mob, to be tarred, feathered, hanged, drawn, quartered, and burnt.—O rare American freedom!" Colonists will have to "open your doors to" prying committeemen and, he later added, "shall probably soon see these lordly Committee-men condescend to go pimping, and peeping, and peering, into tea-canisters." For Seabury, this was inevitable since the Association made it the business of committees to inspect colonists' homes and determine "whether they drink any tea or wine in their families." Only investigations such as what Seabury imagined could enforce the ban. A King's officer needed a warrant to enter a colonist's home. Would Patriots need less? Since there would rarely be cause to obtain a warrant, inspections would be lawless and "arbitrary," as they were in both Withingtons' homes. Hulton likewise worried non-consumption meant oppressive "political inquisitors are appointed in each town to pry into the conduct of individuals" and enforce behavior. Britons will never be slaves. But, "if I must be enslaved," Seabury wrote, "let it be by a KING at least."[54]

Some disparaged Congress for taking their tea. John Ettwein, a Moravian administrator in Bethlehem, Pennsylvania, lamented that "one ought to be afraid even to drink a cup of tea." Eventual Loyalist Hannah Griffitts blamed Congress in a commonplace book (a scrapbook shared among friends who contributed to it). Congress "devis'd the evil Deed / To kill this precious Indian Weed / Come just Resentment guide my Pen / And mark our mad Committee Men . . . Why all their Malice shewn to Tea[?]" Susannah Wright agreed, wondering whether Congress showed "that Sp[ir]it. of D[e]spotism, so loudly complain'd of in America,—I cannot for my Life see the propriety of making this innocent [drink] the chief object of their Vengeance."[55]

The specific focus on tea seemed odd to some. "[W]higs have been extremely partial respecting tea," noted Massachusettensis, which "has been made the shibboleth of party" while "melasses, wine, coffee, indigo, &c, &c, have been unmolested." A rum or "coffee drinker is as culpable . . . viewed in a political light" as a tea drinker, but tea had become a symbol, while coffee and rum had not. Burning it showed fealty to Patriots, refusing to do so showed freedom from Patriot power. This symbolism far exceeded its physical and economic significance. Scotswoman Janet Schaw thought the solemn fetishization of tea absurd. To Jonathan Sewall this meant that Patriots mixed signifiers—"mere sounds"—with what they signified, assuming the "words king, parliament, . . . tea &c carry the idea of slavery with them" while simply uttering "the words congress . . . independence, coffee &c" called up "all the power of necromancy" to overthrow tyranny.[56] Saying "tea" or drinking tea did not, Loyalists noted, cause ministerial oppression to exist. Tea symbolized ministerial evils to the point that Patriots demonized tea itself. To Loyalists, this was a lot of sound and fury, signifying nothing.

Ultimately, Loyalists' fears proved half right. Non-consumption would eventually be enforced, the ban on tea was implemented with show, and the Association would become a tool for finding colonists disaffected from the Patriot cause. But at the same time, the tea ban was not as oppressively or effectively enforced as Seabury feared. Patriots did not go "pimping, and peeping, and peering" into every tea canister. They made a violent example of a few colonists pour encourager les autres. How well this worked is less clear.

CHAPTER 7

Truth in Advertising

How to make sense of the efforts toward a boycott in 1774? The press was part of this collision of merchants and politics. Printers often preformed Patriotism in the press. So while newspapers could be reliable sources of information, they could also serve the political agendas of editors, contributors, and committees. As historians, we have taken at face value too many newspaper accounts of protests, accounts that were far from simple reporting. At the same time, we have largely ignored other parts of protest-era newspapers, especially advertisements. Advertising, not reporting, reveals when and where the boycott became effective. After the Coercive Acts, merchants still advertised tea and British goods even as other colonists protested them. To miss this juxtaposition is to miss that advertisers continued to treat tea as a consumer good even though Patriots insisted it was purely political. To assess its efficacy, boycott talk must be read in the context of consumption talk, the most widely distributed form of which was advertising. Revolutionary-era advertising unlike modern advertising did not try to generate consumption. Yet it spoke about the possibility of consumption. And since in 1774 anti-tea and anti-import news conflated the wish for the deed, we must look to advertising for the truth.[1]

This chapter examines the significance of tea advertising: its prevalence and the varied timing of its disappearance; the types of ads; the dissonance between anti-tea news and tea advertisements; the advertisers themselves; their avoidance of the political significance of tea in their ads; Patriots' and advertisers' interaction in the press, and newspapers' different roles.

Counting Tea Ads

Tea advertisements fall into four periods between October 1773 and June 1776, as seen in figure 7.1. Each period corresponds to a discrete political role for tea, suggesting changes were broadly significant, if not uniform. First, there is the period before the Boston Tea Party, a baseline for measuring change. Second, there is the year or so after the Boston Tea Party. Tea advertisements remained common but less frequent, and the decline varied geographically (e.g., ads disappeared in Boston but continued in Philadelphia). In the third period, beginning March 1, 1775, the Association's non-consumption order was in effect. Almost no tea advertisements appeared in newspapers printed in any territory Patriots controlled during this period. Finally, there is the period beginning April 1776, when tea advertising returned, corresponding to Congress's April 13, 1776 permission for limited tea sales. Advertisements had returned by the time of American independence.

Figure 7.1 depicts the changing frequency of tea ads. Gray bars show the number of tea advertisements found in a given week. The black line represents the number of weekly advertisements per newspaper examined (the rate of tea advertising). Varying survival and availability of newspapers makes the black line the better tool. If the same tea ad appeared in multiple weeks, it is counted each week it appeared, as this figure measures advertisements per newspaper examined.[2]

Shipping was seasonal. This partially explains the high level of ads in the fall of 1773; a wave of autumn imports arrived in October and November, unloading and departing northern ports before harbors froze over.[3] A springtime import wave occasioned a spike of ads in 1774, with vendors advertising new shipments. This seasonal wave pattern occurred in nearly every colony where tea advertising was found. There was also a baseline of constant tea advertisers, usually shopkeepers in mid-Atlantic and New England market towns. The waves were not caused by an increase in the number of newspapers consulted, and there was no fall 1774 wave, as the Patriots' signaling against tea in the summer of 1774 discouraged advertising (the extent to which it successfully discouraged sales is another question).

This figure does not represent every tea advertisement but encompasses enough newspapers to capture the print environment. It is based on the *Readex: America's Historical Newspapers* database, supplemented with other newspapers.

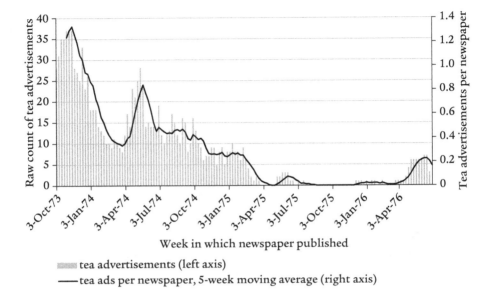

FIGURE 7.1. Tea advertisements in colonial newspapers, October 1, 1773 to July 4, 1776.

The data cover 46 newspapers printed from Nova Scotia to Georgia, including over 4,300 newspaper issues. During this period, 200 merchants or merchant firms advertised tea over 1,230 times. These data provide the first systematic examination of tea advertising in end-of-empire America.[4]

Tea advertising did not appear with the same frequency across newspapers or cities. Table 7.1 shows tea advertising by geography. Although tea ads appeared for similar periods in Philadelphia and New York, significantly more ads appeared in the latter, despite New York being a smaller city with half as many newspapers. The greater number of advertisements in New York may have been a function of the city's tea sellers' preference for advertising as a medium. Virginia merchants largely did not advertise tea. This was not because they eschewed tea but because trade, whether via the factor system or direct order from London, did not necessitate advertising. Norfolk was Virginia's biggest port, but the *Norfolk Intelligencer* ran only one ad mentioning tea on and off for four weeks.[5] In Baltimore and Annapolis, by contrast, tea advertising was more common.

Neither the chart nor the table counts advertisements for generic categories like "East India goods." In 1774 such ads outnumbered tea ads and persisted even as tea ads fell away. They may have been less explicit tea advertisements. The Patriot prohibition on tea extended to these goods at different paces in different places and was not coterminous with the tea ban.[6] Likewise, shopkeepers

Table 7.1   Number of tea ad-weeks by place, October 1, 1773–July 4, 1776

LOCATION	AD WEEKS
Halifax	5
Portsmouth	1
Newburyport & Salem	25
Boston	153
Providence	42
Newport	122
Connecticut	93
New York	284
Philadelphia	205
Annapolis & Baltimore, MD	90
Norfolk & Williamsburg, VA	17
Charleston	176
Savannah	22

Sources: See note 4. An ad-week is one advertisement lasting for one week. While the appearance of an ad marks an initial decision to advertise, some advertisers ran the same ad for several months, while others ran an ad just once. To assess how much tea advertising there was, we must sum up the amount of time each ad appeared. Since most newspapers appeared weekly, an ad appearing in one issue is considered to "last" a week, hence an ad-week. The *Pennsylvania Evening Post* appeared thrice-weekly. For uniformity, these ads are also considered to "last" a week. Tea advertisers did not repeat ads in less than one-week intervals, precluding over-counting of ad-weeks.

listed tea urns, teacups, teapots, tea tables, and teaspoons, ads that signaled tea culture, without advertising tea. Only ads which explicitly mention tea are considered here.

In 1774 many kinds of advertising announced goods and activities the Association would later ban, including British imports, certain British Caribbean products, horse racing, and other games. These did important semiotic work, announcing that the Association remained yet unimplemented. Tea was also not as widely available as is sometimes imagined. Although only some dry goods merchants advertised tea, almost all advertised coffee and sugar, which were easier to acquire. Others advertised British imports or other soon-to-be-banned goods and activities. All these ads, which far outnumbered tea ads, testified to the consumer culture of late-colonial life and the difficulty of a ban.

Cessation of Advertising

Tea advertising disappeared in different places at different times; the campaign against tea was a process. No New Hampshire tea ads survive from 1774 at all. Elsewhere, advertisements for tea continued through May 1774, ending with news of the Coercive Acts. The last tea ads appeared in Williamsburg, Virginia, Annapolis, Maryland, and Salem, Massachusetts papers in May. June saw the last known ads from eastern Connecticut (New London and Norwich). Tea ads continued in Norfolk, Virginia (more conservative than Williamsburg), Baltimore, Maryland (more conservative than Annapolis), and Charleston, South Carolina into July, with a straggling Baltimore ad by James Dagliesh and John Amos listing tea the following February (the Baltimore County committee announced Dagliesh's "incurable emity to his country" in May 1775).[7] The Charleston ads stopped a week after the July general meeting.

Tea ads continued to August 1774 in Providence, though William McKim's February 1775 ad in the *Providence Gazette* was a lone straggler. Most Boston merchants stopped advertising tea in January 1774, as they had agreed to stop selling tea then. Still, huckster Benjamin Davis and shopkeeper Gilbert Deblois continued to advertise, the latter until September. Boston merchants were wary of a boycott unless other towns joined, and other the summer, 137 Boston merchants petitioned against the Solemn League and Covenant, which was a dead letter. Samuel Adams thought the League was almost "totally" opposed by importers.[8] Deblois and Davis risked nothing by advertising tea that they did not already risk with their politics. Deblois had opposed the 1768 nonimportation agreement, helped the defense of Captain Preston (of the Boston "Massacre"), and served as an agent for British transports in Boston in 1774. Davis rented his store to British troops in October 1774 and volunteered for the Associated Loyalists militia company in 1775. Both were addressers to Governor Hutchinson, signing the public letter expressing "satisfaction" with his governance. "Addresser" became an epithet for Loyalist. Politically informed readers would have known Deblois's and Davis's politics. But these two did not pitch tea as a good to be consumed out of Loyalism. They pitched it as a consumer good, and their readers were politically diverse. In September, the Suffolk Resolves silenced their ads, solidified Boston Patriotism, and pushed Congress toward Continent-wide non-importation.[9]

Tea advertising continued elsewhere, as the ban on Dutch tea sales only took effect in March 1775. Tea ads in Newport, Rhode Island (known for its Tories), lasted through December 1774. Tea ads continued into February in New Haven and Hartford, and into March in Philadelphia and New York. Late advertisers probably rushed to offload stock as the ban on sales drew near. In Georgia, tea ads appeared into June 1775. Georgia joined the Association in July. Tea advertising in 1774 follows no one pattern. Even radicals could not agree on whether tea sales and advertising should stop before the Association came into force.[10]

So, what do the tea ads mean? Advertisements are instances of speech, not proof of sales. Even in cases where the end of tea advertising can be linked to a political event, the disappearance of advertising does not mean tea went unsold. Wallace, Davidson, and Johnson sold tea in Annapolis long after the ads stopped there. Patriots policed speech better than they policed behavior.

One must not over-interpret the absence of advertising. Sometimes newspaper issues do not survive. Sometimes tea ads stopped because the merchant ran out of tea, the advertiser ran out of space, or the paper stopped printing. But in larger towns where multiple advertisers and perhaps multiple papers listed tea for sale, it is easier to determine whether the start or stop of advertising reflects one merchant's circumstances or tea's role in the public sphere.

Advertisements cannot be equated to sales, and neither ads nor sales can be easily equated to politics. Neither New Hampshire nor Nova Scotia saw much tea advertising in 1774, yet we know that tea was sold in both colonies that year and that, despite this similarity, the two colonies would take divergent political paths. The sole ad in either colony—run by merchant Andrew Wallace in the *Nova Scotia Gazette* from late June to late July 1774—appeared while Halifax merchants debated tea reshipped from New Hampshire.[11] There is no indication whether Halifax's debate over the New Hampshire tea affected Wallace's sales. Tea ads were similarly rare in Virginia because Virginians got their tea in other ways.

Yet advertisements are deeply useful. They inform our understanding of political events in new ways. They name a much larger group of potential tea sellers than the small coterie of merchants usually discussed by scholars. This group of advertisers hints at a larger group of tea sellers and—a larger group still—their customers.

Type of Advertising

There were two main types of advertisements listing tea: the litany and the "classified." Both discussed tea's consumability without quite proving consumption. Dry goods merchants favored the litany, setting tea among hundreds of items for sale. In these lists, tea was buried in small print, after the "fine Spirits" and before the coffee, one good among many. The South Carolina firm Parker and Hutchings expended dozens of lines listing household goods, with *"Tallow* and *Bees Wax*; *Tea, Coffee, Chocolate*; Loaf and Muscovado *Sugar"* toward the end.[12] The ad ran for nine weeks. (See figure 7.2.) Readers had to search to find things in these catalog-like ads. Nonetheless, advertisers did not leave tea in heedlessly; they removed tea when they ran out, or it

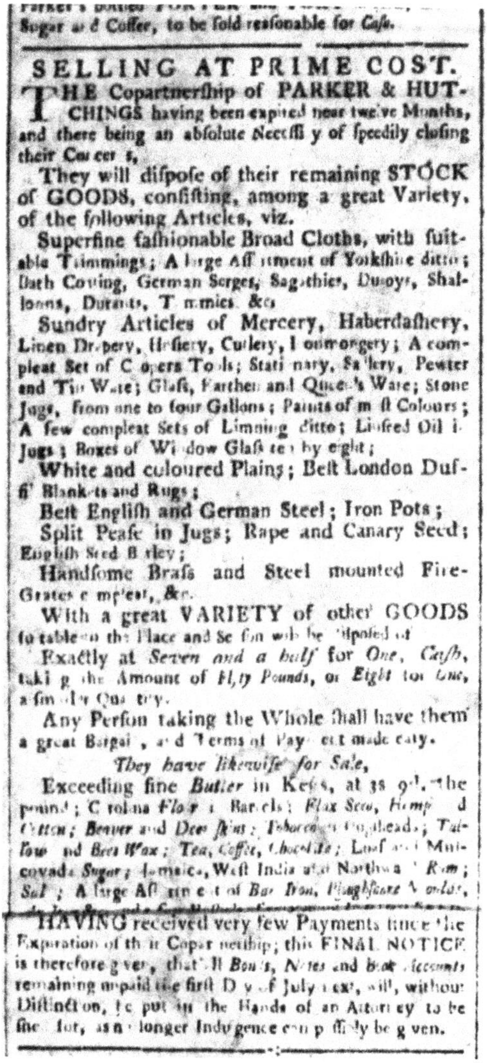
Sugar and Coffee, to be ſold reaſonable for *Caſh.*

SELLING AT PRIME COST.

THE Copartnerſhip of PARKER & HUTCHINGS having been expired near twelve Months, and there being an abſolute Neceſſity of ſpeedily cloſing their Concerns,

They will diſpoſe of their remaining STOCK of GOODS, conſiſting, among a great Variety, of the following Articles, viz.

Superfine faſhionable Broad Cloths, with ſuitable Trimmings; A large Aſſortment of Yorkſhire ditto; Bath Coating, German Serges, Sagathies, Duroys, Shalloons, Durants, Tammies, &c.

Sundry Articles of Mercery, Haberdaſhery, Linen Drapery, Hoſiery, Cutlery, Ironmongery; A compleat Set of Coopers Tools; Stationary, Sadlery, Pewter and Tin Ware; Glaſs, Earthen and Queen's Ware; Stone Jugs, from one to four Gallons; Paints of moſt Colours; A few compleat Sets of Limning ditto; Linſeed Oil in Jugs; Boxes of Window Glaſs ten by eight;

White and coloured Plains; Beſt London Duffil Blankets and Rugs;

Beſt Engliſh and German Steel; Iron Pots;

Split Peaſe in Jugs; Rape and Canary Seed; Engliſh Seed Barley;

Handſome Braſs and Steel mounted Fire-Grates compleat, &c.

With a great VARIETY of other GOODS ſuitable to the Place and Seaſon will be diſpoſed of

Exactly at *Seven and a half* for *One*, *Caſh*, taking the Amount of *Fifty Pounds*, or *Eight* for *One*, a ſmaller Quantity.

Any Perſon taking the Whole ſhall have them a great Bargain, and Terms of Payment made eaſy.

They have likewiſe for Sale,

Exceeding fine *Butter* in Kegs, at 3s 9d. the pound; Carolina *Flour* in Barrels; *Flax Seed, Hemp* and *Cotton; Beaver* and *Deer ſkins; Tobacco* in Hogſheads; *Tallow* and *Bees Wax; Tea, Coffee, Chocolate;* Loaf and Muſcovado *Sugar;* Jamaica, Weſt India and Northward *Rum; Salt;* A large Aſſortment of *Bar Iron, Ploughſhare Moulds,*

HAVING received very few Payments ſince the Expiration of their Copartnerſhip; this FINAL NOTICE is therefore given, that all *Bonds, Notes* and *Book Accounts* remaining unpaid the firſt Day of July next, will, without Diſtinction, be put in the Hands of an Attorney to be ſued for, as no longer Indulgence can poſſibly be given.

FIGURE 7.2. Parker & Hutchings litany ad, 1774. In South Carolina, Parker and Hutchings's litany ad listed dozens of goods. Buried among them is tea, which appears toward the bottom. Source: *SCAGG*, May 13, 1774.

became too impolitic to list by name. Grocers in market towns used litanies to impress readers with the breadth of their wares. Most readers lived in these towns' commercial peripheries; these ads signaled the advertiser was the merchant to see when going to market. Tea and British manufactures were part of the implicit "everything" that the grocer seemed to sell. Their appearance testified to the continued consumability of such goods.

Other advertisements broke goods out for special mention: first billing in boldfaced type, or last in capitals. Smith and Richards of New York headlined their litany advertisement with an illustration of the sign above their shop: a "Tea canister and two sugar loaves" (see figure 7.3). Samuel Gordon of Charleston advertised "JUST OPENED, A CHEST of fine-flavoured HYSON TEA" (see figure 7.4). Some listed tea last: "He has also some very good Hyson TEA, which he will sell low," concluded Philip Marchinton's notice in the *Pennsylvania Packet*. These ads were more like twentieth-century classifieds than modern newspaper advertisements. Such advertisers drew attention to specific products. In April 1774, William Donaldson of Charleston gave a dense paragraph of wares ("Souchong Tea" slipped in between the forks and the coffee), but broke out other goods. Then in May he broke out "Souchong Tea at 60s. the Pound" instead.[13] (See figures 7.5 and 7.6.)

Some tea sellers did not advertise—it was understood they stocked tea. This applied to some dry goods merchants. Innkeepers, tavernkeepers, and coffeehouse owners were also understood to carry tea; therefore, few (only eight) advertised it. John Adams's innkeeper had not advertised tea, but Adams still tried ordering it anyway. Occasionally, when announcing a new inn, a tavernkeeper mentioned he stocked tea, as Duncan Carmichael did upon opening the Red House between Baltimore Town and Philadelphia, but it rarely needed mentioning. Likewise, two apothecaries advertised tea among their balms and elixirs. But apothecaries usually did not need to list it; tea's purported medicinal properties mean it might be assumed.[14]

Advertising as Speech

What did tea advertisements say? Most spoke generically to tea's consumability. What advertisers meant to say about tea origins is less clear. Mid-Atlantic advertisers did not mention from whence their tea came, but perhaps the ubiquity of Dutch tea implied an answer. Boston advertisers avoided discussing their tea's origin, perhaps because it was so contentious, or perhaps so they could sell to either side. Charleston advertisers commonly noted teas came from England. In July, Zephaniah Kingsley described his tea as "from London."[15] Was this an embrace of the idea of consuming British tea, or truth in advertising meant to help consumers make informed choices? It is unclear. Tea prices and varieties, like hyson or bohea, implied certain consumers but were rarely given. Most ads were simply for tea.

Advertisements do not prove tea was sold any more than news of tea protests prove tea was all burned. Ads were speech: statements that tea was for

SMITH RICHARDS,
GROCER and CONFECTIONER,

At the Tea canifter and two fugar loaves, in Queen-ftreet,
Next door but one to Robert Gilbert Livingfton's, Efq; and
over againft Meffrs. Taylor and De Lancey's Vendue-
houfe, fells the following articles at the loweft rates.

FINE hyfon,
    Common green,
Souſhong and Bohea teas of
  the firft qualities.
Double refin'd,
Single do.
Lump and
Mufcovado fugars,
Coffee, chocolate,
Black pepper,

India foy and ketchup,
Italian and other capers,
Olives, anchovies,
Florence oyl,
Oatmeal, vermicelli,
Tamarinds,
Ground ginger,
New rice,
Englifh fplit peafe,
Salt petre, bafket falt,

FIGURE 7.3. Smith, Richards advertisement, New York, 1774. The New York shop of Smith and Richards put tea and sugar at the center of their marketing, with the "tea canister and two sugar loaves" as their street sign, and the sign reproduced in their advertisement. This made their litany ad, which listed dozens of groceries besides tea (not all of which are shown here), stand out. Source: *NYG*, March 28, 1774.

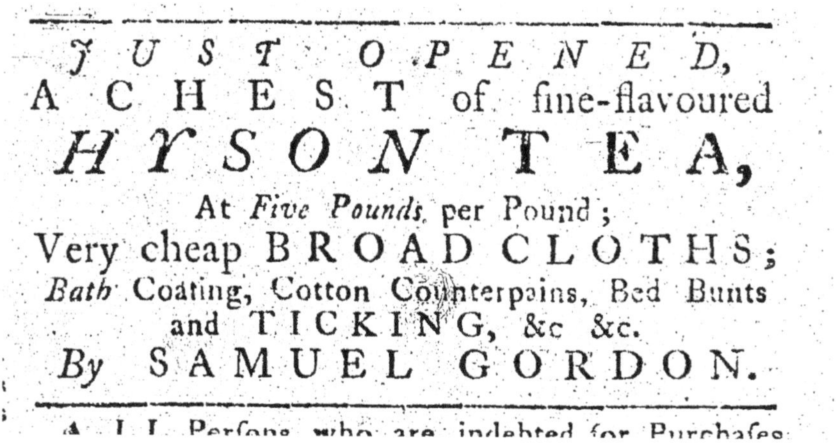

J U S T   O .P E N E D,
A   C H E S T   of   fine-flavoured
H Y S O N   T E A,
At *Five Pounds,* per Pound ;
Very cheap B R O A D   C L O T H S ;
Bath Coating, Cotton Counterpains, Bed Bunts
and T I C K I N G, &c &c.
By S A M U E L   G O R D O N.

A . I. I. Perfons who are indebted for Purchafes

FIGURE 7.4.   Samuel Gordon's tea ad, 1773. In South Carolina, Samuel Gordon's advertisement put tea front and center. Source: *SCG*, November 1, 1773.

sale, often by merchants who left little other writing behind. Because Patriots policed political speech, most advertisements avoided acknowledging the politicization of tea, leaving ads an area of ostensibly commercial discourse where word of consumption might continue.

Printers ran anti-tea editorials and celebrated tea protests while taking tea advertisers' money, simultaneously voicing Patriots' and tea-sellers' discourses. One issue of the *Newport Mercury* ran a letter against the "slavery" that the "East-India company's tea" would bring and also Hezekiah Dayton's tea ad. The same issue of Purdie and Dixon's *Virginia Gazette* informed readers of the Coercive Acts and "very fine Hyson tea." The *Georgia Gazette* announced a "subscription for the Relief of the Suffers in Boston" and Gershon Cohen's tea. The *Pennsylvania Packet* ran the Cumberland County committee's version of the Greenwich tea party and carried Richard Bache's tea ad.[16] The committee spoke to the firebrands. Bache spoke to consumers. These were rival systems of meaning, which, in their juxtaposition, recapture the ambivalence toward boycotts often missed if we look only at Patriotic press releases.

In 1774, not all printers imposed ideological conformity on their pages; fewer did so on paid advertising. Printers had politics, but moderate papers still ran radical content (and vice versa), and Patriot newspapers ran tea advertisements. Patriot Solomon Southwick of the *Newport Mercury* buried his press and fled the British occupation, allegedly claiming the paper "should die, or be free."[17] But in 1774, Newport had many who were less Patriotic, and Southwick catered to readers and advertisers by printing much that was

WILLIAM DONALDSON,

HAS received a CONSIGNMENT of the following Goods, which he will fell at *Seven* and *a Half* for *One*, Cafh, and in Proportion for Credit;

Striped, flowered and plain Muflins; Suits of Tambour worked Ruffles, Handkerchiefs and Aprons; Silk Shoes and Stockings, Striped and plain Luteftrings and Mantuas; Silk and fattin Bonnets, Cloaks, Hats and Petticoats; One Suit of Baby Linen, Printed Gown Pattern, Table China in Setts and by the Dozen; Table Knives and Forks, Souchong Tea, Coffee, Table Cloths, of all Sizes; Fine Fowling Pieces.

Loom Quilting for Petticoats at *Seven* for *One*.

N. B. Good BUTTER in Kegs, at 3s. 9d. the Pound, and a few Barrels of SPANISH INDIGO SEED to be fold cheap.

To be Sold for Coft and Charges,

A CONSIGNMENT of elegant Silks, Muflins and Humhums for Gowns; Silk and Sattin Petticoats, Cloaks, Bonnets and Hats, elegantly trimmed; Worked Ruffles, Silk Shoes and Stockings, Ribbon, Drefs Caps, Cap and Skeleton Wire Table Cloths of all fizes, Table China, Knives and Forks, Copper Saucepans, Linen Drapery, Guns. Mancheffer Stripes for Waiftcoats, Mens fine Hats and Gloves, by

WILLIAM DONALDSON.

Souchong Tea at 6os. the Pound.

Commodious Back Stores and a Cellar, inferiour to few in Town, to be Let. Enquire as above.

FIGURES 7.5. AND 7.6. William Donaldson advertisements listing tea, 1774. In South Carolina, William Donaldson advertised his souchong tea as one of many items in his April 1774 advertisement. A month later he drew special attention to his tea in an addendum. Sources: *SCAGG*, April 15 and May 13, 1774.

inconsistent with a hard Patriot stance. William Bradford hosted in his home the meeting which decided how to oppose the East India Company's shipment to Philadelphia in 1773. His *Pennsylvania Journal* took a strong editorial line against tea, published John Dickinson's denunciation of the 1773 tea scheme and the broadsides from "Committee on Tarring and Feathering," which threatened pilots who brought the *Polly* upriver. He served in two battles in the Patriot militia and published the journals of Congress. But he was also a businessman. He ran the London Coffee House, which had a mercantile clientele, and sold marine insurance. He took money to run tea ads from John Mitchell and Richard Bache in the *Pennsylvania Journal*. Nor were these small ad buys; between May 1774 and March 1775 their ads appeared most weeks. The ultra Benjamin Edes—Patriot, Son of Liberty, member of the Loyal Nine, probable participant in the Boston Tea Party, and publisher of the radical *Boston Gazette*—printed Loyalist Benjamin Davis's tea advertisement in May 1774. Even when they might censor or distort news and opinion about tea, Whig printers Ebenezer Watson (*Connecticut Courant*), John Carter (*Providence Gazette*), John Holt (*New York Journal*), John Dunlap (*Pennsylvania Packet*), William Goddard (*Maryland Journal*), John Dixon (*Virginia Gazette*), Peter Timothy (*South Carolina Gazette*), and Charles Crouch (*South Carolina Gazette and Country Journal*) by and large did not censor tea ads. They ran these ads as long as they were politically permissible in their respective colonies.[18] Business constrained how politically exclusive these publishers could be.

These printers were not hypocrites. In 1774, printers' openness to advertising goods that Patriots wanted to boycott reflected the unclear and contested edges of acceptability and Patriot power. In 1775 and 1776, printers were more circumspect, and papers' division into Loyalist (often "Royal") gazettes and Patriotic "American" gazettes reflected who held local control. But in 1774, discourse and consumption were only partially politicized, and advertisements remained separate from but parallel to political debate. A good part of the colonial political news of 1774 revolved around consuming and banning goods: the tea parties and the calls for non-importation, non-consumption, and, ultimately, compliance with the Association. This gave the presence or absence of advertisements for tea and British manufactures a capacity to speak to politics even when advertisers did not try to.

Advertisers

Tea advertisers varied. They included wholesalers: Anthony Bleecker of New York, Christopher Champlin of Newport, Roger Smith, George Heriot, and

Daniel Tucker in Charleston. Most wholesalers did not advertise tea, even though they probably carried it. The largest group of tea advertisers were minor grocers (John and William Leary of New York and Frederick Bull of Hartford). Some were not merchants at all. Others are impossible to identify and forgotten to history, hardly the politically involved merchants from this period with whom we are familiar.[19]

The variety of colonists offering tea for sale suggests "merchant" is a limited category for understanding them. Printers Isaiah Thomas (Patriot) and James Rivington (Loyalist) used their newspapers to advertise their own tea. New Yorker Thomas William Moore's notices advertised the "private sale" of tea during his real estate auctions. Elnathan Camp offered a "Five Dollars reward" for the return of a stolen barrel with 177 pounds of tea in it. The milliner Margaret Hunter listed tea in the *Virginia Gazette* among the lace and fabric she sold in her Williamsburg shop, and when Mr. Hoar advertised his concert in the *New York Journal,* he noted tea would be served. In Pennsylvania, Walter Hall, advertising for the return of stolen silver, concluded his ad, "N.B. Choice Green Tea . . . to be sold."[20] These ads spoke to tea's enduring consumability, even if the advertisers were neither prominent nor merchants. They announced tea because readers would not normally assume they had any.

Tea advertisers included prominent colonial families: the Wantons of Rhode Island (Loyalists), the Delanceys of New York (Loyalists), the Wadsworths of Connecticut (Patriots), and colonial officials like New Yorker Abraham de Peyster (Loyalist). Patriotic merchant-politicians advertising tea included Richard Bache (Philadelphia), Stephen Higginson (Salem), and Samuel Allyne Otis (Boston). Patriotic merchants advertising tea included George Woolsey (Baltimore), and Abraham Duryee (New York). Connecticut tea advertiser Jesse Leavenworth served in the war on the American side. Tea advertiser Thomas Achincloss later signed a Loyalist counter-association in Portsmouth, New Hampshire. Archibald Cunningham joined the Loyal North British Volunteers in Boston in 1775. Charleston's Brian Cape was a noted Loyalist.[21] The only thing these men had in common was that tea was not their primary endeavor, so they had to advertise it; they were slave traders, merchants, and grandees who speculated in tea. They formed no coherent social or political group. Tea advertiser was not a social class, and tea was incidental to their standing.

The protests about East India Company and other tea in 1773 and 1774 directly targeted between forty and forty-five tea importers, including the various Company consignees and private importers of English tea like Thomas Williams in Maryland. These men are the "usual suspects" in most late-colonial stories about tea, stories which make colonial resistance to tea seems widespread and monolithic. This is what Patriots, who wrote the first edition of those stories, wanted. If we only look at people who got in trouble over tea, we will think tea was troublesome. But if we note the hundreds of people who did *not* get in trouble over tea, we see a very different story. Some importers of du}tied tea and many importers of Dutch tea continued unmolested, as did most tea retailers and advertisers. Advertisers, as a category, most closely tracks retailers rather than importers. Of the over 200 individuals advertising tea in this period, the only ones who faced direct action did so because they imported tea: Thomas Williams (*Peggy Stewart*), Zephaniah Kingsley (*Britannia*), and William Donaldson (*Magna Charta*). Meanwhile, hundreds of others advertised tea for sale without the consequences Williams faced, meaning Williams's experience cannot be representative of tea merchants as a whole. For every importer like Williams, there was a James Nicholson, the importer of du}tied tea to Chestertown on the *Geddes*, who never advertised what he did and skated by; and several Frederick Bulls, minor retailers who advertised tea with little or no consequence. Moreover, it seems likely that most tea sellers did not advertise at all. While twenty tea sellers advertised in the Boston papers in the last quarter of 1773, the town's post-Tea Party gathering of tea sellers counted one hundred among their number, suggesting another eighty tea vendors who did not advertise.[22] Most of these sellers were likely minor vendors, who were an important part of retail networks, further suggesting that a focus on the troubles of a few dozen importers overlooked the varied experiences of hundreds of retailers, whose experiences can be better understood by an analysis of local advertisers rather than of in-hot-water importers, for advertisers' announcement that tea was for sale implied that area merchants were still allowed to sell it.

Tea advertisers were many things: Patriots and Loyalists, big importers and small retailers. They were not demographically representative of colonists. Nor were Patriot and Tory essayists, who were well-off and educated elites. The contest between politicians and advertisers was a context between two different groups of elites over who spoke to the people's concerns. Novanglus (John Adams) debated ideas with his Tory opponent Massachusettensis (Daniel Leonard and Jonathan Sewall). Meanwhile, tea advertisers Zephaniah Kingsley (Charleston) and Anthony Bleecker (New York) advertised things. The contest between politicians and advertisers came down to what would happen when Patriots began to offer the public ideas about things.[23]

Competing Discourses

Advertisers' first approach to the boycott movement was to ignore it. Patriots argued that tea ought to be political, but advertisers did not write essays back

GRENADA RUM.

A FEW hogsheads of choice GRANA-DA RUM, to be sold by JOSEPH P. PALMER, at the lowest store on the south side of the Town-Dock.—Cheese, Coffee, Chocolate, &c. as usual. **N. B. NO TEA.**

FIGURE 7.7. Joseph P. Palmer's "NO TEA" ad, Massachusetts, 1774. Some advertisers announced that they did not carry tea, usually with a simple "no tea" at their end of their litany. Massachusetts vendor Joseph Palmer, however, drew special attention to his adherence to the emerging tea boycott. He also mentioned rum from British Grenada prominently. British West Indian rum and sugar would continue to be consumed after the Association was in force. Source: *Mass Spy*, April 7, 1774.

arguing that tea ought not be politicized. Such essays would have implicitly conceded tea's politicization. Instead, demonstrating the power of the dictum, "show don't tell," tea advertisements demonstrated tea was not exclusively political, without taking a stance on whether it ought to be. Advertisers advanced a consumerist understanding of tea. Ads portrayed tea as just another consumer good. There was more business in speaking of tea as something anyone (even Patriots) could drink than speaking of it as a political symbol. Tea advertisements and anti-tea essays thus appeared side-by-side in the same newspapers but in separate "lanes" that rarely interacted.

A few advertisers acknowledged this contest. Between January 1774 and April 1775, roughly sixty advertisements (in addition to those above) acknowledged tea's politics by signaling compliance with those politics. Some listed groceries with the addenda, "NB: No tea," at the bottom (see figure 7.7). One pledged not to sell tea. Others hawked literature opposed to tea drinking. Such compliance theater was not necessarily actually compliance. Some advertisers who claimed to no longer sell tea probably sold it anyway. But "no tea" ads perpetuated a myth useful for Patriots, of tea's unavailability. Such ads were unusual; most advertisers dropped tea from their merchandise lists without comment. Two-thirds of no-tea ads appeared in Massachusetts. The remainder appeared in other colonies, usually when the Association took effect.[24]

Then there was shopkeeper William Beadle's advert. Beadle had migrated from England to North America and settled in Wethersfield, Connecticut. His neighbors knew him as a man of "strict honor and integrity" who dabbled in dark and ambiguous humor and improved himself with theology and Shakespeare. Was he joking at the expense of the Boston tea partiers or the drinkers deprived of their tea when he advertised his "Best Bohea Tea" in March 1774,

FIGURE 7.8. William Beadle's mocking tea advertisement, Connecticut, 1774. Wethersfield merchant William Beadle's advertisement playfully celebrated the destruction of the tea in Boston and the fact that not all tea was destroyed. Source: *Connecticut Courant*, March 8, 1774.

"Such as Fishes never drink!!"? (See figure 7.8.) The reference to the Boston Tea Party was clear: jokes about fish drinking tea were commonplace. Peter Oliver joked (or perhaps even alleged) that some Bostonians abstained from eating local fish "because they had drank of the *East India Tea*." The further implications of Beadle's joke were also vague. Was he offering Dutch tea? Or was he drawing attention to Connecticut not having a tea boycott? The space for such ambiguity was important: the boundaries of political correctness were inchoate, and Beadle's humor helped negotiate their drawing. Patriots were not always powerful enough to be defied—as opposed to ignored—by tea advertisers in 1774. Tea advertising remained common in Connecticut, and Beadle bore little burden for his cheek: he placed generic advertisements for tea throughout the spring and summer of 1774 and early 1775.[25]

Jokes about selling tea cut in various directions. Beadle joked in a different advertisement about the risibly misogynistic Patriotic trope of women unable to resist tea. Another author wrote in to the *Massachusetts Gazette*, pretending to be a Newport tea importer. Though "T" supported internal taxation and tea sales, he insisted he was a Patriot. To prove it, he denounced "Tea as a Vile, Rotten, Stinking, Lousy, Rascally, Poisonous Drug, fit only for fine ladies and Dutchesses." The letter mocked the pretend-Patriotism of importers and advertisers (many of whom did claim to be Patriots) and Newport merchants.[26] It took more than florid language to be a good Patriot, and T's letter mocked the idea that Patriotism was merely a word game. And yet, Patriots did favor expressive language.

Patriots generally did not comment on tea advertisements. Roger Martyn, a Woonsocket, Rhode Islander, was one exception. Martyn complained to the *Newport Mercury* that the paper advertised tea. This made the publisher an "accessory" to the advertiser's "unjustifiable views." Martyn asked the printer to publish his letter (which the printer did) so that tea sellers "may consider their ways, repent, and amend," and the printer could avoid sharing "their guilt." Martyn's letter appeared on December 19, 1774, the last issue of the *Newport Mercury* to carry a tea ad before the ban and was reprinted as far as Virginia. Irascible Charles Lee likewise noticed that James Rivington, the popular and popular-to-hate New York printer, advertised tea. Rivington's paper circulated widely enough that Lee thought "every body" in Annapolis, "as I dare say they are" in Philadelphia, "is astonish'd that the miscreant Rivington is suffer'd to heap insult upon insult on the Congress with impunity. He has now advertis'd tea to be sold—for God's sake, as the committee of New York is so profound [asleep w]hy does not your Committee" in Philadelphia "wake 'em?"[27]

Ads and News

Patriots gamed the news to support their cause. This came from several sources. First, Patriots made the news more easily than law-abiding colonists did because change and disruption were inherently more newsworthy than continuity and stability. Thus the destruction of private shipments of dutied tea on the *Fortune* (in Boston) and the *London* (in New York) in March and April 1774 were reported in many newspapers. If we assume these protests somehow spoke for colonists who did not attend, we can easily miss the safe landing of tea in Charleston in February and March. These events, not widely celebrated by Patriots, suggested that some colonists were willing to let tea land.

Patriots also made the news in that they wrote press releases forming part of the budding newspaper campaign against tea. Annapolis Patriots declared support for a colony-wide association on May 25. Baltimore Patriots declared for some form of non-importation on May 31. Inhabitants of other Maryland counties met and announced similar views in the press. A meeting in the "upper part" of Frederick County approved a boycott and pledged to "not, after this day, drink any Tea, not suffer the same to be used in their Families." On June 22, a provincial congress announced Maryland-wide non-importation—effective at a later date, to be determined by an inter-colonial congress.[28] Similar news announcements appeared in print weekly, making tea seem broadly opposed. Change, in the form of a new boycott, committee, or resolve was news. Continuity (no boycott, committee, or resolve) was not.

These resolves did not indicate a broad, popular boycott. Households subscribed to the Association only at the end of the year. Frederick County Patriots' resolve was a promise about future tea drinking, not a claim about past abstention. It was unclear whether it bound the Patriots who attended the meeting or everyone. Resolves advocated for tea's politicization and boycott and, as part of that advocacy, depicted tea as more politicized and boycotted than it was.

It was also unclear how Maryland Patriots' meetings were constituted. "Meeting" evoked the New England town meeting, a formal institution of governance. Maryland meetings were informal. Yet what New Englander, reading of a Maryland county meeting, knew this? The upper part of Frederick County was not a political unit in 1774. What geographic and property qualifications determined who could attend? How was the meeting advertised? Who came? Who spoke? Who voted? Who determined this? We do not know. The meeting claimed to include "about 800 of the principal inhabitants," but there is no evidence others felt (or did not feel) bound by it afterward. Patriots claimed the populace broadly supported their policies. But that claim is not, by itself, evidence of support. The road from Patriot claims of colonial support to colonial compliance with Patriot orders was long and twisted. On one level, the meeting was just some guys from Fredrick County who, in claiming to speak for everyone, manufactured consent.[29]

Conservative writers contested the legitimacy of such meetings. Writing in New York, James Rivington pointed to the committee that had sent Captain Lockyer's tea back. "What is the *Committee of Observation*? By whom were they *appointed*? And what *authority* had they to *order* Capt. Chambers or any body else to attend them . . . ? Who says . . . the sense of the *city* was asked, relatively, either to sending away Capt Lockyer, or the destruction of the tea aboard the *London*?" The resolutions of "the people" came from a gathering of perhaps less than one-twentieth of population. How could they speak or represent all?[30]

Rivington's attacks might be dismissed because of their partisanship. Pro-Patriot readers, who increasingly saw Rivington as a conservative hack, might see these queries as signs of Rivington's illegitimacy, not their own. And yet Rivington's queries highlighted the tenuous, contested, and inchoate legitimacy of committees and conventions operating outside of government in 1774. Public discontent was real, but it was not universal.

On the back pages of Maryland's newspapers, a contrary consumerist tea discourse persisted for a few weeks. Tea advertisements appeared in the Baltimore

Maryland Journal and the Annapolis *Maryland Gazette,* often in the same issues that reported on anti-tea resolutions. Thomas Williams and Co. listed "green congo, and bohea tea" "from London" in Annapolis in May 1774. Thomas Hyde advertised "fine hyson tea" at his Annapolis store in the *Maryland Gazette* in March, April, and May 1774. In late May and early June, Christopher Johnson offered tea in Baltimore, and Thomas Brook Hodgkin offered "East India" goods from the *Geddes* in Annapolis. William O'Brien advertised tea in Baltimore in July. The Baltimore committee supported a boycott in principle but had not implemented one, though looking busy with committee work obscured this. These ads and the resolves against tea testified to inconvenient truths: that not all merchant and advertisers were bound by committee resolves, and that there was still tea to boycott.[31]

Boston merchant and Son of Liberty, Harbottle Dorr Jr., indexed Boston newspapers throughout the imperial crisis. His index is sometimes taken as a general handlist of newspaper content, but Dorr's indexing, like Patriot writing, reflected political choices. Dorr focused on the Patriotic *Boston Gazette* to the near exclusion of other Boston papers, cherry-picked Patriot news from other colonies (like tea burnings), and ignored conservative news even from his own town, such as Bostonians' efforts to pay for the East India Company tea. Dorr's index shows what Sons of Liberty wanted readers to glean from colonial newspapers: that tea was widely hated and the Tea Party widely supported. But it does not show how colonists read newspapers. Notably, Dorr omitted tea advertising.[32] Dorr ignored tea's commercial value to focus on its politics, even though, as a shopkeeper, Dorr knew that commercial value well.

Unlike Rivington or Dorr, eighteenth-century advertisers did not persuade or exhort. Unlike modern advertisers, they did not create demand or desire. Their ads were often grocery lists—items for sale, perhaps graded "best" or "fine." Advertisers did not push their wares with the zeal that newspaper polemicists pushed their ideas. To further a political goal, anti-tea news and essays told the public tea was or should be disused. They projected a sense that tea was already broadly opposed, which was only sometimes true. Such essays and news cannot be taken at face value. By contrast, advertisements told a simple truth: that tea was available and that advertisers had not been shut down. The Cumberland committee's version of the Greenwich tea party and Richard Bache's tea ad appeared in the same newspaper. Not only did they have divergent systems of meaning, but the news was much less reliable than the advertisement. The Cumberland committee pretended not to know how tea in its possession was destroyed and feigned outrage at the Greenwich tea party. Bache, lacking special claims, testified weekly to what was: tea for sale. We, as scholars, must read Patriotic news and editorials with greater care. Advertisements reflected reality; news was propaganda.

In South Carolina, the lie of tea news and the truth of tea advertising were starkly contradictory. The *Carolina* arrived from London on March 14, 1774. According to Peter Timothy, Patriotic editor of the *South Carolina Gazette*, the captain "very judiciously refused to bring out what Teas were offered to be shipped by him." But wishing did not make it so. Bonneau and Wilson began advertising "teas" among their goods on April 4, "a Great Part of which arrived in the *Carolina*." Radcliffe and Shepheard also advertised tea brought "by the Carolina, from London" in April. They faced no repercussions. The *Union* arrived from London on April 23, 1774. According to the *Gazette*, it arrived "WITHOUT ANY TEA!" as per the South Carolina committee's nonimportation order, which banned tea from being imported from Britain after April 15. Yet, on April 26, Zephaniah Kingsley began advertising tea "just imported in the *Union*, Capt Coombes, from London." Samuel Douglass & Company began advertising the same in the *Georgia Gazette* a few weeks later. Kingsley's ads ran until mid-July. Timothy's news may have been fake, but the ads debunking its claims never directly challenged Patriots or their authority— which was why they could continue.[33]

When the *Magna Charta* arrived in June, three merchants, Zephaniah Kingsley, George Thomson, and Parker & Hutchings were advertising (other) teas. In November, Kingsley would have to destroy his tea imported on the *Britannia*. But in June Kingsley advertised tea expressly "from London" just fine.[34]

Merchants James Wakefield and William Donaldson imported tea on the *Magna Charta*, not expecting this tea to be any more politicized than previous cargoes. Patriots put words in Donaldson's mouth, optimistically claiming in a July 4 press release that he had "refused to receive" the tea. But Donaldson advertised the tea on July 8, as he had advertised tea in April and May. Yet the turn against tea at the July 6–8 general meeting gave him pause. Donaldson edited his advertisement, and on July 15 it ran again, with tea omitted. A few days later, when a mob attacked Captain Maitland for landing the tea, it left Donaldson alone. Donaldson made no mention of his dropping tea from his advertising. He probably wanted to avoid attention (see figures 7.9 and 7.10). Wakefield's advertisement, appearing on July 12, also omitted tea. The remaining Charleston tea advertisements stopped. Advertisers censored themselves.[35]

Where and when they continued in 1774 and early 1775, tea advertisements suggest merchants thought advertising was worth the risk. These ads were risks: public statements, readable by all, whatever the merchant's or printer's

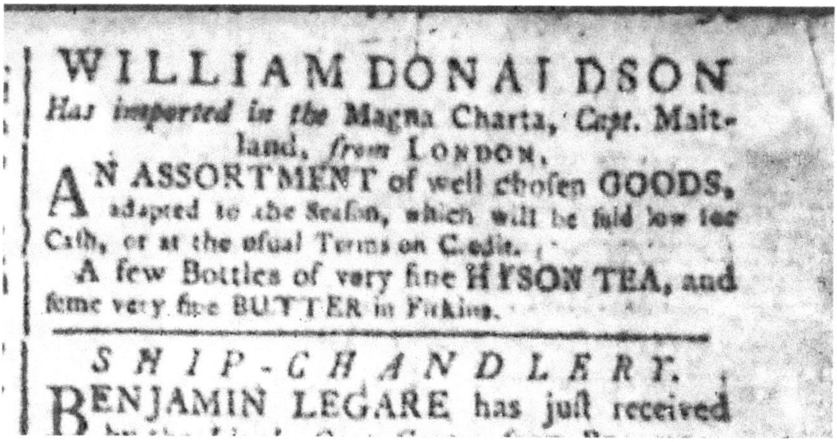

WILLIAM DONALDSON
Has imported in the Magna Charta, *Capt.* Maitland, *from* LONDON,
AN ASSORTMENT of well choſen GOODS, adapted to the Seaſon, which will be ſold low for Caſh, or at the uſual Terms on Credit.
A few Bottles of very fine HYSON TEA, and ſome very fine BUTTER in Firkins.

SHIP-CHANDLERY.
BENJAMIN LEGARE has juſt received

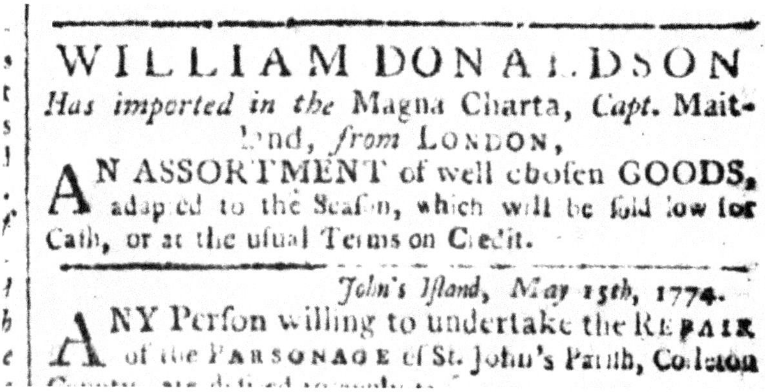

WILLIAM DONALDSON
Has imported in the Magna Charta, *Capt.* Maitland, *from* LONDON,
AN ASSORTMENT of well choſen GOODS, adapted to the Seaſon, which will be ſold low for Caſh, or at the uſual Terms on Credit.

John's Iſland, May 15th, 1774.
ANY Perſon willing to undertake the REPAIR of the PARSONAGE of St. John's Pariſh, Colleton

FIGURES 7.9. AND 7.10. William Donaldson advertisements with and without tea, Charleston, July 1774. Captain Maitland's *Magna Charta* brought tea into Charleston, South Carolina in June 1774, causing considerable consternation. Donaldson advertised this tea on July 8 in the *South Carolina and American General Gazette*, but dropped his role in the tea, and quietly dropped tea from his ad, on July 15. A mob attacked Maitland for his role in this on July 19, which he escaped by reaching HMS *Glasgow*. Sources: *SCAGG*, July 8 and 15, 1774.

or consumer's politics. Tea ads did not give tea political significance; they described tea as a consumer good. Tea advertising's continuation reminds us of Patriots' lagging ability to shut down this alternate understanding of tea. It implies Patriots lacked even the handful of activists needed to cow advertisers and tea sellers in New York, Pennsylvania, and other market colonies. Even in South Carolina and Maryland, tea advertising lasted longer than the resolves against tea would suggest. Advertisers gave their names. What more did the Sons of Liberty need to pull down their shops?

Newspapers' Double Valence: The Political World

A press and type were significant capital costs. Once bought, printers wanted to maximize their use. In addition to newspapers, printers printed anything else they could: stationery (the Caroline County committee recorded its proceedings in a notebook bought from printer Alexander Purdie in Williamsburg), almanacs, psalters, pamphlets, broadsides, ballads, sermons, and books. Printers also sold printed matter imported from London. Colonial legislatures contracted to print government acts, other documents, and paper money. Printers bound books, owned paper mills, ran post offices, vended dry goods, or sold medicine (the printer-apothecary was a common English combination).[36] Printers maximized newspapers' readers and advertisers by running political and commercial news and ads. Notably, it was usually the advertiser, not the printer, who retracted ads.

Newspapers were at the core of a political discourse that extended beyond their pages because they reprinted other media, putting a broader range of content alongside advertising. Newspapers serialized political essays, some of which were sold as stand-alone pamphlets. In the newspaper, these essays had rejoinders or assents that were usually absent from the pamphlet. Newspapers also reprinted ephemera. A Mechanic's Philadelphia broadside against the East India Company's tea first appeared out of doors for passersby to see on December 4, 1773. The printers of the *Pennsylvania Gazette* ran it, giving it a new audience: more-distant colonists who could read it indoors in homes, taverns, and coffeehouses. They also gave the notice a new context; it shared an issue with Mason and Dorsey's ad for smuggled tea. A handbill about the recent tarring and feathering of John Malcom was so vulnerable to being torn down, its text warned that if "any Person should be so hardy as to tear this down, they may expect my severest Resentment." Edes and Gill extended the handbill's life by running it in their radical *Boston Gazette*. They also sharpened its political context. It appeared on the same page as: a few lines directed at tea consignee Benjamin Faneuil, the Salem town meeting's claim to stop the sale of dutied tea there, a veiled threat that Bostonians might walk out to see the consignees at Castle Island if the harbor froze over enough, and no tea ads.[37]

Printers' most important political functions were running local Patriot press releases and re-running stories from out-of-colony newspapers. These combined to distribute Patriotic news across North America. This was not a perfect or systematic effort. Printers did not reprint every handbill or essay. Newspapers were sometimes irregular, as was the mail. Even when a paper was regularly printed, arrived on time, and was promptly read, news traveled with a weeks-long lag. Nevertheless, newspapers linked readers across their circulation areas and interfaced with a larger oral culture.

Larger papers (and, therefore, the ads they carried) had substantial reach. The *South Carolina Gazette* was read from North Carolina to the Floridas. Roger Smith, George Heriot, and Daniel Tucker's advertisement for tea lodged "at a store in George-Town" South Carolina thus reached thousands beyond George Town.[38] *Rivington's New York Gazetteer* spanned the colonies and reached Britain and France, carrying twenty-nine tea ads in 1774. North American German-language prints, catering to a readership widely but thinly distributed across the continent, had particularly broad distribution. The most widely circulated colonial newspaper may have been Henry Miller (Heinrich Muller)'s *Wöchentliche Pennsylvanische Staatsbote*. His tea advertisers included Anglophone merchants Attmore and Hellings and Mason and Dorsey, who also advertised in Philadelphia's Anglophone papers (Muller translated advertisements into German free of charge). Miller's tea advertisers also included Freehauf und Wyntoop, Christoph Becker, and Jacob Schallus, among others, German merchants who did not advertise in the Anglo press, suggesting a category of merchants whose boycott-related activities have been overlooked.[39]

Rivington's and Miller's papers carried tea ads until early 1775, reaching colonies where local tea advertising had already ended. Mid-Atlantic advertising was thus performed before a broadly North American audience.[40] German-speaking colonists are sometimes seen as having been slow to join the cause, but why should Germans in, say, North Carolina, participate in that colony's early non-consumption campaign when they could see Philadelphia merchants—Anglo and German—were still offering tea and English goods? One of the many reasons for Carolina Germans' reticence may be that, as readers of the *Staatsbote* and its advertisements, they were better informed about the progress of non-importation and non-consumption across the continent than their Anglophone neighbors relying on the local *Gazette*.

Newspaper content was read locally in public. Clubs, circulating libraries, taverns, and inns took newspapers. Philadelphia's London Coffee House stocked papers from Rhode Island, South Carolina, Ireland, and England, as well as the proprietor's *Pennsylvania Journal*. This embedded print in a public, oral experience. Nicholas Cresswell "went to the Tavern to *hear*"—not to read—"the Resolves of the Continental Congress." Reading aloud spread news, included the illiterate, and sparked discussion. Taverns and coffeehouses also served as mail and newspaper distribution and collection centers.[41]

In taverns and coffeehouses, colonists responded to tea and boycott news. The Charleston Pope's Day celebration was thus performed once on the ground, a second time in the press, and a third time as it was cheered in a tavern. Tea could be drunk or renounced there too, for, despite their names, taverns and coffeehouses did serve tea. Even Boston Son of Liberty John Marston's tavern kept a tea service.[42] Public tea consumption in such spaces was performative, as John Adams discovered.

Different taverns were for different sorts: travelers, workingmen, politicos, and merchants. In New York, there were Loyalist and Patriot taverns. Taverns served as voting places, army recruiting posts, militia muster points, and perhaps rallying points for the Boston Tea Party, as the epigraph at the start of this book suggests. Charleston taverns hosted half a dozen clubs. In coffeehouses and taverns (the difference between these two blurred), colonists could consume tea and newspapers in a way that linked consumer, mercantile, and political sociability. The "pastry-cook" Francisco Morelli advertised his new "coffee-room," promising posh Charlestonians "Tea or Coffee" and "every News-Paper that can be procured." In New York, Thomas William Moore auctioned tea and land in a public house. At the public house, colonists could drink tea, read the newspaper carrying Moore's adverts, and bid on lots of bohea. In and outside such venues, newspaper advertisements were part of how colonists debated, performed, read, wrote, and spoke about tea.[43]

Newspapers' Double Valence: The Commercial World

Advertisements were an unmissable part of the newspaper reading experience. Parliamentary debates and colonial news were important, but they came in long, undifferentiated columns of small print. For ads, Printers jumbled typefaces, capitalizations, lines and borders, manicules—the ☞ symbol—majuscules (large starting letters), and clip-art style illustrations. When Ebenezer Watson ran William Beadle's tea ad in the *Connecticut Courant* (see figure 7.8), he included three type sizes and two fonts and played with capitalization, italics, and manicules. The ad Peter Timothy set on the front page of the *South Carolina Gazette* announced "HYSON **TEA**" in the largest font outside the masthead (see figures 7.4 and 7.11). Even litany ads were more visually varied than long blocks of news. In a culture where newspapers were pored over carefully and saved for future reference, advertisements were seen.[44]

Advertising took up more column inches than any other component of the colonial newspaper, usually one and a half out of a standard four pages, but sometimes more than half the total page space. Sometimes the front page of the *Boston Gazette* was entirely given to ads. Timothy routinely placed "New Advertisements" on the front page of the *South Carolina Gazette*, perhaps

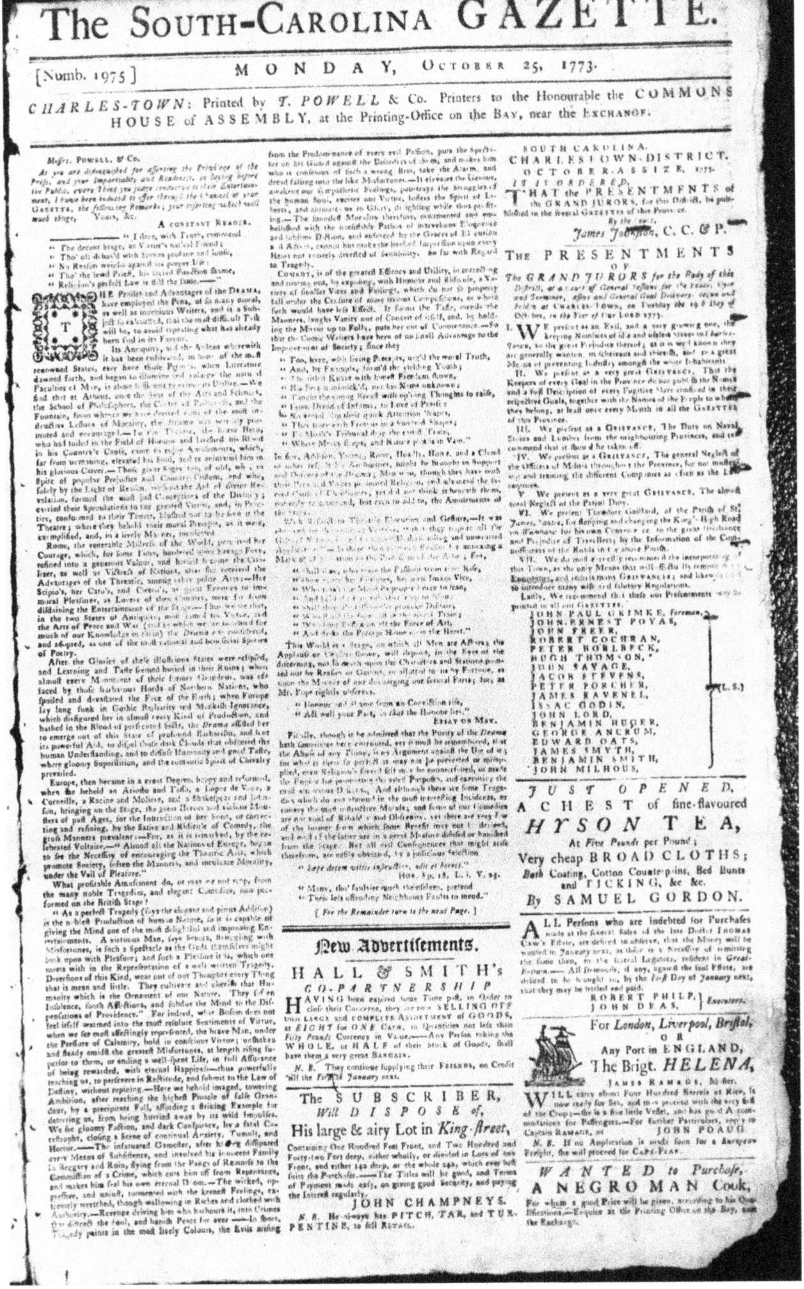

The SOUTH-CAROLINA GAZETTE.

[Numb. 1975]   MONDAY, OCTOBER 25, 1773.

CHARLES-TOWN: Printed by T. POWELL & Co. Printers to the Honourable the COMMONS HOUSE of ASSEMBLY, at the Printing-Office on the BAY, near the EXCHANGE.

FIGURE 7.11. Front page of *South Carolina Gazette* with Gordon's ad, 1773. Some printers gave a substantial part of their front page to advertising, as this front-page of the October 25, 1773 issue of *South Carolina Gazette* shows. Samuel Gordon's tea advertisement, in the right-side column, mentioned tea prominently. Note the specific mention of "New Advertisements," which were of particular consumer and commercial interest. Inside this newspaper, four other merchants or firms advertised tea. Among them was Roger Smith, who was also a consignee for the East India Company's tea arriving on the *London* a little more than a month later. Source: *SCG*, October 25, 1773.

reasoning readers were more interested in this than his news, which he pushed to the inside pages. In 1773, he included two- or four-page supplements, comprising mostly ads. Advertising declined during the war, making up only 25 to 30 percent of page space. This reflected paper shortages (which reduced page size, newspaper frequency, and supplements). Even at this reduced level, advertising, paid for weekly or monthly, provided printers with vital cash flow, as they faced recurring costs for ink and paper but collected subscriptions annually. Printers were not dependent on tea advertisers for their livelihoods. The most common advertisements were for real estate, not dry goods. Yet printers did not want to lose any ads prematurely, even as most printers also sought to ingratiate themselves with Patriots. And so they ran ads for things like tea, English goods, and racing, which were all in the midst of being banned, as long as their advertisers would pay. The presence and absence of these ads speak directly to the coming and going of the Association.[45]

Many advertisements containing vital and timely commercial information functioned like business-to-business classifieds. Gordon's ad did not explain where his store was; his customers knew where to find him. But his ad did indicate the goods he stocked. Charleston advertisers often indicated which ship had carried their goods (which, when cross-referenced with the shipping list indicated when it arrived) and whence it came. This was useful for distant planters considering a new order of goods from town.

Readers sought this sort of news, and some papers announced a specialization in commercial news by calling themselves *Advertisers*. Timothy did not just happen to run an ad on his front cover—the abundance of advertising was one reason readers bought Timothy's *Gazette* at all. Timothy's Patriotic reporting was another reason. Newspapers printed parallel political and commercial discourses because newspapers had political and commercial appeal. This disjuncture was at the heart of the newspaper reading experience in 1774, a disjuncture that emerged forcefully in the anti-tea propaganda that printers ran alongside their tea ads.

CHAPTER 8

Propaganda

Patriots attacked tea with satire, public ritual, excoriation, and misinformation. Whatever its purported rationales, such propaganda served political ends. Sometimes Patriots even lied to each other. In February 1774, one Virginia Patriot urged disuse of tea following the example of "the Northward." However, as Customs Commissioner Benjamin Hallowell explained, "people to the Southward have been taught by the Sons of Liberty here [in Boston], to believe that no Tea has been imported from England" despite Boston being the center of legal tea importation and consumption continuing in many colonies. In 1769, one writer had mocked the anti-tea invectives in the newspapers as ineffectual "deceptives" (propaganda): "As to our people's quitting the use of tea, it is really a Joke."[1]

This chapter considers two attacks on tea. First, Patriots described tea as a medical danger. There were standing concerns about tea's health effects, but the timely distillation and distribution of these concerns was political. A countervailing belief in tea's medical benefits blunted this attack, and some committeemen granted colonists medical dispensation to drink tea. Second, Patriots blamed the King or parliament for introducing or forcing tea upon the colonies. Colonists knew tea was not new. This attack probably aimed not to gaslight colonists about their habits but to re-frame tea drinking as a political choice and virtue, one with sexual or religious overtones.

Tea as Poison

Patriots claimed tea was unhealthy to dissuade tea drinkers. The physician David Ramsay's pamphlet, *A Sermon on Tea*, summed up much of the genre. Ramsay claimed tea caused every ailment, from farting to death. Tea made Europeans "some inches" shorter than their predecessors, "many degrees" weaker in "strength," and inflicted a profusion of "disorders." London tea drinkers were so weakened they could take only "half as much bleeding" as they used to. "Nervous complaints" had skyrocketed—"*weak nerves* are occasioned by *strong tea*"—and the "human frame" was left "so debilitated" from tea "that scarce any disorder" was enough to cause "spasms." Tea's effects were long-term and cumulative. Like opium or arsenic, a person could build up a tolerance but would suffer in the end. Tea "gradually saps the constitution, without surprising us with its immediate effects," though some did have immediate effects, such as stomach pain and "tremors." It caused drowsiness and wakefulness; farting and constipation; hysteria and hypochondria. Pregnant tea drinkers imparted "a whole tribe of diseases" to their children, making "their lives miserably wretched" and risking infant death. Ramsay imagined a tea drinker: "A ghost-like pale face spectre . . . not really dead, though she appears bloodless," too weak to care for her child and bound for an early grave. The "Devil himself" could not make a more pernicious drink. It was a "poison" that "kills."[2]

Ramsay's was one of several essays of this sort. Dr. Thomas Young of the Boston committee of correspondence wrote a similar screed in the *Newport Mercury*. Disguising his political dislike of tea with the pseudonym "A Physician," he warned that tea was a "highly debilitating" stomach "relaxant" and made "nervous ailments" such as "hypochondria, palsies, [and] cachexies [wasting away]," nearly universal. Reverend William Tennent declared tea "has in the Opinion of the best Physician, spread . . . Legions of Diseases, before unknown," and "ruined the Nerves" and "Health" of its drinkers. Tea "fattened the Purse of the Physician and the Sexton, encreased the Number of the Dead, and enfeebled the Living." By abstaining, readers could "save the Remains of your own Constitutions, and secure the Health of your Children." Tennent saw tea's medical ailments as a metaphor for the political diseases it brought: taxation and oppression. Dr. Benjamin Rush, writing as "Hamden," concurred; he considered tea a "slow poison" physically and politically. One newspaper writer thought tea caused "certain feminine disorders." It was "an offense against nature" that caused men to have "lost their stature and comeliness; and women their beauty." It would "shorten your days."[3]

Amateur and professional medical concern for tea's effects on human health both predated and outlasted the Patriot movement. As early as 1731, a New

York editorialist had worried that tea drinking was dangerous to "Health and Happiness" and caused physical and mental distress. Perhaps he had read *A Dissertation upon Tea*, published by the Scottish doctor Thomas Short the previous year. John Wesley, in his well-known *Letter to a Friend, Concerning Tea* (1748), lambasted tea for causing tremors (over-caffeination), which he characterized as a "Paralytick Disorder," albeit one that passed after withdrawal. Wesley likened tea to alcohol in the dependency it created and discussed quitting at length. He recommended sage, green balm, mint, pennyroyal, the herbal mixture "Foltron," and cocoa over the "slow poison" of tea. Jonas Hanway, in *An Essay on Tea: Considered as Pernicious to Health*, thought tea as "injurious" as gin and "pernicious to health, obstructing industry and impoverishing the nation" (Samuel Johnson, however, defended the beverage). Mid-century British middle-class reformers harped on about workingmen consuming too much tea and sugar and needing whole wheat, oats, and potatoes instead. They saw the new diet of tea and sugar as "less substantial" and more costly. Anti-tea ideas persisted in some parts of nineteenth-century Britain. Cobbett compared it to laudanum. Others worried tea "weakens the stomach" and "unbraces the nerves." G. G. Sigmond noted various cases in which tea was thought to have harmed patients (and others where it had helped). The concern for tea's effect on health appeared in France as well.[4]

A naive reader could see the question of tea's effects on health in the Revolution as a sincere intellectual dispute. But it is important to distinguish between the medical tradition examining tea's effects on health and Ramsay's and Tennent's selective drawing from that tradition to suit their politics. Their arguments appeared alongside every other possible reason not to drink tea: that it brought tyranny, monopoly, taxes, and that Chinese peasants packed it with their dirty feet. Perhaps they believed their propaganda, but not everyone did. One writer in the *Massachusetts Spy* deprecated such "scare crow stories." If tea was dangerous, "Why were not these arguments used against the use of [tea] in former times, before it was thought a political evil?" Drs. Rush and Young's urgency about tea's health effects in 1774 was matched by how quickly they forgot about it. They did not campaign about tea's health effects in 1776, after Congress reauthorized tea's use.[5]

Other scare crow stories were obvious lies, like the rumor that the tea the East India Company sent to the colonies was infested with an insect, "which renders it more pernicious to health than usual." Conservatives joked with all these tales of tea poison, Patriotic smugglers would have to claim Dutch tea had "the poisonous quality" "drawn off" before shipment.[6]

In addition to tea's alleged poisonousness, Patriots pointed out the economic savings in abandoning tea—another idea with a long lineage. Wesley, too, had seen tea as a needless expense. The well-off could better use the money as alms; the poor should rather save their funds to escape poverty.[7] Patriots claimed that tea burdened the individual's purse and drained the colonies on a macro-level, mirroring the mercantilist arguments about the East India trade hurting Atlantic economies by exporting specie to Asia.

Just how many readers believed Ramsay is unclear. Ramsay's authorities—doctors—were the last people eighteenth-century Britons called when sick. Dismissing the medical and economic arguments against tea, Hannah Griffitts noted that only "Doctors & Misers" "rail at Tea." To everyone else tea was "Blest." "Tea I must have," she wrote, "or I shall dye."[8]

Tea as Tonic

Some colonists claimed to need tea for medical reasons, suggesting the diversity of medical opinions (official and folk) about tea. Ramsay may have emphasized tea's dangers strenuously because belief in tea's benefits was ubiquitous. Folk remedies often claimed tea was a tonic. Some thought tea prevented scurvy. In 1770, 300 Patriotic women had promised to abstain from tea, "Sickness excepted." The claim, made in the *Boston Evening Post,* was sincere. Medical exemption was not a hypocrite's loophole but a common home remedy. Landon Carter recorded various self-administered medicines in his diary and noted that medical exemptions to boycotts and associations were common. He had come to his own conclusions about tea. Tea had "medical qualities," which he had discovered from his forty years of use. He thought hyson stopped his diarrhea; others agreed green tea did the same. "I speak not this with a desire to indulge," but out of medical experience. He would stick to the boycott—unless, perhaps, his bowels disagreed. Others went further. Conservative John Randolph, in *Considerations on the Present State of Virginia*, argued it would be "dangerous to Health" to stop drinking tea, especially if colonists were to "stop suddenly" after being "long accustomed to" it. Peter Oliver thought tea was fine, but its herbal substitute, Labrador tea, caused "Disorders in Health"—cases, perhaps, of conservatives believing the medical ideas that suited their politics. In the *Norfolk Intelligencer,* "Penelope House-Wife" warned other families about what happened when her "poor deluded" "patriotic Husband" switched the family from tea to "sage and baum." They were "scoured off their feet by the use of these herbs," their two children sick in bed. The cause was "their tender bowels being abraided by a too free use of these acrid plants." Having switched to rosemary and lavender, others supposedly suffered from giddiness and diminished eyesight. Tea, by contrast, was "soothing and agreeable."[9]

High medical discourse also noted tea's health benefits. It was thought to cure ague. Seventeenth-century Dutch treatises argued it cured asthma, colds, constipation, and fatigue. Nahum Tate, British poet laureate, celebrated tea in his mock-heroic "Poem upon tea with . . . Directions in the Uses of It for Health" (1702). In *The Good and Bad Effects of Tea Consider'd* (1745), Simon Mason noted the broader pro-tea British medical literature. It "cools, and allays Drought, helps Digestion, makes clean the Stomach, attenuates Viscidities, augments the Velocity of a sluggish Circulation, invigorates, and gives new Spirits, promotes Secretions, strengthens the Bowels, and prompts natural Evacuations"—the complete opposite of Ramsay. For Mason, though, tea's good was for the better sort. For the poor tea was "very pernicious to their Healths, Circumstances, and Morals." The poor aping their betters put ill ideas of life above their stations in their heads. Writing in the 1820s, New Englander Dr. Edward Holyoke attributed his longevity to tea, among other things.[10]

Even some committeemen thought that tea was not the poison Ramsay suggested. After the Association came into force, Patriot authorities granted medical exemptions to the tea ban. These permissions were popular workarounds. In Wethersfield, Connecticut, magistrate and committeeman Elisha Williams issued medical permits for various people to receive tea from pharmacist Leonard Chester. Mrs. Baxter requested "Liberty to buy" a quarter pound of tea; Williams reasoned that because of her "Age & bodily Infirmities it will not be acting contrary to the Design of our Association," to grant the request—allowing another half-pound for her later. In August, Williams' neighbor, Seaman Riley, said that "one of his Children is very sick and the Doctor advises to the use of Tea." Williams allowed half a pound. A Mr. Samuel Boltwood of Amherst, Massachusetts, indicated that two elderly women in that town needed tea on "physicians" advice. Williams approved the request, and another for a Mrs. Kellogg, who "Beeing sick wants Bohe Tea for med[i]c[in]e."[11]

Williams was not alone. When a cargo of tea was discovered in Salem, Massachusetts, committeeman David Mason found his wife was "in a very low state of health and could take but little nourishment excepting tea," and suggested getting permission to use it (she declined). Though it had publicly resolved against dutied tea, the Westerly, Rhode Island town meeting permitted the "Doctor [to] sell his Tea (now of his property) if he pleases." In Virginia, Colonel Lawrence Taliaferro asked the Orange County, Virginia committee "in behalf of Mother Judah & after inform[in]g them of her situation"— presumably, a medical one—"all agreed that she Might Drink Tea." In Annapolis, Maryland, Charles Willson Peale "beged a little tea of Mrs. Scott for my [ill] mother" in October 1775. Three days later he "got a note from Mr. [William] Paca," a Maryland delegate to Congress, "of leave for Mr. [Thomas] H[y]de to sell my mother what Tea she may really want." Fortunately for Peale, Hyde still had stock. In North Carolina, Elizabeth Catherine De Rosset was "very ill," and asked permission to drink tea, the committee granting "permission in the consideration of my age and infirmities." The presence of "proper" medical advice in some cases and its absence in others suggest tea functioned as formal medicine and folk remedy across the colonies.[12]

Committeeman Williams took these cases seriously. He agonized over Pattison's case—wishing he had brought a doctor's note, or a certificate from his local committee, before allowing it. Williams was a true believer. To him, these permission slips were not bogus excuses but medical needs. Other colonists, caught drinking tea, used illness as a justification. How many applicants saw things the same way is unclear. False claims of infirmity or age could be easy ways to get tea. Peter Oliver, inclined to see the worst in Patriots, suspected as much when he noticed Patriotic Boston women stocking up before the 1770 boycott. They "were cautious enough to lay in large Stocks before" the boycott commenced, and "could be sick just as it suited their Convenience or Inclination" after. Oliver mocked colonists suffering under the "Evasion of Sickness." "They, poor Souls! Were forced to take Turns to be sick & invite their Acquaintance[s] to visit them [for tea], & so the Sickness went on by Rotation." The Continental Association contained no medical exemption for tea, but medical exemptions were part of the broader discussion around the Association. The Virginia Association, for instance, banned all imports from Britain—except medicine—and the medical dispensation to drink tea may have been made in that spirit. Such exemptions make the tea ban less effective as local Patriots bent a Continental Association toward folk customs.[13]

Colonists did abuse the medical permits. According to the Hartford County committee of inspection, the trick was to apply to a committee in another town, as Samuel Boltwood had, to get "permits" to buy tea "under pretence for the use of the sick," since the local committee might realize the applicant was faking. Then colonists presented their local committee with an out-of-town note and received tea. The county committee was displeased—less with the tea drinking and more with the circumvention of its authority. Medical licenses for tea drinking were not to be issued anymore—"except for the use of the sick in their respective towns," which meant that they were.[14] Ramsay's claim that tea was a medical danger was propaganda, pure and simple, and colonists did not believe it.

The Myth of Britain Forcing Tea on the Colonists

Patriots also told the story that Britain had forced tea on the colonists, who did not want it. Taken literally, this is clearly false: colonists liked tea and did not need to be forced to drink it. Usually interpreted as a reference to the tea destroyed in the Boston Tea Party (or the tea shipped by the Company in 1773 generally), it might have been a better fit for the tea from the *William*, stored in Castle William outside Boston. The Boston Port Act required trade be safe and duties be collected as part of Boston's re-opening, which meant the ministry was trying to force the *William's* tea upon colonists. Yet the disappearance of the *William's* tea from colonial public discussion after January 1774 indicates colonists did not make this connection explicitly, if at all. (This disappearance is why we have missed the fate of the *William's* tea for the last 250 years.) Tryon in New York, Wentworth in New Hampshire, and Bull in South Carolina had tried to help land tea cargoes. But as Patriots moved to a generalized opposition to all teas in 1774, a general sense of tea being forced upon colonists was a helpfully simple propaganda point, creating the notion that colonists were against tea while Britain forced it down their throats.

The idea may have originated in a rumor about William Kelly. In 1773, Kelly was said to expect that Governor Tryon would "cram the tea down their throats." Kelly was a prominent New York merchant who had retired to London and helped his partner, Abraham Lott, become a consignee for the New York shipment. The story got Kelly hung in effigy. In 1774, colonial papers expanded on the underlying idea, claiming that the King-in-Council determined, "Bostonians are to be chastised, and are to drink tea, though ever so great an emetic." "We hear that it is intended to ship a fresh Cargo of tea for Boston, and to send it thither with a military force," wrote the *Boston Post-Boy*, reminding readers that, in 1773, the plan had also been, "in case of refusal, the tea was to be crammed down the people's throats."[15]

In "The Able Doctor, or America Swallowing the Bitter Draught" (1774) (see figure 8.1), the cartoonist took this literally, and depicted the King's ministers stripping, holding down, and preparing to gang rape a young female America, as Lord North shoves the tip of his teapot down her throat. The cartoon is crudely sexual. It is also very much about tea. The central action in the image is Lord North forcing the tea upon America. He is violating her with the pot, and she resists by spitting the tea in his face. The cartoon, with a partially denuded woman and a perverted, upskirting Lord Sandwich (a notorious womanizer), was catchy.[16]

Patriots appropriated "The Able Doctor." It was first printed in the *London Magazine* in April 1774 (the journal likely used the image not so much to elicit

FIGURE 8.1.   *The Able Doctor*, 1774. Drawn in Britain as a critique of the ministry, this print shows Lord North assaulting America with a pot of tea. The image took on new meaning in America as a symbol of ministerial aggression and colonial resistance (the tea is being spat back at the prime minister). Source: Library of Congress, Prints and Photographs Division, Cartoon Prints, British.

sympathy for Bostonians as to attack the ministry for the Boston Port Act). Yet it was a compelling image and was soon reproduced throughout the empire, the unwanted tea and victimized America resonating with Patriots' self-image. *The Able Doctor* appeared the next month in Dublin in the *Hibernian Magazine*. In June, Paul Revere rendered it for the Boston-based Patriotic *Royal American Magazine* (printed by Isaiah Thomas). Revere tweaked the image, adding the word "TEA" to the pot. It appeared in Philadelphia as a broadside in August (where it would have likely been put up in taverns), retitled "The Persevering Americans"). It appeared in Salem in 1774, and in late 1775 it appeared on the cover of *Freebetter's New-England Almanack* (New London).[17] Continental soldiers carved it on their powder horns during the war.

There were various conceits here: in London, it criticized the ministry for assuming it could get colonists to buy taxed tea. But the tea in this image is just tea, not taxed tea, and was read as just tea in the colonies through Revere's putting "TEA" on the pot, rather than "EIC," the Company logo, or the rate of duty.

The second conceit conflated taxed tea with all tea. The Tea Party was about dutied tea, but this image helped reimagine the destruction of the tea as a general tea protest. With *The Able Doctor* there was no need to explain why some teas were bad but not others, and it was easy to explain why a cut in the tea tax was bad—it was the ministry's means to force tea upon the colonies.

With a lone avatar, the image simplified Bostonians (indeed, all colonists) into a single unit, even though they were hardly a unitary group—some Patriots, some Loyalists, some willing to buy dutied tea and some not, some ready to reimburse the Company for its losses and some unwilling. It transformed the Boston Tea Party from an act of violence that shocked consciences into spittle on North's face: sympathetic protest and justifiable self-defense.[18]

The final conceit was the other half of the first: colonists did not want tea. The same conceit was imbedded in Henry Laurens's quip to his son in 1775. Even "Our Cherokee Indians . . . blame King George exceedingly for quarreling with his Children about 'the Leaves of a Tree'—they Say 'he is foolish'— 'Why does not he see that the People in America don't Love it' 'if they did, would they have thrown a whole Ship Load of it into the Sea." The revolutionary dislike for tea would be a long-lasting conceit, born of the myths spread by the *Boston Gazette* in the wake of the Boston Tea Party of booming coffee sales, and forming the basis for the unexamined assumption that in the Revolution "Americans were weaned from the teacup to the coffee cup, where . . . their devotion still rests."[19]

The image contained layers of unintentional irony as well. When it was first printed in London, the title, *The Able Doctor*, referenced tea's reputed medical properties. North here was a bungling doctor torturing his patient—a gag that hit home for anyone who had had one too many bloodlettings—but the underlying implication that tea was a tonic, not a risk, remained intact. Isaiah Thomas retained the title when he reprinted it in Boston, even though he could have changed it to "The Rape of America" or another punchy name. Later versions cut the title and simplified the image. Yet Thomas's title retained (accidentally, one presumes) the implication that tea was healthy.

A second layer of unintentional irony, especially in Boston, was the juxtaposition of *The Able Doctor*'s vision of America—a woman held down by force, stripped, tea shoved down her throat—with how Boston Patriots treated customs collector John Malcom in chapter 4: beaten, half-naked, with tea forced down his throat. When Patriots did it, it was supposed to be fitting. When North did it, it was outrageous.

Philadelphian John Leacock's *American Chronicles of the Times* blamed the King for the tea. Leacock lampooned the ministry, but his work was complex, and its humor both mocked and celebrated the Patriot cause (Leacock was a member of the Philadelphia Sons of Liberty). A "biblical parodic satire," as Carla

Mulford terms it, *American Chronicles* recapitulated current events in biblical prose by parodying the tone of the *Geneva* and *King James* bibles and referencing a pastiche of biblical stories in describing contemporary events. *American Chronicles* came out in six chapter-length installments in 1774 and 1775, complete with notation dividing it into "verses." It reflected the latest developments in the crisis engulfing the colonies. Its timeliness, political coverage, and allusion to familiar scripture meant it was widely distributed and avidly followed. Various chapters were printed in Boston, New York, Philadelphia, North Carolina, Connecticut, and Rhode Island, and it came out in more editions than all but a few prints of its era.[20] *American Chronicles* lampooned the ministry's approach to the colonies, framing the colonists as stout Israelites resisting a bad king and his ministers (George III appears as an amalgamation of the darker moments of Kings Saul and David, the kings of Judah, and the kings of Babylon).

American Chronicles described forced tea. "And hast thou not send forth a decree, that all the world should be taxed for the God of the TEA CHEST?" Leacock asked the King in a jeremiad. "And yet, notwithstanding, would we not all to a man . . . sooner agree voluntarily to burn our throats with a ladle of hot mush, our own country produce, and manufacture, than have the nosle of a teapot crammed down our throats, and scalded with the abominable and baneful exotic, without our own consent?"[21]

American Chronicles dwelled not on the image of tea forced upon colonists but on the idea that the King introduced tea to the colonies in the first place. The claim that George III introduced tea is, in its delusion and need to blame Britain for everything, not far off from slaveholder Thomas Jefferson's claim, made in an early draft of the Declaration of Independence, that King George III had forced slavery upon the colonists. The idea that the King introduced tea to the colonies transformed the story.

The *Chronicles* began with the Boston Tea Party:

And behold! When the tidings came to the great city that is afar off, the city that is in the land of Britain, how the men of Boston, even the Bostonites, had arose, a great multitude, and destroyed the TEA, the abominable merchandise of the east, and cast it into the midst of the sea.

[2]That the Lord the King waxed exceedingly wroth, insomuch that the form of his visage was changed, and his knees smote one against the other.

[3]Then he assembled together the Princes, the Nobles, the Counsellors, the Judges, and all the Rulers of the people, even the great Sanhedrim, and when he had told them what things were come to pass,

⁴They smote their breasts and said, 'These men fear thee not, O King! Neither have they obeyed the voice of our Lord the King, not worshipped the TEA CHEST, which thou hast set up, whose length was three cubits, and the breadth thereof one cubit and an half.

The *Chronicles* continued, lamenting the Boston Port Act, which meant Boston would be "made tributary, and bow down to the TEA CHEST, the God of the Heathen: tell it not in Gath, nor publish it in the streets of Askalon." Colonists, however, would not be deceived, and refused to "to sell our birthright for a dish of TEA."²²

Leacock's description of tea parties helped canonize these events as righteous stands of a moral, God-fearing people against the King's iniquity. In Leacock's telling, tea was akin to Exodus's golden calf or the Baal of 1 Kings—a bad king's heresy. Tea was sin, and those who resisted it were righteous. Leacock began Chapter V with the burning of the *Peggy Stewart* (a "free-will offering"), and covered the *Virginia* incident as well. The "Marylandites were like watchmen on the towers," he explained, "they kept a good look out (for the spirit of liberty, of watchfulness and freedom, went throughout the land)." And so when "it came to pass about this time, that there came a ship from the land of Britain afar off, with merchandize and TEA," the vigilant Marylandites were ready for the *Peggy Stewart*. They asked the tea importers, "Wherefore have ye committed this iniquity in the land? behold, ye be but three, and ye be not able to stand before this multitude."

⁹Now they were sore afraid and dismayed, and said until the men of Maryland, We have indeed sinned against the people of the land.

¹⁰Nevertheless, suffer us as we pray ye, to make an atonement, and moreover that we make a sacrifice of the TEA, and a burnt-offering of the ship,

the smoke blowing "onward towards the NORTH."²³

Meanwhile,

⁴⁷ there came another TEA SHIP from the land of Britain, and cast her anchor in the river of York, in the land of the Virginites, and the Sons of Liberty and the Virginia Rangers assembled themselves together, and the TEA and their TEA CHESTS ascended up in a pillar of fire and smoke, and vanished out of sight.

⁴⁸But the ship being innocent, and the owner thereof a righteous man, and knowing nought of the matter, for his sake therefore they suffered her to depart.

Leacock's framing identified Patriotic colonists with God's chosen people, casting these events as demonstrations of colonial virtue and unity, however unjust their actions may have seemed to locals and however divided Patriots and colonists were. This framing made the tea parties into a part of the struggle against the ministry worth chronicling. In such a cause, details (the *Virginia's* tea was drowned, not burned), hardly mattered.[24]

Leacock perpetuated Patriot myths about the *Peggy Stewart*: that the Maryland Patriots were unified, and that the ship owners destroyed their ship freely. Patriot newspapers whitewashed as much, but Leacock went a step further, casting these events as canonical acts of resistance and making the Patriot version canon.

The East India Company had not introduced tea to the colonies in 1773 nor forced tea upon them. Tea was not particularly bad for colonists' health, either. It is unlikely this hoodwinked too many colonists. Perhaps Gordon Wood's optimistic claim that "Propaganda could never move men to revolution" is right. It is hard to convince someone of something they know to be false, and one doubts anyone took up arms in 1775 because they thought the King was forcing the colonists to drink poisoned tea. But this sort of propaganda could have an emotional effect, making the tea drinker marginally more afraid for his health and marginally more likely to follow the Association. Channeling colonists' anger at the ministry toward tea made them less likely to consume it. In evoking fear and anger, Patriot propagandists called upon emotions that many colonists must have felt as they considered the crisis of 1774, giving tea propaganda an emotional truth.[25]

In addition to fear and anger, Patriots preyed upon one other emotion to get readers to boycott tea: pride. Only women, they told men, lacked the strength to boycott it.

CHAPTER 9

Tea's Sex

Tea and women were associated in different but muddled ways in the Revolution. In one way, tea was associated with women as a household good. It was part of women's daily lives, not because they drank it more than men but because women—slaves, servants, mothers, daughters, and wives—often bought tea for the household. With it they bought coffee and other necessities. They also prepared and served it. As a good in households managed by women, tea (like coffee) was part of women's daily lives and of women's history.

In the second way, Patriots created gendered propaganda around tea by making tea feminine. This was a story not about how women lived but how people ought to behave. Patriots thought the boycott required virtue. Virtue meant manly self-sacrifice, or at least self-restraint, for the common good—and though a platitude, "virtue" had meaning with tea. Women, thought to be emotional, weak-willed, and easily moved, were said to lack the self-control to stop drinking tea. This threatened the boycott. Such gendered thinking was hardly original, but Patriot writers played off it innovatively. Rather than bemoan women as weak, they mocked the men who refused to boycott tea as womanly. Patriots cast themselves as paragons of stoic restraint, emasculating Loyalists as effeminate. The Sons of Liberty and their angry mobs were passionate, but Patriot writers re-wrote noisy passion as quiet virtue. Men too reserved to join the Patriots were recast as weak and womanish. Patriotic women also spoke of their boycotting tea. Others asked: if women could give up tea, how weak were the men still drinking it?

Women's Tea Consumption

Despite the song at the beginning of this book, tea was not a particularly female drink. No data suggest that sex affected how much tea or coffee a colonist drank, and we have no reason, save perhaps present bias, to assume otherwise. Correlating tea with women risks buying into the gendered caricature. Tea was drunk socially. Both men and women both drank at tea parties and daily meals. It was served to visitors, shared with the household, and drunk alone. At all these times, men were as likely as women to have it.[1] In a household of means, the table would have a teapot and a coffee pot, and men and women drank from either.

As buyers and household managers, women controlled not just their personal consumption but household use generally. A woman, Pennsylvanian Sarah Mifflin explained, determined what was on her table and served to her family. Captain Chambers had planned to sell his tea to several women who entertained and managed large households in New York. Women were implied when Providence "Families" "discontinued" tea. The proposed December 1773 boycott agreement in South Carolina committed each signatory "him or herself" against "importing, buying, selling or using" tea, recognizing that women could be buyers, not just drinkers.[2]

Tea was prominent at female social events. In some colonies, drinking a cup with each of perhaps a dozen female well-wishers became part of the bride's post-wedding obligations. Charles Beatty recommended tea to his soon-to-be-married sister because the female sociability involved with it would help her make friends in her new home: "If you have tea you will have visitors enough, you will see every old wife in the neighbourhood each week, you will hear all the news that is stirring." More obviously, tea parties—in parlors, not harbors—were feminine affairs. But the existence of tea parties did not mean women drank more tea than men. Other drinks could be served (when Bedford, Rhode Island's Daughters of Liberty resolved against tea, they served a tisane). Men attended tea parties too. Hannah Griffitts noted that both sexes took tea, one getting "Sense," the other, "Politeness," from it. Tea parties were sites of "domesticity and women's sociability," but this sociability included men. Tea parties were feminine because women had social authority there. Female control of the tea table left it open to accusations of domestic frivolity: "idle chatter," gossip, and "tattle and chat," but the presence of gossip hardly meant the absence of men.[3]

Tea was also an important component of male sociability. Men could drink tea at taverns, pubs, and coffee houses. William Caswell did just this at a Philadelphia tavern. These were predominantly male places, where men's consumption did not necessarily have a female counterpart. Elihu Ashley's diary reveals the importance of tea-drinking in his socializing with other men: reverends, merchants, clerks, militia officers, and fellow doctors. Taverns and coffeehouses served more than tea, of course, and Ashley as his friends socialized over other drinks, too, like coffee and flip, but tea remained an important part of this male social world.[4]

The tea table could also serve as a place for courtship, which required men. A suitor, such as the New York man who sought to have "a dish of tea with some one of my female acquaintance," expected other women to be there. This reception was a chance for him to demonstrate gentility and refined conversation and for the women to evaluate him as a match. Ashley's diary frequently recorded groups of several young men and young women taking tea together during his courtship days (coffee or alcohol was also sometimes served). Similar courtship rituals, with young men drinking tea "with an agreeable circle of young ladies," occurred in Connecticut. The poem "A Lady's Adieu to Her Tea-Table" describes a "spruce Coxcomb" suitor at the tea table. Tea could be a part of courtship in other venues, too. "[Y]oung ladies and gentlemen" from New York and New Jersey went about on sleighs after a snowfall. With four people per sleigh and perhaps a dozen sleighs at a time, these "parties of pleasure" rode out "to dine and drink tea"—and court—in January 1775. At Batchelor's Hall, a venue north of Philadelphia on the Delaware River that served as a playground for the city's wealthy youth, "maidens were inveigled and deceived," as one moralist noted, at tea and dancing parties—hardly the stuff of women-only consumption.[5]

Teas served various social functions and men had various roles within them: suitors, family members, church members, neighbors, guests, and hosts. Pennsylvania diarist Hannah Callender Sansom noted "Daddy at tea" and "Daddy and John Thompson at tea" in 1772, as well as "tea at Unkle Robert Smiths." Cousin Catherine "Smith and I drank tea at Neigh[bor] Warners." New Yorker Samuel Seabury also offered tea to "my friendly neighbors when they come to see me." "Besides," he added, "I like a dish of tea too." Sansom went to teas with fellow church members—she noted teas following Quaker meetings. Some were female-only: a tea with "Aunt Fisher" before a meeting or afterward with Betsey Waln, Becky Shoemaker, and Sukey Waln. But Sansom's teas were not exclusively female. When, in September 1772, five women joined her for tea, she had "Daddy Sansom at tea," too.[6]

Men and women discussed tea in their diaries and letters in different ways. Few noted daily tea consumption. Women were more likely to note occasions: coffee klatches, teas, and dinners that were social or family events. These were ways for women to see friends and relatives, markers of women's lives and relationships. Household goods could be such markers, too. When Loyalists valued their estates for reimbursement from the British government after the war, men usually gave lump sums for home goods. Women, however, enumerated these items, implying a sentimental or personal value: a mahogany table, the tablecloth a sister had made, a tea service. This reflected how women, as homemakers, used and owned things. They gave cloth and household goods to other women in wills as gifts. These were products of their labor, heirlooms, holders of sentimental and economic value. For married sisters living apart, gathering for tea or coffee on their mother's tablecloth was worthy of note in diaries in a way that men meeting their regular friends at the tavern and perhaps having tea was not.[7]

Thus, between the time when the *Polly* turned back from Philadelphia in December 1773 and the Association's non-consumption order began in March 1775, Elizabeth Drinker recorded four outings where she "drank tea" with friends and family and four occasions when she drank coffee. The "family" "went to Frankford" and "had tea there," she wrote in August 1774. Sometimes she listed the attendees by name: S. Emlen and wife, Nancy Potts, Sally Parish and daughter Debby Mitchel, and Samuel Plesents "drank coffee with us" in January 1775. Likewise, in South Carolina Eliza Lucas Pinckney noted social calls with Mrs. William Henry Drayton (two teas in February 1775) but did not note tea consumption generally.[8] This meant that ordinary tea consumption went unnoted among the well-to-do and other social classes.

While Drinker and Pinckney noted tea's social value, neither noted its political importance in their discussion of tea visits in 1774 and early 1775, even though both families were at the epicenter of tea politics. Elizabeth Drinker's husband, Henry, and his partner, Abel James, were consignees for the Company tea on the *Polly* in 1773 and had endured political hardship for it. Elizabeth recorded teas with the Jameses but was silent about tea politics, perhaps because she did not accept the Association's authority over her (she also noted having teas while the Association was in effect). Pinckney, by contrast, was a powerful, educated, and independent Patriotic woman, mother to two Patriot statesmen, who took tea with Drayton, wife to a Patriot leader. Pinckney did not say why she stopped having teas; perhaps it was too obvious. Some women mentioned the reason clearly. Sarah Mifflin, wife of Thomas Mifflin, a major Pennsylvania merchant and Patriot leader, noted in mid-1775 that she had "not drank" tea "since last Christmas" because "parties of pleasure, tea-drinking and finery" had been sacrificed to the "great spirit of patriotism."[9] But Sarah Mifflin was the exception. Most women's diaries remained silent on the issue. For Pinckney and Drinker, the politics that affected their lives could go unstated in their diaries and letters.

Many male diarists and lettrists commented on tea drinking: John Andrews, John Adams, Nicholas Cresswell, Robert Honyman, Philip Vickers Fithian, George Washington, Landon Carter, and Charles Willson Peale. But they noted politically significant teas, not purely social or familial gatherings. Andrews joked that he had been drinking tea while listening to the Boston Tea Party. But presumably he had drunk tea on other occasions too banal to joke about; Adams opined that tea should be banned in July 1774. Did he note it because it was the first time he had tried to order tea since the Tea Party, or because he finally got a political response to his order? Cresswell documented the ban and Honyman and Fithian its violations, but they did not mention teas and coffees at other times when they lacked political significance. Carter mentioned a tea party celebrating the end of the tea boycott. Charles Willson Peale's diary entry noting a dish of tea with his family simply as part of their travels was an exception, as was George Washington noting tea with Mrs. Roberdeau—wife of a prominent area Patriot.[10] What the men omitted about tea was as significant as what they said: men were at Elizabeth Drinker's teas, and men went to family gatherings where tea was served, even if they failed to mention it.

Women in Tea Politics

Politics was not just a man's business. Women had been listening to political discussions at home for a decade. "Your husbands, your fathers, and all your dearest friends of the other sex, have no doubt frequently discussed, in your presence, this momentous point" of politics, wrote Virginia's women to the "Ladies of Pennsylvania." So women acted. They cooked for militia musters, made ammunition for the Powder Alarm, joined Patriotic mobs, and encouraged their men. Massachusetts women signed the Solemn League and Covenant. In Edenton, North Carolina, fifty-one women signed their support for their menfolk's resolves. The tea protests discussed in earlier chapters likely included women. Women participated in Charleston's Guy Fawkes Day parade and were part of the "numerous Concourse of People" who watched Robert Lindsay, Zephaniah Kingsley, and Robert Mackenzie toss their tea into Charleston harbor.[11]

Women wrote about tea politics. One Daughter of Liberty, writing in to the *Massachusetts Spy* about the Company tea, urged men, "Don't suffer any tea to land." Tea would "enslave ourselves and Posterity" if women drank it, "A Planter's Wife," thought. Women had to "forego the Use of all Foreign Tea" and "East-India Goods" out of "Regard for our Country," and for the sake of their "Fathers or Brethren, Husbands or Children" who would have to fight any war. For "A Planter's Wife" this was because women, like men, drank tea, and since tea was now political, men's and women's tea drinking was political, too.[12]

Women organized against tea. In August 1774, an "ADVERTISEMENT to the LADIES" appeared in the *South Carolina Gazette and Country Journal*. It announced an upcoming "Meeting" of "a Number of respectable ladies" "to converse and agree upon some general Plan of Conduct with Respect to the Article of TEA." Writing "To the LADIES of South Carolina" as "The HUSBAND of the PLANTER'S WIFE" (a deliberate inversion of who is married to whom), Reverend William Tennent III supported women's anti-tea organizing: "Associate—resolve—burn your tea;—refuse to buy any more. Your country will rise and call you blessed," and women will become "the Deliverers of their Country." In Wilmington, North Carolina, women publicly burned their tea. The Daughters of Liberty in Bedford, Rhode Island, announced their resolve not to "use nor suffer to be used in their houses" duted tea. They would "bid adieu to India stuff/ Before we'll lose our liberty." "We . . . Promise, from this day forth, to reject, and totally renounce" tea, the South Carolinian "Andromache" replied to A Planter's Wife. "[F]riendly Visits" among women would spread the word of the tealess party, and she hoped women would canvass the town "to obtain the Assent of every Mistress of a family" to disuse tea.[13]

By mid-August 1774, the *South Carolina Gazette* reported that the town's "Ladies" had formed an "Association, and are subscribing to it very fast." The Association, reprinted in the South Carolina papers, aspired to "a total Disuse of East-India-Teas" to avoid the "Ruin" of "our Country" and to protect "the Lives of our Fathers" and "the Liberty of our Posterity." Signers promised immediately not to "purchase or buy" any tea (women's primary connection to tea) and, from November on, not to serve or drink it, "counting any little Self-Denial, we may meet with in our Adherence to these Resolutions, as our Pleasure and Glory in the Cause of our Country."[14]

The tea boycott was a "watershed" in women's political consciousness and engagement, and in the public recognition of women's political role, particularly in Southern newspapers, where women's political writing appeared for the first time (Daughters of Liberty had already sent items into northern newspapers earlier in the imperial crisis). Women engaged in an informed and "intelligent public discourse" in an otherwise-male medium. Women wrote to other women about women's roles in politics.[15]

"A Planter's Wife" had written to the *South Carolina Gazette and Country Journal* in July 1774, drawing Charleston women to tea politics and bringing on the townswomen's boycott. Writing to her "Sisters and Countrywomen," she argued that tea was a matter "chiefly" for "our sex" because women's decisions whether to serve, boycott, or burn tea affected the whole household. "Every Mistress of a Family, may prohibit the Use of Tea and East-India Goods in her Family and among her Children." This was an act of "Self-Denial, and public virtue" which "many respectable Families" in Charleston, led by their ladies, had already done. More needed to. This was not a time for women to "be tame Spectators."[16]

"Andromache" replied. She thanked A Planter's Wife for encouraging "Ladies of my Acquaintance" to "rouse from this shameful Stuper" and banish tea from their homes. The boycott was a "Test of our Obedience, our Love, and that Gratitude we owe" men. It required women be political. "I dare answer there will not be found among us, one EVE, who, after Promise . . . [would] touch the forbidden fruit," bring "Infamy" on women, and doom the future. Nor would Charleston's women be Jezebels who misled their husbands. They would be like Esther: the good and Godly wife who protected her husband and saved her people. Andromache had chosen her examples carefully. Eve, Jezebel, and Esther had power because they influenced men: to Andromache, women's choices mattered because women made men's minds for them. As went Eve, so went Adam. Jezebel's man Ahab was "weak and wrongheaded," and Charleston men were as easily led. As planter's wives, Charleston ladies had a political role. Like Esther, they could whisper in their husbands' ears or let the King's ministers destroy their people instead.[17]

Some writers also began to refer, as A Planter's Wife had, to "Countrywomen"—a term that placed women in the polity and evoked the more common "countrymen." Virginia women wrote a "sisterly" open letter to their "countrywomen," the "Ladies of Pennsylvania," urging "public virtue" (a manly trait) to "banish *India tea* from your tables," drink "aromatic herbs," and "cooperate with" men in resisting Parliament. The "fair sex of . . . all America, will be so" "instrumental" in any "redress," that history would be "filled with their praises, and teach posterity to venerate their virtues." The Husband of the Planter's Wife agreed, "Have you the Soul of Englishwomen?" If so, give up tea "for *your* Country"—not for their husbands' country, but their own.[18]

Class, Women, and Tea

Such discourse confined the polity to the upper classes, leveraging conservative class norms to broaden the polity by gender. In this reading, politics was a matter for women who did not have to work, who had time and money for an education (implied in the classical name, "Andromache"), and whose menfolk were property owners (and may not have had to work either). A Planter's Wife was not a cooper's wife and most certainly not a slave or woman of color.[19] Thus while writers used many terms: "sisters," "fair sex," and "your sex," they constantly returned to "lady." A Planter's Wife addressed the town's "ladies." "A Lady's Adieu to her Tea Table," the poem "Written by a LADY, on receiving a handsome Set of TEA CHINA," the "advertisement to the ladies" organizing an anti-tea meeting in Charleston—the term was ubiquitous. Andromache wrote of the "uncommon . . . Ease and Affluence," of South Carolina ladies' social calls, and of their travels in "Chariots." Affluent women traveled in season between Charleston and country plantations with children, extended family, slaves, and servants and entertained a constant stream of visitors. When genteel women banned tea from their tables, they also chose not to serve it to dozens of others. In Pennsylvania, "ladies and gentlemen" referred to households of urban merchants and officials above the hoi polloi—merchant's wives like Sarah Mifflin and Elizabeth Drinker, not cooper's wives, either.[20] The calls to politics for elite women followed the same class norms as for elite men: planters in the Carolinas, Quakers and merchants in Philadelphia. Where ladies led, it was expected common women would follow.

There was a gap between talk of tea as an upper-class item and its generic reality. Tea and the tea table were associated with gentility and refinement. "A Lady's Adieu to her Tea Table" recites the "gaudy attire" of the tea table, its chinaware and equipage, the "pretty" tea "chest that so lately did shine," and the "spruce" guests. Affluent hosts displayed imported finery: mahogany tables, special cloths, and silver services. But alternatives existed for the middling sort: mahogany veneers, homespun cloths, and pewter services. The "Adieu" portrayed an upper-class ideal that may have existed more in colonists' minds than in their daily lives. Housemaids drank tea as well as their ladies.[21] Middling colonists commonly had tea at breakfast. Tea consumption had spread to people who might drink bohea in earthenware even as elites drank hyson in porcelain.

The association of tea with refinement gave tea a class and a gender. By focusing on the high consumerism of elite tea parties and ignoring the bulk of tea consumption among common people, Patriot propagandists disassociated tea from everyday life (in which it was unobtrusive). They associated it with luxury, idleness, and a lack of resolve—a caricature of weak-willed Tory elites. Thus Peter Thatcher, giving the first wartime Boston Massacre oration, could say the British had given in to "luxury which effeminates the mind and body" and exhort colonists to cling to their guns, their boycotts, and their manly virtue.[22]

Gendering Tea

Gender was a key thrust of the Patriot propaganda campaign against tea. Patriots were genuinely concerned about the supposed female weakness for tea. Some women writers pushed back against this. Others—both men and women—wrote under female bylines to talk about the female effort to give up tea. These writers exhorted women to give up tea and emasculated the men who had not. But the exhortation not to drink tea was driven by a concern that women and men still did.

Tea became gendered in the eighteenth century through its association with women-run tea parties and home life, based on which some describe women as the main tea drinkers. Englishman Nicholas Cresswell thought Alexandria, Virginia's "ladies seem very sad about" the "last day Tea is allowed to be drank on the Continent." Connecticut Congressman Oliver Wolcott hoped "The Ladys" could "make themselves contented to live without Tea for the good of their Country," and after Congress allowed tea explained that Congress had "permitted the Ladys to drink" it (for who else would?). Tea was a weakness and women, the weaker sex, gave in to it. Poetess Mercy Otis Warren pondered "weak" women asking why they should give up "female ornaments." Such women considered the "finest muslins that fair India boasts, And the choice herbage from Chinesan coasts" their "sex's due." She imagined Boston's tea going into the harbor and she-nymphs fighting over it, a metaphor for women's ambivalence toward a boycott. Warren was pessimistic about whether women could sustain a boycott, so much so that in 1790 an editor had to explain that Warren's "opinion of the equity" of the Tea Party was not to be found in her Toryesque view of its success.[23]

Wolcott's idea that men let women have tea was a handy conceit. It positioned men as chivalrous heads of households indulging their women. During prohibition, Reading Beatty hoped Enoch Green would "*allow*" his wife tea.[24] Given that tea was brewed and served by the pot, this obscured what the men were doing: indulging themselves by allowing women, as mistresses of the table, to pour tea for everyone.

To characterize tea as a women's problem could be to call upon women to become political to fix it. "If the Ladies in America will agree to use no More

East India tea," Rev. William Tennent III wrote, their men will be saved. Else they would fell men with their womanish sin: for women's "trivial Pleasure" in tea was taken "at the Expense of the Liberties" of their men. "Will any Female American indulge herself in so trifling an Amusement at the Danger of the Lives and Liberties of all she holds dear?" The ministry believes that "rather than give up their darling Tea Dish Ceremony, you will suffer this Empire to be enslaved, and your Husbands Throats to be cut." "My dear Ladies, have you any Spirit? . . . If you thought you could do any Thing to save your Country, I'm sure you would do it . . . if you will only deny yourselves—what? . . . Only a meer" dish of tea. "All America is threatened with a Deluge of Blood from this accursed Tea." It was tea that had caused the port of Boston to be shut, the Administration of Justice Act (aka the "Murder Act") to be passed, armies to be sent to North America "to put you to death if you oppose" them. "I cannot think you so divested of all love to your Country," Tennent told women, as to drink tea. Tea is the "*Hinge* on which our Freedom turns." "Every Ounce of Tea you buy, will I fear be paid for by the Blood of your Sons." Show "American Patriotism extends even to the Fair Sex." Tennent's writing was "obvious hyperbole," but so were all the other evocations of streets running with blood and conspiracies to enslave the populace penned in 1774—the difference was that Tennent thought women could do something about it.[25]

Tennent thought women were stupid. He was over-the-top to be sure women got the point. He was not alone. David Ramsay likewise explained that tea was an "engine of slavery." Parliament offered "Tea, chains and military law." Buying tea constituted "high treason against three million Americans." (A comment that was as much an offense to logic as to math.) A "guardian" spirit had warned colonists against tea: "Taste not the forbidden fruit, for in the day ye eat thereof, ye shall surely die." To be forgetful about the politics of tea now was, well, womanish. Ramsay fretted that "Here and there a silly Eve, regardless of her countries call, stretches forth her unthinking hand, and receives the accursed herb with all its baneful attendants."[26]

Ramsay solved the problem of "silly" and "unthinking" women by explaining tea in terms of beauty and babies, topics he thought women would understand. Stop drinking tea, oh "young and fair," to "attract the notice of the other sex." It "will either suffuse your faces with a deadly paleness, or what is worse, with a sallow hue, to the upper exclusion of the lovely red." And it will endanger the fetus, too. Claims that tea impaired looks were old. In 1737 the *New-England Weekly Journal* alleged that tea contained "Bile"; dried women's faces; "shrivels their Skin"; and caused "Wrinkles" and "Deformity"; but now there were political reasons to repeat this. It is unclear who believed them given tea's prominent role in courtship.[27]

The cartoon *The Able Doctor* gendered tea, too. The image inspired a poem in the *South Carolina Gazette and Country Journal* as South Carolinians were discussing a boycott. The poet reinterpreted the scene from rape to rape resisted, and at least one colonial printing of the cartoon retitled the image "Persevering Americans," to emphasize this. Resistance connoted virtue both in the sense of male politics and female sexual purity. Faced with North's teapot, the virtuous woman did not lie back and think of England; she fought back. Such resistance was dangerous: "because, her Virtue does refuse / Her Country's Poison" "they do her abuse" more. But America virtuously spat the tea back at her assailants anyway—and such perseverance "alone can bring t' our Country Joy." The poet encouraged colonial women to spit out their tea, too. It is "such like her who may our Freedom save / And such, alone" who "are loyal, virtuous, brave." Tea abstainers were the good, unsullied women whom good men would "Love." Tea drinkers, by contrast, were treacherous, craven, cowardly, despoiled, and unloved.[28]

One wonders how compelling women found this. Nominally about women, the poem was by and for men. Much of what survives from the anti-tea campaign comes from male-dominated venues. Newspapers were aimed at male readers. They focused on either politics or business, male subjects. Newspapers included off-color doggerel not just on rape, but on "bigot Papists," pregnant slaves, dead prostitutes, dead Jews, and so on.[29] These were not topics to be discussed in mixed company, let alone at tea parties, but ribaldry meant to be read aloud in male-dominated taverns or coffee shops.

Resisting Gendering

Some Patriotic women argued against the gendering of tea. A Planter's Wife lamented that tea drinking was considered a sign of women's "Vanity, Ambition, and Pride" and not men's. "Don't cast reflections on our sex / Because the weaker sort we be," wrote a member of the Bedford, Rhode Island Daughters of Liberty, "We'll fight it out with courage free / Before we'll lose our liberty." "[M]any unjust Reflections have been cast on us," wrote Andromache. "Our Countrymen have . . . been told, that their greatest Enemies are those of their own Houses, and scruple not to affirm, that their Wives and Daughters" broke the last boycott "and will, most certainly be the Cause of this" one breaking too. But Patriotic women would give the lie to tea's gendering. "We have now an Opportunity to manifest the Fallacy of the Invidious Insinuation, or forever lye under the Imputation of it." For all her pessimism about women's resolve, Mercy Otis Warren thought no higher of men: "Few

manly bosoms feel a nobler flame" than the women who "round folly's vor-
tex play." This left resistance to the few "good Cornelias" and "worthy men"
who would "fight for freedom, and for virtue bleed."[30]

A tea merchant wrote the best riposte to the gendering of tea. William Beadle, whose puckish advert about the Boston Tea Party was noted previously,
satirized the gendering of tea in his tea advertisement "Addressed to the LA-
DIES." Beadle recapitulated the notion that tea was feminine. "Fair Ladies,"
he wrote in early 1775, "'tis not very arch, / To talk about the first of March, /
That woful day, when each of ye, / Must leave your darling Nectar, *TEA!*"
Poor Beadle still had "a hundred Weight, or so" and asked his female readers
to "buy" up his tea before the Association began. Having asked the "LADIES"
to buy, he joked about the stock they might still leave in his shop. "Yet stop a
moment! on my Life! / For now I think on't I've a Wife! / And if she proves
of Eve the Daughter, / To have a Kind of Hank'ring after / This noxious Herb,"
how could he save her? Would not the she-fiend crave her fix, find "Ax or
Hatchet," and "lay on, / With Arm and Will, both bold and stout," open crates
and "find this potent Poison out"? "[H]elp us," Beadle begged his female buyers, "keep our virtue sound / And quickly purchase" every pound.[31]

What did Patriots make of this? Beadle himself had made a public donation
to Boston relief the previous year. That, and the poem's promise that Beadle was
"no Tory" and would "obey" Congress, created space for jest. Did women, buying tea for pharisaical men who blamed women for their own tea drinking,
warm to his mockery of male claims of female "addiction"? Beadle must
have hoped they would, for his poem strikes at the double meaning of tea
consumption—consumption as buying and consumption as drinking—behind
which the slippery idea of a special female taste for tea hid. Beadle, a shopkeeper,
knew women did the buying and appealed to them on this ground, mocking the
idea that they had a special thirst for tea to curry favor with them as shoppers.
His ad had a final irony: though his wife Lydia went crazy with the ax in his
poem, it would be Beadle who, impoverished by the Association, the Patriots'
ever-debasing paper currency, and the war, ultimately snapped, tragically slaugh-
tering his family in 1782 with two pistols, a carving knife, and an ax.[32] They were
causalities of wartime economics, hyperinflation, and maybe tea politics.

Rhetorical Femininity

Many anti-tea essays had female bylines, whether the author was female or
not. "Rhetorical femininity," as Tedra Osell calls this, was hardly new: Benjamin
Franklin wrote as "Silence Dogood" in 1722. The use of female pseudonyms

was an established practice in the British press. Male and female writers both used female "masks." In the colonies, rhetorical women defended tea as healthier than alcohol in the 1720s and 1730s and attacked George Whitfield and the Great Awakening in the 1740s. Both issues combined gender and politics and turned on the blurred boundary between private and public life. Masks obscured authors and presented women as archetypes. Bylines like Silence Dogood, A Planter's Wife, or, as in one 1773 article, "Hannah Hopeful, Sarah Faithful, Mary Truth and Abigail Trust," deployed the authors' female virtue "as a policing force" upon women and men.[33]

Readers recognized pennames as guises. David Ramsay's female voice in his "Sermon on Tea" was blatantly inconsistent; perhaps the pretense was too obvious to bother maintaining. Seeing a female byline, readers often assumed the real author was a man. Nevertheless, rhetorical femininity was useful. The female voice provided another way to address the tea question, as women urging other women to abstain could take a different tone than men urging each other not to drink tea. Male and female authors gained power with anonymous and abstract pseudonyms: "A Lady" was every lady rather than one in particular. Male authors also found the rhetorical value of speaking for a larger group attractive, whether writing as a "Lady" or, as Samuel Seabury and John Dickinson, as "farmers." Rhetorical femininity included real and imaginary women, which makes a tally of female writers difficult. But their gendered discussion of expected male and female behavior mattered regardless of who wrote it.[34]

"A Lady's Adieu to Her Tea-Table" was an idealized portrait of gender norms. The woman lived in domestic refinement, listening to and learning from her man. She was "taught"—by her husband—"(and believe it is fact), / That our ruin is aimed in the late act" (the Tea Act). Enlightened, she bade "FAREWELL" to tea. She swore to "die in the cause" before drinking more, for "we" women "can quit when we please." The author of a poem "Written by a LADY, on receiving a handsome Set of TEA CHINA" regarded her tea set with "Horrour" and swore to "resign" it. Both poems were didactic and demonstrative, their purported authors' archetypes modeling renunciation. By contrast, the essay "Arabella's Complaint," written in the voice of a nagging wife, satirized female desire for tea to encourage women to stick to the boycott. Arabella's question to Congress—"are we forever to be debarred the use of *India* Teas!"—was made shrewish to encourage women who thought this way to hold their tongues.[35]

Whether such strategies succeeded is another question. Exhortation is no proof anyone listened. The "Adieu" appeared in January 1774 after the Boston Tea Party; Virginians did not broadly renounce tea until May. In South Carolina, Patriotic women like Eliza Pinckney and Mrs. William Henry Drayton consumed tea until just before the Association began.[36]

Emasculating with Tea

When Patriots associated tea with women, they often effeminized it to target men. The gendering of tea was a running gag with which men might mock one another by charging effeminacy into abstention. Patriots emasculated male tea drinkers with rhetorical women in a morality tale for, by, and about men. Tea was thus an "evening dish" for women who sat at their "tea-table" (a feminized space) and gossiped—allegedly a female habit. The boycott against tea, according to David Ramsay, faced "a female army" of tea drinkers driven "entirely" by womanish "whim and pride." The *Pennsylvania Journal* ran a mock petition on March 1, 1775, in which "Diverse OLD WOMEN," including "old women of the male gender," requested an exemption from non-consumption. "A Physician" warned the *Newport Mercury* that because of tea "The Bodies of men are enfeebled and enervated" and "hysterics [an affliction of the womb], which used to be peculiar to the women . . . now attack both sexes indiscriminately." Ramsay agreed that tea drinking caused "Histeria" in both sexes and had "reduced the robust masculine habit of men, to a feminine softness." "[I]t has turned the men into women, and the women into—God knows what."[37]

Patriots thought there was something androgynous about moderates who lacked the stuff to stand up for their country. When Middlesex, Virginia Patriots failed to resolve against the Coercive Acts as others had in 1774, one writer punned, "when a number of such creatures, / With womens hearts, and manly features, / Their country's gen'rous schemes perplex, / I own, I hate this MIDDLE-SEX." Such were the "hegemonic norms" of the "grammar of manhood" that Patriots applied to the Revolution. Patriots who conceived of the Revolution in terms of manly strength and virtue versus female indolence, "Luxury and Dissipation" saw tea as part of the world of virtue-less cuckolds and ministerial sybarites, whom real men resisted.[38]

George Washington explained that the Revolution tested whether Americans would "act like men." Manliness might mean, as in the epigraph for this book, defending "our girls and wives" against the King's attempt "to force" them to drink tea. It meant abstaining oneself. Women shamed men who bought tea anyway. In Bedford, Rhode Island, the Sons of Liberty threatened to hand a tea buyer over to the Daughters of Liberty if he did not give his tea up first, for which the Daughters mocked him in the press. There was also the story about virtuous Sarah Boudinot, who, when offered tea by Governor Franklin of New Jersey, tossed the tea out the window: a royal governor shown true grit by a girl. Such incidents were not far removed from the skimmingtons that publicly shamed men who violated matrimonial norms. Women were, as Al Young describes, "exhorters" of men not to drink tea, just as their presence in mobs and riots exhorted or humiliated the mob's target.[39] Patriots made women into rhetorical tools for keeping men in their place.

Women's success in giving up tea was an effective tool, too. The emasculating contrast between the Bedford Daughters of Liberty—who had boycotted tea—and the weaselly little man caught buying it was plain enough. Patriots announced that in response to the Association, Wilmington, North Carolina's "Ladies . . . entirely declined the use of Tea" by March 1775. Their natural weakness made this a "sacrifice by the fair Sex," which "should inspire" men to have at least as much "firmness and public virtue" as their wives (helpfully, the townswomen had already burned some of their husbands' tea for them). In Providence, the women who burned their tea were "worthy" and had "Conviction," meaning men who still drank it were unworthy and irresolute.[40]

Tea itself could be given a gender, as in the campy Patriot description of tea as a prostitute. Thus, "the Funeral of Madam Souchong":

> She came into this Colony about 40 Years ago, and hath been greatly caressed by all Ranks. She lived in Reputation for several Years, but at length became a common Prostitute among the lowest Class of People. She became very poor, and her Price was so lowered that any One might have her Company for almost nothing. The Quality deserted her, and by hard Living in Log Houses and Wigwams, her Health was impaired. Broken Spirits and Hystericks seized her, and she died on the first Day of March 1775, at Midnight.[41]

The "Funeral" implied that female tea drinkers were loose, unlike the "worthy women" who burned tea. It implied that tea was filthy and that men dirtied themselves when they touched it. It implied that tea was widely consumed, even on the frontier. And, by making tea a woman, it made men the consumers who mattered, the ones who might "have her Company for almost nothing" and therefore needed virtue to resist. Tea was a woman because men wanted her.

Madame Souchong's obituary appeared in Rhode Island and Virginia newspapers, ribaldry to be read to the boys in the tavern. It was, to its audience, hilarious: is there a more perfectly misogynistic joke than one about a dead whore read aloud in the pub while the village prostitute is listening? She died implicitly by disease and explicitly by hysteria. Some said tea caused hysteria;

others blamed a lack of sex. The straightforward reading was that the dirty old hag went crazy and died because men would not touch her anymore: men "deserted" her and left her in "Broken Spirits," which killed her.

Loyalists

Loyalists deployed gendered rhetoric around tea, too. The caricature of women yearning for tea could even facilitate the subversion of the Association. When Concord, Massachusetts adopted the Association in January 1775, heads of family (including two single women) signed. Stephen Hosmer, by contrast, signed on condition he was permitted "tea for his wife only."[42]

Samuel Seabury played upon the theme of men protecting and providing for women. He deemed the Patriots scrubs for denying men "a dish of tea to please our wives." "I hate to stint my wife and daughters," he wrote, flinging the caricature of the woman tea drinker back at Congress. Colonists, Seabury warned, would have you "open your doors to" peeping committeemen, "let them examine your tea-cannisters, and molasses-jugs, and your wives and daughters petty-coats." Susanna Wright struck a similar note when she asked how Congress could be "so cruel to the whole female World, to debar them so totally of their favourite Potation?"[43] Patriots could be made out as a threat to women.

"PENELOPE House-Wife" implied Patriots were effete abusers in her letter to her "dear Country Women" in the *Norfolk Intelligencer*. Her "poor deluded" "patriotic Husband" "has broken all the cups, and denies his family their accustomed use of Tea for breakfast." What had he done? Tea was the mark of "civilization." She could not fault a "social cup" among "well-bred" people. She thought the men who declined tea on political grounds suffered a "sentimental delicatesse," and she urged young women not to marry such men. Penelope also claimed to oppose "arbitrary power:"

> But you know, my dear country women, that there are tyrants at the head of little families as well as at the head of great empires; and I always thought that our sex have an undoubted right to carry their resistance as great lengths, if needful, in opposition to domestic tyranny in the one instance, as the men pretend to, in their opposition to state tyranny in the other.

She would elaborate, but hush, the Patriotic brute she married was coming home, so she had to stop.[44]

Other British and Loyalist writers saw women participating in politics as a world turned upside down. One mock letter, appearing in New England and

FIGURE 9.1. Philip Dawe, *A Society of Patriotic Ladies, at Edenton in North Carolina*, 1775. There was no actual Edenton Tea Party, but Philip Dawe's image has made many imagine there was. This is a comic imagining of what the absurd (to Dawe) idea of women in politics looked like. Source: Library of Congress, Prints and Photographs Division, Cartoon Prints, British.

London, pretended to be from the "Daughters of Liberty." Aware that hanging, drawing, and quartering were punishments against high treason, these women were "determined, constantly to assemble at each other's Houses, to HANG the Tea-Kettles, DRAW the Tea, and QUARTER the Toast." For engraver Philip Dawe, a pupil of William Hogarth, political women were nightmarish, fantastic, and silly. In "A Society of Patriotic Ladies" (1775, see figure 9.1), Dawe depicted Edenton women's non-importation agreement as a topsy-turvy world: mannish women, ugly hags, loose ladies, neglected children, even a slave seems to want to join—but the most absurd act, the one Dawe drew front and center, was women signing a boycott. Dawe's women could not control themselves: they sign, dump out their tea canisters, then drink from a giant bowl of tea in the back. They act like animals, hardly better than the dog urinating on a tea canister in the front. The print is didactic and absurd, evoking Hieronymus Bosch, and mocks the Patriot movement by suggesting it was so silly, women joined it. Dawe's "Alternative of Williamsburg" showed black men and white women among the Patriot boycotters, similarly delegitimizing Patriot opposition, casting it as a commoners' charivari, not real politics. Edenton's women did not actually mention tea in their association—it was a generalized non-importation agreement, not specific to tea (the Edenton Tea Party, as it was later called, was a misnomer). But Britons, reading the Edenton agreement, assumed it must have been about tea, hence Dawe's joke. Contemporary Arthur Iredell assumed it was a "protest agst Tea Drinking." "Is there a female congress at Edenton, too?" he laughed—for if congresses were low enough for women to join, that would be hilarious. In *A Dialogue between a Southern Delegate and His Spouse* (1774), James Rivington emasculated Congress further: he described women as knowing better than their husbands and Patriots as contemptible because they were below their women.[45]

Colonial women consumed tea at the same levels their menfolk did. And they engaged in tea politics. Tea fit into a complex array of gender and class roles. These roles gave tea drinking rhetorical power: one could uphold examples of female abstention, attack men who drank tea for having less virtue than their sisters, or admonish Patriots who deprived women of tea as ungentlemanly. These discussions of women's abstention were part of the propaganda attempt to get women and men to abandon the drink and make prohibition possible.

PART THREE

The Tea Ban

March 1, 1775–April 13, 1776

CHAPTER 10

Prohibition as Conformity

On March 1, 1775, the prohibition on tea consumption came into force. The next day Providence Patriots held a rally, calling townsfolk to burn "evil" tea and "testify to their good Disposition" toward Patriot authority. Patriots claimed a "great Number" burned "free-will" tea offerings in "Cheerfulness." They also burned Loyalist newspapers and copies of a speech by Lord North. Tea was "detrimental to our Liberty, Interest, and Health." And so a "spirited Son of Liberty" ran down the street and covered "the Word TEA on the Shop Signs" with "Lampblack."[1]

In Connecticut, the Stamford committee executed a tea chest. Sylvanus Whitney confessed in June 1775 to the "crime" of buying and selling tea. The committee "passed sentence against him." A "grand procession" with a "guard under arms," "the unfortunate Tea hung across a pole, sustained by two unarmed soldiers," and the committee just behind, marched to a gallows. Spectators, drums, and fifes followed. There, in front of "Mr. Weed's" tavern, a hangman tied the chest to a noose and dropped it through the trapdoor while Whitney "behaved himself" and watched. He fled to New Brunswick after the war.[2]

These events were enforcement theater, reminding colonists where their Patriotic duties lay. The Providence show announced tea and Loyalist writings were forbidden, invited townsfolk to agree, and made the ban look effective. It did this a second time as printers ran the Providence committee's press release about it. Printers in other towns re-ran the story, and so by placing the story in the *Providence Gazette*, Patriots spread the story as far as Virginia.[3] A story about burning newspapers, submitted to a newspaper, also sent a message about the virtue of self-censorship. And so the Patriot version of this event became the only one. Most Rhode Islanders, and even more Virginians, would not know whether the tea burners were truly cheerful, or whether colonists attended for the "right" reasons.

We might ask the same questions about the events in Providence and Stamford that we asked of the Charleston Pope's Day celebration. Why was there tea left to burn? Did the "execution" put off Whitney's buyers? Did Providence colonists burn all their tea? Notably, just before the burning, the Providence committee had to "remind" the public "not to purchase or use East India tea." Were there other reasons colonists might show up? (The Stamford tea was the tea that had to be burned after hanging to protect it from "Tea-lovers.") Who went to these rallies because they were believers, and who went just to be seen? (From the over-the-top action and pun in the tavern's name, one might wonder whether the Stamford story was a Loyalist satire of Patriot excess. But the tavern, and the story, were real.)[4]

Prohibition appeared successful. And surely many colonists did give up tea. "There is no more tea to be drank here, but very good coffee," wrote one correspondent from Annapolis at the beginning of non-importation. Robert Honyman, who traveled between Virginia and Boston in March and April 1775, found that only in Newport was tea "commonly & publickly drank," and even there the committee was "striving to abolish the use of it." Shortly after Honyman's visit, the committee succeeded. In Annapolis, Philadelphia, New York, and Boston, Honyman could get coffee publicly but not tea.[5] Nearly all newspaper advertisers stopped listing tea after March 1, 1775. But appearances could be deceiving. Honyman's emphasis on drinking tea "publickly" reminds us that such activities, like tea burnings and tea advertisements, were performances and may not have had a direct bearing on private behavior.

Between March 1, 1775 and April 13, 1776, Patriots promoted the Association enthusiastically. They signed colonists up to the Association in a continent-wide signature campaign. Conformity to the sumptuary provisions of the Association were important indicators of political belief, but Patriots prioritized getting colonists to say they supported the Association (taking it as support for Patriot authority) over checking whether they obeyed it. The Association became a public pledge of allegiance, while Patriots took a don't-ask-don't-tell approach toward private consumer behavior. Patriots came down hardest on public disapproval of their cause or material support for the King's troops, not consumer violations. Enforcement prioritized tea dealers over consumers. Enforcement also prioritized repentance: even major infractions could be forgiven if the violator asked for forgiveness and accepted committee authority. This prioritization of the Association as public rhetoric rather than private reality went hand-in-hand with censoring the press and policing the mail. The public story of tea in 1775 emerged from this environment of censorship, propaganda, and persuasion, which, by its nature, was divorced from lived experience.

Signing Patriotism

With Parliament unmovable and local committees forming, the Association became a means to mobilize the public and assert local Patriot authority rather than to strong-arm Britain. The Association prohibited colonists from buying, selling, or using any tea or British goods. It encouraged frugality and discouraged gambling, plays, and other "expensive diversions." It limited mourning dress at funerals. Like the ban on horse races, the ban on Dutch tea did not affect merchants in Britain, though it did imply the belt-tightening that the boycott was assumed to require. More importantly, signing was, according to James Madison, "the method used among us to distinguish friends from foes." Catharine Crary describes signing as "the most significant early touchstone" for political sympathies after March 1, 1775, forcing a "crisis of allegiance."[6] Yet the extent to which it changed minds or simply encouraged virtue-signaling and conformity is less clear.

Committees went door-to-door asking colonists to sign. Thus the Wilmington, North Carolina committee went out "in a body, to the several house keepers and traders in town," ensuring the Association "was signed by all those of any note." In Pennsylvania, the Cumberland County committee sent one hundred men to collect signatures. In Virginia, as voters and candidates looked on, copies were signed at elections. The Albemarle committee sent militia captains to collect signatures, letting residents say "yes" or "no" to men with guns. Continent-wide, over 7,000 men served on committees or in provincial congresses in the spring of 1775, a sizable number of potential door-knockers.[7]

Signatures were coerced by violence, threats, the shunning of non-signers, and the boycott of their trade. As James Parker, a Loyalist Virginia storekeeper, explained, anyone who refused to sign risked being "delivered over" to a mob. The "furious" Maine mob, which Jacob Bailey encountered, compelled "people, by force of arms, to sign the solemn league." The governor of Georgia thought "Great Numbers have been Intimidated to Sign." "Every body," according to one South Carolina Loyalist, "was obliged to temporize." Virginia merchant

William Allason signed "not from any conviction, but from notions of self-preservation with peace and quietness." Henry Hulton explained, "Many, to save themselves & families from destruction, signed to any articles that were imposed upon them." Philadelphia merchant son James Allen admitted, "My inducement principally to join them is that a man is suspected who does not."[8]

Signing indicated consent to be governed by Patriot authorities, not necessarily agreement with Patriot policy. It was a "statement" of "communal solidarity." Even Congressmen James Duane (New York) and Joseph Galloway (Pennsylvania) disagreed with the Association but signed it to maintain the appearance of "consensus" and the "extraordinary unanimity" of the Continental Congress.[9] Householders looked at a signature sheet and noticed names of people they knew, realizing the presence or absence of their names would be noticed by neighbors in turn. How can we expect them to do differently than Duane and Galloway?

This was conformity, not a "drive for unity achieved through consent." Consider Concord, Massachusetts. The Concord town meeting had approved the Solemn League and Covenant in June 1774. Town leaders "offered" the covenant for townsmen to sign, and about 80 percent did. In September, a mass meeting forced "every person suspected of being a *tory*" (and not signing in June would have been suspicious) "to pass the ordeal of a trial" on the town common. "If found guilty, he was compelled to endure such punishment as an excited multitude might inflict." The town historian called this "humbling the tories." In November, Concord residents approved the Association unanimously in a town meeting—unanimously because the Tories were too humbled to speak. Not all Concordians agreed: revolutionaries had to extend the signing deadline three times to collect all signatures. Ultimately three Concordians refused. On the eve of battle, a government spy asked Patriot authorities whether there were many Loyalists in town. "The answer was," he reported, "they expected there were, but *not openly*." Signing campaigns worked to persuade. Colonists said they were persuaded, but such conformity was a performative kind of consensus.[10]

Colonists on both sides wondered whether there was a "shy Tory" effect. Had all the merchants signed, asked one Patriot? "If they have, I would ask if it is not through compulsion?" One Tory writer wrote of coerced consent, "I shall ever look upon some of those propositions as containing my tar and feathers sentiments, and no farther."[11] Yet even conformity gave Patriots power. And Patriots offered those who acquiesced and signed a good deal: in exchange for public obedience, Patriots left them alone in private.

The committees' concern for public allegiance was part of their concern to uphold their shadow governments' honor and authority. As James Parker termed it, Congress's Association was an "American Constitution," which legitimated the committees. These, in circular fashion, legitimated Congress.[12] Committees responded forcefully to public defiance, concerned that colonists who refused to sign in the face of threats were rejecting the entire architecture of Patriot legitimacy. Thus the committees punished two infractions above all: slander of the committees and open noncompliance toward their diktats.

In July 1775, the mariner John Hopkins drank "Damnation to America" in Savannah and found himself tarred and feathered, carted about, and threatened with a hanging unless he drank "Damnation to all Tories and Success to American Liberty." The problem was not Hopkins's Loyalism, but how he went about it: he "behaved disrespectfully" toward Patriots. Had he simply kept his mouth shut, Patriots probably would have left him alone. The Connecticut General Assembly focused on colonists who "contravene or defame . . . the Resolves of the Hon^le Continental Congress or the Acts of the Gen^al Assembly," especially people accused of calling Congress "Rebels & Traitors" (which was true on its face, but amounted to revolutionary lèse-majesté), who claimed they "would not pay Obedience," or who attacked the assembly as "unconstitutional and oppressive." Patriots punished "speech crimes" with tar and feathers in the spring and summer of 1775 in New York, New Jersey, Pennsylvania, Maryland, Virginia, and South Carolina. As the New York provincial congress explained, "Although this Congress have a tender regard for freedom of speech, the rights of conscience, and personal liberty," anyone denying its authority would be disarmed and possibly confined at his own expense. A "fellow was lately tarred and feathered for treating one [of] our county committees with disre[s]pect," the future constitutional thinker James Madison, then on the Orange County committee, bragged to the printer of the *Pennsylvania Journal*. Thankfully, thought Madison, Virginia was not a place where a minority of colonists could speak their minds and enjoy protection from the majority. They could not "insult the whole colony and Continent with impunity!" As Nantucketer Kezia Coffin noted of Patriots, "It is liberty which they pretend they are fighting for, yet don't allow others liberty to think as they please."[13]

Finally, after a decade of boycott attempts, Patriots brought in a broad-based boycott with real teeth. They enforced it. In many historical accounts, just as the boycott takes effect, the Association falls victim to a bait and switch: attention turns to the battles at Lexington and Concord and the questions of allegiance they raised. The Association had been in effect for less than two months when the war began. What happened to the Association's provisions for tea drinking (or sheep breeding or gambling or slave trading) after that? Such provisions had divergent lives and deaths.[14]

Material acts—joining militias, buying gunpowder, supplying troops, and perhaps signing defense associations (agreements to support the defense of the revolutionary colonial governments)—became new ways to support the common cause. Statements (such as being an "addresser," signing the Continental Association, swearing for rebel or loyal governments in test oaths, or proclaiming independence) were also ways to show allegiance; but in these it was the signing itself that mattered. After Lexington and Concord, tea was still forbidden. But private non-consumption was only loosely linked either to material military acts or public signings. Colonists increasingly disregarded the boycott (see chapter 11), and Congress wrestled with this disregard (see chapter 12). Congress's and the public's priority had, understandably, shifted to the war. When, on March 14, 1776, Congress ordered the Association Test administered, the concern was that public disapproval of Congress might link to Loyalist armed action. Non-signers were to be disarmed, and their guns given to signers.[15] Meanwhile, the boycott was fast shrinking from sight: Congress did not disarm tea drinkers or the users of British goods. It ordered the Association Test while on the verge of repealing the tea ban.

Non-signers to the Continental Association of 1774, the Association Test of 1776, and other documents included Loyalists, sects that were either pacifist or prohibited the swearing of oaths (Quakers, Mennonites, Moravians, Dunkards, Jews, and some Freewill Baptists), and the ornery. Customs clerk William Eddis, who refused to sign, argued non-signers were the real "victims." Non-signers stood up to Patriot power and brought terror down on their heads. Many fled. By late 1775, wealthy Loyalists took "French leave," and announcements of colonists leaving for Britain frequently appeared in colonial papers as Patriots hounded Loyalists out.[16]

During the war, Patriots listed, tracked, and proscribed non-signers to a degree they never did for tea drinkers or theatergoers because, in wartime, non-signers might go from being "a traitor in thought but not in deed," as Thomas Jefferson put it, to taking up arms against Congress. When the Maryland convention threw off the proprietary power of the colony in July 1775, it issued a new association and ordered lists of non-associators to be kept. In December, the Maryland convention reviewed the lists, telling non-associators to sign by April 10, 1776, lest they be disarmed and perhaps forced to give bond against supporting ministerial troops. Similar lists were compiled in Connecticut, New Jersey, New York, Pennsylvania, and South Carolina, making it easier to disarm, punitively tax, and sometimes imprison non-signers.[17]

In such oaths it was military allegiance, not commercial activity, that concerned Patriots. Consider Myer Pollock. Edmund Burke later said that "because he had imported tea contrary to the command of the Americans, he was stripped of all he was worth and driven" from Rhode Island. It was a good story. But there is no other indication Pollock had anything to do with tea. He remained in Rhode Island after Patriots ended their tea ban, which makes it hard to see how they could have expelled him for violating it. Revolutionary authorities did suspect him of being "Inimical to the United Colonies in America" in 1776 and asked him to swear an oath of loyalty. Considering the Jewish prohibition against swearing oaths, revolutionaries came up with an affirmation, a sort of not-quite-an-oath oath, which Pollock found a way to sign. This declaration did not mention tea, British trade, or sumptuary codes. Rather, signatories promised not to "directly nor indirectly afford Assistance" to the "Fleets and Armies" of Britain and that they would "assist in the Defence of the United Colonies." Non-associators mattered because they might aid British troops, not because they might trade with the enemy (a practice that had been previously tolerated).[18]

Committees emphasized declaring loyalty, not proving it since, while committees had "police powers" and watched some merchants, they lacked police.[19] Despite Seabury's fears, committees did not go door to door looking into colonists' tea canisters. Routine, warrantless, and arbitrary searches would have alienated the populace. Instead, Patriots relied on individuals to police themselves: hence their concern with virtue (or, for the more skeptical, virtue signaling) and enforcement theater.

They did not seek out violators, but committees still dealt with the few who came to their attention. Their light-touch policy forgave and forgot even flagrant violators as long as they recognized committee authority. This was not naïveté. Ruthlessness would not win hearts and minds to a cause claiming to oppose tyranny. The appearance of magnanimity was just as important as boycott efficacy for public relations. Public infractions were dealt with harshly. Private violations were largely ignored. Prohibition was thus rhetorical: Patriots said tea was prohibited, and colonists agreed to say so. This worked because the war reduced the boycott's relative value as a symbol and a means of resisting Britain.

Enforcement and Merchants

To the extent that Patriots did inspect, they focused on merchants. This was more efficient and less invasive than household inspections. When focusing on merchants the Philadelphia committee emphasized non-importation (by checking cargo manifests) rather than non-consumption (which would require inspecting accounts and ledgers). The Baltimore committee prepared a form for masters of vessels to "make Oath on the Holy Evangels" not to import goods. The Sons of Liberty inspected warehouses, books, and stores to monitor compliance with non-importation, but only enough to convince merchants they were watching.[20]

In some places, enforcement was more intensive. Virginia merchants were required to get certificates proving they had signed the Virginia Association, and later some Virginia committees checked daybooks and accounts for price gouging. At first, merchants "generally refused," as factor James Robinson explained from Falmouth in January 1775. Port Royal merchants justified their refusal in print. But merchants who refused inspection were considered violators until proven innocent, and eventually the committee forced the merchants to give up their books. Inspections of merchant books occurred in Dunmore and Charlotte counties, Virginia as well. In Norwich, Connecticut, the committee required merchants to display their products' certificates of origin.[21]

Virginia Patriots had a unique opportunity to bring merchants into the Association when several hundred Virginia merchants gathered in Williamsburg in early November 1774. Patriots, led by Peyton Randolph and other congressional delegates, got the merchants to sign. They were aided by Burgess Archibald Cary, who organized an "Occasional Committee." Norfolk merchant Henry Fleming described

> a pole erected upon the parade in Wmsburg when I was there with a Brush a Bag of Feathers & a Tar Barrel at its foot by order of the Burgesses to intimidate such as would dare to broach a sentiment contrary to what is calld the liberties of America, Hanging, Drowning, Ducking, Taring & Feathering, Beating to death & Gouging was threatened . . . many us[e]d very ill . . .

unless they signed. Randolph and others intervened, though whether they genuinely disapproved or used the occasion to appear magnanimous is less clear. (See figure 10.1.) Because Patriots allowed only signatories to the Association to continue exporting until September 1775, merchants also had a financial reason to sign and perhaps adhere to the Association. A muddle of principles, threats, and inducements motivated merchants across the colonies to sign. Since part of conforming is pretending to agree, Virginia merchants claimed to sign "voluntarily and generally" (i.e., unanimously).[22]

Patriots singled out itinerant merchants as uniquely subversive to the Associational order. In Westmorland, Virginia, the committee required "itinerant or casual vendor of goods" to have certificates proving they were imported before the Association began.[23] This focus was strongest in New England, where peddlers were caught carrying tea. Traveling merchants presented a

THE ALTERNATIVE OF WILLIAMS-BURG.

Plate IV.

London Printed for R. Sayer, & J. Bennett Nº 53 Fleet Street as the Act directs 16 Feb 1775.

FIGURE 10.1. Philip Dawe, *The Alternative of Williams-Burg*, 1775. English engraver Philip Dawe did not attend the November 1774 merchant meeting Williamsburg, Virginia. He imagined the violence attendant at the gathering in his print. Here armed Patriots force merchants to sign the Association or endure tar and feathers. The scaffold in the back was a threat all in its own. One man, on the left, is pressured to sign. On the right, men prod the signers with posts. Source: Library of Congress, Prints and Photographs Division, Cartoon Prints, British.

unique problem for geographically structured committees. Peddlers came and went quickly, meaning even the men they caught selling tea had probably gotten away with it in other towns already. As peddlers were not members of the communities to which they sold, social pressure was less able to constrain them.

By the time Captain Edward Clark was caught "purchasing and selling Tea" in September 1775, he had passed through eight Massachusetts towns undetected, leaving a web of colonists violating non-consumption. Clark confessed to buying twenty pounds of tea. He had sold five and a half pounds to "sundry persons," used some himself, and lodged the rest with an associate, with plans to deliver it to others. The committees ordered "all persons who are lovers of their Country . . . break off . . . dealings with him" and published the order in the *Gazette*.[24]

Eleazer Bradshaw had smuggled tea from Albany to Eastern Massachusetts. This journey allowed him to pass through and potentially sell tea in at least twenty towns in western and central Massachusetts before he was caught. This was surely tempting, for Western Massachusetts towns were slow to take up the Association. In Eastern Massachusetts, "[S]undry persons" complained "sundry times" about his selling tea to the Weston committee (suggesting it took a while for anything to be done). Eventually, the Waltham committee, and the Newtown, Watertown, Weston, and Sudbury committees got dragged into his case. His central and western Massachusetts customers, if any, escaped unscathed. In October 1775, Bradshaw defied the five eastern Massachusetts committees, swore he would "do as he tho[ugh]t fit," and promised "the death of any person that should molest him." The committees shunned him, hoping "*Tea Merchants* may be treated as their Merits deserve."[25]

Committees also caught and proscribed a Waltham baker, David Townsend, who had acquired and dealt six pounds of tea from Bradshaw. He sold it to a doctor's wife in Newtown (who had asked him to procure it) and unnamed others but, perhaps having more ties in Waltham than Bradshaw, said he was "heartily sorry." Massachusettsans in Montague, Shrewsbury, Leominster, and Lancaster were also caught buying tea from peddlers, suggesting the limits of prohibition's ability to change consumer behavior.[26]

Itinerants—portraitists, preachers, dancing masters, and language teachers—roved the countryside, but chapmen especially frustrated rural New England elites. These peddlers cut in on local shopkeepers' business. Peddlers operated from taverns or public houses, doing a burst of trade, then moving on. They did not pay upkeep for a country store which, in a small town, might see little trade. Shopkeepers had been trying to keep peddlers out of their communities since the early eighteenth century with little luck. For local merchants abiding by the Association, the arrival of chapmen with banned goods must have been galling. Some committees attempted, as the Newmarket, New Hampshire one did, to restrict "any Hawker, Pedler, or Petty Chapman" from entering its domains, threatening the innkeepers who harbored them. Newmarket followed the New Hampshire convention's recommendation to enforce standing laws against chapmen, and offered to punish "according to Law" any peddler who closed a sale. This suggests the law against itinerants had not been well enforced previously. The Epsom, New Hampshire, committee threatened to tar and feather chapmen selling imported goods. Massachusetts had a similar law to New Hampshire's. But, as the provincial congress lamented in February 1775, it "cannot at present be effectually carried into execution," so travelers were "going from Town to Town selling East India Goods and Teas" and British manufactures. Provincial Patriots recommended town committees "be very violent and industrious" in policing hawkers and "make a thorough and careful search" of their bags when they arrive. If the committees "find any India Teas or European Manufactures" they should prevent the chapmen from selling them.[27] Notably, most of the tea sellers described above sold tea after this order was issued.

Regular merchants were also caught violating the Association. Isaiah Worrell admitted to selling tea to "sundry persons and at sundry times." He had sold tea "imprudently" and "inadvertently" (by which he meant he had sold it negligently and meant nothing political by it, not that he had sold it accidentally). The "I didn't mean it" defense was common, an extension of the "accidental" tea importations of 1774. Ebenezer Withington claimed inadvertency when he collected tea washed ashore from the Boston Tea Party. Salemite John Cook, who brought the salvaged East India Company tea to Castle William, pled "mere Inadvertence" and "ignorance," as did several Truro residents who bought some of the salvaged tea. Philip Vickers Fithian saw Mrs. Carter inadvertently pour tea for her husband. Inadvertency was mentioned only when someone was caught. Worrell was "sincerely sorry" and promised to abide by the Association in the future. He added that he had "no other motive . . . but my own interest, in getting off my hands about 30 or 40 pounds of said Tea"— by which he meant that he sought to profit, not defy the committee, by selling it. Worrell had not spoken ill of Congress. He was just a small, selfish merchant. How many others were there like Worrell?[28]

A theater emerged: if violators recognized Patriot authority and asked forgiveness, they could be absolved. Thus, in October 1775, Providence merchant Nathan Angell was caught selling tea. The committee published his promise to "deliver up" all he had and to obey the Association. "I earnestly ask the forgiveness of the community," Angell pleaded. Such declarations performed committee mercy, power and, occasionally, wrath. But one should not assume they indicated the internal thoughts of committeemen, Angell, or townsfolk. The committee also demanded that anyone else who had tea give it up, suspecting from "frequent complaints from the country" that other people were selling tea, which belied the idea that the community disapproved.[29]

Merchants' defiance was dealt with firmly. The Scituate, Massachusetts committee asked the "refractory shopkeepers," Charles Curtis and Frederick Henderson, to adhere to the Association. "I shall *not* adhere to it," Curtis replied. "I don't know any *Congress*," Henderson added. So the committee ordered the town to break off contact with them. The Ulster County committee proscribed Jacobus Low of Kingston, New York as the sole vendor not to sign the Association. He "declared he had, and would sell Tea." Low retorted that committee members used tea, too. "It was reported by one of the members of the Committee, . . . that he had purchased Tea at my house. [Committee Chairman] Johannes Sleght continued drinking Tea after the 1st of March, in direct violation of the Association; and John Beekman did confess at the meeting, that he had a quantity of Tea, and intended that it should be made use of in his family, contrary to the Association." The committee's charges, Low concluded, were hypocritical "chicanery." The committee denounced Low's "absolutely false" claims and the "wickedness of his heart." Seeing their "characters" "impeached," they compelled him to sign the Association and to appear on June 6, 1775, before the committee of the Town of Kingston and accept its authority. Likewise, Staten Island's Loyalism—the island resisted "obedience" to Congress in 1775—led several New Jersey committees to boycott the island. When the Staten Islander Peter Waglom tried to sell tea in Dover New Jersey, he found himself a "publick enemy" in Dover. This was not simply because he sold tea but because of the Loyalism that selling it from Staten Island implied.[30]

Yet Loyalism's true importance lay in political not commercial matters. Such was the case of Breed Batchelder, who, unlike Low, did not sign the Association. He refused to "comply" with the Packersfield (present-day Nelson), New Hampshire committee's terms and "sine a covenant," arguing such associations were "Aganst the law." He also warned Packersfield Patriots that signers risked the Crown's wrath. Batchelder was an influential man in Packersfield. He was a founding father of the town, a substantial landowner holding thousands of acres, having initiated settlement there in 1767. The settlement's first town meeting had been held in his home in 1772, and after the settlement was incorporated in 1774, Batchelder moderated town meetings. He also ran an inn and commanded the town militia. At this time, the town had less than 200 souls.[31]

He was not on the town's committees in 1775. Not wanting to take up arms against his King, he failed to march with his company to Massachusetts after news of the Battles of Lexington and Concord. The committee claimed he "refused to have anything to do with his Company," but, unarmed, he followed it to Massachusetts a few days later and assumed command in Cambridge for a while before leaving. Some of his men left, too, perhaps with his encouragement. Batchelder, still untouchable, sold tea after his return.[32]

Only after committees from other towns began complaining in early 1776 did Packersfield move against him. The committee of nearby Marlborough, New Hampshire pursued Batchelder on word he had "a quantity of Tea." A Marlborough committeeman caught up to him in Fitzwilliam, where Batchelder tried to evade committeemen from both towns. He fled on horseback with three bags of tea, only to be pursued, fighting off and wounding one committeeman with a club, before being forced to turn around by another. Then he hid one bag "in the Brush a little out of the road" and tried to pretend someone had stolen it. The Fitzwilliam committee complained Batchelder was "bringing in a Large quantity of India Tea and freely offering it for Sale" in their town, at which he was at least partly successful, as one of his customers, Frederick Reed, quickly "Retaild the most of it [the tea] out." He told the committee he "would b[u]y more if he could get it" and threatened anyone who dared "Examine or disturb" him. For such overt denial of Patriot authority, the Fitzwilliam committee deemed Reed and Batchelder "Enemical." The Packersfield committee complained of Batchelder's "bad behueyer [behavior]," including (but not limited to) the "Distorbance" and "trouble" caused by his buying a "lardg" amount of tea and "paddeling it out" throughout the country, and his desultory role in the militia. Despite (or because of) word that he "Damned the Comitteys" and threatened to "kill" anyone who arrested him, they were unable to get rid of him until 1777.[33]

Complaints about Batchelder's tea sales emerged shortly before the tea ban ended. They mattered, even after the ban was lifted, as part of his ongoing denial of the revolutionary order and local authority, which was the real "bad behavior." The Packersfield committee struggled to isolate him in town. Chasing down his tea sales would only create an embarrassing record of local purchases. So the committee gave no indication of where he got his tea or who else bought large parcels, and left no record of who consumed it. Given the back and forth between Batchelder and the committee in 1776, his tea sales likely "disturbed" the town because they offended some while appealing to others.

Consumer Enforcement: "Don't Ask, Don't Tell"

Like merchants caught selling, consumers caught buying or drinking tea could publicly confess their guilt and be reaccepted, or defy the committee and be

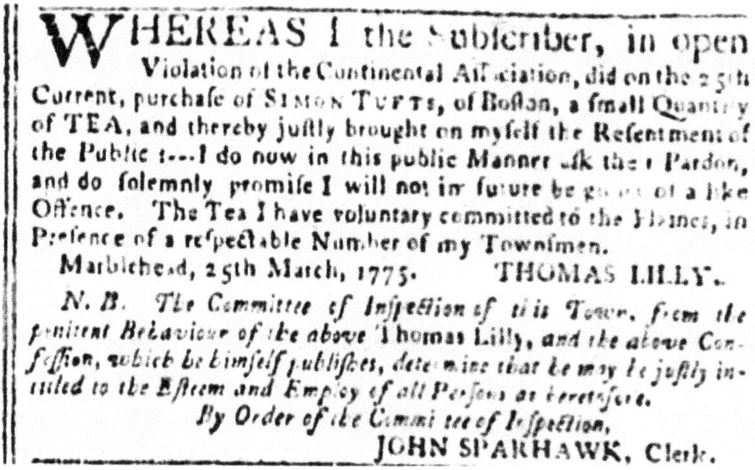

WHEREAS I the Subscriber, in open Violation of the Continental Association, did on the 25th Current, purchase of SIMON TUFTS, of Boston, a small Quantity of TEA, and thereby justly brought on myself the Resentment of the Public :---I do now in this public Manner ask the Pardon, and do solemnly promise I will not in future be guilty of a like Offence. The Tea I have voluntary committed to the Flames, in Presence of a respectable Number of my Townsmen.

Marblehead, 25th March, 1775.   THOMAS LILLY.

N. B. The Committee of Inspection of this Town, from the penitent Behaviour of the above Thomas Lilly, and the above Confession, which he himself publishes, determine that he may be justly intitled to the Esteem and Employ of all Persons as heretofore.

By Order of the Committee of Inspection,
JOHN SPARHAWK, Clerk.

FIGURE 10.2.   Thomas Lilly's apology, March 1775. Marblehead, Massachusetts resident Thomas Lilly's punishment for buying tea in violation of the Association was typical. He was made to destroy it and apologize to his local committee in the press. The committee then appended their forgiveness at the bottom. Colonists who duly bowed to Patriot authority were usually forgiven. Unusually, the Marblehead committee also publicly named Lilly's supplier, Boston merchant Simon Tufts, to spur Boston Patriots to action. Source: *Essex Gazette*, March 28, 1775.

proscribed. Travers Nash of Prince William County, Virginia, confessed in the *Virginia Gazette* "that once since the beginning of last March I made use of tea, contrary to the continental association, for which I am sincerely sorry, and ask pardon of the public." The committee recommended no further action against him. In Farmington, Connecticut, Martha and Solomon Cowles made up for serving tea by apologizing in the papers and naming the drinkers. Marblehead resident Thomas Lilly confessed in the *Essex Gazette* that his buying tea was an "open Violation" of the Association. (See figure 10.2) He "voluntar[il]y" burned his tea, named his supplier, and asked forgiveness; his letter was printed with an endorsement from the committee.[34]

Conversely, a Pittsylvania, Virginia committee heard a complaint that John Pigg had "violated the association, by drinking, and making use of in his family, the detestable *East India* TEA." "Pigg had taken uncommon pains in order to defeat the intention of the said association" by speaking against it. Pigg refused to appear before the committee, ignored its authority, and declared he would "do as he pleased." The committee declared him "a traitor to his country, and inimical to American liberty" and urged others to "break off intercourse and connection" with him.[35] Yet most colonists when called out gave in.

The accusation of tea drinking became a useful tool in neighborly politics and feuds. Benjamin Stiles was the only man referred to the Connecticut General Assembly for tea drinking. As one local explained: "Stiles was a bad man." When pressed whether "yo have some little prejudice against Sd. Stiles," his accuser explained, "I have no Little Prejudice against him but a Great one."[36]

Other accusations served colony-level politics. William Ellery accused Rhode Island Congressman Stephen Hopkins of tea drinking. "Such examples [of tea drinking] are pernicious," Ellery explained to the Rhode Island attorney general, Henry Marchant. "If a delegate of the Congress, who associated, under the ties of honor, virtue, and love of his country, not to use that poisonous plant after the 1st of March, doth drink it, what will not others do?" Ellery opposed the Wanton-Hopkins faction in Rhode Island politics in favor of Hopkins's rival, Samuel Ward. When Ward died in 1776, Ellery took Ward's place in Congress. The evidence against Hopkins was thin: one man had told him that another had told him that Hopkins "drank tea at the Governor's."[37]

Ellery was even more opposed to Governor Wanton. Wanton's family had been prominent in Newport trade and politics for generations. Newport, then the seat of colonial government, was conservative. Rhode Island and imperial customs officials, naval patrols, merchants, and others added up to what Patriots called the "Newport Junto." To oppose Wanton was to oppose this conservatism. In early 1774, Tories were so strong in Newport that Connecticuters gossiped "a Whig dared not open his mouth in favor of liberty" there.[38]

But Newport was moving in the Patriot's direction. It resolved against dutied tea in January 1774 and established a committee of inspection that included Ellery, Ward, and the governor's son, Col. Joseph Wanton Jr. It is unclear how seriously the Wantons took this duty: Two members of the colonel's family—John and Peter Wanton—advertised tea of unknown origin in 1774. Ellery and others attacked the Wantons for their Toryism, causing the younger Wanton to lose the 1774 elections. In 1775, Ellery complained that Governor Wanton continued to serve tea to his guests that March, though Patriots had convinced the governor's son to give up tea, "He was very much afraid . . . that he should be posted, and his father turned out." Eventually, the younger Wanton appeared at a meeting of the very same committee of which he had been a member the previous year, "promising that we would not drink tea, nor suffer it to be used in our families." Ellery pushed on, publishing a broadside accusing Governor Wanton of being a Tory. In May, upset at Wanton's refusal to support raising troops after the Battles of Lexington and Concord, the Assembly expelled its Tory members and governed without Governor Wanton.[39]

Ellery also wanted to "shake" Providence County into action. Newport Patriots had learned that "John Jenck[e]s of Providence drinks tea." Jenckes was a Patriot official on the Providence committee that enforced prohibition. He also represented Providence in the Rhode Island General Assembly. There is no real evidence that Jenckes drank tea, or that Providence Patriots bothered investigating. For Ellery shaking Providence Patriots was the point, whether or not the charge was true.[40]

The most clear-eyed understanding that the politics of tea drinking was more about power than practice came from the Harvard faculty. Patriotic Harvard students tried to enforce the Association upon their classmates. A fight broke out between two sides over breakfast on March 1, 1775. The conventional reading is Josiah Quincy's: tea drinking was a performance of Loyalism. "Tories among the students were in the practice of bringing 'India tea' into commons, and drinking it, to show their loyalty," he wrote. This "gave great offense" to Patriots and their "sensitive patriotism."

Harvard's president and various faculty members were Patriots, and had they been on a revolutionary committee, they may have ruled differently. But on campus, they pursued a "don't ask, don't tell" policy that protected their authority at the Association's expense. Admonishing "both sides as imprudent," the faculty gave no opinion on tea drinking, but took a firm stance against students enforcing anything. Power to regulate "the Hall belongs exclusively to . . . Government of the College," not student protestors, who had no authority to act. Given that the populace found tea "disagreeable," the faculty hoped to avoid "grief" by asking students not to bring tea into the Hall or drink it publicly. As students who "carried Tea into the Hall declare that the drinking of it *in the Hall* is a matter of trifling consequence with them," the faculty "advised" the tea drinkers to drink it in private to preserve "harmony . . . peace & happiness" in the college.[41] Pace Quincy, these students did not subscribe to a gloss in which they drank tea to show Loyalism. They drank tea because they liked it, even if "sensitive" Patriotic snowflakes thought it was all about them.

Press Censorship

Collecting signatures for the Association was part of a campaign to persuade colonists to conform to Patriots' views. Many did so willingly, but it is difficult to believe that printed affirmations of public conformity represented private opinions or actions, whether they concerned tea or other goods. This was partly because Patriots' growing control of the press made it difficult for contrary information to appear in print. In 1775, Patriotic propaganda, censorship, and control of a large majority of North American presses helped ensure only certain information about the Association appeared in print. In print tea drinkers were either (1) inadvertent or apologetic tea drinkers who had promised to stop, or (2) recalcitrant ones who had not. The special permission granted to Harvard's tea drinkers did not appear in print, which was why it could happen. Manuscript sources hint that what colonists meant, and did not mean, with banned goods was more nuanced than the bounds of public rhetoric would allow. In 1774, newspapers printed the thank-you notes local committees received for the relief they sent to Boston to build up the common cause. The public signings, stories of tea burnings, stories of tea's health effects, and stories that gendered tea were all part of Patriots' campaign to persuade colonists to support the Association. This campaign focused most intently on the powers of committees and Congress, but control of the press also helped enforce the Association (by naming and shaming violators) and affected discussions about tea.[42] Tea burnings got more press than efforts to end prohibition. Tea advertising similarly vanished even if tea did not. Tea's supposed ill effects on health were printed widely, but readers still treated tea as a medicine. The revolution was not all propaganda and performance, but propaganda and performance were necessary to create a common cause.

Colonial presses had once published all sides of an issue, but they were heavily censored by 1775. Printers who ran conservative content were politically suspect, relegating such content to a few die-hard Tory printers, whom mobs targeted. When South Carolina printer Robert Wells ran pieces in defense of the Company's tea in 1773, JUNIUS BRUTUS attacked them as *"cloven foot"* work and suggested Wells be quiet. Such a stance was "looked upon, even by the most zealous assertors of the *liberty of the press* . . . as an insult," he explained. But at least Wells could print them. In 1775 one correspondent wrote, "It is but very lately that a Tory writer dare appear, or that a Printer could be prevailed on to publish any thing on the side of Government." When Samuel Loudon was contracted to print a reply to Thomas Paine's *Common Sense*, a mob forced him to surrender the printing plates, 1,500 impressions, and the manuscript, which was burned. Patriots warned New York printers: "if you print . . . anything against the rights and liberties of America . . . death and destruction, ruin and perdition, shall be your portion." This was hardly a basis for free debate and information. No more Loyalist tracts were printed in New York until the British occupation. In December 1776, the Philadelphia committee forbade the printers of the *Germantowner Zeitung* from printing anything.[43]

It was common to publicly destroy Tory newspapers and copies of parliamentary acts. At Charleston's Pope Day celebration, the devil had held a copy of James Rivington's *New York Gazetteer*. The Ulster County, New York committee burned Samuel Seabury's *Free Thoughts*. In Providence, they burned two Tory newspapers with their tea.[44]

Rivington's *Gazetteer* became a particular totem of political identification. "As to my being a Tory it was all a Joke," Charles Beatty explained, "I only *used to* take Rivington's papers." Committees in at least twenty communities from Rhode Island to South Carolina called for boycotts of his *Gazetteer*, and it was burned as a "dirty, scandalous and traitorous" rag. It is unclear how this affected readership—there seemed to have been plenty of copies to burn. Patriots also pressed Rivington's advertisers. Connecticut Patriots urged fellow "Friends of America" to avoid Rivington and his advertisers. A New Jersey mob hung Rivington in effigy in April 1775. The following month, another mob ransacked his shop. Later that year, a third mob wrecked his press and took his type.[45]

The attack on conservative printers was an important step in the revolution. With the start of armed combat, it had military necessity, and with the push for independence, political necessity. But its utility dates back earlier, to the Association. The 1770 non-importation agreement collapsed partly because the conservative press had published evidence proving Bostonians who claimed not to be importing from Britain in fact were. Non-importation was more effective in 1775 than in 1770, partly because Patriots "learned the lessons" of 1770: to make the Association binding on all, enforce it more, and keep its inadequacies out of the press.

Suppressing Loyalist writing was construed as protecting freedom, since a free press was the Patriots' right, not their opponents'. Loyalist writers were imagined to be paid ministerial stooges who neither deserved, nor could be trusted with, a platform. According to the *South Carolina Gazette*, it was "no *Loss of Liberty*, that court-minions can complain of, when they are silenced. No man has a right to say a word, which may lame the liberties of his country." The Newport committee explained, in boycotting Rivington, that a free press meant the right to print "liberal sentiments," not "wrong sentiments." The "press of freedom" allowed "rights which all men are entitled to, of speaking their sentiments," but, as the Philadelphia committee explained in 1775, "raising jealousies among the people" or "counteracting" the revolutionary leadership's "virtuous exertions against . . . oppression" was "licentiousness" that deserved "punishment." "Philadelphius" argued that "censure" of Congress be suppressed from print. As historian Arthur Schlesinger explained, "liberty of speech belonged solely to those who spoke the speech of liberty."[46]

British officials censored, too. Governor Dunmore denounced the *Norfolk Intelligencer*'s "poisoning the minds of the people," seized the press, and began a new paper. But Patriots censored more because there were more presses under their control.[47]

There were two conceptions of the press. One was the free press, which printed only Patriotic writings and was, Robert Martin argues, "violently exclusionary." Then there was the open press, which printed all views, a tradition that continued in Britain (British papers ran Patriotic content, even as Patriot presses excluded Tory views). Under the "free" press, contesting ideas were neither possible nor desirable. No "fair" contest could be had, explained John Holt of the *New York Journal*, since Tory presses were biased and full of lies. This kind of censorship risked a "tyranny within," Myles Cooper lamented. In January 1776, Congress pulled radical Patriots back, instructing them to consider Tory writers misinformed, not evil. By then, most printers had become Patriots or fled.[48] This was not an environment where nuance about boycotts (or much else) could thrive.

Policing the Mail

News and mail were intricately linked. Newspapers came by mail and ran news received by mail; some postmasters printed newspapers. The *Virginia Gazette* was printed "at the POST OFFICE." The *Gazette* also published correspondence exposing an order from Britain by Andrew Sprowle, contrary to the Association, thereby making an example of the man who had once led Virginia's merchant community. By controlling mail and the press, Patriots controlled the metapolitics of speech—who could speak to whom and with what constraints and legitimacy.[49]

Both sides weaponized the mail, further constraining public discourse. Lord Dartmouth intercepted Patriot letters. In early 1774, the Boston committee of correspondence proposed a Patriot-controlled post, which printer William Goddard began. Printers were central in setting up this new postal system. The stated purposes were (1) securing committees' correspondence against ministerial interdiction, and (2) denying revenue to the ministry. Should the Patriot post replace the imperial one, it had the unstated benefit of (3) denying conservatives secure communication. A Continental mail service operated (but was not dominant) in New England and the middle colonies by mid-to-late 1774. However, the King's riders still carried most mail until after the Battle of Lexington, after which local committees stopped and examined the post. In Hartford, Patriots removed General Gage's letters and about 300 copies of Rivington's *Gazetteer* from the mail and burned them. Writing from Philadelphia in May, Samuel Curwen warned a correspondent in Nantucket that the old post was "stopped," with the new one only taking "franked" letters, "the contents of which must be known to one of the Committee." By the end of 1775, Patriots had shut down the "Parliamentary Post" in all thirteen colonies. Meanwhile, the British government opened all mail to or from those colonies by official post. By the end of the year, the ministry began shutting packet services, ordering governors to correspond with Whitehall via the navy. Alarmed colonists increasingly sent letters privately.[50]

The value of controlling information can be seen in the news about the Battles of Lexington and Concord. The Massachusetts provincial congress claimed Gage's troops fired first and "slaughtered the unarmed, the sick, the helpless." Lexington militiamen swore depositions to the same, hoping to sway the newspaper-reading public in London. By contrast, General Gage suggested colonists fired first. Who fired first remains unknown. Yet of the two sides, Gage struggled to distribute his version of events. Gage's account was printed in Boston, which he controlled, and in only one other city in North America. He had sent notices to neighboring governors via gentlemen riders, but Patriots intercepted them. Meanwhile, committees of correspondence ensured their version of the Battles of Lexington and Concord reached as many presses as possible, and that colonists as far away as the Carolinas thought redcoats shot first.[51]

Propaganda

Some of this persuasion campaign involved outright propaganda. At the *Boston Gazette*, Patriots manipulated the news. When John Adams visited, he found two Patriots hard at work, "a curious employment, cooking up paragraphs, articles, occurrences, etc., working the political engine." In such cases, truth did not always matter. "Throw something into the press to convince the people," William Ellery urged Henry Marchant, "of the danger we are in from a Tory administration, and don't be afraid of seasoning it highly. People who have weak appetites must be warmed." In December 1773, Charles Thomson stirred up Philadelphia about the Company's tea. His handbills were "to kindle a flame of resentment." "I do not think it unworthy the cause sometimes to borrow aid from the passions," he added.[52]

Sometimes Patriots lied outright, as with the *Peggy Stewart*. The Continental Congress's *Address to the People of Great Britain* pretended the East India Company could have brought suit for its lost tea in Boston, a claim the Massachusetts delegation knew was false. Virginia Patriots burned down Norfolk, the colony's largest mercantile town and a Tory enclave, and successfully blamed Governor Dunmore's troops. This was a key atrocity pushing colonists to independence. Perhaps it would have been worth asking, why would Dunmore burn a Loyalist town? The lie worked, and colonists, along with generations of US historians, spent the next two centuries falsely believing Dunmore had done it.[53]

Colonists believed what they wanted, and propaganda gave readers an explanation of events that did not challenge their views. The prevalence of rumors made this easier. As Ambrose Serle, secretary to Lord Howe, lamented from British-occupied New York, the times were "fertile Soil for Lying: So many Fals[e]hoods are told on both Sides, [that] one does not know whom to believe." Thus one of the central claims made in the Patriot press about the Tea Act was that it was intended to set the precedent of tax payment, but that precedent had been sent, as colonists had been paying taxes on tea since 1770. Some Patriot writers made the lesser claim that the Tea Act would improve imperial tax revenue and, therefore, fund a larger imperial bureaucracy. But admitting that colonists were already paying tea taxes was inconvenient. It was easier for Patriots to flatter colonists that they had been more virtuous than they were. Similarly, the Patriot press described crowds as orderly even when they were not. The *Massachusetts Spy* could reassure readers that the East India Company tea sent to South Carolina had been "entirely destroyed." Boston Patriots could overstate Halifax Patriotism and invent a tea party, claiming that, on September 22, 1775, a British tea ship reached Halifax, whereupon "liberty boys immediately committed it to the sea." As Nova Scotia historian John Brebner notes, Patriots told themselves "what they wanted to believe about Nova Scotia." For their part, Loyalists could murmur both that colonists were abused for drinking tea and that Patriots drank it extensively. Overall, Patriots' pretenses flattered readers' sensibilities and helped the common cause seem proper.[54]

In 1775, Patriots enforced the ban on tea consumption. Enforcing a ban on something presupposes its commission. So, what did these violations of the Association mean? Does enforcement indicate prohibition's success, or does it indicate the difficulty of getting colonists to comply? Examinations of the boycotts have ignored these questions.

The printed material generated about enforcement is especially bad at answering them, because those prints were part of an effort to encourage colonists to conform to the Association. Genre constrained what such performative texts could say. They were too politic to say the quiet part out loud. To understand colonists' unguarded thoughts and actions, one must examine less public sources: tea sellers' records and colonists' diaries and letters.

CHAPTER 11

Tea Drinkers

Just as Americans drank alcohol during the Pro-
hibition of the 1920s, so colonists drank tea and consumed British goods during the prohibition of 1775. Records show thousands of colonists buying,
selling, and drinking tea in private, despite public declarations of abstinence.
The Harvard students from the previous chapter are one example. Ledgers,
correspondence, and diaries reveal tea's secret life during the ban and the lives
of the colonists who consumed it. Published announcements from the committees that tea consumption had ceased were for show.

Tea consumption continued openly in areas beyond Patriot control and secretly in Patriot areas. Merchants wholesaled it, retailed it, and tried to import more. Loyalists tried to organize against the Association, but the main
thrust of tea consumption was not political. It came from colonists operating
as consumers and merchants rather than as politicos.

Patriots could not even stop their own. Cumberland County, New Jersey
committeeman Silas Newcomb drank tea with his family after March 1, 1775;
his fellow committeemen found out when he blurted out a surprise confession. Newcomb's brother was also a committeeman, and his son had been a
Greenwich tea burner, but it took a public shunning to put Newcomb on the
right path. Charles Beatty, one of the College of New Jersey students who
burned the college's tea in 1774, wrote his sister Betsey in April 1775, hoping
her fiancé was "not such a patriot but will let you have tea." Betsey's fiancé,

the diarist (and possible Greenwich tea burner) Philip Vickers Fithian, also lamented the lack of tea in 1775. Charles Willson Peale, the artist making militia battle flags and portraits of Patriot politicians, was not too Patriotic to buy tea on February 1, 1776, from a Philadelphia vendor, the same day he worked on a miniature of Mrs. Hancock. In Virginia, Patriot Isaac Bowes bought two pounds of hyson from James Hunter Jr.'s store in 1775 and took up a commission in the Stafford county militia that October.[1]

Patriot merchant politicians sold tea, too. Edward Telfair was a Scots merchant. He was part of Georgia's provincial congress, which banned the import of tea (but not its use) beginning March 15, 1775. He also joined Georgia's second provincial congress, which announced an immediate ban on the import, purchase, sale, or use of tea on July 6, 1775. Telfair signed both bans. His firm booked twenty-four tea sales in the two months after the July ban, and he was never outed for it. Telfair was a Patriot: he helped raid a Savannah gunpowder magazine; this helped supply the Continental army besieging Boston. He was a member of the Georgia Council of Safety tasked with, among other things, policing prohibition.[2] He did not police himself.

John Campbell was part of the Virginia county committee governing the Pittsburgh region. He sold tea. Pennsylvania Patriots ran a rival county government in the area. When they heard that Campbell was selling tea, they rushed to Pittsburgh to inform on him. Campbell confessed and delivered up his stash—a box and two ten-gallon containers of tea leaves—to be "Burned at the Liberty pole." Some tea had already been sold. The shipment, which had traveled across the Appalachian Mountains from his partner's store in Lancaster, Pennsylvania, suggested he anticipated real demand in Pittsburgh or down the Ohio River. It was only by virtue of the Virginia-Pennsylvania land dispute that he was caught.[3]

The Albany firm Henry, McClallen and Henry openly advertised tea and other banned goods "Just received" from Continental-occupied Montreal, beginning on March 25, 1776. This seems to have been part of a larger supply of goods the firm bought in Montreal over the winter. One partner, Robert Henry, had been in the Sons of Liberty. Another, Robert McClallen, was investigated for price gouging while he sat on the committee which set prices. After the army helped evacuate the firm's goods from Montreal to Albany, the firm thanked the army by trying to get it to buy the firm's unwanted goods. Advertising tea while sitting on the committee prohibiting it was, at least, in character.[4]

Telfair, Campbell, and McClallen were all tasked with enforcing the ban on tea, which they violated, and helped others violate, by selling and advertising tea to fellow colonists. Hypocrisy is human, and it should hardly be surprising that not every Patriot politician said what he meant or meant what he said.

They were politicians, after all. Are they best understood as merchants who joined committees to limit enforcement, or as Patriots who happened to have mercantile livelihoods? Not one turned himself in. Their committees in Albany, Pittsburgh, and Savannah enforced with a light touch, and did not examine the ledgers of merchants who said they followed prohibition. If local Patriot leaders bought, sold, drank, and advertised tea, how many politically uninvolved colonists also did so?

Areas beyond Patriot Enforcement

Buying and selling tea was easiest in areas outside Patriot control. Georgia ratified the Association late, and the provincial congress ignored non-consumption before July. Tea advertisements and sales continued into June in Georgia. Edward Telfair sold tea before the July ban came into effect (in addition to what he sold during the ban). New tea imports had been banned since March, but merchants could sell existing stock. This is what Telfair did, licitly, Patriotically, and self-interestedly selling into a market from which he had legislated away competition. Edward Telfair & Co made ninety-six tea sales between the ban on tea imports and the ban on tea sales, suggesting extensive tea consumption in 1775 Georgia. Georgia tea advertising stopped in July, after which Telfair continued tea sales underground.[5]

Boston merchants sold tea. Patriot Joseph Barrell sold tea on April 6, 1775. Loyalist James Murray sold in March and early April. Boston Patriots detected neither. Simon Tufts was caught because his customer, Thomas Lilly, was discovered with tea in Marblehead and informed on Tufts. When Boston Patriots finally found out and confronted Tufts, he pled ignorance, blaming his clerk for selling tea without his knowledge. "I will not buy or sell any more" tea without "permission," he promised.[6]

After the Battles of Lexington and Concord on April 19, 1775, Boston ceased to be under Patriot control. British troops freed the city, and most Patriotic colonists fled. The civilian population fell from 15,000 to 3,500, two-thirds of whom were Loyalists. The city's food situation also changed. Patriots across North America had been feeding Boston since the Port Act. Now they besieged and blockaded the town instead. The war made the Port Act, once a matter of contention, pointless. The act mandated that merchants land their cargoes outside Boston, but the only merchants left in Boston were Loyalists who could not land their cargoes elsewhere "on Account of the Rebellion." Fearing their vessels would fall "into the hands of the Rebels," General Gage and Admiral Samuel Graves began letting supply vessels into Boston instead. Shortages persisted, exacerbated by an accidental fire. Bostonians survived on salt meat. Lack of vegetables and milk caused illness among Gage's troops. By fall, bread shortages were severe, as supply vessels were delayed or captured.[7]

Yet the Association was void in Boston. Colonists were free to buy, sell, drink, and advertise tea openly if, shortages allowing, they had any. English merchants shipped 8,055 pounds of tea to "New England" in 1775, most likely to Boston. It was probably then, freed from Patriot control, that Simon Tufts sold more tea. At least three other merchants retailed tea in British Boston. Among the buyers was John Soley, a Patriotic merchant.[8]

The tea salvaged from the *William* was still in the castle in the harbor. But with a wartime rethinking of the restrictions on Boston's port, that tea could sell. On August 8, 1775, those East India Company's consignees still in the city sold more than fifty chests of Company tea at public auction, remitting £1,054 11s8d sterling to London. The tea found ready drinkers among Boston Loyalists and His Majesty's soldiers and sailors.[9] This was the tea that was supposed to have gone to the bottom of Boston Harbor in 1773. It did not. Patriots had been right to oppose landing it: when sold, there were Bostonians who would drink it.

Evidence of tea in British Boston abounds. John Grozart and James Perkins advertised tea—perhaps the Company's—in the *Massachusetts Gazette*, the only paper published in Boston during the siege, throughout the winter. Loyalist William Perry, who probably bought his tea from the consignees' auction, still had tea on hand in early March when his shop was looted by British troops evacuating the city. Tea was movable enough for retreating soldiers to take; bulkier supplies, like salt and sugar, were "thrown into the river." As a result, while Bostonians of all ranks had tea in early March (amid final preparations to evacuate, army engineering officer Archibald Robertson reported being "kindly invited to breakfast and drink a dish of green Tea by a Black" person), the incoming Continental Army found none.[10]

This was just as well, as the freedom to sell tea did not survive the return of the Association. Some tea advertisers and sellers fled with the British evacuation (as did the publisher of the *Gazette*). Perkins stayed behind and was arrested shortly thereafter (but not, it seems, for violating the tea ban). He was briefly exiled to Medfield. Tufts was proscribed in 1778. Selling tea was not the most Loyalist thing these men did. It was, as with Batchelder, a sign of their broader unwillingness to conform to Patriot morality.[11]

The Association was initially void in Marshfield, Massachusetts, too. There, 300 people signed a loyalist association and formed a militia. They dominated the town and were reinforced by some of Gage's troops in January 1775. A Marshfield resident could "freely utter his thoughts, drink his Tea, and kill his sheep as profusely as he pleases." Gage hoped success at Marshfield would encourage other towns suffering rebel oppression to speak out, but Marsh-field's freedom was short-lived. The day after the fighting at Lexington, 1,000 Patriot militiamen swarmed the town. British troops and 100 Loyalists fled, and the Continental Association began.[12]

Nantucket declared neutrality. The island was simultaneously exposed to Royal Navy patrols and dependent on mainland Patriots for supplies and thus could not afford to take sides. Many islanders were Quakers, or Friends, and their pacifism and their eschewal of swearing oaths left the Association unenforced. Mainlanders found Nantucket a haven after fighting began; refugees from Boston and Loyalists from Salem and the North Shore fled to Nantucket as Patriots escaped out of Boston. William Vassall Sr. left Boston on May 10, 1775. "The distressed Situation of the Town of Boston induced me" to move to Nantucket "for the Sake of retiring from Noise, Tumult & War to a place of Peace & Quietness."[13]

A mandamus councillor and wealthy plantation owner, Vassall was a stereotypical "High Tory"; he leased an entire vessel to ferry his family to Nantucket. Dr. Edward Holyoke sent his wife, Mary, and children to Nantucket, continuing his isolated existence as a Loyalist in Salem. On Nantucket, Mary had tea at "old Friend Husseys [who had come from Lynn] with Friend Vassal" (William Vassall's wife, Margaret). Meanwhile, her husband signed (perhaps after being shunned) a public recantation of his Loyalism in Salem. Melatiah Bourn left Boston after the siege began and found Nantucket a convenient place to sell tea. Elizabeth Winslow, the mother to tea consignee Joshua Winslow, relocated with three daughters to Nantucket in June 1775. Her son-in-law, Newport merchant and tea seller Simon Pease, joined them when Continental troops took over Newport at the end of 1775.[14]

The Massachusetts provincial congress boycotted Nantucket in June for fear islanders were supplying British forces, and refugees started to move on. Three months later, the provincial congress entrusted a Falmouth, Cape Cod committee to regulate Nantucket's trade with the mainland. Facing shortages of flour and wood, Nantucketers smuggled supplies from Newport (before Patriots took over the town) and Connecticut—their tea probably made excellent barter. Tea was still available and drunk on the island the following summer. Islanders could get more tea abroad through trade with the Caribbean, particularly at St. Eustatius, where many returning whalers stopped.[15]

Other islands evaded the Association. In South Carolina, the Sea Islands saw rampant smuggling, and the Beaufort committee could not effectively enforce the Association there. The HMS *Scarborough*'s presence off Tybee Island (on the South Carolina-Georgia border) in early 1776 made enforcing the Association hard there, too.[16]

Colonists were reluctant or openly hostile to joining the Patriot movement in the backcountry. This included areas with open skirmishes (Maine), areas with long-standing backcountry/coastal antagonism (the Carolinas), and peoples reluctant to join the Anglos' revolution, including Native Americans and German-speaking Pietists. Many were alienated from coastal elites and had little interest in non-consumption. Prior to the war, colonists in Worthington, Massachusetts, were so divided over the Association and its enforcement that they spent eight hours debating in town meeting whether to punish a man for using tea—with no resolution. The region joined more forcefully with the rest of Massachusetts after warfare began. Moravians brought tea with them when they trekked from Pennsylvania to North Carolina. Having hauled tea along the Appalachians, they were unlikely to give it up. In Salem, North Carolina, Moravians allowed tea sales until March 12, 1775, and permitted home consumption thereafter. Moravians in nearby Bethania, North Carolina did not ban tea either, cherishing it for special occasions. Finding no buns for the Love-feast (a Moravian religious service at which simple food is provided), Reverend John Jacob Ernst and his wife served communicants a meal from their larder "only of bread, salt, and a mug of tea" on July 8, 1775. "Several members," wrote the reverend, "said afterwards that for a long time they had not had so sweet a Lovefeast, and it was dearer to them than if they had had the best of cake," though the reverend attributed this to Christ, not tea.[17] Native Americans were wholly uninterested in the Association. In August 1775, Nicholas Cresswell, surveying land, came upon a town of "Christianized Moravian Indians" called Schoenbrunn (in present-day Ohio). Schoenbrunn had log-and-clapboard homes and a church with shingles, glass windows, a bell, and a German pastor. Cresswell attended evening services, which he thought put any "bigot"'s ideas of Indians to shame. After church he was "Treated with Tea, Coffee and Boiled Bacon at supper."[18]

Even Patriotic colonists consumed tea outside of Patriot territory. Ethan Allen was famous for his capture of Fort Ticonderoga. He was later taken prisoner. In January 1776, he was held aboard HMS *Soledad*, off Cork, Ireland. Allen reported that the Irish populace took up a collection to supply him and thirty-three other rebel prisoners. For Allen, the celebrity, supporters provided a panoply of luxuries. But every man got clothes, sugar, and "two pounds of tea." The captain, declaring "the d—d American rebels should not be feasted at this rate, by the d—d rebels of Ireland," seized some of the goods and gave the prisoners' tea to the crew. In foreign ports, provincial merchant captains also bought tea for personal use.[19]

Tea was an imperfect marker of allegiance. Salemite James Jeffry worked as a mail carrier out of Quebec, where no association was signed. He traveled between Montreal and Massachusetts as non-consumption began. His social engagements were a political mash-up: Patriot sympathizers, Loyal Britons, and Quebequois. He took tea in Montreal and Willsboro, New York. He reached Ticonderoga in April with the Loyalist Major Andrew Skene, taking tea with Captain Delaplace, his wife, and Skene's sisters at the fort, and taking tea again in Salem with a Mrs. Cabot in May. Two months later, on his return, he found Ticonderoga under rebel control and drank chocolate with Benedict Arnold on Lake Champlain. He spent the summer and fall in Quebec City, drinking tea with the Anglophone establishment until General Carleton expelled him for refusing to defend the city.[20]

Tea Consumption in Patriot Lands

Colonists bought and drank tea in Patriot-controlled areas, too. The gap between professed and real adherence to the Association was greatest when merchants thought Patriots were not looking, though how much tea colonists consumed remains unclear.

Norfolk, Virginia merchant Neil Jamieson sold tea on his own account, despite a run-in with Patriots over tea in 1774. He was also resident partner for the Glasgow firm John Glassford and Company. Glassford kept stores in Southern Maryland and Eastern Virginia. Between September 1775 and March 1776, Glassford sold over ninety pounds of tea in forty-eight sales to at least thirty-three buyers. These sales were mostly in Maryland but also in Boyd's Hole and Norfolk, Virginia. This included sales to Glassford subsidiary stores in Bladensburg and Colchester and to another firm. Some retail buyers paid cash; most bought on credit: tea fit into debit and credit relationships that stood for years. Glassford sold to all, and so the ledger entry for Dr. James Huie's pound of hyson in September 1775 sat silently on the page next to the Stafford County, Virginia committee's order of gunflints the following spring. Among the tea buyers was the "Sheriff of Charles County (W. Homson)," who bought two pounds of green tea on January 30, 1776.[21]

In Guilford, North Carolina, John Tate sold tea, and the Byrne general store in Bladen County took payments for tea previously bought. Richard Bennehan and William Johnston's Little River Store inventories show they got rid of four pounds of tea between March 1775 and March 1776. Johnston was active in North Carolina Patriot politics.[22]

In Scarsdale, New York, Benjamin Cornell booked four sales in March 1775. In Lloyd's Neck, Abner Osborn bought tea from the Patriotic merchant James Lloyd II. In Frederickstown (present-day Patterson), one merchant sold tea to eight men between July 1775 and January 1776, most during the autumn, when farmers bartered crops for supplies. In New York City, John Taylor's daybook shows nearly thirty retail sales between March and August 1775, much of it smuggled onto pilot boats for sale along the Hudson River. Taylor risked exposure when selling to each of his sixteen buyers. They risked, perhaps without knowing it, being recorded in a merchant's book. In August 1775, the Westchester committee declared "all persons who shall sell or buy any Tea in this County, and all boatmen and others who shall buy any Tea at New-York or elsewhere . . . contemners of the Resolutions of the Continental Congress," and set a deadline of August 25 for enforcement, suggesting the ban was not well enforced previously.[23] Taylor's last sale of tea was on August 22 to the *Bishop*.

Sales continued in Newport, where merchants had violated the previous non-importation agreement. Philadelphia was a hotbed of tea sales and consumption, too, despite hosting Congress. Though new to the city, Loyalist Samuel Curwen had no trouble finding tea there in May.[24]

At home, colonists violated the ban circumspectly. In Pennsylvania, Patriot Susanna Wright explained in a commonplace book, "I have public sp[ir]it. enough never to taste one drop of what [tea] has p[ai]d. The Duty." But for Dutch tea, "I must venture to use it as the Mahometans do Wine, not openly but in a manner to elude scandal & not to give Offence." Tea could be disguised as "Monongoheley Balsam" or other tisanes. A memoirist recalled her father, a minor Virginia merchant, declared for the Patriot side. He was coming home one day, "laughing and saying . . . 'Well, now, take notice one and all of you, that I have joined the *Association* (against tea), and you must drink no more of it.'" He added, "at least," do not drink it "in my sight." The family "banished the teapot from the table." But they "saw no good to come in spiting ourselves" by actually giving it up, so "we used to sip a little, now and then, by ourselves." Sometimes mother even served tea in front of father. She poured it "from a *coffee pot*, to which, of course, he could make no objection."[25]

In Salem, North Carolina, the Moravian Brother Bonn likewise suggested "Brethren and Sisters should be careful about buying and drinking tea," not because tea was bad, but to "not give occasion for criticism to travelers or visitors." In New Jersey, Reading Beatty hoped his sister and her husband would keep up appearances. Does she "drink <u>Tea</u> yet?," he wrote his brother-in-law Enoch Green. "I hope not," for "if she does, and you allow her, you will perhaps fall under the denomination of a Tory." Reading was not bothered about their tea but about their getting caught. He recalled Enoch's mother. If she were alive, she "would have had a whole Chest laid up in Store against a rainy Day"—she knew how to ride out a boycott.[26]

Violating the boycott could later become a jaunty triumph. Thus the apocryphal story of the wily Vermont widow, Lucretia Houghton, who, years later, was said to have discussed prohibition with a young visitor. Lucretia "had been a warm patriot in Revolutionary times, but such a devoted tea drinker that for many months she said, she used to set her tea table down cellar, lest folks should see her drink it."

"'Oh,' said I, 'you were not as good a patriot as my mother; she would not drink it on any account, but substituted sage and balm.'"

"'More fool she!' said the old lady, 'though I did cheat sometimes and drink Evanroot tea, but I would have my comfortable tea with my husband in the evening, and nobody was the wiser.'"[27] The story cannot be taken as fact, but its assumption (that people violated the Association) and its framing as an amusing (not embarrassing) anecdote are telling.

Tea marked special occasions. Elihu Ashley enjoyed tea with his brothers, sisters, and friends as part of his wedding in November 1775 and had a separate drink of tea with his brother to mark the occasion a couple days prior. This tea, like the tea served at the Moravian Lovefeast or the medical permits discussed previously, may have seemed more acceptable because of the distinctive meaning attached to it and its limited use.[28]

Then there were the permitted sales in the days before prohibition began. The ban on retail tea sales and home consumption began on the same date, March 1, 1775, a flaw (or a feature?) of the Association. Colonists could buy tea in February and drink tea in private in March. In Boston, Caleb Loring bought four pounds of tea (enough to last a household for years) four days before the ban on home consumption began. Why buy, if not to drink it? At their Millstone, New Jersey store, provincial congressman Abraham Van Neste and his partner Frederick Van Liew recorded forty-eight tea sales in February 1775. Similar spikes in sales occurred before the Association began in other colonies.[29] Patriots imagined that political virtue would prevent home consumption. So, were colonists like Loring virtuous and stupid (spending money on tea they did not drink) or naughty and smart?

Merchants knew which; thus, tea advertisements continued right up until prohibition began. William Beadle's ad joking that tea was addictive appeared in the *Connecticut Courant* until late February 1775. Here was an implicit invitation to drink tea during the ban. Other ads in the *Pennsylvania Journal*, *Wöchentliche Pennsylvanische Staatsbote*, *New York Gazette*, *Providence Gazette*, and *Maryland Journal* offered tea for sale weeks before non-consumption began.[30]

Most tea ads stopped during prohibition, but not all. Frederick Bull advertised for "TEA! (I ask pardon)" several times between May and July in the Hartford *Connecticut Courant*. The ad acknowledged the ban while violating it.

Patriot John Mitchell advertised tea in the *Pennsylvania Journal* in March. Other advertisers during the ban included the New York firm of Shaw and Long, which sold banned tea and apparently felt no need to hide it. New Yorkers Remsen and Peters advertised tea as well.[31] None suffered for these invitations to violate the Association, which seem as egregious as they were unremarked upon.

Various merchants were left with unsold tea as the Association began. Some lobbied Congress to lift the ban. Patriots forgave merchants who repented (sincerely or not) for selling tea, sometimes allowing repentant sellers to keep their tea until prohibition ended. Patriots trusted these merchants' promises not to sell. Jacobus Low's troubles with committees in New York disappeared with a simple promise not to sell any more tea rather than with open destruction of his stock.[32] Simon Tufts was not forced to burn his tea and sold it again soon thereafter, though his customer burned what he had bought. Holding tea put a tremendous burden on merchants' virtue. Tea was desired, forbidden, and ever-present, an untenable situation for all.

Wholesale Violations

Wholesale tea trading continued, too. The New York firm Shaw and Long acquired 1,454 pounds of tea in the fall of 1774. During the Association, they bought another 3,000 pounds and sold 2,700. This tea came from other New Yorkers, like Loyalists Hugh & Alexander Wallace. There is no indication Shaw and Long were Loyalists themselves. Rather, they were connected to the Wallaces through the city's Irish business community.[33]

Shaw and Long sold to merchants in other towns: four barrels of tea leaves to Albany committeeman Robert McClallen and additional tea to the Quackenbush and Ten Eyck families. Most of Shaw and Long's tea, nineteen barrels, went to Newport, an even more egregious town, where local merchants sold it on commission. There Samuel Bours sold fifteen barrels, representing thousands of pounds of product.[34]

Bours had been caught selling tea in March 1775. He confessed and was forgiven. Committeeman William Ellery lamented Bours did not name names, and that the committee was "not so firm and severe as I could have wished," but thought it "hath had a good effect" and "gave a home-blow to the baneful herb." Unbeknownst to Ellery, Bours was selling tea again by summer (if he ever really stopped), this time for Shaw and Long. Bours's records do not survive. Shaw and Long's books are the only evidence that Bours sold their tea, and the Newport committee was blissfully unaware of them. Without them, we would be led, as Ellery, to see Bours's story as an example of effective enforcement. Bours repented, but probably to get the committee off his back so he could go back to selling tea, not because he had a change of heart. If he took any lesson from his encounter with the committee, it was probably not to keep records.[35]

Other Newport merchants' books survive, suggesting extensive prohibition tea trade in Rhode Island. Thomas Vernon sold tea in bulk: twenty, forty, one hundred pounds at a time. He sold it by the hogshead to Stephen Smith in Bristol and John Glazier in East Greenwich, by the cask to John Hadwen, and to others by the pound. Hadwen retailed tea in 1775, and in early 1776 bought two casks from Vernon, probably hoping to move up the supply chain.[36]

Bours was not the only seller who kept selling after being caught. In April, the Calvert County, Maryland committee declared merchant Alexander Ogg "enemy to the cause of America" for price gouging. Despite censure, he did well enough to restock tea from Wallace, Davidson, and Johnson in Annapolis that August.[37] The committees may even have inadvertently helped him, signaling to buyers that he was transgressive enough to sell banned goods. Ogg's order survives in his suppliers' books, not in his own: merchants under suspicion keep few records. If Jamieson, Bours, and Ogg successfully sold tea even as Patriots watched, what did unwatched merchants do?

The documents cited here hint at clandestine traffic extending beyond their pages. Shaw and Long's wholesale trades equated to hundreds of retail transactions—but the end buyers are mysteries. Their records point to larger suppliers like the Wallaces. Who else served this role? Where did these suppliers get tea? Not from Britain—New York imported almost no tea from there. Whom else did they supply? Shaw and Long's sales in Albany and Newport hinted at broader trading networks. Philadelphia has its own tea trading network, as evinced by tea discussions between Philadelphian John Pringle and Patriotic Baltimore merchant George Woolsey. Philadelphians Willing and Taylor bought tea from New York Patriot Anthony Bleecker. When they complained it was "Musty & unmerchantable" (implying tea was otherwise "merchantable"), Bleecker tried to settle with his supplier without, crucially, divulging who his supplier was.[38] There is more mystery than revelation here: thousands of pounds of tea changing hands, with its origin, destination, and the broader trade remaining murky, as the names of the thousands of other men and women involved in it.

Bleecker's letters suggest tea may have been imported during prohibition. In May, he ordered twelve chests via St. Eustatius from Amsterdam merchant Jean de Neufville. It is unclear whether de Neufville sent them. Bleecker was more concerned about quality than security, asking the tea be "sent in the original packages" despite British and Patriot patrols. Bleecker discussed the tea trade openly in his letters. Bleecker could discuss violating the Association in his correspondence more easily than Loyalists could (who knew the committees would read their mail), though one imagines Bleecker sent this letter by private conveyance.[39]

Contrast Bleecker's treatment with the Prince Gorham affair. Gorham arrived in Barnstable, Massachusetts with, it was rumored, tea. The county's past reticence to police tea and its rather conservative population gave this rumor weight. "Our Committee take no Notice of it," complained Nathaniel Freeman, asking whether, if Massachusetts Patriots ignored this, would "one man has not as good [a] right as another to break through the resolves of Congress"? He hoped the colony's revolutionary leadership would "put a stop to the disorderly Spirit prevailing or there will be no end to the growing strength of the Tories in this County." Several days later Freeman heard passengers on Gorham's vessel report Gorham carrying "a large quantity of tea." "[I]f there is a Resolve of Congress against emporting this Article it ought to be adhered to or Rescinded this affair I fancy will make much Noise if worked out of Sight." Massachusetts Patriots summoned Gorham. They also ordered the Barnstable sheriff to seize the tea. But though "he had made all due search and inquiry" for it, he found none, nor evidence that any had been imported.[40] It is unclear whether Gorham had imported tea. Yet Patriots' understandable sense that certain people merited watching seems to have let others, like Bleecker, skate by.

The best evidence tea was shipped to the colonies in 1775 comes from imperial customs collectors. On February 1, 1775, Francis Welsh, a customs officer in Philadelphia, attempted to seize the *Isabella* in the Delaware River. She was in from Dunkirk with various goods, including thirty pounds of tea "done up in Bundles" for easy retail. The smugglers fought off the collectors and, in the conventional interpretation, the Chester County sheriffs were too Patriotic to help officers of the Crown. This allowed the smugglers to escape with the tea. Two days later, customs authorities in Philadelphia warned about another vessel with "Tea and War-like Stores from Holland" that had tried to land near Philadelphia and was trying Newport next. Importing tea was forbidden by Patriot authorities. Yet it was His Majesty's Customs Collectors—a handful of understaffed, over-harassed, and ineffective men—not the Philadelphia committee, who intercepted the *Isabella*. In March 1775, the Admiralty added that the *Prosperity* was sailing "from Dunkirk to North America" with more tea.[41]

As imperial customs offices ceased to function, Patriots began to take over their role. In December 1774, individual shipmasters presented themselves to Baltimore customs officials and the Baltimore committee, swearing to the latter that they had brought no tea. By March 1775, the committee kept records of incoming and outgoing ships and formalized an oath for all masters of incoming vessels to take, swearing their cargoes were Association-compliant.[42] It is unclear if they were any more effective at policing trade than imperial customs officers had been.

It is not surprising that merchants like Bleecker tried to import tea. Perhaps some succeeded, as rumors suggested. A "Mr. Adams" was caught with a barrel of imported tea leaves on Long Island in January 1776. In mid-March, the *Virginia Gazette* reported tea being shipped from Holland to St. Eustatius "to be disposed of to the North American vessels, which are continually passing that way."[43] At the very least, tea smuggling was popularly understood to be ongoing.

Thinking about Merchant Ledgers

Why did merchants record tea sales? There were good reasons not to. Selling forbidden goods was risky enough, but a paper trail was riskier, particularly as committees inspected some merchant books. Circumspect customers might avoid black marketeers who kept records, and most merchants who sold illicit goods probably did not record such sales. Yet even after the Norfolk, Virginia committee sought to inspect books, Glassford & Co sold tea in Norfolk and recorded it in their ledger. Keeping books was a bureaucratic necessity for larger firms. Recordkeeping allowed merchants of any size to track stock and balance books. Two main types of records survive. One is daybooks. These chronologically list each day's transactions and were proof of sale in commercial disputes, an important reason for merchants to retain them. The other is ledgers, which tracked debits and credits. These list each customer's account individually, tracking purchases made on loans and subsequent repayments in cash or barter, allowing a merchant to know who owed what. Most buyers bought tea on credit—three-quarters of the Glassford tea sales were on credit—to be paid off months or years later. Without tracking debt, merchants would be giving their goods away. In deciding whether to record illicit sales, merchants had to balance their need to hide what they did against their need to get paid.

There were ways around this. Cash sales were one. Ledgers tracked debt, not transactions; there was no need to record cash sales in debt ledgers. But the shortage of circulating currency prevented most buyers from paying cash. Glassford's Bladensburg Journal records only three out of fourteen tea sales in cash; for two of them, the buyer is unnamed. Cash commanded discretion but only for the few who could afford it.[44]

Another solution was to book the debt but hide what was sold. Ledgers that were detailed in February 1775 suddenly in March 1775 speak in terms of "merchandise" and "sundries" instead of specific goods. A merchant who extended a £10 credit to a customer to buy "merchandise" could track the loan while hiding whether he sold banned goods or evaded price controls. "Sundries" and "merchandise" also appeared in public advertisements, perhaps as a wink and a nod that they sold more than they could admit. William Beadle, who advertised tea right up until March 1, listed many items in an April ad and closed by offering "2 or 3 Hundred other Articles, which I Sell so Cheap that I cannot afford to Pay the Printer for telling you their Names; therefor would be glad you would Please to come and Buy them without my Advertising them at large."[45] This was a wordy way to save words in an ad that charged by the line. Perhaps it hinted at banned goods.

Most surviving merchant records do not show tea sales during the ban. Twenty-three show tea sales out of roughly one hundred prohibition-era merchants whose accounts were examined. It is difficult to determine how many of the remaining merchants would have recorded tea sales were the ban not in place. Still, this number represents a decline in recorded tea sales since some of the ledgers recording no sales during the ban recorded sales just before the ban took effect or right after it ended. The decline in recorded tea sales can be attributed both to compliance with the ban and to selling tea off-books, but these explanations are in tension. The more of this decline we attribute to selling tea off-books, the less we can attribute to non-consumption.[46]

Even if the drop in recorded tea sales was matched by a drop in actual tea sales, such a drop does not prove compliance with the ban. Sales could stop because the merchant obeyed, or because a merchant had difficulty obtaining credit or supplies. The question, how many merchants did not sell tea because of the ban, is impossible to answer. The best we can do here is make an educated guess: perhaps another twenty out of the one hundred would have sold tea, give or take another ten.

Tea prices allow us to look beyond the limits of the few surviving records. In 1775, New York and Philadelphia wholesale prices remained not far from 1773 levels (see figure C.1). In 1775 the Association diminished demand for tea enough to match supply. The high tea prices of 1774 had been potentially embarrassing for Patriots, hinting at popular demand for tea and the possibility that the boycotts might be disastrous. The Association did not stop the tea trade, but partial compliance kept prices steady, which was itself an achievement. The black marketeers of 1775 probably would have charged more for tea if they could have—we know that Ogg, for instance, gouged customers for other goods. The fact that they did not suggests they may not have been able to. The struggles over rising prices for tea and other imports would begin again in the second half of 1776, as the British blockade and Patriot monetary policies took hold.[47]

Although there was no upward or downward trend in tea prices in 1775, there was considerable regional variance: prices in Savannah and Newport were consistently higher than in New York, suggesting Shaw and Long's arbitrage, buying tea cheaply in New York and selling it at a markup in Newport, was good business. (See figures C.1 and C.2.)

Yet the biggest variance was often in the price one merchant would charge different people for the same tea. In Maryland, in January 1776, Glassford & Co sold bohea to five different buyers at varying prices (all on credit and in Maryland currency), some paying double what others did. Perhaps the price fell for damaged tea and rose for customers in arrears on their debt. By contrast, Glassford gave good prices (if not always their best) to buyers who paid in barter or pounds sterling.

Specialized teas had greater variance. Regular green tea varied between 8 shillings in Maryland and 10 shillings in Rhode Island, while hyson varied between 10 shillings sterling in Maryland and 23 in Georgia. With smaller supplies, their prices reflected shortages sooner, providing new, if smaller, arbitrage opportunities. By contrast, in British Boston hyson prices remained steady at 15 shillings a pound, despite the shortage of other goods.[48]

Merchant ledgers whisper a secret truth about tea and British goods: colonists surreptitiously consumed them. The recorded evidence of thousands of colonists buying tea and British goods during the ban created a new category of information that had to be guarded. These secrets were strikingly well kept. Almost none of the transactions in the ledgers discussed here were known to the committees charged with investigating them, though some committees may not have looked too closely.

These hidden truths speak to other lies: the lies of tea sales not booked in ledgers and the lies of colonists who went about with prohibition on their lips and tea in their stomachs. These lies have value. They tell us the social imaginings of colonists: their belief that they needed to pretend to obey the ban shows their belief in the power of the Patriot committees and the social importance of the pretense of non-consumption, even as continued consumption eroded that pretense.

Counter-Associations

The Association signaled allegiance to the Patriot cause; counter-associations signaled allegiance to the government. For Loyalists, the Association and tea riots were not resistance but things to be resisted. In response to Patriot demands that colonists support the boycott and sign the Continental Association, Loyalists formed their own associations. Retreating to British-defended Boston, Timothy Ruggles announced a loyalist counter-association in the press.[49] Signatories agreed to defend each other against the "banditti" who would deprive them of their rights and privileges, "the free exercise, and enjoyment of our undoubted right to Liberty, in eating, drinking, buying, selling, communing and acting what, with whom and as we please." Ruggles appealed to Massachusettsans who deplored the Tea Party and the with-us-or-against-us divisiveness of the Association. But potential signatories, spread out across the land and threatened with violence, remained silent. Before Lexington and Concord, General Gage struggled to get even Loyal Bostonians to sign a counter-association: whenever he asked them to sign, they put him off.[50]

Beverley Robinson of Westchester, New York, formed an association, raising and commanding the Loyal American militia regiment. Robinson valued this sort of militia for the way they left men "free to speak their sentiments." New York's Dutchess County declared an association drawn from Ruggles's text. Ruggles's counter-association and those from Westchester, Dutchess, and Marshfield defended colonists' freedoms to speak, buy, and sell. But such counter-associations were rare. Most counter-associations were about defense and in response to military events.[51] They might implicitly protest on behalf of Loyalists' freedoms, but practically they extended little beyond defending Loyalists' persons and expressing loyalty to the Crown.

Governor John Wentworth of New Hampshire armed an association for "Constitutional Liberty" and "wholesome Laws of the Land" against "Mobs" on January 17, 1775. The Portsmouth Loyalist Protective Association included tea importer Edward Parry and his landlord. Its fifty-nine members were professionals, merchants, and relations or connections of the governor. Their immediate impetus was the danger posed by the 400 Portsmouth men who had stormed Fort William and Mary on December 14, 1774, and taken the arms inside. The Protective Association was probably insufficient. The night after it was formed, Patriots held their tea bonfire in Portsmouth.[52]

In South Carolina, a group of backcountry of "Nonassociators" defied the provincial congress (in which the backcountry was not represented). This counter-association was more concerned with opposing armed struggle against Britain than preserving the freedom to consume. Similar efforts occurred in

North Carolina. In Georgia, Governor James Wright circulated papers to record colonists' disagreement with radicals' resolves. Men in Westchester, New York declared their "abhorrence of all unlawful Congresses and Committees." In Queens County, 136 people signed a resolve denouncing Congress and the Association. Other rural New York counties ignored the Association without forming a counter one.[53]

There was no coordination among counter-associations, which did not communicate with each other and hence did not achieve the Continental, or even colony-wide, scope of Patriot organizations. Conservatives' lack of organization was ironic, given that they stood for the ordered whole, which the rebels fractured, but conservatives and moderates were suspicious of associations, committees, and congresses. They were illegal, unconstitutional bodies. How could one uphold law and order in a lawless, disorderly way? Marshfield counter-associators could not accept they had formed an association, objecting to the word association and expressing "detestation and abhorrence of all assemblies and combinations of men (by whatever specious name they may call themselves)" who oppose the "Government of Great Britain." On March 16, 1775, Sir John Johnson, Guy Johnson, and other Tryon County leaders in New York signed a declaration against the Association. Likewise, in North Carolina, a group of 539 "sundry Inhabitants" (not associators) denounced associations as "dangerous" to "good Government" and bad for the public weal but formed no counter-group. An Association of Nonassociators would be nonsensical, and few Loyalists saw the point of, in their view, stooping to the rebels' level.[54]

Loyalists saw themselves as an oppressed minority suffering from "the multitude," as William Eddis put it, while contradictorily hoping to be part of the silent majority, the "many" whom Eddis also thought shared his views.[55] Perhaps many colonists did not care to obey the Association; perhaps many disliked politics, but time and again, Loyalists mistook apolitical colonists for anti-Patriots. In 1774, tea had been the basis for grand stands against Parliament. But as the banal violations of prohibition in 1775 suggest, using banned goods was not equivalently grand grounds for making a statement of loyalty to the King. The tea buyers and sellers described above generally did not sign counter-associations. Most colonists who bought banned goods avoided attention. The silent majority was not Loyalists but consumers and the politically indifferent.

The Failure of Tea as a Loyalist Symbol

Tea had marginal value as a Loyalist symbol. General Gage sent two spies to survey the road between Boston and Worcester in February 1775. The men were badly disguised. They stayed in known Loyalist taverns and gave themselves away as they went, which led to their being run out of Marlborough and discovered in nearly every other town. Friendly landlords discerned who they were and offered them "either tea or coffee" to hint at their politics. "We immediately found out with whom we were," Ensign D'Bernicre explained, chuffed at working it out. Asking "what he could give us for breakfast . . . tea or any thing else we chose," "that . . . was an open confession" the publican was a "friend to government." Others also gave tea drinking a Loyalist gloss. The New Yorker Benjamin Booth assured fellow Company tea importer James Drinker that "tea is bought, sold and drank as usual, *in defiance of Congress and Committees*" after the Association took effect. In exile in London, Elisha Hutchinson received word of his wife, still in the colonies, who "braves it out; by the last accounts from her in Sept. [1775] she is President of a Club composed of 8 ladies. They meet over a tea table once or twice a week, in opposition to the Rebells."[56]

The boycott could have created a way for Loyalists, particularly through consumption of British manufactures and tea, to express their sentiments, just as in non-consumption it gave Patriots a way to express theirs. Tea drinking, done to express Loyalism, would defy Patriot authority. This was what happened when Captain William Ward and several other men invited Elihu Ashley to tea shortly after the Association came into force. At first thinking it a joke, Ashley finally sat down and "found it to be Tea in reality. I drank none of it," he wrote, as his host revealed himself to be a "High Torey." This was risky for Ward, as there was more defiance and danger in drinking tea in New England than in boycotting it in defiance of a Parliament thousands of miles away.[57]

Yet tea drinking did not have to signal Loyalism. Ashley would have tea at his own wedding half a year later—not out of Loyalism, but because it was nice. To make tea a Loyal symbol, Ward had to imbue it with politics, and there were more direct ways to express one's Loyalism.

Loyalists rarely made tea central to resisting Patriots. William Aitchison, a Scots factor and Tory with a Virginia wife, explained in December 1775 that "Tea is now entirely disused in our Familys," despite tea on hand and his wish to continue it. Mary Rothery recalled of relatively Loyalist Norfolk, Virginia, that "Few people would permit Tea to be drank in their Houses," suggesting most tea drinkers had propitiated Patriots. When others, such as Frances Martin, described serving tea to Mr. and Mrs. Benjamin Hatley Foote, it was without any sense of resisting Patriot power.[58]

Loyalists rarely thought in terms of resistance. Some were reluctant to separate themselves from the politically indifferent. "Resistance" also made little sense to others who saw themselves upholding legitimate order against a Patriot junto. They were supposed to be the mainstream, not the rebels. But, as Loyalists stayed still, the world transformed around them, making them dissenters for the establishment, an impossible position. The best way to undermine Patriot dominance would have been to use Loyalist associations, the same kind of organization that had undermined the empire. But the counterassociations were reluctant shambles. For Loyalists, Patriot-style politics were the problem. This was partly an aesthetic objection. The public display—the mobs, the militias, the street politics, and the showy investment of everyday consumer choices with political meaning (surely many wondered whether anyone's little bit of tea made a difference)—was off-putting. Loyalists did not drink tea "in opposition" to the rebels with the same public display, political savvy, and verve as Patriots burned tea in opposition to Parliament. While Ashley's fellow militiaman treated tea drinking politically, he drank it just as privately as a thousand less-political consumers.[59]

Loyalists' failing would be tea's saving grace. Tea only faintly symbolized Tory resistance. After Lexington, Loyalists followed their Patriot cousins in emphasizing preparations for war, not consumer choices. Forming militias, stocking gunpowder, and declaring for the King were more important than drinking tea or killing sheep. Loyalists were shunned, proscribed, and disarmed, bigger problems than being deprived of tea or British fabrics. Lamenting their condition after the war, they complained of being attained of treason, stripped of their property, tarred and feathered, beaten, and forced to flee for their lives without benefit of trial or common law. When Loyalists tallied up their financial losses and sufferings and sought recompense from the British state, tea was hardly mentioned. Loyalists wanting a symbol for King and Parliament could do as Loyalists in Shawangunk, New York did. They replied to the Association not with a tea barrel but a seventy-six-foot mast with a royal standard on it.[60]

Nor was tea the best way to goad Patriots. As Samuel Johnson noted, patriots had complained that Parliament was trying to make them slaves, but Loyalists knew what really infuriated Patriots was the charge that their own work was fit for "Negroes." "[D]amn them all," Virginia merchant Andrew Leckie said of Virginia's congressmen. When committeemen asked him to sign the Association, Leckie turned to "a Negro Boy" and joked, "Piss Jack, turn about my Boy and sign." The committee, angered by the idea that the Association was fit for Jack, forced Leckie to publish a self-criticism in the newspaper, wherein Leckie apologized for being "so unguarded and imprudent" as to tell a "Negro" slave to sign the Association, which was "indecent" and "contemptuous." In Delaware, Tories took a Patriot constable down a peg by getting a black man to whip him. In Connecticut, Benjamin Stiles was accused of insulting congressmen as "good for nothing Dogs" and, worse, compared them to "his Negro Jeff." This, more than the accusation of tea drinking, was what got him a trial in the colonial legislature. (Stiles had a point: his slave Jeffrey later joined the Continental Army and won his freedom).[61] In general, destroying tea was a better way for Patriots to thumb their noses at Parliament than drinking it was a way for Loyalists to thumb their noses at Congress.

A Loyalist did not have to drink tea because she was Loyalist. She might, like everyone else, drink tea because she liked it. Elizabeth Drinker was the sort of woman who should have found tea politically and symbolically meaningful. Tea had been central to her family's fortunes. In her diary she noted the Patriots hounding her husband over the Company's tea in 1773, and the Patriots closing her brother-in-law's shop in 1776. But she never remarked on the Association's effect on her personal life or gave any sense she was defying it. In 1774, when tea was still allowed, she recorded that the family had gone out riding and "came home all together after Tea." When the Patriots banned tea, she recorded just as prosaically that "Sarah Mitchel and Molly Strench, drank Tea with us," among her regular outings and visits, and added in October 1775, "I drank Tea at Uncle Jerviss" in her diary. She gave no sense that these were politically meaningful acts. Rather, she noted these visits for their social value. Her family probably drank tea at home too, but she did not bother marking this in her diary because these were not special gatherings. Other times during the Association she had coffee. She was careful that "having tea" meant tea. When William Brown visited, she wrote "drank tea with us," in her diary, only to cross out "tea" and write in "coffee" instead.[62] For Elizabeth, tea was part of normal life. It maintained custom and routine (a sentiment at the heart of conservatism), but she gave no sign it was tied up in an active expression of Loyalism.

Briton Janet Schaw lamented finding no "dish of Tea" for a month in Brunswick, North Carolina (her stay overlapped with the Association taking effect). She had had tea in Scotland, on the voyage to the New World, on Antigua and St. Kitts, and would have it later in Portugal; by comparison, the Patriot fetishization of tea seemed absurd. Schaw took her first dish in the colonies at the North Carolina estate of Joseph Eagles, a plantation owner's son just back from an Anglicizing adolescence in Britain, his home an oasis from the Patriots around her.[63] But Schaw gave no sense that tea meant defiance—she and Eagles admitted no Patriot writ to defy. Rather, tea signified normalcy—she drank tea because that is what people did.

A coherent meaning to tea is hard to find because tea drinkers were not a coherent behavioral or social group. There was no distinct class of Loyalist tea drinkers. Loyalist and Patriotic merchants were intermixed, as Patriots and Loyalists generally, by business partnerships, marriages, commerce, and community. These links had doomed Patriot tea politics for a decade. The firm Amory Taylor and Rogers was Loyal enough to stay on in Boston in 1775, but it worked with William Barrell, a confirmed Patriot, in Philadelphia. Tea wholesaler Thomas Vernon of Newport was exiled for Loyalism in 1776. His siblings included the noted Patriots Samuel and William Vernon, who had imported Swedish tea in late 1774. Their sister, Elizabeth, married Elnathan Hammond. Hammond bought tea from his brother-in-law, Thomas, and retailed it to others, including two of Hammond's own sons. One of these sons, John Arnold Hammond, was taken prisoner by the British and died in captivity.[64] The step-uncle, Thomas, exiled for his Loyalism, and the step-nephew, John Arnold, who died for the Patriot cause, were part of the same tea-trading network.

Nor was Telfair, for all his Patriotism, above selling to Loyalists. Georgia Loyalism is tricky: a Loyalist in 1775 was not necessarily the same as one in 1776 or 1779.[65] Yet while an ideological gap separated Telfair and his buyers, trading tea did not, suggesting the ban was not that meaningful.

A tea seller could serve both sides. Christopher Champlin had contracts to supply the Royal Navy at Newport, but Champlin needed supplies from a base of Patriot farmers to do it. Until 1775 he pleased both sides, keeping his politics and tea sales quiet and evading the distinction between Patriot and Tory. He ignored the 1767 boycott and joined the 1770 one but was embarrassed to admit it to his British correspondents. The purser of HMS *Rose* ordered tea from him in February 1775. That year, Champlin sold tea and had Loyal friends and relatives. Yet he ultimately supported the Patriots and fled Newport when British troops arrived.[66]

The poet Hannah Griffitts captures this ambiguity. Rather than siding with Tories or Patriots, she attacked politicians in general. The tea ban was "wicked," and she declared a pox on both houses. Neither "King, nor Parliament nor North," "Nor Congress, nor Committee Muster / With all their Malice, noise & Bluster / Sur will not dare—to hinder me / From getting fresh Recruits of Tea." She also wrote an anti-ministerial poem, "Beware the Ides of March," urging people to "give up Tea." Griffitts was of many minds: she ultimately became a Loyalist but was sympathetic to the issues Patriots raised. She spoke to the nebulous feelings that many people, not just Quakers like herself, felt: to being not on one side or the other, but sometimes both and neither at the same time.[67]

The Hollow Ban

Some colonists embraced the ban. On the first day of prohibition, Christopher Marshall noted in his diary, "departed these parts . . . to the joy and satisfaction of the lovers of freedom, that baneful and detested weed, East India TEA, whose return is never desired . . . by the true sons of American liberty." As a pharmacist, the Philadelphian Marshall could have dispensed tea, but he was active in Patriot politics and took virtue to heart. He did not dispense tea, stuck to coffee, balm, and sage for himself, and wrote in his remembrancer of having "coffee," not tea, with Congressmen Ward, Gadsden, and the Adamses.[68] The propaganda theater that began the last chapter encouraged average colonists to do likewise. Patriots believed colonists who declared for the Association and did not enforce the ban heavily. This created a safe space for tea consumers. Inspection committees did not catch the sales described earlier. The claim that private consumption had stopped was propaganda; the Association could not distinguish between true believers, like Marshall, and Bours, who was just pretending.

The war replaced the boycott as a practical and symbolic way to resist Britain, making the consumption of banned goods easier. In March 1775, the Association's ban on tea, British trade, and cockfighting had value in protests, moral economies, and ways for colonists to signal conformity to a common cause. But, as the war, various test oaths, and independence became stronger ways to express these meanings, the ban on tea seemed as trifling as a cockfight.

Colonists liked tea. Merchants smuggled it past Crown customs collectors and broke Patriot non-importation and non-consumption orders to get it. Neither Parliament nor Congress could stop this. Following the example of the Crown customs collectors they deposed, Patriots largely confined their interdiction to non-importation, ignoring the sale and home consumption of banned goods. It was easier for committees to rule if they were not obnoxious.

The economic importance of the boycott declined as the hope of strong-arming British merchants faded, and as Parliament closed more colonial ports. Since Britain would keep these ports closed whether non-importation continued, the latter became moot. Patriots made various political-economic trade-offs with the Association. They made exceptions to non-importation for strategic goods: salt (to preserve meats) and saltpeter (to make gunpowder). Congress continued to permit the importation of British Caribbean rum and sugar, important trade lines. Conversely, it kept the ban on imported woolens from Britain. Tea was not so economically crucial. It did not have to be acquired, as English woolens, by trading with the enemy. Nor was it as important as sugar. Merchants lobbied against the tea ban, but once denied, they could smuggle in new tea quietly. Loyal merchants' intercepted letters show them contemplating what goods might sell (to British soldiers, Dunmore's slave army, or maybe, once the King's troops won, to the general public). British tea is not among these.[69] The conflict over tea quieted; business continued; tea became, once more, a politically insignificant mid-level trade good. At the height of the ban, all the meaning Patriots had invested in tea evaporated. Colonists responded to the Association with all the tea buying and drinking above, but as consumers, not Loyalists. This left Congress to repeal the ban.

CHAPTER 12

The Drink of 1776

The tea ban fit uneasily in an Association that banned other goods based on where they came from, not what they were. In wartime, trade with Europe was more necessary than ever—to get arms and ammunition, manufactured goods, and other supplies. Since tea could be smuggled in from Europe without affecting the Association's anti-parliamentary posture, the boycotts on tea and Britain might be separated. Merchants with capital tied up in unsellable tea chaffed at the tea ban. They did not debate this in the newspapers; they lobbied Congress, arguing that allowing them to sell existing tea supplies would free up funds to smuggle arms. After months, Congress relented and re-authorized tea. In 1776, the campaign to make tea unpatriotic failed.[1]

After war began in 1775, the value of tea as a symbol of Patriot resistance waned. By 1776, non-importation and non-consumption were no longer the sine qua nons of Patriot authority they had been in early 1775; more colonists accepted Patriot authority than adhered to non-consumption. A key argument for permitting tea once more was that supposedly Patriotic colonists (i.e., ones who had signed the Association) were drinking tea despite the ban. Colonists said they would follow prohibition, yet they did not. Instead of declaring so many colonists unpatriotic, Congress made tea Patriotic. This was a triumph of consumerism.

The war even hollowed out the ban on British tea and British goods. While trading with the enemy was banned, consuming British tea and manufactured goods was allowed, provided those goods were captured from the enemy rather than traded for. Such prizes were a welcome relief from wartime shortages.

In the end, Patriot leaders left the tea affair behind them, allowing colonists to drink and merchants to sell tea. Once re-authorized, tea was openly consumed across the colonies. South Carolina Patriots even went so far as to sell off the East India Company's tea previously held in the Charleston Exchange to support their newly independent state government. Elsewhere, while colonists had once burned tea in protest, Americans now rioted because the tea that was left was too expensive.

The Move against Prohibition in New York

A push to lift the tea ban, often with the interests of mid-Atlantic merchants who had imported Dutch tea in mind, began shortly after non-consumption was implemented. The New York committee considered whether tea selling was as bad as buying it in March 1775.[2] In June, Alexander McDougall wrote to Richard Henry Lee, suggesting those with leftover Dutch tea be permitted to sell their stock and use the proceeds to buy arms. This was less workable in Virginia, where merchants had imported English and Dutch tea, meaning there was less capital to free up by allowing Dutch tea to be sold, and a greater risk that British tea would be sold under Dutch cover. Lee reproached McDougall. He lamented the general want of "public virtue," worrying that if Congress permitted "the sale and the use of what tea is on hand, may not bad men take the advantage" and import new tea as well and "thus render abortive our Association against this article, the hateful cause of the present disagreeable situation in N. America." Perhaps he had the collapse of the 1770 boycott on his mind. Lee commended Virginia merchants to McDougall, whom he imagined were better at "public virtue" than New Yorkers—they had "large quantities of stopt Tea" but bore their "misfortune" for the "public good." "It is more than a year now," Lee smugly told McDougall, "since the use of Tea has been totally banished from Virginia."[3] Lee's conceit overlooked both the reality of tea consumption in Virginia and New York merchants' contribution to keeping British tea out by importing Dutch tea (which helped prevent colonial tea prices from rising enough to make importing British tea worth the risk).

New Yorkers argued that selling stopped tea would free up merchant capital to import arms. The New York committee of safety wanted to import £10,000 of weapons, but importers' money was still tied up in tea, which made the purchase difficult. As tea-holder Christopher Smith explained to Congressman John Alsop, the city's "Chief Dependence" for arms had "always" been upon the "Tea Holders," who had imported tea from Holland, with the Patriotic aim of keeping British tea out. They now had to sell off additional tea to be able to import arms. In July 1775, New York and Philadelphia merchants petitioned Congress for dispensation to sell European tea imported before the Association.[4] The New York provincial congress added that, though they "do not mean to encourage the future introduction of tea into the Colony," "Sundry" merchants still had "a very Considerable quantity of Tea" on hand, which, if sold, could aid the importation of "all kinds of ammunition, of which the Colonies are in the greatest want & which are chiefly Imported by the Tea Traders." In such a situation, "Congress," New York merchant Peter Keteltas explained to his congressman, John Alsop, "ought not to look with so evil an Eye on those Persons whom in contempt they call Smuglers." Alsop was sympathetic. A smuggler himself, he owned considerable stocks of stopped tea.[5]

The New York provincial congress added that the "illicit" trade in tea "undoubtedly" continued in New York. Since there was "general consumption of it throughout the Colony," it made sense to re-authorize and tax this tea, adding revenue to the colony's treasury. The alternative "clandestine" sales (but not so clandestine as to elude provincial congressmen) were no good for the public.[6] Richard Henry Lee's solution—enforcing prohibition—was not discussed.

Congress Debates Prohibition

Rumors of tea consumption reached the Continental Congress. Stories of New York merchants selling tea and mid-Atlantic merchants' inflated reputation for reluctance in previous boycotts helped these stories spread. In Congress, Samuel Chase of Maryland denounced New York for a "breach of the association" "with Respect to Tea." Pennsylvania delegate and merchant Thomas Willing concurred. "New York have broken it, entirely," he said, "ninety-nine in a hundred drink tea" there. In such a climate, it was difficult for the New York Continental Congress delegation to secure permission to sell stopped tea. "[T]ea gives us real Anxiety," the delegation wrote back to New York. We "sincerely wish to relieve our suffering" tea holders, they wrote, but chances were slim, despite a new petition, this time by Isaac Sears. In November, Congress rejected the New York and Philadelphia "tea holders" request to sell stopped tea.[7]

John Jay thought this "strange," "frivolous" decision came about because there was "no Tea" south of Philadelphia, except "what has paid Duty," making southerly delegates unsympathetic to the differentiation between English and Dutch tea and to the tea smugglers' plight.[8] However, it is more likely that Congress was unwilling to give up on prohibition so soon after it had begun.

While the tea ban still stood, chinks in the ban on the tea trade with Europe were appearing. In September 1775, Congress set up a secret committee to import war materiel and granted the first exceptions to non-exportation to ships that returned with arms. Merchants made a strong showing on the committee. These merchants were known for their skills in smuggling goods from Europe, and Congress needed smugglers. To get gunpowder to North America, Dutch merchants disguised their gunpowder in, as mentioned, tea chests. Congress permitted limited trade with Bermuda in November 1775, allowing in salt and military supplies along a route that might also bring in tea. The secret committee dispatched Samuel Mifflin's *Peggy* to Europe in December 1775, probably to purchase ammunition. The cover story included instructions to return with equal parts sail cloth, linen, and tea. The *Peggy's* supercargo would have to have purchased enough of this to hide the real cargo had the HMS *Viper* not intercepted her a week later. Revolutionaries in Boston, New York, the Chesapeake, and elsewhere contracted with merchants for weapons from abroad, and they all needed some way to transmit payment, which meant exports abroad and increased merchant demands to free up their capital in stopped goods, including tea and British manufactures.[9]

Meanwhile, stories of tea drinking abounded. In December 1775, Congress heard "Information" that "sundry persons in" Philadelphia were selling tea. (They may have sold tea under fake labels.) Congressman McKean informed his colleagues that "many Persons in Pennsa., Maryland and Jersey sell tea and drink Tea upon a [false] Report that Congress has granted Leave so to do & he doubted Whether the Committees had Power to restrain them." In Maryland, the provincial convention thought "all India teas" imported before March 1775 "may be sold and used without any prejudice to the cause of America" and instructed its congressional delegation to secure permission from Congress. The same day, Congress heard "Information" had emerged "against persons selling tea." By January 1776, the Philadelphia committee asked Congress for "Directions" for "selling & drinking Tea" in the city where Congress met. One wonders how blind an eye congressmen cast upon the tea illicitly bought, sold, and drunk around them. In January, McKean pressed again to permit pre-Association tea to be sold, but Franklin and Lynch opposed him. The Maryland convention's similar request to Congress was narrowly rejected on January 15, 1776, with New York, New Jersey, Pennsylvania, Delaware, and Maryland losing 5–7. Some described efforts to loosen the ban on tea as representing Dutch-trade merchants and the "smuggler's interest."[10] The description was accurate: the lobbyists asked to authorize Dutch tea, not British tea, and the smugglers with stopped Dutch tea on hand would have benefitted. However, this description tends to dismiss the demands for tea as coming from a narrow interest group rather than reflecting the consumer demand among the populace (for the smuggler's interest was a function of consumers' interests). Such a framing also overlooks the expanding group of colonies which wanted to re-authorize tea. If, as Samuel Chase complained, "ninety-nine in a hundred drink tea"—whether in New York or any other town—it can hardly be said that all the tea drinkers were smugglers. Nor can it be said that tea drinking was constrained to New York.

The ban on tea stood, but delegates slowly yielded as they recognized that pronouncements against tea were unheeded: the end of the Association in tea was not a case of congressional edict but of congressional accession to popular will. The great unstated lie of the Association—that colonists who said they would abide by it did so—became more openly admitted. New lies combatted it. The lie that Congress had permitted tea allowed for open violations of the ban. The ensuing claim that the ban was widely and openly violated played an important role in getting Congress to lift the ban. The social need to keep up the appearance of obeying prohibition collapsed when colonists realized they could stop pretending not to consume tea and pretend instead that they thought it was acceptable. They could claim to have heard the ban had ended or pretend to have "medical" needs. In so doing, they realized prohibition was hollow. Once consumption could be admitted out loud, the secrecy around consumption and the lie of prohibition could be dispensed with.[11]

Three weeks after the Maryland proposal lost and the pro-boycott delegates considered the matter concluded, New Jersey pressed Congress to reconsider, sparking, as Richard Smith noted, renewed "Controversy." In February, the New Jersey convention reminded Congress that "many persons have publicly sold" tea since the first false report of Congress permitting it, and now new, similar reports were trickling in. New Jersey asked for "Directions," reminding Congress that since "People" already "sell and use it on a supposed Connivance of Congress," permission would recognize current practice. Such tales, "often deceitful and always uncertain," Samuel Tucker grumbled, could not be allowed to quash "established regulation." But what could one do? The implicit message from New Jersey and other provinces was that tea could not be stopped. However rumors of congressional connivance began, New Jersey residents were willingly repeating them. Responding to a proposal to "stop" "this growing evil" of tea, more than one New Jersey delegate claimed his colleagues had "agreed in Congress that no notice should be taken of the sale or use of East-India Teas in the Eastern Colonies" at all.[12]

Seeing the extent of the rot, on February 13, 1776, Congress scaled back enforcement in the largest city under its control, urging the Philadelphia committee of inspection to halt "censures on the venders, and users of Tea, till farther orders from Congress." Now Congress was conniving to let tea be sold, for violators no longer risked being blacklisted. March was when Henry, Mc-Clallen and Henry advertised for tea in the *New York Gazette*, suggesting the connivance of Albany Patriots, too.[13]

While enforcement of the tea ban weakened, the rationale vanished. The King proclaimed rebellious ports shut, effective at the end of March 1776. Continuing a trade boycott while the Royal Navy blockaded the colonies would not impress London with the efficacy of the boycott. It would impress London with the efficacy of the British blockade and deny colonists vital supplies to little point. So, on April 6, Congress defied the King and declared its ports open. There were two exceptions: Patriotic colonies remained closed to British goods and all tea. Practically, this was not a big change in what trade Congress permitted, but it was a massive shift in the purpose of non-importation: non-import was no longer expected to affect the British economy since the blockade would have the same effect; rather, it avoided trading with the enemy in wartime. And with the conflict no longer about tea but instead with Britain, the question of Dutch tea came into sharper relief. The same day Congress reaffirmed the boycott on Britain, John Jay, Robert Morris, and Thomas McKean were asked "to bring in a resolution for disposing of and using the Tea now in these colonies." They pled the tea merchants' case: merchants had imported Dutch tea to undermine the East India Company but could not sell it before the Association took hold; now good, Patriotic tea vendors faced ruin. Merchants should, they urged, be permitted to sell tea imported before non-importation took effect (December 1, 1774), provided it was not British. As explained in the press, "zealous friends to the American cause" had smuggled in "large quantities" of Dutch tea in 1774. This not only enriched themselves but "counteract[ed] the plan . . . to sell tea in these colonies subject to a duty." With tea stopped, Adams's honest smugglers were "great sufferers," and Congress would give them relief. On April 13, 1776, Congress permitted tea be "sold and used" again, and published notice of this in the *Pennsylvania Gazette* four days later.[14]

Here, for once, the debate about whether the Patriot leadership acted out of openly stated ideological reasons or unstated economic ones evaporates: Congress meant what it said, and it said it was helping tea merchants. This shift had practical effects: Congress helped tea smugglers because they could smuggle gunpowder. After the King declared rebel ports shut, Congress relied on the "much-maligned" merchant-smugglers for supplies. Whether directly from Europe or indirectly via the Caribbean, arms sailed on the same routes, capital, and connections as tea.[15]

Two pretenses stood: only tea imported before December 1, 1774, was allowed, and this tea would not be from Britain. As one tea merchant commented in his journal, "Should be glad if Congress would inform me which way they are to distinguish between that which payed duty and that which has not; or whether the stock of Tea which I have now on had has paid duty or not unless I inform on myself." The commenter, John Weatherburn, was Patriot enough—he joined a toy militia for Baltimore's posher Patriots. Congress now reasoned that the three months between non-importation (December 1, 1774) and non-consumption (March 1, 1775) had been "too short." Congress now argued the lag had been intended to allow "all India tea" smuggled in before December 1774 to be "sold and consumed." (The congressional record from 1774 does not reflect this.) Allowing merchants who had smuggled tea before December 1774 to sell unsold stock was now said to fulfill the original plan. That tea, and only that tea, could "be sold and used." All tea imported from the East India Company, from Britain, or which had paid duty remained banned, and "future importation" of any tea—smuggled or otherwise—remained "prohibited." Underscoring this, the final resolve emphasized the continued "desire of Congress to exclude all teas." Congress urged local committees of inspection to remain vigilant and ensure no new tea was imported.[16] The one way new tea could be imported was if it were part of a prize cargo.

Despite ostensibly banning new tea imports, Congress was understood to allow them. This was partly because of the contemporary debate over independence, one argument for which was the need to trade and form military alliances with foreign powers. In this context, "A Virginian" wondered in print whether an alliance and trade agreement with France would allow the French to take North American produce and "furnish us with teas" and other consumer goods. The author worried that the trade agreement "will not be made soon enough," not that French tea would be forbidden.[17] It made sense to allow such tea in, as stopping it had no economic or symbolic value in the struggle against Parliament or Britain. The assumption that such tea was allowed was so thoroughly shared that Congress forgot to repeal its formal ban on tea imports. Instead, new tea masqueraded as old, or as tea taken in prize, just as legal tea had masqueraded as smuggled in 1770, and just as Richard Henry Lee had worried.

Merchants immediately took advantage of the exception for prizes. James Hunter's Virginia merchant firm listed "Goods most in demand in Virginia," including various British manufactures and East India goods, among them hyson tea. The firm explained that "All Goods of British Manufacture" needed a falsified "Certificate of their being Prize Goods" to prevent seizure. New tea imports were still illegal when Dutch merchant Jean de Neufville supplied Newporter Christopher Champlin with tea in Newport in 1779 or 1780. De Neufville, who was important as a lender to and supplier for the rebel cause and a key intermediary in negotiating relations with the Dutch, traded with other North American merchants, including Anthony Bleecker, which gave him ample opportunity to ship to tea. Champlin also imported tea from Gothenburg in 1780, following the old smuggling routes that had brought tea from Sweden and the Netherlands in the 1760s. The tea ban still formally stood when the first American merchantmen sailed to China in 1783 and after. It never was repealed, which means, if one takes the Continental Congress's resolves as standing law, tea imports are still forbidden to this day—that they were never actually stopped is a sign of how thoroughly the ban has been forgotten. Congress acceded to popular will: the people were drinking tea despite what the Association said, and in 1776 congressional "decriminalization" of tea gave consumers a wink and a nod to buy and drink as they wished.[18]

Tea's Return

Congressmen, like other colonists, loved tea. Relieved of the obligation to maintain a virtuous face, they began drinking it and sending it home immediately, some even before they declared independence. Caesar Rodney, who had enforced the Association as a member of the committee of observation and inspection in Kent County, Delaware, in 1775 between stints in Congress, sent a pound of "Green-Tea" to his brother and sister-in-law as soon as Congress permitted. "Tell Betsey to taste it," he told Thomas Rodney in May 1776, "and if She likes it, I will Send her a pound by the next post." He promised to send along another "ten or twelve" pounds of "Good Bohea Tea" by water, for even though tea prices were "most abominable high," he "Could not do without." In September 1776, John Adams sent a "Pound of Green Tea" to his wife Abigail. "I flattered my self, you would have the poor Relief of a dish of good Tea," he wrote, a balm amid her worries about smallpox inoculations for the children. Learning the tea had been delivered to Samuel Adams's wife, Elizabeth, instead, he urged Abigail "send a Card to Mrs. S.A., and let her know the Cannister was intended for You," though he suspected the other Mrs. Adams might not give it up. "[V]exed" by the awkwardness of the situation, John bought and sent "another Cannister" at what seemed the "amazingly dear" price of 40 shillings "Lawfull Money" a pound, to be sure Abigail got any.[19]

Nor were congressmen any more abstemious in their official duties. Arriving in Continental-occupied Montreal, the congressional commission sent to persuade Canadians to join their cause in 1776, which included Benjamin Franklin, Charles Carroll, and Samuel Chase, took tea en route on Lake George and Lake Champlain and was greeted upon arrival in Montreal by "a large assemblage" of French women, with whom the congressmen set down to tea. (Apparently, Henry, McClallen and Henry were right to have eyed the town's supply.[20])

Tea's social role—as a shared drink and a beverage good hosts provided guests—re-emerged in topsy-turvy ways. When the Connecticut brig *Defence* put in at Plymouth in June, Abigail Adams spent the afternoon aboard at tea. By contrast, Rhode Island had a sheriff exile Thomas Vernon and other Loyalists who refused the test oath to the farm of Stephen Keech in Glocester, Rhode Island. They enjoyed tea daily in June and July 1776, supplied by Keech as host, and paid for by the now-State of Rhode Island as a necessary expense. These political prisoners drank tea at state expense on the fourth of July.[21]

Virginians were just as tea mad. James Hunter, whose firm had tried to break into tea smuggling a few years earlier, was trading tea in bulk in 1776. When he learned that tea could once again be "indulged," Virginian Landon Carter had guests over to celebrate. "Not one of them could be satisfied but with two dishes," he wrote. The ten of them found it so "inebriating" they got nearly "drunk with it."[22] A tea party was, once again, just that.

Meanwhile, tea's medical role could be openly reaffirmed. It is unclear whether, in 1775, Robert Dixon's surgeon carried banned tea across the Maine wilderness to treat wounded soldiers in Quebec. But in 1776, Nathaniel Shaw ordered chocolate, coffee, and a bit of tea when laying in orders for the "Hospitle for the Sik" of the Continental fleet.[23]

The rapidity with which tea reappeared in shops and taverns reaffirms that some tea had been held aside, not burned. There was not enough time for tea appearing in April and May to be imported after Congress re-authorized it. William Barrell began booking tea sales again in Philadelphia on April 24. Charles Willson Peale took the stage boat from Philadelphia to Wilmington with his family on April 17, 1776, four days after Patriots lifted the ban. They went ashore in Chester, Pennsylvania and had "Coffee & tea at a Tavern." Peale bought tea in Philadelphia three times in May. Abraham Van Neste sold tea in New Jersey by June 1. By then, the Patriot and tea speculator Isaac Sears had already sold tea in New York. Sears's ideological credentials were impeccable: member of the New York committee of correspondence; the committees of 51, 60, and 100; and the New York provincial congress, Sears commanded the sloop that policed non-importation in New York Harbor. He also led the mob that destroyed James Rivington's press. Sears had obtained thirty-nine chests of tea and had already sold ten by May.[24] Sears was no hypocrite; tea's politics had changed.

Tea advertising resurfaced as well. In June, the Patriotic Benjamin Andrews (brother to the John Andrews mentioned in previous chapters) offered tea in

Table 12.1   Tea advertisers, April–June 1776

LOCATION	ADVERTISER
Newburyport:	price auction
Boston:	Benjamin Andrews
	prize auction
New York:	John Amiel Jr.
	Abraham Brinkerhoff
	Henry, M'Callen and Henry
	William Leary
	Stephen Rapalje
	Stockholm and Dickson
	John Young
Philadelphia:	Attmore and Hellings
	Ezekiel Brown
	Dominick Joyce
	Samuel Garrigues, Jun. & Co.
	Walter Hall
Williamsburg:	Alexander McAulay

Sources: *New York Gazette* (March 25–April 15; April 29–May 6; May 20–June 17, 1776). *New York Journal* (April 25–June 13, 1776). *Pennsylvania Packet* (April 22, May 6, June 3, 1776). *Pennsylvania Evening Post* (May 16, May 23, May 30, June 6, June 11, June 20, June 22, 1776). *Essex Journal* (Newburyport, May 10–24, 1776). *New-England Chronicle* (Boston, May 16, 1776). *Continental Journal* (Boston June 13–27, 1776). *Virginia Gazette* (Purdie and Dixon, June 22–29, 1776).

Boston, only a few months after Loyalist John Grozart had. Andrews had fled Boston after the Battles of Lexington and Concord, returning after the Continental Army retook the city, at which point it was Grozart's turn to flee, in his case to Nova Scotia. Both Grozart and Andrews had owned tea in 1775. The difference was when they sold it openly.[25]

Between April and June 1776, fifteen advertisers in four separate colonies took out twenty-eight discrete tea ads. These spanned eight newspapers. The return of tea advertising was hardly universal, and not every merchant holding tea advertised it. But the ads were as widely distributed as the papers they ran in, and they announced the end of the ban wherever they went. Seeing a Philadelphia advertiser list tea in the *Pennsylvania Packet*, a New Jersey reader might check whether local vendors had stock. (See table 12.1.)

The advertisements were heaviest in New York and Philadelphia, affirming that traders in those cities had large stocks. The Philadelphia advertisements helpfully directed Adams and other congressmen to shops where they could find tea for their families. Some advertisers were Patriotic: Abraham Brinkerhoff was a member of the committee of 100. On the other hand, Alexander McAulay was probably a Tory.[26] Only three of these advertisers had also advertised tea before the ban: Rapalje, Garrigues, and Leary, suggesting some had acquired black market tea during the ban, perhaps on speculation prohibition would end.

War Erodes the Association

Congress authorized tea consumption to allow previously imported Dutch tea to be sold. But it also allowed new tea to come in as prize. Rebels had been looting their opponents since the war began. Prize-taking deprived ministerial troops of sustenance and provided Continental troops with supplies. Parliament's Trade Act constricted colonial shipping, and its Prohibitory Act declared colonial vessels legitimate prizes for British privateers and naval forces. Colonists' making prizes of British shipping was an important riposte that might broaden the economic reach of the conflict (by depriving the British Caribbean of food and fuel), while eschewing confrontation with the stronger vessels of the Royal Navy.

And yet neither side had a coherent and effective form of economic warfare. While Continental and colonial (later state) navies took some prizes, privateers (licensed private raiders) took most prizes on the rebel side. This prize-taking enabled a form of trading with the enemy, since by definition legitimate prizes (1) came from Britain or non-Associating colonies, from which the Association banned goods, (2) were owned by local non-Associators with whom colonists were not supposed to trade, or (3) included banned cargoes, like British manufactures and tea. [27]

Using goods taken from the enemy was a triumph. Patriots reveled in using British-sourced ships, guns, blankets, and food. Henry Knox famously transported British cannons taken from Fort Ticonderoga to Boston, forcing His Majesty's troops to withdraw from the city. When Ethan Allen's Green Mountain Boys took Fort Ticonderoga, they looted the nearby estate of William Friend, commander of one of His Majesty's sloops on Lake Champlain. They took wine, sugar, rum, feather beds, sheets, and twenty-eight pounds of "Bohe Tea." [28] The rest of the tea in the area probably met a similar fate, including tea in the fort (which Captain Delaplace had recently served to James Jeffry) and at nearby Skenesborough House. Allen's men were no more abstemious about British tea than Knox was about British cannon—and why should they be? The only real difference between taking British tea and British guns, flour, nails and coal was that there was more of the latter. In the context of so many other seized British goods, some often quite mundane, British tea was normalized.

In late 1775 Captain Manly, commanding the *Lee*, captured the *Little Hannah* and brought the vessel into Beverly, Massachusetts. The *Little Hannah* had sailed from Antigua with provisions for the Royal Navy. Her two small cannons and her powder were valuable, and her liquor and tropical produce considered a necessity. Beverly townsfolk and various ships' crew looted the brig before Continental agent William Bartlett could inventory it. Bartlett forwarded what bit of *Little Hannah's* supplies he could get hold of to George Washington, including a barrel of tea, which Washington noted, had "two Canisters only" in it. Looters seem to have taken the rest. Ever careful about his public image, Washington returned the canisters without using them, but what happened to them when they got back to Beverly is unclear.[29]

The *Little Hannah* was one of two cargoes Manly took in quick succession. The other, the *Nancy*, carried 2,000 muskets plus ammunition and ordinance for British troops in Boston. The *Little Hannah* and *Nancy* captures were celebrated in woodcut and song, and Washington placed Manly in charge of his fleet. Other cargoes of tea arrived. The *Sukey*, in from Cork, Ireland, was taken with beef, butter, potatoes, and "2 large Canisters of Tea." In September 1776, the privateer *Hawke*, owned by Rhode Island Governor Nicholas Cooke and merchant John Brown captured the *Thomas* en route from London to Quebec with blankets, wine, and, among other things, tea. Newburyport man Enoch Hale captured the *Friends*, a "courageous" act that yielded tea.[30]

Tea was a rarely noted part of these captures. Washington was the only one we know of who expressed any sense that the *Little Hannah's* tea should be held back. Published summaries of the *Little Hannah's* cargo rarely mentioned tea (though newspapers relished printing lists of looted goods), and songs celebrating Manly never did. When Sailor Ashley Bowen directly compared the Boston Tea Party to Manly's taking the *Nancy*, referring to Manly having "another sort of tea at Cape Ann," he probably had no idea that his fellow North Shore residents were actually having tea. The *Sukey* was another noted capture in which the tea escaped note. The *Essex Journal* relished the loss to the *Sukey's* owner (Lewis Gray, son to Tory, and former colonial treasurer, Harrison Gray). A painting even commemorated the capture (but not the tea).[31]

Tea was a small part of the goods taken from British vessels and stores, but there were enough such captures for this to add up. In the first two years of the war, over 700 British merchant vessels were captured, and privateers spread out to the Caribbean and beyond. Precise information about these cargoes does not exist, but vessels supplying British consumers carried some tea often enough. Colonists found this tea unremarkable. Prize-taking subverted the logic of the boycott by providing banned goods, making British manufactures, or British tea, acceptable. Armed victories (Allen's at Ticonderoga, Manly's at sea) supplanted boycotts as a focus of colonial celebration. Tea did not make victory less honorable; victory made tea less forbidden. When Congress authorized tea to be taken as a prize, it validated this standing practice. Such prizetaking was so pronounced that in January 1776, the London *Public Advertiser* joked that provincial ships would soon cruise against the East India Company's China fleet, so "that they will still drink Tea Duty free."[32]

War was not merely a new, more dramatic theater for abstaining from tea and British goods, as the tales about Robert Dixon dying before Quebec at the beginning of this book might suggest. War was a way to get banned goods. Soldiers could buy tea in Montreal, or Montreal tea could be evacuated to and advertised in Albany. Seizures of Loyalist properties might yield tea, such as the 336 pounds of tea recovered from a raid on Abraham Van Buskirk's property in January 1777 or the 600 pounds of tea found in a Paramus, New Jersey field that May. Raids on Loyalist property by land, like privateering at sea, had obvious appeal: revolutionary leaders could defray war costs, and individual soldiers or seamen might get some small share of the booty. These were valuable finds. The State of New York sold Van Buskirk's tea to the men who captured it (one pound of tea per man). The Paramus tea was carefully handed over to George Washington's quartermaster for distribution. Defying Britain changed from not using British goods to using British goods on American terms. Legitimacy by capture also informed how Patriot authorities rationalized selling and profiting from the massive East India Company tea shipment from the *London*, sent in 1773, still in the cellar under the Exchange.[33] Patriots began selling it in 1776.

The Company's Charleston Tea

One consequence of the end of tea prohibition was the sale of the East India Company's tea in Charleston. In July 1776, Patriot debate about this tea centered on who would profit from it. South Carolina's President Rutledge sought congressional permission for the state of South Carolina to sell it, but some congressmen wanted to use the money for Continental purposes, or to reimburse Americans whose properties in England might be seized. South Carolina congressional delegates argued the tea had become the King's property when customs officers seized it in 1773; after independence, it became the state's, not Congress's, just as Crown lands and the King's forts now belonged to the state, not Congress. South Carolina's congressional delegation convinced their fellow congressmen of this, urging their state's assembly to sell the tea "immediately," and "apply the profits" to South Carolina's budget before Congress changed its mind. They chided Rutledge for asking; it was better to seek forgiveness than permission.[34]

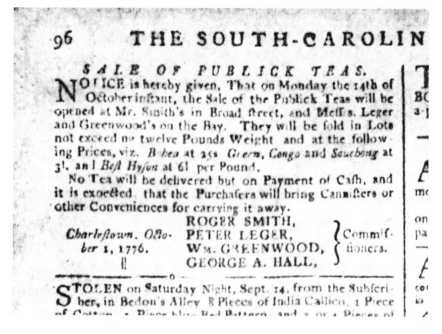

FIGURE 12.1. South Carolina sells the East India Company's tea, 1776. This October 1776 advertisement announced the sale of the East India Company's tea, originally imported on the *London* in 1773 but in 1776 deemed "PUBLICK" property. Proceeds went to the State of South Carolina. Source: *SCAGG*, October 9, 1776.

The South Carolina legislature authorized the sale on September 27, 1776. Ads for the "Publick Teas" sale appeared in the *South Carolina and American General Gazette* in early October; the first sale took place on October 14 and sales continued into 1777, with the last payment to the state treasury made at the end of that year. (See figure 12.1.) Buyers were limited to twelve pounds each, enough for a small retailer, and prices for all grades of tea were fixed to prevent merchants from buying up the stock and re-selling it at a markup. Impressively, South Carolina Patriots allowed the original tea consignees from 1773, Roger Smith, Peter Leger, and William Greenwood, along with George A. Hall, a South Carolina State Congressman and the new US customs collector for Charleston, to conduct the sales.[35]

The State of South Carolina received 61,603 South Carolina pounds from tea sales, as valued in 1776 currency. This was a small contribution to the state budget. The sales in the last quarter of 1776 covered only 3 percent of the state's expenditure for that period. Funds raised by loans, taxes, the South Carolina Insurance Company, or by issuing paper money, were far greater, but the money raised by selling tea in the last quarter of 1776 was enough to fund expenditure on one of the smaller militia regiments (like the Sixth) for that period. In 1777, the tea money was roughly enough to fund the fortification of Charleston. More importantly, funds generated by selling assets rather than printing money did not contribute to the debasement of the state's currency and the resulting hyperinflation. It took 5,245 South Carolina pounds to buy in May 1780 what 100 pounds had bought in January 1777, which suggests just how desperate the state was for revenue. As such, the tea sales had the fingerprints of the state's leading Patriots: the state president, the congressional delegation, and the attorney general, along with Colonel Charles Pinckney and the majority of the state legislature, not to mention the covetous, if spurned, members of much of the Continental Congress. All favored selling the East India Company's tea. In 1776 and 1777, the East India Company's tea helped Patriots pay for the war.[36]

Tea Price Controls and Tea Riots

Tea prices rose even before wartime inflation set in, partly because of the shortages of supply brought on by Patriot action. To check "exorbitant prices," Patriot authorities set tea prices. Congress capped the price for bohea, the most widely commoditized and consumed variety, at three-fourths of a dollar a pound on April 13, 1776. This spoke to the needs of most common consumers to receive supplies of tea and affordable prices. Congress let local and state committees regulate other types of tea, which, due to their smaller markets, might require tailoring to local conditions. The Philadelphia committee of inspection set the price of "the best Green Tea" at 32 shillings 6 pence a pound. The New York committee set prices for congo, souchong, and hyson, and the State of New York took care to sell Van Buskirk's tea at the Continental price. A Patriot-fixed price further endorsed tea as no Tory thing to buy, a point Attmore and Hellings's advertisement implied when it offered "Tea at the price limited by Congress."[37] These fixed prices picked up on the just price theory enshrined in the Association (which had barred vendors from raising prices as a result of non-importation), but they may not have had much effect on the black market.

The new set price for bohea came to 3s 4½d sterling, substantially lower than what merchants in Newport and Savannah had been charging during prohibition and lower than what merchants elsewhere soon tried to charge.[38] Colonists described price increases in moral terms, seeing them as evidence of merchants taking advantage rather than the consequence of their own demand and a dwindling supply. Similarly, Patriots were unwilling to admit that cutting supplies (by destroying tea and stopping new imports) affected price. The fundamental conflict over tea in 1776 was thus between, on the one hand, consumers' demand for cheap and plentiful tea and other imported goods (expressed in revolutionary just-price language) and, on the other hand, the shortages caused by revolutionary action and British blockades.

Price controls were not always successful. In May, Isaac Sears complained that New York merchants were charging so much that it pushed New Haven merchants away from the controlled price. Sears averred that he sold tea at the fixed price but worried that speculators would re-sell it on the black market for triple the value. In April, the Albany committee, faced with shortages, set prices for tea, coffee, molasses, sugar, rum, and salt. Within a month, the Albany committee found before it a merchant accused of overcharging for tea. He was found guilty and held up "to the public view as an Enemy to his Country." Another merchant charged the set price but added two shillings "for his trouble in weighing." The committee ordered him to be boycotted and punished several others for not supplying Albany's tea addiction cheaply enough.[39]

Congressman and merchant John Alsop was called before the New York City committee for offering tea wholesale at the set retail price and demanding half the money in specie (vendors were required to accept paper money). In explaining how retailers could profit in such a situation, Alsop also recommended they overcharge. Alsop was let off on the grounds that though he offered tea for sale under these terms, the committee could not prove a transaction had occurred. Mangil Minthorne, a New York shopkeeper with a captaincy in the militia, admitted overcharging. He was proscribed, but restored, and his commission returned by June 1776. Andrew Gautier confessed to demanding payment in specie but was pardoned because besides this, he was a good Associator. Gautier and Alsop's demands for specie also pointed to the currency problem. Merchants importing tea might have to buy it with hard money. If so, they understandably wanted to be paid in hard money, especially as the rapid printing of Continental and state currencies debased those monies.[40]

The most egregious case of price gouging in New York was Jonathan Lawrence's. Lawrence was a provincial congressman and commissioner overseeing works at Fort Constitution, intended to command access to the upper Hudson. The New Windsor committee found that Lawrence's wife was overcharging for tea and that Mr. Lawrence had been using the fort to store the family's horde of it. Other merchants not part of the Patriot movement were also caught up in the scandal. In September, responding to this wave of price gouging scandals, the New York State Congress formed a committee to investigate "abuses committed in withholding of Tea" and selling it "at higher prices than that limited by Congress."[41]

Barbara Clark Smith has documented over thirty food riots in 1776–1779 and found tea well-represented among them. In August 1776, a "committee of ladies" in Fishkill, New York forced Jacobus Lefferts to open his store and sell them his tea at "the Continental price." Perhaps he resisted too much; in the end, they confiscated the tea and sold it themselves (at the Continental price), with the proceeds going to the local revolutionary committee. That same month, the women of Kingston, New York went as far as to demand tea from the revolutionary committee as a condition of their husbands' and sons' continued military service: Tea could be more popular than Patriotism.[42]

In response to this and other incidents, in October 1776, the New York State Congress declared the tea holders' practices "unjustifiable and mercenary" and ordered local committees to seize stocks of tea over twenty-five pounds and sell them at the fixed price. The goal was to break up wholesale lots and get tea to consumers. As in South Carolina, buyers were limited to twelve pounds each—enough for a small shop, while preventing wholesalers from flipping large stocks on the black market. The committees followed through, even going after the tea supplies of merchants who were passing through. Connecticut merchant John Thomas needed an order from the New York State Congress to prevent the Kingston committee from redistributing the 2,000-pound supply he was transshipping through the state.[43]

Meanwhile, mobs took direct action against tea hoarders and price gougers, seizing and redistributing tea at the set price with little direction from revolutionary authorities. On November 18, 1776, the Kingston committee chairman, Johannes Sleght, lamented that the countyfolk "are now daily alarmed," with "streets filled with mobs" hunting for "that detestable article called *tea*," probably Thomas's supply. (The state congress had allowed Thomas to proceed with his tea, but it was unclear whether the people of Kingston would.) Tea was, for Sleght, detestable not because it was a sign of taxation without representation, monopoly, or tyranny but because the people had gone mad for it: whenever they found any, the people "divided or distributed" it among themselves. Seizing goods to secure a just price was the most popular form of direct action in England.. In France it was called *taxation populaire*. Nor was it unusual in America.[44]

Tea remained a focus of direct action in 1777 (but not after, perhaps because adequate supplies were finally had). The women of Poughkeepsie, New York thrice forced Peter Messier to sell them tea that year. In New Windsor, a mob seized a tea shipment and sold it to themselves, claiming the owners overcharged. This was probably an excuse to take the tea (there is no indication that the owners even offered the tea for sale in New Windsor at all, and every reason to expect the cargo was just passing through). A correspondent relayed the story to the tea's absent owner, James Caldwell: A wagoner had "put up at Mr. Shults's tavern" and "called for tea for his supper." The innkeeper had none, to which the wagoner replied that some was coming. Townsfolk overheard. Now thirty "women! in this place have risen in a mob, and are now selling a box of tea of yours at 6s per lb." Caldwell had obtained the tea in Philadelphia, where it seems to have been obtained by capture. But Caldwell paid a "very high price" for the tea, and the New Windsor sale forced him to take a major loss.[45] The writer suggested taking special precautions with such an article next time.

Patriotic New Yorkers faced many difficulties in 1776. New York City, their main port, was under British control after September of that year, which made getting supplies upstate difficult. That fall, Albany faced severe shortages. All but one of Smith's food riots involving tea between 1776 and 1779 were in New York State. Smugglers may have carried tea from occupied New York City over British lines in exchange for food and fuel, but it is unclear how much since shortages in British New York forced Tryon to cap the price of tea there as well in 1777.[46]

High tea prices (and failed price controls) were not confined to New York. During prohibition, the Wilmington-New Hanover committee had seized British cargoes and fixed prices for imports in North Carolina.[47] Post-Association, prices were high inland. In May 1776, Moravians noted that "tea, coffee and sugar" for use in Lovefeasts were "very expensive." This was hard for a people used to buns and tea at church. The following year, tea was sold in the state only at an "impossible price."[48]

When Norton & Sons received word that Virginians had also begun openly "to drink tea again," they learned it was "selling very High." Charles Willson Peale found tea prices skyrocketing despite Patriots' efforts to control them, and John Adams made similar observations. In Salem, Massachusetts, residents objected to high tea prices in December 1776. Tea was one of several necessities, along with sugar and bread, which became dear during the war—partly because of the British blockade, but also because of the Association, which had first cut supply, and particularly because of the Americans' taste for printing money. In 1777 a crowd of Boston women seized Thomas Boylston's coffee because he charged beyond the "regulated Price." In 1779, Philadelphians protested weekly increases in prices of "rum, sugar, flour, coffee and tea," and formed a committee to investigate the cause. The same year, a Williamsburg, Virginia committee set various prices, including on tea. Rumors of hoarding and artificial scarcity abounded.[49]

After 1776, Patriots no longer saw tea as a counter-revolutionary political symbol, but as a consumer good to be seized and redistributed to the people.

Ironically, these episodes of redistribution had grown from earlier tea parties—as acts of commercial enforcement, protests against high prices, and expressing a sense that proper modes of consumption and sale signaled revolutionary economic and consumer propriety. Now consumption could be about equality: that merchants not raise prices and hoard goods so much that only the rich could consume, but rather that everyone was entitled to some small taste of the Atlantic commercial world. This contrasted starkly with the anti-tea tone of the riots and committees of 1774–1775. The tea protests of 1776 and after still constituted an "enforcement of patriotism," but tea had lost its old symbolic value. Merchants were never happy when rioters came to their doors—but food rioters were arguing on the premise that tea was a consumer necessity, not a political symbol. In the spirit of 1776, consumers had taken the tea sellers' logic further: now consumers, not merchants, governed tea discourse. American tea drinkers demanded large amounts at low prices and seized tea stocks. Everyone could be customers. And woe to the merchant or revolutionary official who got in their way. To tea colonists applied that most revolutionary and American formulation: the customer is always right.

Conclusion

Tea and politics took many turns between 1773 and 1776. The connection between the tea protests of 1773 and American independence in 1776 was indirect. The popular memory of 1773 was rewritten multiple times. Consider the case of Loyalist shopkeeper and tea seller John Hook. Hook found himself in trouble with the Bedford, Virginia County committee in June 1775 not because he had sold tea, but for saying that "the Bostonians did not behave well in Destroying the Tea" and that they deserved to "get well flog'd." Worse, he distributed Loyalist pamphlets, and his failure to sign the Association left him a Tory. A year and a half later, by which time Virginia had declared independence from Britain, a magistrate led a "mob association" to attack his house and take him "dead or alive," "Law or no law." They charged him with treason, jailed him, and forbade him to sell goods until he answered the charges. "I should have known," Hook wrote. "I am truly sorry for" having "given offence." But while the Tea Party was *now* "universally" seen "throughout this whole Continent" as being for "American Liberty," it had not been *then*. At the time, many colonists abhorred the Tea Party. Hook explained that back when he had wished the Bostonians "a scurging for destroying the Tea," the destruction of the tea "was generally condemned," but it has "since been justified by the representatives of America," remade A Good Thing. Hook's opinion of Boston mattered to Patriots because of what it implied about his Loyalism. In the winter of 1776–1777, his allegiance was to a foreign power with which Virginia was at war. Hook resolved the matter by signing a "Certificate of Fidelity" to the Virginia assembly, which made his opinions about Boston irrelevant. Hook's opinion matters to us because it suggests public memory can change. After signing his loyalty oath, Hook was free to sell tea (if he had any) to the people of Bedford County. Tea's past destruction was to be lauded while its present consumption resumed.[1]

Most Patriots had preferred to return the Company's tea, not destroy it. In 1773, Philadelphia, Patriots forced the ship carrying the Company's tea to turn around. This was the most widely approved-of response. Paul Revere brought news of the Boston Tea Party to Philadelphia on December 24. That news was celebrated, and the *Polly*, with the Company's tea, was sighted the next day. But Philadelphia Patriots did not destroy that tea. Even the Boston committee of correspondence conceded (or felt it had to pretend) that the destruction of the tea was lamentable, blaming the consignees, the governor, and customs officers for preventing the tea from returning and forcing Patriots to destroy it. News from Charleston may have encouraged Philadelphians to return their tea. Details of Charleston's December 3 meeting, including the report that Charleston Patriots preferred to send their tea back, reached Philadelphia by December 22.[2] Pound for pound, most of the Company's tea was safely returned, with no risk that impounded tea might be released or, as John Adams noted of the Boston Tea Party, that someone might get too rough. When the tea ship *Nancy* reached New York in April 1774, that city's Patriots could have destroyed the Company's tea on board, as they did a private shipment of dutied tea reaching New York at the same time. But they sent the *Nancy* back. The destruction of the tea in Boston may have been done by "the people," but it was not that popular.[3]

Many across the continent, even prominent Patriots, agreed with Hook that Bostonians "did not behave well" in destroying the tea, leaving an unexploited opening for Lord North and the ministry to pit colonists or Patriots against one another. In defending their actions, Boston Patriots' could not acknowledge Charleston's successful alternative—letting customs officers lock the tea up—without acknowledging their own double failure: their violence in response to tea on the *Dartmouth, Eleanor*, and *Beaver* and their lack of a response to the tea from the *William*. There was a high risk that any Company tea stored in Boston would eventually be sold, which was why Patriots downplayed news of the *William*'s tea. Maintaining a perpetual boycott on Company tea was impractical, because, unlike New York and Charleston, the Boston consignees were not reconciled to the Patriot committees. Unlike Leger and Greenwood, the Clarkes and Hutchinsons had imported dutied tea extensively during the last boycott and could be expected to do so again.[4]

News that the *William* had wrecked off Cape Cod reached Boston on the evening of December 15, 1773. The next day a notice appeared in the *Massachusetts Gazette* informing that the crew and "most of the Cargo" were "saved." The Boston Tea Party occurred on December 16, timed to destroy the tea on the *Dartmouth, Beaver,* and *Eleanor* before customs collectors could seize it, but also in the knowledge that even as this tea was being destroyed, tea from the *William* was likely safe and, for the time being, out of reach. The Boston Tea Party was incomplete from its inception, and Boston Patriots likely knew the *William's* tea might undo their work. They initially hoped Cape "Indians" would destroy the *William's* tea, but it was soon stored and landed in the castle.[5]

The debate over the destruction of the tea drew attention away from the tea that survived. Yet this surviving tea was important. It was part of why Boston Patriots remained implacably hostile to the Boston consignees in early 1774. To prevent them from bringing suit in court or landing the remaining tea, Patriots hounded them out of Boston.

The Coercive Acts heightened the all-or-nothing conflict between Boston Patriots and the Boston consignees. Either Boston would defy Parliament or: the destroyed tea would be paid for; the *William's* tea would be landed; new dutied tea would be allowed in; Parliamentary supremacy would be accepted; and the Tea Act, Coercive Acts, the American Board of Customs, and various trade regulations would function. Payment became a performance of obeisance. For North, the principle mattered more than the money, just as the principle of committee authority embedded in the Association would matter more than any little bit of tea that got through. If average colonists were happier to sign the Association than Boston Patriots were to accept the Coercive Acts, it was because average colonists were less principled.

The Port Act helped Patriots rally colonists to a common cause and made the destruction of tea worth copying. The excess and the incompleteness of the Boston Tea Party were forgotten, as was the response to the Company's tea in Charleston and Philadelphia. One sign of how quickly popular memory forgot other cities' role in the tea can be seen in John Leacock's *The First Book of the American Chronicles of the Times.* Leacock was a member of the Philadelphia Sons of Liberty, the body which helped send the *Polly* back.[6] His story featured tea prominently, even beginning with the Boston Tea Party. Leacock omitted the Philadelphia Sons of Liberty, ignored the Philadelphia mass meeting that forced the captain of the *Polly* to turn around (a meeting he probably attended himself), and wrote out Philadelphia generally. Leacock did not once mention the fate of the Company's tea from the *William* or the *London,* let alone the *Nancy* or the *Polly.* Whereas there had once been many responses to the Company's tea with many possible outcomes, there was now just one: the Company sent its tea, Bostonians destroyed it, and Parliament passed the Coercive Acts.

In its post-Coercive Acts symbolism, destroying tea acquired a political "truth" detached from what had actually happened. It symbolized the common cause and resistance to what Patriots saw as a dangerous new constitutional settlement. The Acts made the Boston Tea Party seem heroic and justified, a stance reiterated in other tea parties and in the press. In case, as with the *Peggy Stewart*, locals went so far as to burn the ship itself, Patriots lied and claimed the ship owner did it "voluntarily," a lie that worked because readers wanted to believe it. Granular local realities—that colonists did not burn all their tea, that they sometimes showed up to tea parties to steal it, and that the alleged destruction of some tea supplies, like in York, Maine, may never have happened at all—these were sacrificed to the greater political truth of unity against Parliament. Imbued with a kernel of truth and facing an audience wanting to believe it, Patriot propaganda thrived.

Meanwhile, the old distinctions that defined how tea was consumed daily faded away. It did not matter whether tea was black or green, bohea or souchong, cheap or expensive, dutied or smuggled, owned directly by the Company or by private English merchants. As a symbol, tea became generic, abstracted from the idiosyncrasies of actual use. This made it easier to pledge to boycott tea (the abstraction) while secreting a small cache for Lovefeasts, courtship, or medicine.

The Association was both the apotheosis of the anti-tea movement and the start of its collapse. Its story of resistance to ministerial oppression let colonists be the protagonists in their own narratives and centered political action in the colonies. It ended imports of tea and other goods from England, thereby ending opportunities for most harborside tea parties. This left the Association as the most visible totem of resistance to the ministry. Dutch tea imports, which were also supposed to stop, were harder to police, less often protested, and may have continued. The Association allowed colonists to publicly *say* they would not consume tea and banned goods, which, ironically, freed them to continue consuming them in private.

James Thatcher, a Massachusetts military surgeon, begrudgingly acknowledged this. His journal was published in the 1820s, which was probably when, before his first entry, he added an explanation of the coming of the revolution, including the destruction of the tea. Thatcher explained that news of the "Boston Vindictive Port Bill" caused "merely the name of tea" to become "associated with ministerial grievances, and tea drinking is almost tantamount to an open avowal of toryism." Men "who are anxious to avoid the odious epithet of enemies to their country, strictly prohibit the use of tea in their families." This was how people wanted to remember the event, but then Thatcher added that others "secretly steal indulgence in their favorite East India beverage" anyway.[7]

Signing the Association worked as a sort of test oath. Yet Patriots enforced actual non-consumption lightly. This is apparent once we realize that much of Patriotic writing about tea was propaganda. This came in the form of press releases and news stories portraying events in a certain light; in the form of claims about tea's medical dangers and jibes to the effeminacy of tea drinkers; in the form of exhortations not to drink tea; and in the form of rumors promising that the tea in the Charleston Exchange was unusable. But talk is cheap, and it is unclear how many colonists believed it. Even the Patriot colonists who convinced themselves or sincerely believed that tea was unhealthy in 1774 forgot these medical dangers by 1776. Perhaps we should focus more on the hundreds of advertisers who put their money where their mouth was in 1774 and paid to announce that they had tea in their shops while suffering little to no repercussion, or on the falling tea prices of that year, which suggest importers risked their capital and credit to bring in more tea. We might consider the tea holders who, in 1775, lobbied Congress for permission to sell their supplies; the colonists who asked for "medical" exemptions from the tea ban; and the vendors who sold tea under the table, along with the thousands of colonists who bought it. Overlooking all this consumption helped make the Association appear successful.

The war robbed non-importation and non-consumption of meaning. Many of the items captured from British forces were British goods, and they were all—guns, produce, and tea—useful. The war, especially the Battle of Bunker Hill, also made the suggestion that Dartmouth repeal the tea tax as a conciliatory measure laughably too little, too late. Both sides had moved on.[8] Military service was a better tool than non-consumption for James Thatcher and Robert Dixon to oppose the ministry.

Congress gave up its prohibition on tea in April 1776. Americans—led as always by the good examples of their congressmen—rushed to buy some. Non-consumption failed because it became irrelevant to the resistance, and the end of the tea ban fit into the broader preparation for declaring independence. The tea ban was not formally ended, but Congress created two categories of permitted tea: Dutch tea imported by 1774, and tea taken as prize, categories which were interpreted broadly. After the war, many Loyalists disappeared into the background of American life, as did tea and British goods.[9]

The through-line for tea in the Revolution, the underlying logic that gave it various political meanings—and eventually none—was its significance as a consumer good. Late colonial tea smuggling, the Townshend Acts, and the Company's shipment of tea in 1773 were recognitions of the small but growing consumer demand for tea in the colonies. Only because colonists consumed tea was it an object of taxation and regulation. Even the Boston Tea Party was not an anti-tea moment per se: it destroyed some tea so that, hopefully, in future years tea could come without unjust taxation and East India Company monopoly. The "virtuous" destruction of tea often implied the existence of less-virtuous colonists who would drink it. Tea prohibition and propaganda were premised on tea being part of how the public participated in the Atlantic consumer world. So, too, was the voyage of the first American tea ship to China a decade later. In all this, merchants, advertisers, and consumers spoke more to public wants about tea than politicians. When South Carolina politicians sold their Company tea, they acknowledged public desire for it.

Later generations added to the myths around the tea protests. One such addition was probably the song in the epigraph at the start of this book, allegedly sung before the Boston Tea Party. It claimed King George would "force our girls and wives" to drink tea. This was laughable, for in 1773, Bostonians decried North and the ministry, not the King. The song was probably written well after the Boston Tea Party (its sourcing is unclear). But with time, it was easy to re-remember the Boston Tea Party as a protest against a King trying to force colonists' wives to drink tea, even if it was as apocryphal as prima nocta. Family genealogists "discovered" ancestors who participated in the Boston Tea Party. Some surely participated, but verifying participation in a criminal conspiracy that silenced witnesses, avoided record-keeping, and used laborers who could skip town has proven difficult. Chestertown, Maryland town historians "discovered" their town's little piece of the American pageant, just as John Joseph Henry "remembered" Sargent Robert Dixon's last words. Americans invented traditions which glorified these protests and gave them latter-day meanings. Yet for people in 1776 and 1777, the protests against rising prices and the lack of imported goods mattered just as much, perhaps more as the protests against tea had.

The fleetingness of tea's ban recalls the fleetingness of some other consumer movements centering on symbolic actions, such as renaming sauerkraut as liberty cabbage in 1917 and French fries as freedom fries in 2003; neither stuck. Not every boycott or every prohibition fails, but the inadequacy of the prohibition on tea recalls the inadequacy of others: the prohibition of alcohol in the 1920s failed to end alcohol consumption; the drug war that began in the late twentieth century failed to eliminate marijuana. Patriots' great virtue was in how quickly they realized the futility and ridiculousness of their efforts.

Tea's final act in American politics would be as a symbol of economic independence. In 1784, the *Empress of China* was the first US merchant vessel to reach China. Its voyage from New York was marked with newspaper essays, thirteen-gun salutes, and poems. In "On the First American Ship That explored the Rout to China and the East-Indies after the Revolution," Philip Freneau waxed about the vessel's sailing "without the leave of Britain's king."[10] In finally getting for America the sort of tea previously sourced from Britain and Europe, the *Empress of China*'s voyage reminds us of tea's enduring commercial appeal.

The history and the popular memory of tea in the Revolution diverged. The simplified version of the latter was easy enough: Britain imposed tea taxes on America, Bostonians vigorously opposed it, and when Parliament cracked down the colonies united to throw off the British yoke. This left out the detours, the almost-might-have-beens, and the actually-were: how differently Charleston, Philadelphia, and Boston responded to the Company's tea, how much British tea Bostonians had been drinking, and the likelihood that, had the tea from the *Dartmouth*, *Eleanor*, and *Beaver* been landed, it would have been drunk. It left out how close Boston came to paying for the tea and how the end of a meaningful difference between English and Dutch tea shifted New York and Philadelphia from being the most virtuous (having almost no British tea at all) to the least (being awash in Dutch), even as those Dutch importations lowered prices and kept British tea out. It usually forgot how the Association was violated and ignored the Association's end. It forgot that tea from the *William* and the *London* was landed and ultimately consumed. Both vessels belied the neat little story that the Company's tea met its end at the bottom of Boston Harbor and that Americans drank coffee and Britons drank tea because Parliament taxed America. Tea's fast-changing role was mirrored by the rapid changes that terms like Association, Patriot, and Tory underwent between 1773 and 1776.

It is tempting to impose an artificially American reading of the events from Tea Party to independence, to write America as being made in Boston Harbor, but we know the thirteen colonies were not yet distinct from the rest. The question of which colonies would join or not join the rebellion was contested. Tea crisscrossed the rebellion's lines. Continental soldiers marched into Quebec, a province that had not joined the Association but seemed, for a time, that it might rebel. Quebec had tea and British goods (especially for the fur trading industry). Nova Scotians received cargoes of tea originally destined for Massachusetts and New Hampshire and tried to re-sell some of them back to New England. Other Nova Scotians protested that very same tea. Massachusettsans shipped tea to Barbados and Grenada and back again, and the East

India Company's tea destined for New York stood a fair chance to be landed in Antigua or Halifax instead. In the journey of unbecoming British, tea protests were a funny way to start.

The original East India Company consignees were hardly representative of tea sellers, but the way tea politics passed some of them by is indicative of the way the Revolution moved on from tea. To be sure, in Boston, the Hutchinsons and their in-laws, the Clarkes, left. But they left because of more than tea—the Hutchinsons' father was hated for his governorship. Thomas Hutchinson Jr. had been appointed a mandamus councillor in 1774 (though he did not take the oath of office) and was an addresser of Gage, and both the Hutchinsons and the Clarkes were prominent Loyalists. Massachusetts Patriots banished both Hutchinsons as well as Richard and Jonathan Clarke in a general banishment order, claiming they had "left this state . . . and joined the enemies thereof." Yet Massachusetts Patriots let another Boston consignee, Benjamin Faneuil, live out his days in the state; perhaps he was too elderly to be offensive (he died in 1785 at age eighty-four).

Abraham Lott, treasurer of the Colony of New York, served on the committee of 51 and lived out his days in the United States. Benjamin Booth served on the same committee. New Yorker Henry White was friendly to the Crown but tried to avoid trouble from Patriots. He departed New York, returning once the city was safely in British hands. In Philadelphia, consignees Thomas Wharton Sr. and Henry Drinker were arrested in 1777 on vague charges. The arrests stemmed from the Patriot reoccupation of Philadelphia following the evacuation of British troops. Wharton's and Drinker's arrests related to their roles as leading Quakers as much as to their old roles in the tea. They were sent into internal exile in Virginia but returned the next year. Abel James, Drinker's partner, avoided arrest. Wharton's health soon faded. James and Drinker stayed on in post-war Philadelphia.

In South Carolina, Peter Leger remained in Charleston until his death in the 1780s, having made his peace with Patriots. Carolina consignee Roger Smith went from serving on Patriotic committees to taking up a post in the new state treasury. Despite rumors he was a "Ministerial Agent," William Greenwood took an oath to the American cause and served in the rebel forces. He later served in a Loyalist militia during the British occupation of Charleston, fleeing when the British evacuated in 1782. Military service, not tea, made him a Loyalist. If Patriots found some of these men irredeemably odious, it had more to do with their taking up arms for the King, their fleeing to British lines, or their Quaker reticence to declare any allegiance at all than it did with the Company's tea.[11]

In the Years That Followed

Where available, tea was a normal drink in revolutionary America. Thus, the week after independence, Englishman Nicholas Cresswell, then in Alexandria, Virginia, could complain in his diary, "This cursed Independence has given me great uneasiness," even as on July 14 he "Drank tea" at committeeman "Mr. [James] Kirk's." Politics, but not tea, was the difference between the men. Cresswell noted elsewhere in his diary: "(Mem. Never to enter into Political disputes with Mr. Kirk. He has rebellious principles.)" Foreign visitors to Philadelphia remarked on Americans' continued tea consumption in 1777. Now a prisoner, Baroness de Riedesel, wife of the Hessian general surrendering with General John Burgoyne at Saratoga, found that Americans refused to sell food to her and her daughters. "[Y]ou come out of your land to kill us," they grumbled, and "it is, therefore, our turn to torment you." Yet the Baroness found even this implacability melted with a bribe of tea. Rachel Graydon made the dangerous journey across the front, from Patriot-controlled Pennsylvania to British-occupied New York, to see her son, an American POW, and to plead with General Howe for his release. By the time the general would see her, she had already thrown "one or two tea-drinkings, at which the rebel clan"—prisoners and Whig sympathizers in the city—attended. In 1778, Grace Galloway, seeking to prevent her family property from being confiscated because of her Loyalist husband, invited the Patriot leader Thomas McKean to discuss the matter—over tea. American prisoners of war in London (who might have more reason than most to make some emotive connection, however faint, with home) asked for monetary relief so that they might buy tea. American General Charles Lee, a prisoner aboard the HMS *Centurion*, invited Cresswell to chat over tea. One lieutenant in Rochambeau's army thought Americans' "favorite drink seems to be tea." George Washington took it daily while at the Constitutional Convention.[12] Distaste for tea had nothing to do with the creation of a uniquely American identity, even at this, the most anti-British (or at least counter-British) moment in American formation.

The fiction continued that the tea sold after 1776 had been "honestly smuggled" before the Association—but only because tea had become so innocuous that Congress forgot to revisit the issue. In the meantime, the United States signed commercial treaties with European powers, and new tea from Europe reached the United States. The latter began to lay excise taxes. Massachusetts taxed wine, rum, brandy, wheeled carriages, and tea—6 pence on every pound of bohea—with tavernkeepers and tea retailers required to buy licenses. This license regime increased costs for consumers but generated revenue for the state. In 1781, Beverly, Massachusetts resident Joseph Baker paid £50 for a tea seller's license, valid for one year. (See figure 13.1.) By 1783, the discussion

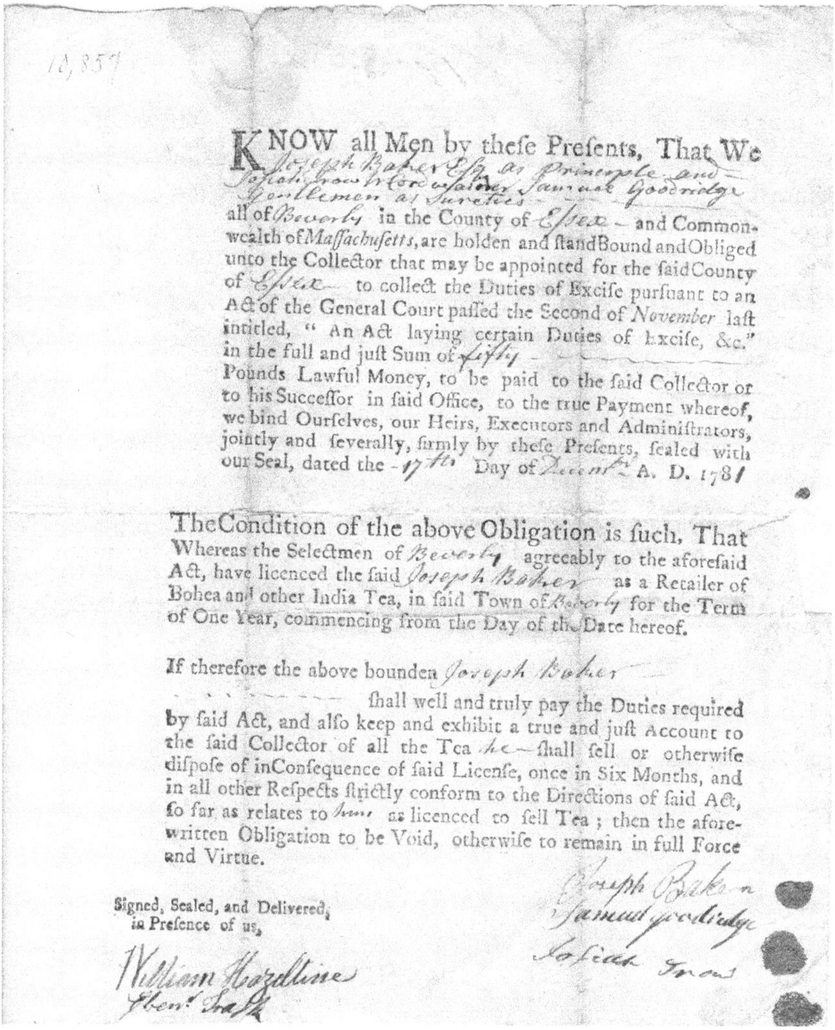

KNOW all Men by these Presents, That We *Joseph Baker Esq.* as *Principle and Gentlemen* as *Sureties Samuel Goodridge* all of *Beverly* in the County of *Essex* — and Commonwealth of *Massachusetts*, are holden and stand Bound and Obliged unto the Collector that may be appointed for the said County of *Essex* to collect the Duties of Excise pursuant to an Act of the General Court passed the Second of *November* last intitled, " An Act laying certain Duties of Excise, &c." in the full and just Sum of *fifty* Pounds Lawful Money, to be paid to the said Collector or to his Successor in said Office, to the true Payment whereof, we bind Ourselves, our Heirs, Executors and Administrators, jointly and severally, firmly by these Presents, sealed with our Seal, dated the *17th* Day of *December* A. D. 178*1*

The Condition of the above Obligation is such, That Whereas the Selectmen of *Beverly* agreeably to the aforesaid Act, have licenced the said *Joseph Baker* as a Retailer of Bohea and other India Tea, in said Town of *Beverly* for the Term of One Year, commencing from the Day of the Date hereof.

If therefore the above bounden *Joseph Baker* shall well and truly pay the Duties required by said Act, and also keep and exhibit a true and just Account to the said Collector of all the Tea *he* shall sell or otherwise dispose of in Consequence of said Licenfe, once in Six Months, and in all other Respects strictly conform to the Directions of said Act, so far as relates to *him* as licenced to sell Tea ; then the afore-written Obligation to be Void, otherwise to remain in full Force and Virtue.

Signed, Sealed, and Delivered, in Presence of us,

William Hazeltine
Eben.r Frazk

Joseph Baker
Samuel Goodridge
Josiah Snow

FIGURE 13.1. Tea seller's license, Joseph Baker, Beverly, Massachusetts, 1781. In 1781 the state of Massachusetts created a licensing regime for tea sellers. Towns would authorize vendors, who would pay a £50 license fee to the state (valid for one year) and be responsible for collecting excise duties on tea as laid out by the state. Licensees were also responsible for keeping a tally of tea sales for biannual inspection. Evidently, Baker expected profits from tea sales to outweigh the burdens of this system. Source: Courtesy of Historic Beverly.

about tea assumed a nation awash in tea and demanding more. Congress not only forgot to finish lifting the prohibition on tea, it also jumped right to taxing it.[13]

Tea's return did not signal an end to hardship. After 1776, tea, as coffee, was scarce and dear. Homemade brews—made of paucity, not politics—could substitute for both. But tea could be all the more fine in a homespun age. As tea lost its role in non-consumption, its role as a consumer good shone—and access to tea, not the boycott of it, became the issue that upset the Americans rioting in late 1776 for tea to be distributed at a just price. Patriots, as Loyalists, had other ways to show their allegiance. When Patriots arrested the Mayor of Albany, Abraham Cornelius Cuyler, it was for his celebration of the King's birthday (June 4), not for the tea sent to him a few days prior. Similarly, with no sense of impropriety, Thomas Jefferson could sip tea poured by his slave Richard while drafting the Declaration of Independence. As vital as tea and tea politics had been, Jefferson did not mention tea or the East India Company in that document's list of grievances against the King.[14] Once more, tea was a consumer good, not a political symbol. For colonists, Patriot, Tory, and otherwise, consumption *was* the pursuit of happiness.

Tea Sale Records—Ledgers and Daybooks Showing (and Not Showing) Tea Transactions during Prohibition

Only holdings with ledgers, daybooks, account books, waste books, or other accounts primarily detailing mercantile activity are considered here. Holdings are included even if they only cover part of the ban period. For the sake of counting merchants who sold tea, merchants with multiple ledgers, even if held at different archives, are counted as once. A single catalog holding with ledgers belonging to multiple merchants is counted once per merchant.

Holdings without tea sales include:

Baker Library, Harvard Business School: Jacob and William Wildes Records, 1772–1815. Hancock Family Papers, 1664–1854 [Mss:766 1712–1854 H234]. Samuel Abbot Business Papers, 1754–1819 [Mss:761 1754–1819 A122]. Frost Family Business Records, 1727–1884 [Mss:77 1727–1884]. Reynell & Coates Records, 1744–1828 [Mss:766 1744–1828].

Columbia University Library: Ludlow Family Papers. Gay-Otis Family Papers.

Duke University Library: John Hook Papers. Thomas Adams Account Books. William Graham and Simpson Company Papers. New Bern (NC) Merchant's Ledger C, 1767–1785, bulk 1767–1776.

Johns Hopkins University Library: John Weatherburn Collection.

Library of Congress: Oliver Pollock Papers. The Papers of Stephen Collins and Son. The Papers of Stephen Collins and Son—William Barrell. The Papers of

Stephen Collins and Son—Solomon Fussell. The Papers of Stephen Collins and Son—James Mullan.

Library of Virginia: David and William Allason Papers, 1722–1847. Accession 13.

Maryland Center for History and Culture: McCulloh Family Papers, 1773–1848 MS2110. Anonymous Account Book, Alexandria, Virginia, 1775–1778 (Vertical File). William Russell Account Book 1774–1783 MS 1989. Wallace, Davidson and Johnson account book 1771–1777 MS 499. Hall Collection. Goodwin and Russell Letterbook; Account book 1774–1781. Sasquehanna Shipping Company Account Book 1773–1776 MS 2393. Ridgely Papers, Box 4, Bills and Receipts 1767–1789. Cooke Papers. Accounts of William Cooke 1761–1798 and William Cooke Cash Book c. 1775–1777. Cheston Galloway Papers, 1684–1961 MS 1994.

Massachusetts Historical Society: Increase Sumner Papers, 1769–1798 [Ms. N-1642]. Benjamin Greene Account Books, 1734–1805 [Ms. N-2064 (XT); P-489]. John Tudor Papers, 1732–1793 [Ms. N-1683]. Benjamin Goodwin Account Books, 1767–1796 [Ms. N-1300]. Samuel Russell Gerry Papers, 1769–1843 [Ms. N-1282; P-362]. Boylston Family Papers, 1688–1979 [Ms. N-4]. John Boylston Ledger. Boylston Family Papers, 1688–1979 [Ms. N-4]. Thomas Boylston Wastebook. Patrick Tracy Jackson Papers, 1766–1869 [Ms. N-408 (Tall)].

Newport Historical Society: Papers of the following: Stephen Ayrault, William Channing, Freedbody (Family), Archimedes George, Aaron Lopez, William Manley, David Moore, Henry Peckham, Thomas Robinson, Thomas Tew, Job Townsend.

New-York Historical Society: Bayard-Campbell-Pearsall Family Papers (Bayard accounts). Hudson Collection. Tayler-Cooper Family Papers. Thomas Cobbs Ledger. Brailford Receipt Book. Charles Nicoll ledgers.

New York Public Library: Hooe, Stone & Company. William Smith's Store Ledger (Kakiat, NY). Gilbert Livingston papers. Bancker family papers. Hasbrouck family papers.

Princeton University Library: Abraham Van Neste, Ledger B 1775–1779 and Daybook C. Ledger 1770–1775, CO199. Howell Daybook. Thomas Patterson, Account Book. Thomas Gordon Account Book.

Rhode Island Historical Society: Anthony Low Account Book, 1774–1801 [MSS 9001 L]. Ward Family Papers, 1714–1879 [MSS 776]. Moses Brown (1738–1836) Papers, 1636–1836 [MSS 313]. Samuel Nightingale I Papers, 1740–1786 [MSS 588 Sub Group 1]. Samuel Nightingale II Papers, 1759–1802 [MSS 588, Sub Group 2]. Papers of William Greene (1743–1826), 1775–1826 [MSS 469]. Christopher Champlin Papers, 1700–1840 [MSS 20]. Jonathan Peck Papers, 1728–1783 [MSS 610].

State Archives of North Carolina: John Cockton Daybook and Ledger. Thomas Oldham Ledger. John Hogg Company Papers. John Allen Papers.

University of North Carolina at Chapel Hill Library: Hayes Collection, 1694–1928. Robert Hogg Account Books, 1762–1787. William Hargrove Papers, 1773–1930. Robert Wilson Account books, 1777–1888. Wilson and Hairston Family Papers, 1757–1928.

Holdings with tea sales include:

Baker Library, Harvard Business School: Papers of: Joseph Barrell, 1770–1803. Cornelius Fellows, 1775–1791. Melatiah Bourn Papers, 1728–1803 [Mss:733 1728–1803 B775].

Duke University Library: Telfair & Co. Journal, 1774–1775; 1775–1781. Byrnes Account.

Library of Congress: Glassford Records. Neil Jamieson Financial Papers, 1771–1782.

Maryland State Archives: Wallace, Davidson and Johnson Accounts MSA S 528–27/28, 1771–1775. http://mdhistory.net/msaref06/wdj_order_bks/html/index.html.

Massachusetts Historical Society: James Murray Papers, 1732–1781 [Ms. N-571; P-141]. Amory Family Papers, 1697–1894 [Ms. N-2024 (Tall)]. Amory, Taylor, and Rogers, 1769–1784, Wastebook, 1774–1784 [Vol. 13].

Newport Historical Society: Papers of: Christopher Champlin; John Hadwen; Elnathan Hammond; Pierce, Clothier & Howard Potter; Henry Potter; Thomas Vernon.

New-York Historical Society: John Taylor Daybook (BV Taylor, John). Shaw and Long Wastebook (BV Shaw). Benjamin Cornell Daybook (BV Scarsdale).

State Archives of North Carolina: Matthew and Margaret Byrne Collection.

University of North Carolina at Chapel Hill Library: Cameron Family Papers.

University of Pennsylvania Library: Manuscript Farmer's Ledger, 1774–1777 Ms. Codex 1587.

University of Virginia Library: Papers of R. M. T. Hunter. Hunter-Garnett Collection [aka Papers of the Hunter and Garnett families] Accession No 38-45.

Two merchants had papers in multiple archives, with tea sales in one and not in the other: Christopher Champlin (sales in NHS records, not in RIHS) and Wallace, Davidson and Johnson (no sales at MDHS, but sales at mdhistory.net). These have been counted once in chapter 8, as records with tea sales, but are listed separately here.

APPENDIX B

Tea and Coffee Consumption Estimates

Americans did not turn from tea after the Revolution. Trade data, though far from perfect, show this. The CUST 16/1 file records colonial imports, 1768–1772. Net tea imports into the thirteen colonies from this data set (imports minus exports) show consumed tea. Population data for 1760, 1770, and 1780 are drawn from *Historical Statistics of the United States* and interpolated to provide annual population estimates. Dividing consumed tea by population gives estimated per-capita tea consumption. This yields an average of 373,000 pounds of legally imported tea for 2.168 million colonists over the 1768–1772 period at 0.17 pounds per year, with annual levels varying, depending on non-importation. (If one wished to determine tea consumption per free person, one would divide imported tea by 1.712 million, the estimated free population circa 1770, resulting in a legal tea consumption level of 0.22 pounds per free person. Late colonial per-capita consumption figures can be multiplied by 1.25 to estimate per-free-person consumption.)[1]

An alternative data set, CUST 3, recounts English tea *exports* to the thirteen colonies over a longer period, 1761–1775, and corroborates the above data.[2] (See figure B.1.) This set has been adjusted to remove the tea shipped by the Company to North America in 1773 (none of which was consumed in 1773), with the tea from the *William* added back in 1775. Adjusted numbers are indicated in bold in table B.1.[3] Averaging the CUST 3 data over its longer

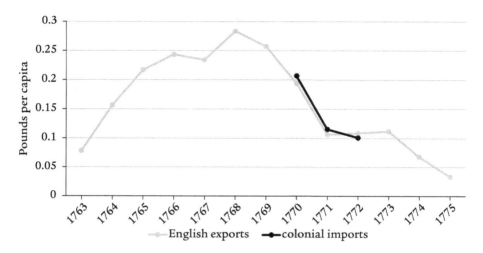

FIGURE B.1. Late colonial consumption of *legal* tea, three-year moving average. Source: PRO CUST 16/1 and PRO CUST 3/61-75, the latter and population data via Carter et al., *Historical Statistics*, http://dx.doi.org/10.1017/ISBN-9780511132971.Eg.ESS.01.

Table B.1 British tea and coffee shipments to the thirteen colonies, compared (pounds weight)

YEAR	TEA EXPORTED FROM BRITAIN TO THIRTEEN COLONIES (CUST 3)	CUST 3 ADJUSTED	TEA LEGALLY IMPORTED INTO THIRTEEN COLONIES (CUST 16)	THREE-YEAR MOVING AVERAGE	BRITISH COFFEE IMPORTED INTO THIRTEEN COLONIES (CUST 16)	THREE-YEAR MOVING AVERAGE
1761	56,110	56,110				
1762	161,588	161,588				
1763	188,785	188,785				
1764	489,180	489,180				
1765	518,424	518,424				
1766	360,329	360,329				
1767	479,961	479,961				
1768	868,791	868,791	877,191		298,495	
1769	226,778	226,778	309,871		446,402	
1770	108,629	108,629	99,498	428,853	451,512	398,803
1771	359,153	359,153	342,092	250,486	263,821	387,245
1772	263,140	263,140	237,062	226,217	484,171	399,835
1773	738,408	**139,758**				
1774	70,731	70,731				
1775	16,830	**28,192**				

Sources: PRO CUST 16/1 and PRO CUST 3/61-75.

time series gives 0.14 pounds of legal tea per person a year, but this average obscures significant variance.

The CUST data omit smuggling, with CUST 16 giving a suspiciously low zero pounds of tea imported into Philadelphia in 1771. The CUST data are thus a bottom threshold for tea consumption.

Actual consumption was more, but how much more? One way to estimate this would be to look at the drop off in legal tea imports in response to the Townshend Acts using the CUST 3 series. From 1763 through 1767, average annual exports of legal tea from England to America amounted to 407,336 pounds (0.216 pounds per capita). From 1768 through 1772—between the Townshend and the Tea Acts—legal English tea exports fell to 365,298 pounds (0.168 pounds per capita), a drop in per-capita consumption of 22 percent.[4]

Smuggled tea can be estimated by positing that colonists smuggled tea to make up this difference. This is a conservative estimate, as it does not attempt to factor in the base level of tea smuggling common to the 1763–1767 era, which may have been considerable. There were various estimates of this, as discussed in chapter 2. Dutch sales and export records, which could, in theory, shed light on this, are unavailable.[5]

The question of how much tea was smuggled is impossible to answer definitively. Assuming smuggled tea merely compensated for the 20 percent drop off in legal supply gives a low estimate. Assuming half the tea in the colonies was smuggled, which would match the assumption that roughly half of tea in Britain was smuggled, would yield a colonial consumption level of 0.33 pounds of tea per capita from the CUST 3 data (and 0.34 from the CUST 16 data). Assuming three-quarters were smuggled (the highest plausible scholarly estimate) gives 0.67 pounds per capita from the CUST 3 data and 0.69 from the CUST 16 data.

These estimates can be paired with US federal customs records, which provide reliable runs of tea import and export data beginning in the mid-1790s.[6] A three-year moving average of net tea imports removes year-on-year volatility. These figures are divided by population data from the decennial US census, interpolated to fill in missing years. Between 1797/98 and the start of the War of 1812, this three-year moving average of per capita tea consumption fluctuated between 0.36 and 0.76 pounds. The variance seems to be due to changes in supply—the dates coincide with the Jeffersonian Embargo and the War of 1812, suggesting that supply constraints, not a distaste for tea, caused the lower data points in this series. There is little indication of tea smuggling in this period, meaning net legal tea imports in the US period can stand for all tea imports. This gives us post-independence tea consumption levels in the 1790s and early 1800s as high as or higher than the various late colonial estimates.[7]

Table B.2   US net tea and coffee imports on all vessels, foreign and domestic (pounds weight), 1795/96–1814/15

YEAR	NET TEA IMPORTS	NET COFFEE IMPORTS
1795/96	2,355,755	−1,244,066
1796/97	1,786,761	4,969,615
1797/98	1,894,368	8,141,698
1798/99	4,992,732	−2,008,518
1799/1800	3,938,708	8,792,472
1800/1801	2,414,556	12,277,410
1801/1802	2,339,838	4,380,863
1802/1803	3,265,042	6,543,800
1803/1804	1,971,595	4,965,316
1804/1805	3,283,360	8,781,026
1805/1806	5,017,248	8,992,126
1806/1807	4,938,551	34,712,238
1807/1808	5,182,604	29,709,905
1808/1809	−299,082	11,152,908
1809/10	6,370,476	−553,593
1810/11	1,824,238	19,801,230
1811/12	2,555,111	18,192,101
1812/13	831,726	5,147,490
1813/14	202,236	7,538,139
1814/15	2,269,688	12,095,193

Source: *American State Papers*. Commerce and Navigation 1, 1789–1815. Each tax year in this series runs from October 1 of one year to September 30 of the next. These dates are associated with the latter year in figures B.2 and B.3.

Americans after independence liked tea as much as or more than before (see table B.2 and figure B.2).

Coffee trade data provides another way to consider the problem. The assumption tends to be that Americans shifted away from tea to coffee, tea's nearest, most measurable substitute. Yet during the Townshend Act boycotts we see no substantial shift in colonial coffee consumption to match tea's decline. The Townshend Act did not change the tariff on coffee; there was no American coffee boycott commensurate to that on tea; coffee smuggling is not known to have had particular growth or decline in this era. CUST 16's coffee import data are thus a good starting point for determining coffee consumption.[8] CUST 16 shows a relatively stable level of American net coffee imports during the 1768–1772 period. (See table B.1.)

Looking at figure B.3, it is also clear that Americans consumed more tea than coffee in the late colonial period, and more coffee than tea in the early

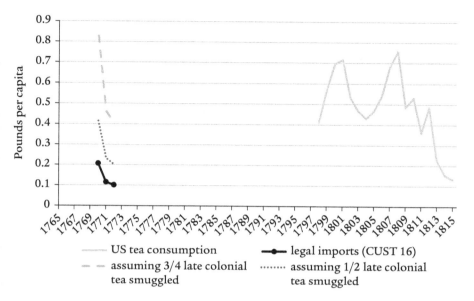

FIGURE B.2. American tea consumption, 1760s–1810s, three-year moving average. Sources: PRO CUST 16/1. *American State Papers*. Commerce and Navigation 1, 1789–1815 Population data: Carter et al., *Historical Statistics*.

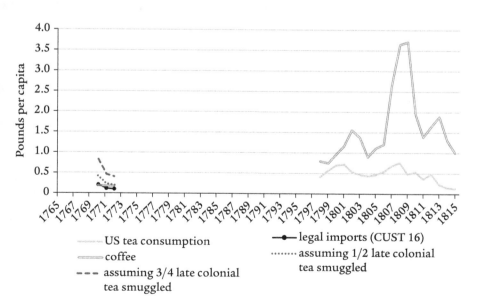

FIGURE B.3. American tea and coffee consumption, 1760s–1810s, three-year moving average. Sources: PRO CUST 16/1. *American State Papers*. Commerce and Navigation 1, 1789–1815 Population data: Carter et al., *Historical Statistics*.

republic. The increase in per capita coffee consumption by the 1790s was greater than the increase in tea.[9] In the early republic, Americans consumed more than twice as much coffee as tea. But the increase in coffee consumption was not at tea's expense. Consumption of tea had returned to, or exceeded, late colonial levels by the 1790s. In the quarter-century between 1772 and 1797, the switch was not from the teacup to the coffee cup, but to both—with both growing in absolute terms, and coffee growing relatively more. Whatever the reason for rising coffee consumption, being anti-tea is not one of them.

So why the increase in coffee consumption? There was perhaps a generational transition in taste, although more data on the tea and coffee trades in the 1770s and 1780s would be needed to prove this. Changes in tariffs, prices, and quality of tea and coffee might be at work. Certainly new trade networks and supplies, from the growth in coffee planting in Jamaica and other British colonies to American commercial access to French, Spanish, and Dutch coffee colonies (notably Saint Domingue and Cuba) during the French Revolution, encouraged the switch. It is thus possible that the French and Haitians Revolutions had more influence on this shift in American tastes than the American Revolution did. Habits formed during the Continental Association and persisting after the spirit of '76 had passed did not dissuade Americans from drinking tea in the 1790s. The tea parties of 1774 did not cause an abrupt and lasting switch to coffee as a distinctly national taste, since for all their coffee, the Americans of John Quincy Adams's generation drank no less tea than their fathers had. And yet with coffee consumption burgeoning around them, one can see how Americans of the 1820s, attempting to remember the Revolution as the men of John Adams's generation faded away, might have latched onto the myth that shunning tea for coffee was part of what made the Revolution so American.[10]

APPENDIX C

Tea Prices, 1773–1776

Tea prices reflect variations in the supply and demand of tea. They may also hint at shifts in supply and demand of banned goods generally.

Prices for bohea, the most widely consumed tea and the best indicator of the general tea market, are considered here. Other grades were more expensive and sold at lower volumes, with price changes less reflective of a general market and more reflective of local idiosyncrasies.

Prices are in sterling shillings. Shillings were divided into twelve pence but are expressed in table C.1 in decimal format to allow easier comparison with figure C.1.

How to Read Figure C.1

Figure C.1 shows wholesale prices for bohea tea in various colonial locations. Prices have been converted to pounds sterling using McCusker's conversion data.[1] The 1773 price increases occurred after news of the Company's shipments were known, reflecting a tea shortage as merchants canceled orders in anticipation of a large supply of Company tea. Since that tea never landed, tea prices remained high at the beginning of 1774. Tea prices fluctuated throughout 1774 but reveal a visible downward trend. This indicates that new supplies of Dutch

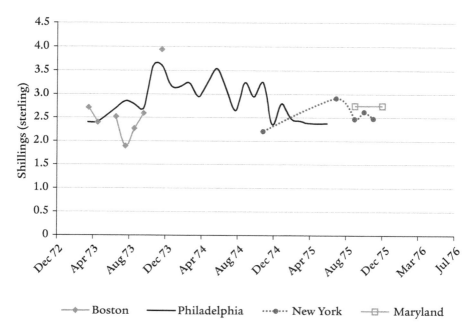

FIGURE C.1. Colonial bohea prices, 1773–1776 (wholesale). Sources: Philadelphia and Boston: Cole, *Wholesale Commodity Prices*. Maryland: LoC Glassford and Company Papers, Maryland Ledger, 1775. New York: NYHS. Shaw & Long Wastebook, 1771–1789.

Table C.1   Dutch and English wholesale bohea prices, annual averages, 1772–1776

YEAR	DUTCH WHOLESALE PRICES (EXPRESSED IN ENGLISH SHILLINGS/ENGLISH POUND)	BRITISH WHOLESALE PRICES (SHILLINGS/POUND)
1772	1.96	2.59
1773	1.72	2.18
1774	1.52	2.24
1775	1.44	2.24
1776	1.51	2.21

Dutch prices and conversions: Posthumus, *Inquiry into the History of Prices in Holland*, 190, 605–606. British prices: House of Commons, "Returns showing the number of pounds weight of tea sold by the East India Company . . ." Labaree gives the Dutch price as 2.25 shillings in 1773. He may not have converted from the 494 g. Amsterdam to the 453 g. English pound (Labaree, *Boston Tea Party*, 332–333).

tea, smuggled into mid-Atlantic ports, were eventually able to meet continued demand. Prices returned to earlier levels in 1775, probably from the combined effect of new tea supplies and reduced tea demand as the Association took hold. Note that while prices here are in sterling, prices described in chapter 1 of 6/6 a pound are in Pennsylvania currency, which converts to roughly 3/11 (or 3.9) sterling. The New York price series from Cole, *Wholesale Commodity Prices*, has

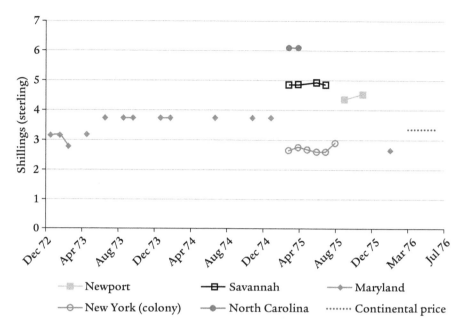

FIGURE C.2.   Colonial bohea prices, 1773–1776 (retail). Sources: Newport: NHS, John Hadwen Day Book (1771–1779). Savannah: Duke, Edward Telfair. Edward Telfair Papers. "Telfair, Edward, and Company, Journal, 1775–1781." Maryland: LoC, Glassford and Company Papers, Maryland Ledgers, 1773–1776. New York (colony): NYHS, John Taylor Papers, 1743–1775. Daybook 1774–1775. North Carolina: UNC, Robert Wilson Account Books, 1772–1888, oversize volume SV-1896/1. Continental: *JCC*, 4: 278.

not been used here. That series gives an unchanging price for bohea from July 1773 to May 1775 of 4.5 New York shillings per pound. In 1774 this converted to 2.49 shilling sterling. These numbers are apparently extracted from the *New York Gazette* price current and likely reflect customary and/or regulated prices rather than market transactions, which have more variance.

How to Read Figure C.2

Retail prices remained remarkably consistent within each region. Prices remained higher in certain towns, suggesting the attractiveness of shipping tea from New York to Newport, for example. Stable pricing suggests that during 1775, reduced demand (from partial compliance) and reduced supply (from partial non-importation) roughly and consistently matched. Newport prices also may have been affected by the shutdown of supply from Boston. Whether merchants in Savannah, Newport, and other towns would have to take a loss by selling tea at the Continental price is unclear, as their cost of acquiring the tea is not always known.

Maryland data come from Glassford & Company's Chesapeake factors. They sourced their tea from Britain and may have been less affected by changes in the Philadelphia price than merchants in Chesapeake market towns. Yorktown, Virginia, merchant William Reynolds reported in December 1774 that tea had returned to "a very moderate price" from, implicitly, a higher one. Glassford factors recorded sales in different monies, usually either "currency" (Maryland colonial currency) or "sterling goods" (purchases on loan, with the debt denominated in sterling). This was repaid by the customer in tobacco or other goods. Occasional sales were recorded in "cash" (i.e., for Spanish silver dollars). Separate "currency" and "sterling goods" price series have been generated from Glassford records. However, the ledgers do not imply a conversion rate that works across grades of tea or is consistent with McCusker. As such, "currency" sales have been excluded in preference for "sterling goods," which can be readily compared to prices in other colonies.[2]

The old East India Company tea was sold in Charleston, South Carolina, in 1776. While there is no 1776 conversion rate, the 1775 South Carolina/sterling conversion rate shows 25s South Carolina currency per pound of bohea converts to 3.4 shillings, which is close to the Continental price (3s 4½ d sterling or ¾ of a dollar). It is unclear, however, how far off from the 1775 rate the 1776 rate was. In May 1775, John Amory sold three pounds of bohea at 5 shillings Massachusetts currency a pound in Boston, which converts to 4.26 shillings in decimal pounds sterling.[3]

ABBREVIATIONS

AHR   *American Historical Review*

Am Arch   Peter Force, ed., *American Archives . . . A Documentary History* (Washington, DC: 1837–1851).

Amer Chron   Carla Mulford, ed., *John Leacock's The First Book of the American Chronicles of the Times, 1774–1775* (Newark: University of Delaware Press, 1987).

ANB   John A. Garraty and Mark C. Carnes, *American National Biography* (New York: Oxford University Press, 1999).

Aspinwall 2   "Aspinwall Papers II," Massachusetts Historical Society. *Collections of the Massachusetts Historical Society* (Boston: The Society, 1881) (Series 4 Vol. X) (Boston, 1881).

Baker   Harvard Business School, Baker Library Historical Collections.

BPL   Boston Public Library

Cont Assoc   "Articles of Association, October 20, 1774." https://avalon .law.yale.edu/18th_century/contcong_10-20-74.asp.

CRI   Worthington Chauncey Ford, ed., Commerce of Rhode Island 1726–1800, 2 vols. (*Collections of the Massachusetts Historical Society*, 7th Ser., vol 9–10, 1914–1915).

CRNC   The *Colonial Records of North Carolina*, ed. William L. Saunders. Raleigh, NC: P. M. Hale, Printer to the State, 1886–1890. https://docsouth.unc.edu/csr/index.php/volumes.

DAB   *Dictionary of American Biography*, Dumas Malone., ed. (Charles Scribner's Sons for the American Council of Learned Societies (1928–1936), 22 vols.

DAR   K. G. Davies, ed., *Documents of the American Revolution 1770– 1783* (Dublin: Irish University Press, 1975).

Dartmouth	Historical Manuscripts Commission. *The Manuscripts of the Earl of Dartmouth*. Volumes 1–3. (London: Her Majesty's Stationery Office, 1887–1896).
DCB	*Dictionary of Canadian Biography* / Dictionnaire biographique du Canada (University of Toronto / Université Laval, 2003–). http://www.biographi.ca/en/.
DNB	*Oxford Dictionary of National Biography* (Oxford: Oxford University Press, 2004).
Duke	Duke University Rubenstein Library
EAS	*Early American Studies*
Egerton	British Library, Egerton Manuscripts
EHR	*Economic History Review*
EIHC	*Essex Institute Historical Collections*
FO	*Founders Online*, National Historic Publications and Records Commission. founders.archives.gov.
HSP	Historical Society of Pennsylvania
HUNTER	University of Virginia Library. Papers of R. M. T. Hunter. Hunter-Garnett Collection [aka Papers of the Hunter and Garnett families] Accession No 38-45.
IOR	British Library, India Office Records
JAH	*Journal of American History*
JCC	Worthington Chauncey Ford, ed., *Journals of the Continental Congress 1774–1789* (Washington, DC: Government Printing Office, 1904–1937), 34 vols. American Memory. https://memory.loc.gov/ammem/amlaw/lwjclink.html.
JPCNY	*Journals of the Provincial Congress, Provincial Convention, Committee of Safety and Council of Safety of the State of New York, 1775–1776–1777* (Albany: 1842), 2 vols.
LDC	Paul H. Smith, ed., *Letters of Delegates to Congress, 1774–1789* (Washington, DC: Library of Congress, 1976–2000). American Memory. https://memory.loc.gov/ammem/amlaw/lwdg.html.

L&G	University of Michigan, William L. Clements Library, Leger & Greenwood Letterbook
LoC	Library of Congress
LVa	Library of Virginia
Mass Spy	*Massachusetts Spy*
MHS	Massachusetts Historical Society
NARA	National Archives and Records Administration
NDAR	William Bell Clark and William James Morgan, eds., *Naval Documents of the American Revolution* (Washington, DC: U.S. Government Printing Office, 1964–1970), 5 vols.
NEHGR	*New England Historical and Genealogical Register*
NEQ	*New England Quarterly*
NHA	Nantucket Historical Association
NHS	Newport Historical Society
NYG	*New York Gazette and the Weekly Mercury*
NYHS	New-York Historical Society
NYPL	New York Public Library
NYJ	*New York Journal*
PAG	*Pennsylvania Gazette*
PA Jrnl	*Pennsylvania Journal*
PBF	William B. Willcox, ed., *Papers of Benjamin Franklin* (New Haven: Yale University Press).
PHL	Henry Laurens, *The Papers of Henry Laurens* (Columbia: University of South Carolina Press).
PMHB	*Pennsylvania Magazine of History and Biography*
PRO	British National Archives
PUL	Princeton University Library, Rare Books & Manuscript Collections
RISA	Rhode Island State Archives

RNYG   *Rivington's New York Gazetteer*

Sabine   Lorenzo Sabine, *Biographical Sketches of Loyalists of the American Revolution* (Boston: Little, Brown & Co, 1864).

SCAGG   *South Carolina and American General Gazette*

SCG   *South Carolina Gazette*

SCGCJ   *South Carolina Gazette and Country Journal*

SCHM   *South Carolina Historical Magazine*

SCPRO   Public Record Office, Colonial Office. Filmed by South Carolina Department of Archives and History. *Records in the British Public Record Office Relating to South Carolina, 1663–1782.*

Scribner   Robert L. Scribner and Brent Tarter, *Revolutionary Virginia. The Road to Independence* (Virginia Independence Bicentennial Commission, University Press of Virginia, 1973–1983), 7 vols.

UNC   University of North Carolina Libraries

UPenn   University of Pennsylvania Libraries

UVa   University of Virginia, Albert and Shirley Small Special Collections Library

VMHB   *Virginia Magazine of History and Biography*

VMHC   Virginia Museum of History and Culture

Winslow   Isaac Winslow and Margaret Catherine Winslow, transcribed and edited by Robert Newsom, *Family Memorial. The Winslows of Boston* (Boston, MA: 1837?–1873?) 1. MHS.

Winterthur Winterthur Museum, Gardens, & Library

WMQ   *William and Mary Quarterly*

WPS   *Der Wöchentliche Pennsylvanische Staatsbote*

NOTES

Front Matter

1. "Rally Mohawks! . . .": Drake, *Tea Leaves: Being a Collection of Letters and Documents Relating to the Shipment of Tea to the American Colonies in the Year 1773, by the East India Tea Company*, clxxvi. "For since . . .": Granger, *Political Satire*, 235.

2. Note on Currency: For more, see McCusker, *How Much Is That in Real Money?*

Introduction

1. On national identity: Parkinson, *The Common Cause*. McDonnell, "National Identity and the American War for Independence Reconsidered," 3–17. Peskin, *Captives and Countrymen*. Waldstreicher, *In the Midst of Perpetual Fetes*. Young, *Shoemaker and the Tea Party*. Yokota, *Unbecoming British*.

2. Truxes, *Defying Empire*, 2–5.

3. Cont Assoc. LVa. Charles Steuart Papers Misc., Reel 3703, f291.

4. On print culture: Adelman, *Revolutionary Networks* and Parkinson, *The Common Cause*. On performance and spectacle, see Waldstreicher, *Perpetual Fetes*.

5. Breen, "Baubles of Britain," 74, 75, 77, 88, 93, 96, 98.

6. There is no evidence, pace Breen, that committees monitored home consumption. Breen, "Baubles of Britain," 102. Carp, *Defiance of the Patriots*. "assumes . . .": Castronovo, *Propaganda 1776*, 103.

7. See, e.g., Rakove, *The Beginnings of National Politics*, 50. The most important recent economic analysis of the Association remains Holton, *Forced Founders*, 121–124, upon which this analysis builds.

8. Though some were Loyalists who got into trouble for their Loyalism more generally.

9. Cont Assoc.

10. This book does not address the imported material culture (tea tables, tea services, and other tea ware) surrounding tea consumption, for which see Yokota, *Unbecoming British*, 62–114.

11. Hancock, *Oceans of Wine*, 95, 120–122. The other item to be specifically banned was foreign indigo. Bear and Stanton, eds., *Jefferson's Memorandum Books*, 1: 408.

12. Fichter, "Collecting Debts." *Norfolk Intelligencer*, August 23, 1775. Colonial Williamsburg, John Norton and Sons Papers, MS 36.3, folder 102. Norfolk County committee orders to Mr. Andrew Sprowle, August 9, 1775. Sprowle was a personal friend of Dunmore. Butt, *Portsmouth Under Four Flags*, 8–15.

13. Fichter, "Collecting Debts."

14. "Repatriated" is Merritt's term. On tea in post-independence United States: Merritt, *The Trouble with Tea*, 125–146.

15. His Majesty's customs officers struggled to stop arms imports (PRO T 1/513, 20, 24–26, 28, 38–39). On the secret committee, see *JCC*, "Secret Committee Minutes of Proceedings," various dates.

16. Barck Jr., *New York City*, 99, 133. Smith, "Food Rioters."

17. Jane Merritt, *The Trouble with Tea*. Norton, *1774*. Norton generously corresponded with the author, sharing her expertise and insight during the drafting of this manuscript, which has been further updated in light of *1774*.

18. Glickman, *Buying Power*, 56. "the People": Sullivan, *Disaffected*, 36.

19. The assumption of continuity between the 1769–1770 and 1775–1776 non-consumption movements is usually the product of a compressed discussion of the boycotts in a book focused on other matters.

20. Ammerman, *In the Common Cause*, 5.

21. Glickman, *Buying Power*, 35–36.

1. The Tea Party That Wasn't

1. Fraser Jr., *Patriots Pistols and Petticoats*, 52. Schafer, *Zephaniah Kingsley Jr.*, 13. *SCG*, December 27, 1773.

2. Butler, *Votaries of Apollo*, 129.

3. "UNCONSTITUTIONAL," "WITHOUT . . ." "Several" "We, the underwritten . . .": *SCG*, December 6, 1773. Rogers, "The Charleston Tea Party," 158. Walsh, *Charleston's Sons of Liberty*, 4–9, 60.

4. Fraser Jr., *Patriots Pistols and Petticoats*, 53–54. *PHL*, 9: 593 n 3. Refusal: *SCG* December 6, 1773. Fraser Jr., *Charleston! Charleston!*, 136. In the Patriot version of events, Smith announced, "HE had determined some weeks before . . . not to have any concern" in the tea. However, when the consignees, including Smith, wrote the Company on December 4, they noted the large crowd opposing them, not Smith's decision. Smith declined to sign the first draft of a letter written by Leger and Greenwood on December 3 but co-signed their second draft, written on December 4; it is unclear why. The first draft was more pessimistic; the second suggested that mercantile discontent with the meeting on December 3 might aid the Company, an addition which did not make sense if Smith were trying to duck having to deal with the tea. (L&G, 137–139). "Great majority" and "to Wink . . ." from PRO CO 5/133 f61 (old f40d). Consignees to Company December 4, 1773. "every thing . . ." "Inconsistency" "Merchants . . .": L&G, 138–139. Timothy's politics: Cohen, *South Carolina Gazette*, 244.

5. "upwards of" "a little more . . ." "import . . .": *SCG*, December 6, 1773. Labaree, *Boston Tea Party*, 153. McDonough, *Christopher Gadsden and Henry Laurens*, 133.

6. *SCG*, December 6, 1773.

7. PRO CUST 16/1. "nothing . . .": L&G, 138. "that will . . ." "a *total disuse* . . ." "made . . .": *SCG*, December 6, 1773. Smith's advertisement: *SCG*, October 25 to November 8, 1773. Other advertisements: Hawkins, Petrie & Co., John Benfield, and Alexander Gillon & Co. *SCG*, December 6, 1773.

8. "Disputes . . .": "Rules of the Charlestown Chamber of Commerce," 4. Rogers, "The Charleston Tea Party," 161. Fraser, *Patriots Pistols and Petticoats*, 55. Sellers, *Charleston Business*, 222. "when . . ." "the moment . . ." "every Man . . .": L&G, 138–139. "unless . . ." "be . . .": PRO CO 5/133 f61. Consignees to Company December 4, 1773. Though dated to December 4, this sentiment seems to be part of what was expressed at the Chamber of Commerce. Egnal, *A Mighty Empire*, 266, 366.

9. "private" "parcels of tea" "the meeting . . .": Drayton, *Memoirs*, 1: 98. PRO CO 5/133 f62. "had not *desisted* . . .": *SCG* December 20, 1773. Emphasis original.

10. "unpopular" "very few" "ought . . .": *SCG*, December 20, 1773. "Many friends . . ." "always . . ." Drayton, *Memoirs*, 1: 98. Sellers, *Charleston Business*, 223. SCPRO Reel 11. Vol. 33, 350–354. Charles Town. December 24, 1773. Bull to Dartmouth.

11. "unjust" "to the Company" "others . . ." "Injurious" "by depriving . . ." "every argument": L&G, 140–141.

12. "Enemys . . .": PRO CO 5/133 f62. Smith: Higgins, "Charles Town Merchants." Leger and Greenwood tried to enter the slave trade but remained marginal in it.

13. "same footing" "to consume . . ." "no Teas . . .": PRO CO 5/133 f62. Schlesinger, *Colonial Merchants*, 297. "ought": *SCG*, December 20, 1773. The exact number of months may have been unresolved. Leger and Greenwood left a blank in their letter book for the number of months and filled in "Six" later (L&G, 141). Timothy did not mention a six-month lag at the time (*SCG*, December 20, 1773), and the issue was revisited the following March. British exports: PRO CUST 17/1 and 17/2.

14. "to be entered . . ." "*no Teas* . . ." "import . . ." "any": *SCG*, December 20, 1773. PRO CO 5/133 f62. *SCG* March 21, 1774. Drayton, *Memoirs*, 1: 100.

15. "Forfeiting": L&G, 139–140. "Difficulties": *SCG*, December 6, 1773. Curling's bond was ultimately cancelled (IOR B/90, 196).

16. Maier, "The Charleston Mob and the Evolution of Popular Politics in Revolutionary South Carolina, 1765–1784," 180–181. Marguerite Steedman, "Charleston's Forgotten Tea Party," *Georgia Review* 21, no. 2 (Summer 1967): 247. Drayton, *Memoirs*, 1: 99.

17. "There was not . . .": Schlesinger, *Colonial Merchants*, 298. "the warmth . . ." "hasty": SCPRO Reel 11, 33: 350–354. Charles Town. December 24, 1773. Bull to Dartmouth. Walsh, *Charleston's Sons of Liberty*, 60. Steedman, "Charleston's Forgotten Tea Party," 248. Rogers, "The Charleston Tea Party," 162. *SCG*, July 25, 1774. Weir, *Colonial South Carolina*, 313. Northernmost: L&G, 168.

18. "greatest . . .": PRO CO 5/133 f36. Labaree, *Boston Tea Party*, 158. PRO CO 5/133 f43-44. *DAR*, 7: 27–28. Norton. "The Seventh Tea Ship," 681–710.

19. "embarrassed": McDonough, *Gadsden and Laurens*, 133. Maier, "The Charleston Mob," 179. "Since . . ." "Our People . . ." "under . . .": L&G, 156. "were . . ." "did" "do still . . .": *SCG*, December 27, 1773. Emphasis original. "the Bostonians . . .": PHL, 9: 391.

20. Rao, *National Duties*, chapter 1.

21. Butterfield, ed., *Diary and Autobiography of John Adams*, 2: 86.

22. "Huzzai": Roche, *The Colonial Colleges*, 60. "No one . . ." "universally Resented here": Baker Hancock family papers. Series II. Letterbook JH-6, 424. John Hancock to

Hayley and Hopkins, December 21, 1773. Krusell, *Of Tea and Tories*, 8. Charlestown: Cunningham, ed., *Letters and Diary of John Rowe*, 259.

23. "gross immoral" "malignant atrocious" "diabolical": Gray, "The two congresses cut up," 3–4. Schlesinger, *Colonial Merchants*, 303–304. Weir, *Colonial South Carolina*, 313. "Not that we approve their conduct in destroy[in]g the Tea," Washington wrote in June 1774 (Labaree, *Boston Tea Party*, 234). "an Act . . .": Schlesinger, *Colonial Merchants*, 299. Dabney and Dargan, *William Henry Drayton*, 22–23. Scots factors noted Patrick Henry's and Richard Henry Lee's disapproval. Dabney, "Letters from Norfolk," 116. Schlesinger suggests Henry was ambivalent (Schlesinger, *Colonial Merchants*, 331). "wily Cromwellians" "prudent": McDonough, *Gadsden and Laurens*, 134. "discretion": Norton, *1774*, 37. "substantial thinking part": Schlesinger, *Colonial Merchants*, 291. "generally condemned": Adair and Schutz, eds., *Peter Oliver's Origins & Progress*, 103.

24. "the divided sentiments . . .": Norton, *1774*, 48. Brown sees New England towns united in support of the Tea Party (Brown, *Revolutionary Politics*, 167–168). Norton notes division in Masschusetts, Virginia, and elsewhere (Norton, *1774*, 47–57). Schlesinger, *Colonial Merchants*, 331. "The affair . . ." "a Disastrous . . .": Cunningham, ed., *Letters and Diary of John Rowe*, 258.

25. Krusell, *Of Tea and Tories*, 9. Olson, "Pictorial Representations," 18. *Massachusetts Spy*, February 23, 1774. Young, *Shoemaker and the Tea Party*. This myth is most recently encapsulated in Carp, *Defiance of the Patriots*, 161–181.

26. Norton, *1774*, 47–83.

27. "bloodshed": Norton, *1774*, 49. "The people . . .": Boyle, "Boyle's Journal of Occurrences in Boston," *NEHGR*, 84 (1930) 371. "because Governor Hutchinson . . .": *JCC* 1: 98. Boston committee: NYPL. Boston Committee of Correspondence Records, 1772–1784 Boston committee to New York and Philadelphia, December 17, 1773.

28. Anderson, *The Martyr and the Traitor*, 77. Parkinson, *The Common Cause*.

29. Labaree, *Boston Tea Party*, 156.

30. Lincoln, ed. *Journals of Each Provincial Congress of Massachusetts*, 27–28. Ingersoll, *The Loyalist Problem*, 72 n 43, 166. Williams, *A Discourse*. Lyman, "A Sermon Preached at Hatfield." Young, *Shoemaker and the Tea Party*, 108–120, 155–165. Norton, *1774*, 240, 248–252.

31. "COFFEE" "NO TEA": "The One Hundredth Anniversary of the Destruction of Tea," 231. Drake, *Tea Leaves*, cxi. Young, *Shoemaker and the Tea Party*, 88–89, 108–120, 155–165. "rascally" "Convened . . .": PRO CO 5 / 133 f62.

32. "advis'd . . ." "I would not . . ." "Noble spirit'd": Roberts, *March to Quebec*, 265. "English gentleman" "lady of the house" "No, madam" Roberts, *March to Quebec*, 358–359. Some sources offer the alternative spelling, Dickson.

33. "great . . .": Meigs, *Journal*, 23. "agonies": Stone, ed., *Invasion*, 20. Stone gives Dixon's as the "first blood shed before Quebec," though some men had died in the wilderness en route (Ibid., 20). Smith, *Arnold's March*, 33–38. Hale and Wolfe: Guthke, *Last Words*, 21, passim. I am indebted to Virginia DeJohn Anderson for this reference. Hale: Anderson, *The Martyr and the Traitor*. Accounts of Dixon's death by Barney (Darley, *Voices Waiting to Be Heard*, 17), Greenman (Ibid., 67), Meigs (Meigs, *Journal*, 23), Thayer (Stone, ed., *Invasion*, 20), Senter (Senter, *Journal*, 44), Haskell (Withington, ed., *Caleb Haskell's Diary*, 13), Humphrey (Humphrey, "A Journal Kept by William Humphrey," 101). Topham (Roberts, *March to Quebec*, 265) and Henry (Ibid., 358–359) mention the tea.

34. "ideas . . ." "countrymen" "Hence . . .": Roberts, *March to Quebec*, 359. Dixon and Henry both served in Smith's Company ("Roll of Captain Matthew Smith's Company," 39–42). Ellis and Evans, *History of Lancaster County*, 43. On the use of the term "country," Ingersoll, *Loyalist Problem*, 126–127.

35. "English": Humphrey, "Journal" 100. "died . . ." "worthy . . .": Ibid., 108. "Provincials": Ibid., 117. "Provincial" could describe many of the men defending Quebec as well. "old country men": Darley, *Voices*, 71, 167. In 1776, when prisoners escaped to the Provincial siege lines around the city, deserters from His Majesty's lines sometimes came along (Withington, ed., *Caleb Haskell's Diary*, 17). Frost: "A Journal Kept by William Humphrey," 99. Gilje, "Loyalty and Liberty." William Tennent III likewise described Patriotic American women as having "the Soul of Englishwomen" (*SCGCJ*, August 2, 1774).

36. Norton, *1774*, 20. Ellison, "Montgomery's Misfortune," 602–614. Purcell, *Sealed with Blood*, 24–33.

37. "Enslow the baker": UPenn, Franks ledger. Zitt, "David Salisbury Franks," 77–95. "Sugar . . .": Darley, *Voices Waiting to Be Heard*, 72. On Frost, see Ibid., 310. "several . . ." "as the majority . . .": Darley, *Voices Waiting to Be Heard*, 47–48. Henry on his and others' tea purchases: Roberts, *March to Quebec*, 404, 417, 423.

38. Conroy, *In Public Houses*, 262. Hartigan-O'Connor, *The Ties That Buy*, 2. Chesapeake indentured servants may have consumed little tea. Virginian Walter Jones thought "Vulgar" people "used none of it" (McDonnell, *The Politics of War*, 34. Also Rhys Isaac, *Transformation of Virginia*, 46). "even . . .": Norton, "The Seventh Tea Ship," 685. Shammas, *The Pre-Industrial Consumer*, 144, 183. Ligon, "The Fashionable Set." Miller, *Sam Adams*, 285. Wharton, "Observations upon the Consumption of Teas," 139. The Delaware Indians of Ohio. Yokota, *Unbecoming British*, 83. "tea, coffee and chocolate" Guild, *Early History of Brown University*, 274.

39. Shammas, *The Pre-Industrial Consumer*, 78, 85. For the 0.5 pound estimate, see Mason, *Road to Independence*, 4.

40. Shammas, *The Pre-Industrial Consumer*, 85, 137, 144. Mintz, *Sweetness and Power*, 115–117, 121, 141. James, *Two Centuries*, 4.

41. Breen, "Baubles of Britain," 73–104.

42. "Boycott" as a term dates from the 1880s. In the 1770s the term was nonconsumption, which meant not to use or buy. Glickman, *Buying Power*, 33.

43. "If a Commodity . . ." Randolph and Nicholas, *Considerations*, 28. "why should . . ." "Many . . .": Ibid., 52. "renounce": Miller, *Sam Adams*, 285. Butterfield, ed., *Letters of Benjamin Rush*, 84. "if not . . .": Scribner, 3: 130–131.

44. "Our credit . . .": Miller, *Sam Adams*, 288.

45. *CRI*, 1: 451–452.

46. "there was no tea . . .": PRO CO 5/133 f136. "almost invincible temptation": Akers, *The Divine Politician*, 164. "Temptation of . . .": Randolph and Nicholas, *Considerations*, 52.

47. "AN OLD PROPHET" "TO USE NO TEA" "any Person . . .": *PAG*, December 8, 1773. Labaree, *Boston Tea Party*, 157. Labaree gives a price of 3/6 but the *Gazette*, his source, gives 6/6. Norton, "The Seventh Tea Ship," 688.

48. "extortion": Patterson, *Political Parties*, 114 n 46. *Newport Mercury*, February 14, 1774. Seabury, *Free Thoughts*, 10. Yet merchant Neil Jamieson still thought he needed

to spell out the effects of supply on price to Thomas Jefferson in 1784 (Boyd, ed., *Papers of Thomas Jefferson*, 7: 365–375).

49. MHS Misc. Bd. 1773 Dec 31. Many thanks to Mary Beth Norton for this reference. The customs commissioners also spent part of December in the castle (PRO T 29/43, 150) but seem to have returned to Boston by January. Quibbles: PRO CO 5/769, 48–49.

50. "utterly . . ." "steps": PRO T 1/505, 73. Thomas and Elisha Hutchinson, Richard Clarke & Sons and Benjamin Faneuil Jr. to Richard Harrison and Robert Hallowell. January 1, 1774.

51. "gentlemen . . .": *Pennsylvania Chronicle*, February 1, 1774. "our Duty . . .": PRO T 1/505, 89. Richard Harrison and Robert Hallowell to Customs Commissioners, January 6, 1774.

52. "unsafe . . .": PRO T 1/505, 81. Richard Harrison and Robert Hallowell to Governor Hutchinson. "destroyed . . ." "the Key . . .": PRO T 1/505, 89. Richard Harrison and Robert Hallowell to Customs Commissioners, January 6, 1774. "in the Custody . . .": PRO T 1/505, 71. Samuel Mather to John Robinson, January 21, 2774. Montagu: PRO T 1/505, 75–77.

53. News of the salvage on Cape Cod reached Boston on December 15 and appeared in the *Massachusetts Gazette* on December 16, the day of the Tea Party. At this time it was unclear what would happen to the *William*'s tea next. "most . . .": *Massachusetts Gazette*, December 16, 1773. Norton, "Seventh Tea Ship," 682 n4.

54. "people" "immersed" "cast . . .": NYPL Boston Committee of Correspondence Records, 1772–1784. Boston committee to New York and Philadelphia, December 17, 1773.

55. "none": SCG January 17, 1774. "How . . ." "Grand . . .": NYPL. Boston Committee of Correspondence Records, 1772–1784. Boston committee to Charleston. January 20, 1774. The Boston committee did not specify that this was in reference to landing the *London*'s tea, but it remains the most plausible explanation. New York: Rogers, "The Charleston Tea Party," 164.

56. Norton, "The Seventh Tea Ship," 681–710. Egerton 2661 f5. Reporting of storage at Castle William: *Boston Evening-Post*, January 17, 1774. *Connecticut Courant*, January 20, 1774. *NYJ*, January 27, 1774. *RNYG* January 20, 1774. "original design" "watchfulness . . .": *Boston Gazette*, January 17, 1774. "seems . . ." "What shall . . .": *NYJ* January 13, 1774.

57. After the feint of customs seizing the *William*'s tea, perhaps the Boston consignees hoped to buy it back at auction. *William* tea: IOR B/91 290. *London* tea: SCAGG, October 2 to 9, 1776. *Records of the South Carolina Treasury*, Roll 1: Public Ledger, 1775–1777, "Money Received from the Commissioners on the Sales of Tea," 152. Weights: Labaree, *Boston Tea Party*, 335. The tea consumed in Charleston included the 70,304 pounds shipped by the East India Company in 1773, plus several chests seized in 1774. Allan, *John Hancock*, 141–142. The *London*'s tea was said to have been damaged. Labaree, *Boston Tea Party*, 335. Cf. invoice values in PRO CO 5/133, 101.

58. Schafer, *Zephaniah Kingsley*, 17. Richard Walsh, *Charleston's Sons of Liberty*, 4–9, 60. The use of "propaganda" as a term has been rehabilitated in, among others, Castronovo, *Propaganda 1776*, 87–115 and passim.

2. Before

1. Mui and Mui, "Smuggling and the British Tea Trade before 1784," 45, 48. Labaree, *Boston Tea Party*, 6. Kent, *War and Trade in Northern Seas*, 113–114. Dillo, "Made to Measure?" 61.

2. British home consumption of legal tea: House of Commons, "Returns . . ." Home consumption includes Great Britain but not Ireland and the Americas. Slightly different figures are derived in Mui and Mui, "Smuggling and the British Tea Trade before 1784," 68. British smuggled tea: Cole, "Trends in Eighteenth-Century Smuggling," 405 and Thomas, *The Townshend Duties Crisis*, 18. "growing consumption . . .": Cross, ed., *Eighteenth Century Documents*, 237. The Company estimated 7.7 million pounds of smuggled tea to 6.7 million pounds legal tea a year (IOR L/AG/18/2/1, 11). British population estimate of 8.4 million: Rickman, "Observations," 9–10. Lee and Schofield, "British Population in the Eighteenth Century," 21. Lockwood, *To Begin the World over Again*, 14–19.

3. Legal tea imports: PRO CUST 16/1. Calculations assume a population of 2.168 million. Were 75 percent of tea smuggled, it would use up much of the European supply. Hutchinson, Wharton, and Palmer: Thomas, *Townshend Duties Crisis*, 247.

4. Kent, *War and Trade*, 119. Mui and Mui, "Smuggling and the British Tea Trade" 50. Hodacs, *Silk and Tea in the North*, 49.

5. de Vries and van der Woude, *First Modern Economy*, 457–462. Mui and Mui, "Smuggling and the British Tea Trade," 48. Writers claiming that Europeans did not drink tea rarely cite evidence about European consumption. VOC director Cornelis van Oudermeulen thought Frieslanders and Groningeners loved tea and coffee so much they drank the whole Dutch supply (De Vries and van der Woude, *First Modern Economy*, 458). On Amsterdam: McCants, "Poor Consumers as Global Consumers," 182–185. German tea consumption was great enough for one author to recommend import substitution. Rumpf, *Deutschlands Goldbrube*. European demand helped make a deeper tea market.

6. Dermigny, *La Chine et l'Occident*, 2: 616, 636. Dutch expatriates in other cities often had prominent roles trading tea. Ibid., 2: 613.

7. Müller, "The Swedish East India Trade," 32–33. Kent, *War and Trade*, 122. Kjellberg, *Svenska Ostindiska Compagnierna*, 218. Hodacs, *Silk and Tea*, 37. In 1770, two-thirds of Swedish East India re-exports by value (largely tea) went to the Netherlands, one-quarter to France and German states, and 3 percent went directly to Britain (Lind, *Göteborgs Handel*, 184. Lindblad, *Sweden's Trade with the Dutch Republic*, 160. Nyström, *De svenska ostindiska kompanierna*, table 4. Cf. for 1771–1777: Dermigny, *La Chine et l'Occident*, 2: 605). Sweden exported little directly to North America in the 1760s and 1770s. Few ships sailed from Gothenburg directly to North America between 1771 and 1775. Högberg, *Utrikeshandel*, 63, 73. Arrivals to Sweden could come indirectly via the Caribbean, and departures were similarly circuitous (*CRI*, 1: 519).

8. Heckscher, *Economic History of Sweden*, 195–196. Kent, *War and Trade*, 120. Dermigny, *La Chine et l'Occident*, 2: 604. On European tea consumption, see note 5. Some Lübeck tea was re-shipped to Britain. Müller, "Swedish East India Trade" 35. Hodacs, *Silk and Tea*, 2.

9. Pourchasse, "Roscoff, un important centre de contrebande," 147–156. "monied men": HUNTER Archibald Hunter to James Hunter Jr., June 7, 1774, Dunkirk. "only time . . .": HUNTER Archibald Hunter to James Hunter, May 13, 1774, Dunkirk. "all kinds . . ." HUNTER Archibald Hunter to James Hunter, June 10, 1774, Dunkirk. Smuggling from Iberia: PRO T 1/513, 16.

10. "whole Navy of England": *South Carolina Gazette*, December 27, 1773. Wharton, "Observations," 140. Harrington, *New York Merchant*, 268. HUNTER Archibald Hunter to James Hunter Jr., Account, February 15, 1774. "I shall . . .": HUNTER Archibald Hunter to James Hunter, March 4, 1774, Dunkirk. Box 1. Hammond: *CRI* 1: 332, 519–520.

11. Smuggling to the British Caribbean is difficult to glean from shifts in legal British tea re-exports, as such shifts were as likely to be affected by changing naval and military deployments as by changes in smuggling (PRO CUST 17/8 and CUST 17/9). Westergaard, *Danish West Indies*, 250. Jensen, *Maritime Commerce*, 133. Vernons: Norton, *1774*, 5–6.

12. Norton, "The Seventh Tea Ship," 686. Labaree, *Boston Tea Party*, 10. Harrington, *New York Merchant*, 268. York, ed., *Hulton*, 115–116. Clark, "American Board of Customs," 793–794.

13. New York customs: *DAR*, 8: 224–225, Lt Gov Colden to Dartmouth, November 2, 1774. Labaree, *Boston Tea Party*, 54–55. "Stoping . . .": Hersey, "Tar and Feathers," 462. Irvin, "Tar, Feathers, and Enemies of American Liberties," 205 n 18, 210.

14. "Weltring . . ." "very cruelly" "beating out . . ." "great Magnitude & Enormity": Cross, ed., *Eighteenth Century Documents*, 308–313.

15. Thomas, *Townshend Duties Crisis*, 26–28. Indemnity Act, 1767, 7 Geo. 3, c. 56. Bowen, *Revenue and Reform*, 109. Cole, "Trends in Eighteenth-Century Smuggling," 401. Labaree, *Boston Tea Party*, 13, 21. Clark, "American Board of Customs," 781. York, ed., *Hulton*, 113.

16. Hutchinson thought the Townshend duties still gave smugglers an advantage. Thomas, *Townshend Duties Crisis*, 11, 19, 247, 252. Bowen, *Revenue and Reform*, 121–123.

17. Bowen, *Revenue and Reform*, 103, 122, 125.

18. Nierstrasz, *Rivalry for Trade*, 55, 60, 54–66. Mui and Mui, "Smuggling and the British Tea Trade," 55.

19. IOR B/86, 344. Bowen, "'So Alarming an Evil,'" 7, 12, 14. Mui and Mui, "Smuggling and the British Tea Trade," 46, 47, 67. Some of the increase was actual Irish demand, which post-Commutation Act tea exports to Ireland show was real (PRO CUST 17/9).

20. Labaree, *Boston Tea Party*, 13, 22–24, 33–35. York, ed., *Hulton*, 126. Hoffman, *Spirit of Dissention*, 86. "obstinate": Labaree, *Boston Tea Party*, 33.

21. York, ed., *Hulton*, 142. Boston. "At a meeting . . ." Labaree, *Boston Tea Party*, 31–34.

22. Irving and Mein, *A State of Importations*. Labaree, *Boston Tea Party*, 26. Schlesinger, *Colonial Merchants*, 159–170.

23. Labaree, *Boston Tea Party*, 25. Barbara Clark Smith, *The Freedoms We Lost*, 100.

24. York, ed., *Hulton*, 138. Brown, "Shifting Freedoms," 371–376. Martin, *Free and Open Press*, 80.

25. Labaree, *Boston Tea Party*, 25, 47–50. Patterson, *Political Parties*, 69. L&G, 1.

26. "Mr. John Hancock . . .": Stevens, *Facsimiles*, Document 2029, 5. Palfrey: *New-York Journal*, December 23, 1773. Palfrey denied that Hancock "paid the Revenue Duty" on tea, leaving the possibility that his ships carried dutied tea belonging to others. For ownership of vessels carrying tea: MHS British North American customs papers, 1765–1774, "An Account of what Tea has been imported into Boston since the year 1768." Shared ownership linked these men across the Atlantic; thus, Bostonian Nathaniel Wheatley owned the Harmony with Nantucketer William Roach and Londoners Isaac Buxton and Samuel Enderby, into whose family he would later marry. Dennie: Day, "Another Look at the Boston 'Caucus,'" 33, 36. Hancock imported tea from the Netherlands in 1772 as one-fourth owner of the *Neptune*. Hancock even named a vessel *Undutied Tea*. Labaree, *Boston Tea Party*, 10. Akers, *Divine Politician*, 160. Miller, *Sam Adams*, 285. Hancock sold tea during the non-import agreement in April 1769, August 1769, and January 1770. Hancock also kept a mistress, Dorcas Griffiths, who had a "Grocery and Tea shop" on his wharf, selling tea probably supplied by him. Hersey, "The Misfortunes of Dorcas Griffiths," 13–25. Schlesinger, *Colonial Merchants*, 299. Reed, ed., *Life and Correspondence of Joseph Reed*, 1: 52, 56.

27. L&G, 6, 128.

28. Cole, *Wholesale Commodity Prices . . . Statistical Supplement*, 55–64.

29. Miller, *Sam Adams*, 287–288.

30. Thomas, *Townshend Duties Crisis*, 255. Jensen, *Maritime Commerce*, 198. The rebate of the 25 percent duty lapsed in 1772. Tea sent to the colonies that year paid a 10 percent re-export duty (Drawback Act, 1772, 12 Geo. 3, c 60. Bowen, *Revenue and Reform*, 125). Re-exported tea was fully rebated from this tax again in 1773 (Thomas, *Townshend Duties Crisis*, 248, 251). The drawback on tea re-exported to Ireland ceased. The Company instructed its consignees to sell singlo at 2 / 8 and hyson at 5 / .. Labaree thinks the Company would not necessarily have undersold smugglers (Labaree, *Boston Tea Party*, 76–77). Thomas disagrees (Thomas, *Townshend Duties Crisis*, 255).

31. Bowen, *Revenue and Reform*, 151, 159. The VOC's shareholders were similarly reluctant to cut dividends. van Zanden and van Riel, *The Strictures of Inheritance*, 78.

32. Bowen, *Revenue and Reform*, 152. While North America received smuggled tea from elsewhere, it was too far away to re-distribute smuggled tea back to Britain or Ireland. Ship captains had to give bond for the delivery of dutied teas in North America (whether shipped by the Company or not). To cancel the bond, they had to return to Britain with a certificate from a North American customs house verifying the tea's landing. It was not worth smuggling tea from Britain to New York and then back to Ireland when smugglers could supply the Irish market from cheaper sources close by. This gave shipping to North America a particular appeal.

33. Labaree, *Tea Party*, 335.

34. Tea Act, 1773, 13 Geo. 3, c. 44, Article VI. Tea sales: Mui and Mui, "Smuggling and the British Tea Trade," 68. Tea imports: Nierstrasz, *Rivalry for Trade*, 62 (chart) and data table, private correspondence with Nierstrasz, based on IOR sources. The Company reduced tea imports after 1773 because of London oversupply, not because it lost access to the thirteen colonies. IOR L / AG / 18 / 2 / 1, 7, 11. Mui and Mui, "The Commutation Act," 235. European purchases of tea for European use continued after 1784.

35. Labaree, *Boston Tea Party*, 76. Jensen, *Maritime Commerce*, 198. Drake, *Tea Leaves*, xii, 245. The Company shipped 598,659 pounds of tea to North America in 1773, of

which the New York and Philadelphia shipments comprised 211,778 pounds each (Labaree, *Boston Tea Party*, 335). Doerflinger, *Vigorous Spirit of Enterprise*, 193.

36. "lenient Principle": Adair and Schutz, eds., *Peter Oliver's Origins & Progress*, 101. Schlesinger, *Colonial Merchants*, 282. Hutchinson tea sales: Allen, *An Account*, 5–7.

37. Shammas, *The Pre-Industrial Consumer*, 66. "if the tea comes . . .": Thomas, *Townshend Duties Crisis*, 257.

38. "absolute Sovereign," *New-York Journal*, October 22, 1772. Agents: Kammen, *A Rope in the Sand*. Tax in the form of port dues was paid in silver to the Swedish state (Kjellberg, *Svenska Ostindiska Compagnierna*, 317). Anti-monopoly sentiment: Fichter, *So Great a Profit*, chapter 1. Mui and Mui, "Smuggling and the British Tea Trade," 48. Kent, *War and Trade*, 113–114.

3. Tea Politics

1. "It is Tea . . . ": "To the LADIES of South Carolina," *SCGCJ* August 2, 1774. Carp, *Rebels Rising*, 159. "the fatal cause . . .": LDC, 1: 51. James Duane speech to Committee on Rights, September 8, 1774. Lester Olson, "Pictorial Representations," 26.

2. Schlenger, *Colonial Merchants*, 300–301. Dealers agreed to a maximum 4d/lb profit on tea until January 20 (*Massachusetts Spy*, December 30, 1773, cf. *Boston Evening Post*, January 17, 1774). "A True Whig" doubted whether Patriots could maintain this price control even until January 20 (*Boston Evening Post*, January 10, 1774). There may have been only six chests of tea in the city, which may have affected prices (Labaree, *Boston Tea Party*, 162–163).

3. "if undutied . . ." "disperse" "the East India Company's . . ." "different parts of America": *Boston Evening Post*, February 7, 1774. On Massachusetts in 1774, see Norton, *1774*. Bell, *The Road to Concord*. Raphael, *First American Revolution*. Colonists in Rhode Island towns resolved against duted tea in early 1774, but left alone Dutch tea, which could have reached Boston. Bartlett, ed., *Records of the Colony of Rhode Island*, 272–279. Hedges, *Browns of Providence Plantations*, 210–211. Rappleye, *Sons of Providence*, 143.

4. "by Uniting . . .": NYPL Boston Committee of Correspondence Records, 1772–1784, Boston committee to Charleston, January 20, 1774. The Boston committee probably based this assessment upon information supplied by Gadsden or Timothy, both of whom occasionally corresponded with the Boston committee without formal sanction, expressing their frustration with moderate colleagues.

5. Progation: *SCG*, January 17, 1774. Committee formation: *SCG*, January 24, 1774. Committee membership: NYPL Boston Committee of Correspondence Records, 1772–1784, Charleston committee to Boston, June 1774. "diligently": *SCG*, January 24, 1774.

6. McDonough, *Christopher Gadsden and Henry Laurens*, 133. "general meeting" "Every . . .": *SCG*, February 28, 1774. "NO TEAS" "Agreement": *SCG*, March 21, 1774. The import ban allowed tea ordered before December 3, 1773 and arriving before April 16, 1774 to be landed and sold (*SCG*, March 21, 1774). The January 7, 1774 meeting was postponed until March 16 (*SCG*, December 20, 1773; December 27, 1773; January 24, 1774; March 7, 1774). Fraser, *Patriots Pistols and Petticoats*, 56. Notice by Timothy printed on March 15 for meeting that evening. The March 16 meeting also ordered the Company's tea remain in the Exchange, and that anyone who imported,

bought, or sold tea be shunned (*SCG*, March 21, 1774). Rogers, "The Charleston Tea Party," 164–165. For a list of committee members: NYPL Boston Committee of Correspondence Records, 1772–1784, Charleston committee to Boston committee, June 1774. The one-month delay for non-importation may have been because dutied tea was imported on March 15 (*SCG*, March 21, 1774).

7. "publick Meetings" "separated themselves . . ." "overvirtuous" "treasonous": Walsh, ed., *Writings of Christopher Gadsden*, 93. Christopher Gadsden to Samuel Adams May 23, 1774. PRO CO 5 133 f62.

8. "Association . . .": Schlesinger, *Colonial Merchants*, 292.

9. Ammerman, *Common Cause*, 10.

10. Ryerson, *Revolution Is Now Begun*, 43. Aspinwall 2: 703, 718. *SCG*, June 13, 1774. On Franklin: Dabney and Dargan, *William Henry Drayton & the American Revolution*, 22–23. Brown, *Revolutionary Politics*, 199.

11. Brown, *Revolutionary Politics*, 188. Gross, *Minutemen and Their World*, 50–51. Schlesinger, *Colonial Merchants*, 323. Brown, *Revolutionary Politics*, 200–201, 213. Some towns and counties had their own covenants.

12. Jensen, *Maritime Commerce*, 208. Ryerson, *Revolution Is Now Begun*, 40–41. "risque . . .": Olton, *Artisans for Independence*, 58, citing *Pennsylvania Gazette*, August 14, 1774. Rosswurm, *Arms, Country, and Class*, 21.

13. Port Act: *SCG*, June 3, 1774. "overhasty . . ." "Principal . . ." "deter . . .": NYPL Boston Committee of Correspondence Records, 1772–1784. Christopher Gadsden to Samuel Adams, June 5, 1774. "even . . .": NYPL Boston Committee of Correspondence Records, 1772–1784. Charleston committee to Boston committee, June 13, 1774. Emphasis original. "the people . . .": NYPL Boston Committee of Correspondence Records, 1772–1784. Charleston committee to Boston committee, June 28, 1774. July 6 meeting: *SCG*, July 11, 1774. Donnan, *Documents Illustrative of the History of the Slave Trade to America* 4: 470 n1.

14. "Fasting . . .": Labaree, *Tea Party*, 233. "recommend it strongly": Kennedy, *Journals of the House of Burgesses*, 13: xiv. "tyrannically" "Bostonians": Poston, "Ralph Wormeley V of Rosegill," 35. "tea of any kind": "Association of the Virginia Convention, Aug 1–6, 1774." The North Carolina provincial congress (August 25–27, 1774) declared non-importation to begin on January 1, 1775, and a cessation of tea consumption on September 10, 1774 (CRNC, 9: 1046). The Massachusetts provincial congress declared non-importation of "all kinds of East India teas" on October 28, having not yet heard of the Continental Congress's Association. (Schlesinger, *Colonial Merchants*, 324). On Fredericksburg: James Robinson to W. Cuninghame & Co. June 7, 1774, in Devine, ed., *Scottish Firm in Virginia*, 142. Labaree, *Tea Party*, 251.

15. "no legal authority": Marston, *King and Congress*, 77. The New York committee of fifty-one did include some conservatives, including tea consignee Benjamin Booth (Labaree, *Tea Party*, 228). Gage wrote to the Massachusetts provincial congress, "Whilst you complain of acts of parliament that make alterations in your charter . . . by your assembling, you are yourselves subverting that charter, and now acting in *direct* violation of your own constitution" (Lincoln, ed., *Journals of Each Provincial Congress of Massachusetts*, 21). On delegate selection: Norton, *1774*, 148–159. Marston, *King and Congress*, 74–77.

16. "We don't . . .": Marston, *King and Congress*, 113. Scribner, 2: 104–105. No tea was bought back. Henry Fleming described buying back canvas at "prime cost" with

"no further expense" than the auctioneer's commission. (*British Records Relating to America . . . Papers of Henry Fleming*. Fleming to Turners & Woodcock, Norfolk, January 26, 1775.) If there was a bid-up, profits went to Boston relief. Virginia had previously set non-importation for November 1. South Carolina also imposed non-consumption of tea on that date (Schlesinger, *Colonial Merchants*, 525).

17. "we can . . .": PRO CO 5/160 Copy of proceedings of the committee of correspondence at Worcester, August 9, 1774. "by their sufferings": PRO CO5/396 Bull to Dartmouth July 31, 1774. Maier, *From Resistance to Revolution*, 235, 252–255.

18. Sosin, *Agents and Merchants*, 199. Maryland State Archives, Port of Entry Book, SE 71-1, 220, 228–229, 304, 314–315.

19. "especially . . ." Suffolk Resolves, http://www.masshist.org/database/696.

20. Schlesinger, *Colonial Merchants*, p. 428, called the Association a "quasi-law." Marston, *King and Congress*, 100–130. Norton, *1774*.

21. "no tea . . ." "What right . . ." "acceptable & pleasing" "Sounds . . .": *PHL*, 9: 428. Emphasis original. "Violent, Arbitrary & Unjust," McDonough, *Gadsden and Laurens*, 135. "Surely some Judas . . .": *PHL*, 9: 434–435. Schafer, *Zephaniah Kingsley*, 14. "him or herself": *SCG*, December 20, 1773. "private Persons . . ." "what is lawfull . . ." "Indian Liberty Sons" "Liberties destroyd": Norton, "The Seventh Tea Ship," 702.

22. Phillips, *1775*, 309. Countryman, *People in Revolution*, 101. Norton, *1774*, 249–252.

23. "could never last" "refuse . . .": Thomas, *Tea Party to Independence*, 139.

4. Paying for the Tea

1. Bailyn, *Ordeal*, 262–263. Labaree, *Boston Tea Party*, 146, 221. Schlesinger, *Colonial Merchants*, 289, 300. "justice demanded . . .": Adair Schutz, eds., *Peter Oliver's Origins & Progress*, 103. "sober . . ." "disclaimed" "no steps" "show . . .": Gray, "The two congresses cut up . . ." 4. "compulsive": *PBF*, 21: 75–76. *PBF*, 21: 153. Olson, "Pictorial Representations of British America Resisting Rape," 17, 27. "the Province . . ." "the Town . . ." "acting . . .": *Boston Post-Boy*, January 31, 1774. Krusell, *Of Tea and Tories*, 9.

2. "Attack upon Property": Butterfield, ed., *Diary and Autobiography of John Adams*, 2: 86.

3. Labaree, *Tea Party*, 144, 149. Allison, *The Boston Tea Party*, 39. Brown, *Revolutionary Politics*, 166. "solemnly Protest": PRO CO 5/133 f89. Young, *Shoemaker*, 43. Lemisch, "Jack Tar in the Streets," 371–407. "the People": NYPL Boston Committee of Correspondence Records, 1772–1784, Boston committee to New York and Philadelphia committees, December 17, 1773.

4. PRO CO 5/133 f64–65. Hersey, "Tar and Feathers," 442. "hardships . . .": IOR B/90, 339.

5. Irvin, "Tar, Feathers, and Enemies of American Liberties," 205 n 18, 210. "drenching Horn": Hersey, "Tar and Feathers," 452. Respectable Patriots disavowed the assault. Young, *Shoemaker*, 50–51. "in Stakes": Cunningham, ed., *Letters and Diary of John Rowe*, 261. Hulton, *Letters of a Loyalist Lady*, 70–72.

6. "pelted . . ." "I took . . ." "And I . . ." York, ed., *Henry Hulton*, 282. "There is no spirit . . ." *DAR*, 8: 27. Walmsley, *Thomas Hutchinson*, 151. "likely . . ." "for the Mob . . .": PRO T 1/505, 109. "very cold place": Kamensky, *Revolution in Color*, 215. "not one . . .": Egerton 2661 f18 Hutchinson to Company Directors, March 19, 1774.

"Mill-Stone . . .": *Boston Gazette*, January 10, 1774. "base treatment" "My friends . . ." "generally . . .": Egerton 2659 f62.

7. "very silent" "I think . . .": Egerton 2661 f14. On *Fortune*: Labaree, *Boston Tea Party*, 164–167. DAR 8: 62–63. Cunningham, ed., *Letters and Diary of John Rowe*, 264. *Mass Spy*, March 10 and 17, 1774. The owners offered to send the tea back, but wanted to wait for a full cargo for the return trip. Loyalist Henry Lloyd was the recipient of sixteen chests and also a supplier for British troops in Boston. Tyler, *Smugglers and Patriots*, 207–208. Sabine, 2: 24. Akers, *The Divine Politician*, 172–173. The "Massacre" was marked on March 4 because some considered the evening of March 5 a Sabbath. Thomas, *Tea Party to Independence*, 46. Bailyn, *Ordeal*, 265–266, 270. Kamensky, *A Revolution in Color*, 215–220. DAR, 8: 115–116. Jonathan Clarke left the castle briefly in January. DAR, 8: 23–24. Only with Gage's arrival could John Greenough safely travel to Boston for business. Norton, "The Seventh Tea Ship," 726. Bailyn, *Ordeal*, 263. Adair and Schutz, eds., *Peter Oliver's Origins & Progress*, 115.

8. Younger, "Grand Juries and the American Revolution," 257, 261. Labaree, *Boston Tea Party*, 146, 149. PBF, 21: 137 n 9. Thomas, *Townshend Duties*, 226–230. Thomas, *Tea Party*, 24. "Grand Jurors . . .": Egerton 2261 f10. Hutchinson, ed., *Diary and Letters of Thomas Hutchinson* 1: 114. A few sources give the story of a man, Eckley or Ackley, arrested for the Boston Tea Party and released for lack of evidence. (Labaree, *Boston Tea Party*, 149–150. Drake, *Tea Leaves*, cx.) No evidence of this appears in Massachusetts newspapers or Suffolk court records (Suffolk County Court of General Sessions of the Peace. Supreme Judicial Court Archives, Massachusetts Archives).

9. Younger, "Grand Juries," 258. Longley, "Mob Activities in Revolutionary Massachusetts," 114–115. Brown's claim that "regular criminal procedures were available" is thus moot. Brown, *Revolutionary Politics*, 199.

10. Baxter, *House of Hancock*, 285. IOR B/89, 961. Massachusetts Archives, Supreme Judicial Court Archives, Washburn, *Sketches of the Judicial History of Massachusetts*, 168–169, 319–320, 332, 335. The East India Company's Court of Directors sent its Boston consignees instructions on recovering compensation through the Boston Port Act. The instructions were forwarded to Thomas Gage on April 11, 1774; however, only the covering letter survives (PRO CO 5/765, 308 and University of Michigan, Clements Library, Thomas Gage papers, J. Pownall to Thomas Gage, April 11, 1774).

11. Ubbelohde, *Vice-Admiralty Courts*, 13, 16.

12. "Screen . . ." "flame . . ." "it is thought . . .": Edgerton 2659 f70. "prevent . . ." *Dartmouth* 1: 348. *Catalog of the Records*, 93. Bailyn, *Ordeal*, 265–266, 270. Adair and Schutz, eds., *Peter Oliver's Origins & Progress*, 110, 112.

13. Staples, *Destruction of the Gaspée*, 102–107.

14. "Dependence . . .": PRO CO 5/396 Dartmouth to Bull, February 5, 1774. "reducing . . .": PRO CO 5/763 f77 Dartmouth to Gage, April 9, 1774. Simmons and Thomas, *Proceedings and Debates*, 4: 211.

15. DAR, 8: 37–41. Thomas, *Tea Party*, 72.

16. Thomas, *Tea Party*, 24. "insult . . ." DAR, 8: 45. "private . . .": DAR, 8: 103.

17. "an attempt . . ." "concerted . . .": Labaree, *Boston Tea Party*, 174–175. Donoughue, *British Politics*, 54. DAR, 8: 47–48. Akers, *The Divine Politician*, 161. "were of such . . .": PRO CO 5/763 f78–79. Dartmouth to Gage, April 9, 1774. Warner, *Protocols of Liberty*, 113–119.

18. "Tea . . .": PRO CO 5/763 f99. PRO CO 5 763 f105. "what more . . .": PRO CO 5/763 f95-96. Raphael, "The Signal of Sam Adams."

19. "mark out . . .": Labaree, *Tea Party*, 178. Thomas, *Tea Party to Independence*, 44.

20. Donoughue, *British Politics*, 57-59, 61. Depositions at PRO CO 5/763 f175-216. PRO CO 5/763 f85-89, 95-96, 98-99, 105. Labaree, *Boston Tea Party*, 174-178. *PBF*, 21: 153 n 5. Captain Scott of the *Hayley* helped bring the news of the Tea Party to England. Donoughue, *British Politics*, 29, 57.

21. Marston, *King and Congress*, 40.

22. "full satisfaction" "reasonable satisfaction": Boston Port Act, 1774, 14 Geo. 3, c. 19. 4 Am Arch, 1: 362. May 28, 1774. "sum . . .": Patterson, *Political Parties*, 78.

23. Labaree, *Boston Tea Party*, 222-223. Dartmouth's July note was similarly unclear. PRO CO 5/763 f191 Dartmouth to Gage, July 6, 1774. Whitehall. Real losses: PRO CO 5/133 f101.

24. "peace . . ." "the trade . . .": Boston Port Act, 1774, 14 Geo. 3, c. 19. Cobbett, *Parliamentary History*, 17: passim.

25. Norton, "Seventh Tea Ship," 691, Thomas, *Tea Party to Independence*, 61. The Port Act passed on March 31, 1774. The Treasury, with North in attendance, read a report on the tea's survival on March 17, 1774 (PRO T 29/43 f165), though it dated the item itself as received April 2, 1774 (PRO T 1/505, 72). Hutchinson wrote Dartmouth of the tea's survival on January 4, 1774, though when Dartmouth received Hutchinson's letter is unclear (*Dartmouth*, 1: 346.) IOR B/90.

26. *Dartmouth*, 2: 246-247.

27. Labaree, *Boston Tea Party*, 219. "suffer": 4 Am Arch, 1: 361. "If your . . .": *PHL*, 9: 533.

28. The merchants were Hayley and Hopkins, Alexander Champion and Thomas Dickason, Lane, Son & Fraser, [Thomas or Henry] Bromfield, and a Mr. Harrison. Sellers, *Patience Wright*, 64-65. Sosin, *Agents and Merchants*, 175-176. "the future . . .": PRO PRO 30/8/97, 260-61.

29. Patterson, *Political Parties*, 82. Schlesinger, *Colonial Merchants*, 317-318. "to pay . . .": *JCC*, 1: 114.

30. "has had . . ." "persons . . ." "have been . . .": Winslow, 100.

31. PRO CO 5/247, 186. Memorial of Court of Directors to Lord Dartmouth, February 16, 1774. "of a bad Quality" "Out of Time . . ." "and so often refused" "could . . .": PRO PRO 30/8/97, 261. "Damagd . . ." "not merchantable" "Many . . .": Charles Coleman Sellers, *Patience Wright*, 65. "three . . ." "mouldy . . .": *PAG*, February 9, 1774. Labaree, *Tea Party*, 335. *DAR*, 7: 46. There was no discussion then, or since, about the security merchants who had guaranteed the Company's tea shipments could be asked to pay for the lost cargo.

32. The teas would have been several years older than the usual shelf life of black and green teas today. Green tea oxidizes as it ages, and so the greens would likely have tasted blackish. Yet what "normal" bohea or hyson was thought to taste like remains unclear, making it hard to determined how different these teas would have seemed.

33. "most," "silent approval": Labaree, *Tea Party*, 144.

34. Labaree, *Boston Tea Party*, 187-188. O'Shaughnessy, *Empire Divided*, 129. "lenity": Thomas, *Townshend Duties*, 258. The Company's losses included £9659 6s 4d for the tea in Boston, £1168 10s 3d in shipping costs and damages for the Philadel-

phia tea, and £1458 4s 9d for New York. *DAR*, 7: 46, 280. *DAR*, 8: 72–73. PRO CO 5/115 f37–39. Porteous Riots: Phillips, *1775*, 251. "rotten and useless" "damp cellar": Cobbett, *Parliamentary History of England*, 17: 1180. Rumors of the Charleston tea being destroyed by damp continued in the colonial press in 1774. Tea Act: *PHL*, 9: 421 n 2.

35. Berkin, *Jonathan Sewall*, 101. Massachusetts Government Act, 1774, 14 Geo. 3, c. 45. art. V, VIII. Adair and Schutz, eds., *Peter Oliver's Origins & Progress*, 114. Thomas, *Tea Party to Independence*, 42–43.

36. Coleman, *Thomas McKean*, 88. The Reed correspondence lasted from December 1773 to February 1775. Reed, ed., *Life and Correspondence of Joseph Reed*, 1 (1847).

37. "ringleaders . . .": *DAR*, 7: 58. March 9, 1774. Whitehall. Dartmouth to Gov Hutchinson. Carter, ed., *The Correspondence of General Thomas Gage*, 2: 161. "one thing . . ." "punishment . . .": Donoughue, *British Politics*, 62. "difficult . . ." "in the ordinary . . ." "there is a probability . . ." "a very necessary . . ." "prejudices of the people" "disgraceful": PRO CO 5/763 f79–80. Dartmouth named individuals sometimes only by a surname, and sometimes with a misspelling, indicating the striking ignorance of personages and facts around which charges of treason were considered.

38. "not yet favorable": *DAR*, 8: 137. Gage furnished Oliver with the Attorney and Solicitor General's reports on the February 5 narrative, which included Dartmouth's interrogatories and their replies. Carter, ed., *Correspondence of General Thomas Gage*, 1: 358–359. "tho' . . ." "the usurpation . . ." "free and impartial . . ." "the chief thing wanting" PRO CO 5/763 f212–213. "thousands" "spectators of it" "only one . . .": Gage, "Queries of George Chalmers, with answers of General Gage . . . ," 371. It is unclear who this witness was. Adair and Schutz, eds., *Peter Oliver's Origins & Progress*, 114. Labaree, *Boston Tea Party*, 224.

39. "obedience . . ." *Dartmouth*, 1: 358. Dartmouth to Gage, August 3, 1774. "Civil government . . ." *DAR*, 8: 181. September 2, 1774 Boston Gage to Dartmouth. "civil authority . . .": *DAR*, 8: 191. Benjamin Hallowell to Grey Cooper, September 5, 1774. Adair and Schutz, eds., *Peter Oliver's Origins & Progress*, 117–118, 152–153. York, ed., *Henry Hulton*, 178. "no Obedience": Suffolk Resolves. http://www.masshist.org/database/696. "refuse obedience to the law": *Dartmouth*, 1: 365 Dartmouth to Gage, October 17, 1774. "This is very . . .": Brown, *Revolutionary Politics*, xvi.

40. "the general sense . . .": Gray, "The two congresses cut up . . . ," 4–5. *Boston Town Records*, 173. "the revenge . . ." Labaree, *Boston Tea Party*, 221. Cunningham, ed., *Letters and Diary of John Rowe*, 8, 256, 278. On merchant meetings, see "The merchants and traders of this town . . ." May 24, 1774. Rowe owned one of the tea ships but not the tea. He served on a committee in December 1773 to determine a Patriotic response to the tea's arrival. Labaree, *Boston Tea Party*, 152. He is sometimes credited with suggesting the tea be thrown in the water. Drake, *Tea Leaves*, lxiii. Patterson, *Political Parties*, 76.

41. "many among us . . ." "though he urged . . .": Sargent, ed., *Letters of John Andrews*, 16. Patterson, *Political Parties*, 76. Labaree, *Tea Party*, 222. *Boston Town Records*, 174–176.

42. *Boston Town Records*, 175. Griffin, *Old Brick*, 153. Patterson, *Political Parties*, 79. Schlesinger, *Colonial Merchants*, 315. "whose importance . . .": Gray, "The two congresses cut up," 5.

43. "disavowed" "lawless" "outrage" "yet considering . . .": Stark, *Loyalists of Massachusetts*, 123–125. Patterson, *Political Parties*, 76–78. 4 Am Arch, 1: 361–363. "all the Colonies . . .": *Boston Post-Boy*, May 16, 1774.

44. Signers who advertised tea: Benjamin Davis, Gilbert Deblois, William Jackson, James Perkins, both Isaac Winslows. Sometimes described as written by merchants, the address was written by merchants *and others*. 4 Am Arch, 1: 362–364. Patterson, *Political Parties*, 79. "Whereas a great number of people . . ." Evans. 13767.

45. "We have found . . ." "their own . . ." "not buying . . .": Thomas and Peach, eds., *The Correspondence of Richard Price*, 1: 170. Emphasis original. Patterson, *Political Parties*, 80–81. Brown, *Revolutionary Politics*, 198.

46. "wanting to pay . . .": Brown, *Revolutionary Politics*, 194. Labaree, *Boston Tea Party*, 225. Cunningham, ed., *Letters and Diary of John Rowe*, 276–277. Carter, ed., *Correspondence of General Thomas Gage*, 1:358–359. *Boston Town Records*, 176–178. "not one" "unanimity": *Boston Gazette*, June 20, 1774. Labaree, *Boston Tea Party*, 218, 236. Compare 4 Am Arch, 1: 429–430. Patriot members of the General Court may have discussed repayment of the tea by day to decoy conservatives, then discussed congressional delegates with committeemen by night. Tea repayment is not mentioned in *Journals of the House of Representatives of Massachusetts* for May or June 1774. Alden, *General Gage in America*, 207. Tradesmen, meeting on June 15, were divided on the issue. (Cunningham, ed., *Letters and Diary of John Rowe*, 275)

47. "that the Inhabitants . . ." "to sell . . .": IOR B/90, 200. They had previously updated the Company in June (IOR B/90, 117).

48. "silly": 4 Am Arch, 1: 430.

49. "controversy" "constitutional liberty": Schlesinger, *Colonial Merchants*, 344. Ryerson, *The Revolution Is Now Begun*, 43. Doerflinger, *Vigorous Spirit*, 194. Champagne, *Alexander McDougall*, 52. "weighty . . ." "it would . . ." "agreed by most" "Restitution" "ought to be made": Jensen, *Maritime Commerce*, 214.

50. "an Invasion . . ." Rutland, ed., *The Papers of George Mason*, 1: 205, 210. Ragsdale, *Planter's Republic*, 191–193. "I truly hope . . ." *PHL*, 9: 392. "an American cause" "from five . . ." *PHL*, 9: 387–388. McDonough, *Christopher Gadsden and Henry Laurens*, 135–136 n 11. *PHL*, 9: 389–92, 414–15. "at most a trespass" "healed . . .": *PHL*, 9: 392. "must be paid for" "I say *must* . . .": *PHL*, 9: 387–388.

51. "what every . . ." "that you regard . . ." "pay for . . ." "ought to . . ." "virtue . . ." "hint given you" "have induced . . ." "are indeed . . .": *Massachusetts Gazette*, July 14, 1774.

52. "conscientious Americans": "Address to the People of Boston." June 27, 1774. 4 Am Arch, 1: 487–489. Labaree, *Boston Tea Party*, 261.

53. "chastisement . . ." "intimidation . . ." "suffering . . .": *DAR*, 8: 142. Lee: Ford, ed., *Letters of William Lee*, 1: 87. "wasted" "now Say . . .": Labaree, *Boston Tea Party*, 221. "it should be granted . . .": Mays, *Pendleton Biography*, 1: 272. "warranted" "we know not . . ." "have made . . .": Schlesinger, *Colonial Merchants*, 311. "we shall not . . ." "despotick Measures" "cause of Boston . . .": Abbot, ed., *The Papers of George Washington. Colonial Series*, 10: 96. "UNITED . . .": *Virginia Gazette* (Rind), July 28, 1774.

54. "more an hand . . .": Griffin, *Old Brick*, 154.

55. Gervais: *PHL*, 9: 533.

56. Quotations: "Address to the People of Boston." June 27, 1774. 4 Am Arch, 1: 487–489. Emphasis original.

57. "1. Because . . .": BF to William Franklin *PBF*, 21: 287. September 7, 1774.

58. *SCG*, June 27, 1774. PRO CO 5/763 f196. Coleman, *Thomas McKean*, 137. "We will . . ." "not pay . . .": Walsh, ed., *Writings of Christopher Gadsden*, 95, 99. Breen, *American Insurgents American Patriots*, 110–127.

59. *Norfolk Intelligencer*, March 9, 1775. Hamilton, *John Ettwein*, 146. "Minutes of the Committee of Safety of Bucks County," 268. Scott, "Tory Associators of Portsmouth," 508. "Their bountiful . . ." "Waggons . . ." "The cause . . .": Thomas and Peach, eds., *Correspondence of Richard Price*, 1: 171–172. Marston, *King and Congress*, 318.

60. "daily bread": Thomas and Peach, eds., *Correspondence of Richard Price*, 1: 201.

61. Boyle, "Boyle's Journal of Occurrences," 5–28.

62. Marston, *King and Congress*, 71, 318. 4 Am Arch, 1: 551–552, 587–602, 624–625. Schlesinger, *Colonial Merchants*, 353, 357. Though recently returned from England, Adams had already signed the May 27, 1774, Virginia declaration against the Coercive Acts ("Association of the Members of the Late House of Burgesses." "Americans" "undoubtedly . . .": VMHC Thomas Adams Papers. Thomas Adams to Thomas Hill, June 22, 1774.

63. *Lee Papers*, 1: 126. Thomas Gamble to Charles Lee, July 1, 1774. Schlesinger, *Colonial Merchants*, 407. "opinion . . .": *DAR*, 8: 151. Gage to Dartmouth, Boston July 20, 1774. "might prevail . . .": Upton, *Revolutionary Versus Loyalist*, 46. Schlesinger, *Colonial Merchants*, 394. "accommodation": *DAR*, 8: 222. "without . . ." Carter, ed., *Correspondence of General Thomas Gage*, 1:380.

64. "expressly justify": *LDC*, 1: 133. Scribner, 1: 233. Ragsdale, *Planter's Republic*, 205. In New York's case the boycott was to fight the tea tax. Ranlet, *New York Loyalists*, 46. Willard, *Letters on the American Revolution*, 4–5.

65. "proposal to pay . . .": Winslow, 109. Carter, ed., *Correspondence of General Thomas Gage*, 1:391 Boston. January 27, 1775. Gage to Dartmouth. Congressional knowledge of tea consumption: *LDC*, 1: 87.

66. Pendleton: *LDC*, 1: 488–489. By this time North sought to stop trade at ports that tried to boycott Britain. "Trade of . . ." Boston Port Act, 1774, 14 Geo. 3, c. 19.

67. "trespass" "committed . . ." "Even supposing . . ." "unauthenticated . . ." "persons . . .": *John Jay Papers*, 1: 104. *JCC*, 1: 86.

68. Barnes and Barnes, *The American Revolution through British Eyes*, 1: 8. *PBF*, 21: 366, 381, 383, 385, 444–445, 466, 492–493, 553–554. John Fothergill reported a private offer from Franklin to pay for the tea in early February (*Dartmouth*, 2: 266, 270). Sosin, *Agents and Merchants*, 208, 213, 214. "they never could . . .": York, ed., *Henry Hulton*, 184–185. Thanks to Mary Beth Norton for this reference. Greene, *History of Boothbay*, 215. Bauman, Dent, et al., *Lively Stones*, 33–41, 58.

5. Toward Non-importation

1. PRO CO 5/133, 101, 117–118.

2. "it will cast . . .": Egerton 2661 f6 Boston, January 7, 1774. "new tumults": Egerton 2661 f18 Hutchinson to Court of Directors, March 19, 1774. Norton, "Seventh Tea Ship."

3. "by degrees . . .": Thomas, *Tea Party*, 29. Thomas, *Tea Party*, 14, 29, 31.

4. Tryon: PRO CO 5/1105 f47–48d Tryon to Dartmouth, January 3, 1774. "your property . . .": PRO CO 5/133 f70. Thomas, *Tea Party to Independence*, 16, 22. Labaree,

Boston Tea Party, 90, 154–156. Labaree indicates Pigou's son as the Company director, but see *PBF*, 38: 425–429 n 2. Drake, *Tea Leaves*, 226. Norton, *1774*, 37–38.

5. "declared . . .": *Boston Gazette*, January 3, 1774.

6. PRO T 1/509, 90–122. Naval Office, Antigua. Lists of entrances and clearances, October 1, 1773 to September 30, 1774. Lockyer's arrival in Antigua on or before February 15 and at Sandy Hook on April 19 leaves time for more than twenty days in Antigua.

7. Merritt, *Trouble with Tea*, 69.

8. PRO CUST 17/1, 17/3.

9. "British colonies . . .": The Revenue Act (1767). Clark, "The American Board of Customs," 781 n 20. O'Shaughnessy, *Empire Divided*, 81, 106, 107. Putting different parts of British America under different tea tax regimes would have encouraged smuggling. Some Antiguan planters did refuse business with a captain who had taken tea to Boston in 1773. This seems to have been *after* the Coercive Acts. (O'Shaughnessy, *Empire Divided*, 43–47, 149.)

10. "acquainted," "sentiments," "fatality": *Rivington's New York Gazetteer*, December 23, 1773, *New York Gazette*, December 27, 1773, *Massachusetts Gazette*, December 30, 1773. Lockyer letter: Norton, *1774*, 39.

11. "properest . . .": IOR B/89 679. Labaree, *Boston Tea Party*, 35, 172. On the proposal to send Company tea to Nova Scotia in 1773: Brebner, *Neutral Yankees*, 167.

12. "give all proper . . .": Nova Scotia Archives. RG1 vol. 32 doc 18. Dartmouth to Legge February 5, 1774. "every other . . ." and "to remove . . .": Thomas, *Tea Party*, 29. "more prudent . . ." Speech by Lord North, March 14, 1774. Simmons and Thomas, *Proceedings and Debates*, 4: 79. "insult": *DAR*, 7: 36, Dartmouth to Wright, February 5, 1774. Dartmouth to Tryon, February 5, 1774. *DAR*, 7: 37 Dartmouth to Bull February 5, 1774. *DAR*, 8: 45 Dartmouth to Penn, February 5, 1774.

13. "resigned": Norton, *1774*, 20. "Liberty Boys" "Secret" "we should . . .": Sabine, ed., *Historical Memoirs*, 1: 173. PRO CO 5/133, 22–26. Norton, *1774*, 20, 37–39. Lockyer payment: IOR B/90 98, 123. "ringleaders": Simmons and Thomas, *Proceedings and Debates*, 4: 79. Swan: *RNYG*, April 7, 28, May 5, 1774. Lott sold one chest of bohea to Jacob C. Ten Eyck and another to Gerardus Beekman, both of Albany, in July 1774. (Lott, "A Journal," 65.) Pigou was in London at this time (Godbeer, *World of Trouble*, 111, 124).

14. Colden: *DAR*, 8: 108–109. Colden to Dartmouth May 4, 1774. Colden also left vague exactly when he received Dartmouth's February 5 instructions regarding the tea, indicating that these instructions arrived after Tryon's departure on April 7 but not whether they arrived before or after the *Nancy*. The directors approved further orders to consignees on February 22, 1774. Minutes of the Court of Directors mention these, as well as letters from the New York and Nova Scotia consignees, but not their content. IOR B/89, 797; B/90, 76, 85, 166. Chambers: Sabine, *Historical Memoirs*, 1: 184–185.

15. Quotations: *RNYG*, April 28, 1774. August 11, 1774. *NYG*, April 25, 1774.

16. "further orders": PRO 5/410 Bull to Dartmouth, December 24, 1773. "be kept . . ." "further Orders": Treasury Out-letter books. February 5, 1774. PRO T 28/1, 397.

17. IOR B/89 717, 736. PRO T 1/509, 174-177. "other Relief": IOR E/1/217, 76. Court of Directors, East India House to Lords Commissioners of HM Treasury. February 16, 1774.

18. PRO T 29/43 f152, 154, 161. PRO T 1/509, 174–177.

19. Receipt of February order in America: PRO T 29/43 f200. Quotations: PRO CO 5/396 Bull to Dartmouth, May 25, 1774.

20. "Insult": PRO CO 5/396 Dartmouth to Bull, February 5, 1774. Thomas, *Tea Party to Independence*, 14.

21. Awareness: *Massachusetts Spy* March 31, 1774. *NYG*, April 4, 1774. "Tea Commissioners": *Pennsylvania Packet*, May 23, 1774. *Boston Post-Boy*, May 30, 1774.

22. *London*: 4 Am Arch, 1: 248–249. Colden to Dartmouth. May 4, 1774. *Rivington's New York Gazetteer*, April 28, 1774. Mason, *Road to Independence*, 20–21. The second vessel appears to be the *Britannia*. This vessel is referred to by Timothy as Captain Ball's *Friendship* (*SCG*, March 21, 1774) "from London and St. Augustine," but comparing the captain and place of origin with shipping lists in the same newspaper suggests it was actually the *Britannia*. The *Britannia*, Captain Ball, arrived March 15 from St. Augustine. Timothy gives the cargo as a half-chest only, but he should be read with caution. William Gibbons advertised tea for sale in March (*SCG*, March 7, 1774) from the *Suky and Katy*, which arrived February 4, 1774 from Providence (*SCG* February 14, 1774). It is unclear whether the *Suky and Katy* tea was dutied or smuggled. The *Britannia* tea was likely dutied.

23. Labaree, *Boston Tea Party*, 164–167. "devoted . . .": MHS Misc Bd. 1774 March 8. Nathaniel Taylor to Isaac Clarke. Many thanks to Mary Beth Norton for this reference. MHS Misc Bd. 1769 Aug 14. "An Alphabetical List of the Sons of Liberty who din'd at Liberty Tree, Dorchester."

24. New Hampshire: Maguire, ed., "Parry's Journal," xiv–xvi. DAR, 8: 186–197. Charleston: *SCG*, July 25, 1774. Chesapeake: Scribner, 3: 429 fn 16, Scharf, *History of Maryland*, 2: 159. Salem: PRO T 1/505, 391–396. Felt, *Annals of Salem*, 490. DAR, 8: 196. 4 Am Arch, 1: 783. Wroth et al., *Province in Rebellion*, 61, 694, 695 and documents 289, 290. It was thirty chests and three half chests. NARA (Waltham). Salem Custom House Letter Book. Salem Customs House to American Board of Customs, December 5, 1774. Annapolis: Hoffman, *Spirit of Dissention*, 133–135. Norton, *1774*, 203–206.

25. "Oblation . . .": *SCG*, November 21, 1774. *Virginia*: Mason, *John Norton & Sons*, 368. Scribner, 2: 164. *Ross*: *Virginia Gazette* (Pinkney), December 1, 1774. *Sally*: CRNC, 9: 1089–1090. *Greyhound*: Sickler, *Tea Burning Town*, 38–41.

26. Annapolis: Norton, *1774*, 203. Portsmouth: PRO CO 5/938 Wentworth to Dartmouth, July 4, September 13, 1774. Salem: NARA (Waltham) Salem Customs House Letter Book. Salem Customs House to American Board of Customs, December 5, 1774. If the Boston consignees could have given bond that the duty would be paid elsewhere, the events of December 1773 could have proceeded quite differently in Boston; but this was another example of post–Boston Tea Party innovation on the part of customs officials. It took the destruction of the tea in Boston to make them this creative in the first place. Cape Cod: Norton, "The Seventh Tea Ship," 681–710.

27. "Violent . . .": Sickler, *Tea Burning Town*, 42. Gerlach, *Prologue to Independence*, 198–200. The owners of the tea shipment were Stacey Hepburn and John Duffield.

28. "virtue enough . . .": Seabury, *Congress Canvassed*, 22. Matson, *Merchants & Empire*, 308.

29. "Upon . . ." "to declare . . ." "unanimously" "stigmatized": *Maryland Gazette*, June 2, 1774. Adam Goodheart debunked the myth that Chestertown held a tea party

akin to Boston's but was unsure whether Patriots destroyed tea surreptitiously. Good-heart, "Tea & Fantasy," 21–34.

30. "E[ast] I[ndia]": Maryland State Archives, Port of Entry Book, SE 71-1, 218. Departure date: Goodheart, "Tea & Fantasy."

31. Hodgkin: *Maryland Gazette*, May 19, 26, and June 16, 1774. Committee membership: *Maryland Gazette*, June 9, 1774.

32. Hodgkin signed bills on behalf of the Maryland convention in 1776. *Proceedings of the Conventions of the Province of Maryland*, 88. Dating of resolves: *Maryland Gazette*, June 2, 1774. Coercive Acts in Maryland: Norton, *1774*, 97–98.

33. Maryland State Archives, Port of Entry Book, SE 71-1, 219–221. "has . . .": *Maryland Journal*, June 11–18, 1774.

34. "voluntarily": *New York Gazette*, October 31, 1774. Land, *Letters from America*, 93, 95. Hoffman, *Spirit of Dissention*, 133–136. John Hancock had opposed a similar proposal to burn the *Dartmouth* in December 1773 (PRO CO 5/763 f95–96).

35. "absurdity": Land, *Letters from America*, 97. "I went to . . .": Labaree, *Boston Tea Party*, 168. "burning . . .": Sargent, ed., *Letters of John Andrews*, 69.

36. Carroll: McWilliams, *Annapolis*, 90. Grahame: Hoffman, *Spirit of Dissention*, 134.

37. Land, *Letters from America*, 91.

38. "Americanus": *Maryland Gazette*, April 13, 1775. "I should not . . .": Price, ed., "Joshua Johnson's Letterbook," 157b. Papenfuse, *In Pursuit of Profit*, 49 n 36 notes Wallace, Davidson, and Johnson may have played a role. McWilliams, *Annapolis*, 78. Price indicates Wallace took a "leading part" in burning the brig; Galloway claims Wallace tried to save it. (Jacob M. Price, "Johnson, Joshua [1742–1802]," *DNB*. Galloway, and Ringgold, "Account of the Destruction of the Brig "Peggy Stewart,"" 250.) "scarce . . .": Land, *Letters from America*, 98.

39. *Maryland Gazette*, April 13, 1775. Maryland State Archives, Port of Entry Book, SE 71-1, 219. Maryland State Archives, Wallace, Davidson, and Johnson order books, 330, 356, 385, 458. "not to be . . .": Charles Carroll of Carrollton to Wallace, Davidson, and Johnson January 8, 1775 in Hoffman, ed., *Dear Papa, Dear Charley*, 2: 778.

40. PRO CUST 17/2 and CUST 17/3. Shipments of British goods to the thirteen colonies increased from £1.777 million to £2.336 million, 1773–1774. Shipments to colonies outside the Association, such as Quebec and Jamaica, did not substantially change. Shipments to New York increased 82 percent, to Pennsylvania 63 percent. "I learned . . .": "A Real Associator," *Virginia Gazette* (Purdie and Dixon), December 15, 1774. Gage: Matson, *Merchants & Empire*, 307. Rodney and Frank: Marston, *King and Congress*, 120–121.

41. Boyd: *Maryland Gazette*, September 29, 1774.

42. Fichter, "Collecting Debts," 200.

43. "Great Stock of Goods" "Interest" "become a Burthen": Guttridge, ed., "Letters of Richard Champion," 30. Richard Champion to Willing Morris & Co. May 30, 1774. Schlesinger, *Colonial Merchants*, 473–474. "have imported . . .": Seabury, *Free Thoughts*, 12. "Stocks have risen . . .": Pauline Maier, *The Old Revolutionaries*, 99–100.

44. 4 Am Arch, 1: 248–249. Lt. Gov Colden to Dartmouth. May 4, 1774. "numerous . . .": *DAR*, 8: 224. Lt Gov Colden to Dartmouth, November 2, 1774. "a small . . .": *Virginia Gazette* (Rind), August 25, 1774. Enforcement: PRO T 1/513, 12, 24–26, 38–39.

45. *Dartmouth*, 2: 227. James Ireland to Dartmouth, September 30, 1774. *DAR*, 7: 182. Extract of letter dated Boston August 31, 1774. *DAR*, 7: 193 Emmanuel Mathias to Earl Suffolk, October 14, 1774. *DAR*, 7: 199. Dartmouth to Admiralty, November 1, 1774. *DAR*, 7: 207 November 1, 1774. Extract of letter from Mr. De Laval to Earl of Suffolk. *Dartmouth*, 2: 233. Emanuel Mathis to Earl of Suffolk, November 15, 1774. *DAR*, 7: 215. Extract of letter from Hamburg, November 22, 1774. Huibrechts, "Swampin' Guns," 179. "a mask": *DAR*, 7: 243 Sir Joseph Yorke to Earl Suffolk, January 6, 1775. "North America," "intervals": PRO CO 5/138 f430. Extract of a letter from M. De Laval to Earl of Suffolk, November 1, 1774.

46. *DAR*, 7: 239 October 30, 1774. Vice Admiral Samuel Graves to Philip Stevens. "to meet . . .": *Dartmouth*, 2: 227. James Ireland to Dartmouth, September 30, 1774. Rumors to the same effect were cheered on in Virginia. *Virginia Gazette* (Pinkney), December 22, 1774. Augur, *The Secret War of Independence*, 22. Phillips, *1775*, 305. Huibrechts, "Swampin' Guns," 180. Tea Party chest count: Fichter, "The Tea That Survived the Boston Tea Party," note 1.

47. "trifling": Huibrechts, "Swampin' Guns," 172. Davies, *DAR*, 8: 246. Magra, *The Fisherman's Cause*, 161–176. Phillips, *1775*, 305. PRO T 1/513, 20. *CRI*, 1: 519. "New England": Winterthur. Vernon family records. Folder 8. Bill of Lading from Scott and Fraser, August 31, 1774. 4 Am Arch, 4: 1695. December 22, 1774.

48. "the colonists . . .": *Lee Papers*, 1: 168. Lee to Constantine John Phipps. 1773–74. "honestly smuggled": John Adams to Abigail Adams, July 6, 1774. Butterfield, ed., *Adams Family Correspondence*, 1: 129–30. "Sawney Sedition" "published . . .": "To the Agents of Their High Mightinesses the Dutch East India Company, at St. Eustatia," New York Broadside, October 28, 1773 in Granger, *Political Satire*, 59.

49. Amor Patriae: *Maryland Journal*, June 11–18, 1774. This price spike does not appear in the Glassford records; see appendix C. "at Half the Price": Randolph and Nicholas, *Considerations*, 28.

50. "authentick Lists": UVa. Papers of the Lee Family, 1750–1809. MSS 38–112 box 4. George Washington to Richard Henry Lee. August 9, 1774. "observe . . .": "Articles of Association." Fichter, "Collecting Debts." Rao, *National Duties*, 45–46.

51. Norton, "The Seventh Tea Ship," 694. *Newport Mercury*, February 14, 1774. A minority of advertisements mentioned tea had arrived from a particular port, implicitly marking it as "English" or "Dutch."

52. Fichter, *So Great a Proffit*, 14. Baldwin: *Mass Spy*, December 23, 1773 to January 20, 1774.

53. Matson, *Merchants & Empire*, 306. "All . . ." "is smuggled . . .": Seabury, *Free Thoughts*, 10. Knollenberg, ed., *Correspondence of Governor Samuel Ward*, 24. "Agreement" "NO TEAS": *SCG* March 28, 1774. An exception was made for tea ordered before December 7, 1773.

54. "any kind . . .": Boyd, ed., *Papers of Thomas Jefferson*, 1: 108. "tea of any kind": "Association of the Virginia Convention." "with a Caution . . ." "this proves . . .": *SCG*, November 21, 1774. Schlesinger, *Colonial Merchants*, 526. Maier, "Charleston Mob," 180–181.

55. PRO CUST 17/1, 17/3, 16/1. John J. McCusker, "Tea exported from England, by importing colony: 1761–1775."

56. On survival of Salem letter books and loss of other Salem and Boston customs records: Webber, "Lost Customs Records."

57. NARA (Waltham) Salem Custom House Letter Book. Salem Customhouse to Board of Commissioners, June 8, 1774, February 10, 1775. *Essex Gazette*, June 14, 1774. "Extracts from the Interleaved Almanacs of William Wetmore of Salem, 1774–1778," *EIHC*, 43 (1907), 116. PRO T 1/505, 342-343. Commissioners of Customs to Treasury, September 20, 1774. Raphael, *First American Revolution*, 142. Felt, *Annals of Salem*, 2: 197. Winslow, 105–106, 112.

58. *SCG*, July 25, 1774, September 19, 1774.

59. "as a mart . . .": *DAR*, 7: 183. PRO CUST 17/1, 17/2, 17/3.

60. "no proper . . ." "platform . . ." "great want" "Coasting Schooners": PRO CO 5/115 f19–20. Volo, *Blue Water Patriots*, 38.

61. PRO CUST 17/2, 17/3, 17/4. Innis., ed., *Diary of Simeon Perkins*, 118–120. Norton, *1774*, 67. Labaree, 173–174. IOR B/89, 743.

62. "When Quebec . . .": Labaree, *Boston Tea Party*, 172. PRO CUST 17/2, 17/3.

63. PRO CUST 17/1, 17/2, 17/3.

64. Kerr, "The Merchants of Nova Scotia," 20. "unjust and oppressive": Legge to Dartmouth. Halifax September 20, 1774. Nova Scotia Archives. RG1 vol. 44 doc 45. Kerr, *Maritime Provinces*, 56. A. A. Mackenzie, "FILLIS, JOHN," in *DCB*. *Boston Evening Post*, August 15, 1774. Truckman James Crayton carried the twenty-seven chests to the storage offered by Robert Campbell. "against his principles": Kerr, "Merchants of Nova Scotia," 30.

65. "unwelcome . . ." "the same spirit . . .": Sargent, ed., *Letters of John Andrews*, 45. "regularly landed": NARA (Waltham). Salem Custom House Letter Book, Halifax Customs to Boston Customs, September 14, 1774.

66. "prejudiced" "the Governor . . .": Brebner, *Neutral Yankees*, 169. Kerr, "Merchants of Nova Scotia," 30–31. "persons . . ." "disorder": *DAR*, 8: 199 Legge to Dartmouth September 20, 1774.

67. Earlier shipments: Mancke, *Fault Lines of Empire*, 95. Innis, ed., *Diary of Simeon Perkins*, 83. Hurd, *History of Plymouth*, 142. *Boston Post-Boy*, September 26, 1774. *Boston Evening Post*, October 3, 1774. *Mass Spy*, October 6, 1774. Massachusetts newspapers indicate this tea came from Halifax; Perkins indicates Liverpool. "to buy Tea" "and carry . . .": *Boston Gazette*, October 3, 1774. Tea may have been imported by Captain [James] Donnel[l] for his uncle, Jonathan Sayward. *Boston Evening Post*, October 3, 1774. *Boston Post-Boy*, September 26, 1774. Sayward gives the tea as from Newfoundland. Banks, *History of York, Maine*, 1: 386. "two days later . . .": Ernst, *New England Miniature*, 76.

68. Barnes, "Francis Legge," 425–429. Nova Scotia Archives, RG1 Calendar vol. 32. Dartmouth to Legge. July 1, 1775. Nova Scotia Archives. RG1 vol. 44 doc 38. Mfm 15234. Legge to Dartmouth, July 6, 1774. Fischer, "Revolution without Independence," 99, 111, 122. Cahill, "The Treason of the Merchants," 69. Barnes, "Francis Legge," 420–447.

69. "without . . .": Maguire, "Parry's Journal" xiv. "quite unexpected" "Part of . . .": *SCG*, July 25, 1774 emphasis original. "an entire Stranger . . .": *SCG*, November 21, 1774. Maier, "Charleston Mob," 180–181.

70. "acquainted . . .": 4 Am Arch, 1: 703–704. Scharf, *History of Maryland*, 2: 159. *Virginia Gazette* (Rind), September 1, 1774.

71. "he relied . . ." "submitted": 4 Am Arch, 1: 704–705. Emphasis original. PRO CUST 16/1.

72. "submitted . . ." 4 Am Arch, 1: 704–705. Sullivan, *Disaffected*, 34.

73. "thanks" "candid . . .": 4 Am Arch, 1: 705. Wertenbaker, *Father Knickerbocker Rebels*, 34. *Virginia Gazette* (Purdie and Dixon), May 5, 1774. Mason, *Road to Independence*, 20. Labaree, *Boston Tea Party*, 167.

74. "his life": *RNYG*, April 28, 1774. Mason, *Road to Independence*, 21. Labaree, *Boston Tea Party*, 167. "agitated": *DAR*, 7: 175. Maguire, "Parry's Journal," xiv–xvi. "promised . . ." "Stranger" "the Sense . . ." "since he . . .": *SCG*, July 25, 1774. Emphasis original. *PHL*, 9: 524, 527 n 2. Fraser, *Charleston!*, 138. Maitland, Curling, and Urquhart all did the Charleston-London run, were all familiar with Charleston tea politics, and in that sense should have "known better." Each got caught with tea on board once, but only once.

75. *PHL*, 9: 525.

76. *SCG*, July 25, September 19, 1774. The customs collector seized and stored the *Briton*'s tea under the exchange as Maitland's. The *Briton* left on August 18 without incident. *PHL*, 9, 438 n 6. The Patriots' July 6–8 meeting, called in response to the Coercive Acts, stirred up Charlestonians while Maitland was in port. Fraser Jr., *Patriots Pistols and Petticoats*, 58.

77. "had no . . .": *SCG*, July 25, 1774. "I am unwilling . . ." Maguire, "Parry's Journal," xiv.

78. Maguire, ed., " Parry's Journal," vii, ix, xix, l. *DAR*, 7: 175. "recover" "esteem" "friends . . ." "not the least . . .": *Virginia Gazette* (Purdie), May 12, 1775. 4 Am Arch, 1: 965. Moses Robertson reported in June 1775, the "Tea Affair Seems to have blown Over" (Mason, *John Norton and Sons*, xxix–xxx, 381). Norton had lived in Virginia for two decades, married a Virginian, and served in the House of Burgesses. His son married the daughter of the colonial treasurer. Evans, *Thomas Nelson*, 42. Ragsdale, *A Planter's Republic*, 224–225. Price, "Who Was John Norton?," 406 n 35. Scribner, 2: 164 n 2. Fichter, "The Mystery of the 'Alternative of Williamsburg'"; Fichter, "Collecting Debts."

79. "to make . . .": *Adams Family Papers. Diary of John Adams*, March 7, 1774. Brown, *Revolutionary Politics*, 184. "inhabitants . . ." "into . . ." "highly approve . . .": *Virginia Gazette*, November 24, 1774 (Pinkney). "committed . . .": 4 Am Arch, 1: 965. Marston, *King and Congress*, 127. Thomas Nelson's biographer agrees with Dunmore. Emory Evans, *Thomas Nelson of Yorktown*, 42. *DAR*, 8: 268.

80. "surprise" "the tea . . ." "entirely . . ." "not . . ." "at least . . .": Cushing, *History of the Counties*, 536–537. Gerlach, *Prologue to Independence*, 198–199. Smith, *Freedoms We Lost*, 126. Ver Steeg, "Stacey Hepburn and Company," 1–5. Cushing, *History of the Counties*, 537. A new sheriff convened another, more conservative, grand jury in the autumn of 1775. It made a presentment—a statement of (potentially indictable) facts but did not indict. Smith, *The Freedoms We Lost*, 126.

81. Norton, *1774*, 203–206. Schlesinger, *Colonial Merchants*, 389–392. Maier, *From Resistance to Revolution*.

82. "presumed . . .": Smith, *The Freedoms We Lost*, 125. Smith, "Social Visions," 41–42. On mobs, see Wood, "Mobs in the Revolution," 641. Lemisch, "Jack Tar in the Streets." Schlesinger, "Political Mobs and the American Revolution." Aptheker, *American Revolution*, 81. Plebian crowds came into greater conflict with Patriot elites in 1775

and 1776. McDonnell, *The Politics of War*. Ryerson, *The Revolution Is Now Begun*. Steven Rosswurm, *Arms, Country, and Class*.

83. "three hearty . . .": *SCG*, November 21, 1774. "direct action . . .": Maier, "Charleston Mob," 180–181. Steedman, "Charleston's Forgotten Tea Party," 251. Scribner, 2: 159–160. Schlesinger, *Colonial Merchants*, 302–303. "two Drums . . ." "a number of Men . . .": Wroth et al., *Province in Rebellion*, 527. Governor Wentworth blamed three "mariners" for rallying people with drums to destroy tea and its ship. (*DAR*, 8: 139.)

84. "keep the tea . . .": *Virginia Gazette* (Pinkney), December 1, 1774. "lives were threatened": Benson, "Wealth and Power in Virginia, 1774–1776," 166. Crary, *Price of Loyalty*, 59. "spoke . . .": National Library of Scotland, Charles Steuart Papers MSS #5028 f287r. [James Parker] to Charles Steuart, November 27, 1774. Special Thanks to Mary Beth Norton for this reference. Ragsdale, *Planter's Republic*, 228.

85. "What . . .": Smith, *The Freedoms We Lost*, 125. "Sons of Anarchy" "horrid Crime . . .": Egerton 2659 149 Peter Oliver Jr. to Mrs. Elisha Hutchinson. May 26, 1775. "Committee . . .": *PHL*, 9: 525. PRO AO 13/133 March 25, 1784. Sarah was Richard Maitland's wife. Maguire, "Parry's Journal," xiv. *"free* and *voluntary Offer"* "at his own Cost": *SCG*, July 25, 1774. "whilst some . . ." "our property . . .": *British Records Relating to America . . . Papers of Henry Fleming*. Henry Fleming to Fisher & Bragg. Norfolk November 17, 1774. Frantz and Pencak, *Beyond Philadelphia*, xvii.

6. Toward Non-consumption

1. "Oblation . . .": *SCG*, November 21, 1774. Schlesinger, *Colonial Merchants*, 525. Shaw, *Rituals of Revolution*, 204–226. Gilje, "Republican Rioting," 204–205.

2. *Boston Evening Post*, November 10, 1774. "Brethren . . ." "overlooked": *SCG*, November 21, 1774. Cogliano, "Deliverance from Luxury," 15–28. Paul A. Gilje, "Republican Rioting," 204–205.

3. Cogliano, *No King, No Popery*.

4. All quotations: *SCG*, November 21, 1774. Steedman, "Charleston's Forgotten Tea Party," 254–259.

5. But not too low: boys, not slaves, collected the tea. Shaw, *Rituals of Revolution*, 9. Gilje, *Rioting in America*, 48. Irvin, "Tar, Feathers," 197–238. Thomas S. Wermuth "The Central Hudson Valley," in Tiedemann and Fingerhut, *The Other New York*, 132. Withington, *Toward a More Perfect Union*, 228.

6. Mentor: *Newport Mercury*, February 14, 1774.

7. "thirteen . . ." Adams, ed., *Works of John Adams*, 10: 283. Loughran, *Republic in Print*, 9, 33–103. Gould, "The South Carolina and Continental Associations," 32.

8. Brown, *Revolutionary Politics*, 168 argues these resolves signaled popular support for radicalism. It is unclear when Boston's ban was practically effective. The Boston committee thought the tea boycott was effective by May, but Boston still appointed a committee to enforce the Continental Association in December. Brown, *Revolutionary Politics*, 189. Wroth et al., *Province in Rebellion*, 95. Schlesinger, *Colonial Merchants*, 301.

9. Raphael, *A People's History*, 48. "total disuse of tea . . .": "An oration: delivered March 5, 1774 . . ." Early American Imprints, Series 1, no. 14097, 19. "renounce consumption": *DAR*, 7: 130. Wroth, *Province in Rebellion*, 34. "total disuse": Lincoln, ed., *Journals of Each Provincial Congress of Massachusetts*, 26. Wroth, *Province in Rebellion*, 85.

10. "enquire if . . .": Wroth, *Province in Rebellion*, 1303. Ibid., 778, 946. Norton, "Seventh Tea Ship." Cf. Hoerder *Crowd Action*, 268.

11. "have nothing to do . . .": *Newport Mercury*, February 14, 1774. "Drank Coffee" "they . . .": Farish, ed., *Fithian*, 147. Groce Jr., "Eliphalet Dyer," 298. Caroline, Dunmore, Essex, Gloucester, Isle of Wight, Richmond, and Westmoreland Counties. Main, ed., *Rebel versus Tory*, 24–25. Schlesinger, *Colonial Merchants*, 369. 4 Am Arch, 2: 76. Harwell, ed., *Committees of Safety of Westmoreland and Fincastle*, 30. "all persons . . .": *CRNC*, 9: 1046.

12. *DAR*, 7: 160. "boys and sailors" "who had tea . . ." "entirely": *DAR*, 8: 169. Scott, "Tory Associators of Portsmouth," 508. *Boston Gazette*, January 23, 1775, *New-Hampshire Gazette*, January 20, 1775. Schlesinger, *Colonial Merchants*, 484–485.

13. *Newport Mercury*, January 24, 1774. "As for Tea . . .": Riley, ed., *Journal of John Harrower*, 56. "gave a ball . . .": Cresswell, *Journal*, 28. LoC, Reynolds papers, William Reynolds to Samuel Rogers, August 16, 1774. "I have not drunk . . ." Riley, ed., *Journal of John Harrower*, 73.

14. "prodigious shouts" "drinking . . ." "went . . .": Andrews: Sargent, ed., *Letters of John Andrews*, 13. "16 Pounds . . ." "Send . . .": Sheffield City Archives, Vassall Letterbooks. William Vassall Sr. to James Syme January 7, 1774. *Massachusetts Spy*, December 30, 1773. "Liberty Matters": Miller and Riggs, eds., *Journal of Dr. Elihu Ashley*, 72. Matson, *Merchants & Empire*, 305–307. *Pennsylvania Packet*, April 11, 1774. Schlesinger, *Colonial Merchants*, 434 n 1. Lott, "Journal," 65–74. "coffee . . .": Sargent, ed., *Letters of John Andrews*, 41. Ibid., 29. LVa. Allason Papers, Misc. Reel 1373. Inventories of Goods on hand October 1, 1773 and September 10, 1774. "Drank Tea . . .": Cresswell, *Journal*, 45. *CRI*, 1: 383.

15. "three or four": Yale University Library, Beinecke Library, Medad Rogers Diary, December 24, 1774. Roche, *Colonial Colleges*, 61. Peckham, "Collegia Ante Bellum," 58. "Number of Families . . .": *Newport Mercury*, February 14, 1774.

16. Glickman, *Buying Power*, 39, 49. "What Good": Norton, *1774*, 60. "already in . . ." "the Overflowing . . .": Scribner, 1: 215. "never to purchase . . .": *CRNC*, 9: 1038–1041. Norton, "Seventh Tea Ship," 689, 696, 702, 706. "any kind . . .": Wroth, *Province in Rebellion*, 1326, 1324.

17. Roth, "Tea Drinking," 67, 78. Quotations: Farish, ed., *Fithian*, 189, 257. Travel: Ibid., 131, 144, 273.

18. "tolled the bell" "many spirited resolves" "to show . . .": PUL. Beatty Collection. Box 1 Folder 5. AM 1590. Charles Beatty to Enoch Green, January 31, 1774. "Officers and Students": Gerlach, *Prologue to Independence*, 197–198. Wertenbaker, *Princeton*, 57.

19. Beatty, ed., "Beatty Letters," 231 Charles Beatty to Erkuries Beatty, February 23, 1774. "spent . . .": PUL. Beatty Collection Box 1 Folder 5 Folder Precis p. 2. Beatty, ed., "Beatty Letters," 233 n 11. "fine frolick" "all drest . . ." "who used . . ." "made him . . ." "I am . . .": Beatty, ed., "Beatty Letters," 235, Charles Beatty to Erkuries Beatty, June 8, 1774.

20. "lawful . . .": John Adams to Abigail Adams, July 6, 1774. Butterfield, ed., *Adams Family Correspondence*, 1: 129–130.

21. Irvin, *Clothed in Robes of Sovereignty*, 39. John Adams diary, *Adams Family Papers: An Electronic Archive*, August 21, 22 1774. "never . . ." "acquitted": Ellis and Evans, *History of Lancaster*, 35–36, 369. The Lockharts also furnished lead balls and powder to

their local committee. *FO*. Diary of George Washington October 22, 1774. "drank Tea": *CRNC*, 9: 1066.

22. Scribner, 1: 215.

23. "a Dignity . . .": Fichter, *So Great a Proffit*, 11. "amidst . . .": *Boston Evening Post*, January 24, 1774. "small . . .": York, ed., *Hulton*, 158. "conspicuous *non* consumption": Smith, *The Freedoms We Lost*, 101.

24. Brooke, "Consumer Virtues in Revolutionary America?" 336. Breen notes "coercive settings" in *Marketplace of Revolution*, 296. "they say . . .": Berkin, *Revolutionary Mothers*, 23.

25. "burnt . . .": Carter, ed., *The Correspondence of General Thomas Gage*, 1: 391. "so far . . ." "he put . . .": *Boston Gazette*, January 23, 1775. Smith, "Social Visions," 46.

26. "raging . . .": Maguire, "Parry's Journal," xlvi–xlvii. "Committees . . .": Cresswell, *Journal*, 43–44. Mays, *Pendleton Biography*, 1: 304.

27. "a great number . . ." "not to . . ." "utter inability . . .": *Boston Evening Post*, August 15, September 12, 1774. "much against . . ." "Tea is sold there": *New York Gazette*, August 1, 1774. "Spirit of Liberty": *Boston Evening Post*, September 12, 1774. "inhabitants in general . . ." "tea has been . . .": Kerr, "Merchants of Nova Scotia," 30–31. Kerr, *Maritime Provinces*, 58. Sargent, ed., *Letters of John Andrews*, 45. "small" "Inhabitants are but few": Nova Scotia Archives, RG1 vol 44 doc 47 Legge to Dartmouth, October 18, 1774.

28. "our American . . .": *Boston Evening Post*, August 15, 1774

29. *Boston Post-Boy*, June 17, July 11, 1774. "Negro fellow," "the Fellow . . .": *Essex Gazette*, October 4, 1774. "obliged," "contrary . . .": *Essex Gazette* October 11, 1774. Boston: *Massachusetts Spy*, October 6, 1774. Special thanks to J. L. Bell for consulting on this.

30. Andrews and Andrews, eds., *Journal of a Lady of Quality*, 155. "every ounce": Norton, *1774*, 61.

31. Maguire, "Parry's Journal," xlvi–xlvii. There were two mobs near Georgetown. Their relationship is unclear.

32. "careful . . .": Drake, *Tea Leaves*, lxxix. "small Boats . . .": Upton, "Proceedings of Ye Body Respecting the Tea," 299. Drake, *Tea Leaves*, cxvi. Glickman, *Buying Power*, 40.

33. Adair and Schutz, eds., *Origins*, 102. Hoerder, *Crowd Action*, 263. "Captain Conner" "ript . . ." "nearly .." "handled . . ." "filled . . .": Sargent, ed., *Letters of John Andrews*, 13. Or "O'Connor." The spelling and mythologies of his treatment differ. Cf. Akers, *Divine Politician*, 166. Fischer, *Paul Revere's Ride*, 26. Labaree, *Boston Tea Party*, 144. Drake, *Tea Leaves*, lxxvii. Young, *Shoemaker*, 45. Glickman, *Buying Power*, 40. "think themselves . . .": MHS Misc Bd. 1773 Dec 31. MHS. "Tea leaves from the Boston Tea Party." "Boston Tea Party tea in a glass bottle."

34. "Well . . .": Drake, *Tea Leaves*, lxxiv. Labaree, *Boston Tea Party*, 143, 145. Drake, *Tea Leaves*, cxxix, clix.

35. Sickler, *Tea Burning*, 40. Gerlach, *Prologue to Independence*, 199. "dangerous . . .": 4 Am Arch, 2: 920. "a Quantity . . ." "strowed . . .": *Boston Post-Boy*, July 11, 1774. "for safe keeping": Smith, "Biographical Sketch of Col. David Mason," 203. Maier, "Charleston Mob," 179.

36. Versions of this story appear in Stackpole, *History of New Hampshire*, 4: 306 and Morison, *Maritime History*, 13.

37. "made . . ." "found . . .": *SCG*, November 21, 1774. Steedman, "Charleston's Forgotten Tea Party," 246, 251. Breen, *Marketplace of Revolution*, 327.

38. "pursuing . . ." "were stumbled on" "to fill . . .": *Boston Evening Post*, November 7, 1774. "contained . . ." Sargent, ed., *Letters of John Andrews*, 70. Conroy, *In Public Houses*, 279.

39. *Boston Gazette*, February 14, March 7, 1774. Conroy, *In Public Houses*, 279. Labaree, *Tea Party*, 161. *Providence Gazette*, April 2, 1774. Norton, "The Seventh Tea Ship," 695. "remotest . . ." "pedling Trader" "honest Savages": *Connecticut Gazette* (New London), September 2, 1774. News came via Cohos, suggesting Haverhill, New Hampshire rather than Haverhill, Massachusetts.

40. *Maryland Gazette*, December 22, 1774. Schlesinger, *Colonial Merchants*, 507.

41. "divers Persons" "proceeded . . ." "Harm": *Massachusetts Spy*, January 13, 1774. Breen, *Marketplace of Revolution*, 294–296. Withington found the tea on a Saturday; it is unclear which one. (BPL, Dorchester Town Records, 3: 414.) Destruction date: *Boston Gazette*, January 3, 1774, Cunningham, *Letters and Diary of John Rowe*, 259.

42. "one Common Cause" "Several Persons . . ." "just Indignation": BPL: Dorchester Town Records, 3: 407.

43. "old . . .": *Boston Gazette*, January 3, 1774. "Captain . . ." "Labourer": BPL Dorchester Town Records, 3: 414. "Narragansett-Indians" "consent": *Boston Gazette*, January 3, 1774. "East-India Teas" BPL Dorchester Town Records, 3: 437. Career: Ibid., 406–439. The captain had already served on various committees in 1773. Without evidence, the two men are given as father and son in Breen, *Marketplace of Revolution*, 294–296. The genealogy, Withington, "Henry Withington," 149–150, gives second cousins. The *Gazette* probably used "old" and "Captain" to disambiguate the men rather than imply parentage. (Neither the *Gazette* nor the town meeting used the suffixes "Sr." and "Jr." for these men.)

44. "Satisfaction" "discovered . . ." "Tea said . . ." "deliver" "publickly posted": BPL. Dorchester Town Meeting, 3: 414–415.

45. "simple old men": Breen, *Marketplace of Revolution*, 296. At 54 or 55, he was not that old: a few years older than Samuel Adams but young enough to be canny of the opportunity and move a heavy box. Age: Withington, "Henry Withington," 149. Weights and prices calculated from Fichter, "The Tea That Survived the Boston Tea Party," n 1, PRO CO 5/133, 89–93, Labaree, *Boston Tea Party*, 335. A "half chest" was a specific container. He may have had half of a half chest (one possible reading) of the cheapest tea or as much as a proper half chest of hyson. Boston Tea Party Ship Museum, https://www.bostonteapartyship.com/partners/a-box-worth-keeping.

46. "Marshes" "if . . .": BPL. Dorchester Town Records, 3: 414–415. "below . . .": *Boston Gazette*, January 3, 1774.

47. Rowe gives "half [of] a chest" (Cunningham, *Letters and Diary of John Rowe*, 259). The *Gazette* gave "a Chest" and "a half chest" (*Boston Gazette*, January 3, 1774). "Some Gentlemen . . ." "harm" "neighbours": BPL. Dorchester Town Records, 3: 414. York, ed., *Hulton*, 157. *Massachusetts Spy*, January 6, 13, 1774.

48. Merchants' buyback: *Massachusetts Spy*, December 30, 1773. Town buyback: Brown, *Revolutionary Politics*, 168.

49. Ragsdale, *Planter's Republic*, 193. "publickly burn'd": Rutland, ed., *George Mason*, 1: 205.

50. Quotations: *Newport Mercury*, February 7, 1774. Westerly, Rhode Island, Town Meeting Minutes. February 2, 1774.

51. "Ordered . . ." "Proceedings of the Committees of Safety of Caroline and Southampton Counties," 128. Mays, *Pendleton Biography*, 1: 300–301. "all . . ." "is . . .": *SCG*, April 3, 1775. " to be . . ." 4 Am Arch, 1: 705. *Virginia Gazette*, (Rind) September 1, 1774. "deliver . . ." *Norfolk Intelligencer*, January 19, 1775. 4 Am Arch, 4: 1695, 1724–1725. Likewise, John Ferguson and Robert Peter offered to hand over tea from the *Mary and Jane*, were it landed. *Virginia Gazette* (Rind), September 1, 1774.

52. Labaree, *Patriots & Partisans*, 37. "Intend . . ." "to sell . . ." "general Association: Scribner, 7: 747.

53. Huntington Library. Tea Permits. Special thanks to Mary Beth Norton for this reference. "Secrieted . . .": Norton, "Seventh Tea Ship," 703.

54. Papas, *That Ever Loyal Island*, 28. "required . . .": Potter, *Liberty We Seek*, 30. "Will you . . ." "You must . . ." "have ordered . . ." "shall be . . ." "open your . . .": Seabury, "Free thoughts," 17–19. "shall probably . . ." Seabury, "An alarm to the legislature," 6. "Whether they drink . . ." Seabury, "Free thoughts" 18. "arbitrary" Seabury, "Free thoughts," 4. "political inquisitors . . .": Hulton to Robert Nicholson February 21, 1775, in York, ed., *Hulton*, 311. "if I . . ." "let it . . .": Seabury, "Free thoughts," 18.

55. "one ought . . ." Hamilton, *John Ettwein*, 147. "devis'd . . ." "that Sp[ir]it . . .": Blecki and Wulf, eds., *Milcah Martha Moore's Book*, 247.

56. "[W]higs . . ." "has been . . ." "melasses . . ." "coffee . . .": Massachusettensis, "Present state of the province of Massachusetts Bay," 83. Schaw, *Journal of a Lady of Quality*, 155. "mere sounds" "words king . . ." "the words . . ." "all the power . . .": Calhoon, "The Character and Coherence of the Loyalist Press," 116.

7. Truth in Advertising

1. Keyes's "A Revolution in Advertising" and "Early American Advertising Marketing and Consumer Culture in Eighteenth-Century Philadelphia" are the main studies of revolutionary advertising. Keyes does not look closely at tea. E. M. Gardner's *The Business of News in England, 1760–1820* considers how ads financed the press. For the relationship between advertising and consumption in Britain, see Ferdinand, "Selling it to the provinces."

2. October to December 1773 is an imperfect baseline—campaigns against the East India Company tea had begun—but earlier times are unwieldy since advertising can be affected by season, business cycle, and newspaper availability. These three months are a least-bad control set.

3. Heaton, "The American Trade," 199.

4. No newspapers were printed in Delaware, New Jersey, or the Floridas from October 1773 to June 1776. Nor were any printed in Patriot-controlled Quebec. Some ads ran for multiple weeks; there were just over 580 discrete decisions to advertise. Readex sources: *American Gazette* (Salem, MA), *Boston Evening-Post, Boston Gazette, Massachusetts Gazette, Boston Post-Boy, Connecticut Courant* (Hartford), *Connecticut Gazette* (New London), *Connecticut Journal* (New Haven), *Constitutional Gazette* (New York), *Continental Journal* (Boston), *Essex Gazette* (Salem, MA), *Essex Journal* (Newburyport, MA), *Freeman's Journal* (Portsmouth, NH), *Mass Spy* (Boston, continued in Worcester),

New-England Chronicle (Cambridge, continued in Boston), *New-Hampshire Gazette* (Portsmouth), *Newport Mercury* (RI), *NYG* (New York City), *NYJ* (New York City), *Norwich Packet* (CT), *Pennsylvania Chronicle* (Philadelphia), *Pennsylvania Evening Post* (Philadelphia), *PAG* (Philadelphia), *Pennsylvania Ledger* (Philadelphia), *Story and Humphreys's Pennsylvania Mercury* (Philadelphia), *Pennsylvania Packet* (Philadelphia), *Providence Gazette* (RI), *RNYG* (New York City), and the *Maryland Gazette* (Annapolis).

Data was collected with a full-text search for "tea" among items classified by Readex as "advertisements." This introduced classification errors (Readex may not have classed an advertisement as such) and text recognition errors. Hits were individually checked. Preceding and succeeding issues of newspapers containing tea ads were checked to see if the search missed advertisements in those weeks. The resultant perusal of newspapers yielded fewer than two dozen additional tea advertisements, allowing confidence in Readex's search tool.

"Bohea" was also searched for. However, the first twenty sample hits for "bohea" only returned ads already found in the search for "tea." Searches for "bohea," "hyson," "souchong," and "congo" or "congou" were abandoned.

The *Maryland Gazette* was also consulted online at the Maryland State Archives, http://aomol.msa.maryland.gov/html/mdgazette.html. All three Williamsburg-based Virginia gazettes were consulted at Colonial Williamsburg at https://research .colonialwilliamsburg.org/DigitalLibrary/va-gazettes/. *Nova Scotia Gazette* (Halifax), *PA Jrnl* (Philadelphia), *Dunlap's Maryland Gazette* (Baltimore), the *Maryland Journal* (Baltimore), *Virginia Gazette, or Norfolk Intelligencer* (Norfolk), *North Carolina Gazette* (New Bern), *SCG*, *SCAGG*, *SCGCJ* (all Charleston), and *Georgia Gazette* (Savannah), were consulted on microfilm. The *fraktur* typeface used for the *Germantowner Zeiting* (PA) and the *Wöchentliche Pennsylvanische Staatsbote* (Philadelphia) was illegible to the search engine. Issues were read individually.

If a merchant advertised in separate newspapers, the two ads are counted separately. Advertisements placed by partnerships and individual partners are counted separately. In rare instances, two versions of a newspaper were published on the same day (*Newport Mercury*, August 1, 1774). These are treated as one newspaper, as one version appears to be an incomplete version of the other. Sometimes (also rarely), the same ad appears twice in the same issue of the same paper, perhaps to fill space, as Gould Marsh's tea ad in the *Newport Mercury*, August 1, 1774. These are treated as one ad. In counting newspaper issues, "Postscript" and "Supplement" pages are considered part of the main issue if printed on the same day or holding the same issue number as the main issue. Newspapers giving a range as publication date are taken as being published on the earlier date. The forty-six newspapers counts separately the Cambridge and Boston editions of the *New-England Chronicle* and the Worcester and Boston versions of the *Massachusetts Spy*, which papers moved in or out of Boston because of the siege.

5. *Norfolk Intelligencer*, June 30 to July 7, 1774, July 21, 1774.

6. Lewis Ogier & Co's ad of November 22, 1774, in the *SCGCJ* (after the Pope's Day celebrations that began the last chapter) lists Indian cloth from the "Company's" auctions in London. Joseph Reed suggested that smugglers imported "calicoes, spices, and other India commodities" with Dutch tea. (Reed to Dartmouth, December 27, 1773. Reed, ed., *Joseph Reed*, 1, 52.) A cursory examination indicates that advertisements for

East India goods persisted in Maryland longer than advertisements for tea did. Wallace, Davidson, and Johnson advertised "East-India goods" (*Maryland Gazette*, May 19, May 26, June 9, June 23, July 7, and August 4, 1774). Thomas Williams advertised "East-India goods" also (*Maryland Gazette*, June 2, June 23, July 7, and July 21, 1774). Jonathan Hudson did the same (*Maryland Gazette*, September 22, 1774). James Christie and John Boyd advertised East Indian spices (Christie: *Maryland Gazette*, August 18 and 25, 1774, Boyd: *Maryland Gazette*, September 19, 1774). The very vagueness of these ads renders efforts to quantify them unilluminating.

7. "incurable emity . . .": Sabine, 2: 503. *Maryland Journal*, February 13–27, 1775.

8. *Providence Gazette*, August 13, 1774, February 18, 1775. *Boston Post-Boy*, May 30, 1774, September 12, 1774. Solemn League: Nash, *Urban Crucible*, 358. "Whereas a great number of people have express'd. . . .": Boston. 1774 Evans 13767. "totally": Egnal, *Mighty Empire*, 277–278.

9. Davis: Sabine, 2: 359–60. Sargent, ed., *Letters of John Andrews*, 61. Boyle, "Boyle's Journal," *NEHGR*, 85 (Apr 1931): 123–124. Jones, *Loyalists of Massachusetts*, 113. Deblois: Sabine, 1: 362. Egnal, *Mighty Empire*, 343. Jones, *Loyalists of Massachusetts*, 116. "satisfaction": "Address of the Merchants and Others of Boston to Gov. Hutchinson" Boston. May 28, 1774, in Stark, *Loyalists of Massachusetts*, 123–125. This address also offered to pay for the destroyed tea. Addresser: Oliver, ed., *Journal of Samuel Curwen*, 1: 6. Suffolk Resolves: Ammerman, *In the Common Cause*, 15, 26–32, 39–40, 75, 81.

10. *Newport Mercury*, December 19, 1774. *Connecticut Journal*, February 2, 1775. *Connecticut Courant*, February 20, 1775. *NYG*, March 20, 1775. *PA Jrnl*, March 29, 1775. Newport Tories: Edelberg, *Jonathan Odell*, 25.

11. NH sales: *DAR*, 8: 169. NS sales: Kerr, "Merchants of Nova Scotia," 30–31. *Nova Scotia Gazette*, June 28 to July 26, 1774. Wallace: Gwyn, "Female Litigants," 327. Only one issue of the *Nova Scotia Gazette* survives between November 5, 1775 and July 4, 1776. Other ads may have appeared in missing issues. *New Hampshire Gazette* stopped on January 7, 1776.

12. "fine Spirits": Moses Morss: *Connecticut Gazette*, January 28, 1774. Parker & Hutchings: *SCAGG*, May 6 to July 1, 1774.

13. Smith, Richards: *NYG*, March 28, 1774. Gordon: *SCG*, October 25 to November 8, 1773. Marchinton: *Pennsylvania Packet*, January 17, 1774. Donaldson: *SCAGG*, April 26, May 13, 1774. Price is in South Carolina currency. 1 British shilling bought 7.25 South Carolina shillings in 1774. This made it a normal price in sterling. McCusker, *How Much Is That in Real Money?*, 70.

14. Carmichael: *Pennsylvania Packet*, August 1, 1774. Waugh: *Newport Mercury*, November 1, 1773.

15. Kingsley: *SCAGG*, July 15, 1774. *SCGCJ*, July 12, 1774.

16. *Newport Mercury*, "To the true SONS of LIBERTY," February 21, 1774. *Virginia Gazette* (Purdie and Dixon), May 26, 1774. *Georgia Gazette*, September 28, 1774. *Pennsylvania Packet*, January 9, 1775.

17. Brigham, *American Newspapers*, 998. Loyalists dug up the press and type to print a *Gazette* during the British occupation. *Newport Mercury*, June 12, 1858.

18. Bradford: Thomas, *History of Printing in America*, 1: 242–243. Labaree, *Boston Tea Party*, 94, 98, 101. *Pa Jrnl*, June 15, 22, July 6, 20, 27, August 17, 24, September 7, December 21, 1774; January 1, 11, February 1, 15 March 1, 8, 15, 29, 1775. Edes: *ANB*, s.v., "Edes,

Benjamin." Humphrey, *"This Popular Engine,"* 38. *Boston Gazette*, May 16, 1774. Printer politics: Thomas, *History of Printing*, 191 (Watson), 204 (Carter), 258–259 (Dunlap), 303–304 (Holt), 344–345 (Crouch). Brigham, *American Newspapers*, 654. Goddard: Miner, *William Goddard*, 147. Dixon: Reardon, *Peyton Randolph*, 55. Timothy: Cohen, *South Carolina Gazette*, 244.

19. Bleecker: *NYG*, December 12 to 19, 1774. Champlin: *Newport Mercury*, October 25 to November 1, 1773. Lough, "The Champlins of Newport." Smith, Heriot and Tucker: *SCG*, October 25 to November 8, 1773. Smith would soon be known as a Company tea consignee, but this advertisement was not for Company tea. Leary: *NYG*, January 31 to February 14, 1774. Bull: *Connecticut Courant*, July 10, 1775.

20. Thomas: *Mass Spy*, December 30, 1773. Rivington: *RNYG*, September 2, 1774. Moore: *RNYG*, January 13, 1774. Camp: *Connecticut Journal*, March 18 to April 1, 1774. Hunter: *Virginia Gazette* (Purdie and Dixon), May 12, 1774. Hoar: *NYJ*, August 11 to 18, 1774. Hall: *Pennsylvania Evening Post*, May 16, 1776.

21. John Wanton: *Newport Mercury*, December 27, 1773 to January 10, 1774. Peter Wanton: *Newport Mercury*, April 11 to April 25, 1774. Taylor and Delancey: *NYG*, October 4, December 6, 1773. Amos and Fenn Wadsworth: *Connecticut Courant*, July 19 to August 2, August 23, 1774. de Peyster: *RNYG*, August 11–18, 1774. Countryman, *People in Revolution*, 98. Bache: *Pennsylvania Packet*, April 4, 1774. *ANB*, s.v. "Bache, Richard." Higginson: *Essex Gazette*, November 16–23, 1773. Higginson became a Congressman at war's end. Higginson, *Stephen Higginson*, 49. Otis: *Boston Evening Post*, October 4–25, December 20, 1773. *Boston Gazette*, October 4, 1773. Egnal, *Mighty Empire*, 341. Waters, *Otis Family*, 188. Woolsey: *Maryland Journal*, February 10, 1774. Hoffman, *Spirit of Dissention*, 139. Duryee: Ranlet, *New York Loyalists*, 191. *RNYG*, November 4, 1773, October 13 to 20, 1774. *NYJ*, September 15 to October 27, 1774, November 10 to December 1, December 22, January 5 to 26, 1775, February 9, 1775. Leavenworth: *ANB*, s.v. "Leavenworth, Henry." *Connecticut Journal* (New Haven), November 5–26, 1773. Achincloss: *New Hampshire Gazette*, October 15, 1773, Scott, "Tory Associators," 512. Cunningham: *Boston Gazette*, October 25 to November 1, 1773. Jones, *Loyalists of Massachusetts*, 105–106. Cape: *SCG*, October 4 to 25, November 8, 1773. Egnal, *Mighty Empire*, 367.

22. Kingsley: *SCAGG*, April 26 to May 20 and June 3 to July 15, 1774, *SCGCJ*, April 26 to May 3, May 24, June 21, and July 12, 1774. One hundred and seventy merchants or merchant firms advertised tea from October 1773 to December 1774; counting firm members yields at least 210 individuals involved in tea advertising, almost all by name. Boston vendors: Fichter, *So Great a Proffit*, 14.

23. Shalev, "Ancient Masks," 163. Nicolson et al., "A Case of Identity," 651–682.

24. Palmer: *Mass Spy*, October 27, 1774. Literature: *New Hampshire Gazette*, July 22, 1774. Dropping tea: Nathaniel Sparhawk, *Essex Gazette*, May 17, 24, 1774. Some, such as Alexander Donaldson, also announced that their retail goods were "agreeable to the resolve of the Continental Congress." *Dunlap's Maryland Gazette*, May 9, 1775.

25. "Narrative of the Life of William Beadle," 4–5, 13, 14, 28. Fishes: *Connecticut Courant*, March 1–8, 1774. Oliver: Adair and Schutz, eds., *Origins & Progress*, 103. "defiant": Ammerman, *Common Cause*, 5.

26. Beadle: *Connecticut Courant*, January 30, February 13–20, 1775. "To the Worthy Patriots of Boston" by T.: *Massachusetts Gazette*, February 10, 1774. Irvin, "Tar, Feathers, and Enemies of American Liberties," reads "T's" letter literally.

27. *Virginia Gazette* (Pinkney), January 19, 1775. *Newport Mercury*, December 19, 1774. Advertisement by Gould Marsh. Lee: Charles Lee to Benjamin Rush. December 15, 1774, "Lee Papers," 1: 143–144.

28. Annapolis: Land, ed., *Letters from America*, 85. Scharf, *Chronicles of Baltimore*, 126. Frederick county: Scharf, *History of Maryland*, 2: 155. Provincial congress: Scharf, *History of Maryland*, 2: 158. This may have been meant as a guideline for a future intercolonial congress's use. Schlesinger, *Colonial Merchants*, 362.

29. Walter Lippmann described "the manufacture of consent" as, in part, an official deciding "what facts, in what setting, in what guise he shall permit the public to know." (Walter Lippmann, *Public Opinion*, 248.) In later usage, "manufacturing consent" suggested that advertisers manipulated news. (Herman and Chomsky, *Manufacturing Consent*.) In this case the news was manipulated and the advertisers told the truth. The July 2 meeting for the "upper part" of Frederick County was held at Elizabeth Town (later Hagerstown). It included Jonathan Hager, area patriarch, which helped build support for the cause among German speakers. It was the second meeting in that county. On June 20 in Frederick Town, Maryland, the county seat, a meeting agreed to join an Association but did not mention tea. Scharf, *History of Maryland*, 2: 154–156.

30. *RNYG* April 28, 1774. As Marston noted, "those colonists who did not attend the meetings, whether for reasons of apathy or disapproval" did not have their views included. Marston, *King and Congress*, 317.

31. Williams: *Maryland Gazette*, November 4 to December 9, 1773, May 5 to 26, 1774. Hyde: *Maryland Gazette*, March 3 to May 19, 1774. Johnson: *Maryland Journal*, May 28 to June 11, 1774. Hodgkin: *Maryland Gazette*, May 19 to 26, June 16, 1774. O'Brien: *Maryland Journal*, June 11, July 2, 1774.

32. Dorr, *Annotated Newspapers*, 2: introduction, iii, https://www.masshist.org/dorr/. The MHS claims Dorr covered Patriotic and Loyalist papers, but in 1774 Dorr indexed forty-four copies of the radical *Boston Gazette*, nine issues of the more-neutral *Boston Evening Post*, and one issue of the Loyalist *Massachusetts Gazette*. Dorr did not include issues of the *Boston Post-Boy* or the *Massachusetts Spy* from that year. Dorr noted London merchants' offer to pay for the tea, indexed from a Patriotic story in the September 19, 1774 *Boston Evening-Post*. This story disputes the "wicked" claim "no offers had been made to government" for the tea. Dorr omitted disputes around whether the town of Boston should pay, though Boston papers covered these disputes. See *Massachusetts Gazette*, July 14, 1774, which Dorr does not index. Dorr, *Annotated Newspapers*, 4: 581.

33. "very judiciously": *SCG*, March 14, 1774. Bonneau and Wilson quote: *SCG*, April 4, May 16, 1774. Also ads in *SCAGG*, April 15 to 29, 1774. *SCGCJ*, April 12 & 26, 1774. Radcliffe & Shepheard: *SCGCJ*, April 5 to 12, 1774. "WITHOUT . . .": *SCG*, April 25, 1774. Caps in original. "just imported . . .": *SCGCJ*, April 26, May 3, May 24, June 21, July 12, 1774. A similar Kingsley ad appeared in *SCAGG*, April 26 to May 20, June 3 to July 15, 1774. Samuel Douglass & Company: *Georgia Gazette*, May 11 to 25, 1774.

34. *SCAGG*, June 24, 1774. *SCGCJ*, June 21, 1774. *SCG*, June 20, 1774.

35. "refused": *SCG*, July 4, 1774. Donaldson ads: *SCAGG*, July 8, 15, 1774. On *Magna Charta*, see *PHL*, 9: 525–527. Wakefield: *SCGCJ*, July 12, 1774.

36. "Proceedings of the Committees of Safety of Caroline and Southampton Counties," 124. Humphrey, *"This Popular Engine,"* 38, 41–42, 79–81. Botein, "Meer Mechanics," 144–145. Miner, *William Goddard*, 4. Botein "Printers and the American Revolution," 17.

37. Schlesinger, *Prelude to Independence*, 46. Davidson, *Propaganda*, 210. Jensen, *Founding of a Nation*, 128. Weir, "The Role of the Newspaper," 119. Clark, "Early American Journalism," 364–365. Lucas, *Portents of Rebellion*, 7–8, 282 n 31. Irvin, "Tar, Feathers," 212. Broadside: *PAG*, December 8, 1773. Handbill quote: Hersey, "Tar and Feathers," 458. *Boston Gazette*, January 31, 1774.

38. Cohen, *South Carolina Gazette*, 11. Sellers, *Charleston Business*, 3. *SCG*, October 25 to November 8, 1773.

39. Rivington: Crary, "The Tory and the Spy," 66–67. German papers: Adams, "The Colonial German-language Press," 165, 167, 169, Stoudt. "The German Press," 86. Attmore and Hellings: *Pennsylvania Evening Post*, June 22, 1776. *WPS*, August 30 to September 13, 1774, June 21–28, 1776. Mason and Dorsey: *Pennsylvania Packet*, December 8, 1773, April 4, 18, May 9, 30, September 5, October 4, 1774. *WPS*, October 3, December 7 to 14, December 28, 1773, January 11 to 25, 1774. Freehauf und Wyntoop: *WPS*, November 16, 30, December 14, 1773. Becker: *WPS* June 21 to July 5, 1774. Schallus: *WPS*, October 19, November 9, 1773, February 15 to 22, March 15, April 26, 1774. Adams, "The Colonial German-language Press," 170.

40. Ryerson, *Revolution is Now Begun*, 44.

41. Quotation: Cresswell, *Journal*, 45. The "First Newspaper in New Jersey," the "Plain Dealer" was a hand-written series of weekly essays. Needing to post it in one location where it would be readily seen, its authors chose a tavern. Brigham, *American Newspapers*, 492–493. Loughran, *The Republic in Print*, 6, 22. Padelford, ed., *Colonial Panorama*, 16. Thomas, *History of Printing*, 242–243. Isaac, "Dramatizing the Ideology of Revolution," 358–359. Weir, "The Role of the Newspaper in the Southern Colonies," 134, 137. Shields, *Civil Tongues*, 60. Salinger, *Taverns and Drinking*, 56.

42. Patrons who kept a tab at the One Tun Tavern in Philadelphia bought £395.02 in drinks, of which tea and coffee comprised £5.80. Most bought toddies, punch, and beer. Thompson, *Rum Punch & Revolution*, 71, table 3. Carp, *Rebels Rising*, 66. Marston kept the Golden Ball Tavern and took over the Bunch of Grapes in 1775, where the Sons of Liberty likely met and where he served tea with a fancy tea service. Conroy, *In Public Houses*, 257–258.

43. Maier, *Old Revolutionaries*, 72–74. Crary, ed., *Price of Loyalty*, 32. Warden, "Chester County," 2. Thompson, *Rum Punch & Revolution*. Shields, *Civil Tongues*, 57. There were also, rarely, teahouses—Abigail Stoneman ran a coffeehouse, tavern, and teahouse in Newport and Middletown, Rhode Island. Mason, *Reminiscences of Newport*, 179. Fraser, *Charleston!*, 130. Salinger, *Taverns*, 56, 76–82. Morelli: *SCGCJ*, October 19 to 26, 1773, *SCG*, October 4 to 18, 1773. Moore: *NYJ*, January 20 to February 24, 1774, *NYG*, January 10 to April 25, 1774, *RNYG*, January 13 to February 3, 1774.

44. Botein "Meer Mechanics," 146–147.

45. *Boston Gazette*, January 3, 1774. Humphrey, *"This Popular Engine,"* 41–42, 96. Lucas estimates one-quarter of page space devoted to ads over this period. Lucas, *Portents of Rebellion*, 5. *Dunlap's Maryland Gazette* was roughly 25–30 percent ads. In response to paper shortages printers cut page size and the number of columns (sometimes printing the last column sideways). Shortages affected the *Pennsylvania Packet*,

SCG, *Newport Mercury*, and *Maryland Journal*, among others. Hawke, *In the Midst of a Revolution*, 48. Rogers, "The Charleston Tea Party," 164. Lovejoy, *Rhode Island Politics*, 187. Miner, *William Goddard*, 150. Botein, "Meer Mechanics," 150.

8. Propaganda

1. Granger, *Political Satire*, 70. "the Northward": *Newport Mercury*, February 7, 1774. "people to the Southward . . .": Stevens, *Facsimiles*, document 2029, 5. "deceptives" "As to . . .": Labaree, *Tea Party*, 31.

2. All quotations: David Ramsay, *A Sermon on Tea*. For SC printing: *SCGCJ*, September 13–20, 1774. Reprinted by Francis Bailey in Lancaster, PA, assigned Evans number 13606.

3. "highly debilitating" "relaxant" "nervous ailments" "hypochondria . . .": *Newport Mercury*, February 28, 1774. Norton, *1774*, 63. "has in the Opinion . . ." "ruined the Nerves" "Health" "fattened the Purse . . ." "save the Remains . . .": *SCGCJ*, August 2, 1774. Jones, "Writings of the Reverend William Tennent," 135–136. Carp, *Rebels Rising*, 159. "slow poison": Butterfield, ed., *Letters of Benjamin Rush*, 84. "certain feminine disorders": *Norfolk Intelligencer*, September 29 to October 6, 1774. "an offense . . ." "lost their . . ." "shorten your days": *Norfolk Intelligencer*, October 6–13, 1774.

4. "Health and Happiness": Singleton, *Social New York*, 378. Dermigny, *La Chine et l'Occident*, 2, 621 n 6. "Paralytick Disorder" "Foltron" "slow poison": Wesley, *A Letter to a Friend*, 3–4, 7, 9. Donat, "The Rev. John Wesley's Extractions from Dr. Tissot," 285. "pernicious . . ." "injurious": Hanway, *An Essay on Tea*, title page, 204. "less substantial": Shammas, *The Pre-industrial Consumer*, 137. "weakens . . ." "unbraces . . .": Torr, *Small Talk at Wreyland*, 144. Sigmond, *Tea*. Gassicourt, *Le thé est-il plus nuisible qu'utile?*

5. "scare crow stories" "Why . . .": Norton, *1774*, 62–63. Labaree, *Boston Tea Party*, 164.

6. "which renders . . .": Ragsdale, *Planter's Republic*, 177 n 7, citing *Virginia Gazette* (Rind), December 16, 1773. "poisonous quality" "drawn off": Granger, *Political Satire*, 58–59.

7. Wesley, *Letter to a Friend*, 5.

8. "Doctors . . ." "rail . . ." "Blest": Blecki and Wulf, eds., *Milcah Martha Moore's Book*, 299. "Tea . . ." "or I shall dye": Blecki and Wulf, eds., *Milcah Martha Moore's Book*, 247.

9. Tea as tonic discussed in *Norfolk Intelligencer*, September 29 to October 6, 1774. "Sickness excepted": Norton, *Liberty's Daughters*, 161, citing *Boston Evening Post*, February 12, 1770. "I speak not . . .": Greene, ed., *The Diary of Colonel Landon Carter*, 2: 825. June 12, 1774. Carter's use of the word, tea, is vague. Often by "tea" he meant herbal tisanes. This is one of the few mentions of *camellia sinensis*, which he had sworn off because of the Coercive Acts. "dangerous to Health" "stop suddenly" "long accustomed to": Randolph and Nicholas, *Considerations*, 31. "Disorders in Health": Adair and Schutz, eds., *Peter Oliver's Origins & Progress*, 75. "poor deluded" "patriotic Husband" "sage and baum" "scoured . . ." "their tender bowels . . ." "soothing and agreeable": *Norfolk Intelligencer*, August 11–18, 1774.

10. Shields, *Civil Tongues*, 113 n 21. Kowaleski-Wallace, "Tea, Gender, and Domesticity," 132. "cools, and allays Drought . . ." Mason, *The Good and Bad Effects of Tea*, 1–2. "very pernicious . . .": Mason, *The Good and Bad Effects of Tea*, 3. Essex Southern District Medical Society, *Memoir of Edward A. Holyoke*, 40–41.

11. "Liberty to buy" "age & bodily Infirmities . . ." "one of his Children . . ." "physicians" "Beeing sick . . .": Huntington Library, Mss HM 70291-70302. Elisha Williams, Tea Permits. Special thanks to Mary Beth Norton for this reference. Ukers, *All about Tea*, 1: 54.

12. "in a very low . . .": Smith, "Biographical Sketch of Col. David Mason," 203–204. "Doctor sell . . .": Westerly, Rhode Island, Westerly Town Clerk's Office. Town Meeting Minutes, August 9, 1774. "In behalf . . ." "all agreed . . .": HUNTER. Lawrence Taliaferro to James Hunter Jr., March 2, 1776. Mother Judah may have been an older slave. Special thanks to Anne Causey at UVa libraries for help tracking this reference. "beged . . ." "got a note . . ." "of leave . . .": Miller, ed., *The Selected Papers of Charles Willson Peale*, 1: 148, 150. *Maryland Gazette*, March 3 to May 19, 1774. "very ill" "permission . . .": Elizabeth Catherine De Rosset to John Burgwyn [1775]. Battle, ed., *Letters and Documents*, 28. Norton, *Liberty's Daughters*, 160.

13. Elisha Williams: Huntington Library. Tea Permits. Mss HM 70292. Seth Bird, confronted for drinking tea at Solomon and Martha Cowles's house in Connecticut, claimed to be a good Patriot who only drank tea because he had a cold. (Anderson, *The Martyr and the Traitor*, 87.) Young, "The Women of Boston," 208. "were cautious enough . . ." "lay in large Stocks . . ." "could be sick . . ." "Evasion of Sickness" "They, poor Souls! . . .": Adair and Schutz, eds., *Peter Oliver's Origins & Progress*, 73. The ban on British imports, "medicines excepted," caused a dispute in Norfolk, Virginia, when Doctor Alexander Gordon imported medicines under the provincial exception but was caught out because the *Continental* Association did not provide such an exception. The committee argued that Continental rules superseded provincial ones. (*Norfolk Intelligencer*, February 9–23, 1775.) David John Mays, *Edmund Pendleton*, 1: 352 n 22.

14. "permits" "under pretence . . ." "except . . .": *Connecticut Courant*, April 8, 1776.

15. "cram . . .": Truxes, "Ireland, New York, and the Eighteenth-Century Atlantic World," 30. "Bostonians . . .": NYG, April 18, 1774, *Massachusetts Spy*, April 28, 1774. "We hear . . ." "in case . . .": *Boston Post-Boy*, May 16, 1774.

16. Olson, *Emblems of American Community*, 112, 141.

17. Olson, "Pictorial Representations," 1–2, 5, 10, 15, 19, 21, 24.

18. Olson, "Pictorial Representations," 17, 27.

19. "Or Cherokee Indians . . .": PHL, 10: 325. "Americans were weaned . . .": Miller, *Origins*, 352. Berkin, *Revolutionary Mothers*, 20 alludes to this as well. There are no econometric data on tea and coffee consumption to back Miller up. *Boston Gazette*, December 20, 1773 and February 14, 1774. Labaree, *Boston Tea Party*, 164.

20. "biblical parodic satire": *Amer Chron*, 29. *Amer Chron*, 11, 15, 18. Slauter, "Reading and Radicalization," 14, 40.

21. "And hast . . .": *Amer Chron*, 76. "And yet . . .": *Amer Chron*, 77. Granger, *Political Satire*, 69.

22. "And behold! . . .": *Amer Chron*, 51. "She that . . ." "made tributary . . .": *Amer Chron*, 54. "to sell . . .": *Amer Chron*, 63.

23. "free-will offering": *Amer Chron*, 70. The *Peggy Stewart* and *Virginia* were covered in chapter 5, which appeared in February 1775. *Amer Chron*, 38–39. "Marylandites . . ." "they kept a good . . ." "it came to pass . . ." "Wherefore . . ." "Now they were . . .": *Amer Chron*, 70. "onward . . .": *Amer Chron*, 71.

24. "there came . . .": *Amer Chron*, 75. Some of Leacock's passages are meant to be read as mocking how Patriots spoke about their conduct; however, no evidence exists that these passages meant to frame Patriots as intentionally ironic.

25. "Propaganda . . .": Wood, "Rhetoric and Reality," 31.

9. Tea's Sex

1. There has been some study of women and tea. Norton, *Separated by Their Sex*. Kierner, *Beyond the Household*. Norton, *Liberty's Daughters*, 157–163. Kerber, *Women of the Republic*, 37–44. On gender and advertising: Keyes, "Early American advertising." On women tea sellers: Smith, "Social Visions," 40. Norton, *Separated by Their Sex*, 170. Shields, *Civil Tongues*, 116.

2. Egle, *Some Pennsylvania Women*, 127. Labaree, *Boston Tea Party*, 167. "Families" "discontinued": *Newport Mercury*, February 14, 1774. "him or herself" "importing . . .": SCG, January 24, 1774. Emphasis added.

3. Norton, *Separated by Their Sex*, 146, 167. "if you have tea . . .": PUL Beatty Collection, Box 1, Folder 4 AM 9640, Charles Beatty to Cleona (Betsey) Beatty, April 6, 1775. *Newport Mercury*, February 7, 1774. "Sense" "Politeness": Blecki and Wulf, eds., *Milcah Martha Moore's Book*, 299. "domesticity . . .": Kierner, *Beyond the Household*, 78. Kowaleski-Wallace, "Tea, Gender, and Domesticity," 132. Dillard, *Historic Tea-Party*, 10. Shields, *Civil Tongues*, 104. "idle chatter": Ingrassia, "Fashioning," 289. "tattle and chat": Roth, "Tea Drinking in 18th Century America," 68.

4. Miller and Riggs, eds., *Journal of Dr. Elihu Ashley*, 41, 43, 72, 75, 79, 82, 96, 109, 114, 137. Taverns: Miller and Riggs, *Journal of Dr. Elihu Ashley*, 74. Shields, *Civil Tongues*, 59. CRNC, 10: 1066.

5. "a dish of tea . . .": Singleton, *Social New York*, 383. Ashley: Miller and Riggs, eds., *Journal of Dr. Elihu Ashley*, 42, 73, 76, 77, 80, 86, 107, 118. "with an agreeable . . .": Anderson, *Martyr and the Traitor*, 107. "spruce Coxcomb": *Virginia Gazette* (Purdie and Dixon), January 20, 1774. "young ladies . . ." "parties of pleasure" "to dine . . .": M'Robert, *Tour*, 34. "maidens . . .": Crane, ed., *Diary of Elizabeth Drinker*, 1: 208, Watson, *Annals of Philadelphia*, 1: 432–433, PA Jrnl, April 5, 1775.

6. "Daddy at tea" "Daddy and John . . ." "tea at . . ." "Smith and I . . ." "Aunt Fisher" "Daddy Sansom . . .": Klepp and Wulf, eds., *Diary of Hannah Callender Sansom*, 262–263. "Daddy" was her father-in-law, Samuel Sansom Sr. "my friendly . . ." Besides, I like a dish of tea too": Seabury, *Free Thoughts*, 9.

7. Norton, *Separated by Their Sex*, 165. Norton, "Eighteenth-Century American Women," 396. However, when James Pitts's estate was inventoried at death, it listed tea kettles, tea stands, a tea board, tea table, and other tea accouterments. (MHS. Ms. N-726. Pitts Family Papers, 1648–1960. Box 1: Inventory of the Estate of the Honble James Pitts, May 1776.) Hartigan-O'Connor, "Measure of the Market," 297–298. Ulrich, *Age of Homespun*, 299–300.

8. Crane, ed., *The Diary of Elizabeth Drinker*, 1: 198, 199, 203, 204. "family went to Frankford" "had tea there": Ibid., 202. "drank coffee with us": Ibid., 207. Schulz, ed., *Papers of Eliza Lucas Pinckney*. Pinckney to Harriott Pinckney Horry, February 1775, February 12, 1775.

9. "not drank" "since last Christmas" "parties of pleasure . . ." "great spirit of patriotism": Egle, *Some Pennsylvania Women*, 127.

10. Mary Bostwick Roberdeau (d. 1777) was wife of Daniel Roberdeau, a Philadelphia merchant and Patriot.

11. "Your husbands . . .": *Virginia Gazette* (Rind), September 15, 1774. Norton, *Liberty's Daughters*, 157. Young, "The Women of Boston," 192–193, 203–205. Kierner, *Beyond the Household*, 81. *Morning Chronicle and London Advertiser*, January 16, 1775. SCG, November 21, 1774.

12. "Don't . . .": *Massachusetts Spy*, December 2, 1773, as cited in Young, "Women of Boston," 203–204. "enslave . . ." "forego . . ." "East-India Goods" "Regard . . ." "Fathers . . .": SCGJ, July 19, 1774.

13. "ADVERTISEMENT . . ." "Meeting" "a Number . . ." "to converse . . ." "Associate . . .": SCGJ, August 2, 1774. "use nor suffer . . .": *Newport Mercury*, February 7, 1774. "bid adieu . . .": *Newport Mercury*, February 14, 1774. Hartigan-O'Connor, "Measure of the Market," 327. "We . . . Promise . . ." "friendly Visits" "to obtain . . .": SCGJ, August 16, 1774.

14. "Ladies" "Association . . ." "a total Disuse . . ." "Ruin" "our Country" "the Lives . . ." "the Liberty . . ." "purchase or buy" "counting . . .": SCG, September 19, 1774, Hartigan-O'Connor, "Measure of the Market," 328.

15. "watershed" "intelligent public discourse": Kierner, *Beyond the Household*, 78.

16. "Sisters and Countrywomen" "chiefly" "our sex" "Every Mistress . . ." "Self-Denial . . ." "many respectable Families" "be tame Spectators": SCGJ, July 19, 1774. Many thanks to Mary Beth Norton for digging up a copy of this otherwise missing issue in PRO CO 5/663 f138. "A Planter's Wife" was germinal. Its existence can be inferred by the references in later articles, written "To the Planter's Wife" (SCGJ, August 16, 1774) or by "The Husband of the Planter's Wife" (SCGJ, August 2, 1774), but has not been seen by most scholars. The exception is Cynthia Kierner, *Beyond the Household*, 79–80, who found a reprinted version in Rind's *Virginia Gazette*, September 15, 1774.

17. "Ladies . . ." "rouse . . ." "Test . . ." "I dare . . ." "Infamy" "weak . . .": SCGJ, August 16, 1774.

18. "Countrywomen": SCGJ, July 19, 1774. "sisterly" "countrywomen" "Ladies of Pennsylvania" "public virtue" "banish . . ." "aromatic herbs" "cooperate with" "fair sex . . ." "instrumental" "redress" "filled . . .": *Virginia Gazette* (Rind), September 15, 1774. Kierner, *Beyond the Household*, 79. "Have you . . ." "your Country": SCGJ, August 2, 1774 Emphasis added.

19. "Planter" could refer to smallholders who worked their own farms (Holton, *Forced Founders*, 49). However the term could also refer to grandees, as in the "principal planters and landholders" of the province. (SCG, December 6, 1773.) Classical references in "A Planter's Wife" suggest the latter was meant. "Ladies" also sometimes referred to all free women, but the lady who received "a handsome Set of TEA CHINA" was not an everywoman. On uses of "lady," see Brown, *Good Wives*. In the *Iliad* Andromache, Hector's wife, was described as a perfect wife and good mother.

20. "a Lady's Adieu . . .": *Virginia Gazette* (Purdie and Dixon), January 20, 1774. "Written by a LADY . . .": *Virginia Gazette* (Purdie and Dixon), June 16, 1774. "uncommon . . ." "Chariots": SCGJ, August 16, 1774. Jones, *Wealth of a Nation to Be*.

21. "gaudy attire" "pretty" chest . . ." "spruce": Roth, "Tea Drinking," 68. Ingrassia, "Fashioning," 288–290. Anderson, *Mahogany*. Norton, *Separated by Their Sex*, 165.
Kowaleski-Wallace, "Tea, Gender, and Domesticity," 137.

22. Hartigan-O'Connor, "Measure of the Market," 328–329. "luxury . . .": Bloch,
"The Gendered Meanings of Virtue," 45.

23. Norton, *Separated by Their Sex*, 164, 144–145. "ladies . . ." "last day . . .": Cresswell, *Journal*, 58. "The Ladys . . . make themselves . . .": *LDC*, 3: 192. Oliver Wolcott
to Samuel Lyman. February 3, 1776. "permited . . .": *LDC*, 3: 546. Wolcott to Thomas
Seymour. April 16, 1776. Warren, *Poems*, 201–205, 210. "weak" "finest muslins . . ." sex's
due": Ibid., 211. "female ornaments": Ibid., 208. "opinion . . .": Ibid., 202.

24. "allow": PUL. John Beatty Family Collection 1768–1804. Box 1 Folder 19 AM
1601. Reading Beatty to Enoch Green. December 19, 1775. Emphasis added.

25. Tennent: *SCGCJ*, August 2, 1774. "obvious hyperbole": Norton, *Liberty's
Daughters*, 159.

26. "engine of slavery" "Tea, chains . . ." "high treason . . ." "'Taste . . ." "Here and
there . . .": Ramsay, "Sermon on Tea," 6.

27. "young and fair" "attract . . ." "will either suffuse . . .": Ramsay, Sermon on Tea,"
7. "Bile" "shrivels . . ." "Wrinkles" "Deformity": Shields, *Civil Tongues*, 115–116.

28. *SCGCJ*, September 6, 1774. Olson, "Pictorial Representations," 19.

29. Norton, *Separated by Their Sex*, 154. Some women read newspapers, though fe-
male literacy lagged male literacy. Lockridge, *Literacy in Colonial New England*. *SCGCJ*,
September 6, 1774. *Virginia Gazette* (Dixon and Hunter), June 3 and 24, 1775, *Providence
Gazette*, March 4, 1775, reprinted *Virginia Gazette* (Purdie), April 7, 1775.

30. "Vanity . . .": *SCGCJ*, July 19, 1774. "Don't . . ." "We'll . . .": *Newport Mercury*, February 14, 1774. "many unjust . . ." "Our Countrymen . . ." "and will . . ." "We have
now . . .": *SCGCJ*, August 16, 1774. "Few manly . . ." "round . . ." "good Cornelias"
"worthy men" "fight . . .": Warren, *Poems*, 212.

31. "Advertisement, Addressed to the LADIES": *Connecticut Courant*, February 13,
1775.

32. "no Tory" "obey": *Connecticut Courant*, February 13, 1775. Smart, "A Life William Beadle," 110, 114. Halttunen, *Murder Most Foul*, 52–53. "A Narrative of the Life of
William Beadle," 5, 21.

33. "Hannah Hopeful . . .": Young, "Women of Boston" 203–304. Norton, *Separated
by Their Sex*, 144, 159, 160. Kierner, *Beyond the Household*, 78. Osell, "Tatling Women
in the Public Sphere," 283–4, 286. "as a policing force": Ibid., 293.

34. Ramsay, "Sermon on Tea," 6. Kierner, *Beyond the Household*, 78, 82. Cleary, *Elizabeth Murray*, 201–202. Norton, *Separated by Their Sex*, 144, 159.

35. Various versions of the "Adieu" appeared. The version in Roth, "Tea Drinking,"
68 is quoted here. Roth's version is longer than the version in *Virginia Gazette* (Purdie
and Dixon), January 20, 1774. In both, the woman is "taught" (by men) what to think
about politics, and "Girls," "old maids," and the "spruce coxcomb" "laugh" like fools.
Cf. Norton, *Liberty's Daughters*, 159. "Written by a LADY" "Horrour" "resign" *Virginia
Gazette* (Purdie and Dixon), June 16, 1774. "are we forever . . .": Benjamin H. Irvin, "Of
Eloquence 'Manly' and 'Monstrous,'" 204.

36. Schulz, ed., *Papers of Eliza Lucas Pinckney*. Eliza Lucas Pinckney to Harriott
Pinckney Horry, February 1775 and February 12, 1775.

37. "evening dish" "tea-table" "a female army" "entirely" "whim and pride": Ramsay, "Sermon on Tea," 3, 6. "Diverse . . ." "old women . . .": Smith, "Social Visions," 53. "The Bodies . . ." "hysterics . . .": Hartigan-O'Connor, "Measure of the Market," 328. *Newport Mercury*, February 28, 1774. "Histeria" "reduced . . ." "it has turned . . .": Ramsay, "Sermon on Tea," 4.

38. "when a number . . .": *Virginia Gazette* (Rind), August 11, 1774. "hegemonic norms" "grammar of manhood": Kann, *A Republic of Men*, 3. "Luxury . . .": *Virginia Gazette* (Purdie and Dixon), January 20, 1774.

39. "act like men": Kann, *Republic of Men*, 31. Drake, *Tea Leaves*, clxxvi. *Newport Mercury*, February 7, 1774. Kerber, *Women of the Republic*, 39, citing Milton Halsey Thomas, ed., *Elias Boudinot's Journey to Boston*, x. Thomas gives no sourcing. The incident is possibly a didactic myth. "exhorters": Young, "Women of Boston," 203–204.

40. "Ladies . . ." "sacrifice . . ." "should inspire" "firmness . . .": SCG, April 3, 1775. "worthy" "Conviction," *Providence Gazette*, March 4, 1775.

41. *Providence Gazette*, March 4, 1775.

42. "tea for . . .": Shattuck, *History of the Town of Concord*, 92–93. Ammerman, *Common Cause*, 114. Gross, *Minutemen and Their World*, 59.

43. "a dish of tea . . ." "I hate . . ." "open . . ." "let them examine . . .": Seabury, "Free thoughts," 20, 8, 19. "so cruel . . .": Blecki and Wulf, eds., *Milcah Martha Moore's Book*, 247. Marginal note by Wright.

44. PENELOPE House-Wife: *Norfolk Intelligencer*, August 11–18, 1774.

45. "determined . . .": *New Hampshire Gazette*, February 4, 1774. *Connecticut Gazette*, February 11, 1774. *London Chronicle*, March 31, 1774, reprinted Halsey, *The Boston Port Bill*, 308–309. Kierner, *Beyond the Household*, 82. The misnomer came from later generations seeking a revolutionary heritage they could connect to Boston. Norton, *Liberty's Daughters*, 161. These later North Carolinians thought, as their Loyalist predecessors, that since it was a women's protest it *had to be* about tea. "protest . . ." "Is there . . .": Higginbotham, ed., *Papers of James Iredell*, 1: 282–284. On conservative satire: Norton, *1774*, 64. Irvin, "Of Eloquence 'Manly' and 'Monstrous,'" 207.

10. Prohibition as Conformity

1. All quotes: *Providence Gazette*, March 4, 1775. The papers were RNYG and *Boston Post-Boy*.

2. Quotations: 4 Am Arch, 2: 920. Sabine, 2: 426. On threat by metonymy, Withington, *Toward a More Perfect Union*, 234.

3. *Virginia Gazette* (Purdie), April 7, 1775. Glickman, *Buying Power*, 48–50.

4. "remind" "not to purchase . . .": Guild, *Early History of Brown University*, 283. The New York committee reminded its constituents similarly (4 Am Arch, 1: 1269). Weed was a common surname around Stamford. Mead, *Historie*. Huntington, *History of Stamford*. On Weed Tavern: Jenkins, *The Old Boston Post Road*, 165. Mock executions: Withington, *Toward a More Perfect Union*, 144–184.

5. "There is . . .": Willard, *Letters on the American Revolution*, 22. "commonly . . ." "striving . . .": Padelford, ed., *Colonial Panorama 1775*, 37

6. "expensive diversions": Cont Assoc. "the method . . .": *Sullivan, Disaffected*, 33. "the most significant . . ." "crisis . . .": Crary, *Price of Loyalty*, 2, 56. Schlesinger, "The American Revolution Reconsidered," 77.

7. "in a body . . ." "was signed . . .": *SCG*, April 3, 1775. Crist, "Cumberland County," 119–120. Albemarle: Ragsdale, *Planters' Republic*, 227. Bear and Stanton, eds., *Jefferson's Memorandum Books*, 1: 381. Ammerman, *Common Cause*, 109, 111–124. Committees had high membership levels in Massachusetts, Connecticut, South Carolina, and Virginia. Phillips, *1775*, 260.

8. Withington, *Toward a More Perfect Union*, 219–220. Meroney, *Inseparable Loyalty*, 119. Parker: Benson, "Wealth and Power in Virginia," 165. Bailey: Maguire, "Parry's Journal," xlvi–xlvii. Georgia: Schlesinger, *Colonial Merchants*, 551. The governor referred to the defense association, which was signed together with the commercial association in Georgia in the summer of 1775. "Every body": Norton, *British-Americans*, 35. Allason: Ragsdale, *Planter's Republic*, 230. Hulton: Crary, *Price of Loyalty*, 30. Allen: Aptheker, *American Revolution*, 82.

9. "statement" "communal solidarity": Glickman, *Buying Power*, 46. Duane and Galloway: Becker, *History of Political Parties*, 150. Burnett, *Continental Congress*, 55. "consensus," "extraordinary unanimity": Ammerman, *Common Cause*, 101.

10. Norton uses "conformity": Norton, "The Seventh Tea Ship," 708. "drive . . .": Brown, *Revolutionary Politics*, 180, see also 203. Unity required the end of opposition, which was achieved, according to Brown, when "overwhelming popular majorities" could "compel harmonious behavior," which does not seem harmonious. "offer": Gross, *Minutemen and Their World*, 50. "every person . . ." "to pass . . ." "If found guilty . . ." "humbling . . .": Shattuck, *A History of the Town of Concord*, 89. Gross, *Minutemen and Their World*, 50–51, 55, 58, 63. Gross implies that Concord was unified at this time. Spy: Gross, *Minutemen*, 111. Emphasis added. Signing campaigns: Ryerson, *The Revolution Is Now Begun*, 98. Sullivan, *Disaffected*, 10–11, 29.

11. "If they have . . .": Schlesinger, *Colonial Merchants*, 510. "I shall ever . . .": Benson, "Wealth and Power in Virginia," 166. Sullivan, *Disaffected*, 8.

12. "American Constitution": LVa, Charles Steuart Papers. f288 Parker to Steuart, November 27, 1774.

13. "Although . . .": Schlesinger, *Colonial Merchants*, 546. Denying Congress's authority was a step beyond merely not signing the Association. Madison: Irvin, "Tar, Feathers, and Enemies of American Liberties," 217. Coffin: NHA. Kezia Coffin Fanning Papers. MS2 folder 5, December 29, 1775. Hopkins: Crary, *Price of Loyalty*, 63–64. Connecticut: Connecticut State Archives, Revolutionary War, 1st Series, vol. 1, 390a, 395, 396–8. "speech crimes": Irvin, "Tar, Feathers, and Enemies of American Liberties," 216. Thompson, *Rum Punch & Revolution*, 165–166.

14. Cont Assoc.

15. Mays, *Edmund Pendleton 1721–1803. A Biography*, 1: 302. On Congress: *JCC*, 4: 205.

16. Irvin, "Tar, Feathers, and Enemies of American Liberties," 223. Hamilton, *John Ettwein*. Mekeel, *Quakers and the American Revolution*. Ryerson, *The Revolution Is Now Begun*. Adelman, "Strangers," 114. Eddis: Land, *Letters from America*, 100. "French leave": Land, *Letters from America*, 122. Terror included force, violence, and public humiliation, but not (yet) torture or death. Coleman, *Thomas McKean*, 141. Emigration: Norton, *British Americans*, 25–26, 34, 38. Schlesinger, *Colonial Merchants*, 393–431, 552–559.

17. "a traitor . . .": Levy, *Emergence*, 178. Jefferson meant this liberally: Tories that opposed the common cause but had not taken up arms against it. Yet it still meant politics became a crime. *Proceedings of the Conventions of the Province of Maryland*, 47, 109–111. 4 Am Arch, 2: 76; 3: 593. Scharf, *History of Maryland*, 2: 184–185. Hamilton, *John Ettwein*, 154–155. Ireland, "Bucks County," 33. "Minutes of the Committee of Safety of Bucks County," 265, 277–278. In New York, anti-Loyalist riots pushed disarmed non-associators underground. Barck Jr., *New York City*, 43. Schlesinger, *Colonial Merchants*, 543. Flick, *American Revolution in New York*, 318. Venables, "Tryon County," 186–187.

18. "because . . .": Speech of Edmund Burke in Cobbett, *Parliamentary History of England*, 22: 225. Pollock would eventually become a Loyalist, staying when the British took Newport at the end of 1776. He left when the British evacuated in 1779, but there is no indication tea (as opposed to staying for the British occupation) was his crime. RISA General Assembly Papers. Revolutionary War. Suspected Persons, 1775–1783. Trading with enemy: Truxes, *Defying Empire*. Parliament recognized the non-juring status of various religious minorities. Past British practice informed the revolutionary use of affirmations. Meanwhile, the contest for minority religious communities' support constrained how aggressive revolutionaries' attitudes on oaths could be.

19. Police powers: Gerlach, *Prologue to Independence*, 249.

20. "make Oath . . .": NDAR, 3: 1367. HSP Am.817 Cargo manifests conveyed to the Committee of Observation of Philadelphia, Northern Liberties, and Southwark 1774. NDAR, 1: 6. Ward, *The War for Independence*, 11. Smith, *Freedoms We Lost*, 114.

21. Schlesinger, *Colonial Merchants*, 370, 486, 517. "generally refused": Devine, ed., *A Scottish firm in Virginia*, 173–174. Mays, *Pendleton Biography*, 1: 301–302. Benson, "Wealth and Power in Virginia," 162.

22. Fichter, "Collecting Debts." "a pole erected . . .": *British Records Relating to America . . . Papers of Henry Fleming*. Fleming to Fisher & Bragg, November 17, 1774. Cf. Crary, *Price of Loyalty*, 58–59. "voluntarily and generally": *Virginia Gazette* (Purdie and Dixon), November 10, 1774.

23. "itinerant . . .": Ragsdale, *A Planters' Republic*, 234. Peddlers were active in Appalachia but received less attention because committees took longer to form in this area. Virginia peddlers timed their arrivals to court days. Martin, *Buying into the World of Goods*, 46.

24. 4 Am Arch, 3: 729.

25. "Tea Merchants . . .": *Boston Gazette* October 2, 1775. All other quotes: *Boston Gazette*, October 16, 1775.

26. Smith, "Social Visions," 44. "heartily sorry": *Boston Gazette*, October 16, 1775. Breen, *Marketplace of Revolution*, 311–312. Schlesinger, *Colonial Merchants*, 302 n 2. 4 Am Arch, 2: 1678.

27. Jaffee, "Peddlers of Progress." Benes and Benes, *Itinerancy in New England and New York*, 7. Tea peddling occurred in Britain, too. Mui and Mui, "Smuggling and the British Tea Trade," 51. Wright, *Hawkers & Walkers*, 89–91. "any Hawker . . .": Ammerman, *Common Cause*, 119. "according to Law": *New Hampshire Gazette*, January 20, 1775. Schlesinger, *Colonial Merchants*, 484–485. Epsom: 4 Am Arch, 1: 1105–6. Irvin, "Tar, Feathers, and Enemies of American Liberties," 214. "cannot . . ." "going from Town to Town . . ." "be very violent . . ." "make a thorough . . ." "find any India . . .": 4 Am Arch, 1: 1339–1340. Schlesinger, *Colonial Merchants*, 482.

28. Worrell: *PA Jrnl*, May 17, 1775. Withington: *Massachusetts Spy*, 13, 1774. Cook: Norton, "Seventh Tea Ship," 692, 695. Truro: NYPL, Boston Committee of Correspondence Records, Truro to Boston committee, February 28, 1774. Breen, *Marketplace of Revolution*, 294–296. *Oxford English Dictionary Online*, s.vv. "inadvertency," "inadvertent," http://www.oed.com/view/Entry/93041. Patriots later accused Worrell of treason for aiding the British army at Philadelphia. Pennsylvania, *Minutes of the Supreme Executive Council*, 11: 515.

29. Angell: *Pennsylvania Mercury*, October 20, 1775. "frequent complaints . . .": 4 Am Arch, 3: 975–976. Schlesinger, *Colonial Merchants*, 581. Withington, *Toward a More Perfect Union*, 222–224. Norton, *British-Americans*, 23.

30. "refractory shopkeepers" "I shall . . ." "I don't . . .": Deane, *History of Scituate*, 134–135. "declared . . .": 4 Am Arch, 2: 298. "It was reported . . ." "chicanery": 4 Am Arch, 2: 448. "absolutely false" "wickedness . . ." "characters" "impeached": 4 Am Arch, 2: 548, 3: 584, 2: 917. "publick enemy": Papas, *That Ever Loyal Island*, 30. Ibid., 28, 33.

31. "comply" "sine a covenant" "Aganst the law": New Hampshire State Archives. Petitions to the General Court. Tory: Packersfield: Breed Batchelor, Confiscated Estate (1775–92). Packersfield Committee to New Hampshire General Assembly, March 19, 1776. Nelson Picnic Association et al., *Celebration*, 10, 12, 19, 21–24. The surname is standardized as "Batchelder" here.

32. "refused . . .": New Hampshire State Archives. Petitions to the General Court. Tory: Packersfield: Breed Batchelor, Confiscated Estate (1775–92). Packersfield Committee to New Hampshire General Assembly, March 19, 1776.

33. "a quantity of Tea" "in the Brush . . ." "bringing . . ." "Retaild . . ." "would . . ." "Examine or disturb" "Enemical": New Hampshire State Archives. Petitions to the General Court. Fitzwilliam Committee to New Hampshire General Assembly. March 6, 1776. "bad behueyer" "Distorbance" "trouble" "lardg" "paddeling . . .": New Hampshire State Archives. Petitions to the General Court. Packersfield Committee to New Hampshire General Assembly, March 19, 1776. "Damned . . ." "kill": New Hampshire State Archives. Petitions to the General Court. Petitions to the General Court. Tory: Packersfield: Breed Batchelor, Confiscated Estate (1775–92). Josephus Rugg statement, March 19, 1776. Norton, *History of Fitzwilliam*, 218–219. Knouff, "That Abundant, Infamous Roach," 152.

34. "that once since . . .": *Virginia Gazette* (Pinkney), June 1, 1775. Cowles: Crary, *Price of Loyalty*, 56. *Connecticut Gazette*, April 14, 1775. Breen, *Marketplace of Revolution*, 327–329. "open Violation" "voluntary": *Essex Gazette*, March 28, 1775. Lilly: Smith, "Social Visions," 45. 4 Am Arch, 2: 234.

35. "violated . . ." "Pigg . . ." "do as he pleased" "a traitor . . ." "break off . . .": Scribner, 2: 300.

36. "Stiles . . ." "yo . . ." "I have . . .": Connecticut State Archives. Revolutionary War. 1st Series, vol. 1: 376. Deposition of David Wood, May 2, 1776.

37. "Such examples . . ." "If a delegate . . ." "drank . . .": MHS, *Proceedings*, 4: 382–383. William Ellery to Henry Marchant, March 27, 1775. Lovejoy, *Rhode Island Politics*, 180.

38. "a Whig dared not . . .": Lovejoy, *Rhode Island Politics*, 188.

39. "He was . . ." "promising . . .": MHS, *Proceedings*, 4: 381. Ellery to Marchant, March 27, 1775. Fowler, *William Ellery*, 16, 18. Broadside appeared on April 17. Lovejoy, *Rhode Island Politics*, 176–177, 179, 182, 184. Bartlett, ed., *Records of the Colony of Rhode Island*, 274. *Newport Mercury*, January 10, April 25, 1774.

40. "shake" "John Jencks . . .": MHS, *Proceedings*, 4: 382. Ellery to Marchant, March 27, 1775. Staples, *Annals*, 246, 651–652.

41. "Tories . . ." "gave great offense" "sensitive patriotism": Quincy, *History of Harvard University*, 2: 164. "both sides . . ." "the hall . . ." "disagreeable" "grief" "carried . . ." "advised" "harmony . . .": Harvard University Archives. Faculty minutes, 1806–1994 (inclusive) (UAIII 5.5.2, IV: 4–5). Emphasis added. Destler, *Joshua Coit*, 13.

42. Stout, *The Perfect Crisis*, 151.

43. Clark, "Early American Journalism," 1: 357. Botein "Printers and the American Revolution," 19, 32–49. Weir, "The Role of the Newspaper in the Southern Colonies," 114. Humphrey, *"This Popular Engine,"* 37–38. Martin, *Free and Open Press*, 87. Botein, "'Meer Mechanics,'" 214, 217. *"cloven foot"* "looked upon . . .": *SCG*, November 29, 1773. The offending items appear to have run in Robert Wells's *SCAGG*, November 26, 1773; however, this issue has not been found. Timothy suggested Wells was not a real Carolinian (*SCG*, April 30, 1774). Lambert, *South Carolina Loyalists*, 25–26. Brown, "Shifting Freedoms of the Press," 373. "It is but . . .": William Glanville Evelyn to Revd Dr. Evelyn, February 18, 1775, in Barnes and Barnes, *The American Revolution through British Eyes*, 1: 16. "if you print . . .": Levy, *Emergence of a Free Press*, 175. Mob was led by Alexander McDougall, John Morin Scott, Isaac Sears, and John Lamb. Charles Inglis's *Deceiver Unmasked* was later printed in Philadelphia. Clark, *Thomas Paine*, 195–196. Loudon beseeched the New York committee for protection, arguing that, as a Patriot, he was entitled to press freedom. Thomas, *History of Printing*, 312. Brigham, *American Newspapers*, 675. Loudon printed Paine's *American Crisis* (1777). Martin, *Free and Open Press*, 90. Schlesinger, *Prelude*, 257–258. Teeter, "'King' Sears," 543. Adams, "The Colonial German-language Press," 214–216. Sullivan, *Disaffected*, 23–24. Gould, "Loyalist Responses to Common Sense," 105–127.

44. Wermuth, "The Central Hudson Valley," 137. Smith, *The Freedoms We Lost*, 111, 126–127. Ranlet, *New York Loyalists*, 49. Withington, *Toward a More Perfect Union*, 226. 4 Am Arch, 2: 35–36. 4 Am Arch, 1: 1013. Sabine, 1: 302, https://www.episcopalchurch.org/library/glossary/chandler-thomas-bradbury.

45. "As to . . ." "I only . . .": Beatty: Beatty, ed., "Beatty Letters," 235. "dirty . . ." "Friends of America": Pomerantz, "The Patriot Newspaper and the American Revolution," 316. Ford, ed., *Correspondence and Journals of Samuel Blachley Webb*, 1: 46–47. 4 Am Arch, 2: 12–13, 36–37. Crary, "The Tory and the Spy," 66–67. Mason, *Road to Independence*, 54. Martin, *Free and Open Press*, 87–88. Teeter, "King' Sears," 543. Maier, *The Old Revolutionaries*, 87–88.

46. Levy, *Emergence of a Free Press*, 83–88. Martin, *Free and Open Press*, 78. "no Loss . . .": Martin, *Free and Open Press*, 88, citing *SCG*, December 19, 1774. Newport: 4 Am Arch, 2: 12–13. Buel, "Freedom of the Press in Revolutionary America," 61–62. Levy, *Emergence*, 174. "press of freedom": *Pennsylvania Gazette*, September 27, 1775, as cited in Martin, *Free and Open Press*, 89. "censure": Sullivan, *Disaffected*, 25. Schlesinger, *Prelude*, 189.

47. "poisoning . . .": Botein, "'Meer Mechanics,'" 225. Humphrey, *"This Popular Engine,"* 89.

48. "violently exclusionary": Martin, *Free and Open Press*, 81. Ibid., 83, 88, 90. Bickham, *Making Headlines*. Potter and Calhoon, "The Character and Coherence of the Loyalist Press" 231, 250. Holt: Martin, *Free and Open Press*, 86. Cooper: *RNYG*, November 18,

1773. Clark, "Early American Journalism" 1: 362. Weir, "The Role of the Newspaper in the Southern Colonies," 138. Botein, "Printers and the American Revolution," 36. Humphrey, *This Popular Engine,* 37.

49. Some printers organized their own couriers. Miner, *William Goddard*, 112. Clark, "Early American Journalism." Humphrey, *This Popular Engine,* 35, 79. "at the POST OFFICE": *Virginia Gazette* (Purdie and Dixon), November 10, 1774. Sprowle: Schlesinger, *Colonial Merchants*, 511. *Virginia Gazette* (Purdie), December 22, 29, 1775. Warner, *Letters of the Republic*, xi.

50. On British government opening mail, see Mason, ed., *Norton and Sons*, 378 and Sellers, *Patience Wright*, 69. On the new post: Brown, *Revolutionary Politics*, 179, 181. Thomas, *History of Printing*, 258. Adelman, "A Constitutional Conveyance," 711–754. Hartford: "Journal Kept in Quebec in 1775 by James Jeffry," *EIHC*, 50 no 2 (April 1914) 109–110. Curwen: Oliver, ed., *Samuel Curwen*, 1: 11 n 17. "Parliamentary Post": Miner, *William Goddard*, 136. Marston, *King and Congress*, 228, 230. Miner, *William Goddard*, 114–136, 147. Adelman, *Revolutionary Networks*, 188–126. Parkinson, *Common Cause*. See also LVa. Virginia Convention, Intercepted letters, December 5, 1775. Accession 30003. Land, *Letters from America*, 117, 119. Packets and navy: PRO CO 5/76, 287.

51. "slaughtered . . .": Lee, *Crowds and Soldiers*, 140. CRNC, 10: 51. Letter from Massachusetts to the Committee of South Carolina, June 30, 1775, in *Cape Fear Mercury*, July 28, 1775. Depositions: 4 Am Arch, 2: 491–494. Miner, *William Goddard*, 146. Mary Goodard printed "General Gage's account . . .": Evans 14192. Gage's account may have reached South Carolina. This is implied by the Massachusetts provincial congress's reference to Gage's account in its letter to the South Carolina committee, cited above. Fischer, *Paul Revere's Ride*, 269–280. Adelman, *Revolutionary Networks*, 131–137.

52. Schlesinger, *Prelude to Independence*. Davidson, *Propaganda*. Adams: Irvin, "Tar, Feathers, and Enemies of American Liberties," 212 n 33. Ellery: MHS, *Proceedings*, 4: 382. William Ellery to Henry Marchant, Newport, March 27, 1775. Thomson: Labaree, *Boston Tea Party*, 157.

53. McDonnell, *The Politics of War*, 169–170, 173. At Norfolk, both sides started fires, but the wind favored the Patriot fires, which destroyed 1331 buildings to Dunmore's 51.

54. "fertile Soil . . .": Tatum Jr., ed., *The American Journal of Ambrose Serle*, 140. Labaree, *Boston Tea Party*, x, 90. The idea that the Tea Act was intended to establish a precedent originated in England—where writers knew less about how things worked in the colonies. York, *Henry Hulton*, 157–158. Willard, *Letters on the American Revolution*, 26–27. "entirely destroyed": *Massachusetts Spy*, March 10, 1774. Boston Patriots so overstated William Smith's and John Fillis's Patriotism that these men had to defend their loyalty to Governor Legge. "liberty boys . . .": 4 Am Arch, 3: 780. "what they wanted . . .": Brebner, *Neutral Yankees*, 170 n 177. Weir, "The Role of the Newspaper in the Southern Colonies," 125. Smith, *The Freedoms We Lost*, 121.

11. Tea Drinkers

1. *Minutes of the Provincial Congress and the Council of Safety of the State of New Jersey*, 94–95. Gerlach, *Prologue to Independence*, 198–199, 250. "not such a patriot . . .": PUL. Beatty Collection, Box 1, folder 4, AM 9640. Charles Beatty to Betsey Beatty, April 6, 1775. Fithian: Beatty, ed., "Beatty Letters, 1773–1782," 231, 234 n 12. Farish, ed., *Jour-*

nal and Letters of Philip Vickers Fithian, 282. There is no proof Fithian broke the ban for his bride. Miller, ed., *Selected Papers of Charles Willson Peale*, 1: 137, 170. HUNTER. Box 2. Isaac Bowes Memoranda, 1775. Item dated 1775 on folder, no date on document.

2. White, *Historical Collections*, 58–61, 65–68. Georgia's first provincial congress represented only a few parishes. "Proceedings of the Georgia Council of Safety," 15. *DNB*, s.v. "Telfair, Edward (c.1735–1807)." *ANB*, s.v. "Telfair, Edward." Duke. Edward Telfair Papers. Edward Telfair and Company Journal, 1775–1781.

3. Virginia governed the region as the District of West Augusta. Pennsylvania governed it as Westmorland county. "Burned . . .": Scribner, 4: 48. Buck and Buck, *The Planting of Civilization in Western Pennsylvania*, 180.

4. *New York Gazette*, March 25–April 15, 1776. McClallen's committee membership: Sullivan, ed., *Minutes of the Albany Committee of Correspondence*, 1: 367. Origin of goods: Ibid., 350, 383. Price gouging: Ibid., 363, 387. Sales of other goods: 4 Am Arch, 5: 857. The third partner was Robert Henry Jr., Colonial Albany Social History Project, Stefan Bielinski, "Robert Henry," *The People of Colonial Albany*, http://exhibitions.nysm .nysed.gov//albany/bios/h/rhenry8425.html. Stefan Bielinski, "Robert Henry, Jr.," Ibid., http://exhibitions.nysm.nysed.gov//albany/bios/h/rhenry8426.html. Stefan Bielinski, "Robert Mc Clallan," Ibid., http://exhibitions.nysm.nysed.gov//albany/bios /m/romccl725.html. Surname standardized as McClallen. Countryman, *A People in Revolution*, 142.

5. Schlesinger, *Colonial Merchants*, 472, 548. Coleman, *American Revolution in Georgia*, 45–47, 50, 61. Only one Georgia parish—St. John's—signed the Association in 1774. Hall, *Land and Allegiance*, 21. Duke. Edward Telfair Papers. "Telfair, Edward, and Company, Journal, 1775–1781." *Georgia Gazette*, June 14, 1775.

6. Barrell: Baker. Barrell Company Account Books, 1770–1803, B271, vol. 1: 440–441. Barrell's Patriotism: Ford, ed., *Boston in 1775*, 3. Murray: MHS. James Murray Papers, P-141, Reel 2: Account Book 1766–1781. Stark, *Loyalists of Massachusetts*, 283. Tufts: Schlesinger, *Colonial Merchants*, 481–482. 4 Am Arch, 2: 234. Charles Hamilton used the same excuse in Lancaster, Pennsylvania. Ellis and Evans, *History of Lancaster*, 36–37. "I will not . . .": 4 Am Arch, 2: 282. Thomas, "A List of Graduates of Harvard Who Were Tories," 79. Sabine, 2: 367.

7. "on account . . ." "into the hands . . .": PRO T 29/43, f179. Young, "The Women of Boston," 206. Boyle, "Boyle's Journal," *NEHGR*, 85: 5–28. Cain, "Anxiety and Distress." Thomas and Peach, eds., *Correspondence of Richard Price*, 1: 222, 228.

8. PRO CUST 17/4. Tufts: Thomas, "A List of Graduates," 79. MHS. Amory Family Papers 1697–1894 Ms. N-2024 (Tall) Wastebook 1774–1784 (vol. 13). MHS. James Murray Papers, P-141 Reel 2: Account Book 1766–1781. Soley: MHS. Gilbert Deblois ledger book, 1769–1792. Ms. N-2258. 1, 2, 5, 46, 48, 49. One wonders why Soley was in Boston. He may have wanted to guard his stores against British troops. Sargent, *Letters of John Andrews*, 95.

9. IOR B/91 206, 290. At minimum, this seems to have included Richard Clarke.

10. *Massachusetts Gazette*, December 14 to 28, 1775; January 11 and 25, February 1 and 22, 1776. Sabine, 1: 386–387. £120 sterling of tea, rum, and sugar looted from William Perry. Cunningham, ed., *Letters and Diary of John Rowe*, 302–304. Stark, *Loyalists of Massachusetts*, 125. Sabine, 2: 565. On looting: Cain, "Anxiety and Distress," and Boyle, "Boyle's Journal," 117–133. "thrown . . .": New York Public Library. Newell, "Diary of

the Siege of Boston," 22. "kindly . . .": Robertson, *Archibald Robertson*, 78. Cargoes of Loyalist looters (like Crean Brush) seized by Patriots often went un-enumerated. They may have included tea. Continental Army: Frothingham, *History of the Siege of Boston*, 306–307, 406–408.

11. Grozart: Sabine, 2: 524. Perkins: Ibid., 2: 177 and Cunningham, ed., *Letters and Diary of John Rowe*, 315. Deblois: Sabine, 1: 362.

12. "freely . . .": 4 Am Arch, 1: 1177–78. Ibid., 125, 1249. Schlesinger, *Colonial Merchants*, 442, 477–478. Barnes and Barnes, eds., *American Revolution through British Eyes*, 1: 15. Gage to Dartmouth. February 17, 1775. French, *Siege of Boston*, 219.

13. Stackpole, *Nantucket in the American Revolution*. NHA MS2 folder 5, Kezia Coffin Fanning Papers. Diary. April 26, April 29, May 5, 1775. "Journal Kept in Quebec in 1775 by James Jeffry," 111. Oliver, ed., *Samuel Curwen*, 1: 11. "The distressed . . ." "for the Sake . . .": Sheffield City Archives. William Vassall Letterbooks, 96–97.

14. Bowen, *James Lloyd II*, 139–140. Vassall departed Nantucket for London in early August. Sheffield City Archives. Vassall Letterbooks, 100. Vassall was appointed mandamus councillor in 1774 and owned estates in Rhode Island and Jamaica. Bell, *George Washington's Headquarters*, 10. Stark, *Loyalists*, 137–140. Sabine, 2: 382–385. Recantation not related to tea drinking. Stark, *Loyalists of Massachusetts*, 127, 131. Essex Southern District Medical Society, *Memoir of Edward A. Holyoke*, 9, 26–28, 77. "old Friend . . .": William P. Upham, "Extracts from Letters Written at the Time of the Occupation of Boston by the British, 1775–6," *EIHC*, 13, no. 3 (July 1876), 207. Holyoke was an addresser of Hutchinson and Gage. Baker. Melatiah Bourn Papers [Mss. 733 1728–1803 B775], Box 2, folder 26 Melatiah Bourn Memoranda Book, May 31, 1775. Winslow, 41, 64, 126. Lovejoy, *Rhode Island Politics*, 190.

15. Stackpole, *Nantucket*, 16, 18, 27, 49. NHA. MS2 folder 5. July 5, 1776. There were almost no trees on the island which made mainland wood a necessity. Vassall Letterbooks, 98 William Vassall to Wedderburn Nantucket June 19, 1775. Pease supplied goods from Newport in the second half of 1775. Winslow, 64. Obed Macy, *History of Nantucket*, 83, 84, 87.

16. Rowland et al., *History of Beaufort County*, 1: 205, 206.

17. Schlesinger, *Colonial Merchants*, 493. Worthington: Miller and Riggs, eds., *Journal of Dr. Elihu Ashley*, 181–182. Several Hampshire county towns did not send delegates to the second provincial congress, which began sitting in February 1775 (Worthington was so divided it asked not to have to send a delegate), but all Hampshire towns sent delegates to the third provincial congress, which was a wartime gathering (Lincoln, ed., *Journals of the Provincial Congress of Massachusetts*, 79–80, 275–276). Moravians' and Mennonites' caution toward the common cause seems to have been as much a function of language as religion. Martin, *Buying into the World of Goods*, 83. Fries, *The Road to Salem*, 69, 198. Fries, *Records of the Moravians*, 2: 895. "only . . ." "Several . . .": Ibid., 2: 909.

18. "bigot" "Treated . . .": Cresswell, *Journal*, 107. This was real tea; Cresswell specifically noted tea made from other plants. Native American tea consumption is also noted in Rachel B. Herrmann, *No Useless Mouth*, 27, 128.

19. "two pounds of tea": NDAR, 3: 546–547. "the d—d . . .": Moore, *Memoir of Col. Ethan Allen*, 132. Cornelius Fellows ordered three pounds of tea in Ireland in 1775. Baker. Cornelius Fellows ledger, 1775–1791, Mss. 766. F332, 2. Captain Allan Hallet bought two pounds of tea in St. Domingue. NDAR, 4: 658.

20. Jeffry was born in Salem and educated in Quebec. "Journal Kept in Quebec in 1775 by James Jeffry," *EIHC*, 50 no 2 (April 1914) 97, 104, 107, 108, 110, 111, 114, 121, 129, 130, 132, 133, 135, 136, 138, 141, 142, 146, 149, 150. Mrs. Cabot may have been Mrs. George Cabot. Lodge, ed., *Life and Letters of George Cabot*, 11.

21. LoC Papers of Neil Jamieson, film # 17575, reel 8. Neil Jamieson Financial Papers, 1771–1782, 279. Sale February 26, 1776, to Logan Gilmour & Co. Jamieson had been part owner of a shipment on the *Mary and Jane* in 1774. Jamieson joined the Norfolk borough committee (probably to forestall effective enforcement): *Norfolk Intelligencer*, June 15, 1774. In several locations in Virginia, including Norfolk, Patriots used a broader county committee to prevent a merchant-friendly borough committee from being too lax. Patriots later seized Jamieson's property. Charles Lee to Edmund Pendleton, May 4, 1776, in "The Woodford, Howe, and Lee Letters," *Richmond College Historical Papers*, 1, no 1 (June 1915): 154–155. LoC John Glassford & Company Papers, MF#18978, Reel 3, Bladensburg Journal 1775–1777; Reel 17, Maryland Ledger, 1775 and Maryland Ledger, 1775–1776; Reel 57, Boyd's Hole Ledger, 1775–1776; Reel 70, Norfolk Day Book, 1775–1776. Sheriff: Reel 17, Maryland Ledger, 1775–1776 (1776), 46. Huie: Boyd's Hole Ledger, 1775–1776, 186.

22. Tate: UNC. Robert Wilson Account Books, 1772–1888, John Tate Journal. SV-1896/1. Byrne: North Carolina State Archives. Matthew and Margaret Byrne Collection, AB.76, General Store Ledger. Johnston: UNC. Cameron Family Papers, 1757–1978 Folder 3633, Invoice Book, 1773–1801, March 1775 and 1776 instore inventories. Powell, ed., *Dictionary of North Carolina Biography*, s.v. "William Johnston" and "Richard Bennehan."

23. Cornell: NYHS. Richard and Benjamin Cornell Account Book. Mss Collection BV Scarsdale Account book. Osborn: Barck, ed., *Papers of the Lloyd Family*, 2: 534. July 16 and October 10, 1775. Osborn appears to have been a tradesman. Lloyd later fled to Stamford and supplied the revolutionary army. Bowen, *James Lloyd II*, 134. Frederickstown: University of Pennsylvania: Manuscript Farmer's Ledger, 1774–1777. Ms. Codex 1587 http://hdl.library.upenn.edu/1017/d/medren/4919617. Ledger mislabeled by a librarian as a farmer's ledger; however, it is a merchant's ledger showing purchases of farm goods and sales of supplies. Six of the tea buyer residents of Frederickstown, New York, were probably farmers on the Philipse patent. Pelletreau, *History of Putnam County*, 122–127, 150, 437, 697. Taylor: NYHS MSS Collection BV John Taylor Papers, 1743–1775. Daybook 1774–1775. "all persons . . .": Judd, "Westchester County," 115 citing 4 Am Arch, 3: 150.

24. Sellers included Christopher Champlin, Elnathan Hammond, and Pierce and Potter. NHS. Christopher Champlin Shop Waste Book (1774–1775). Elnathan Hammond Day Book (1774–1790). Pierce, Clothier & Howard Potter Day Book, 1774–1730. Crane, *A Dependent People*, 117. Oliver, ed., *Samuel Curwen*, 1: 9.

25. Wright: Blecki and Wulf, eds., *Milcah Martha Moore's Book*, 247, item 82. Marginal note. "Monongoheley Balsam": Miller and Riggs, eds., *Journal of Dr. Elihu Ashley*, 188, 301. Memoirist: Maxwell, "My Mother," 98–99.

26. "Brethren . . ." "not give . . .": Fries, ed., *Records of the Moravians*, 2: 895. "drink . . ." "I hope not" "if she does . . ." "would have . . .": PUL John Beatty Family Collection Box 1, Folder 19. Reading Beatty to Enoch Green AM 1601. Brunswick December 19, 1775. Emphasis original. The Greens took the Beatty family in after Mary

and her brothers were orphaned; Readings' brother-in-law was a surrogate father. (Beatty, ed., "Beatty Papers," 224.)

27. Quotations: Tupper and Brown, *Grandmother Tyler's Book*, 236–237. This source is presented as a yarn. The encounter was set in Guilford, Vermont. "Madam Houghton" would likely be Lucretia Richardson Houghton, and her husband would be Edward, https://www.findagrave.com/memorial/89043996/edward-houghton and https://www.findagrave.com/memorial/135298326/leucretia-houghton.

28. Miller and Riggs., eds., *Journal of Dr. Elihu Ashley*, 259, 260.

29. Loring: MHS Benjamin Goodwin Account Books Ms N-1300 Vol. 2. February 25, 1775. PUL Van Neste and Van Liew, Day Book C 1774–1775, CO199, AM 12800, No. 1430. *Minutes of the Provincial Congress . . . of the State of New Jersey*, 169. LoC Glassford, Maryland Ledger, 1775. NHS William & Mary Channing Accounts (1771–1778). Duke Edward Telfair Papers. Telfair & Co. Journal, 1774–1775; 1775–1781.

30. *Connecticut Courant*, February 20, 1775. *PA Jrnl*, February 15, 1775. *Wöchentliche Pennsylvanische Staatsbote*, February 28, 1775. *New York Gazette*, February 20, 1775. *Providence Gazette*, February 18, 1775. *Maryland Journal* (Baltimore), February 27, 1775.

31. Bull: *Connecticut Courant*, May 15–June 26, 1775, July 10, 1775, July 24, 1775. Mitchell: *PA Jrnl*, March 1–15, March 29, 1775. Mitchell later served as a naval contractor and deputy quartermaster general in the Revolution. (Doerflinger, *Vigorous Spirit*, 144–145.) Remsen and Peters: *New York Gazette*, February 20 to March 6, March 20, 1775.

32. 4 Am Arch, 2: 448.

33. Sabine, 2: 392–393. Shaw was a member of the St. Patrick Society, the Wallaces, Irish-born, fled to Ireland after the war. Barrett, *Old Merchants*, 2: 250. Thomas M. Truxes, *Irish-American Trade, 1660–1783*, 115.

34. Shaw and Long brought in Henry Mitchell to speculate on the trade. NYHS Mss Collection BV Shaw. Shaw & Long Wastebook, 1771–1789. Bours purchased one barrel of tea from Shaw and Long and retailed the other fifteen barrels of tea on commission.

35. Ellery: *MHS Proceedings*, 4: 382. Bours was placed on a list of suspected persons in July 1776, but it is unclear why. RISA. General Assembly Papers. Revolutionary War. Suspected Persons, 1775–1783.

36. NHS Thomas Vernon Day Book, 1767–1776; John Hadwen Day Book (1771–1779).

37. "enemy . . .": 4 Am Arch, 2: 281. Wallace, Davidson and Johnson order books, Maryland State Archives, August 1, 1775, 481, http://mdhistory.net/msaref06/wdj_order_bks/html/index.html.

38. LoC Peter Force Papers. Film # 17137, Reel 95, 186. Woolsey and Salmon to Pringle, April 13, 1776. The partnership was "active in support of the Patriot cause." Woolsey also smuggled to France and St Eustatius. (Truxes, *Irish-American Trade*, 124, 141.) Pringle, also Irish, was part of the Newry-Philadelphia partnership John & Hamilton Pringle. (Hoffman, *Princes of Ireland, Planters of Maryland*, 336.) "Musty & unmerchantable": NYHS Anthony L. Bleecker Letterbook. Mss Collection, BV Bleecker. New York. Bleecker to Willing and Taylor April 20, 1775. Bleecker remained outside the city during the British occupation. (Barrett, *Old Merchants*, 4: 220.)

39. "sent . . .": NYHS Anthony L. Bleecker Letterbook. Mss Collection, BV Bleecker. New York to John DeNeufville, Amsterdam. May 4, 1775. Blok and Molhuysen, eds.,

Nieuw Netherlandsch Biografisch Woordenboek, 8: 1211–1214. Bleecker ordered high-end teas worth the risk. Philip Lott waited for tea to be re-authorized, writing to Copenhagen, "No sale for this tea at present. If times change expect to consign a vessel to his house." (*Dartmouth*, 2: 297. Becker, *History of Political Parties*, 169.) Patriot authorities were on guard for tea imports via the Dutch Caribbean but found no evidence this trade occurred. (Ryerson, *The Revolution Is Now Begun*, 98–99.)

40. Gorham had received permission to export fish to St. Eustatius in 1775. (4 Am Arch, 3: 309–310.) "Our Committee . . ." "one man . . .": *NDAR*, 4: 677. "a large . . ." "if there . . .": *NDAR*, 4: 734. "he had made . . .": 4 Am Arch, 5: 1286. 4 Am Arch, 5: 1272. *NDAR*, 4: 746.

41. "done up in Bundles": *NDAR*, 1: 83. *Minutes of the Provincial Council of Pennsylvania*, 10: 230–232. *NDAR*, 1: 458–459. "Tea and War-like . . .": *CRI*, 2: 5. "from Dunkirk . . .": *NDAR*, 1: 418.

42. *NDAR*, 1: 6. *NDAR*, 3: 1367.

43. Smith, "Social Visions," 42. "to be disposed of . . .": *Virginia Gazette* (Pinkney), March 16, 1775.

44. Some cash transactions are noted in ledgers, but we have no idea what proportion of cash sales was omitted. LoC Glassford, MF#18978, Reel 3, Bladensburg Journal, 1775–1777, 150, 153. The Association required merchants to accept paper currency, but the debasement of paper money by late 1776 led merchants to prefer payment in silver coin, pounds sterling, or barter credit.

45. William Beadle: *Connecticut Courant*, April 24, 1775, as cited in Smart, "A Life of William Beadle," 139.

46. Some merchants kept separate books for separate lines of business, which leaves the possibility of a "black" book of prohibited trades, which could be destroyed. Ledgers from merchants and tradesmen in other lines of business have generally been excluded.

47. LoC. Reynolds papers, William Reynolds to Courtney Norton. December 24, 1774. Colonial currencies converted to sterling as a basis of comparison (and expressed in sterling here) following McCusker, *How Much Is That in Real Money?*, 70. Duke Edward Telfair Papers. Telfair & Co. Journal, 1774–1775; 1775–1781. NYHS BV Shaw and Long. NHS John Hadwen, Pierce and Potter papers. LoC Glassford.

48. Maryland green tea: LoC Glassford, Maryland Ledger, 1775–1776. Rhode Island green tea: NHS John Hadwen Day Book, 1771–1779. Maryland hyson: LoC Glassford, Bladensburg Journal, 1775–1777. Georgia hyson: Duke Edward Telfair & Co Journal, 1775–1781. Boston hyson: MHS Gilbert Deblois ledger book, 1769–1792. Ms. N-2258, f1, 2, 5, 46, 48, 49. Tea sales in Deblois's ledger largely cover the period between May 1775 and the sale of the *William*'s tea in August. William Cheever reported "Fresh Provisions" as "scarce and high." August 12 and November 30, 1775. (William Cheever Diary, 1775–1776. MHS Online, 4, 7, https://www.masshist.org/online/siege/doc-viewer.php?item_id=1909&mode=nav.)

49. Potter, *The Liberty We Seek: Loyalist Ideology in Colonial New York and Massachusetts*, 136–137. Schlesinger, *Colonial Merchants*, 477. Sabine, 2: 245.

50. "banditti" "the free exercise . . .": Jackson T. Main, *Rebel versus Tory*, 33–35. Potter, *Liberty We Seek*, 156. Barnes and Barnes, *American Revolution through British Eyes*, 1: 8. Gage to Dartmouth. January 18, 1775.

51. "free . . .": Winslow, 109–109½. Sabine, 2: 221–225. Potter, *Liberty We Seek*, 156. Cf. *Rivington's Gazetteer*, February 9, 1775, and March 2, 1775, with *Massachusetts Gazette*, December 29, 1774. Robert M. Calhoon, "Loyalism and Neutrality," 238.

52. *Boston Gazette*, January 23, 1775. *DAR*, 7: 253. Separate anti-Congress organizing proceeded in nearby Hillsborough County. Maguire, "Parry's Journal," xiv–xvi. "Constitutional Liberty" "wholesome . . ." "Mobs": Scott, "Tory Associators of Portsmouth," *WMQ*, 3rd Ser., 17 (1960), 507. January 1775. For Hillsborough: Schlesinger, *Colonial Merchants*, 442.

53. "Nonassociators": Edgar, *South Carolina*, 223. Lambert, *South Carolina Loyalists*, 36, 39. Schlesinger, *Colonial Merchants*, 451, 452, 463, 493. McMurtrie, "Pioneer Printing in Georgia," 91. "abhorrence . . .": Judd, "Westchester County," 114. Becker, *History of Political Parties*, 172. Staudt, "Suffolk County," 65. Crary, *Price of Loyalty*, 33–34. Shy, "The Loyalist Problem," 6.

54. Potter, *Liberty We Seek*, 147. *Massachusetts Gazette*, December 29, 1774. *Rivington's New York Gazetteer*, February 9, 1775. "detestation . . ." "Government . . .": 4 Am Arch, 1: 1250. February 20, 1775. Venables, "Tryon County," 183. In 1775, Tryon County had 2,000 colonists and 500 Mohawks. Twenty percent of colonists were Johnson family tenants. "sundry Inhabitants" "dangerous" "good Government": *CRNC*, 9: 1160. *New Hampshire Gazette*, March 31, 1775, and Schlesinger, *Colonial Merchants*, 440.

55. "many" "multitude": Upton, *Revolutionary Versus Loyalist*, 50, 52. On the illusive Loyalist silent majority, see Norton, *British-Americans*, 256. This often involved imagining that Patriots' superior propaganda obscured swaths of Loyal sentiment and that armed forays into the countryside would attract the Loyal to the King's standard. (Selby, *Revolution in Virginia*, 19.) Other times it involved imagining the Patriots pretended to but did not speak for the people. (Mason, *Road to Independence*, 86–88. Schlesinger, *Colonial Merchants*, 340–341.)

56. "either . . ." "We immediately . . ." "what he could . . ." "that . . . was an open confession" "friend to government": Brown and D'Bernicre, "Narrative, &c," 207–208. Conroy, *In Public Houses*, 293–295. "tea is bought . . .": Ammerman, *Common Cause*, 114. Emphasis added. "braves it out . . .": Brown, *King's Friends*, 30–31.

57. "found it . . ." "High Torey": Miller and Riggs, eds., *Journal of Dr. Elihu Ashley*, 197. Norton, *1774*, 278.

58. Aitchison: Dabney, "Letters from Norfolk," 118. Rothery: Brown, *The King's Friends*, 182. *NDAR*, 2: 529. Martin: Scribner, 4: 25.

59. Potter, *The Liberty We Seek*, 27. Norton, *British-Americans*, 7–8.

60. Barthes, *Mythologies*, 109–159. Norton, *British-Americans*. PRO AO 12, AO 13. Becker, *History of Political Parties*, 171.

61. "a Negro Boy" "Piss Jack . . ." "so unguarded . . ." "indecent" "contemptuous": *Virginia Gazette* (Purdie and Dixon), November 3, 1774. Calhoon, "Loyalism and Neutrality," 242. "good for nothing dogs" "his Negro Jeff": Connecticut State Archives. Revolutionary War. 1st Series, vol. 1 374a, 383. Deposition of Moses Stocklin (or Stricklen). Winter, *The Blind African Slave*, 48–51. In Virginia, Patriots returned the favor, handcuffing a Scots Tory to his fellow black "brother . . . cattle." (Withington, *Toward a More Perfect Union*, 235.)

62. Crane, ed., *The Diary of Elizabeth Drinker* [unabridged], 1: 196–197, 214–215. "came home . . ." "Sarah Mitchel . . .": Crane, ed., *The Diary of Elizabeth Drinker*

[abridged], 52, 54. On her partisanship, see Crane, ed., *Diary* [unabridged], 1: xxi. Drinker's politics in 1775 are hard to pin down, but were somewhere on a spectrum of Toryism. "drank tea . . ." "I drank tea . . ." Crane, ed., *Diary* [unabridged], 1: 210–211.

63. Andrews and Andrews, eds., *Journal of a Lady of Quality*, 25, 32, 52, 76, 81, 86, 99, 117, 118, 121, 146, 221. "dish of Tea": Ibid., 147.

64. Sargent, ed., *Letters of John Andrews*, 5. William Vernon would become President of the Continental Navy Board. Hammond, *History and Genealogy*, 195–197. Elizabeth Vernon married Elnathan Hammond. Hammond's daybook gives tea sales to two sons and a son-in-law, [John] Arnold Hammond, Nathaniel Hammond, and Nathaniel Sprague (who married Elnathan's daughter, also named Elizabeth), among others. Elnathan's children were from a previous marriage. John Arnold's death: *NEHGR*, XXX (1876) 31. Vernon family: *NEHGR*, (1879) 33: 315–316. Vernon, *Diary of Thomas Vernon*, 2. NHS Thomas Vernon Day Book, 1767–1776, February 15, 1776. NHS Elnathan Hammond Day Book, 1774–1790, September 8, 1775.

65. Telfair's Loyalist buyers included John Mullryne, William Colville, James Habersham, and Lewis Johnson. Sabine, 1: 503, 2: 111, 498, 537. Basil Cowper, Telfair's business partner, voted for the Association in July 1775 as a member of the second Georgia provincial congress but later became a Loyalist. (Telfair's brother, William, was a London merchant.) Kellock, "London Merchants," 121–122.

66. Lough, "Champlins of Newport," 142, 146, 153. NHS Christopher Champlin Day book (1774–1781). *NDAR*, 1: 77.

67. "wicked" "King . . ." "Nor Congress . . .": Blecki and Wulf, eds., *Milcah Martha Moore's Book*, 247, item 82. "give up Tea": Ibid., 246, item 81. Ibid., 44.

68. "departed . . .": Duane, ed., *Extracts from the Diary of Christopher Marshall*, 14. "coffee": HSP. Christopher Marshall Papers (Collection 395), Marshall Diary photocopies, September 20, 1775. See also August 1, 8, 10.

69. LVa David and William Allason Papers, 1722–1847 Accession 13. LVa Papers (Intercepted letters), December 5, 1775 Accession 30003, State government records collection.

12. The Drink of 1776

1. Bliven, *Under the Guns*, 261.

2. NYHS, Alexander McDougall Papers, Murray Confessions, March 27, 1775.

3. Lee: *LDC*, 1: Richard Henry Lee to Alexander McDougall, July 24, 1775. New York's legislature did not approve the Association before March 1, 1775, though the New York City committee did adopt a subsequent colony-wide convention (Schlesinger, *Colonial Merchants*, 452–453). Lee did not question New Yorkers' allegiances here, but Virginians suspected that New Yorkers were weak adherents to the Association. See "Draft Resolution concerning Adherence of New York to Articles of Association," March 24, 1775, in Boyd, ed., *Papers of Thomas Jefferson*, 1: 159–160.

4. "Chief Dependence" "always" "Tea Holders": NYHS. John Alsop Collection. Christopher Smith to John Alsop. n.d. [1775]. *JCC*, 2: 235. Becker, *History of Political Parties*, 217, citing 4 Am Arch, 2: 1805.

5. "do not . . ." "Sundry": *JPCNY*, 1: 92. "a very Considerable . . ." "all kinds . . .": *The Selected Papers of John Jay*, 1: 141–142. Letter from Provincial Congress, September 1,

1775. The version in the Jay papers appears to be a re-wording of the *JPCNY* version. "Congress" "ought . . .": Ketchum, *Divided Loyalties*, 330, citing NYHS Misc. Mss of John Alsop. Bliven, *Under the Guns*, 273. A good discussion of the New York petitions to sell tea can be found in "Operating under the Continental Boycott" *Selected Papers of John Jay*, 1: 138–141.

6. "illicit" "undoubtedly" "general . . ." "clandestine": *JPCNY*, 1: 92.

7. "breach . . ." "with respect . . ." "New York . . ." "ninty-nine . . .": *LDC*, 2: 472, September 23, 1775. See also Schlesinger, *Colonial Merchants*, 582. "Tea gives . . ." "sincerely . . .": *JPCNY*, 2: 18. Ward suggests Sears's petition was received while the New York and Philadelphia letters were being considered. ("Diary of Governor Samuel Ward," 554.) *JCC*, 3: 389.

8. "strange" "frivolous" "no Tea" "what has paid Duty": *Selected Papers of John Jay*, 1: 164–165.

9. Jameson, "St. Eustatius in the American Revolution," 688. The use of tea chests to smuggle ammunition might explain why Bleecker was willing to have his smuggled tea come in such chests. Bermuda: Kerr, *Bermuda and the American Revolution*, 55. Nuxoll, *Congress and the Munitions Merchants*, 36–37. Mifflin got supercargo Samuel Davison released from his duties as captain of a Pennsylvania row galley by claiming the *Peggy*'s voyage was "in the Service of the Congress" (*NDAR*, 2: 1183, 1236. *NDAR*, 3: 38–39). New York merchants trading with the Netherlands (and Britain) had been importing arms before the Association began in 1774 (Wertenbaker, *Father Knickerbocker Rebels*, 41). In the winter of 1774–1775, Boston agents sought to smuggle gunpowder, and in 1776 smugglers brought in gunpowder from St. Eustatius to the Chesapeake (Jameson, "St. Eustatius," 685, 687).

10. "information" "sundry persons in": *JCC*, 3: 427. Cometti, "Women in the American Revolution," 337, citing *Connecticut Courant*, March 6 and April 24, 1775. Watson, *Annals of Philadelphia*, 2: 327–328. "many persons": *LDC*, 2: 484. "all India teas" "may be sold . . .": *Proceedings of the Conventions of the Province of Maryland, 1774–1776*, 57, December 23, 1775, http://aomol.msa.maryland.gov/megafile/msa/speccol/sc2900/sc2908/000001/000078/html/index.html. "Information" "against . . .": *JCC*, 3: 455. "Directions" "selling . . .": *LDC*, 3: 38. McKean: *LDC*, 3: 86. Maryland petition: 4 Am Arch, 4: 723, 887. *LDC*, 3: 87. The New York delegation was grateful for Maryland's efforts (*LDC*, 3: 410). "smuggler's interest": Matson, *Merchants and Empire*, 308.

11. White, "Telling More," 11–23.

12. "Controversy": *LDC* 3: 215. "many persons . . .": *Minutes of . . . State of New Jersey*, 351. "Directions" "People" "sell . . .": *LDC*, 3: 219. "often . . ." "established regulation" "stop" "this . . ." "agreed . . .": 4 Am Arch, 4: 948.

13. "censures . . .": *JCC*, 4: 133. Congress had Thomas McKean place the request with the Philadelphia committee of inspection and observation. Though a Delaware congressman McKean also served on the Philadelphia committee and was a useful intermediary between Congress and the committee governing the city where Congress sat. John M. Coleman, *Thomas McKean*, xi, 129, 145. Henry, McClallen and Henry: *New York Gazette*, March 25 through April 15, 1776. Manhattan papers like the *Gazette* served Albany as there was no Albany newspaper. The goods may have been considered war booty and allowed by the Albany committee for this reason.

14. With the British blockade, Congress faced a situation analogous to what the Confederacy would face ninety years later. "to bring . . .": *JCC*, 4: 259. "zealous . . ."

"large quantities" "counteract . . ." "great sufferers": *Virginia Gazette* (Purdie), April 26, 1776, Supplement. "sold and used": *JCC*, 4: 278.

15. The debate between New Whigs and economic explanations is long. Cf. Schlesinger, *Colonial Merchants* and Wood, "Rhetoric and Reality," 3–32. Smuggling frustrated the British ambassador to The Hague to no end (Jameson, "St. Eustatius," 688). After the British conquest of New York City, the New York Congress noted that if merchants had "been permitted to vend" tea sooner, "they would have employed the moneys arising from the sale of it in importing divers commodities" for "defence of the Colonies" sooner as well (*JPCNY*, 1: 682–683).

16. "Should be glad . . .": Johns Hopkins University. John Weatherburn collection: 1766–1816, Ms. 44, Box 1, c. 1, Journal 2. John Weatherburn: 1772–1811, 106 "too short" "all India tea" "sold and consumed" "be sold and used" "future importation" "prohibited" "desire . . .": *JCC*, 4: 277–278.

17. "furnish . . ." "will not . . .": *Virginia Gazette* (Purdie), March 29, 1776.

18. "Goods most . . ." "All Goods . . ." "Certificate . . .": HUNTER "Memorandum of goods most in demand in Virginia." n.d. Estimated 1775 by archivists; however, likely 1776, as the original Association did not make exceptions for prize goods. Congress declared all British vessels valid prizes on March 23, 1776 (*JCC*, 4: 231). Lough Jr., "The Champlins of Newport," 154–155, 158–162. There is no record of either a repeal of the Association or the ban on tea imports in the *JCC*. The Associational boycott against Britain evaporated with the Peace of Paris (1783), but a peace with Britain only did not repeal the ban on tea from other locations.

19. "Green-Tea" "Tell . . ." "and if . . ." "ten . . ." "Good Bohea Tea": *LDC*, 3: 643. "most . . ." "Could . . .": *LDC*, 4: 99. "a Pound . . ." "I flatter . . ." "send a Card . . ." "vexed" "another Cannister" "amazingly dear" "Lawful Money": *LDC*, 5: 107.

20. Mayer, ed., *Journal of Charles Carroll*, 65, 82. "a large assemblage": Hanley, ed., *John Carroll Papers*, 1: May 1, 1776.

21. *NDAR*, 5: 584. Perry, *Brief History*, 21. Vernon, *Diary*, 8.

22. James Hunter's memoranda for Foulk & Burkhard. 1776. Box 3 HUNTER. "indulged" "not one . . ." "inebriating" "drunk with it": Greene, ed., *Diary of Colonel Landon Carter*, 2: 1028.

23. "Hospitle . . .": *NDAR*, 5: 913–914.

24. LoC Papers of Stephen Collins and Son, Memorandum and accounts, 1772–1776, William Barrell. MSS 16436, Box 136. "Coffee & Tea . . .": Miller, ed., *The Selected Papers of Charles Willson Peale*, 1: 179 and 182, 183, 185, 186. PUL Abraham Van Neste, *Ledger B 1775–1779*, CO199, AM 12800, No. 1428. 4 Am Arch, 5: 1503, 1175. Bliven, *Under the Guns*, 261–262. Maier, *Old Revolutionaries*, 63, 65. Sears also served as supercargo on an early China trade voyage (*DAB*, s.v. "Isaac Sears").

25. Schlesinger, *Colonial Merchants*, 590. *Continental Journal*, June 13 to 27, 1776. Hanson, ed., *Papers of Robert Treat Paine*, 3: 46 n 1.

26. Ranlet, *New York Loyalists*, 191. Beals, *Coin, Kirk, Class and Kin*, 231. Sabine, 2: 548. Macaulay, "Journal of Alexander Macaulay."

27. It is also possible that some prize-taking may have been collusive—trade between the two sides covered up by a pretextual capture, though there is no direct evidence of this. Truxes, *Defying Empire*. Price, *France and the Chesapeake*, 683. Paullin, "The Navy of the American Revolution," 322–333.

28. "Bohe Tea": NYPL. Schuyler Papers, Military Papers, Box 49, f4 Benedict Arnold. May 9, 1775. Account of Sundries the Property of William Friend, Taken at Ticonderoga by Col. Allen's Green Mountain Boys (Taken on May 1, 1775).

29. *NDAR*, 3: 17, 45, 46, 93. "two Canisters only": *NDAR*, 3: 110. Nelson, *George Washington's Secret Navy*, 237–238.

30. *Nancy: Pennsylvania Evening Post*, December 12, 1775. Woodcut: "Manly. A favorite new song, in the American fleet." Salem, 1776. Evans 43057. The lyrics appeared in the *New-England Chronicle* (Cambridge, December 7, 1775), *Essex Journal* (Newburyport, December 22, 1775), *Providence Gazette* (December 23, 1775), and *Constitutional Gazette* (New York, January 7, 1776). "2 large . . .": *NDAR*, 3: 1010. Prize of *Hawke: Providence Gazette*, October 19, 1776. Auction: *Providence Gazette*, November 2, 1776. Cooke and Brown: American War of Independence at Sea, https://www.awiatsea.com/Privateers/H/Hawke%20Rhode%20Island%20Sloop%20[Crawford%20Phillips].pdf. "courageous": Ulrich, *Age of Homespun*, 175. *New England Chronicle*, January 18, 1776. *Friends* auction: May 24, 1776. Taken in January, the cargo was auctioned in May. It is unclear whether the delay was because of the tea ban or issues in Massachusetts Admiralty Courts (Nelson, *George Washington's Secret Navy*, 270). Auction notices: *Essex Journal*, May 10 to 24, 1776. *New-England Chronicle*, May 16, 1776.

31. "another sort . . .": Nelson, *George Washington's Secret Navy*, 216. *NDAR*, 3: 843, 855.

32. Volo, *Blue Water Patriots*, 46–47. "that they . . .": *NDAR*, 3: 481.

33. Buskirk: Knight, comp., *New York in the Revolution*, 82. In 1775, Buskirk served on the Bergen county committee of correspondence and as a doctor in the local militia, before taking command of the Fourth Battalion of New Jersey Volunteers, a Loyalist militia, after the arrival of British forces in the county in November 1776. (Todd W. Braisted, "Bergen County's Loyalist Population," https://www.bergencountyhistory.org/loyalists-in-bergen. Paramus: *Virginia Gazette* (Purdie), June 13, 1777. The Paramus tea was likely the property of Loyalist William Bayard, or Gerard Dewindt of New York (Tchen, *New York before Chinatown*, 4). The New London-based *Oliver Cromwell* sent a prize into Bedford with tea in 1777 (*Virginia Gazette* [Purdie], October 3, 1777). Despite rumors that it was rotting, at least some of the *London*'s tea survived. "Extract of a letter from a gentleman in Charles-Town, South Carolina to his Friend in New York," *Pennsylvania Journal*, March 16, 1774. Thanks to Mary Beth Norton for this reference. Leger and Greenwood addressed rumors of "the teas being in a damp ware House," writing, "We Cannot think that is altogether the Case." The tea was stored in one of the three cellars on the lower floor of the Exchange. The cellar was not completely underground and had small windows looking out onto the street. Halliday, the customs collector, was "very Carefull in hav[in]g the Celler air'd twice a week." One of the other cellars was even used as a wine cellar, which, as Leger and Greenwood explained, "would not Answer was it in the least damp." (L&G, 168). The tea seized in 1774 from the *Magna Charta* and *Briton* may have been sold as well.

34. "immediately" "apply the profits": *JCC*, 4: 278–279 note. South Carolinians also argued that the tea was their property because Parliament had already indemnified the Company for the tea. However, nothing in the public or private acts of Parliament, 1773–1776, indicates that Parliament granted such an indemnification.

35. Hemphill et al., eds., *Journals of the General Assembly*, 64–65, 104. "Publick Teas": *SCAGG*, October 2 to 9, 1776. On Hall: "To George Washington from George Abbott

Hall, March 31, 1789," *FO*, https://founders.archives.gov/documents/Washington/05 -01-02-0365. Hall may have had a business relationship with Smith previously; a Hall and Smith (first names unclear) had previously been partners (*SCG*, November 8, 1773.) If one applies the 1775 South Carolina/sterling conversion rate, the bohea price in South Carolina currency, 25s, converts close to the Continental price of ¾ of a dollar or 3s 4½d sterling; however, it is not necessarily reasonable to apply the 1775 rate to the second half of 1776.

36. The raw value, a total income of £76,013 11s 6d, was paid to the state in installments between October 1776 and December 1777. The South Carolina pound devalued in 1777 because the state emitted too much paper money. The adjustment for inflation is made according to the monthly currency devaluation table in McCusker, *How Much Is That in Real Money?*, 78. £61,603 represents the deflated sum, rounded to the nearest pound. For South Carolina tea sales, see *Records of the South Carolina Treasury*, Roll 1: "Public Ledger, 1775–1777," 152. "Money Received from the Commissioners on the Sales of Tea." The fortification of Charlestown, unadjusted for inflation, cost SC £71,359 in 1777. Tea revenue, unadjusted for inflation, was SC £58,481. Most of the tea funds were raised by June 1777, when the South Carolina pound still had 80 percent of its January 1777. The pound would collapse to less than half its January value by December 1777. If most of the fortification costs were paid out in lower-value of late 1777 money, the tea may have been worth more than the fortifications (McCusker, *How Much Is That in Real Money?*, 78). Fourth quarter of 1776 revenue and expenditures: *Records of the South Carolina Treasury*, Reel 1: 161. 1777 revenue: Ibid. "A True State of the Public Treasury of South Carolina on the 31st Decem[be]r 1777." South Carolina monetary policy: Hemphill and Wates, eds., *Extracts*, 130–131, 224–66. Hemphill, Wates, and Olsberg, eds., *Journals of the General Assembly*, 5, 79–80, 82. Steedman, "Charleston's Forgotten Tea Party," 259. Edgar, *South Carolina*, 219.

37. "exorbitant prices": *JCC*, 4: 278. *Virginia Gazette* (Purdie), April 26, 1776. Price controls had been linked to the re-authorization of tea as early as 1775 (*JPCNY*, 1: 92). "the best Green Tea": 4 Am Arch, 6: 669. New York: 4 Am Arch, 5: 1128–1129. "Tea . . .": Attmore and Hellings, *Pennsylvania Evening Post*, June 22, 1776. Yet set prices for hyson did track across the colonies. Without having to convert, one notes that the ratio of set hyson to set bohea prices in New York was roughly the same as the ratio of hyson and bohea prices in state sales of tea in South Carolina. In both locations, hyson was roughly five times bohea's price in local currency.

38. At a rate of 4s6d sterling to 1 Spanish dollar. (McCusker, *How Much Is That in Real Money?*, 33.)

39. Sears: Bliven, *Under the Guns*, 261–262. 4 Am Arch, 5: 1503, 1175. *JPCNY*, 1: 440. Albany: Countryman, *A People in Revolution*, 142. "to the public view . . ." "for his trouble in weighing": Ibid., 180.

40. Alsop's prospective buyer (who was also his in-law) ratted him out before the sale; if anyone else had bought from him on those terms, they kept quiet. Gautier ran Ten Eyck and Simmons's store. (Bliven, *Under the Guns*, 273–275.) The original congressional order allowing tea did not mention specie or paper money (*JCC*, 4: 278). South Carolina tea sales required "cash," i.e., specie, not paper money or "currency." The issue of paper money came more sharply to the fore in later 1776 and 1777, but the details varied by state (*JPCNY*, 1: 789–790).

41. Bliven Jr., *Under the Guns*, 295. *JPCNY*, 1: 494–495. "abuses . . ." "at higher . . .":
5 Am Arch, 3: 208.

42. "committee of ladies" "the Continental price": Smith, "Food Rioters," 7. Smith,
"Food Rioters," 18. *JPCNY*, 1: 590.

43. "unjustifiable and mercenary": *JPCNY*, 1: 682. Ibid., 609, 669. Smith, "Food Rioters," 18. Thomas had bought his tea in New York City in June and spirited it up the
Hudson for safekeeping. He returned in November to bring the tea to Connecticut to
find the committee had seized his tea and was demanding an order from the state congress to release it, which he got (5 Am Arch, 3: 305, 603–604).

44. The state congress issued its order to the Kingston county committee on behalf of Thomas on November 11, 1776; Sleght wrote back to the congress notifying
them of the new tea disturbances on November 18. The events, while not explicitly
linked, fit chronologically. Thomas's was the supply the state congress had exempted
from its order that all tea caches be distributed to the people at set prices. Smith, "Food
Rioters," 18. "are now daily alarmed" "streets . . ." "that detestable . . .": *JPCNY*, 1: 714.
"divided or distributed": Countryman, *A People in Revolution*, 182.

45. "put up . . ." "called . . ." "women! . . .": *JPCNY*, 2: 506. "very high price" *JPCNY*,
1: 1008. Wermuth, "The Central Hudson Valley," 139–140. Also Countryman, *A People
in Revolution*, 182–183. Smith, "Food Rioters," 34. Caldwell sought recompense from
state authorities, who "highly disapprove of such violent and disorderly proceedings"
and the way a man was "divested of his property" "in a free country" outside the protection of the law; but they did not want to get on the wrong side of the public, so
they urged he go to court (*JPCNY*, 1: 1010). This was one of the few teas openly defended for being "captured" rather than imported, and therefore not "within the resolution of Congress" to ban new tea imports (*JPCNY*, 1: 1008).

46. Cometti, "Women in American Revolution," 337. Stefan Bielinski, "Albany
County," in Tiedemann and Fingerhut, *The Other New York*, 160. Barck Jr., *New York
City*, 99, 103, 133.

47. Schlesinger, *Colonial Merchants*, 590. Hugh Talmage Lefler and Albert Ray New-
some, *North Carolina. The History of a Southern State*, 191.

48. "tea, coffee, and sugar" "very expensive": Fries, *Records of the Moravians*, 3: 1085.
"impossible price": Ibid., 1411.

49. "to drink tea again" "selling very High": Mason, ed., *John Norton and Sons*, 398.
Miller, ed., *Papers of Charles Willson Peale*, 1: 179, 182, 183, 185, 186. "regulated Price":
Boyle, "Boyle's Journal," 85: 129–130. Boylston was known to be cheap. "John Adams
to John Boylston, 5 July 1782," FO, https://founders.archives.gov/documents/Adams
/04-04-02-0227. Editor's note. "rum . . .": *Virginia Gazette* (Dixon and Nicholson),
June 12, 1779. *Virginia Gazette* (Dixon and Nicholson), July 10, 24, 1779. Salem: Smith,
"Food Rioters," 35–36.

Conclusion

1. "the Bostonians . . ." "get well . . .": LVa. John Hook Records, Accession 22174,
Box 1, folder 6, item 42. Answer of John Hook to Charges of Charles Lynch at the
Bedford Committee, June 1775. All other quotations: Fauntleroy, "John Hook as a
Loyalist," 400–403. The chronology is vague. Hook's complaint against the mob is

dated January 18, 1777 [misstated in Martin, *Buying into the World of Goods*, 35 and Fauntleroy, "John Hook" 402–403 as being June 18, 1777. Cf. Library of Virginia, John Hook Records, Accession 22174, Box 1, folder 6, item 47, "Complaint of John Hook against Colonel William Mead, et. al., 18 January 1777"]. Hook was released from jail the next day, but only signed a "certificate of fidelity" on October 10, 1777. (LVa Hook Records, Box 1, folder 6, item 49.) Hook's partial apology is undated. It appears in Fauntleroy, "John Hook," 403, adjacent to the complaint against Mead. It may have been written then or in 1775. Though most of Fauntleroy's documents appear in the LVa's Hook Records, the apology does not. Virginia only created the oath of allegiance in 1777, so Hook could not have signed it in 1775 (George Mason proposed one, but the legislature did not take it up. Rutland, ed., *Papers of George Mason*, 1: 249 n.) Hook sold tea before 1773; it is unclear whether he made tea sales in 1777, which would have depended on his supply (Martin, *World of Goods*, 55). Labaree, *Boston Tea Party*, 155.

2. News of the destruction of the tea reached New York on December 21 (Labaree, *Tea Party*, 155. Fischer, *Paul Revere's Ride*, 299). *Pennsylvania Gazette*, December 24, 1773. Charleston: *Pennsylvania Gazette*, December 22, 1773. Much of this coverage is a verbatim copy of *SCG*, December 6, 1773. In New York, William Smith seems to have been reacting to this news in his December 20 diary entry, noting that South Carolina Patriots had resolved to send the tea back. Sabine, ed., *Historical Memoirs*, 1: 162.

3. "the people": *Pennsylvania Gazette*, December 24, 1773.

4. Labaree, *Boston Tea Party*, 105.

5. "most of the cargo" "saved": *Massachusetts Gazette*, December 16, 1773. Norton, "Seventh Tea Ship," 682. Labaree, *Boston Tea Party*, 150.

6. *Amer Chron*, 15, 38.

7. "Boston . . ." "merely . . ." "associated . . ." "who . . ." "secretly . . .": Thatcher, *Military Journal*, 14.

8. *DAR*, 10: 57

9. Brannon, *From Revolution to Reunion*, 140–168.

10. "without . . .": Fichter, *So Great a Proffit*, 45–46.

11. Sabine, 1: 560. Addresser: Stark, *Loyalists of Massachusetts*, 132. Mandamus councillor: Whitmore, *The Massachusetts Civil List*, 64. Spelled "Clark" in Stark, *Loyalists of Massachusetts*, 137. "left this . . .": Stark, *Loyalists of Massachusetts*, 140. Benjamin Faneuil Jr., however, was proscribed (Sabine, 1: 418. Stark, *Loyalists of Massachusetts*, 137). Jonathan Clarke left for England in spring 1774 (Kamensky, *Revolution in Color*, 216). Richard and Isaac Clarke departed Boston on December 8, 1775, arriving December 29. (New England Historical and Genealogical Society, Richard Clarke and Sons Records, 1756–1775, Finding Aid. Oliver, ed., *Samuel Curwen*, 1: 102). There are several Abraham Lotts, but they all seem to have died in the United States (Sabine, 2: 29. Abraham Lott to George Washington, 7 August 1789," *FO*, https://founders.archives.gov/documents/Washington/05-03-02-0235. Phillips, *The Lott Family in America*.) Booth: Labaree, *Tea Party*, 228. Godbeer, *World of Trouble*, 5, 212. Sullivan, *Disaffected*. Anderson, "Thomas Wharton." "Ministerial Agent": Richard Genry Lee to Landon Carter, April 24, 1775. *NDAR*, 1: 215. Greenwood and Leger: University of Michigan, Clements Library, "Leger & Greenwood letterbook (1770–1775; 1788)" Finding Aid. https://quod.lib.umich.edu/c/clementsead/umich-wcl-M-2066leg?id=navbarbrowselink;view=text. Smith: "Records

of the South Carolina Treasury: 1775–1780, 1787." Library Catalog. https://loyalist
.lib.unb.ca/node/4724.

In 1775, White supplied Royal Navy vessels with committee permission (it could
be risky not to supply them) (4 Am Arch, 5: 270). He also explained to the committee
that he had declined North Carolina Governor Martin's invitation to assist in setting
up a royal standard (4 Am Arch, 2: 1346). Conversely, Frederick Pigou Jr. was so British-
based, it was less that he was Loyalist or Patriot and more that he returned to Britain
and wrote off the Revolution as a loss. Pigou's father was an East India Company director. He seems to have secured the contracts to sell tea for Abel and James and his
firm, Pigou and Booth. Kellock, "London Merchants," 140–141. PBF, 38, 425–429 n 2.

12. Cresswell, Journal, 149 (July 14, 1776), 59 (March 22, 1775 note on Kirk). Kirk
was Cresswell's sponsor-mentor, the man to whom Cresswell presented his letters of
introduction when he arrived from Britain, who encouraged him to take business ventures, and so on. James Kirk arrived in Virginia sometime before 1762. A prominent
merchant in Alexandria, he signed the Fairfax non-importation association in 1770 and
was a member of the Fairfax County committee of safety from 1774 to 1775 (Curtis
and Gill, "A Man Apart," 171 n 4). Echeverria, "The American Character," 401. "you
come . . ." "it is . . .": Cometti, "Women in the American Revolution," 339. "one or
two . . .": Graydon, Memoirs, 281. McKean, a congressman from Delaware who had
served in Philadelphia's revolutionary committee, was a "fixer" for people in trouble
with the committees). Woloch, Early American Women, 173. Diary of Grace Galloway,
August 16, 1778 (Sunday). Coleman, Thomas McKean, xi. Prelinger, "Benjamin Franklin," 268. Cresswell, Journal, 246. "favorite drink . . .": Jean-Francois-Louis, Comte de
Clermont-Crevecoer, "Journal," October 1780, in Rice and Brown, trans. and eds. The
American Campaigns of Rochambeau's Army, 1: 20. I am indebted to Gregory Unwin for
this reference. Shields, Civil Tongues, 116.

13. Merritt, Trouble with Tea, 124. "An Act Laying Certain Duties": Acts and resolves
passed by the General Court (Boston: 1781), 525–528. License: Beverly Historical Society "document announcing the licensure of Joseph Baker as retailer of tea in Beverly, December 17, 1781," 10857. JCC, 25: 918, 920, 927.

14. Cuyler: DCB, s.v. "Cuyler, Abraham, Cornelius." Patriots seem to have seized
the tea along with the covering letter. NYPL, Schuyler Papers, Military Papers, Box
50. Intercepted letters of Loyalists and others, 1775–1777. Richard Dobie to A. C. Cuyler, May 23, 1776. Arrest: Bielinski, "Abraham C. Cuyler," https://exhibitions.nysm
.nysed.gov//albany/bios/c/abccuyler359.html. Bielinski, "The Beginning of the End"
https://exhibitions.nysm.nysed.gov//albany/or/or-be.html. Jefferson: Egerton, Death
or Liberty, 42.

Appendix B

1. PRO CUST 16/1. Not all tea retained in one year was consumed. But such tea
would be sold first in the next year, meaning that over time imports less exports be-
comes an accurate measure of tea consumed. Only the thirteen colonies are considered. Colonies recorded in CUST 16/1 that did not join the Continental Association
are left out. This includes the Floridas, which are included in Historical Statistics of the
United States. Historical Statistics gives data on the colonial-era Black population but

not the colonial-era slave population. The slave population is estimated as a percentage of the Black population, following Hacker, "From '20. and odd,'" 851–852. One might exclude slaves from consumer counts if (1) one felt they were not even potential tea consumers or (2) one wished to compare consumption among the free population, of all races, between the colonies and Britain. These data exclude Native American populations. It is tempting to compare *adult* tea-drinking populations; however, information about the age at which people began consuming tea remains sparse.

2. PRO CUST 3/61-75. The two sets' variance may be ascribed to the difference between the departure and arrival dates. Dickerson, *The Navigation Acts*, 87–91, 99–100 n 80.

3. Export data from 1773 includes the Company's tea on the *London, Polly, Beaver, Dartmouth, Eleanor, William, and Nancy*, none of which was consumed in North America that year. This leaves 151,962 of the 738,408 pounds of tea exported from Britain available. IOR B/91 206 and 290 do not indicate how many pounds of tea were sold from the *William* (they indicate only auction value). The best estimate is 54/58ths of the *William* tea. Norton, "The Seventh Tea Ship," 681–710. Totals for tea imported in 1773 from Labaree, *Boston Tea Party*, 335.

4. This varies slightly from the 373,000 pounds given in CUST 16/1.

5. Figures for Dutch re-exports are not readily available due to the decentralized administration of the United Provinces. There was no central tariff, leaving no central accounting of Dutch imports and exports. VOC records are likewise decentralized. VOC records at the *kamer* (chamber, the major administrative unit of the VOC within the Netherlands) level may provide import or export records, though a preliminary search through the Amsterdam records did not find any. Liu, *Dutch East India Company's Tea Trade*, 141–142.

6. Good data begins with the year October 1, 1795–September 30, 1796, in *American State Papers* (Commerce & Navigation). Export data for 1790/91, 1791/92 and 1794/95 are in chests of tea, while import data is in pounds (making net tea import impossible to calculate). There is no import data set for October 1, 1791–September 30, 1794. There is no viable data set for the 1780s. Tea imported on all vessels, foreign and domestic, is considered here. For the 1780s US economy, see Bjork, *Stagnation and Growth*.

7. Census data taken from United States Bureau of the Census, *Historical Statistics*, 9. Tea data from *American State Papers* (Commerce & Navigation). Since this population included children, slaves, and others who may not have drunk tea, one should not assume every American drank half a pound of tea each year; the average amount of tea consumed by those who consumed tea was higher, a caveat that applies to coffee as well. The higher estimate of late-colonial smuggling is a ceiling. It runs close to using up the total amount of all tea imported into the Atlantic world by the European importers. The high-bound estimate that more than three-quarters of colonial tea was smuggled makes implicit assumptions about how little tea was consumed elsewhere. European importers brought 10.9 million pounds of tea into the Atlantic world between 1769 and 1772. Britain legally imported (but did not necessarily consume) 10.1 million pounds (Dermigny, *La Chine et l'Occident*, 2: 679). Of Continental Europe's 10.9 million pounds, 4.4 million were imported by the VOC (Nierstrasz, *Rivalry for Trade*, 62). But the VOC reported (as noted in chapter 2) considerable Dutch home

consumption of tea. If we assume half of VOC imports were used domestically, that would leave 8.7 million pounds of European imports for re-export. Of that, 4 to 6 million were imported into Britain (see chapter 2), leaving 2.7 to 4.7 million for consumption in North America and everywhere in Europe except the British Isles and the Netherlands. The thirteen colonies imported roughly a quarter million pounds of legal tea during this period. An assumption that smuggled tea comprised three-quarters of North American consumption would require three-quarters of a million pounds of smuggled tea, leaving 2 to 4 million pounds to be distributed to the rest of the Atlantic world. This tea would also have to meet demand in other *British* colonies (like Quebec and Jamaica). Mason, *Road to Independence*, estimates colonial tea consumption of 1.5 million pounds per year by extrapolating per capita consumption levels from the 1790s back to the 1770s. This would require 1.25 million pounds of smuggled tea to be allocated to the North American market, an implausibly high amount.

8. For more on the coffee trade, see McDonald, "From Cultivation to Cup." CUST 16/1 also gives a total of 7,272 pounds of "foreign" coffee imported between 1768 and 1772. This amount has not been included here, so as to allow a like-for-like comparison of British goods, and because it is unclear how much foreign coffee was also exported. Whatever coffee smuggling there may have been, the coffee import data suggest it did not move in relationship to tea smuggling.

9. Coffee data from 1807–1809 (see table B2) includes abnormally high amounts of coffee remaining in the United States due to a collapse of coffee exports in 1806/7 and 1807/8. This was related to the Embargo; some of this coffee may not have been consumed. Nevertheless, coffee consumption consistently exceeded tea consumption in the United States even without the numbers from these years.

10. Dutch coffee came in from Java. By the mid-1800s, Brazil would emerge as the major coffee producer. Britain would have its own booming interest in coffee in the 1820s. Smith, "Accounting for Taste."

Appendix C

1. McCusker, *How Much Is That in Real Money?*, 70.

2. " a very moderate price": LoC. Reynolds papers, William Reynolds to Mrs. Courtney Norton. December 24, 1774.

3. Charleston prices: *SCAGG*, October 2 and 9, 1776. Conversion: McCusker, *How Much Is That in Real Money?*, 70. Amory: MHS, Amory Family Papers, 1697–1894, Ms. N-2024, Amory, Taylor and Rogers Wastebook, 1774–1784, vol. 13.

BIBLIOGRAPHY

Primary Sources

Archival Sources

Baker Library Historical Collections. Harvard Business School:
  Barrell Company Account Books, 1770–1803
  Cornelius Fellows ledger, 1775–1791
  Hancock family papers. Series II. Letterbook JH-6
  Melatiah Bourn Papers
Beverly Historical Society, Beverly, MA:
  document announcing the licensure of Joseph Baker as retailer of tea in Beverly,
    December 17, 1781
Boston Public Library:
  Dorchester Town Meeting and Selectmen's Records, Boston, Massachusetts,
    1632–1826, volume 3, 1740–1779
British Library:
  Egerton Manuscripts
  India Office Records
British National Archives:
  American Loyalist Claims
  Chatham Papers
  Colonial Office Series
  Records of the Board of Customs
  Treasury
Colonial Williamsburg:
  John Norton and Sons Papers
Connecticut State Archives:
  Revolutionary War. 1st Series
Duke University, Rubenstein Library:
  Edward Telfair Papers. "Telfair, Edward, and Company, Journal, 1775–1781"
Harvard University Archives:
  Faculty minutes, 1806–1994 (inclusive) (UAIII 5.5.2, Volume 4)
Historical Society of Pennsylvania:
  Am 817 Cargo manifests conveyed to the Committee of Observation of
    Philadelphia, Northern Liberties, and Southwark, 1774
  Christopher Marshall Papers
  James & Drinker Business Papers

Huntington Library:
  Tea Permits. Mss HM 70291–70302
Johns Hopkins University, Milton S. Eisenhower Library:
  John Weatherburn collection: 1766–1816. Ms. 44. Special Collections
Library of Congress:
  John Glassford & Company Papers
  Matthew Irwin Journal, 1769–1784 (MMC-1027)
  Papers of Neil Jamieson
  Papers of Stephen Collins and Son, Memorandum and accounts, 1772–1776
  Peter Force Papers
  William Reynolds papers, 1771–1796
Library of Virginia:
  Charles Steuart Papers, 1758–1798, Microfilm
  David and William Allason Papers, 1722–1847. Accession 13. Day Books,
    1770–1800
  John Hook Records
  Virginia. Convention. Papers (Intercepted letters), 1775 Dec. 5.
Maryland State Archives:
  Port of Entry Record, 1744–1797. SE 71-1
  Proceedings of the Conventions of the Province of Maryland, 1774–1776. http://aomol
    .msa.maryland.gov/megafile/msa/speccol/sc2900/sc2908/000001/000078
    /html/index.html
  Wallace, Davidson and Johnson order books. http://mdhistory.net/msaref06
    /wdj_order_bks/html/index.html
Massachusetts Archives, Supreme Judicial Court Archives:
  Suffolk County Court of General Sessions of the Peace
Massachusetts Historical Society:
  Amory Family Papers 1697–1894 Ms. N-2024 (Tall) Wastebook 1774–1784 (Vol 13)
  Benjamin Goodwin Account Books Ms N-1300
  "Boston Tea Party tea in a glass bottle." Artifact. Animal/Botanical 02.008
  British North American customs papers, 1765–1774: "An Account of what Tea
    has been imported into Boston since the year 1768"
  Gilbert Deblois ledger book, 1769–1792. Ms. N-2258
  Isaac Winslow and Margaret Catherine Winslow, transcribed and edited by
    Robert Newsom, *Family Memorial. The Winslows of Boston* (Boston, MA:
    1837?–1873?)
  James Murray Papers, P-141
  List of items belonging to Henry Howell Williams destroyed in 1775, 10
    March 1787. MHS online, https://www.masshist.org/online/siege/img
    -viewer.php?item_id=1918&img_step=1&tpc=&pid=21&mode
    =transcript&tpc=&pid=21#page1
  Misc. Bd. Various years.
  Ms. N-726. Pitts Family Papers, 1648–1960
  "Tea leaves from the Boston Tea Party." Artifact. Animal/Botanical 02.007
  William Cheever Diary, 1775–1776. MHS online. https://www.masshist.org
    /online/siege/doc-viewer.php?item_id=1909&mode=nav

Nantucket Historical Association:
  Kezia Coffin Fanning Papers. MS2 folder
National Archives and Records Administration, Waltham, MA:
  Salem, Massachusetts Custom House Letter Book, 1772–1775. Microfilm
National Library of Scotland:
  Charles Steuart Papers
New England Historic and Genealogical Society
  Richard Clarke and Sons records, 1756–1775
New Hampshire State Archives:
  Petitions to the General Court. Tory: Packersfield: Breed Batchelder, Confiscated
    Estate, 1775–1792
Newport Historical Society:
  Christopher Champlin Shop Waste Book, 1774–1775
  Elnathan Hammond Day Book, 1774–1790
  John Hadwen Day Book, 1771–1779
  Pierce, Clothier & Howard Potter Day Book, 1774–1730
  Thomas Vernon Day Book, 1767–1776
  William & Mary Channing Accounts, 1771–1778
New-York Historical Society:
  Alexander McDougall Papers
  Anthony L. Bleecker Letterbook
  John Alsop Collection, 1733–1792
  John Taylor Papers, 1743–1775. Daybook, 1774–1775
  Scarsdale Account book: Richard and Benjamin Cornell Account Book
  Shaw & Long Wastebook, 1771–1789
New York Public Library
  Boston Committee of Correspondence Records, 1772–1784
  Schuyler Papers
  Timothy Newell. Diary of the Siege of Boston, 1775–1776
North Carolina State Archives:
  Matthew and Margaret Byrne Collection, AB.76, General Store Ledger
Nova Scotia Archives:
  Record Group 1
Princeton University Library:
  Abraham Van Neste, *Ledger B 1775–1779*
  John Beatty Family Collection 1768–1804, C1010, Rare Books & Manuscript
    Collections, Princeton University Library, Princeton, NJ
  Thomas Maan, account book, 1774–1796
  Princeton University Trustee Minutes I, 1746–1894 http://pudl.princeton.edu
    /objects/7w62f826z
  Van Neste and Van Liew, Day Book C 1774–1775
Rhode Island State Archives:
  General Assembly Papers. Revolutionary War. Suspected Persons, 1775–1783
Sheffield City Archives, Great Britain:
  William Vassall Letterbooks
University of Michigan, William L. Clements Library:

Leger & Greenwood Letterbook, 1770–1775; 1788.
Samuel and William Vernon Collection
Thomas Gage Papers
University of North Carolina Libraries:
Cameron Family Papers, 1757–1978
Robert Wilson Account Books, 1772–1888
University of Pennsylvania Libraries:
David Salisbury Franks ledger. MS 56, Codex 008.1 https://colenda.library.upenn
.edu/catalog/81431-p3wh2dk6g
Manuscript Farmer's Ledger, 1774–1777. Probably New England. Ms. Codex
1587. https://colenda.library.upenn.edu/catalog/81431-p3cv4br5z
University of Virginia, Albert and Shirley Small Special Collection Library:
Papers of the Lee Family, 1750–1809. MSS 38-112
Papers of R. M. T. Hunter. Hunter-Garnett Collection [aka Papers of the Hunter
and Garnett families], Accession no. 38-45
Virginia Museum of History and Culture:
Thomas Adams Papers
Westerly, Rhode Island Town Clerk's Office:
Town Meeting Minutes 3, 1745–1778
Winterthur Museum, Gardens & Library:
Vernon Family Records
Yale University, Beinecke Rare Book and Manuscript Library
Medad Rogers Diary

Newspapers

American Gazette, or, the Constitutional Journal (Salem, MA)
Boston Evening-Post
Boston Gazette
Boston Post-Boy
Cape Fear Mercury
Connecticut Courant (Hartford)
Connecticut Gazette (New London)
Connecticut Journal (New Haven)
Constitutional Gazette (New York)
Continental Journal, and Weekly Advertiser (Boston)
Dunlap's Maryland Gazette or the Baltimore General Advertiser
Essex Gazette (Salem, MA)
Essex Journal (Newburyport, MA)
Freeman's Journal (Portsmouth, NH)
Georgia Gazette
Germantowner Zeitung
Maryland Gazette (Annapolis)
Maryland Journal (Baltimore)
Massachusetts Gazette; and the Boston Weekly News-Letter
Massachusetts Spy (Boston and Worcester)
Morning Chronicle and London Advertiser

New-England Chronicle, or Essex Gazette
New-Hampshire Gazette
Newport Mercury
New-York Gazette, and Weekly Mercury
New-York Journal
North Carolina Gazette (New Bern)
Norwich Packet (CT)
Nova Scotia Gazette
Pennsylvania Chronicle
Pennsylvania Evening Post
Pennsylvania Gazette
Pennsylvania Journal
Pennsylvania Ledger: or the Virginia, Maryland, Pennsylvania, and New-Jersey Weekly
    Advertiser
Pennsylvania Packet
Providence Gazette
Rivington's New York Gazetteer
South Carolina and American General Gazette
South Carolina Gazette
South Carolina Gazette and Country Journal
Story & Humphreys's Pennsylvania Mercury
Virginia Gazette (Rind, 1773–1774, Pinkney, 1774–1776)
Virginia Gazette (Purdie and Dixon, 1773–1774, Dixon and Hunter, 1775–1776)
Virginia Gazette (Purdie, 1775–1776)
Virginia Gazette, or, Norfolk Intelligencer
Der Wöchentliche Pennsylvanische Staatsbote

Acts of Parliament

Boston Port Act, 1774, 14 Geo. 3, c. 19.
Drawback Act, 1772, 12 Geo. 3, c 60.
Indemnity Act, 1767, 7 Geo. 3, c. 56.
Massachusetts Government Act, 1774, 13 Geo. 3, c. 45.
Revenue Act, 1767. 7 Geo. 3, c. 46.
Tea Act, 1773, 13 Geo. 3, c. 44.

Printed Primary Sources

Abbot, W. W., ed. The Papers of George Washington. Colonial Series (Charlottesville:
    University Press of Virginia, 1995).
"The able doctor, or, America swallowing the bitter draught." Boston Massachusetts
    United States, 1774. [London: May 1]. Photograph. https://www.loc.gov
    /item/97514782/.
"Acts and resolves passed by the General Court" (Boston: 1781).
Adair, Douglass and John A Schutz, eds. Peter Oliver's Origins & Progress of the
    American Rebellion. A Tory View (San Marino, CA: The Huntington Library,
    1961).
Adams, Charles Francis, ed. Works of John Adams (Boston: Little, Brown, 1850–1856).

Adams Family Papers: An Electronic Archive. Massachusetts Historical Society. http://
www.masshist.org/digitaladams/.

Allen, Jolley. *An Account of a Part of the Sufferings and Losses of Jolley Allen, a Native of
London* (Boston, 1883).

"An alarm to the legislature of the province of New-York . . ." 1775. Readex. Early
American Imprints, Series 1, no. 14453.

Andrews, Evangeline Walker and Charles McLean Andrews, eds. *Journal of a Lady of
Quality* (New Haven, CT: Yale University Press, 1923).

"Articles of Association, October 20, 1774." https://avalon.law.yale.edu/18th
_century/contcong_10-20-74.asp.

"Articles of Confederation: March 1, 1781." http://avalon.law.yale.edu/18th
_century/artconf.asp.

"Association of the Members of the Late House of Burgesses." https://founders
.archives.gov/documents/Jefferson/01-01-02-0083.

"Association of the Virginia Convention, Aug 1–6, 1774." http://avalon.law.yale.edu
/18th_century/assoc_of_va_conv_1774.asp.

Barck, Dorothy C., ed., *Papers of the Lloyd Family of the Manor of Queens Village,
Lloyd's Neck, Long Island, New York, 1654–1826* (New York, 1927).

Barnes, James J. and Patience P. Barnes. *The American Revolution through British Eyes.
A Documentary Collection* (Kent, OH: The Kent State University Press, 2013).

Barrett, Walter. *Old Merchants of New York City* (New York: Thomas R. Knox, 1885),
5 vols.

Bartlett, John Russell, ed. *Records of the Colony of Rhode Island and Providence
Plantations in New England* (Providence: A. Crawford Greene, 1862).

Battle, Kemp P., ed. *Letters and Documents Relating to the Early History of the Lower
Cape Fear*, James Sprunt Historical Monograph no. 4 (Chapel Hill: University
of North Carolina Press, 1903).

Bear, James A., Jr. and Lucia C. Stanton, eds. *Jefferson's Memorandum Books, Volume 1:
Accounts, with Legal Records and Miscellany, 1767–1826* (Princeton: Princeton
University Press, 1997).

Beatty, Joseph M., ed. "Beatty Letters, 1773–1782," *Proceedings of the New Jersey
Historical Society* (October 1962): 223–235.

Blecki, Catherine La Courreye and Karin A. Wulf, eds. *Milcah Martha Moore's Book. A
Commonplace Book from Revolutionary America* (University Park: Pennsylvania
State University Press, 1997).

Boston. "At a Meeting of the Merchants & Traders, at Faneuil-Hall, on the 23rd January 1770." Evans 11576.

Boyd, Julian P. et al., eds. *Papers of Thomas Jefferson.* (Princeton: Princeton University
Press, 1950—).

Boyle, John. "Boyle's Journal of Occurrences in Boston." *NEHGR* 84 (1930): 142–171,
248–272, 357–832; 85 (January and April 1931): 5–28, 117–133.

*British Records Relating to America in Microform. The Papers of Henry Fleming 1772–
1795 in the Cumbria Record Office Carlisle* (E P Microform Lts, Yorkshire, 1978).

Brown, Capt. and Ensign D'Bernicre. "Narrative, &c," *Collections of the Massachusetts
Historical Society*, 2nd Series, vol. 4 (Boston, 1816), 204–219. (Originally
published: Boston: J. Gill, Court St. 1779.)

Brumbaugh, Gaius Marcus. *Maryland Records, Colonial, Revolutionary, County and Church, from Original Sources* (1915).

Butterfield, L. H., ed. *Adams Family Correspondence* (Cambridge, MA: Harvard University Press, 1963–1993).

Butterfield, L. H., ed. *Diary and Autobiography of John Adams*, vol. 2 (Cambridge, MA: Harvard University Press, 1961).

Butterfield, L. H., ed. *Letters of Benjamin Rush* (Princeton: Princeton University Press, 1951).

Carter, Clarence Edwin, ed. *The Correspondence of General Thomas Gage with the Secretaries of State, 1763–1775* (New Haven, CT: Yale University Press, 1931).

Clark, William Bell and William James Morgan, eds. *Naval Documents of the American Revolution* (Washington, DC: U.S. Government Printing Office, 1964–1970), 5 vols.

Cobbett, W., Hansard, Thomas Curson, Great Britain. Parliament. *The Parliamentary History of England from the Earliest Period to the Year 1803.* London: Printed by T. C. Hansard.

Crane, Elaine Forman, ed. *The Diary of Elizabeth Drinker*, vol. 1 [unabridged] (Boston: Northeastern University Press, 1991).

Crane, Elaine Forman, ed. *The Diary of Elizabeth Drinker. The Life Cycle of an Eighteenth-Century Woman* (Boston: Northeastern University Press, 1994).

Crary, Catherine S., ed. *The Price of Loyalty: Tory Writings from the Revolutionary Era* (New York: McGraw-Hill, 1973).

Cresswell, Nicholas. *The Journal of Nicholas Cresswell 1774–1777* (New York: Dial Press, 1924). Digitized version http://hdl.loc.gov/loc.gdc/lhbtn.30436.

Cross, Arthur Lyon, ed. *Eighteenth Century Documents Relating to the Royal Forests the Sheriffs and Smuggling* (New York: Macmillan, 1928).

Cunningham, Anne Rowe, ed. *Letters and Diary of John Rowe Boston Merchant 1759–1762, 1764–1779* (Boston: W. B. Clarke Company, 1903).

Darley, Stephen. *Voices Waiting to Be Heard. Nineteen Eyewitness Accounts of Arnold's 1775 March to Quebec* (Bloomington, IN: AuthorHouse, 2021).

Davies, K. G., ed. *Documents of the American Revolution 1770–1783* (Dublin: Irish University Press, 1975).

Dawe, Philip. "The Alternative of Williams-burg." London: 1775. Printed for R. Sayer & J. Bennett. Library of Congress. https://www.loc.gov/item/97514624/.

Dawe, Philip. "A Society of Patriotic Ladies, at Edenton in North Carolina." London: 1775. Printed for R. Sayer & J. Bennett. Library of Congress. https://www.loc.gov/item/96511606/.

Devine, T. M., ed. *A Scottish Firm in Virginia 1767–1777. W. Cuninghame and Co.* (Edinburgh: Clark Constable for the Scottish History Society, 1984).

"Diary of Governor Samuel Ward." *Magazine of American History* 1, part 2 (1877): 438–442, 503–506, 549–561.

Donnan, Elizabeth. *Documents Illustrative of the Slave Trade to America* (Washington, DC: Carnegie Institution of Washington, 1930–1935), 4 vols.

Dorr, Harbottle, Jr. "The Annotated Newspapers of Harbottle Dorr, Jr." MHS. https://www.masshist.org/dorr/.

Drake, Francis S. *Tea Leaves: Being a Collection of Letters and Documents Relating to the Shipment of TEA . . .* (Boston: A. O. Crane, 1884).

Drayton, John. *Memoirs of the American Revolution, from Its Commencement to the Year 1776, Inclusive; as Relating to the State of South-Carolina* . . . (Charleston: A. E. Miller, 1822).

Duane, William, ed. *Extracts from the Diary of Christopher Marshall* . . . (Albany: John Munsell, 1877).

Echeverria, Durand. "The American Character: A Frenchman Views the New Republic from Philadelphia, 1777." *WMQ*, 3rd Series, vol. 16, no. 3 (July 1959): 376–413.

Essex Southern District Medical Society. *Memoir of Edward A. Holyoke* (Boston: Perkins & Marvin, 1829).

"Extracts from the Interleaved Almanacs of William Wetmore of Salem, 1774–1778." *EIHC* 43 (1907): 115–120.

Extracts from the Journals of the Provincial Congress of South-Carolina. Held at Charles-Town, November 1st to November 29, 1775. Published by Order of the Congress (Charles Town, 1776).

Farish, Hunter Dickinson, ed. *Journal and Letters of Philip Vickers Fithian, 1773–1774: A Plantation Tutor of the Old Dominion* (Willliamsburg: Colonial Williamsburg, 1945).

Force, Peter, ed. *American Archives* . . . *A Documentary History* (Washington, DC: 1837–1851).

Ford, Worthington Chauncey, ed. *Boston in 1775. Letters from General Washington, Captain John Chester, Lieutenant Samuel B. Webb, and Joseph Barrell* (Brooklyn, NY, 1892).

Ford, Worthington Chauncey, ed. *Commerce of Rhode Island 1726–1800* (*Collections of the Massachusetts Historical Society*, 7th Series, vols. 9–10 [1914–1915]).

Ford, Worthington Chauncey, ed. *Correspondence and Journals of Samuel Blachley Webb* (New York: Wickersham Press, 1893), 3 vols.

Ford, Worthington Chauncey, ed. *Journals of the Continental Congress 1774–1789* (Washington, DC: U.S. Government Printing Office, 1904–1937), 34 vols. American Memory. https://memory.loc.gov/ammem/amlaw/lwjclink.html.

Ford, Worthington Chauncey, ed. *Letters of William Lee* . . . (Brooklyn, NY: Historical Printing Club, 1891), 3 vols.

Fries, Adelaide, L., ed. *Records of the Moravians in North Carolina*, vol. 2 (Raleigh, 1922).

Gage, Thomas. "Queries of George Chalmers, with answers of General Gage . . . ," in *Collections of the Massachusetts Historical Society*, Series 4, vol. 4 (Boston: Little, Brown & Co, 1858), 367–372.

Gassicourt, Charles-Louis, Cadet de. *Le thé est-il plus nuisible qu'utile?* (Paris, 1808).

"General Gage's account of the late battle at Boston. Baltimore, April [i.e., May] 15. Annapolis, May 12, 1775. The following was this day received by the post, included in letter from General Gage, dated Boston, April 29, 1775, which we give to the public by authority." Evans 14192.

Gray, Harrison. "The two congresses cut up: or A few remarks upon some of the votes and resolutions of the Continental Congress, held at Philadelphia in September, and the Provincial Congress, held at Cambridge in November 1774" (Boston; reprint New York, 1775). Evans 14074.

Graydon, W. *Memoirs of a Life Chiefly Passed in Pennsylvania within the Last Sixty Years* (Harrisburgh: John Wyeth, 1811; reprint Edinburgh 1822).

Greene, Jack P., ed. *The Diary of Colonel Landon Carter of Sabine Hall, 1752–1778* (Richmond: Virginia Historical Society, 1987; reprint of 1965 edition), vol. 2.

Guttridge, G. H., ed. "The American Correspondence of a Bristol Merchant 1766–1776, Letters of Richard Champion." *University of California Publications in History* 22, no. 1 (1934).

Hamilton, Kenneth Gardiner. *John Ettwein and the Moravian Church during the Revolutionary Period* (Bethlehem, PA: Times Publishing, 1940).

Hammond, Roland. *A History and Genealogy of the Descendants of William Hammond* (Boston: 1894).

Hanley, Thomas O'Brian, ed. *The John Carroll Papers* (Notre Dame: University of Notre Dame Press, 1976).

Hanson, Edward W., ed., *The Papers of Robert Treat Paine*, vol. 3 (Boston: Massachusetts Historical Society, 2005).

Hanway, Jonas. *An Essay on Tea: Considered as pernicious to health, obstructing industry, and impoverishing the nation: With a short account of its growth, and great consumption in these kingdoms: with several political reflections: in twenty-five letters addressed to two ladies* (London, 1756).

Harwell, Richard Barksdale, ed. *Proceedings of the County Committees, 1774–1776, the Committees of Safety of Westmoreland and Fincastle* (Richmond: Virginia State Library, 1956).

Hemphill, William Edwin and Wylma Anne Wates, eds. *Extracts from the Journals of the Provincial Congresses of South Carolina, 1775–1776* (Columbia, 1960).

Hemphill, William Edwin, Wylma Ann Wates, and R. Nicholas Olsberg, eds. *Journals of the General Assembly and House of Representatives 1776–1780* (Columbia: University of South Carolina Press or the South Carolina Department of Archives and History, 1970).

Higginbotham, Don, ed. *The Papers of James Iredell* (Raleigh: Division of Archives and History, Department of Cultural Resources, 1976).

Historical Manuscripts Commission. *The Manuscripts of the Earl of Dartmouth*, vol. 1, Eleventh Report; appendix, part 5 (London: Her Majesty's Stationery Office, 1887).

Historical Manuscripts Commission. *The Manuscripts of the Earl of Dartmouth*, vol. 2, American papers. Fourteenth Report; Appendix Part 10 (London: Her Majesty's Stationery Office, 1895).

Historical Manuscripts Commission. *The Manuscripts of the Earl of Dartmouth*, vol. 3, Fifteenth Report; Appendix Part 1 (London: Her Majesty's Stationery Office, 1896).

Hoffman, Ronald, ed. *Dear Papa, Dear Charley. The Papers of Charles Carroll of Carrollton, 1748–1782* (Chapel Hill: University of North Carolina Press for the Omohundro Institute of Early American History and Culture), 3 vols.

House of Commons. "Returns showing the number of pounds weight of tea sold by the East India Company, for home consumption, in each year from 1740 down to the termination of the Company's sales; &c." *House of Commons Sessional Papers*, 1845, vol. 46, paper 191.

Hulton, Ann. *Letters of a Loyalist Lady. Being the Letters of Ann Hulton, Sister of Henry Hulton, Commissioner of Customs at Boston, 1767–1776* (Cambridge, MA: Harvard University Press, 1927).

Humphrey, William. "A Journal Kept by William Humphrey." *Magazine of History with Notes and Queries*, Extra no. 166 (Tarrytown, NY: William Abbatt, 1931): 87–122.

Hutchinson, Peter Orlando, ed. *The Diary and Letters of Thomas Hutchinson* (London, 1883).

Innis, Harold A., ed. *The Diary of Simeon Perkins, 1766–1780* (Toronto: The Champlain Society, Greenwood Press Reprint, 1969).

Irving, T., & J. Mein, J. *A State of importations from Great-Britain into the port of Boston. From the beginning of January 1770: To which is added an account of all the goods that have been re-shipt from the above port for Great-Britain, since January 1769: The whole taken from the Custom-House of the Port of Boston* (Boston, 1770) Readex. Early American Imprints, Series 1, no. 11744.

Jay, John. Elizabeth M. Nuxoll, ed. *The Selected Papers of John Jay, 1760–1799* (Charlottesville: University of Virginia Press, 2010).

Journal Kept by Hugh Findlay, Surveyor of the Post Roads on the Continent of North America during His Survey of the Post Offices between Falmouth and Casco Bay in the Province of Massachusetts and Savannah in Georgia; Begun the 13th Septr. 1773 and Ended 26th June 1774 (Brooklyn, NY: Frank H. Norton, 1867).

"Journal Kept in Quebec in 1775 by James Jeffry." *EIHC* 50, no. 2 (April 1914): 97–150.

Journals of the Continental Congress, 1774–1789 (Washington, DC: U.S. Government Printing Office, 1904–1937), American Memory, https://memory.loc.gov/ammem/amlaw/lwjc.html.

Journals of the House of Representatives of Massachusetts 1773–1774 (Boston: Massachusetts Historical Society, 1981).

Journals of the Provincial Congress, Provincial Convention, Committee of Safety and Council of Safety of the State of New York, 1775–1776–1777 (Albany, 1842).

Kennedy, John Pendleton. *Journals of the House of Burgesses of Virginia, 1773–1776*, vol. 13 (Richmond, VA, 1913).

Kimball, James, ed. "The One Hundredth Anniversary of the Destruction of Tea in Boston Harbor: With a Sketch of William Russell, of Boston, one of the 'Tea Destroyers,'" *EIHC* 12 (1874): 197–239.

Klepp, Susan E. and Karin Wulf, eds. *The Diary of Hannah Callender Sansom. Sense and Sensibility in the Age of the American Revolution* (Ithaca, NY: Cornell University Press, 2010).

Knight, Erastus C., comp. *New York in the Revolution as Colony and State. Supplement* (Albany: Oliver A. Quayle, 1901).

Knollenberg, Bernard, ed. *Correspondence of Governor Samuel Ward May 1775–March 1776* (Providence: Rhode Island Historical Society, 1952).

Land, Aubrey C., ed. *Letters from America. William Eddis* (Cambridge, MA: Belknap Press, 1969).

Laurens, Henry. *The Papers of Henry Laurens* (Columbia: University of South Carolina Press, 1968–2003).

The Lee Papers, 4 vols., *Collections of the New-York Historical Society*, Series 3 (New York, 1871).

"Letters of John Andrews, Esqr., of Boston," *Proc. MHS* 8 (1864): 314–430.

Lincoln, William, ed. *The Journals of Each Provincial Congress of Massachusetts in 1774 and 1775* (Boston, 1838).

Lodge, Henry Cabot, ed. *Life and Letters of George Cabot* (Boston, 1878).

Lott, Abraham. "A Journal of a Voyage to Albany, etc., Made by Abraham Lott, Treasurer of the Colony of New York, 1774." *Historical Magazine* 8, no. 2 (Aug 1870): 65–74.

Lyman, Joseph. "A Sermon Preached at Hatfield December 15th 1774. Being the Day Recommended by the Late Provincial Congress to be Observed as a Day of Thanksgiving" (Boston, 1775).

Macaulay, Alexander. "Journal of Alexander Macaulay." *WMQ* 11, no. 3 (January 1903): 180–191.

Maguire, James H. ed. "A Critical Edition of Edward Parry's Journal, March 28, 1775 to August 13, 1777" (PhD diss., Indiana University, 1970).

Main, Jackson T., ed. *Rebel versus Tory: The Crisis of the Revolution, 1773–1776* (Chicago: Rand McNally, 1963).

Mason, Frances Norton. *John Norton and Sons: Merchants of London and Virginia* (Devon: David & Charles, Newton Abbot, 1968).

Mason, George Champlin. *Reminiscences of Newport* (Newport, RI, 1884).

Mason, Simon. *The Good and Bad Effects of Tea Consider'd* (London, 1745).

Massachusettensis. "Present State of the Province of Massachusetts Bay," 1775. Readex. Early American Imprints, Series 1, no. 14157.

Massachusetts Historical Society. "Aspinwall Papers II," *Collections of the Massachusetts Historical Society*, Series 4, vol. 10 (Boston: The Society, 1881).

The Massachusetts Vital Records Project. http://ma-vitalrecords.org/.

Maxwell, William. "My Mother: Memoirs of Mrs. Helen Read," *Lower Norfolk County Virginia Antiquary* 1: 96–102 (1895–1896).

Mayer, Brantz, ed. *Journal of Charles Carroll of Carrollton* (Baltimore, 1876).

Mays, David John, ed. *The Letters and Papers of Edmund Pendleton, 1734–1803* (Charlottesville: Virginia Historical Society, University of Virginia Press, 1967).

Meigs, Return. *Journal of the Expedition against Quebec: Under Command of Col. Benedict Arnold in the Year 1775* (New York, 1864).

"The merchants and traders of this town . . . ," May 24, 1774. Boston. Early American Imprints, Series 1, no. 13156.

Miller, Amelia F., and A. R. Riggs. *Romance, Remedies, and Revolution: The Journal of Dr. Elihu Ashley of Deerfield, Massachusetts, 1773–1775* (Amherst: University of Massachusetts Press, 2007).

Miller, Lillian B., ed. *The Selected Papers of Charles Willson Peale and His Family*, vol. 1 (New Haven, CT: Yale University Press, 1983).

"Minutes of the Committee of Safety of Bucks County, Pennsylvania, 1774–1776." *PMHB* 15, no. 3 (1891): 257–290.

Minutes of the Provincial Congress and the Council of Safety of the State of New Jersey (Trenton: Naar, Day & Naar, 1879).

Minutes of the Provincial Council of Pennsylvania 10 (Harrisburg, 1852).

Moore, Hugh. *Memoir of Col. Ethan Allen* (Plattsburgh, NY, 1834).

M'Robert, Patrick. *A Tour through Part of the North Provinces of America 1774–1775* (Edinburgh, 1776), Pamphlet Series. Narratives & Documents. Historical Society of Pennsylvania, no 1.

Mulford, Carla, ed. *John Leacock's The First Book of the American Chronicles of the Times, 1774–1775* (Newark, DE: University of Delaware Press, 1987).

A Narrative of the Life of William Beadle (Bennington, VT: Haswell,1794).

Nixon, John, John Kidd, John Cox, Joseph McIlvain, James Benezet, and Thomas Harvey. "Minutes of the Committee of Safety of Bucks County, Pennsylvania, 1774–1776." *PMHB* 15, no. 3 (1891): 257–290.

Oliver, Andrew, ed. *Journal of Samuel Curwen, Loyalist* (Cambridge, MA: Harvard University Press, 1972).

"An oration: Delivered March 5, 1774, at the request of the inhabitants of the town of Boston . . . By the Honorable John Hancock, Esquire." Readex. Early American Imprints, Series 1, no. 14097.

Padelford, Philip, ed. *Colonial Panorama 1775. Dr. Robert Honyman's Journal for March and April* (San Marino, CA: Huntington Library, 1939).

Page, Thomas Hyde, Sir. *Boston, Its Environs and Harbour, with the Rebels Works Raised Against That Town in 1775; from the Observations of Lieut. Page of His Majesty's Corps of Engineers and from those of other Gentlemen* [?, 1775], Map. LoC, https://www.loc.gov/item/gm71000623/.

Palfrey, William. "An Alphabetical List of the Sons of Liberty who din'd at Liberty Tree, Dorchester," 1769, https://www.masshist.org/database/viewer.php?item_id=8&pid=3.

Pennsylvania, State of. *Minutes of the Supreme Executive Council of Pennsylvania*, vol. 11 (Harrisburg: Theo. Fenn, 1852).

Price, Jacob M., ed. "Joshua Johnson's Letterbook: 1774 (July & Aug)," in *Joshua Johnson's Letterbook, 1771–1774: Letters from a Merchant in London to his Partners in Maryland*, (London: London Record Society, 1979), 145–156.

"Proceedings of the Committees of Safety of Caroline and Southampton Counties, Virginia, 1774–1776." *Bulletin of the Virginia State Library* 17, no. 3 (November 1929): 119–164.

"Proceedings of the Georgia Council of Safety," *Collections of the Georgia Historical Society*, vol. 5, part 1 (Savannah, 1901).

Public Record Office, Colonial Office. Filmed by South Carolina Department of Archives and History, *Records in the British Public Record Office Relating to South Carolina, 1663–1782*.

Ramsay, David. *A Sermon on Tea* (Charleston, SC and Lancaster, PA, 1774).

Randolph, John and Robert Carter Nicholas. *Considerations on the Present State of Virginia and Considerations on the Present State of Virginia Examined* (New York, 1919).

Records of the South Carolina Treasury, 1775–1780 (Columbia, SC: Department of Archives and History, 1969).

Reed, William, ed. *Life and Correspondence of Joseph Reed*, vol. 1 (1847).

A Report of the Record Commissioners of the City of Boston Containing the Boston Town Records, 1770 through 1777 (Boston, 1887).

Rice, Howard C., Jr., and Anne S. K. Brown, trans. and eds. *The American Campaigns of Rochambeau's Army, 1780, 1781, 1782, 1783* (Princeton: Princeton University Press, 1972), 2 vols.

Riley, Edward Miles, ed. *The Journal of John Harrower: An Indentured Servant in the Colony of Virginia, 1773–1776* (Williamsburg, VA, 1963).

Roberts, Kenneth. *March to Quebec: Journals of the Members of Arnold's Expedition* (New York: Doubleday, 1938).

Robertson, Archibald. *Archibald Robertson: His Diaries and Sketches in America, 1762–1780* (New York: New York Public Library, 1971 reprint of 1930 edition).

"Roll of Captain Matthew Smith's Company." *Pennsylvania Archives*, ed. John Blair Linn and William Henry Egle, Series 2, vol. 10 (1895): 39–42.

"Rules of the Charlestown Chamber of Commerce" (Charleston, 1774). Evans 13194.

Rumpf, J. D. F. *Deutschlands Goldgrube oder durch welche inlaendischen Erzeugnisse kann der fremde Kaffee, Thee und Zucker ersetzt? . . .* (Berlin, 1799).

Rutland, Robert A., ed. *The Papers of George Mason 1725–1792*. Vol 1, *1749–1778* (Chapel Hill: University of North Carolina Press, 1970).

Sabine, William H. W., ed. *Historical Memoirs . . . of William Smith* (New York: 1956, 1958; reprint 1969).

Sargent, Winthrop, ed. *Letters of John Andrews, Esq, of Boston, 1772–1776* (Cambridge, MA: John Wilson and Sons, 1866; reprinted from the Proceedings of the Massachusetts Historical Society).

Saunders, William, L. *The Colonial Records of North Carolina*, vols. 9–10 (Raleigh, NC: P. M. Hale, Printer to the State, 1886–1890).

Schulz, Constance, ed. *The Papers of Eliza Lucas Pinckney and Harriott Pinckney Horry*, digital edition (Charlottesville: University of Virginia Press, Rotunda, 2012).

Scribner, Robert L., and Brent Tarter. *Revolutionary Virginia. The Road to Independence.* (Virginia Independence Bicentennial Commission, University Press of Virginia, 1973–1983), 7 vols.

Seabury, Samuel. *AN ALARM to the LEGISLATURE OF THE Province of New-York OCCASIONED BY The Present Political Disturbances, IN NORTH AMERICA: ADDRESSED To the Honourable Representatives IN GENERAL ASSEMBLY CONVENED* (New York, 1775).

Seabury, Samuel. *The Congress Canvassed: Or, an Examination into the Conduct of the Delegates, at Their Grand Convention, Held in Philadelphia, Sept. 1, 1774* (New York, 1774).

Seabury, Samuel. *Free thoughts, on the proceedings of the Continental Congress, held at Philadelphia Sept. 5, 1774: wherein their errors are exhibited, their . . .* (New York, 1774)

Selig, Robert A. "A German Soldier in America, 1780–1783: The Journal of Georg Daniel Flohr." *WMQ* 3rd Series, vol. 50, no. 3 (July 1993): 575–590.

Senter, Isaac. *The Journal of Isaac Senter . . .* (Philadelphia: Historical Society of Pennsylvania, 1846; reprint Tarrytown, NY, William Abbatt, 1915).

Shattuck, Lemuel. *A History of the Town of Concord . . .* (Boston, 1835).

Sigmond, G. G. *Tea: Its effects, Medicinal and Moral* (London, 1839).

Simmons, R. C., and P. D. G. Thomas. *Proceedings and Debates of the British Parliaments Respecting North America, 1754–1783* (New York: Kraus International Publications, 1985).

Smith, Paul H., ed. *Letters of Delegates to Congress, 1774–1789* (Washington, DC: Library of Congress, 1976–2000), American Memory, https://memory.loc .gov/ammem/amlaw/lwdg.html.

Smith, Susan. "Biographical Sketch of Col. David Mason, by His Daughter, Mrs. Susan Smith," *EIHC* 48, no 3 (July 1912): 197–216.

Staples, William R. *The Documentary History of the Destruction of the Gaspée* (Providence, Knowles, Vose, and Anthony, 1845, 1900 reprint, 2001 web version: http://gaspee.org/StaplesGaspee.htm).

Stevens, Benjamin Franklin. *Facsimiles of Manuscripts in European Archives Relating to America, 1773–1783* (London, 1889–1898).

Stone, Edwin Martin, ed. *The Invasion of Canada in 1775: Including the Journal of Captain Simeon Thayer* (Providence, 1867).

Suffolk Resolves. http://www.masshist.org/database/696.

Sullivan, James, ed. *Minutes of the Albany Committee of Correspondence* (Albany: University of the State of New York, 1923).

Tatum, Edward H. Jr., ed. *The American Journal of Ambrose Serle, Secretary to Lord Howe 1776–1778* (San Marino, CA: The Huntington Library, 1940).

Taylor, Robert J., ed. *The Adams Papers*, Papers of John Adams, vol. 4, *February–August 1776* (Cambridge, MA: Harvard University Press, 1979).

Thatcher, James. *A Military Journal During the American Revolutionary War: From 1775 to 1783* (Boston, 1827).

Thomas, D. O. and Bernard Peach, eds. *The Correspondence of Richard Price, Volume 1: July 1748–March 1778* (Durham, NC: Duke University Press, 1983).

"To the Inhabitants of the city and county of New-York." 1775. Evans #14505.

"The Tradesmen's Protest against the Proceedings of the Merchants . . ." November 3, 1773. Boston. Printed by E Russell. Evans 13046.

"Treaty of Amity and Commerce between the United States and France; February 6, 1778." http://avalon.law.yale.edu/18th_century/fr1788-1.asp#art2.

Tupper, Frederick, and Helen Tyler Brown. *Grandmother Tyler's Book. The Recollections of Mary Palmer Tyler (Mrs. Royall Tyler) 1775–1866* (New York: G. P. Putnam's Sons, 1925).

Upton, Leslie F. S. "Proceedings of Ye Body Respecting the Tea." *WMQ*, 3rd Series, vol. 22, no. 2 (April 1965): 287–300.

Upton, Leslie F. S. *Revolutionary versus Loyalist. The First American Civil War, 1774–1784* (Waltham, MA: Blaisdell Publishing, 1968).

Vernon, Thomas. *The Diary of Thomas Vernon* (Providence, RI, 1881).

Walsh, Richard, ed. *The Writings of Christopher Gadsden 1746–1805* (Columbia: University of South Carolina Press, 1966).

Warren, Mercy Otis. *Poems Dramatic and Miscellaneous* (Boston, 1790).

Wesley, John. *A Letter to a Friend, Concerning Tea* (London, 1748; reprint 1825).

Wharton, Samuel. "Observations upon the Consumption of Teas in North America, by Samuel Wharton, 1773." *PMHB* (1901): 139–141.

"Whereas a great number of people have express'd a desire that the names of the addressers to the late Gov. Hutchinson, and protesters against the solemn league and covenant might be made publick, the following is a true list of the same, viz." Boston. 1774 Evans 13767.

White, George. *Historical Collections of Georgia . . .* (New York, 1855).

Willard, Margaret Wheeler. *Letters on the American Revolution 1774–1776* (Port Washington, NY: Kennikat Press, 1925).

Willcox, William B., ed. *Papers of Benjamin Franklin* (New Haven, CT: Yale University Press, 1959). www.franklinpapers.org.

Williams, Samuel. A *Discourse on the Love of Our Country; Delivered on a Day of Thanksgiving* (Salem, MA, 1775).

Winslow, Isaac, and Margaret Catherine Winslow, transcribed and edited by Robert Newsom. *Family Memorial. The Winslows of Boston* (Boston: 1837?–1873?). MHS.

Winter, Kari J. *The Blind African Slave, Or Memoirs of Boyrereau Brinch, Nicknamed Jeffrey Brace* (Madison: University of Wisconsin Press, 2004).

Withington, Lothrop, ed. *Caleb Haskell's Diary. May 5, 1775–May 30, 1776.* (Newburyport, MA, 1881).

Woloch, Nancy. *Early American Women. A Documentary History, 1600–1900.* (Belmont, CA: Wadsworth, 1992).

Wroth, L. Kinvin, et al. *Province in Rebellion. A Documentary History of the Founding of the Commonwealth of Massachusetts 1774–1775* (Cambridge, MA: Harvard University Press, 1975).

York, Neil Longley, ed. *Henry Hulton and the American Revolution. An Outsider's Inside View* (Colonial Society of Massachusetts, University of Virginia Press, 2010).

Secondary Sources

Adams, Willi Paul. "The Colonial German-Language Press and the American Revolution," in *The Press & the American Revolution*, ed. Bernard Bailyn and John B. Hench, 151–228 (Boston: Northeastern University Press, 1980).

Adelman, David C. "Strangers: Civil Rights of Jews in the Colony of Rhode Island." *Rhode Island Jewish Historical Association*, Notes I, no. 2 (December 1954): 104–118.

Adelman, Joseph M. "'A Constitutional Conveyance of Intelligence, Public and Private': The Post Office, the Business of Printing, and the American Revolution." *Enterprise & Society* 11, no. 4 (2010): 711–754.

Adelman, Joseph M. *Revolutionary Networks: The Business and Politics of Printing the News, 1763–1789* (Baltimore: Johns Hopkins University Press, 2019).

Akers, Charles W. *The Divine Politician. Samuel Cooper and the American Revolution in Boston* (Boston: Northeastern University Press, 1982).

Alden, John Richard. *General Gage in America. Being Principally A History of His Role in the American Revolution* (Baton Rouge: Louisiana State University Press, 1948).

Allan, Herbert S. *John Hancock. Patriot in Purple* (New York: Beechhurst Press, 1953).

American State Papers. (Washington, DC: Gales and Seaton, 1832–1861). https://memory.loc.gov/ammem/amlaw/lwsp.html.

American War of Independence at Sea. https://www.awiatsea.com/Privateers/H/Hawke%20Rhode%20Island%20Sloop%20[Crawford%20Phillips].pdf.

Ammerman, David. *In the Common Cause: American Response to the Coercive Acts of 1774* (Charlottesville: University Press of Virginia, 1974).

Anderson, James Donald. "Thomas Wharton, Exile in Virginia, 1777–1778." *VMHB* 89, no. 4 (October 1981): 425–447.

Anderson, Jennifer. *Mahogany: The Cost of Luxury in Early America* (Cambridge, MA: Harvard University Press, 2012)

Anderson, Virginia DeJohn. *The Martyr and the Traitor. Nathan Hale, Moses Dunbar, and the American Revolution* (Oxford: Oxford University Press, 2017).

Aptheker, Herbert. *The American Revolution 1763–1783: A Marxist Interpretation* (New York: International Publishers, 1960).

Augur, Helen. *The Secret War of Independence* (New York: Duell, Sloan and Pearce, 1955).

Bailyn, Bernard. *Ordeal of Thomas Hutchinson* (Cambridge, MA: Harvard University Press, 1974).

Banks, Charles Edward. *The History of York, Maine* (Boston: Calkins Press, 1931).

Barck, Oscar Theodore, Jr. *New York City during the War for Independence* (New York: Columbia University Press, 1931).

Barnes, Viola F. "Francis Legge, Governor of Loyalist Nova Scotia 1773–1776." *NEQ* 4, no 3 (1931): 420–447.

Barthes, Roland. *Mythologies*. Trans. Annette Lavers (New York: Noonday Press, 1972).

Bauman, John F. Robert W. Dent, et al. *Lively Stones: The Evolution of the Congregational Church of Boothbay Harbor, Maine, from Its Origins in 1766 to 2016* (Congregational Church of Boothbay Harbor, 2015).

Baxter, W. T. *The House of Hancock. Business in Boston, 1724–1775* (Cambridge, MA: Harvard University Press, 1945).

Beals, Melodee H. *Coin, Kirk, Class and Kin. Emigration, Social Change and Identity in Southern Scotland* (Oxford: Peter Lang, 2011).

Becker, Carl Lotus. *The History of Political Parties in the Province of New York, 1760–1776* (Wisconsin, 1909, reprint 1968).

Bell, J. L. "George Washington's Headquarters and Home, Cambridge, Massachusetts: Longfellow House-Washington's Headquarters National Historic Site." National Park Service, Department of the Interior report, 2012).

Bell, J. L. *The Road to Concord: How Four Stolen Canon Ignited the Revolutionary War* (Yardley, PA: Westholme Publishing, 2016).

Benes, Peter and Jane M. Benes. *Itinerancy in New England and New York* (Boston: Boston University Press, 1986).

Benson, Dale Edward. "Wealth and Power in Virginia, 1774–1776: A Study of the Organization of Revolt" (PhD diss., University of Maine, 1970).

Berkin, Carol. *Jonathan Sewall, Odyssey of an American Loyalist* (New York: Columbia University Press, 1974)

Berkin, Carol. *Revolutionary Mothers. Women in the Struggle for America's Independence* (New York: Knopf, 2005).

Bickham, Troy. *Making Headlines: The American Revolution as Seen through the British Press* (DeKalb: Northern Illinois University Press, 2009).

Bielinski, Stefan. "Abraham. C. Cuyler." https://exhibitions.nysm.nysed.gov//albany/bios/c/abccuyler359.html.

Bielinski, Stefan. "Albany County," in *The Other New York: The American Revolution beyond New York City, 1763–1787*, ed. Joseph S. Tiedemann and Eugene R. Fingerhut, 155–174 (Albany: SUNY Press, 2005).

Bieliski, Stefan., "The Beginning of the End." https://exhibitions.nysm.nysed.gov//albany/or/or-be.html.

Bjork, Gordon C. *Stagnation and Growth in the American Economy, 1784–1792* (New York: Garland, 1985).

Bliven, Bruce, Jr. *Under the Guns. New York, 1775–1776* (New York: Harper & Row, 1972).

Bloch, Ruth H. "The Gendered Meanings of Virtue in Revolutionary America." *Signs* 13, no. 1 (Autumn 1987): 37–58.

Blok P. J. and P. C. Molhuysen, eds. *Nieuw Netherlandsch Biografisch Woordenboek.* 10 vols. (Leiden: A. W. Sijthoff, 1911–1937).

Boston Tea Party Ship Museum. Accessed July 1, 2023. https://www.bostontea partyship.com/partners/a-box-worth-keeping.

Botein, Stephen. "'Meer Mechanics' and the Open Press: The Business and Political Strategies of Colonial American Printers." *Perspectives in American History* 9 (1975): 127–228.

Botein, Stephen. "Printers and the American Revolution," in *The Press & the American Revolution*, ed. Bernard Bailyn and John B. Hench, 11–57 (Boston: Northeastern University Press, 1980).

Bowen, George Loveridge. *James Lloyd II, M.D.: And His Family on Lloyd Neck* (Privately Printed, 1988).

Bowen, Huw V. *Revenue and Reform: The Indian Problem in British Politics, 1757–1773* (Cambridge: Cambridge University Press, 1991).

Bowen, Huw V. "'So Alarming an Evil': Smuggling, Pilfering and the English East India Company, 1750–1810." *International Journal of Maritime History* 14, no. 1 (2002): 1–31.

Braisted, Todd W. "Bergen County's Loyalist Population." Accessed July 1, 2023. https://www.bergencountyhistory.org/loyalists-in-bergen.

Brannon, Rebecca. *From Revolution to Reunion: The Reintegration of the South Carolina Loyalists* (Columbia: University of South Carolina Press, 2016).

Brebner, John. *The Neutral Yankees of Nova Scotia. A Marginal Colony during the Revolutionary Years* (New York: Columbia University Press, 1937).

Breen, Timothy Hall. *American Insurgents, American Patriots: The Revolution of the People* (New York: Hill and Wang, 2010).

Breen, Timothy Hall. "'Baubles of Britain': The American and Consumer Revolutions of the Eighteenth Century." *Past and Present* 119 (May 1988): 73–104.

Breen, Timothy Hall. *The Marketplace of Revolution: How Consumer Politics Shaped American Independence.* (Oxford: Oxford University Press, 2004).

Brigham, Clarence S. *History and Bibliography of American Newspapers, 1690–1820* (Worcester, MA: American Antiquarian Society, 1947).

Brooke, John L. "Consumer Virtues in Revolutionary America?" *Reviews in American History* 32, no. 3 (September 2004): 329–340.

Brown, Kathleen M. *Good Wives, Nasty Wenches, and Anxious Patriarchs: Gender, Race, and Power in Colonial Virginia* (Chapel Hill: University of North Carolina Press for the Omohundro Institute of Early American History and Culture, 1996).

Brown, Richard D. *Revolutionary Politics in Massachusetts. The Boston Committee of Correspondence and the Towns, 1772–1774* (New York: Norton, 1970).

Brown, Richard D. "The Shifting Freedoms of the Press in the Eighteenth Century," in *A History of the Book in America I: The Colonial Book in the Atlantic World*, ed.

Hugh Amory and David D. Hall, 366–376 (Chapel Hill: American Antiquarian Society and University of North Carolina Press, 2007).

Brown, Wallace. *The King's Friends. The Composition and Motives of the American Loyalist Claimants* (Providence: Brown University Press, 1965).

Buck, Solon J. and Elizabeth Hawthorn Buck. *The Planting of Civilization in Western Pennsylvania* (Pittsburgh: Pittsburgh University Press, 1939, reprint 1967).

Buel, Richard, Jr. "Freedom of the Press in Revolutionary America: The Evolution of Libertarianism, 1760–1820," in *The Press & the American Revolution*, ed. Bernard Bailyn and John B. Hench, 59–98 (Boston: Northeastern University Press, 1980).

Burnett, Edmund Cody. *The Continental Congress* (New York: Macmillan, 1941).

Butler, Nicholas Miller. *Votaries of Apollo: The St. Cecilia Society and the Patronage of Concert Music in Charleston, South Carolina, 1766–1820* (Columbia: University of South Carolina Press, 2007).

Butt, Marshall. *Portsmouth under Four Flags, 1752–1970* (Portsmouth, VA: Portsmouth Historical Association & the Friends of the Portsmouth Naval Shipyard Museum, 1971).

Cahill, Barry. "The Treason of the Merchants: Dissent and Repression in Halifax in the Era of the American Revolution." *Acadiensis* 26, no. 1 (Autumn 1996): 52–70.

Cain, Alexander. "Anxiety and Distress: Civilians Inside the Siege of Boston." *Journal of the American Revolution*, February 13, 2017. https://allthingsliberty.com/2017/02/anxiety-distress-civilians-inside-siege-boston/#_ednref18.

Calhoon, Robert M. "The Character and Coherence of the Loyalist Press," in *The Loyalist Perception and Other Essays* (Columbia: University of South Carolina Press, 1989), 229–272.

Calhoon, Robert M. "Loyalism and Neutrality," in *A Companion to the American Revolution*, ed. Jack. P. Greene and J. R. Pole (Malden, MA: Blackwell, 2000), 235–247.

Carp, Benjamin L. *Defiance of the Patriots: The Boston Tea Party and the Making of America* (New Haven, CT: Yale University Press, 2010).

Carp, Benjamin L. *Rebels Rising: Cities and the American Revolution* (Oxford: Oxford University Press, 2007).

Carter, Susan B., Scott Sigmund Gartner, Michael R. Haines, Alan L. Olmstead, Richard Sutch, and Gavin Wright, eds. *Historical Statistics of the United States, Earliest Times to the Present: Millennial Edition* (New York: Cambridge University Press, 2006).

Castronovo, Russ. *Propaganda 1776: Secrets, Leaks and Revolutionary Communications in Early America* (Oxford: Oxford University Press, 2014).

Catalog of the Records and Files of the Office of the Clerk of the Supreme Judicial Court for the County of Suffolk (Boston, 1897).

Champagne, Roger J. *Alexander McDougall and the American Revolution in New York* (Schenectady, NY: New York State American Revolution Bicentennial Commission, Union College Press, 1975).

Clark, Charles E. "Early American Journalism: News and Opinion in the Popular Press," in *A History of the Book in America I: The Colonial Book in the Atlantic*

World, ed. Hugh Amory and David D. Hall, 347–365 (Chapel Hill: American Antiquarian Society and University of North Carolina Press, 2007).

Clark, Dora Mae. "The American Board of Customs, 1767–1783." *AHR* 45, no. 4 (1940): 777–806.

Clark, J. C. D. *Thomas Paine: Britain, America, and France in the Age of Enlightenment and Revolution* (Oxford: Oxford University Press, 2018).

Cleary, Patricia. *Elizabeth Murray: A Woman's Pursuit of Independence in Eighteenth-Century America* (Amherst: University of Massachusetts Press, 2000).

Cogliano, Francis D. "Deliverance from Luxury: Pope's Day, Conflict and Consensus in Colonial Boston, 1745–1765." *Studies in Popular Culture* 15, no. 2 (1993): 15–28.

Cogliano, Francis D. *No King, No Popery. Anti-Catholicism in Revolutionary New England* (Westport, CT: Greenwood Press, 1995).

Cohen, Hennig. *The South Carolina Gazette 1732–1775* (Columbia: University of South Carolina Press, 1953).

Cole, Arthur Harrison. *Wholesale Commodity Prices in the United States, 1770–1861 Statistical Supplement* (Cambridge, MA: Harvard University Press, 1938).

Cole, W. A. "Trends in Eighteenth-Century Smuggling." *EHR* 10, no. 3 (1958): 395–410.

Coleman, John M. *Thomas McKean. Forgotten Leader of the Revolution* (Rockaway, NJ: American Faculty Press, 1975).

Coleman, Kenneth. *The American Revolution in Georgia, 1763–1789* (Athens: University of Georgia Press, 1958).

Cometti, Elizabeth. "Women in the American Revolution." *NEQ* 20, no. 3 (September 1947): 329–346.

Conroy, David W. *In Public Houses. Drink and the Revolution of Authority in Colonial Massachusetts.* (Chapel Hill: University of North Carolina Press for the Omohundro Institute of Early American History and Culture, 1995).

Countryman, Edward. *A People in Revolution. The American Revolution and Political Society in New York, 1760–1790* (Baltimore: Johns Hopkins University Press, 1981).

Crane, Elaine Forman. *A Dependent People. Newport, Rhode Island in the Revolutionary Era* (New York: Fordham University Press, 1985).

Crary, Catherine Snell. "The Tory and the Spy: The Double Life of James Rivington." *WMQ*, 3rd Series, vol. 16, no. 1 (January 1959): 61–72.

Crist, Robert G. "Cumberland County," in *Beyond Philadelphia: The American Revolution in the Pennsylvania Hinterland*, ed. John B. Frantz and William Pencak, 107–132 (University Park: Pennsylvania State University Press, 1998).

Curtis, George M., III, and Harold B. Gill Jr. "A Man Apart: Nicholas Cresswell's American Odyssey, 1774–1777." *Indiana Magazine of History* 96, no. 2 (June 2000): 169–190.

Cushing, Thomas. *History of the Counties of Gloucester, Salem and Cumberland, New Jersey* (Philadelphia, 1883).

Dabney, William M. "Letters from Norfolk, Scottish Merchants View the Revolutionary Crisis," in *The Old Dominion. Essays for Thomas Perkins Abernethy*, ed. Darrett B. Rutman, 109–121 (Charlottesville: University of Virginia Press, 1964).

Dabney William M., and Marion Dargan. *William Henry Drayton & the American Revolution* (Albuquerque: University of New Mexico Press, 1962).

Davidson, Philip. *Propaganda and the American Revolution, 1763–1783* (Chapel Hill: University of North Carolina Press, 1941).

Day, Katherine. "Another Look at the Boston 'Caucus.'" *Journal of American Studies 5*, no. 1 (1971): 19–42.

Deane, Samuel. *History of Scituate, Massachusetts, from its First Settlement to 1831* (Boston, 1831).

Dermigny, Louis. *La Chine et l'Occident. Le Commerce à Canton au XXVIIe siècle, 1719–1833*, vol. 2 (Paris: S. E. V. P. E. N., 1964).

Destler, Chester McArthur. *Joshua Coit. American Federalist, 1758–1798* (Middletown, CT: Wesleyan University Press, 1962).

de Vries, Jan, and Ad van der Woude. *The First Modern Economy: Success, Failure and Perseverance of the Dutch Economy, 1500–1815* (Cambridge: Cambridge University Press, 1997).

Dickerson, Oliver M. *The Navigation Acts and the American Revolution* (Philadelphia: University of Pennsylvania Press, 1951).

Dillard, Richard. *The Historic Tea-Party of Edenton* (Edenton?, 1898?).

Dillo, Ingrid G. "Made to Measure? A Comparative Approach to the System and Costs of the English and Dutch Shipping to Asia in the 18th Century," in *Anglo-Dutch Mercantile Marine Relations 1770–1850*, ed. J. R. Bruijn and W.F.J. Mörzer Bruyns (Amsterdam: Rijksmuseum Nederlands Scheepvaartmuseum, 1991).

Doerflinger, Thomas. *A Vigorous Spirit of Enterprise: Merchants and Economic Development in Revolutionary Philadelphia* (Chapel Hill: University of North Carolina Press, 1986).

Donat, James G. "The Rev. John Wesley's Extractions from Dr. Tissot: A Methodist Imprimateur," *History of Science 39*, no 3 (September 2001): 285–298.

Donoughue, Bernard. *British Politics and the American Revolution: The Path to War, 1773–75* (London: Macmillan, 1964).

Edelberg, Cynthia D. *Jonathan Odell: The Loyalist Poet of the American Revolution* (Durham, NC: Duke University Press, 1987).

Edgar, Walter. *South Carolina: A History* (Columbia: University of South Carolina Press, 1998).

Egerton, Douglas R. *Death or Liberty: African Americans and Revolutionary America* (Oxford: Oxford University Press, 2009).

Egle, William Henry. *Some Pennsylvania Women during the War of the Revolution* (Harrisburg, PA: Harrisburg Publishing, 1898).

Egnal, Marc. *A Mighty Empire: The Origins of the American Revolution* (Ithaca, NY: Cornell University Press, 1988).

Ellis, Franklin and Samuel Evans. *History of Lancaster County, Pennsylvania* (Philadelphia: Everts & Peck, 1883).

Ellison, Amy Noel. "Montgomery's Misfortune: The American Defeat at Quebec and the March toward Independence, 1775–1776." *EAS 15*, no 3 (Summer 2017): 591–616.

Ernst, George. *New England Miniature: A History of York, Maine* (Freeport, ME: Bond Wheelwright Company, 1961).

Evans, Emory. *Thomas Nelson of Yorktown: Revolutionary Virginian* (Charlottesville: Published for the Colonial Williamsburg Foundation by the University Press of Virginia, 1975).

Fauntleroy, Juliet. "John Hook as a Loyalist." *Virginia Magazine of History and Biography* 33, no. 4 (October 1925): 399–403.

Felt, Joseph B. *Annals of Salem* (Salem, MA, 1845).

Ferdinand, C. Y. "Selling It to the Provinces: News and Commerce Round Eighteenth-Century Salisbury," in *Consumption and the World of Goods*, ed. John Breer and Roy Porter, 393–411 (New York: Routledge, 1997).

Fichter, James. "Collecting Debts: Virginia Merchants, the Association, and the Meetings of November 1774." *VMHB* 130, no 3 (2022): 172–217.

Fichter, James. "The Mystery of the 'Alternative of Williamsburg.'" *Journal of the American Revolution*, April 22, 2019. https://allthingsliberty.com/2019/04/the-mystery-of-the-alternative-of-williams-burg/.

Fichter, James. *So Great a Proffit: How the East Indies Transformed Anglo-American Capitalism* (Cambridge, MA: Harvard University Press, 2010).

Fichter, James. "The Tea That Survived the Boston Tea Party." *Journal of the American Revolution*, June 20, 2019. https://allthingsliberty.com/2019/06/the-tea-that-survived-the-boston-tea-party/.

Fischer, David Hackett. *Paul Revere's Ride* (Oxford: Oxford University Press, 1994).

Fischer, Lewis R. "Revolution without Independence: The Canadian Colonies, 1749–1775," in *The Economy of Early America, The Revolutionary Period, 1763–1790*, ed. Ronald Hoffman, John J. McCusker, Russell R. Menard, and Peter J. Albert, 88–125 (Charlottesville: University Press of Virginia, 1988).

Fowler, William M., Jr. *William Ellery: A Rhode Island Politico and Lord of Admiralty* (Metuchen, NJ: The Scarecrow Press, 1973).

Frantz, John B., and William Pencak. *Beyond Philadelphia. The American Revolution in the Pennsylvania Hinterland* (University Park: Pennsylvania State University Press, 1998).

Fraser, Walter J., Jr. *Charleston! Charleston! The History of a Southern City* (Columbia: University of South Carolina Press, 1989).

Fraser, Walter J., Jr. *Patriots Pistols and Petticoats: "Poor Sinful Charles Town" during the American Revolution*, 2nd ed. (Columbia: University of South Carolina Press, 1993).

French, Allen. *The Siege of Boston* (Boston: Macmillan, 1911).

Fries, Adelaide L. *The Road to Salem* (Chapel Hill: University of North Carolina Press, 1944).

Frothingham, Richard. *History of the Siege of Boston* (Boston, 1851).

Galloway, John, and Thomas Ringgold. "Account of the Destruction of the Brig 'Peggy Stewart', at Annapolis, 1774." *PMHB* 25, no. 2 (1901): 248–254.

Gerlach, Larry R. *Prologue to Independence: New Jersey in the Coming of the American Revolution* (New Brunswick, NJ: Rutgers University Press, 1976).

Gilje, Paul A. "Loyalty and Liberty: The Ambiguous Patriotism of Jack Tar in the American Revolution." *Pennsylvania History: A Journal of Mid-Atlantic Studies* 67, no. 2 (Spring 2000): 165–193.

Gilje, Paul A. "Republican Rioting," in *Authority and Resistance in Early New York*, ed. William Pencack and Conrad Edick Wright, 202–225 (New York: New-York Historical Society, 1988).

Gilje, Paul A. *Rioting in America* (Bloomington: Indiana University Press, 1999).

Glickman, Lawrence B. *Buying Power: A History of Consumer Activism in America* (Chicago: University of Chicago Press, 2009).

Godbeer, Richard. *World of Trouble: A Philadelphia Quaker Family's Journey through the American Revolution* (New Haven, CT: Yale University Press, 2019).

Goodheart, Adam. "Tea & Fantasy: Fact, Fiction, and Revolution in a Historic American Town." *American Scholar* 74, no. 4 (Autumn 2005): 21–34.

Gould, Christopher. "The South Carolina and Continental Associations: Prelude to Revolution." *SCHM* 87, no. 1 (January 1986): 30–48.

Gould, Philip. "Loyalist Responses to Common Sense: The Politics of Authorship in Revolutionary America, " in *The Loyal Atlantic: Remaking the British Atlantic in the Revolutionary Era*, ed. Jerry Bannister and Liam Riordan, 105–127 (Toronto: University of Toronto Press, 2012).

Granger, Bruce Ingham. *Political Satire in the American Revolution, 1763–1783* (Ithaca, NY: Cornell University Press, 1960).

Greene, Francis Byron. *History of Boothbay, Southport and Boothbay Harbor, Maine. 1623–1905: With Family Genealogies* (Portland, ME, 1906).

Griffin, Edward M. *Old Brick: Charles Chauncy of Boston, 1705–1787* (Minneapolis: University of Minnesota Press, 1980).

Groce, George C., Jr. "Eliphalet Dyer: Connecticut Revolutionist," in *The Era of the American Revolution*, ed. Richard B. Morris, 290–304 (New York: Harper & Row, 1939).

Gross, Robert A. *The Minutemen and Their World* (New York: Hill and Wang, 1976).

Guild, Reuben Aldridge. *Early History of Brown University, including the Life, Times and Correspondence of President Manning, 1756–1791* (Providence, 1897).

Guthke, Karl. *Last Words. Variations on a Theme in Cultural History* (Princeton: Princeton University Press, 1992).

Gwyn, Julian. "Female Litigants before the Civil Courts of Nova Scotia, 1749–1801." *Histoire sociale / Social History* 3, no. 72 (2003): 311–346.

Hacker, J. David. "From '20. and Odd' to 10 Million: The Growth of the Slave Population in the United States." *Slavery & Abolition* 41, no. 4 (2020): 840–855.

Hall, Leslie. *Land and Allegiance in Revolutionary Georgia* (Athens: University of Georgia Press, 2001).

Halpenny, Francess G., and Jean Hamelin, eds. *Dictionary of Canadian Biography* (Toronto: University of Toronto/Université Laval, 1983).

Halsey, R. T. Haines. *The Boston Port Bill, as Pictured by a Contemporary London Cartoonist* (New York, 1904).

Halttunen, Karen. *Murder Most Foul. The Killer and the American Gothic Imagination* (Cambridge, MA: Harvard University Press, 1998).

Hancock, David. *Oceans of Wine: Madeira and the Emergence of an American Trade and Taste* (New Haven, CT: Yale University Press, 2009).

Harrington, Virginia D. *The New York Merchant on the Eve of the Revolution* (New York, 1935).

Hartigan-O'Connor, Ellen. "The Measure of the Market: Women's Economic Lives in Charleston, SC and Newport, RI, 1750–1820" (PhD diss., University of Michigan, 2003).

Hartigan-O'Connor, Ellen. *The Ties That Buy: Women and Commerce in Revolutionary America* (Philadelphia: University of Pennsylvania Press, 2009).

Hawke, David. *In the Midst of a Revolution* (Westport, CT: Greenwood Press, 1961).

Heaton, H. "The American Trade," in *The Trade Winds: A Study of British Overseas Trade during the French Wars 1793–1815*, ed. C. N. Parkinson, 194–226 (London, 1948).

Heckscher, Eli F. *An Economic History of Sweden.* Trans. Göran Ohlin (Cambridge, MA: Harvard University Press, 1954).

Hedges, James B. *The Browns of Providence Plantations. The Colonial Years.* (Providence: Brown University Press, 1968).

Herman Edward S., and Noam Chomsky. *Manufacturing Consent. The Political Economy of the Mass Media* (New York: Pantheon Books, 1988).

Herrmann, Rachel B. *No Useless Mouth* (Ithaca, NY: Cornell University Press, 2019).

Hersey, Frank W. C. "The Misfortunes of Dorcas Griffiths." *Colonial Society of Massachusetts Publications* 34 (1937): 13–25.

Hersey, Frank W. C. "Tar and Feathers. The Adventures of Captain John Malcom." *Transactions of the Colonial Society of Massachusetts* 34 (1941): 429–473.

Higgins, W. Robert. "Charles Town Merchants and Factors Dealing in the External Negro Trade 1735–1775," *SCHM* 65, no. 4 (1964): 205–217.

Higginson, Thomas Wentworth. *Life and Times of Stephen Higginson* (Boston: Houghton Mifflin, 1907).

Hodacs, Hanna. *Silk and Tea in the North. Scandinavian Trade and the Market for Asian Goods in Eighteenth-Century Europe* (London: Palgrave, 2016).

Hoerder, Dirk. *Crowd Action in Revolutionary Massachusetts, 1765–1780* (New York: Academic Press, 1977).

Hoffman, Ronald. *Princes of Ireland, Planters of Maryland: A Carroll Saga, 1500–1782* (Chapel Hill: University of North Carolina Press for the Omohundro Institute of Early American History and Culture, 2002).

Hoffman, Ronald. *A Spirit of Dissention: Economics, Politics, and the Revolution in Maryland* (Baltimore: Johns Hopkins University Press, 1973).

Högberg, Staffan. *Utrikeshandel och sjöfart på 1700-talet* (Stockholm: Bonnier, 1969).

Holton, Woody. *Forced Founders: Indians, Debtors, Slaves, and the Making of the American Revolution in Virginia* (Chapel Hill: University of North Carolina Press for the Omohundro Institute of Early American History and Culture, 1999).

Huibrechts, Marion. "Swampin' Huns and Stabbing Irons: The Austrian Netherlands, Liege Arms and the American Revolution, 1770–1783" (PhD diss., Catholic University of Leuven, 2009).

Humphrey, Carol Sue. *"This Popular Engine" New England Newspapers during the American Revolution, 1775–1789* (Newark: University of Delaware Press, 1992).

Huntington, E. B. *History of Stamford, Connecticut, from Its Settlement in 1641, to the Present Time* (Stamford, CT, 1868).

Hurd, D. Hamilton. *History of Plymouth County Massachusetts* (Philadelphia: J. W Lewis, 1884).

Ingersoll, Thomas. *The Loyalist Problem in Revolutionary New England* (Cambridge: Cambridge University Press, 2016).

Ingrassia, Catherine. "Fashioning Female Authorship in Eliza Haywood's 'The Tea-Table,'" *Journal of Narrative Technique* 28, no. 3 (Fall 1998): 287–304.

Ireland, Owen S. "Bucks County," in *Beyond Philadelphia: The American Revolution in the Pennsylvania Hinterland*, ed. John B. Frantz and William Pencak, 23–45 (University Park: Pennsylvania State University Press, 1998).

Irvin, Benjamin H. *Clothed in Robes of Sovereignty. The Continental Congress and the People Out of Doors* (Oxford: Oxford University Press, 2011).

Irvin, Benjamin H. "Of Eloquence 'Manly' and 'Monstrous': The Henpecked Husband in Revolutionary Political Debate, 1774–1775," in *New Men: Manliness in Early America*, ed. Thomas A. Foster 195–216 (New York: New York University Press, 2011).

Irvin, Benjamin H. "Tar, Feathers, and Enemies of American Liberties, 1768–1776." *NEQ* 76, no. 2 (June 2003): 197–238.

Isaac, Rhys. "Dramatizing the Ideology of Revolution: Popular Mobilization in Virginia, 1774 to 1776." *WMQ*, 3rd Series, vol. 33, no 3 (July 1976): 357–385.

Isaac, Rhys. *Transformation of Virginia, 1740–1790* (Chapel Hill: University of North Carolina Press for the Omohundro Institute of Early American History and Culture, 1982).

Jaffee, David. "Peddlers of Progress and the Transformation of the Rural North, 1760–1860." *JAH* 78, no. 2 (September 1991): 511–535.

James, H. H. *Two Centuries. The Story of David Lloyd Pigott and Company of London. Tea and Coffee Merchants 1790–1960* (London: Harley Publishing, 1960).

Jameson, J. Franklin. "St. Eustatius in the American Revolution." *AHR* 8, no. 4 (July 1903): 683–708.

Jenkins, Stephen. *The Old Boston Post Road* (New York: G. P. Putnam's Sons, 1913).

Jensen, Arthur L. *The Maritime Commerce of Colonial Philadelphia* (Madison: Department of History of University of Wisconsin, 1963).

Jensen, Merrill. *The Founding of a Nation* (Oxford: Oxford University Press, 1968).

Jones, Alice Hanson. *Wealth of a Nation to Be: The American Colonies on the Eve of the Revolution* (Columbia: University of South Carolina Press, 1980).

Jones, Edward Alfred. *The Loyalists of Massachusetts; Their Memorials, Petitions and Claims* (London: The Saint Catherine Press, 1930).

Jones, Newton B. "Writings of the Reverend William Tennent, 1740–1777." *SCHM* 61, no. 3 (July 1960): 129–145.

Judd, Jacob. "Westchester County," in *The Other New York: The American Revolution beyond New York City, 1763–1787*, ed. Joseph S. Tiedemann and Eugene R. Fingerhut, 107–126 (Albany: SUNY Press: 2005).

Kamensky, Jane. *A Revolution in Color. The World of John Singleton Copley* (New York: Norton, 2016).

Kammen, Michael G. *A Rope in the Sand: The Colonial Agents, British Politics, and the American Revolution* (Ithaca, NY: Cornell University Press, 1968).

Kann, Mark E. *A Republic of Men: The American Founders, Gendered Language, and Patriarchal Politics* (New York: New York University Press, 1998).

Kellock, Katharine, A. "London Merchants and the pre-1776 American Debts." *Guildhall Studies in London History* 1, no. 3 (October 1974): 109–149.

Kent, H. S. K. *War and Trade in Northern Seas. Anglo-Scandinavian Economic Relations in the Mid-Eighteenth Century* (Cambridge: Cambridge University Press, 1973).

Kerber, Linda K. *Women of the Republic: Intellect & Ideology in Revolutionary America* (New York: Norton, 1986).

Kerr, Wildred Brenton. *Bermuda and the American Revolution: 1760–1783* (Princeton: Princeton University Press, 1936).

Kerr, Wilfred Brenton. *The Maritime Provinces of British North America and the American Revolution* (New York: Russell & Russell, 1970 reprint of 1940 edition).

Kerr, Wilfred Brenton. "The Merchants of Nova Scotia and the American Revolution." *Canadian Historical Review* 13, no. 1 (March 1932): 20–36.

Ketchum, Richard M. *Divided Loyalties, How the American Revolution Came to New York* (New York: Henry Holt and Company, 2002).

Keyes, Carl Robert. "Early American Advertising Marketing and Consumer Culture in Eighteenth-Century Philadelphia" (PhD diss., Johns Hopkins University, 2008).

Keyes, Carl Robert. "A Revolution in Advertising: 'Buy American' Campaigns in the Late Eighteenth Century," in *We Are What We Sell: How Advertising Shapes American Life . . . And Always Has*, ed. Danielle Sarver Coombs and Bob Batchelor, 1–25 (Santa Barbara, CA: Praeger, 2014).

Kierner, Cynthia A. *Beyond the Household. Women's Place in the Early South, 1700–1835* (Ithaca, NY: Cornell University Press: 1998).

Kjellberg, Sven T. *Svenska Ostindiska Compagnierna, 1731–1813* (Malmö: Allhem, 1974)

Knouff, Gregory T. "'That Abundant Infamous Roach': Breed and Ruth Batcheller, Moderate Loyalism, Language, and Domestic Power in Revolutionary New Hampshire," in *The Consequences of Loyalism. Essays in Honor of Robert M. Calhoon*, ed. Rebecca Brannon and Joseph S. Moore (Columbia: University of South Carolina Press, 2019).

Kowaleski-Wallace, Beth. "Tea, Gender, and Domesticity in Eighteenth-Century England." *Studies in Eighteenth-Century Culture* 23 (1994): 131–145.

Krusell, Cynthia Hagar. *Of Tea and Tories. The Story of Revolutionary Marshfield* (Marshfield, MA: Marshfield Bicentennial Committee, 1976)

Labaree, Benjamin Woods. *The Boston Tea Party* (Boston: Northeastern University Press, 1964).

Labaree, Benjamin Woods. *Patriots & Partisans: The Merchants of Newburyport, 1764–1815* (Cambridge, MA: Harvard University Press, 1962).

Lambert, Robert Stansbury. *South Carolina Loyalists in the American Revolution* (Columbia: University of South Carolina Press, 1987).

Lee, Ronald D., and R. S. Schofield, "British Population in the Eighteenth Century," in *The Economic History of Britain Since 1700*, ed. Roderick Floud and Donald McCloskey, vol. 1: 17–35. (Cambridge: Cambridge University Press, 1981).

Lee, Wayne E. *Crowds and Soldiers in Revolutionary North Carolina. The Culture of Violence in Riot and War* (Gainesville: University Press of Florida, 2001).

Lemisch, Jesse. "Jack Tar in the Streets: Merchant Seamen in the Politics of Revolutionary America." *William and Mary Quarterly*, 3rd Series, vol. 25, no. 3 (July 1968): 371–407.

Levy, Leonard. *Emergence of a Free Press* (New York: Oxford University Press, 1985).

Ligon, Samantha M. "The Fashionable Set: The Feasibility of Social Tea Drinking in 1774" (MA thesis, College of William and Mary, 1999).

Lind, Ivan. *Göteborgs Handel och Sjöfart 1637–1820* (Göteborg, 1923).

Lindblad, J. Thomas. *Sweden's Trade with the Dutch Republic, 1738–1795* (Assen: Van Gorcum, 1982).

Lippmann, Walter. *Public Opinion.* (London: Allen & Unwin, 1922).

Liu, Yong. *The Dutch East India Company's Tea Trade with China, 1757–1781* (Leiden: Brill, 2007).

Lockridge. Kenneth A. *Literacy in Colonial New England: An Enquiry into the Social Context of Literacy in the Early Modern West* (New York: Norton, 1974).

Lockwood, Matthew. *To Begin the World Over Again: How the American Revolution Devastated the Globe* (New Haven, CT: Yale University Press, 2019).

Longley, R. S. "Mob Activities in Revolutionary Massachusetts." *NEQ* 6, no. 1 (1933): 98–130.

Lough, George Joseph, Jr. "The Champlins of Newport: A Commercial History" (PhD diss., University of Connecticut, 1977).

Loughran, Trish. *The Republic in Print: Print Culture in the Age of U.S. Nation Building, 1770–1870* (New York: Columbia University Press, 2009).

Lovejoy, David S. *Rhode Island Politics and the American Revolution, 1760–1776* (Providence: Brown University Press, 1958).

Lucas, Stephen. *Portents of Rebellion: Rhetoric and Revolution in Philadelphia, 1765–1776* (Philadelphia: Temple University Press, 1976).

Magra, Christopher P. *The Fisherman's Cause. Atlantic Commerce and the Maritime Dimensions of the American Revolution* (Cambridge: Cambridge University Press, 2011).

Maier, Pauline. "The Charleston Mob and the Evolution of Popular Politics in Revolutionary South Carolina, 1765–1784." *Perspectives in American History* 4 (1970): 173–196.

Maier, Pauline. *From Resistance to Revolution: Colonial Radicals and the Development of American Opposition to Britain, 1765–1776* (New York: Knopf, 1972).

Maier, Pauline. *The Old Revolutionaries: Political Lives in the Age of Samuel Adams* (New York: Knopf, 1980).

Malone, Dumas, ed. *Dictionary of American Biography* (Charles Scribner's Sons for the American Council of Learned Societies, 1928–1936), 22 vols.

Mancke, Elizabeth. *The Fault Lines of Empire. Political Differentiation in Massachusetts and Nova Scotia, ca 1760–1830* (London: Routledge, 2005).

Marston, Jerrilyn Greene. *King and Congress. The Transfer of Political Legitimacy, 1774–1776* (Princeton: Princeton University Press, 1987).

Martin, Ann Smart. *Buying into the World of Goods: Early Consumers in Backcountry Virginia* (Baltimore: Johns Hopkins University Press, 2008).

Martin, Robert W. T. *The Free and Open Press: The Founding of American Democratic Press Liberty, 1640–1800* (New York: New York University Press, 2001).

Mason, Bernard. *The Road to Independence. The Revolutionary Movement in New York 1773–1777* (Lexington: University of Kentucky Press, 1966).

Matson, Cathy. *Merchants and Empire: Trading in Colonial New York* (Baltimore: Johns Hopkins University Press, 1998).

Mays, David John. *Edmund Pendleton 1721–1803. A Biography* (Cambridge, MA: Harvard University Press, 1952; Virginia State Library Reprint 1984).

McCants, Anne E. C. "Poor Consumers as Global Consumers: The Diffusion of Tea and Coffee Drinking in the Eighteenth Century." *Economic History Review* 61 (2008): 172–200.

McCusker, John J. *How Much Is That in Real Money?* (Worcester, MA: American Antiquarian Society, 1992).

McCusker, John J. " Tea Exported from England, by Importing Colony: 1761–1775," Table Eg1152–1159 in *Historical Statistics of the United States, Earliest Times to the Present: Millennial Edition*, ed. Susan B. Carter, Scott Sigmund Gartner, Michael R. Haines, Alan L. Olmstead, Richard Sutch, and Gavin Wright (New York: Cambridge University Press, 2006), http://dx.doi.org/10.1017/ISBN -9780511132971.

McDonald, Michelle Craig. "From Cultivation to Cup: Caribbean Coffee and the North American Economy, 1765–1805" (PhD diss., University of Michigan, 2005).

McDonnell, Michael. "National Identity and the American War for Independence Reconsidered." *Australasian Journal of American Studies* 20, no. 1 (July 2001): 3–17.

McDonnell, Michael. *The Politics of War: Race Class and Conflict in Revolutionary Virginia* (Chapel Hill: University of North Carolina Press for the Omohundro Institute of Early American History and Culture, 2007).

McDonough, Daniel J. *Christopher Gadsden and Henry Laurens: The Parallel Lives of Two American Patriots* (Sellinsgrove: Susquehanna University Press, 2000).

McMurtrie, Douglas C. "Pioneer Printing in Georgia." *Georgia Historical Quarterly* 16, no 2 (June 1932): 77–113.

McWilliams, Jane W. *Annapolis: City on the Severn: A History* (Baltimore: Johns Hopkins University Press, 2011).

Mead, Spencer P. *Ye Historie of Ye Town of Greenwich, County of Fairfield and State of Connecticut* (New York: Knickerbocker Press, 1911).

Meekel, Arthur J. *The Quakers and the American Revolution* (York, England: Sessions Book Trust, 1996).

Meroney, Geraldine M. *Inseparable Loyalty. A Biography of William Bull* (Norcross, GA: Harrison Company, 1991).

Merritt, Jane. *The Trouble with Tea. The Politics of Consumption in the Eighteenth-Century Global Economy* (Baltimore: Johns Hopkins University Press, 2017).

Miller, John C. *Origins of the American Revolution* (Boston: Little, Brown, 1943).

Miller, John C. *Sam Adams: Pioneer in Propaganda* (Boston: Little, Brown, 1936).

Miner, Ward L. *William Goddard, Newspaperman* (Durham, NC: Duke University Press, 1962).

Mintz, Sidney W. *Sweetness and Power. The Place of Sugar in Modern History* (New York: Penguin Books, 1985).

Morison, Samuel E. *The Maritime History of Massachusetts, 1783–1860* (Cambridge: Riverside Press, 1961).

Mui, Hoh-cheung and Lorna H. Mui. "The Commutation Act and the Tea Trade in Britain 1784–1793." *HER* 16, no. 2 (1963): 234–253.

Mui, Hoh-cheung and Lorna H. Mui. "Smuggling and the British Tea Trade before 1784." *AHR* 74, no. 1 (October 1968): 44–73.

Müller, Leos. "The Swedish East India Trade and International Markets: Re-Exports of Teas, 1731–1813." *Scandinavian Economic History Review* 51, no. 3 (2003): 22–44.

Nash, Gary B. *The Urban Crucible: Social Change, Political Consciousness and the Origins of the American Revolution* (Cambridge: Harvard University Press, 1979).

Nelson, James. L. *George Washington's Secret Navy. How the American Revolution Went to Sea* (New York: McGraw-Hill, 2008).

Nelson Picnic Association, Ebenezer Tolman, and Simon Goodell Griffin. *Celebration by the Town of Nelson, New Hampshire: (originally Called "Monadnick No. 6" and Incorporated as "Packersfield") of the One Hundred And Fiftieth Anniversary of Its First Settlement, 1767–1917* (New York, 1917).

Nicholson, Colin, et al. "A Case of Identity: Massachusettensis and John Adams." *NEQ* 91 (2018): 651–682.

Nierstrasz, Chris. *Rivalry for Trade in Tea and Textiles: the English and Dutch East India Companies (1700–1800)* (New York: Springer, 2015).

Norton, John F. *History of Fitzwilliam, New Hampshire, from 1752 to 1887* (New York, 1888).

Norton, Mary Beth. *1774: The Long Year of Revolution* (New York: Knopf, 2020).

Norton, Mary Beth. *The British-Americans: The Loyalist Exiles in England, 1774–1789* (Boston: Little, Brown, 1972).

Norton, Mary Beth. "Eighteenth-Century American Women in Peace and War: The Case of the Loyalists." *WMQ* 33, no. 3 (July 1976): 386–409.

Norton, Mary Beth. *Liberty's Daughters: The Revolutionary Experience of American Women, 1750–1800* (Ithaca: Cornell University Press, 1980).

Norton, Mary Beth. *Separated by Their Sex: Women in Public and Private in the Colonial Atlantic World* (Ithaca: Cornell University Press, 2011).

Norton, Mary Beth. "The Seventh Tea Ship." *William and Mary Quarterly*, 3rd Series, vol. 73, no. 4 (October 2016): 681–710.

Nuxoll, Elizabeth Mules. *Congress and the Munitions Merchants: The Secret Committee of trade during the American Revolution, 1775–1777* (New York: Garland, 1985).

Nyström, Johan Fredrik. *De svenska ostindiska kompanierna: historisk-statistisk framställning* (Göteborg, 1883).

Olson, Lester. *Emblems of American Community in the Revolutionary Era: A Study in Rhetorical Iconology* (Washington, DC: Smithsonian Institution Press, 1991).

Olson, Lester. "Pictorial Representations of British America Resisting Rape: Rhetorical Re-Circulation of a Print Series Portraying the Boston Port Bill of 1774." *Rhetoric & Public Affairs* 12, no. 1 (2009): 1–35.

Olton, Charles S. *Artisans for Independence. Philadelphia Mechanics and the American Revolution* (Syracuse, NY: Syracuse University Press, 1975).

Osell, Tedra. "Tatling Women in the Public Sphere: Rhetorical Femininity and the English Essay Periodical." *Eighteenth-Century Studies* 38, no. 2 (Winter 2005): 283–300.

O'Shaughnessy, Andrew Jackson. *An Empire Divided: The American Revolution and the British Caribbean* (Philadelphia: University of Pennsylvania Press, 2000).

Papas, Phillip *That Ever Loyal Island: Staten Island and the American Revolution* (New York: New York University Press, 2007).

Papenfuse, Edward. *In Pursuit of Profit: The Annapolis Merchants in the Era of the American Revolution, 1763–1805* (Baltimore: Johns Hopkins University Press, 1975).

Parkinson, Robert G. *The Common Cause. Creating Race and the Nation in the American Revolution* (Chapel Hill: University of North Carolina Press for the Omohundro Institute of Early American History and Culture, 2016).

Patterson, Stephen E. *Political Parties in Revolutionary Massachusetts* (Madison: University of Wisconsin Press, 1973).

Paullin, Charles O. "The Navy of the American Revolution. Its Administration, Its Policy and Its Achievements." PhD diss., University of Chicago, 1906)

Peckham, Howard. "Collegia Ante Bellum. Attitudes of College Professors and Students Toward the American Revolution." *PMHB* 95, no. 1 (1971): 50–72.

Pelletreau, William S. *History of Putnam County, New York: With Biographical Sketches of Its Prominent Men* (Philadelphia: 1886).

Perry, Elizabeth A. *A Brief History of the Town of Gloucester, Rhode Island* (Providence, 1886).

Peskin, Lawrence. *Captives and Countrymen. Barbary Slavery and the American Public, 1785–1816* (Baltimore: Johns Hopkins University Press, 2009).

Phillips, A. V. *The Lott Family in America, Including the Allied Families: Cassell, Davis, Graybeal, Haring, Hegeman, Hogg, Kerley, Phillips, Thompson, Walter and Others* (Ann Arbor, MI: Edwards Brothers, 1942).

Phillips, Kevin. *1775. A Good Year for Revolution* (New York: Viking, 2012).

Pomerantz, Sidney I. "The Patriot Newspaper and the American Revolution," in *The Era of the American Revolution*, ed. Richard B. Morris, 305–331 (Harper, 1939).

Posthumus, N. W. *Inquiry into the History of Prices in Holland* (Leiden: Brill, 1946), 2 vols.

Poston, Jonathan H. "Ralph Wormeley V of Rosegill: A Deposed Virginia Aristocrat, 1774–1781" (MA thesis, College of William and Mary, 1979).

Potter, Janice, and Robert M. Calhoon, "The Character and Coherence of the Loyalist Press," in *The Press & the American Revolution*, ed. Bernard Bailyn and John B. Hench, 229–272 (Boston: Northeastern University Press, 1980).

Pourchasse, Pierrick. "Roscoff, un important centre de contrebande entre la France et l'Angleterre à la fin du XXIIIe siècle," in *Territoires de l'Illicite et identitités portuaires et insulaires. Du XVIe siècle au XXe siècle*, ed. Marguerite Figeac-Monthus and Christophe Lastécouères, 147–156 (Paris: Armand Colin, 2012).

Powell, William S., ed. *Dictionary of North Carolina Biography* (Chapel Hill: University of North Carolina Press, 1979–1996).

Prelinger, Catherine M. "Benjamin Franklin and the American Prisoners of War in England during the American Revolution." *WMQ*, 3rd Series, vol. 32, no. 2 (April 1975): 261–294.

Price, Jacob M. *France and the Chesapeake: A History of the French Tobacco Monopoly, 1674–1791, and of Its Relationship to the British and American Tobacco Trades* (Ann Arbor: University of Michigan Press, 1973).

Price, Jacob M. "Who Was John Norton? A Note on the Historical Character of Some Eighteenth-Century London Virginia Firms." *WMQ* 19, no. 3 (1962): 400–407.

Purcell, Sarah J. *Sealed with Blood: War, Sacrifice and Memory in Revolutionary America* (Philadelphia: University of Pennsylvania, 2002).

Quincy, Josiah. *History of Harvard University* (Boston, 1860).

Rakove, Jack N. *The Beginnings of National Politics: An Interpretive History of the Continental Congress* (Baltimore: Johns Hopkins University Press, 1979).

Ragsdale, Bruce A. *A Planter's Republic. The Search for Economic Independence in Revolutionary Virginia* (Madison: Madison House Publishers, 1996).

Ranlet, Philip. *The New York Loyalists* (Knoxville: University of Tennessee Press, 1986).

Rao, Gautham. *National Duties. Custom Houses and the Making of the American State* (Chicago: University of Chicago Press, 2016).

Raphael, Ray. *The First American Revolution. Before Lexington and Concord* (New York: New Press, 2002).

Raphael, Ray. "The Signal of Sam Adams," *Journal of the American Revolution* (January 23, 2014). https://allthingsliberty.com/2014/01/sam-adams-signal/#_edn1.

Rappleye, Charles. *Sons of Providence: The Brown Brothers, the Slave Trade, and the American Revolution* (New York: Simon & Schuster, 2006).

Reardon, John J. *Peyton Randolph, 1721–1775. One Who Presided* (Durham, NC: Carolina Academic Press, 1982).

Rickman, John. "Observations on the Results of the Population Act, 41 Geo. III." (London: 1802).

Robson, David W. *Educating Republicans: The College in the Era of the American Revolution, 1750–1800* (Westport, CT: Greenwood Press, 1985).

Roche, John. F. *The Colonial Colleges in the War for American Independence* (New York: National University Publications, Associated Faculty Press, 1986).

Rogers, George C. "The Charleston Tea Party: The Significance of December 3, 1773." *SCHM* 75 (July 1974): 153–168.

Rosswurm, Steven. *Arms, Country, and Class. The Philadelphia Militia and "Lower Sort" during the American Revolution, 1775–1783* (New Brunswick, NJ: Rutgers University Press, 1987).

Roth, Rodris. "Tea Drinking in 18th Century America: Its Etiquette and Equipage." *United States National Museum Bulletin* Paper 14 (Washington, DC, 1961).

Rowland, Lawrence S., Alexander Moore, and George C. Rogers Jr. *The History of Beaufort County, South Carolina, 1514–1861*, vol. 1 (Columbia: University of South Carolina Press, 1996).

Ryerson, Richard Alan. *The Revolution Is Now Begun. The Radical Committees of Philadelphia, 1765–1776* (Philadelphia: University of Pennsylvania Press, 1978).

Sabine, Lorenzo. *Biographical Sketches of Loyalists of the American Revolution* (Boston: Little, Brown, 1864).

Salinger, Sharon V. *Taverns and Drinking in Early America* (Baltimore: Johns Hopkins University Press, 2002).

Schafer, Daniel L. *Zephaniah Kingsley Jr. and the Atlantic World. Slave Trader. Plantation Owner. Emancipator* (Gainesville: University Press of Florida, 2013).

Scharf, J. Thomas. *The Chronicles of Baltimore* (Baltimore: Turnbull Brothers, 1874).

Scharf, J. Thomas. *History of Maryland* (Baltimore, 1879), 2 vols.

Schlesinger, Arthur M. "The American Revolution Reconsidered." *Political Science Quarterly* 34, no. 1 (March 1919): 61–78.

Schlesinger, Arthur M. *The Colonial Merchants and the American Revolution* (New York: Frederick Ungar, reprint 1957).

Schlesinger, Arthur M. "Political Mobs and the American Revolution, 1765–1776." *Proceedings of the American Philosophical Society* 99, no 4 (August 30, 1955): 244–250.

Schlesinger, Arthur M. *Prelude to Independence: The Newspaper War on Britain, 1764–1776* (New York: Knopf, 1958).

Scott, Kenneth. "Tory Associators of Portsmouth." *WMQ*, 3rd Series, vol. 17, no. 4 (1960): 507–515.

See, Scott. "Aspirations and Limitations: 'Peace, Order and Good Government' and the Language of Violence and Disorder in British North America," in *Violence, Order, and Unrest. A History of British North America, 1749–1876*, ed. Elizabeth Mancke, Jerry Bannister, Denis McKim, and Scott W. See, 17–29 (Toronto: University of Toronto, 2019).

Selby, John E. *The Revolution in Virginia 1775–1783* (Williamsburg: Colonial Williamsburg Foundation, 1988).

Selig, Robert A., "A German Soldier in America, 1780–1783: The Journal of Georg Daniel Flohr." *WMQ*, 3rd Series, vol. 50, no. 3 (July 1993): 575–590.

Sellers, Charles Coleman. *Patience Wright: American Artist and Spy in George III's London* (Middletown, CT: Wesleyan University Press, 1976).

Sellers, Leila. *Charleston Business on the Eve of the American Revolution* (Chapel Hill: University of North Carolina Press, 1934).

Shalev, Eran. "Ancient Masks, American Fathers: Classical Pseudonyms during the American Revolution and Early Republic." *JER* 23, no. 2 (Summer 2003): 151–172.

Shammas, Carole. *The Pre-Industrial Consumer in England and America* (Oxford: Clarendon Press, 1990).

Shaw, Peter. *American Patriots and the Rituals of Revolution* (Cambridge, MA: Harvard University Press, 1981).

Shields, David S. *Civil Tongues and Polite Letters in British America* (Chapel Hill: University of North Carolina Press for the Omohundro Institute of Early American History and Culture, 1997).

Shy, John. "The Loyalist Problem in the Lower Hudson Valley: The British Perspective," in *The Loyalist Americans. A Focus on Greater New York*, ed. Robert A. East and Jacob Judd, 3–13 (Tarrytown, NY: Sleepy Hollow Restorations, 1975).

Sickler, Joseph. *Tea Burning Town Being the Story of Greenwich on the Cohansey in West Jersey* (New York: Abelard Press, 1950).

Singleton, Esther. *Social New York under the Georges, 1714–1776: Houses, Streets, and Country Homes, with Chapters on Fashions, Furniture, China, Plate, and Manners* (D. Appleton, 1902).

Slauter, Eric. "Reading and Radicalization: Print, Politics, and the American Revolution." *EAS* 8 (2010): 5–40.

Smart, James R. "A Life William Beadle" (Senior thesis, Princeton University, 1989).

Smith, Barbara Clark. "Food Rioters and the American Revolution." *WMQ*, 3rd Series, vol. 51, no. 1 (January 1994): 3–38.

Smith, Barbara Clark. *The Freedoms We Lost. Consent and Resistance in Revolutionary America* (New York: New Press, 2010).

Smith, Barbara Clark. "Social Visions of the American Resistance Movement," in *The Transforming Hand of Revolution: Reconsidering the American Revolution as a Social Movement*, ed. Ronald Hoffman and Peter J. Albert (Charlottesville: University of Virginia Press, 1995).

Smith, Justin H. *Arnold's March from Cambridge to Quebec. A Critical Study* (New York: G. P. Putnam's Sons, Knickerbocker Press, 1903).

Smith, S. D. "Accounting for Taste: British Coffee Consumption in Historical Perspective." *Journal of Interdisciplinary History* 27, no. 2 (Autumn 1996): 183–214.

Sosin, Jack M. *Agents and Merchants. British Colonial Policy and the Origins of the American Revolution, 1763–1775* (Lincoln: University of Nebraska Press, 1965),

Stackpole, Edouard A. *Nantucket in the American Revolution* (Falmouth, MA: Nantucket Historical Association, 1976),

Stackpole, Everett. *History of New Hampshire IV* (New York: American Historical Society, 1916).

Staples, William R. *Annals of the Town of Providence* (Providence, 1843).

Stark, James H. *Loyalists of Massachusetts and the Other Side of the American Revolution* (Boston, 1910).

Staudt John G. "Suffolk County," in *The Other New York: The American Revolution beyond New York City, 1763–1787*, ed. Joseph S. Tiedemann and Eugene R. Fingerhut, 63–82 (Albany: SUNY Press, 2005).

Steedman, Marguerite. "Charleston's Forgotten Tea Party." *Georgia Review* 21, no. 2 (Summer 1967): 244–259.

Stoudt, John Joseph. "The German Press in Pennsylvania and the American Revolution." *PMHB* 59, no. 1 (1935): 74–90.

Stout, Neil R. *The Perfect Crisis: The Beginning of the Revolutionary War* (New York: New York University Press, 1976).

Sullivan, Aaron. *The Disaffected. Britain's Occupation of Philadelphia during the American Revolution* (Philadelphia: University of Pennsylvania Press, 2019).

Tchen, John Kuo Wei. *New York before Chinatown: Orientalism and the Shaping of American Culture, 1776–1882* (Baltimore: Johns Hopkins University Press, 1999).

Teeter, Dwight L. "'King' Sears, the Mob and Freedom of the Press in New York, 1765–76." *Journalism Quarterly* 41 (1964): 539–544.

Thomas, Isaiah. *History of Printing in America*. In *Transactions and Collections of the American Antiquarian Society*, vol. 5 (1874).

Thomas, Peter D. G. *Tea Party to Independence. The Third Phase of the American Revolution, 1773–1776* (Oxford: Clarendon Press, 1991).

Thomas, Peter D. G. *The Townshend Duties Crisis. The Second Phase of the American Revolution 1767–1773* (Oxford: Clarendon Press, 1987).

Thomas, R. S. "A List of Graduates of Harvard Who Were Tories in the American Revolution, Residing in Massachusetts." *WMQ* 7, no. 2 (October 1898): 76–81.

Thompson, Peter. *Rum Punch & Revolution. Taverngoing & Public Life in Eighteenth-Century Philadelphia* (Philadelphia: University of Pennsylvania Press, 1999).

Torr, Cecil. *Small Talk at Wreyland* (Cambridge: Cambridge University Press, 1918).

Truxes, Thomas M. *Defying Empire: Trading with the Enemy in Colonial New York* (New Haven: Yale University Press, 2008).

Truxes, Thomas M. "Ireland, New York, and the Eighteenth-Century Atlantic World." *American Journal of Irish Studies* 8 (2011): 9–40.

Truxes, Thomas M. *Irish-American Trade, 1660–1783* (Cambridge: Cambridge University Press, 1988).

Tyler, John W. *Smugglers & Patriots: Boston Merchants and the Advent of the American Revolution* (Boston: Northeastern University Press, 1986).

Ubbelohde, Carl. *The Vice-Admiralty Courts and the American Revolution* (Chapel Hill: University of North Carolina Press, 1960).

Ukers, William H. *All About Tea* (New York: The Tea and Coffee Trade Journal Company, 1935).

Ulrich, Laurel. *The Age of Homespun: Objects and Stories in the Creation of an American Myth* (New York: Knopf, 2001).

United States Bureau of the Census. *The Statistical History of the United States, From Colonial Times to the Present: Historical Statistics of the United States, Colonial Times to 1970.* (New York: Basic Books, 1976).

van Zanden, Jan Luiten, and Arthur van Riel. Ian Cressie, trans. *The Strictures of Inheritance. The Dutch Economy in the Nineteenth Century* (Princeton: Princeton University Press, 2004).

Venables, Robert W. "Tryon County," in *The Other New York: The American Revolution beyond New York City, 1763–1787*, ed. Joseph S. Tiedemann and Eugene R. Fingerhut, 179–198 (Albany: SUNY Press: 2005).

Ver Steeg, Clarence L. "Stacey Hepburn and Company: Enterprisers in the American Revolution." *SCHM* 55, no. 1 (1954): 1–5.

Volo, James M. *Blue Water Patriots: The American Revolution Afloat* (Westport, CT: Praeger, 2007).

Waldstreicher, David. *In the Midst of Perpetual Fetes: The Making of American Nationalism, 1776–1820* (Chapel Hill: University of North Carolina Press, 1997).

Walmsley, Andrew Stephen. *Thomas Hutchinson and the Origins of the American Revolution* (New York: New York University Press, 1999).

Walsh, Richard. *Charleston's Sons of Liberty: A Study of the Artisans, 1763–1789* (Columbia: University of South Carolina Press, 1959).

Ward, Harry M. *The War for Independence and the Transformation of American Society* (London: UCL Press, 1999).

Warden, Rosemary S. "Chester County," in *Beyond Philadelphia. The American Revolution in the Pennsylvania Hinterland*, ed. John B. Frantz and William Pencak, 1–22 (University Park: Pennsylvania State University Press, 1998).

Warner, Michael. *The Letters of the Republic: Publication and the Public Sphere in Eighteenth-Century America* (Cambridge: Harvard University Press, 1990).

Warner, William B. *Protocols of Liberty. Communication, Innovation, & the American Revolution* (Chicago: University of Chicago Press, 2013).

Washburn, Emory. *Sketches of the Judicial History of Massachusetts* (Boston: Little, Brown, 1840).

Waters, John J., Jr. *The Otis Family in Provincial and Revolutionary Massachusetts* (Chapel Hill: University of North Carolina Press, 1968).

Watson, John F. *Annals of Philadelphia, and Pennsylvania, in the Olden Time* (Philadelphia, 1898)

Webber, Sandra L. "The Lost Customs Records of Colonial Massachusetts." *Coriolis: The Interdisciplinary Journal of Maritime Studies* 8, no. 2 (2019): 1–24.

Weir, Robert M. *Colonial South Carolina, A History* (Millwood, NY: KTO Press, 1983).

Weir, Robert M. "The Role of the Newspaper in the Southern Colonies on the Eve of the Revolution: An Interpretation," in *The Press & the American Revolution*, ed. Bernard Bailyn and John B. Hench, 99–150 (Boston: Northeastern University Press, 1980).

Wermuth Thomas S. "The Central Hudson Valley: Dutchess, Orange and Ulster Counties," in *The Other New York: The American Revolution beyond New York City, 1763–1787*, ed. Joseph S. Tiedemann and Eugene R. Fingerhut, 127–155 (Albany: SUNY Press, 2005).

Wertenbaker, Thomas Jefferson. *Father Knickerbocker Rebels. New York City during the Revolution* (New York: Charles Scribner's Sons, 1948).

Wertenbaker, Thomas Jefferson. *Princeton, 1746–1896* (Princeton: Princeton University Press, 1946).

Westergaard, Waldemar. *The Danish West Indies under Company Rule (1671–1754)* (New York: Macmillan, 1917).

White, Luise. "Telling More: Lies, Secrets, and History." *History & Theory* 39, no. 4 (December 2000): 11–23.

Whitmore, William Henry. *The Massachusetts Civil List for the Colonial and Provincial Periods, 1630–1774* (Albany: J. Munsell, 1870).

Withington, Ann Fairfax. *Toward a More Perfect Union: Virtue and the Formation of American Republics* (New York: Oxford University Press, 1991).

Withington, Frederic Scherer. "Henry Withington of Dorchester, Mass., and Some of His Descendants." *NEHGR* 75 (April 1921): 142–154.

Wood, Gordon S. *Creation of the American Republic* (Chapel Hill: University of North Carolina Press for the Omohundro Institute of Early American History and Culture, 1969).

Wood, Gordon S. "A Note on Mobs in the American Revolution." *WMQ* 23, no. 4 (1966): 635–642.

Wood, Gordon S. "Rhetoric and Reality in the American Revolution" *WMQ* 23, no. 1 (1966): 4–32.

Wright, Richardson. *Hawkers & Walkers in Early America* (Philadelphia: J. B. Lippincott Company, 1927).

Yokota, Kariann Akemi. *Unbecoming British: How Revolutionary America Became a Postcolonial Nation* (Oxford: Oxford University Press, 2011).

Young, Alfred F. *Shoemaker and the Tea Party. Memory and the American Revolution* (Boston: Beacon Press, 1999).

Young, Alfred F. "The Women of Boston: 'Persons of Consequence' in the Making of the American Revolution, 1765–1776," in *Women and Politics in the Age of the Democratic Revolution*, ed. Harriet B. Applewhite and Darline G. Levy, 181–226 (Ann Arbor: University of Michigan Press, 1990).

Younger, Richard D. "Grand Juries and the American Revolution." *VMHB* 63, no. 3 (July 1955): 257–268.

Zitt, Hersch L. "David Salisbury Franks, Revolutionary Patriot (c. 1740–1793)." *Pennsylvania History: A Journal of Mid-Atlantic Studies* (1949): 77–95.

INDEX

Note: Figures and tables are indicated by page numbers in *italics*.